ROAD ATLAS

2022 BRITAIN IRELAND

CW00507271

www.philips-maps.co.uk

First published in 2009 as
Complete Road Atlas Britain and Ireland by Philip's,
a division of Octopus Publishing Group Ltd
www.octopusbooks.co.uk
Carmelite House, 50 Victoria Embankment
London EC4Y 0DZ
An Hachette UK Company
www.hachette.co.uk

Thirteenth edition 2021
First impression 2021

ISBN 978-1-84907-566-4 spiral-bound
ISBN 978-1-84907-567-1 perfect-bound

Cartography by Philip's
Copyright © 2021 Philip's

This product includes mapping data
licensed from Ordnance Survey®,
with the permission of the Controller
of Her Majesty's Stationery Office.
© Crown copyright 2021.
All rights reserved. Licence number 100011710.

The map of Ireland on pages XVI–
XVII is based upon the Crown
Copyright and is reproduced with
the permission of Land & Property
Services under delegated authority
from the Controller of Her Majesty's Stationery Office,
© Crown Copyright and database right 2021,
PMLPA number 100503, and on Ordnance Survey
Ireland by permission of the Government
© Ordnance Survey Ireland / Government of Ireland
Permit number 9240.

No part of this publication may be reproduced, stored
in a retrieval system or transmitted in any form or by
any means, electronic, mechanical, photocopying,
recording or otherwise, without the permission of the
Publishers and the copyright owner.

While every reasonable effort has been made to
ensure that the information compiled in this atlas
is accurate, complete and up-to-date at the time
of publication, some of this information is subject
to change and the Publisher cannot guarantee its
correctness or completeness.

The information in this atlas is provided without any
representation or warranty, express or implied and the
Publisher cannot be held liable for any loss or damage
due to any use or reliance on the information in this
atlas, nor for any errors, omissions or subsequent
changes in such information.

The representation in this atlas of any road, drive or
track is no evidence of the existence of a right of way.

Information for National Parks, Areas of Outstanding
Natural Beauty, National Trails and Country Parks in
Wales supplied by the Countryside Council for Wales.

Information for National Parks, Areas of Outstanding
Natural Beauty, National Trails and Country Parks
in England supplied by Natural England. Data for
Regional Parks, Long Distance Footpaths and Country
Parks in Scotland provided by Scottish Natural
Heritage.

Gaelic name forms used in the Western Isles provided
by Comhairle nan Eilean.

Data for the National Nature Reserves in England
provided by Natural England. Data for the National
Nature Reserves in Wales provided by Countryside
Council for Wales. Darparwyd data'n ymwneud â
Gwarchodfeydd Natur Cenedlaethol Cymru gan
Gyngor Cefn Gwlad Cymru.

Information on the location of National Nature
Reserves in Scotland was provided by Scottish
Natural Heritage.

Data for National Scenic Areas in Scotland provided
by the Scottish Executive Office. Crown copyright
material is reproduced with the permission of the
Controller of HMSO and the Queen's Printer for
Scotland. Licence number C02W0003960.

Printed in China

*Data from Nielsen Total Consumer Market 2020
weeks 27–39

CONTENTS

II **Key to map symbols**

III **Smart motorways and motorway service areas**

IV **Restricted motorway junctions**

VI **Route planning maps**

XVI **Road map of Ireland**

XVIII **Tourism and transport**

XX **Distances and journey times**

1 **Key to road map pages**

2 **Road maps of Britain**

161 **Urban approach maps**

161 Bristol *approaches*
162 Birmingham *approaches*
164 Cardiff *approaches*
165 Edinburgh *approaches*
166 Glasgow *approaches*
167 Leeds *approaches*
168 London *approaches*
172 Liverpool *approaches*
173 Manchester *approaches*
174 Newcastle *approaches*

175 **Town plans**

175 Aberdeen, Ayr, Bath
176 Birmingham, Blackpool, Bournemouth
177 Bradford, Brighton, Bristol
178 Bury St Edmunds, Cambridge, Canterbury, Cardiff
179 Carlisle, Chelmsford, Cheltenham, Chester
180 Chichester, Colchester, Coventry, Derby
181 Dorchester, Dumfries, Dundee, Durham
182 Edinburgh, Exeter, Gloucester
183 Glasgow, Grimsby, Harrogate
184 Hull, Inverness, Ipswich, Kendal
185 King's Lynn, Lancaster, Leeds
186 London
188 Leicester, Lincoln, Liverpool
189 Llandudno, Llanelli, Luton, Macclesfield
190 Manchester, Maidstone, Merthyr Tydfil
191 Middlesbrough, Milton Keynes, Newcastle, Newport
192 Newquay, Northampton, Norwich, Nottingham
193 Oxford, Perth, Peterborough, Plymouth
194 Poole, Portsmouth, Preston, Reading
195 St Andrews, Salisbury, Scarborough, Shrewsbury,
196 Sheffield, Stoke-on-Trent (Hanley), Southampton
197 Southend, Stirling, Stratford-upon-Avon, Sunderland
198 Swansea, Swindon, Taunton, Telford
199 Torquay, Truro, Winchester, Windsor
200 Wolverhampton, Worcester, Wrexham, York

201 **Index to town plans**

213 **Index to road maps of Britain**
Inside back cover:
County and unitary authority boundaries

£1.99

Road map symbols

M3	Motorway, toll motorway
5 / 8	Motorway junction – full, restricted access
S / S	Motorway service area – full, restricted access
	Motorway under construction
A303	Primary route – dual, single carriageway
S / ○ / ○	Service area, roundabout, multi-level junction
4 / 5	Numbered junction – full, restricted access
	Primary route under construction
	Narrow primary route
Newbury	Primary destination
A303	A road – dual, single carriageway
	A road under construction, narrow A road
B3089	B road – dual, single carriageway
	B road under construction, narrow B road
	Minor road – over 4 metres, under 4 metres wide
	Minor road with restricted access
2	Distance in miles
TOLL	Toll, steep gradient – arrow points downhill
	Tunnel
	National trail – England and Wales
	Long distance footpath – Scotland
	Railway with station
	Level crossing, tunnel
	Preserved railway with station
	National boundary
	County / unitary authority boundary
	Car ferry, catamaran
	Passenger ferry, catamaran
	Hovercraft
CALAIS	Ferry destination
Ferry	Car ferry – river crossing
	Principal airport, other airport
	National park, Area of Outstanding Natural Beauty – England and Wales National Scenic Area – Scotland Forest park / regional park / national forest
	Beach
	Linear antiquity
	Roman road
✕ 1643	Hillfort, battlefield – with date
▲ 261	Viewpoint, nature reserve, spot height – in metres
	Golf course, youth hostel, sporting venue
	Camp site, caravan site, camping and caravan site
🛒 / P&R	Shopping village, park and ride
29	Adjoining page number – road maps

Approach map symbols

M6	Motorway
	Toll motorway
6 / 5	Motorway junction – full, restricted access
S	Service area
	Under construction
A6	Primary route – dual, single carriageway
S	Service area
○	Multi-level junction
	roundabout
	Under construction
A195	A road – dual, single carriageway
B1288	B road – dual, single carriageway
	Minor road – dual, single carriageway
	Ring road
3	Distance in miles
	Congestion charge area
COSELEY	Railway with station
LOXDALE	Tramway with station
M ⊖ ⊖ ●	Underground or metro station

Town plan symbols

	Motorway
	Primary route – dual, single carriageway
	A road – dual, single carriageway
	B road – dual, single carriageway
	Minor through road
→	One-way street
	Pedestrian roads
	Shopping streets
	Railway with station
City Hall	Tramway with station
	Bus or railway station building
	Shopping precinct or retail park
	Park
	Building of public interest
	Theatre, cinema
P	Parking, shopmobility
Bank	Underground station
West St	Metro station
H	Hospital, Police station
PO	Post office

Tourist information

Symbol	Description	Symbol	Description	Symbol	Description
✝	Abbey, cathedral or priory	🐎	Farm park		Race course
🏛	Ancient monument	❀	Garden		Roman antiquity
	Aquarium	⚓	Historic ship		Safari park
	Art gallery	🏠	House		Theme park
	Bird collection or aviary		House and garden	i	Tourist information
🏰	Castle		Motor racing circuit		Zoo
	Church	🏛	Museum	✦	Other place of interest
	Country park England and Wales Scotland		Picnic area		
			Preserved railway		

Road map scales

1 : 200 000 • 1cm = 2km • 1 inch = 3·15 miles

0 1 2 3 4 5 6 7 8 9 10 km

0 1 2 3 4 5 6 miles

Parts of Scotland

1 : 265 000 • 1 cm = 2.65 km • 1 inch = 4.18 miles

0 2 4 6 8 10 km

0 1 2 3 4 5 6 miles

Scottish Highlands and Islands

1 : 332 000 • 1 cm = 3.32km • 1 inch = 5.24 miles

0 2 4 6 8 10 12 km

0 1 2 3 4 5 6 7 8 miles

Orkney and Shetland Islands 1:400 000 • 1cm = 4 km • 1 inch = 6.31 miles

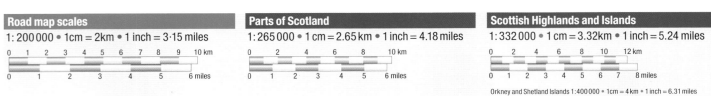

Smart motorways and motorway service areas

Smart motorways

M1

J6a–J10	Controlled, 4-lane
J10–J13	Dynamic hard shoulder
J16–J13	All lane running
J19–J16	All lane running
J23a–J24	Controlled, 4-lane
J24–J25	All lane running
J25–J28	Controlled, 4-lane
J28–J31	All lane running
J31–J32	Controlled, 4-lane
J32–J35a	All lane running
J39–J42	All lane running

M3

J2–J4a	All lane running
J9–J14	All lane running

M4

J3–J12	All lane running

M4–M5 interchange

M4 J20 / M5 J15

Dynamic hard shoulder*

M5

J4a–J6	All lane running

M6

J2–J4	All lane running
J4–J5	Dynamic hard shoulder
J5–J8	Dynamic hard shoulder
J8–J10a	Dynamic hard shoulder
J10a–J11a	Controlled, 3-lane
J11a–J13	All lane running
J13–J15	All lane running
J16–J19	All lane running

M20

J3–J5	All lane running
J4–J5	Controlled, 3-lane
J5–J7	Controlled, 4-lane

M23

J8–J10	All lane running

M25

J2–J3	Controlled, 4-lane
J5–J7	All lane running**
J7–J10	Controlled, 4-lane
J10–J12	Controlled, 4-lane
J12–J14	Controlled, 4-lane
J16–J23	Controlled, 4-lane
J23–J27	All lane running
J27–J30	Controlled, 4-lane

M27

J4–J11	All lane running

M40–M42 interchange

M42 J3a	All lane running

M42

J3a–J7	Dynamic hard shoulder
J7–J9	Controlled, 4-lane

M56

Juncs 6–8	All lane running

M60

J8–J12	Controlled, 3-lane
J12–J17	Controlled, 4-lane

M62

J10–J12	All lane running
J18–J20	All lane running
J20–J25	All lane running
J25–J26	All lane running
J25–J30	Dynamic hard shoulder
J28–J29	Controlled, 4-lane

Undergoing conversion to smart motorway

*Scheme full name: M4 Junctions 19–20 M5 Junctions 16–17

**Junctions 6 to 7 eastbound: controlled motorway 4-lane

Information for smart motorways supplied by Highways England

Legend

Sedgemoor — Motorway services

Smart motorways
— Operational
= Undergoing conversion
— Operational, dynamic hard shoulder
ALR — All lane running
CM3 — Controlled motorway, 3-lane
CM4 — Controlled motorway, 4-lane
DHS — Dynamic hard shoulder

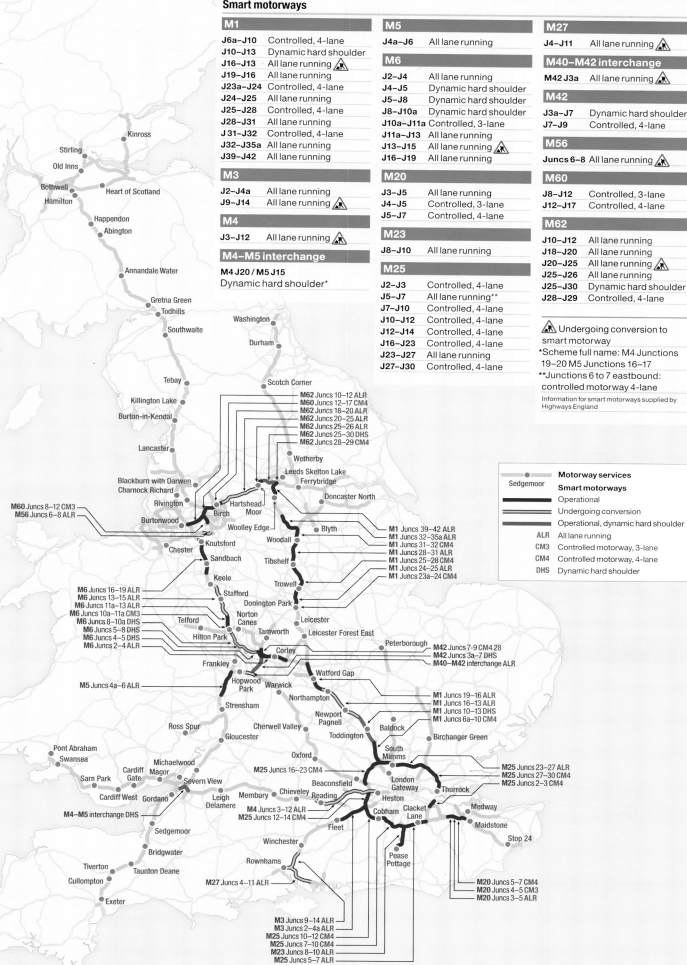

Map labels (clockwise / by region):

Kinross, Stirling, Old Inns, Bothwell, Hamilton, Heart of Scotland, Happendon, Abington, Annandale Water, Gretna Green, Todhills, Southwaite, Washington, Durham, Tebay, Killington Lake, Burton-in-Kendal, Lancaster, Scotch Corner, Wetherby, Leeds Skelton Lake, Ferrybridge, Doncaster North, Blackburn with Darwen, Charnock Richard, Rivington, Birch, Hartshead Moor, Burtonwood, Woolley Edge, Blyth, Woodall, Knutsford, Chester, Sandbach, Tibshelf, Keele, Trowell, Stafford, Donington Park, Norton Canes, Leicester, Telford, Tamworth, Leicester Forest East, Hilton Park, Corley, Frankley, Watford Gap, Hopwood Park, Warwick, Northampton, Strensham, Newport Pagnell, Peterborough, Ross Spur, Cherwell Valley, Toddington, Baldock, Birchanger Green, Gloucester, Oxford, South Mimms, Pont Abraham, Swansea, Michaelwood, Cardiff Gate, Magor, Severn View, Beaconsfield, London Gateway, Sarn Park, Leigh Delamere, Membury, Chieveley, Reading, Heston, Thurrock, Cardiff West, Gordano, Cobham, Clacket Lane, Medway, Maidstone, Fleet, Stop 24, Sedgemoor, Winchester, Rownhams, Bridgwater, Pease Pottage, Tiverton, Taunton Deane, Cullompton, Exeter

Motorway scheme labels on map:

M62 Juncs 10–12 ALR
M60 Juncs 12–17 CM4
M62 Juncs 18–20 ALR
M62 Juncs 20–25 ALR
M62 Juncs 25–26 ALR
M62 Juncs 25–30 DHS
M62 Juncs 28–29 CM4
M60 Juncs 8–12 CM3
M56 Juncs 6–8 ALR
M1 Juncs 39–42 ALR
M1 Juncs 32–35a ALR
M1 Juncs 31–32 CM4
M1 Juncs 28–31 ALR
M1 Juncs 25–28 CM4
M1 Juncs 24–25 ALR
M1 Juncs 23a–24 CM4
M6 Juncs 16–19 ALR
M6 Juncs 13–15 ALR
M6 Juncs 11–13 ALR
M6 Juncs 10a–11a CM3
M6 Juncs 8–10a DHS
M6 Juncs 5–8 DHS
M6 Juncs 4–5 DHS
M6 Juncs 2–4 ALR
M5 Juncs 4a–6 ALR
M42 Juncs 7–9 CM4 28
M42 Juncs 3a–7 DHS
M40–M42 interchange ALR
M1 Juncs 19–16 ALR
M1 Juncs 16–13 ALR
M1 Juncs 10–13 DHS
M1 Juncs 6a–10 CM4
M25 Juncs 16–23 CM4
M25 Juncs 23–27 ALR
M25 Juncs 27–30 CM4
M25 Juncs 2–3 CM4
M4 Juncs 3–12 ALR
M25 Juncs 12–14 CM4
M4–M5 interchange DHS
M20 Juncs 5–7 CM4
M20 Juncs 4–5 CM3
M20 Juncs 3–5 ALR
M27 Juncs 4–11 ALR
M3 Juncs 9–14 ALR
M3 Juncs 2–4a ALR
M25 Juncs 10–12 CM4
M25 Juncs 7–10 CM4
M23 Juncs 8–10 ALR
M25 Juncs 5–7 ALR

Restricted motorway junctions

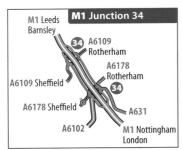

M1 Junction 34

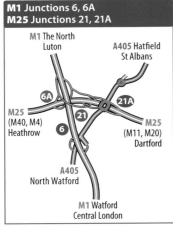

M1 Junctions 6, 6A
M25 Junctions 21, 21A

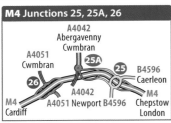

M4 Junctions 25, 25A, 26

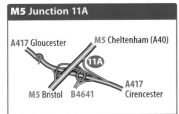

M5 Junction 11A

M8 Junctions 8, 9 · M73 Junctions 1, 2
M74 Junctions 2A, 3, 3A, 4

M1	Northbound	Southbound
2	No exit	No access
4	No exit	No access
6A	No exit. Access from M25 only	No access. Exit to M25 only
7	No exit. Access from A414 only	No access. Exit to A414 only
17	No access. Exit to M45 only	No exit. Access from M45 only
19	No exit to A14	No access from A14
21A	No access	
23A		Exit to A42 only
24A	No exit	No access
35A	No access	No exit
43	No access. Exit to M621 only	No exit. Access from M621 only
48	No exit to A1(M) southbound	

M3	Eastbound	Westbound
8	No exit	No access
10	No access	No exit
13	No access to M27 eastbound	
14	No exit	No access

M4	Eastbound	Westbound
1	Exit to A4 eastbound only	Access from A4 westbound only
2	Access from A4 eastbound only	Access to A4 westbound only
21	No exit	No access
23	No access	No exit
25	No exit	No access
25A	No exit	No access
29	No exit	No access
38		No access
39	No exit or access	No exit
41	No access	No exit
41A	No access	No exit
42	Access from A483 only	Exit to A483 only

M5	Northbound	Southbound
10	No exit	No access
11A	No access from A417 eastbound	No exit to A417 westbound

M6	Northbound	Southbound
3A	No access.	No exit. Access from M6 east-bound only
4A	No exit. Access from M42 south-bound only	No access. Exit to M42 only
5	No access	No exit
10A	No access. Exit to M54 only	No exit. Access from M54 only
11A	No exit. Access from M6 Toll only	No access. Exit to M6 Toll only
20	No exit to M56 eastbound	No access from M56 westbound
24	No exit	No access
25	No access	No exit
30	No exit. Access from M61 northbound only	No access. Exit to M61 southbound only
31A	No access	No exit
45	No access	No exit

M6 Toll	Northbound	Southbound
T1		No exit
T2	No exit, no access	No access
T5	No exit	No access
T7	No access	No exit
T8	No access	No exit

M8	Eastbound	Westbound
6	No exit	No access
6A	No Access	No exit
7	No Access	No exit
7A	No exit. Access from A725 northbound only	No access. Exit to A725 southbound only
8	No exit to M73 northbound	No access from M73 southbound
9	No access	No exit
13	No exit southbound	Access from M73 south-bound only
14	No access	No exit
16	No exit	No access
17	No exit	
18		No exit
19	No exit to A814 eastbound	No access from A814 westbound
20	No exit	No access
21	No access from M74	No exit
22	No exit. Access from M77 only	No access. Exit to M77 only
23	No exit	No access
25	Exit to A739 northbound only. Access from A739 southbound only	
25A	No exit	No access
28	No exit	No access
28A	No exit	No access
29A	No exit	No access

M9	Eastbound	Westbound
2	No access	No exit
3	No exit	No access
6	No access	No exit
8	No exit	No access

M11	Northbound	Southbound
4	No exit	No access
5	No access	No exit
8A	No access	No exit
9	No access	No exit
13	No access	No exit
14	No exit to A428 westbound	No exit. Access from A14 westbound only

M20	Eastbound	Westbound
2	No access	No exit
3	No exit. Access from M26 eastbound only	No access. Exit to M26 westbound only
10	No access	No exit
11A	No access	No exit

M23	Northbound	Southbound
7	No exit to A23 southbound	No access from A23 northbound
10A	No exit	No access

M25	Clockwise	Anticlockwise
5	No exit to M26 eastbound	No access from M26 westbound
19	No access	No exit
21	No exit to M1 southbound. Access from M1 southbound only	No exit to M1 southbound. Access from M1 southbound only
31	No exit	No access

M27	Eastbound	Westbound
10	No exit	No access
12	No access	No exit

M40	Eastbound	Westbound
3	No exit	No access
7	No exit	No access
8	No exit	No access
13	No exit	No access
14	No access	No exit
16	No access	No exit

M42	Northbound	Southbound
1	No exit	No access
7	No access Exit to M6 northbound only	No exit. Access from M6 northbound only
7A	No access. Exit to M6 southbound only	No exit
8	No exit. Access from M6 southbound only	Exit to M6 northbound only. Access from M6 southbound only

M45	Eastbound	Westbound
M1 J17	Access to M1 southbound only	No access from M1 southbound
With A45	No access	No exit

M48	Eastbound	Westbound
M4 J21	No exit to M4 westbound	No access from M4 eastbound
M4 J23	No access from M4 westbound	No exit to M4 eastbound

M49	Southbound	Northbound
18A	No exit to M5 northbound	No access from M5 southbound

M53

	Northbound	Southbound
11	Exit to M56 eastbound only. Access from M56 westbound only	Exit to M56 eastbnd only. Access from M56 westbound only

M56

	Eastbound	Westbound
2	No exit	No access
3	No access	No exit
4	No exit	No access
7		No access
8	No exit or access	No access
9	No access from M6 northbound	No access to M6 southbound
15	No exit to M53	No access from M53 northbound

M57

	Northbound	Southbound
3	No exit	No access
5	No exit	No access

M58

	Eastbound	Westbound
1	No exit	No access

M60

	Clockwise	Anticlockwise
2	No exit	No access
3	No exit to A34 northbound	No exit to A34 northbound
4	No access from M56	No exit to M56
5	No exit to A5103 southbound	No exit to A5103 northbound
14	No exit	No access
16	No exit	No access
20	No access	No exit
22		No access
25	No access	
26		No exit or access
27	No exit	

M61

	Northbound	Southbound
2	No access from A580 eastbound	No exit to A580 westbound
3	No access from A580 eastbound. No access from A666 southbound	No exit to A580 westbound
M6 J30	No exit to M6 southbound	No access from M6 northbound

M62

	Eastbound	Westbound
23	No access	No exit

M65

	Eastbound	Westbound
9	No access	No exit
11	No exit	No access

M66

	Northbound	Southbound
1	No access	No exit

M67

	Eastbound	Westbound
1A	No access	No exit
2	No exit	No access

M69

	Northbound	Southbound
2	No exit	No access

M73

	Northbound	Southbound
2	No access from M8 eastbound	No exit to M8 westbound

M74

	Northbound	Southbound
3	No access	No exit
3A	No access	No access
7	No access	No access
9	No exit or access	No access
10		No exit
11	No exit	No access
12	No access	No exit

M77

	Northbound	Southbound
4	No exit	No access
6	No exit	No access
7	No exit	
8	No access	No access

M80

	Northbound	Southbound
4A	No access	No exit
6A	No access	No access
8	Exit to M876 northbound only. No access	Access from M876 southbound only. No exit

M90

	Northbound	Southbound
1	Access from A90 northbound only	No access. Exit to A90 southbound only
2A	No access	No exit
7	No exit	No access
8	No access	No exit
10	No access from A912	No exit to A912

M180

	Eastbound	Westbound
1	No access	No exit

M621

	Eastbound	Westbound
2A	No exit	No access
4	No exit	
5	No exit	No access
6	No access	No exit

M876

	Northbound	Southbound
2	No access	No exit

A1(M)

	Northbound	Southbound
2	No access	No exit
3		No access
5	No exit	No exit, no access
14	No exit	No access
40	No access	No exit
43	No exit. Access from M1 only	No access. Exit to M1 only
57	No access	No exit
65	No access	No exit

A3(M)

	Northbound	Southbound
1	No exit	No access
4	No access	No exit

A38(M) with Victoria Rd, (Park Circus) Birmingham

Northbound	No exit
Southbound	No access

A48(M)

	Northbound	Southbound
M4 Junc 29	Exit to M4 eastbound only	Access from M4 westbound only
29A	Access from A48 eastbound only	Exit to A48 westbound only

A57(M)

	Eastbound	Westbound
With A5103	No access	No exit
With A34	No access	No exit

A58(M)

	Southbound
With Park Lane and Westgate, Leeds	No access

A64(M)

	Eastbound	Westbound
With A58 Clay Pit Lane, Leeds	No access from A58	No exit to A58

A74(M)

	Northbound	Southbound
18	No access	No exit
22		No exit to A75

A194(M)

	Northbound	Southbound
A1(M) J65 Gateshead Western Bypass	Access from A1(M) northbound only	Exit to A1(M) southbound only

M3 Junctions 13, 14 · M27 Junction 4

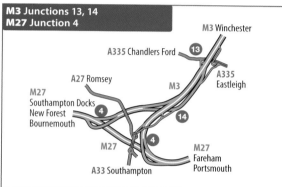

M6 Junctions 3A, 4A · M42 Junctions 7, 7A, 8, 9 · M6 Toll Junctions T1, T2

M6 Junction 20 · M56 Junction 9

M62 Junctions 32A, 33 · A1(M) Junctions 40, 41

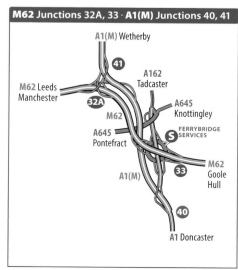

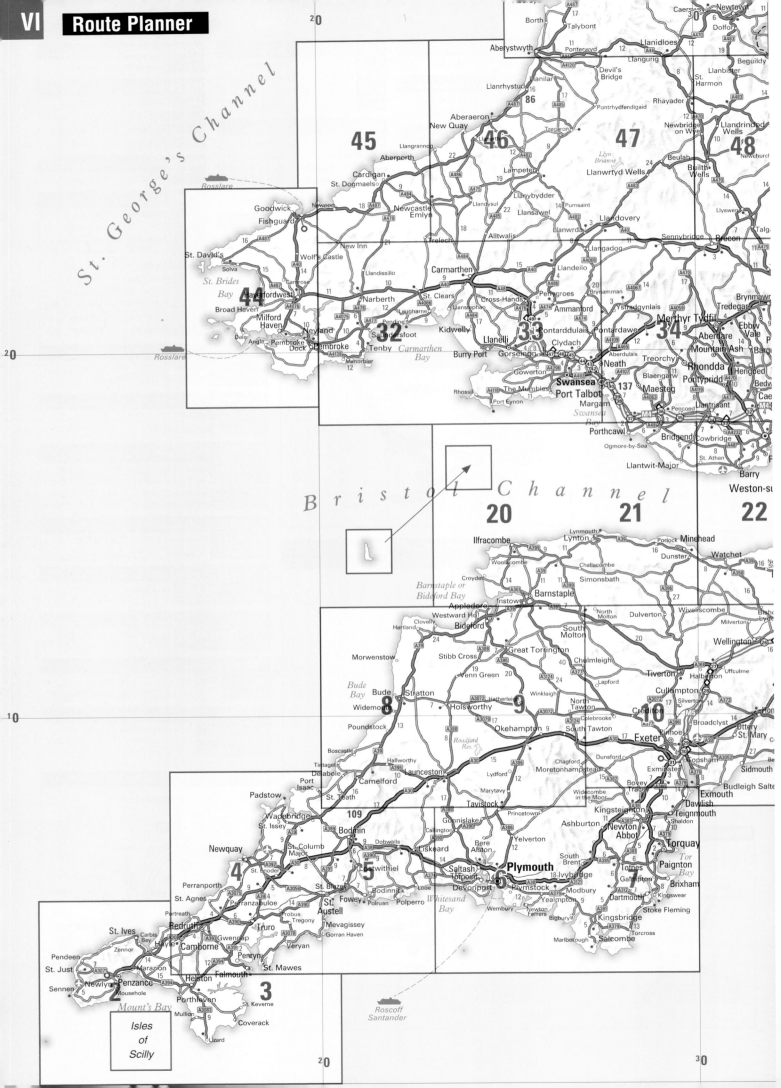

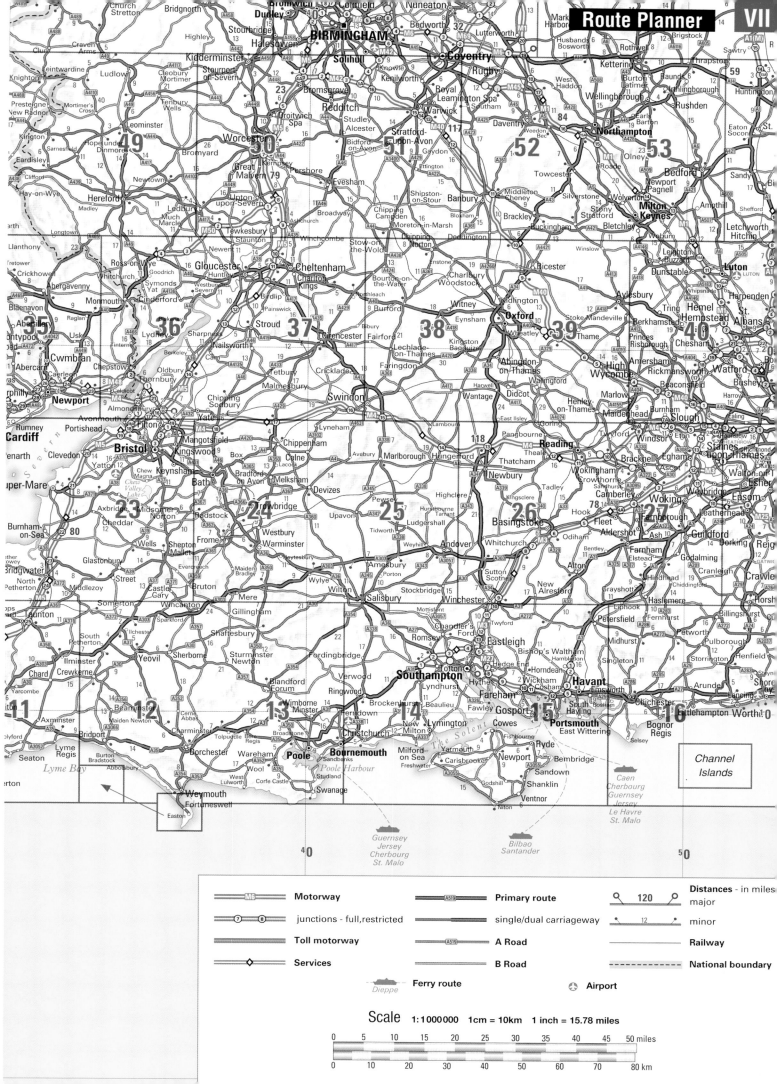

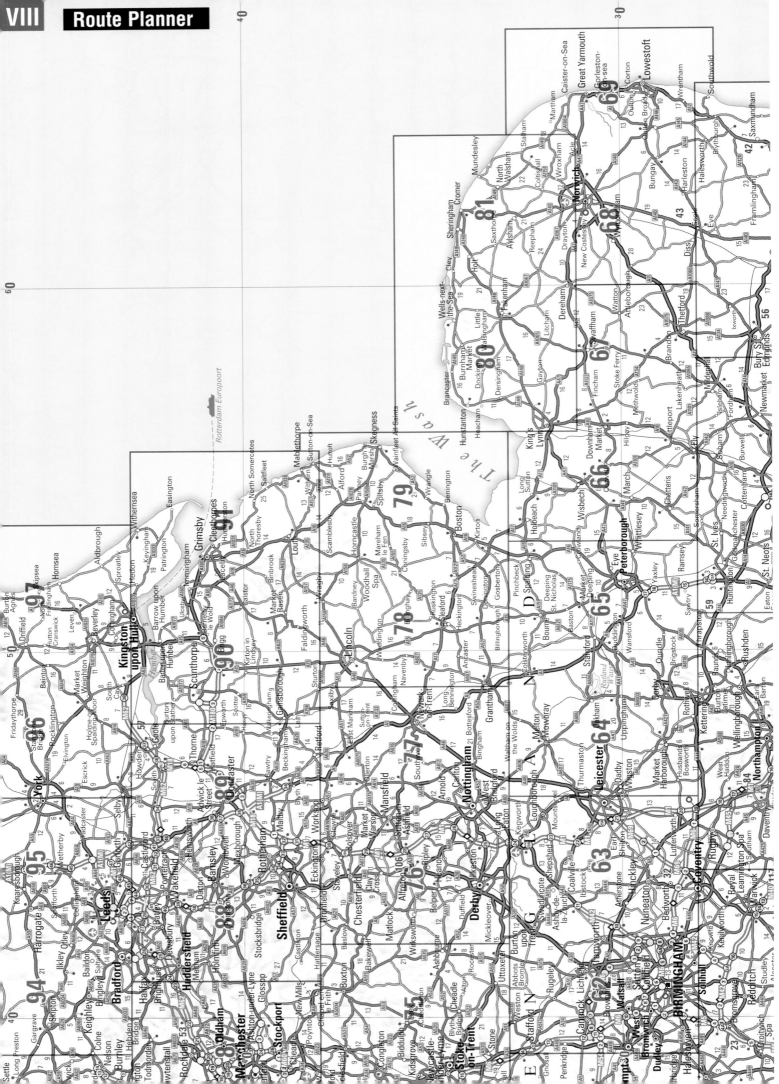

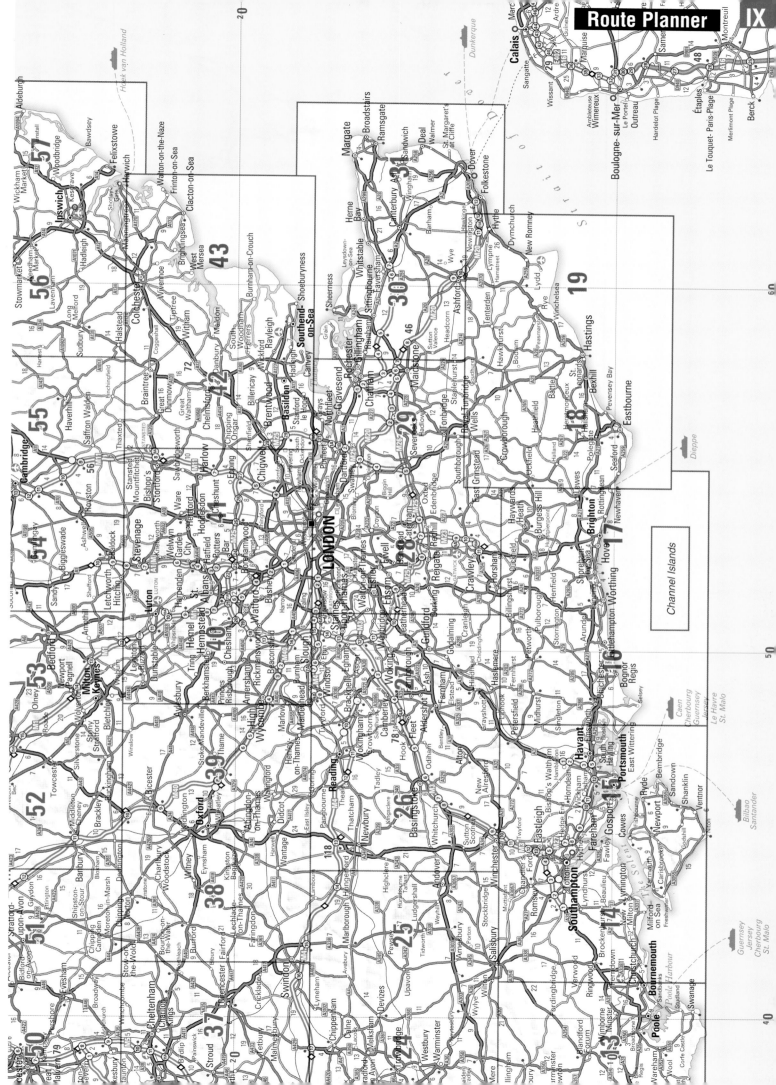

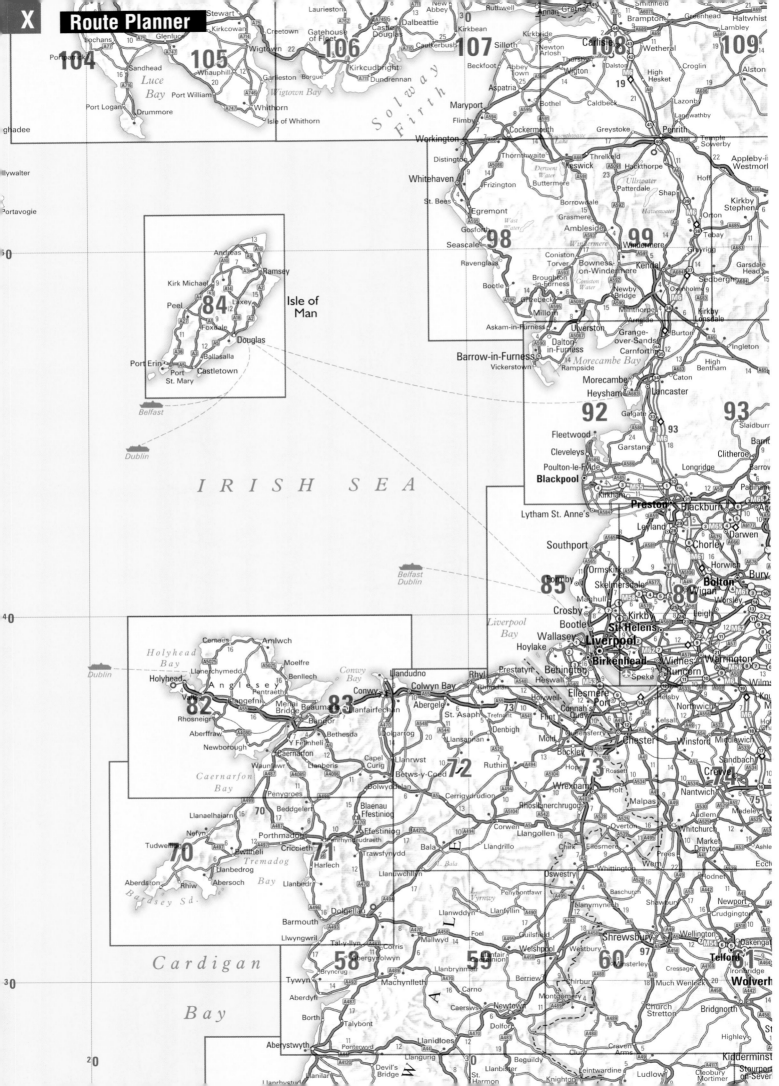

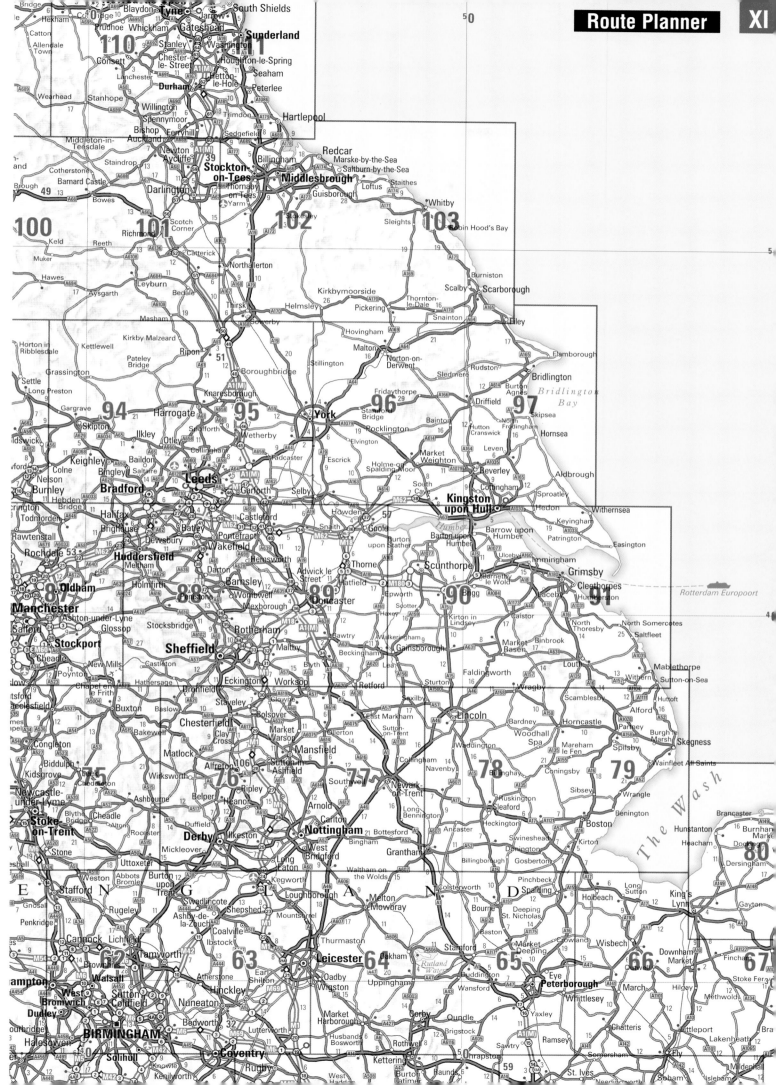

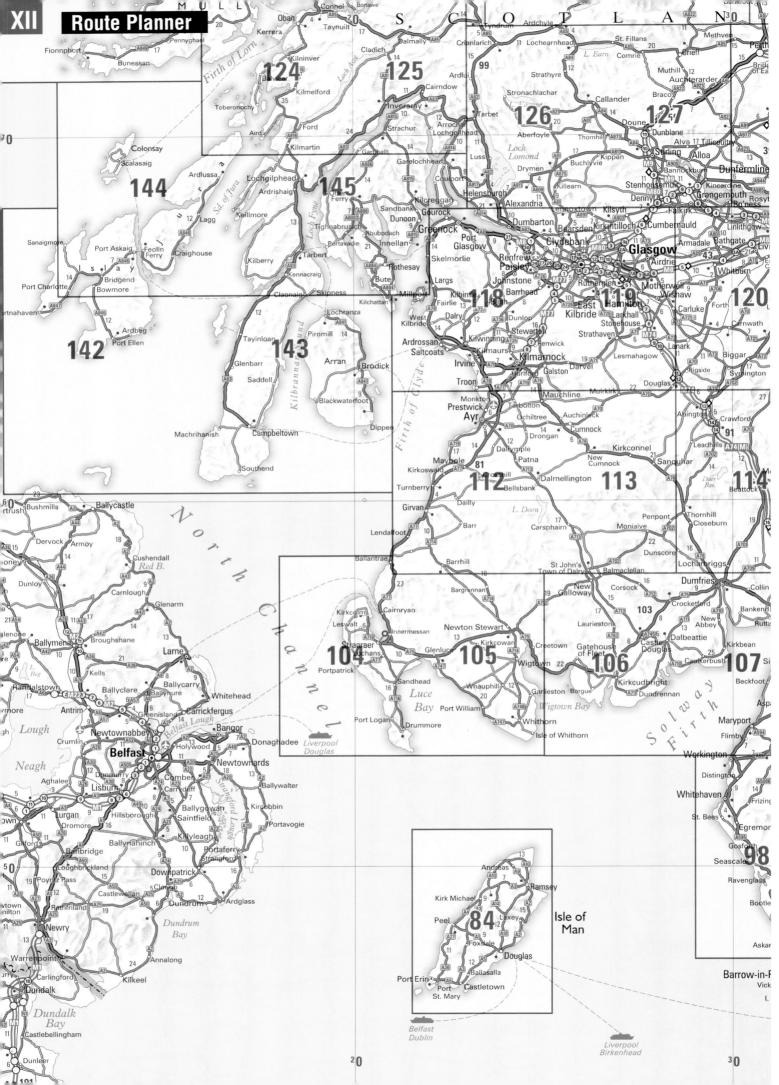

NORTH

SEA

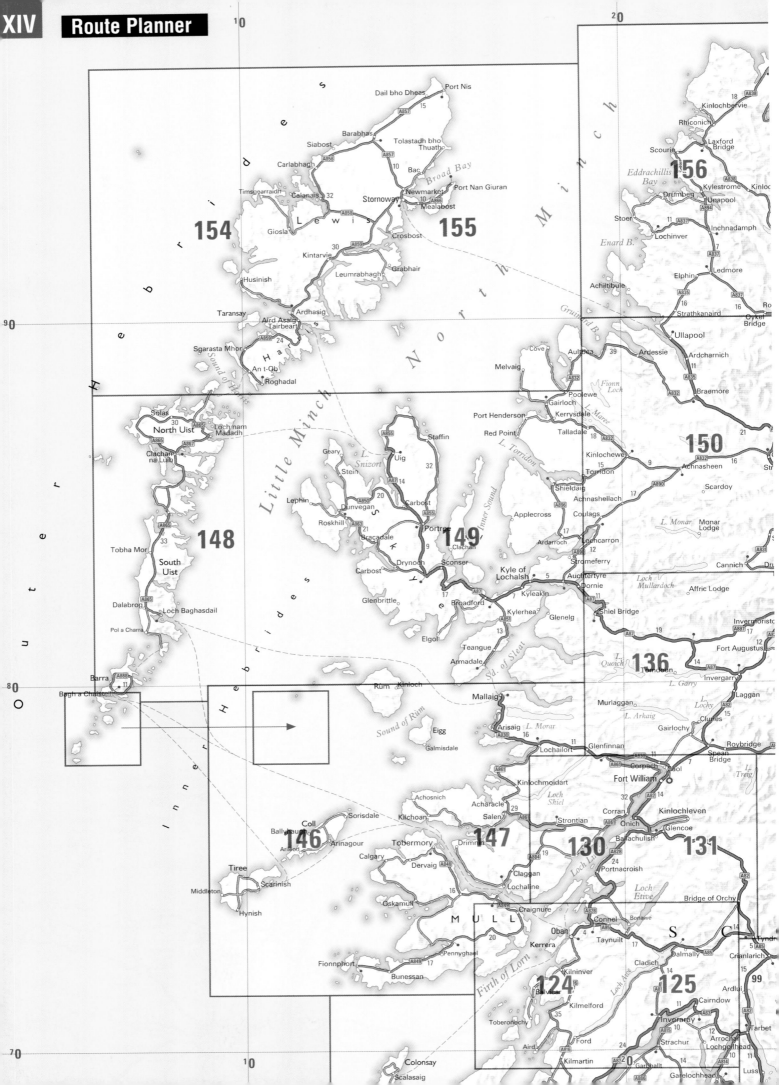

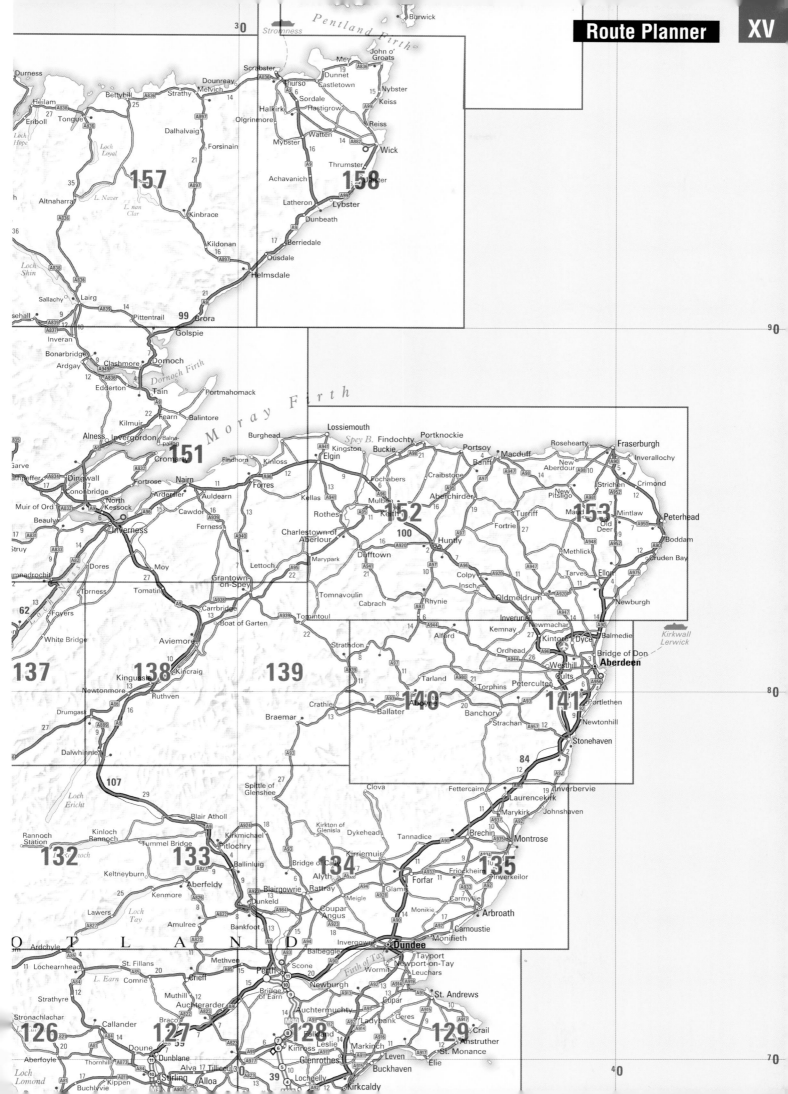

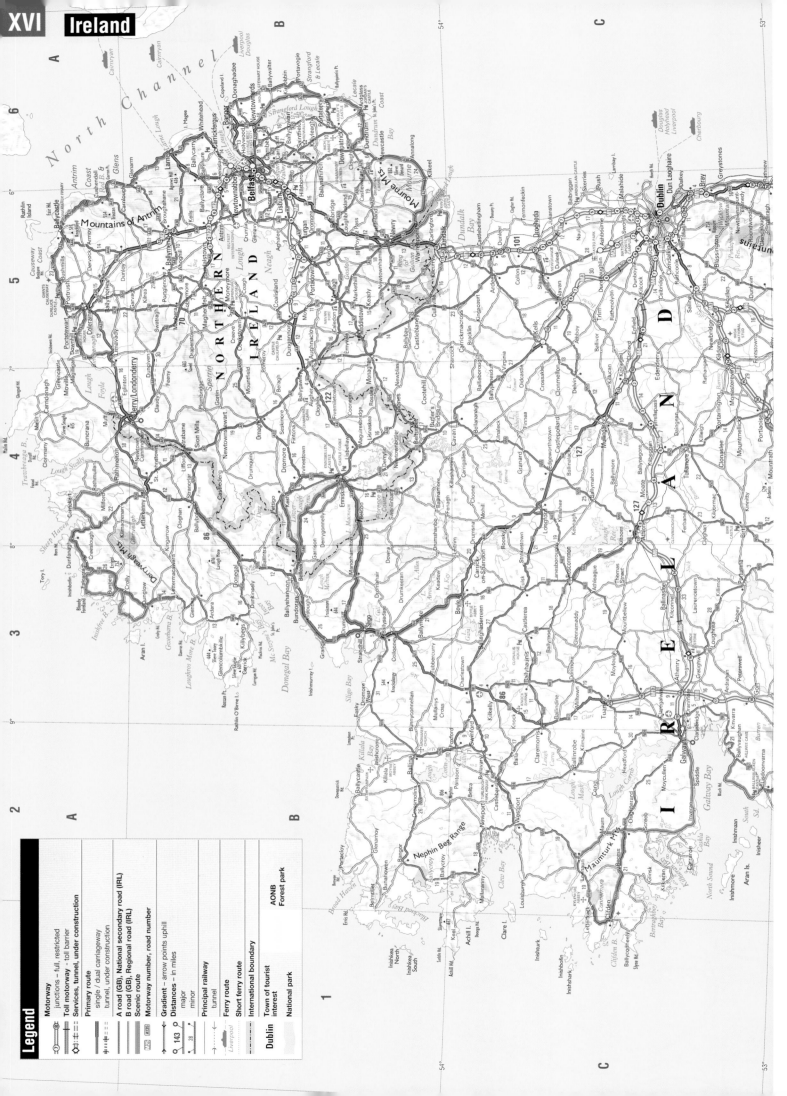

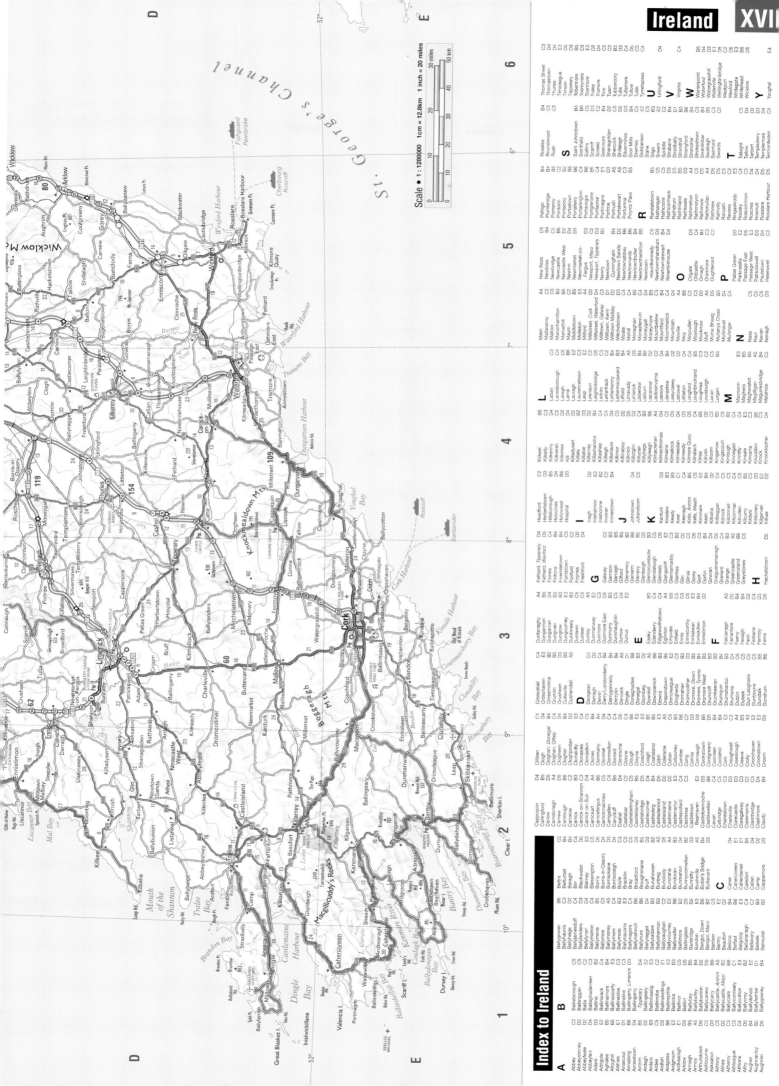

Tourism

- ▨ National Park
- ▨ Area of Outstanding Natural Beauty
- ▨ National Scenic Area
- ▨ Built-up area
- — Long distance footpath
- ● Town of tourist interest
- ◆ Other tourist attraction
- ○ Other town

Top Ireland Tourist Attractions

		Visitors in millions (2019)
1.	Guinness Storehouse, Dublin	1.7
2.	Cliffs of Moher Visitor Experience, Clare	1.6
3.	Dublin Zoo, Dublin	1.3
4.	The Book of Kells, Dublin	1.1
5.	Castletown House Parklands, Kildare	1.0
6.	Kilkenny Castle Parklands, Kilkenny	0.9
7.	National Gallery of Ireland, Dublin	0.8
8.	Glendalough Monument & Site, Wicklow	0.7
9.	Tayto Park, Meath	0.7
10.	National Botanic Gardens, Dublin	0.7

Top UK Tourist Attractions

		Visitors in millions (2019)
1.	British Museum, London	6.2
2.	Tate Modern, London	6.1
3.	National Gallery, London	6.0
4.	Natural History Museum, London	5.4
5.	Southbank Centre, London	4.4
6.	Victoria & Albert Museum, London	4.0
7.	Science Museum, London	3.3
8.	Tower of London	3.0
9.	Royal Museums, Greenwich	2.9
10.	Somerset House, London	2.8
11.	Royal Botanic Gardens, Kew	2.3
12.	National Museum of Scotland, Edinburgh	2.2
13.	Edinburgh Castle	2.2
14.	Chester Zoo	2.1
15.	Kelvingrove Art Gallery & Museum, Glasgow	1.8
16.	Tate Britain, London	1.8
17.	Royal Albert Hall, London	1.7
18.	St Paul's Cathedral, London	1.7
19.	National Portrait Gallery, London	1.6
20.	Stonehenge, Wiltshire	1.6

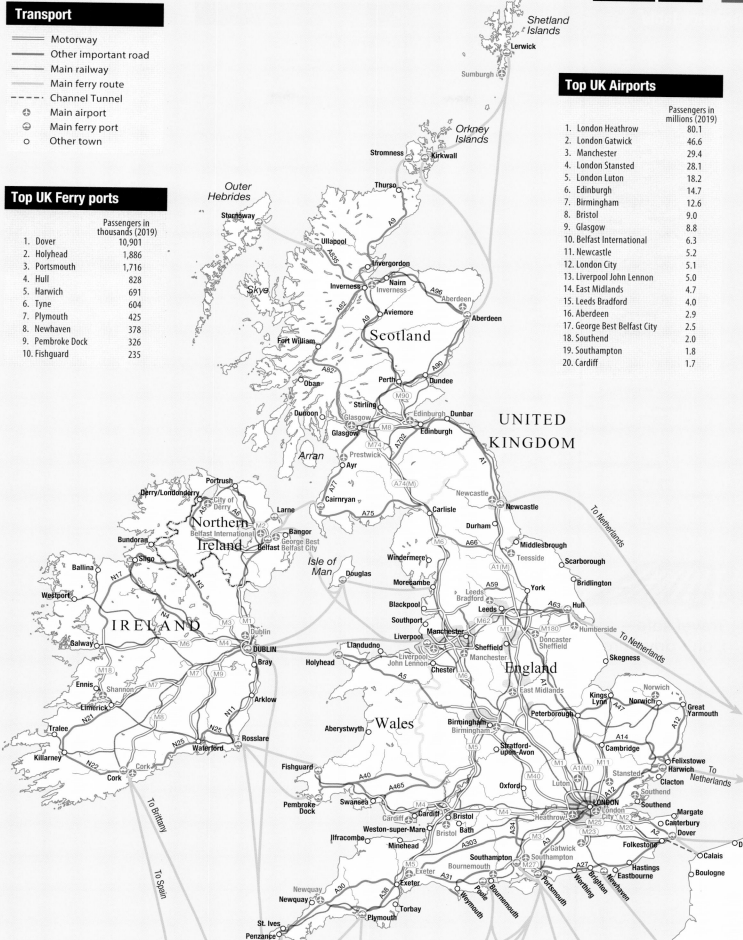

Transport

═══	Motorway
───	Other important road
───	Main railway
───	Main ferry route
- - -	Channel Tunnel
✈	Main airport
⛴	Main ferry port
○	Other town

Top UK Ferry ports

		Passengers in thousands (2019)
1.	Dover	10,901
2.	Holyhead	1,886
3.	Portsmouth	1,716
4.	Hull	828
5.	Harwich	691
6.	Tyne	604
7.	Plymouth	425
8.	Newhaven	378
9.	Pembroke Dock	326
10.	Fishguard	235

Top UK Airports

		Passengers in millions (2019)
1.	London Heathrow	80.1
2.	London Gatwick	46.6
3.	Manchester	29.4
4.	London Stansted	28.1
5.	London Luton	18.2
6.	Edinburgh	14.7
7.	Birmingham	12.6
8.	Bristol	9.0
9.	Glasgow	8.8
10.	Belfast International	6.3
11.	Newcastle	5.2
12.	London City	5.1
13.	Liverpool John Lennon	5.0
14.	East Midlands	4.7
15.	Leeds Bradford	4.0
16.	Aberdeen	2.9
17.	George Best Belfast City	2.5
18.	Southend	2.0
19.	Southampton	1.8
20.	Cardiff	1.7

COPYRIGHT PHILIP'S

Distance table

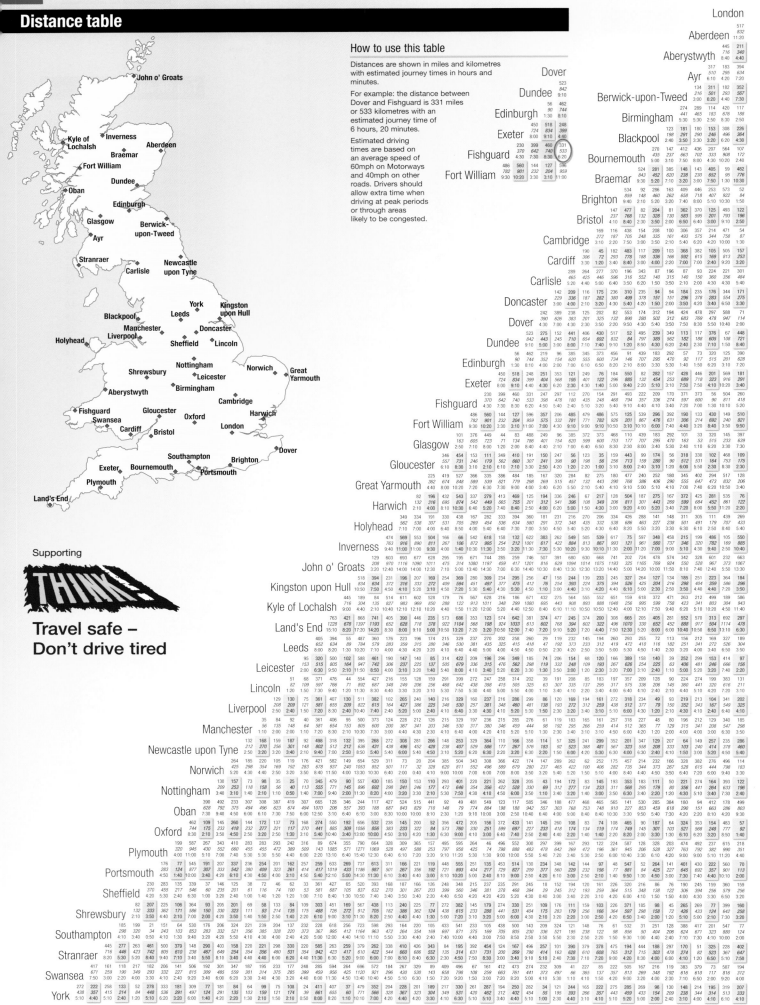

How to use this table

Distances are shown in miles and kilometres with estimated journey times in hours and minutes.

For example: the distance between Dover and Fishguard is 331 miles or 533 kilometres with an estimated journey time of 6 hours, 20 minutes.

Estimated driving times are based on an average speed of 60mph on Motorways and 40mph on other roads. Drivers should allow extra time when driving at peak periods or through areas likely to be congested.

Supporting

THINK!

Travel safe –
Don't drive tired

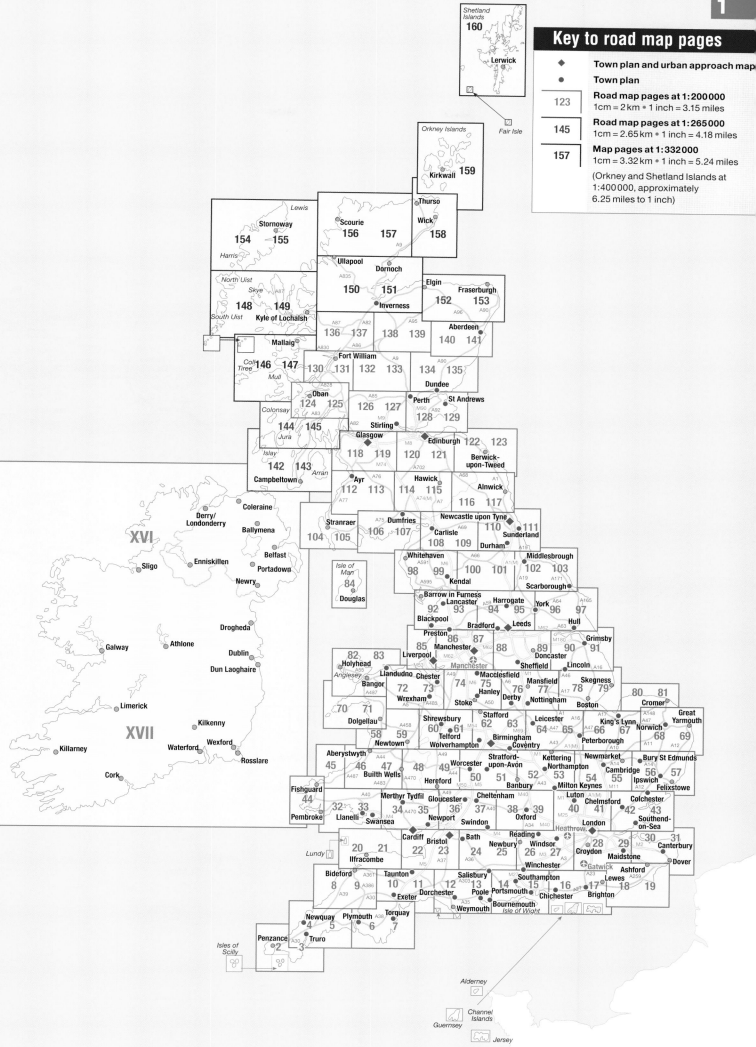

Key to road map pages

◆	Town plan and urban approach map
●	Town plan
123	**Road map pages at 1:200 000** 1 cm = 2 km • 1 inch = 3.15 miles
145	**Road map pages at 1:265 000** 1 cm = 2.65 km • 1 inch = 4.18 miles
157	**Map pages at 1:332 000** 1 cm = 3.32 km • 1 inch = 5.24 miles

(Orkney and Shetland Islands at 1:400 000, approximately 6.25 miles to 1 inch)

Shetland Islands **160** Lerwick

Fair Isle

Orkney Islands **159** Kirkwall

Thurso
Wick **158**

Lewis
Stornoway **154 155**
Harris

Scourie **156 157**
A9

North Uist
Skye A87 **150 151** Ullapool Dornoch
South Uist **148 149** Kyle of Lochalsh
A835 Inverness

Elgin Fraserburgh **152 153**
A96 A90

Coll Tiree **146 147** Mallaig Fort William **130 131 132 133 134 135**
A830 A86 A87 A82 A9 A90
136 137 138 139
A95
Aberdeen **140 141**

Mull
Oban **124 125 126 127** Perth St Andrews
A828 A85 Dundee
Colonsay **144 145** Stirling **128 129**
Jura A83 A82 M9
Islay **142 143** Glasgow Edinburgh **122 123**
Arran **118 119 120 121** Berwick-upon-Tweed
Campbeltown M74 A702

Ayr Hawick **114 115 116 117** Alnwick
112 113 A74(M) A7
A77 A76 A68

Stranraer Dumfries Newcastle upon Tyne **110 111** Sunderland
104 105 106 107 Carlisle **108 109** Durham
A75 A69 A19

Whitehaven **98 99** Kendal **100 101 102 103** Middlesbrough
A591 M6 A66 A1(M) A19 A171 Scarborough
A595 Barrow in Furness Lancaster **92 93 94 95 96 97** A165
Blackpool Harrogate York A64
Preston **86 87 88 89 90 91** Grimsby
Manchester Bradford Leeds A63 Hull
85 M62 M180
Liverpool Manchester Sheffield Doncaster Lincoln
M53 A49 Macclesfield M1 A46 Skegness
Holyhead **82 83** Llandudno Chester **74 75 76 77 78 79**
Anglesey Bangor A55 Hanley Derby Mansfield Boston
A487 Wrexham **72 73** Stoke A50 Nottingham A17
70 71 A5 A483 Leicester A16 Cromer **80 81**
Dolgellau Shrewsbury Stafford **62 63 64 65 66 67** Great Yarmouth
58 59 60 61 Telford M54 King's Lynn Norwich **68 69**
Newtown Wolverhampton Birmingham Peterborough A11 A12
Aberystwyth **45 46 47 48 49** Worcester Coventry A43 Bury St Edmunds
A44 Stratford-upon-Avon Kettering Newmarket A14
Builth Wells Hereford **50 51 52 53 54 55** Ipswich **56 57**
A487 A470 Northampton Cambridge Felixstowe
Fishguard **44** Merthyr Tydfil Gloucester Banbury Milton Keynes Colchester
Pembroke A40 **34 35 36 37 38 39** Luton Chelmsford **42 43**
32 33 Cheltenham M40 **40 41** Southend-on-Sea
Llanelli Newport Oxford M25 London
Swansea Swindon Reading Heathrow **30 31**
20 21 Cardiff Bristol **22 23 24 25 26 27 28 29** Canterbury
Ilfracombe Bath Newbury Windsor Croydon Maidstone Dover
Lundy Bideford A37 A36 Winchester Gatwick Ashford
8 9 10 11 12 13 14 15 16 17 18 19
Taunton Salisbury Southampton Lewes Brighton
Dorchester Poole Portsmouth Chichester
Exeter A30 A35 Bournemouth Isle of Wight
Newquay Plymouth Torquay Weymouth
4 5 6 7
Penzance Truro
2 3
Isles of Scilly

Isle of Man **84** Douglas

XVI
Derry/Londonderry Coleraine
Ballymena
Sligo Enniskillen Belfast Portadown
Newry

XVII
Galway Athlone Drogheda
Dublin Dun Laoghaire
Limerick
Kilkenny
Killarney Wexford
Waterford Rosslare
Cork

Alderney
Channel Islands
Guernsey Jersey

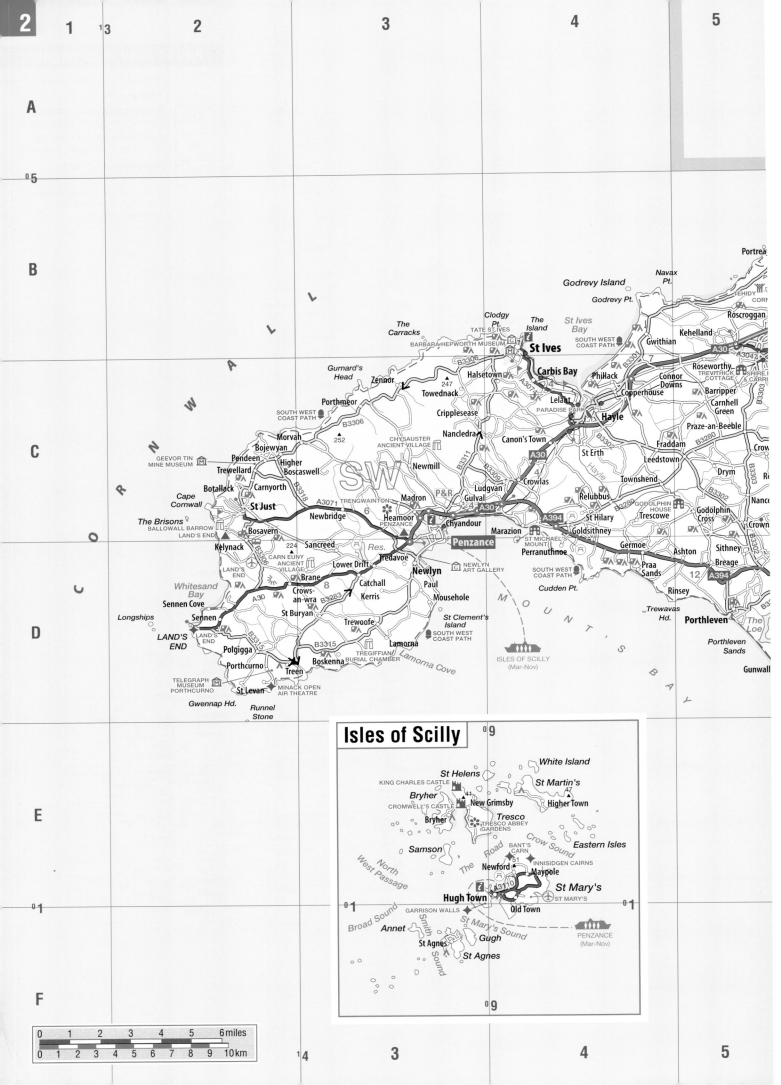

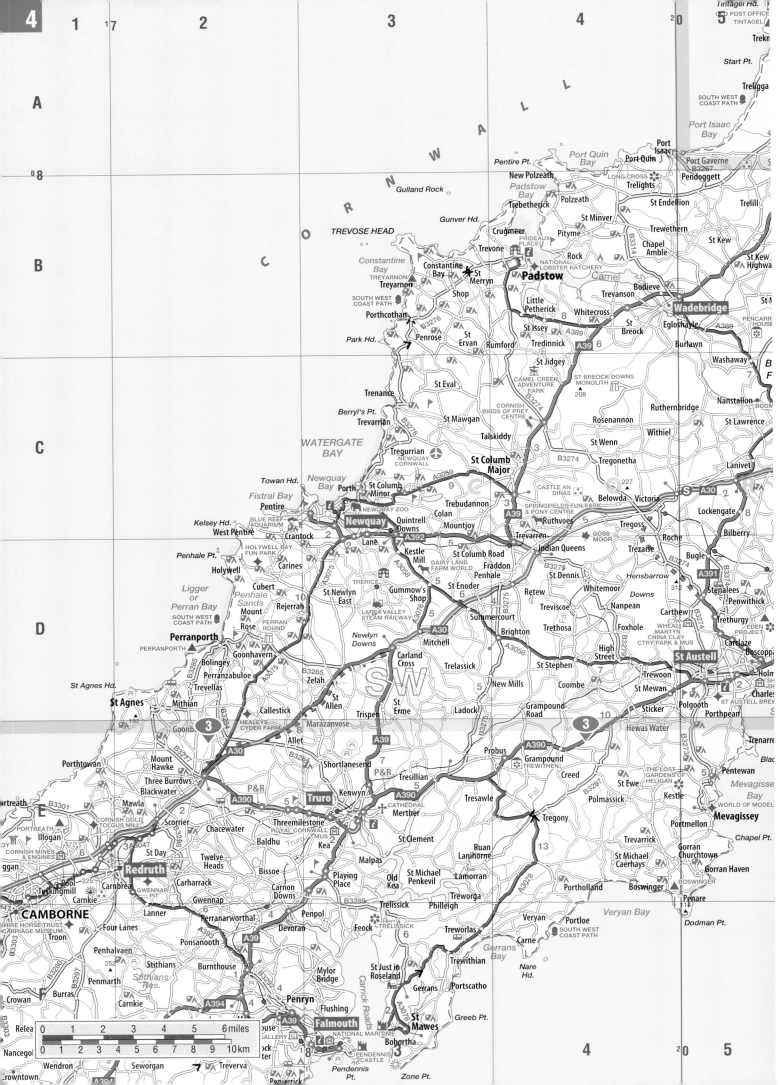

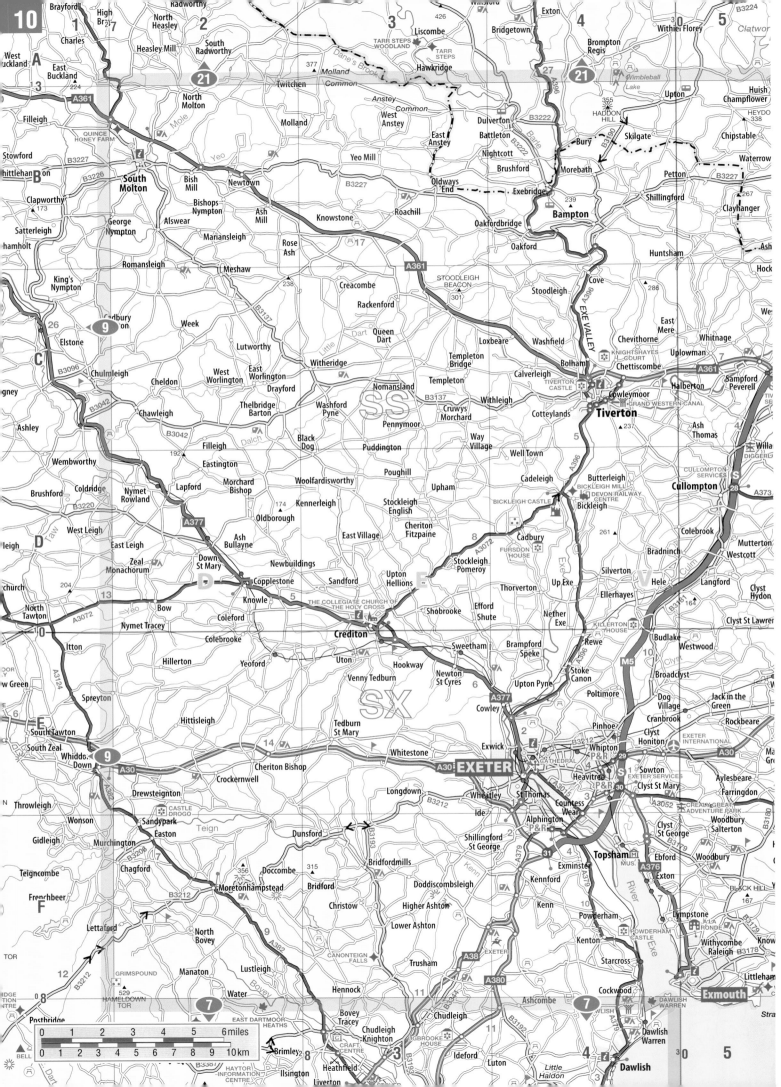

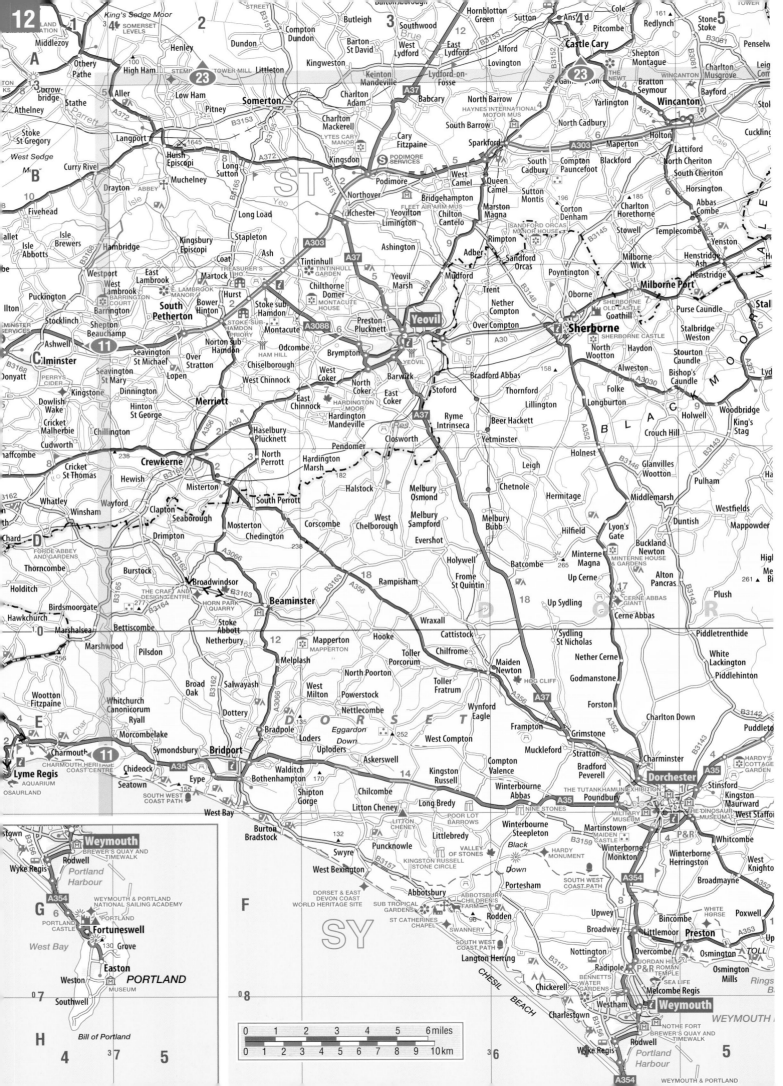

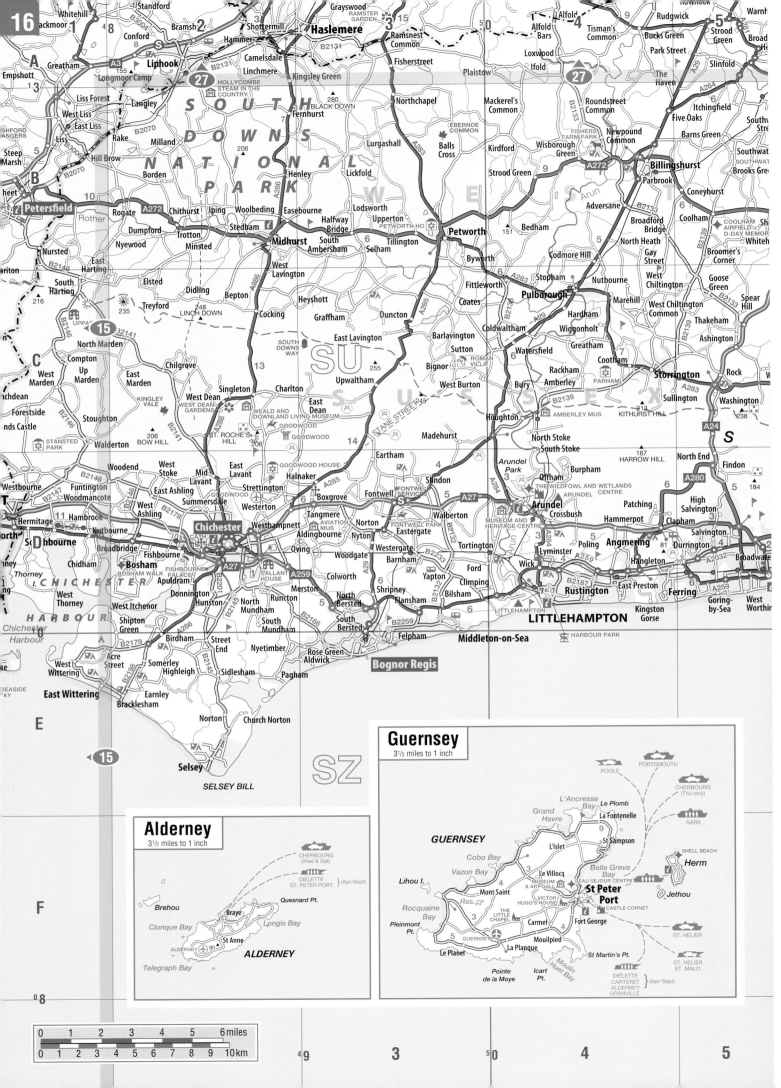

Smarden
Bell 5
Maltman's Hill 6 Great
Chart
HEADCORN
Thorne
GODINTON
HOUSE
CONNINGBROOK
LAK. 7
Elham
Smarden
Haffenden
Quarter
Wissenden
Ashford
Willesborough
Hinxhill
Willesborough Lees
Brabourne
Lymbridge
Green
Rhodes
Minnis
Ottinge
Swingfield
Minnis
Densole
Lashenden
Standen
Bethers 30
Sevington
Kingsnorth
Mersham
Smeeth
Sellindge
Brabourne Lees
KENT BATTLE
OF BRITAIN MUSEUM
Paddlesworth
Hawkinge
Capel le
Ferne
Biddenden
Stubbs
Cross
Cheeseman's
Green
Aldington
Frith
Clap Hill
Sellindge
Lees
Sellindge
Stanford
Beachborough
Postling
Etchinghill
CHANNEL
TUNNEL
Folkes
Tenterden
BIDDENDEN
VINEYARD
St Michael's
KENT & EAST
SUSSEX RAILWAY
13
Shadoxhurst
Henghurst
Shirkoak
Woodchurch
Orlestone
Bromley
Green
Aldington
Bonnington
Court-at-Street
Lympne
PORT LYMPNE
WILD ANIMAL PARK
AND GARDENS
Newingreen
Newington
Pedlinge
Cheriton
ELHAM VALLEY
RLY MUS
Saltwood
Sandgate
CLIFF LIFT
Leigh
Green
COLONEL
STEPHENS
RAILWAY MUSEUM
High Halden
Reading
Street
Kenardington
Warehorne
HAM STREET
WOODS
Ruckinge
Hamstreet
Bilsington
West Hythe
BROCKHILL
Palmarsh
Hythe
Small
Hythe
SMALLHYTHE PLACE
Appledore
Heath
HORNE'S PLACE CHAPEL
Snave
Newchurch
Burmarsh
A259
ROMNEY, HYTHE AND
DYMCHURCH RAILWAY
ISLE OF OXNEY
Appledore
Stone
Snargate
Brenzett
ROMNEY MARSH
St Mary
in the Marsh
AERONAUTICAL
MUSEUM
Ivychurch
ROMNEY WARREN
ROMNEY MARSH
VISITOR CENTRE
Dymchurch
MARTELLO TOWER
St Mary's Bay
Peening Quarter
Wittersham
Ham
Green
The
Stocks
Brookland
Old Romney
New
Romney
Littlestone on Sea
Romney
Sands
Greatstone on Sea
ROTHER LEVELS
FARM WORLD
Four Oaks
9
Iden
Houghton
Green
A259
Walland Marsh
Lydd
LYDD
(LONDON
ASHFORD)
Lydd on Sea
Peasmarsh
Rye
Foreign
Playden
East Guldeford
Rye
RYE HERITAGE CENTRE
Camber
CAMBER CASTLE
Denge
Marsh
LYDD INTERNATIONAL
RACEWAY
DUNGENESS
Denge Beach
DUNGENESS
Winchelsea
WINCHELSEA
COURT HALL
MUSEUM
Rye Harbour
Winchelsea
Beach
Rye Bay
DUNGENESS
POWER STATION
& INFORMATION CENTRE
THE OLD LIGHTHOUSE
Icklesham
Pett
Guestling
Green
Cliff End
Fairlight
Fairlight Cove
HASTINGS
CAVES

ENGLISH CHANNEL

TR

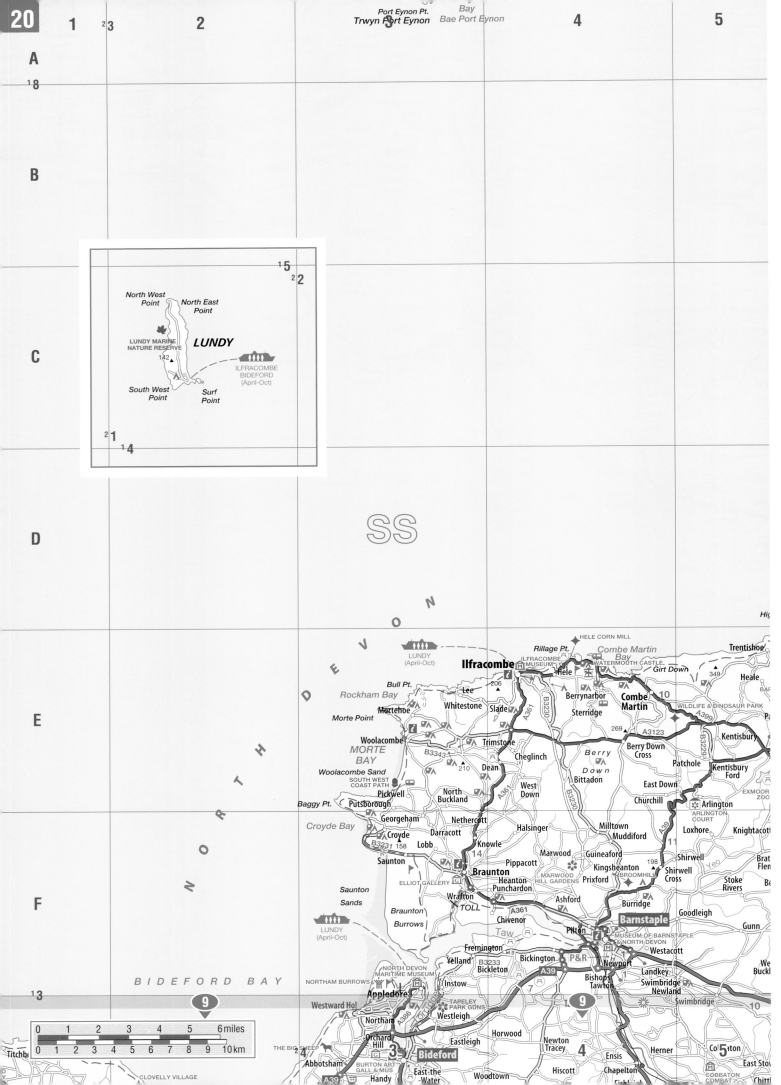

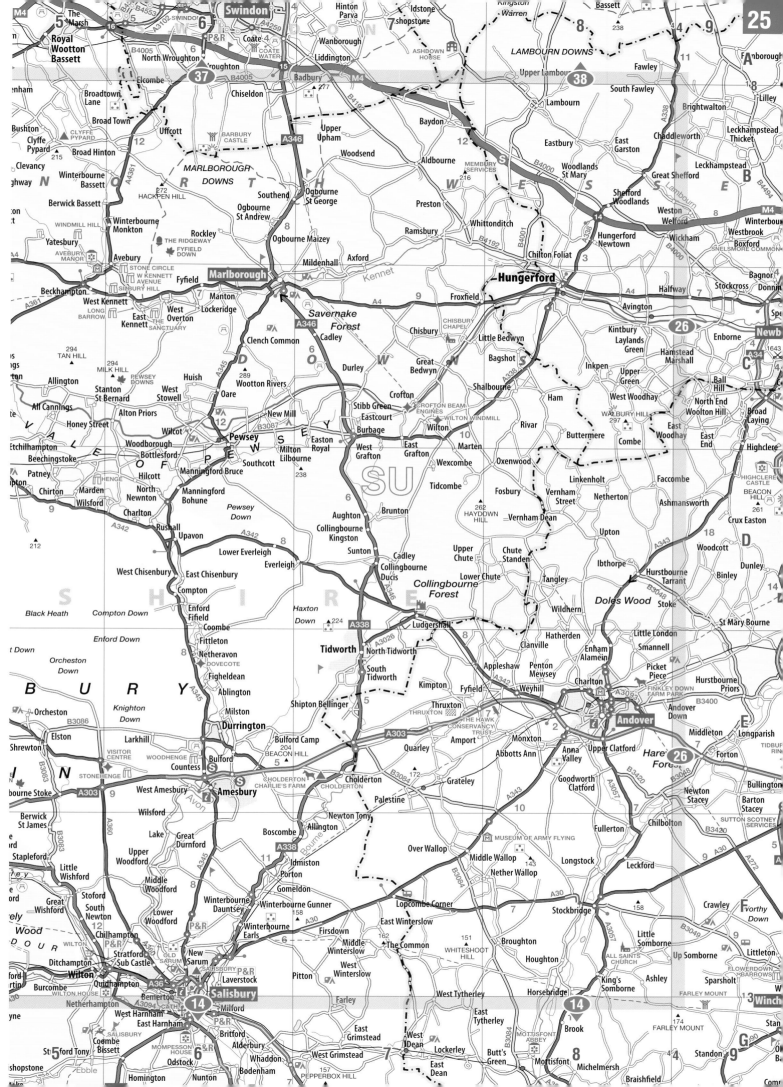

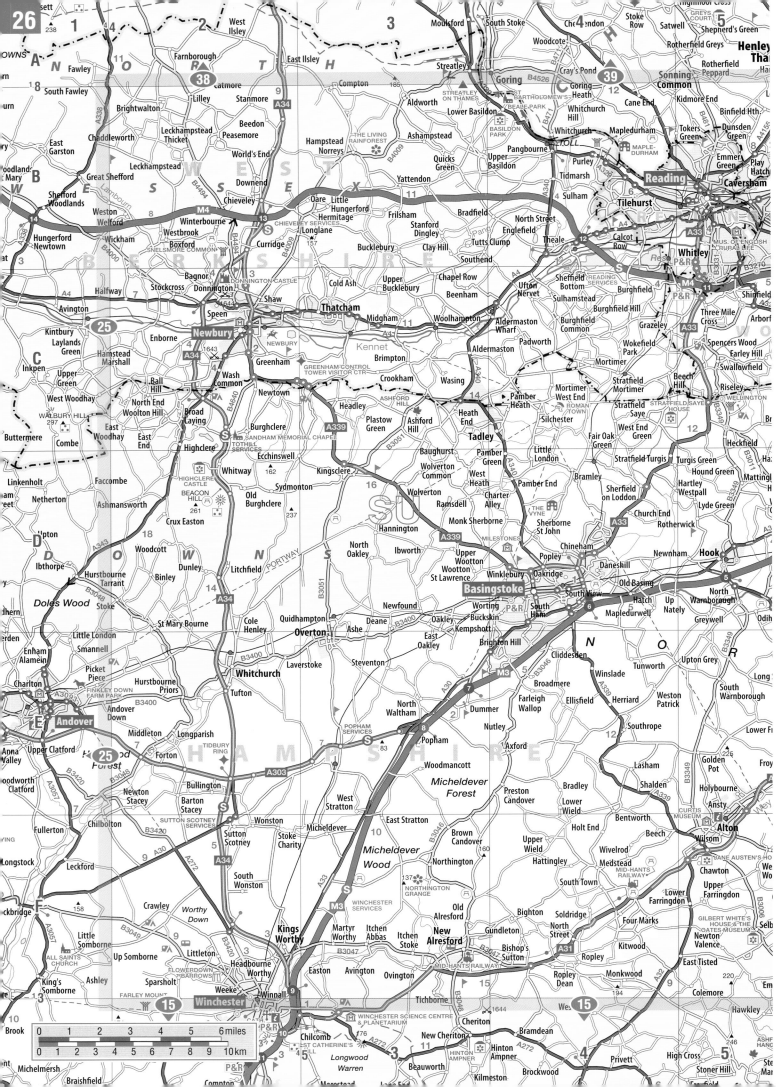

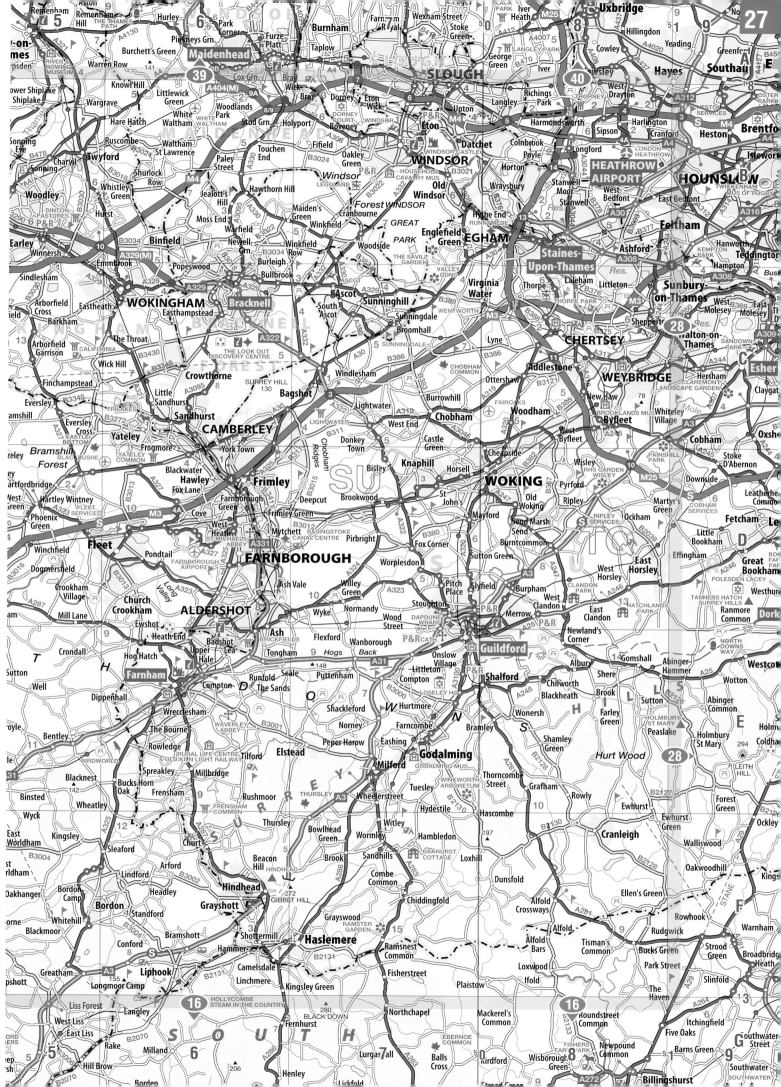

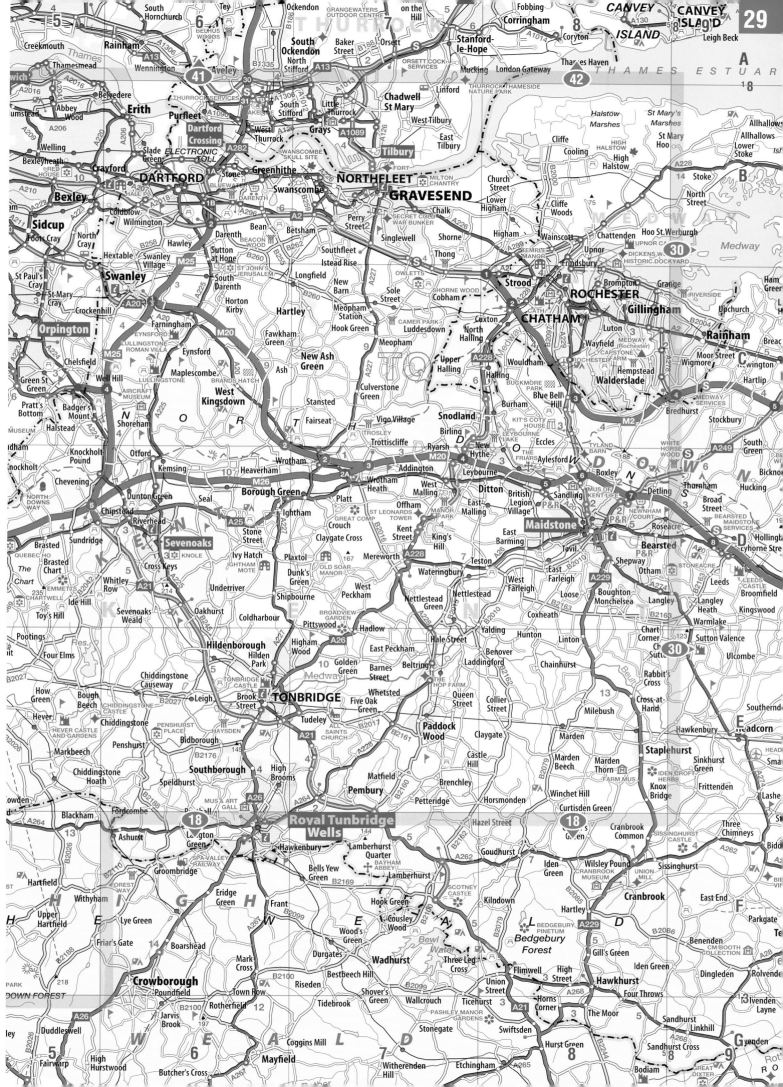

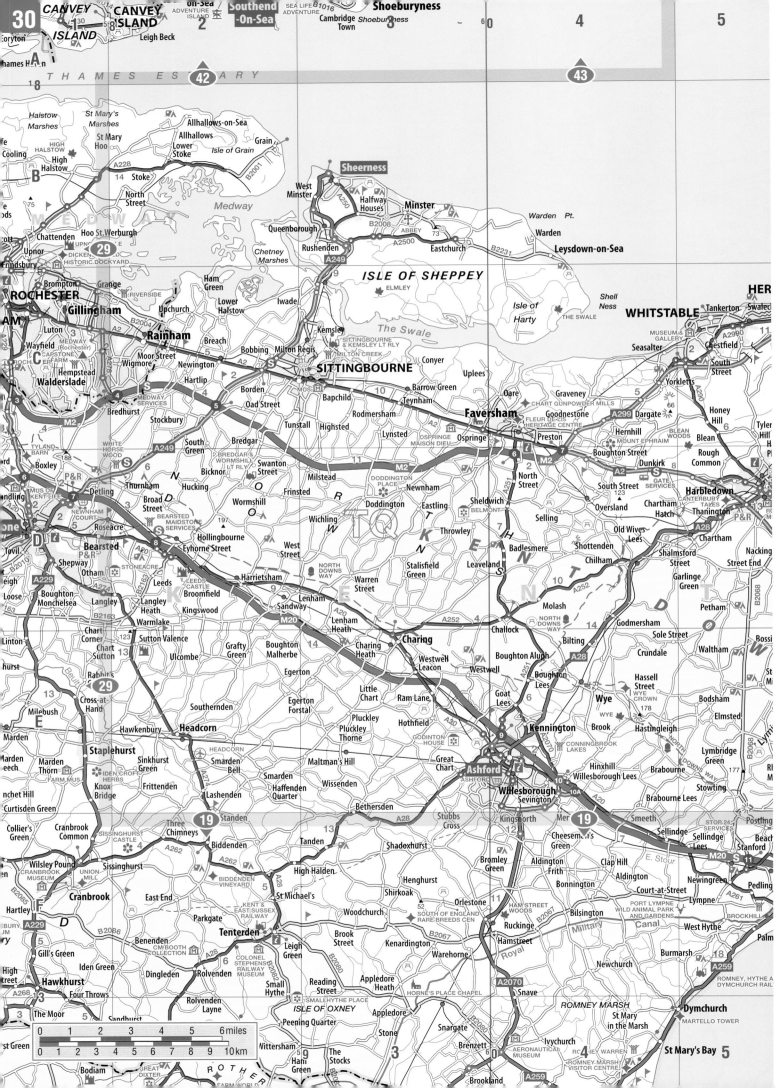

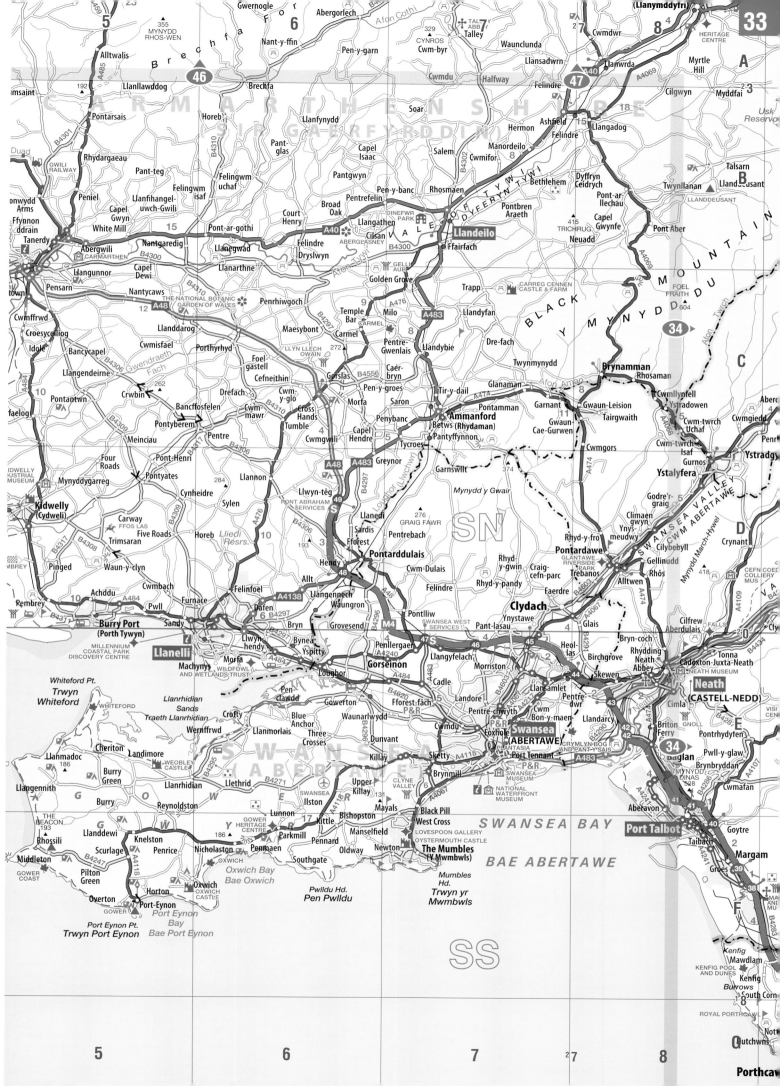

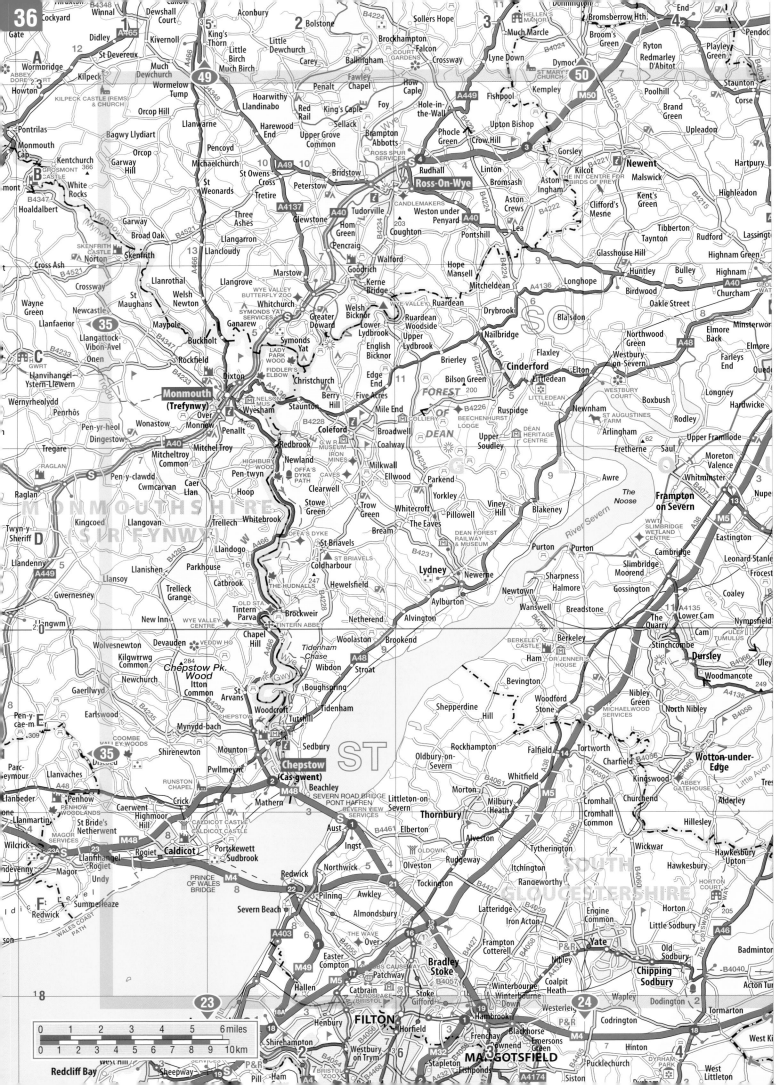

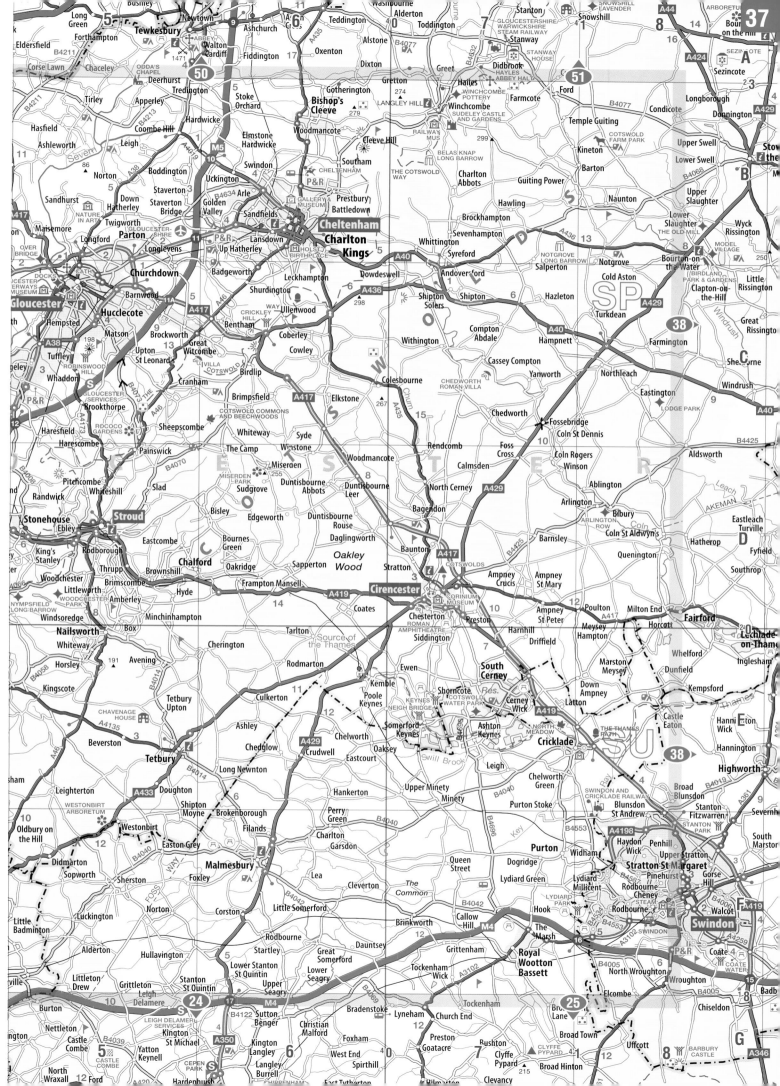

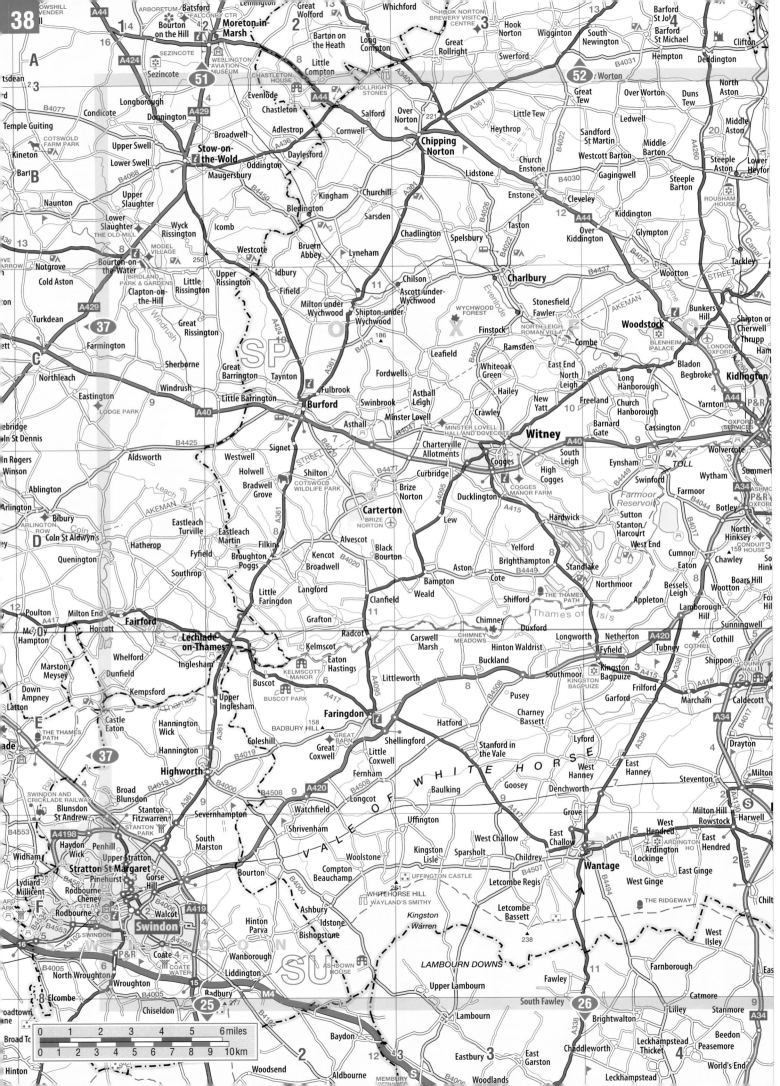

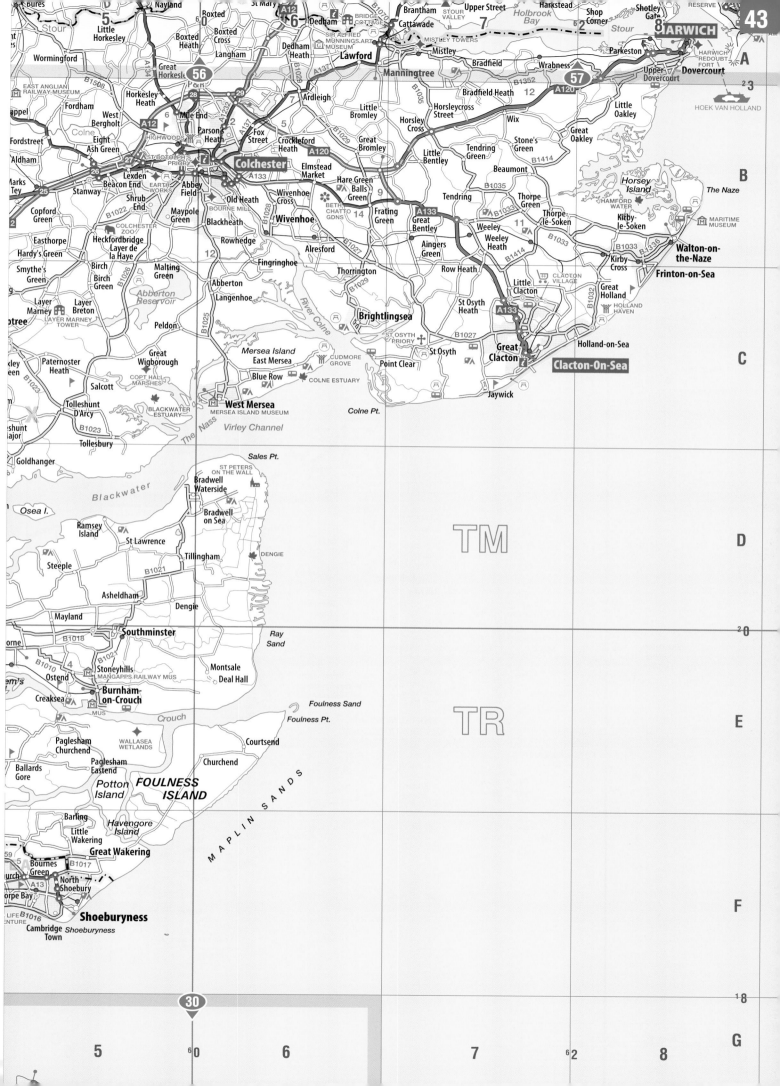

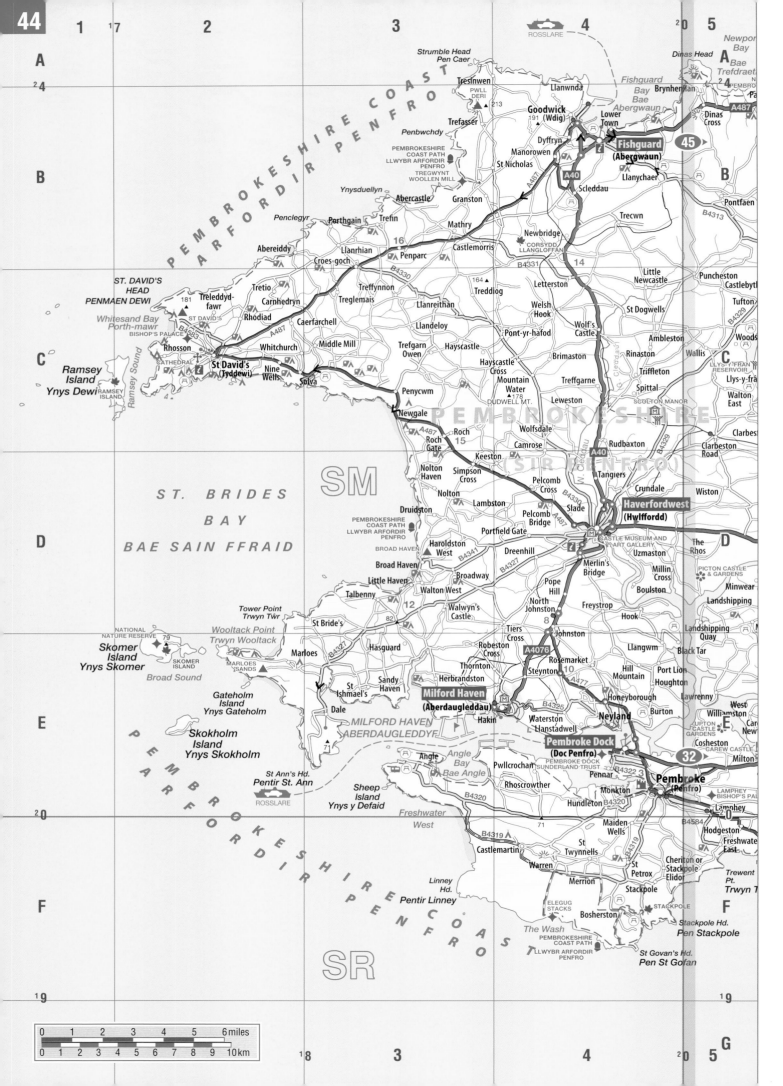

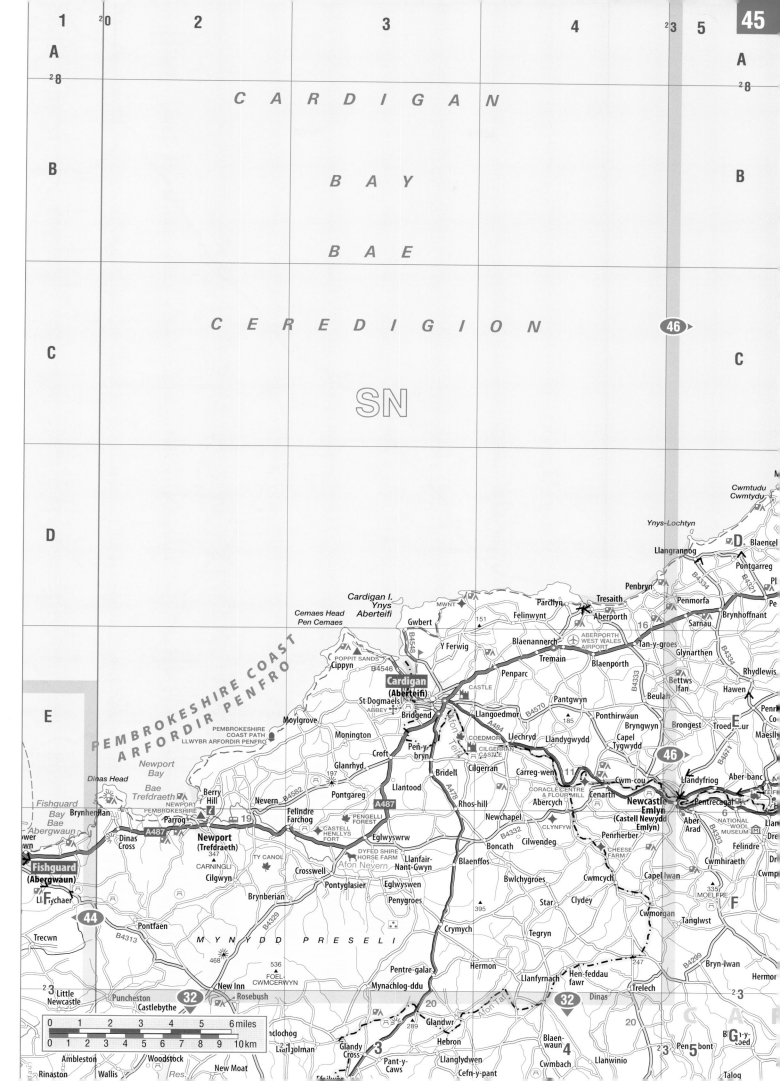

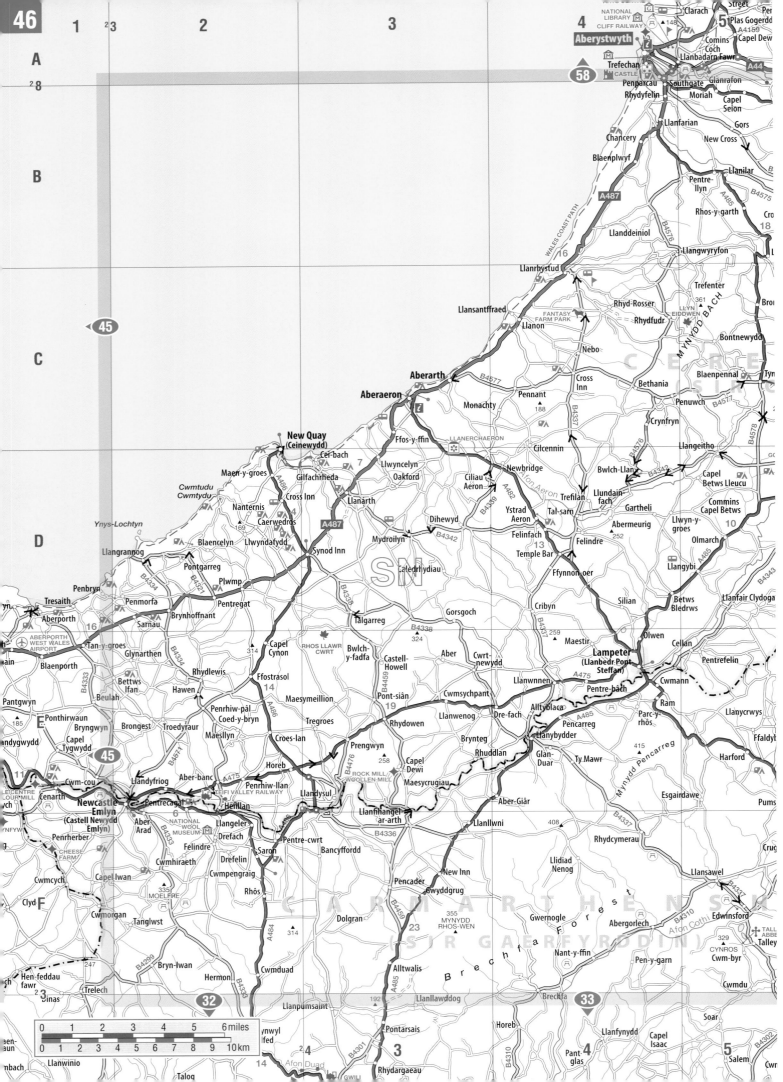

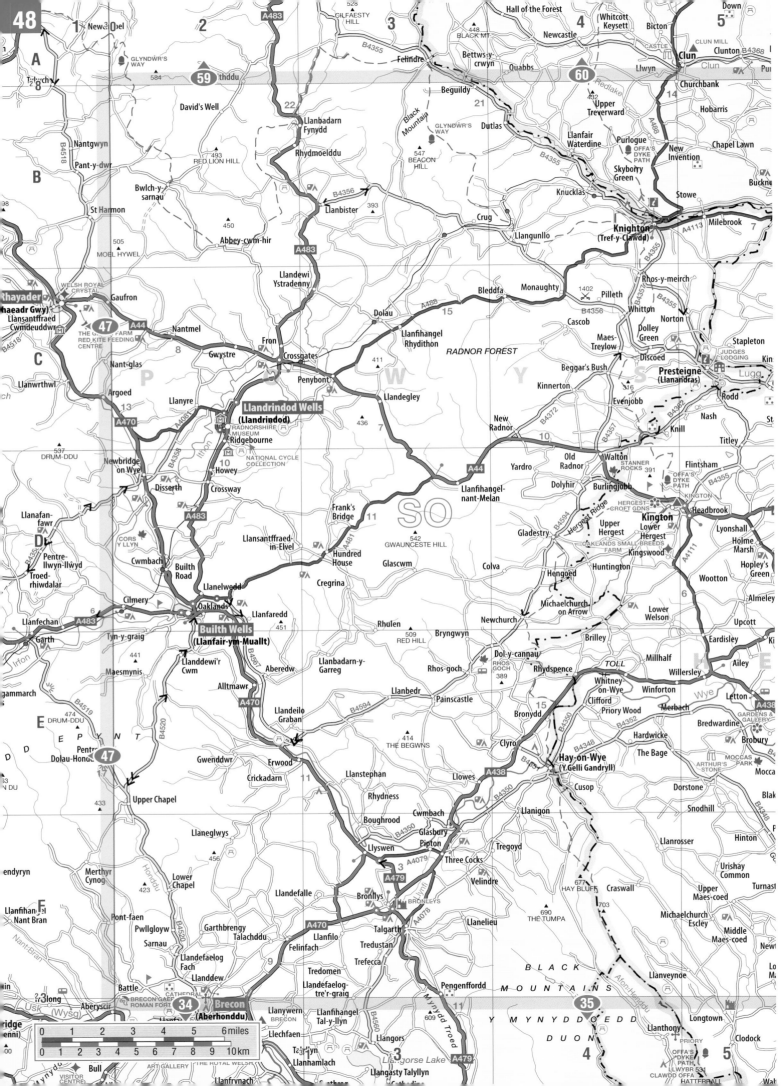

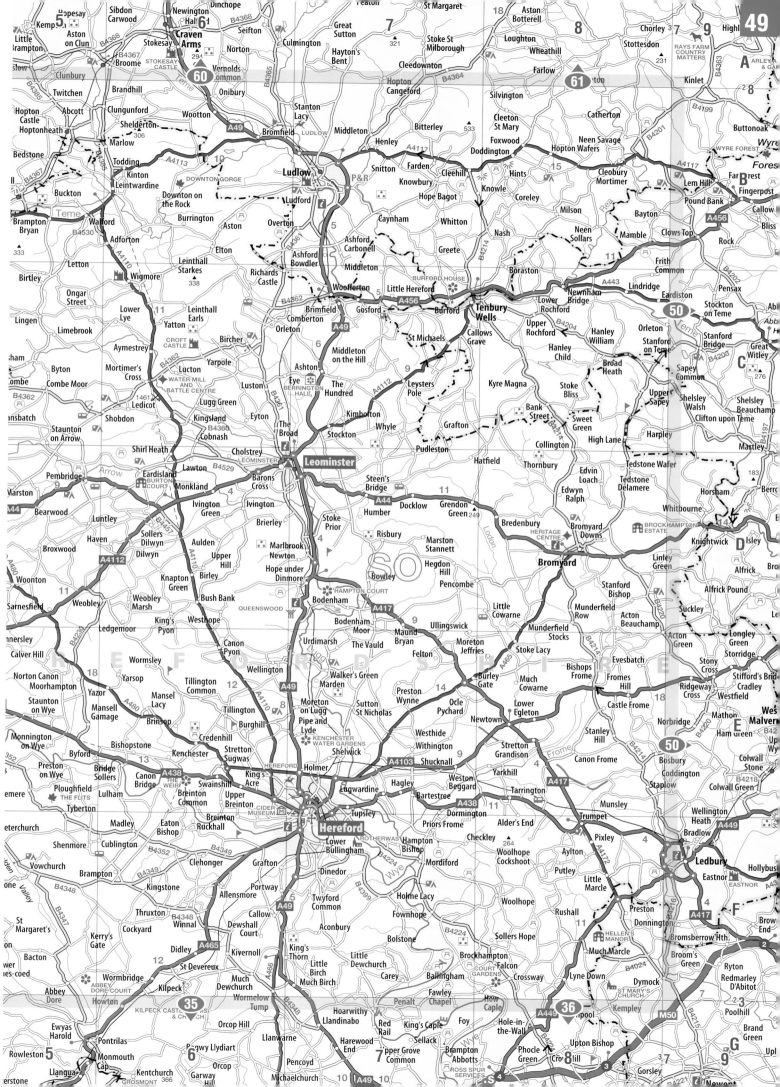

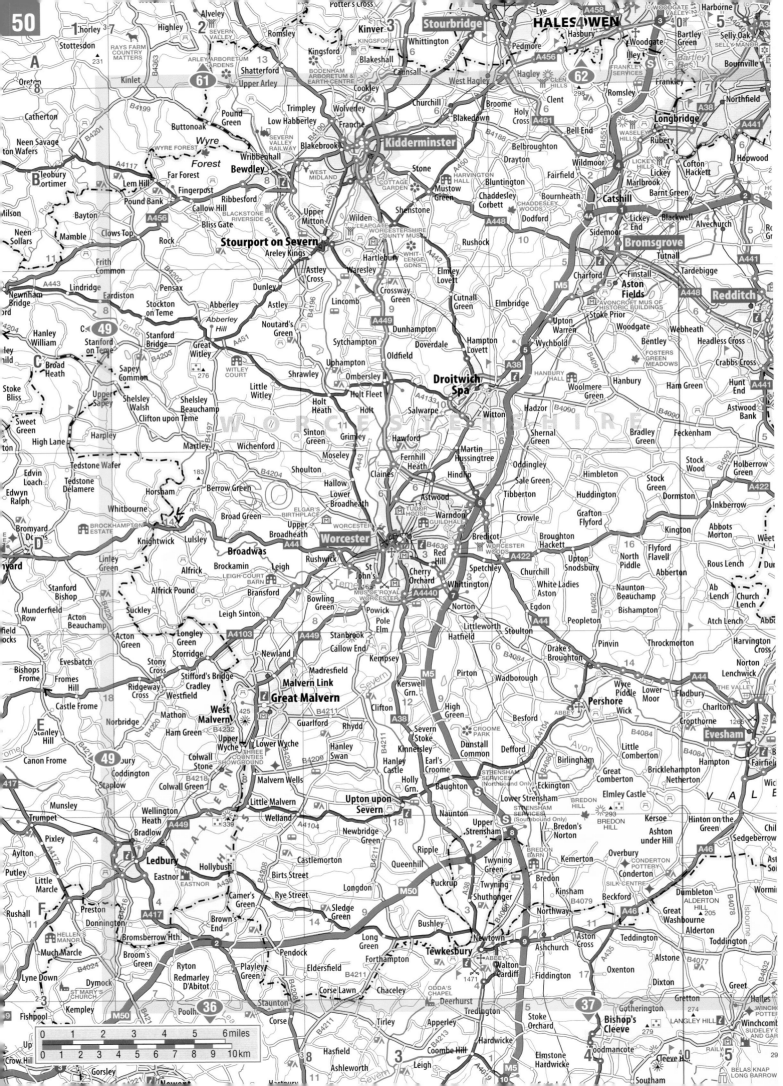

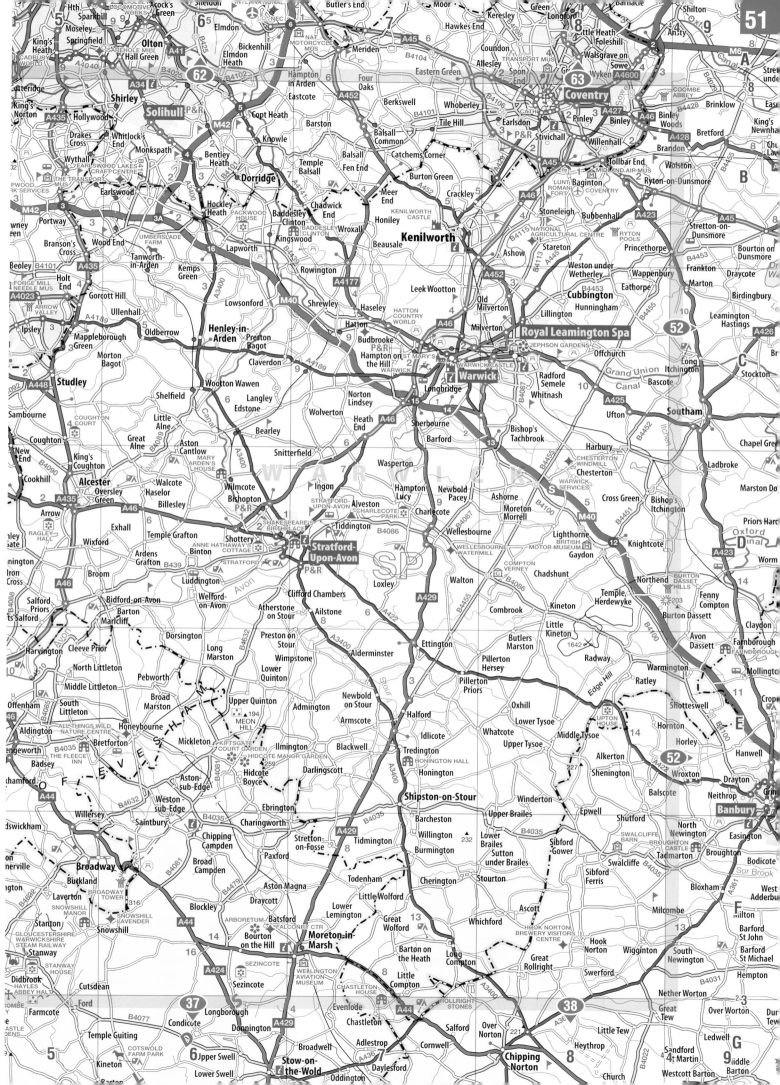

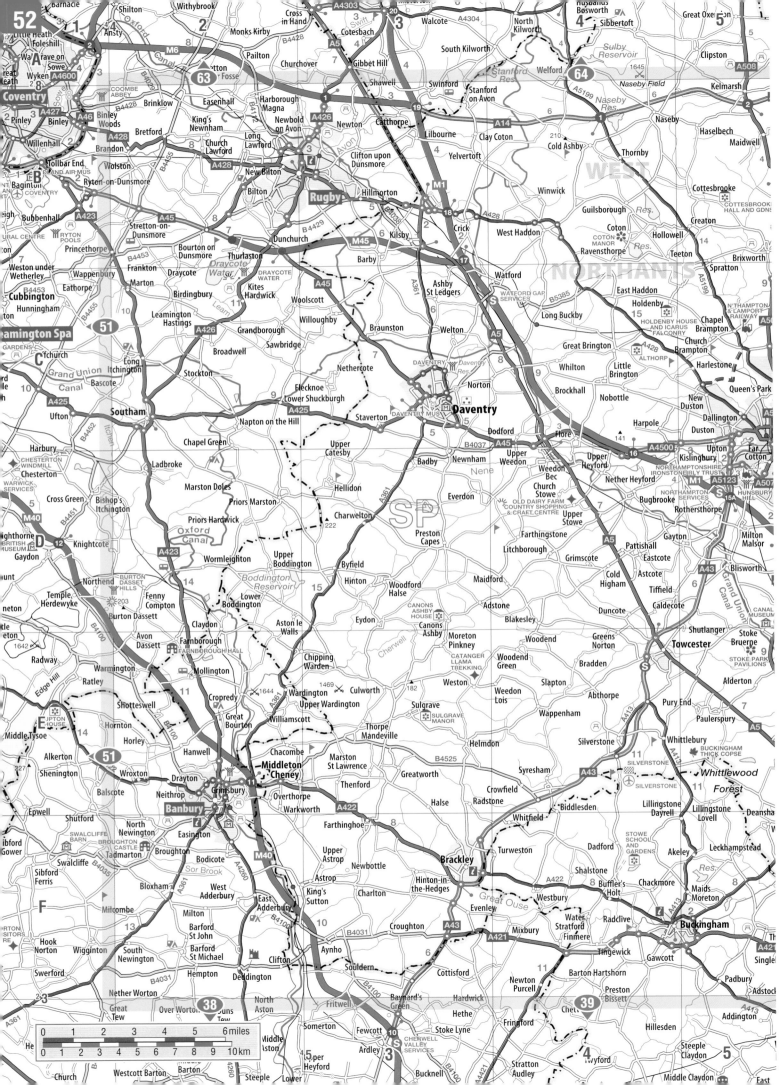

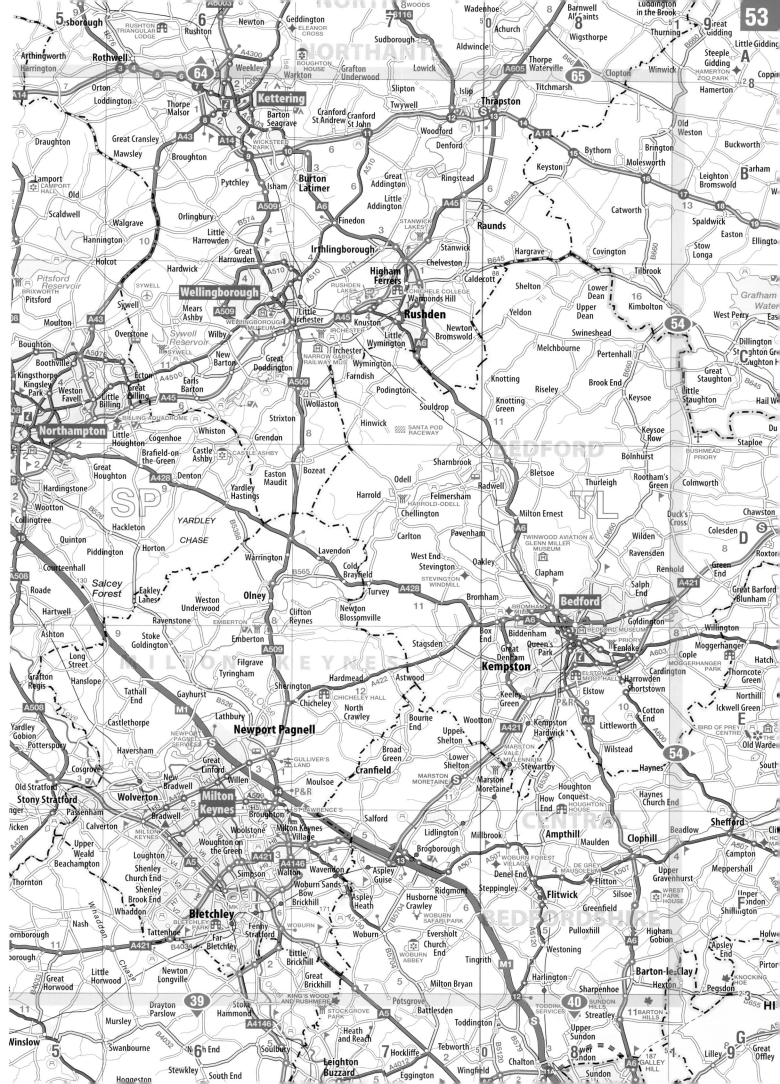

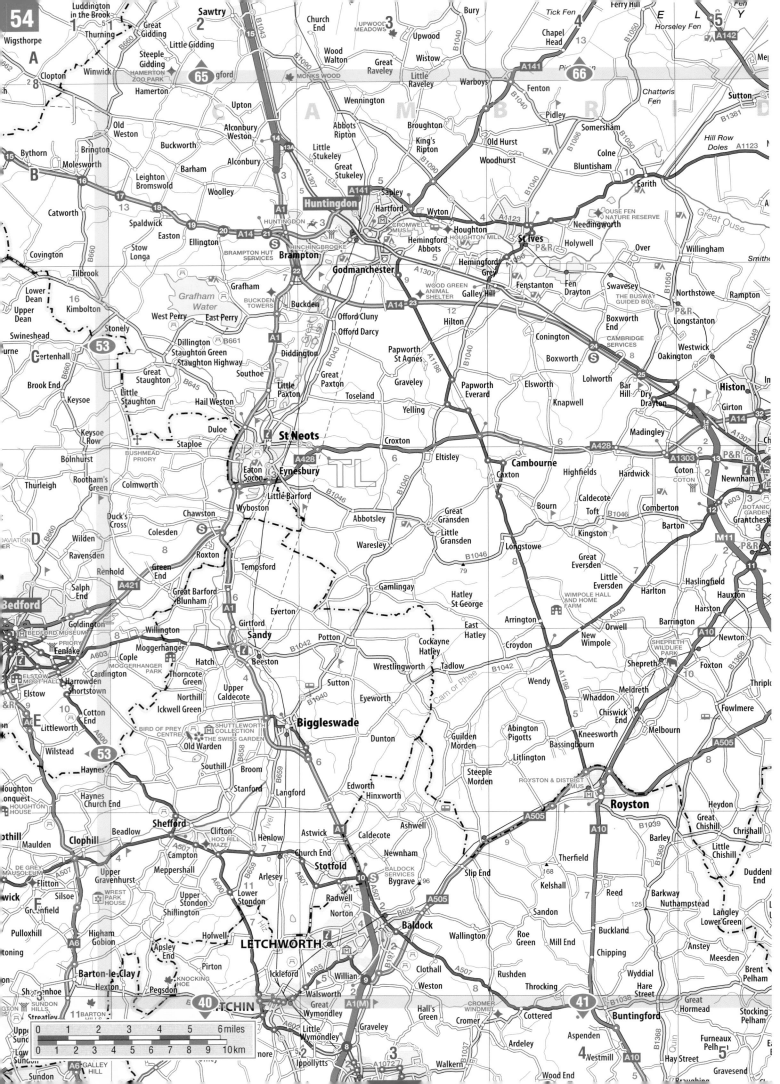

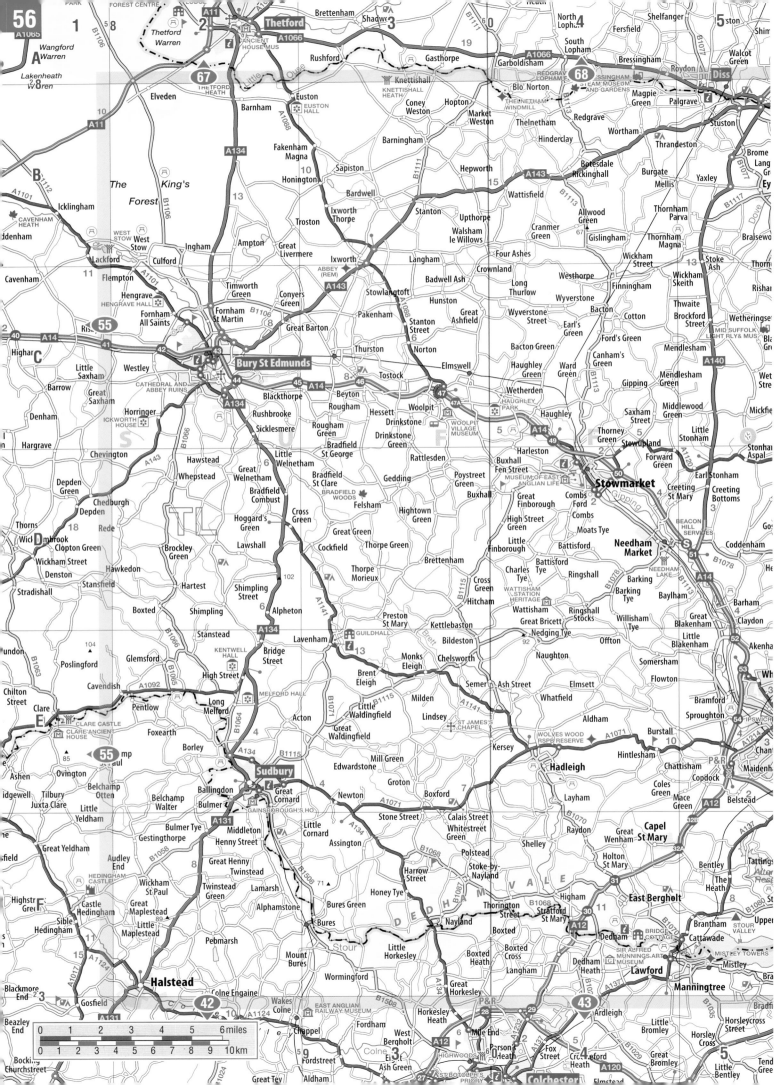

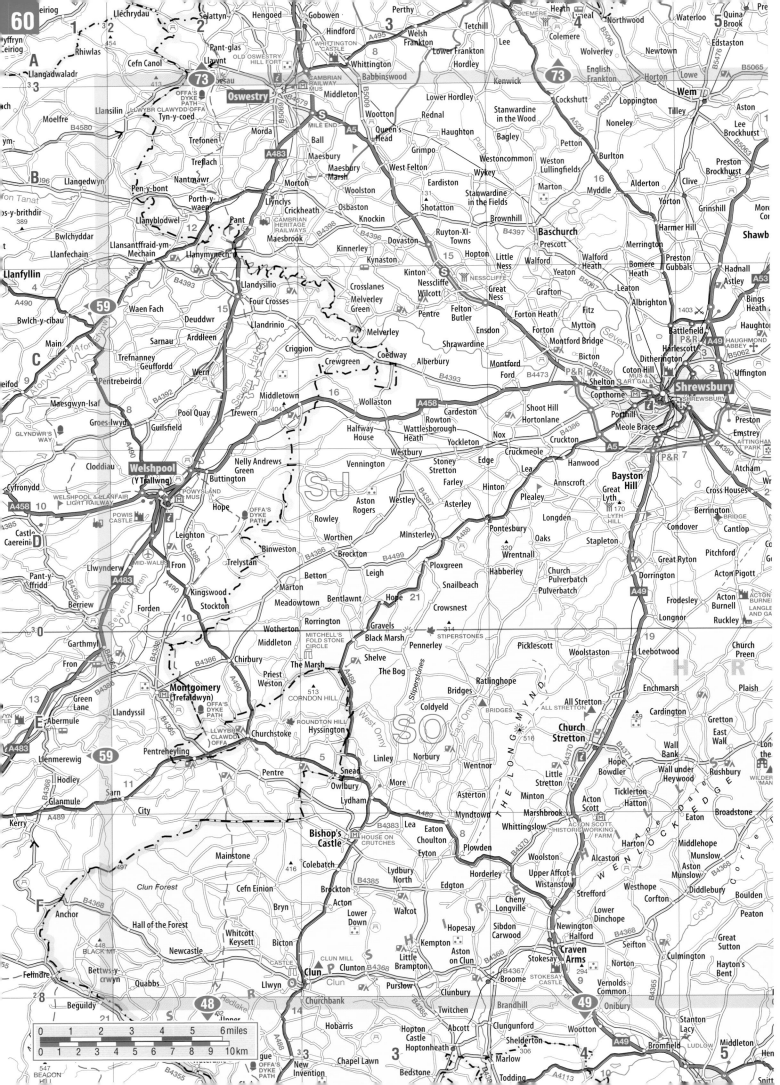

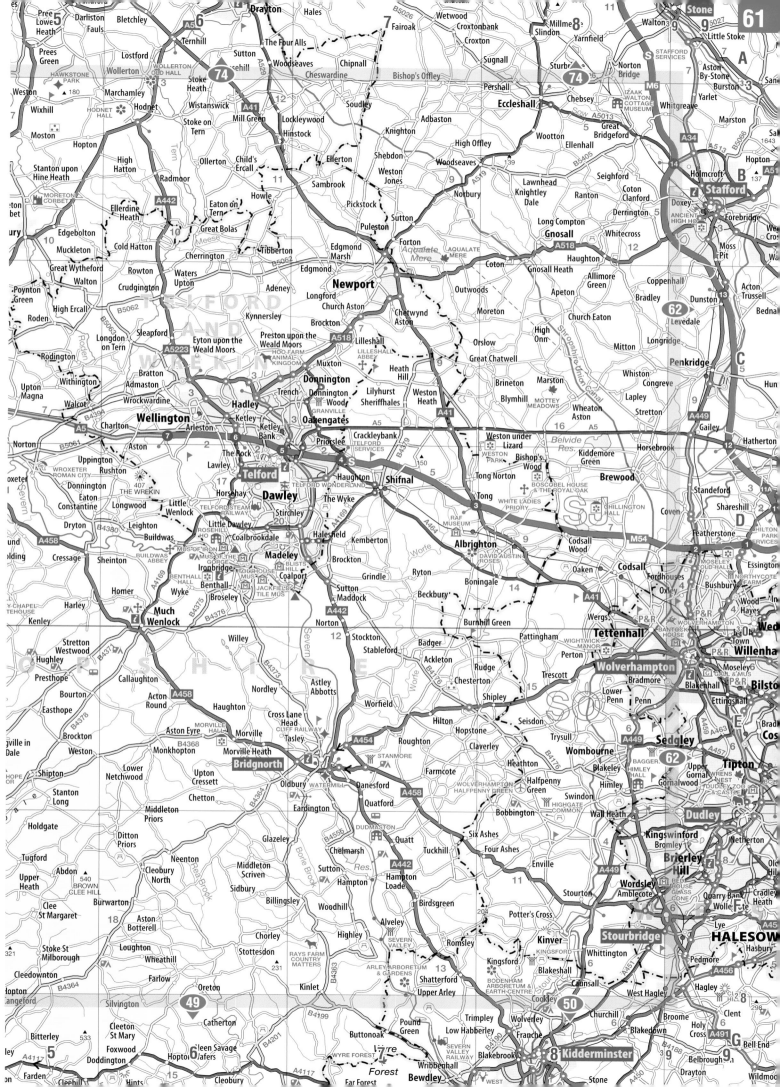

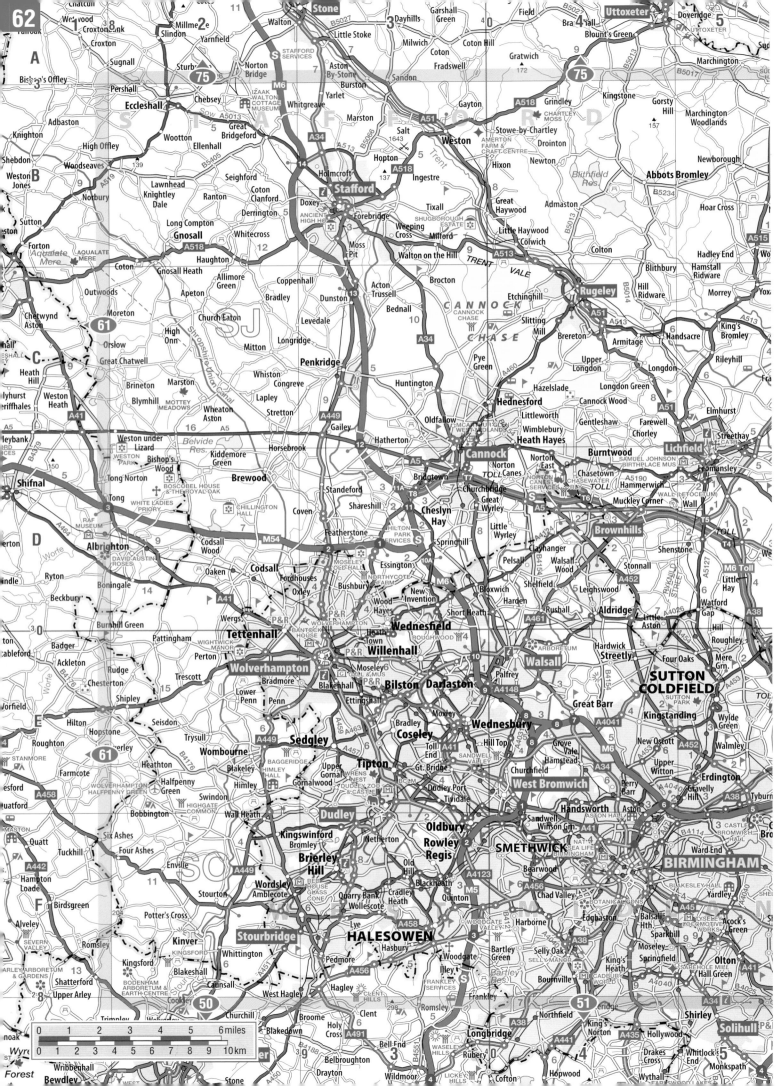

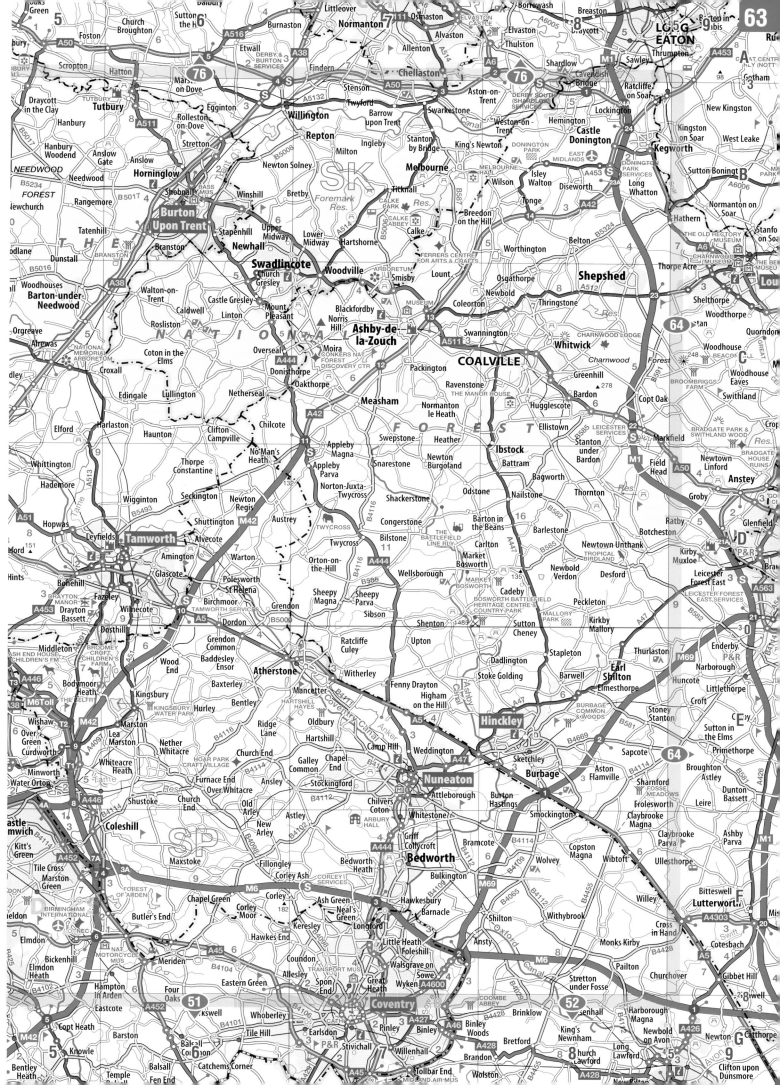

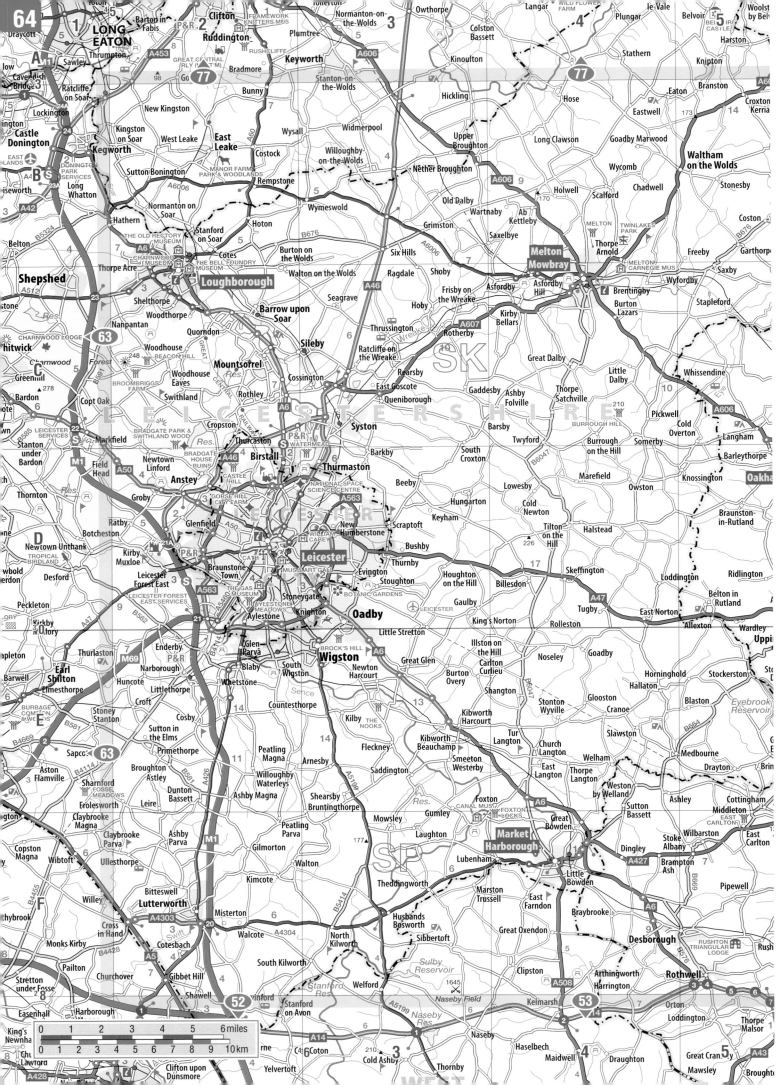

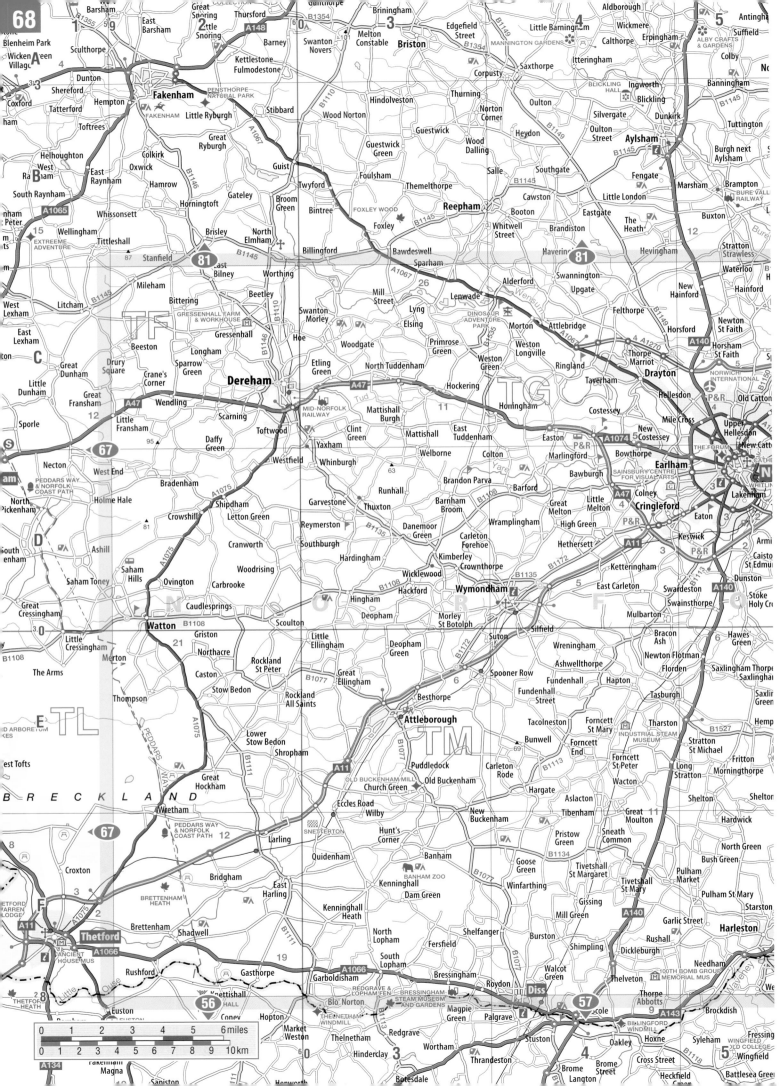

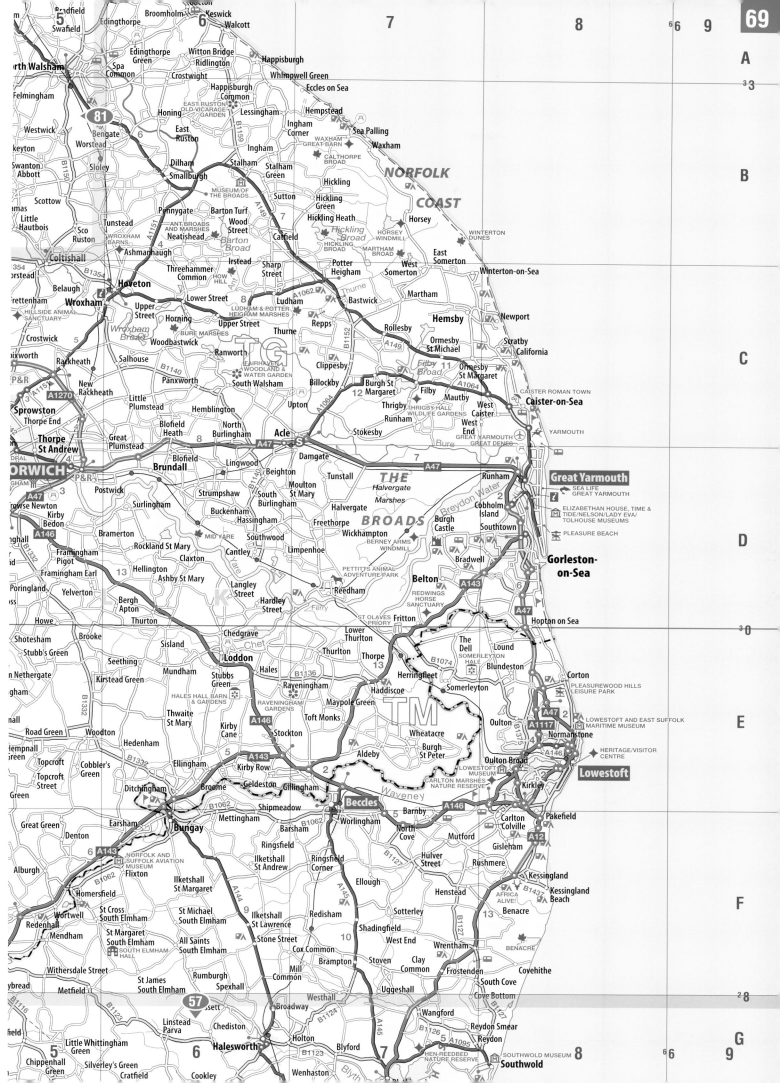

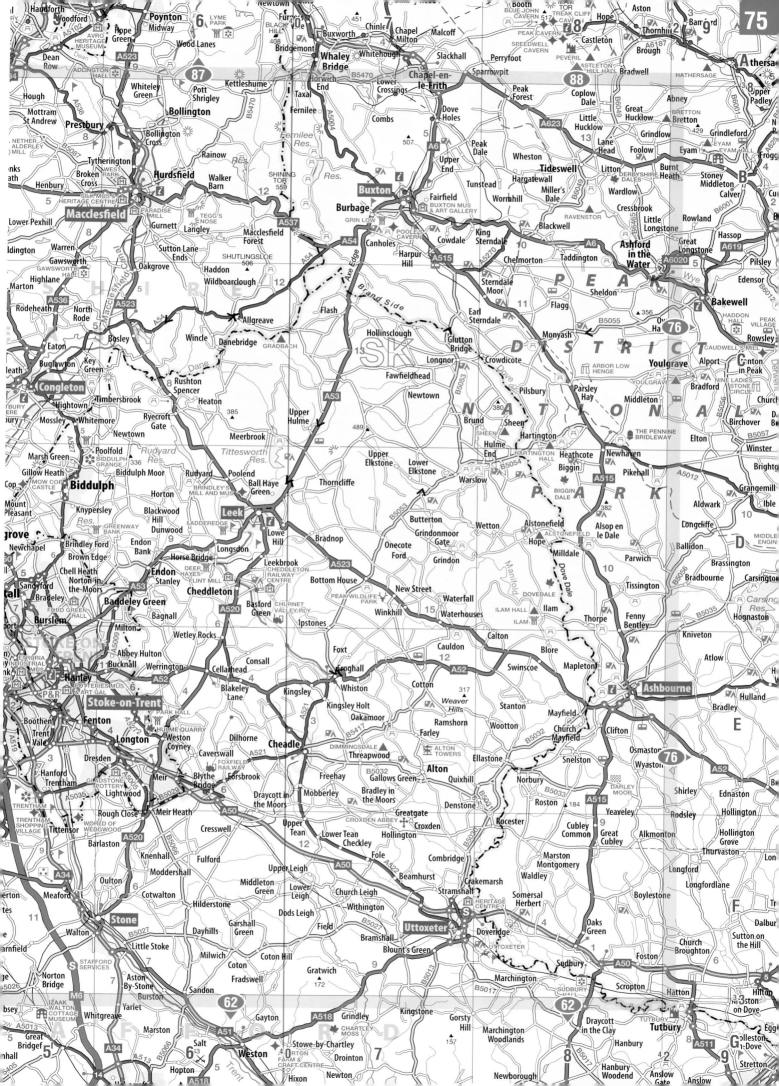

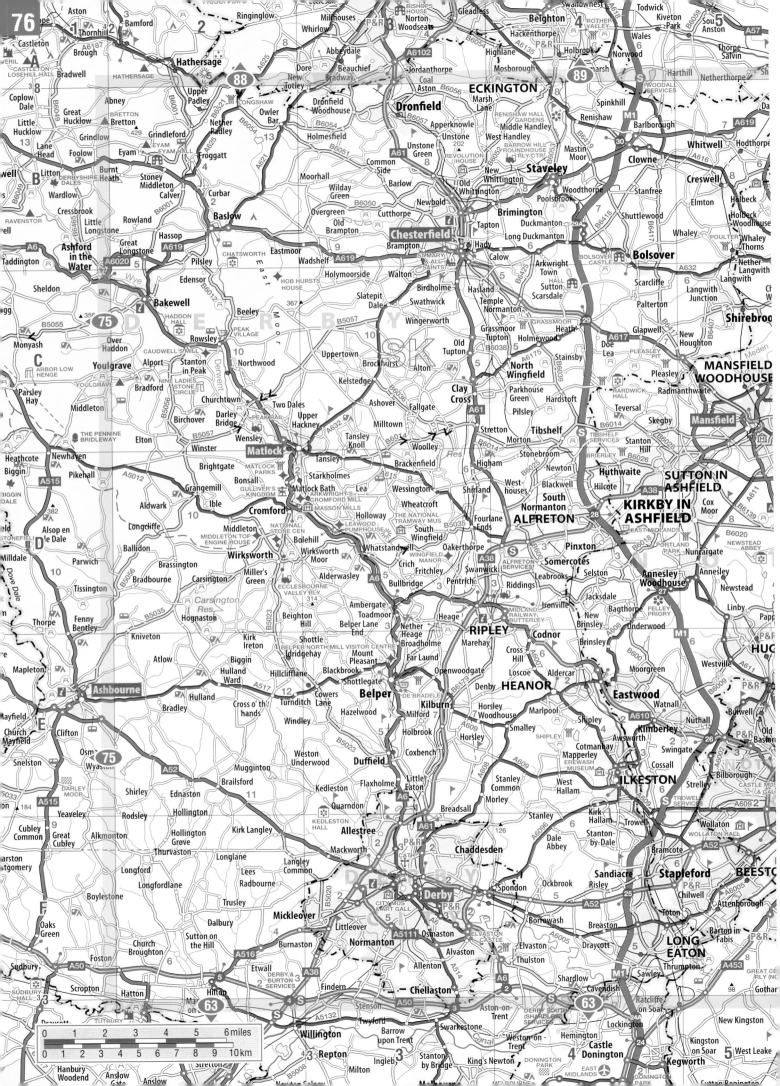

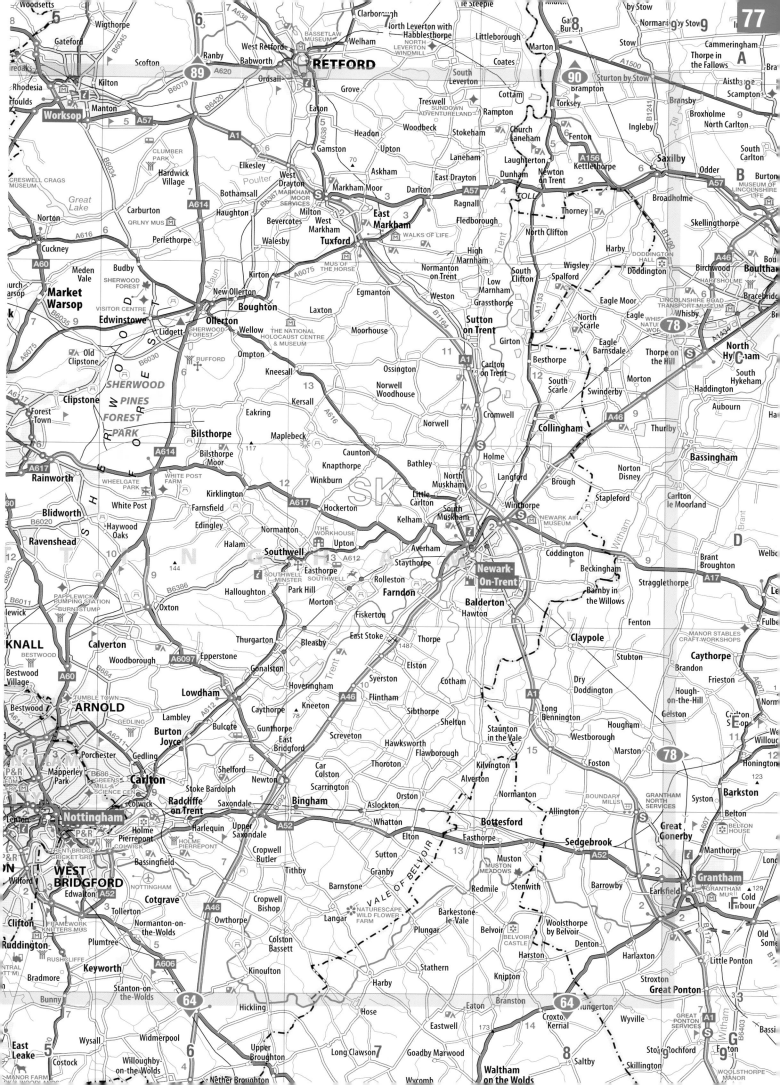

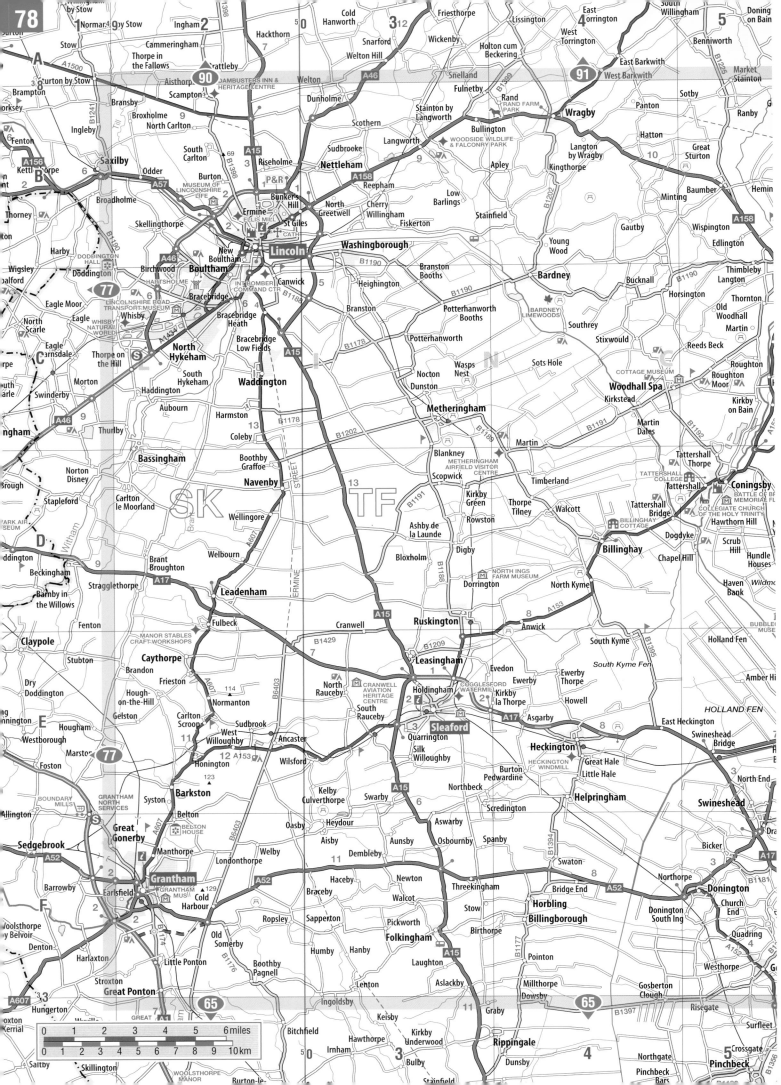

A
B
C
D
E
F

1   2   3   4   5

Skegness
SANCTUARY
THE LIFEBOAT STATION
AQUARIUM
Seacroft
sh
GIBRALTAR POINT
ainfleet
Sand

TF

NORFOLK COAST

BRANCASTER ROADS

LYNN DEEPS
79

SCOLT HEAD ISLAND
Holkham Bay

Brancaster Bay
HOLME DUNES
HOLME BIRD OBSERVATORY
Holme next the Sea
Titchwell
Thornham
Brancaster Staithe
Brancaster Deepdale
Burnham Deepdale
PEDDARS WAY & NORFOLK COAST PATH
WELLS-NEXT-THE-SEA
HOLKHAM
Wells-next-the-Sea

Old Hunstanton
17
Burnham Norton
Westgate
Burnham Overy Staithe
Burnham Overy Town
Holkham
HOLKHAM HALL
Hunstanton
SEA LIFE SANCTUARY
Ringstead
HUNSTANTON
B1153
Burnham Thorpe
Burnham Market
New Holkham
WELLS AND WALSINGHAM LIGHT RAILWAY
Wigh
Heacham
NORFOLK LAVENDER
Summerfield
PEDDARS WAY & NORFOLK COAST PATH
Docking
CREAKE ABBEY
North Creake
B1355
SHIREHALL MUS
79
Little Walsingham
Gre
Sedgeford
B1454
88
Stanhoe
South Creake
Waterden
North Barsham
Houghton St Giles
Fring
12
Bircham Newton
B1155
Barmer
Syderstone
West Barsham
B1355
East Barsham
Gre
Snc
Li
Snettisham
SNETTISHAM PARK
Ingoldisthorpe
62
Great Bircham
B1153
Bircham Tofts
Bagthorpe
Blenheim Park
Wicken Green Village
Sculthorpe
SNETTISHAM NATURE RESERVE
Shepherd's Port
Shernborne
BIRCHAM MILL
West Rudham
4
Dunton
Shereford
Hempton
Fakenham
B1440
10
Dersingham
PEDDARS WAY
Anmer
HOUGHTON HALL
Tattersett
Coxford
Tatterford
Toftrees
FAKENHAM
67
DERSINGHAM BOG
SANDRINGHAM
Sandringham
New Houghton
A148
East Rudham
Wolferton
West Newton
Harpley
Helhoughton
West Raynham
East Raynham
Colkirk
Oxwick
North Wootton
Castle Rising
CASTLE RISING
Flitcham
13
Little Massingham
PEDDARS WAY & NORFOLK COAST PATH
Great Massingham
South Raynham
Hamrow
Horni
B1146
Ongar Hill
ton Marsh
Hillington
Congham
CONGHAM HALL HERB GARDEN
Weasenham St Peter
A1065
Whissonsett
South Wootton
A1078
Roydon
ROYDON COMMON
Weasenham All Saints
15
EXTREEME ADVENTURE
Wellingham
Tittleshall
King's Lynn
TRUE'S YARD FISHERFOLK-MUS
GUILDHALL
Gaywood
Grimston
Massingham Heath
87
Stanfield
A149
West Lynn
Fairstead
Pott Row
Rougham
67
Mileham
Clenchwarton
Hardwick
4
Gayton
B1145
95
Litcham
Bittering
Terrington St Clement
Leziate
Ashwicken
West Lexham
B1145
GRESSEN
& W
Tilney All Saints
Fair Green
Tower End
Gayton Thorpe
East Lexham
Beeston
Tilney High End
A10
Middleton
B1153
West Acre
CASTLE ACRE PRIORY
Newton
Great Dunham
Drury Square
Crane's Corner
Long
Sparrow
Green
A47
West Winch
North Runcton
East Winch
14
East Walton
CASTLE ACRE
South Acre
Little Dunham
terrington t John
Saddle Bow
Wiggenhall St Germans
Blackborough End
West Bilney
Pentney
Great Fransham
Little Fransham
Wendling
Tilney St Lawrence
Wiggenhall St Mary the Virgin
Setchey
Narborough
Great Palgrave
Sporle
12
95
A47
Wiggenhall St Mary Magdalen
Watlington
Tottenhill Row
Wormegay
S
Necton
West End
Tottenhill
Marham
Shouldham
A47
Swaffham
PEDDARS WAY & NORFOLK COAST PATH
Holme Hale
Marshla
Runcton Holme
11
Beachamwell Warren
A1065
rth Pick ham
Bradenham
West Head
Wimbotsham
Bardolph
A1122
Fincham
Barton Bendish
Beachamwell
Crowshill

0 1 2 3 4 5 6 miles
0 1 2 3 4 5 6 7 8 9 10km

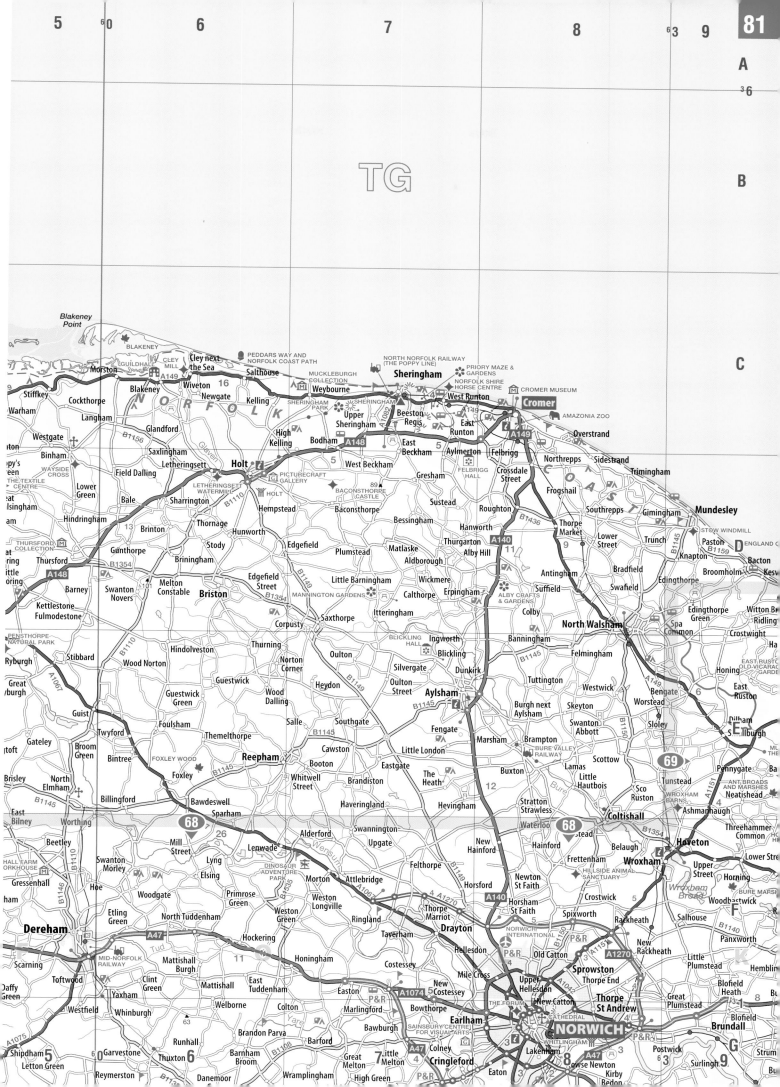

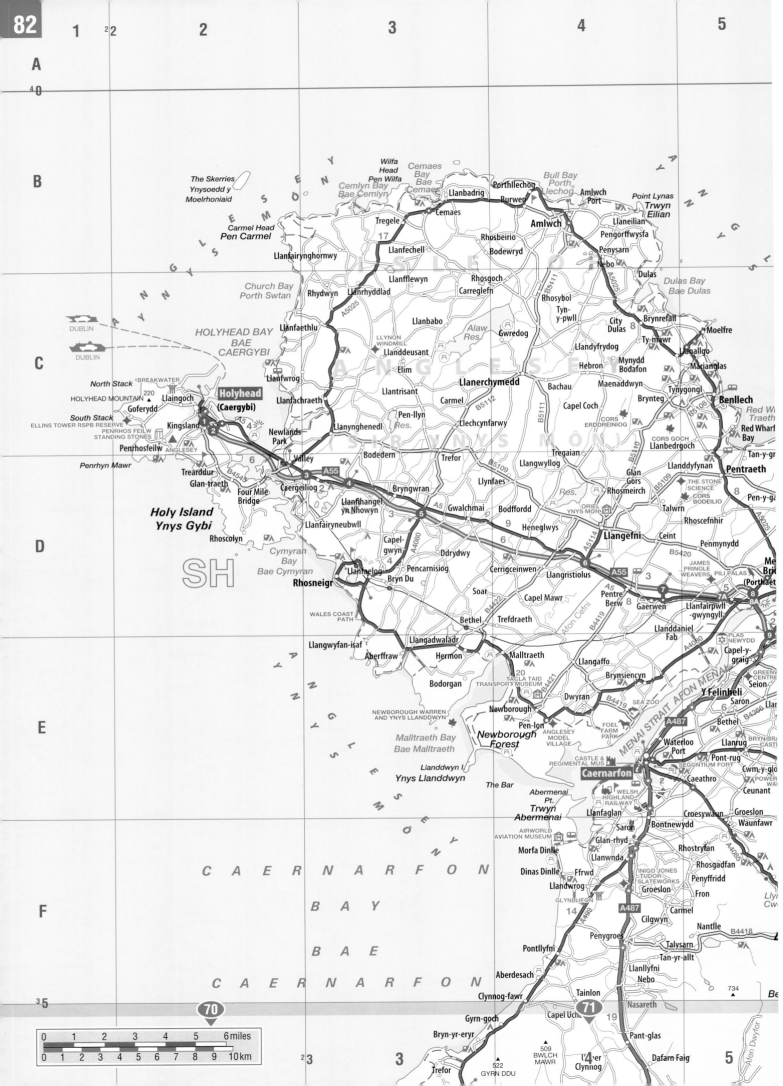

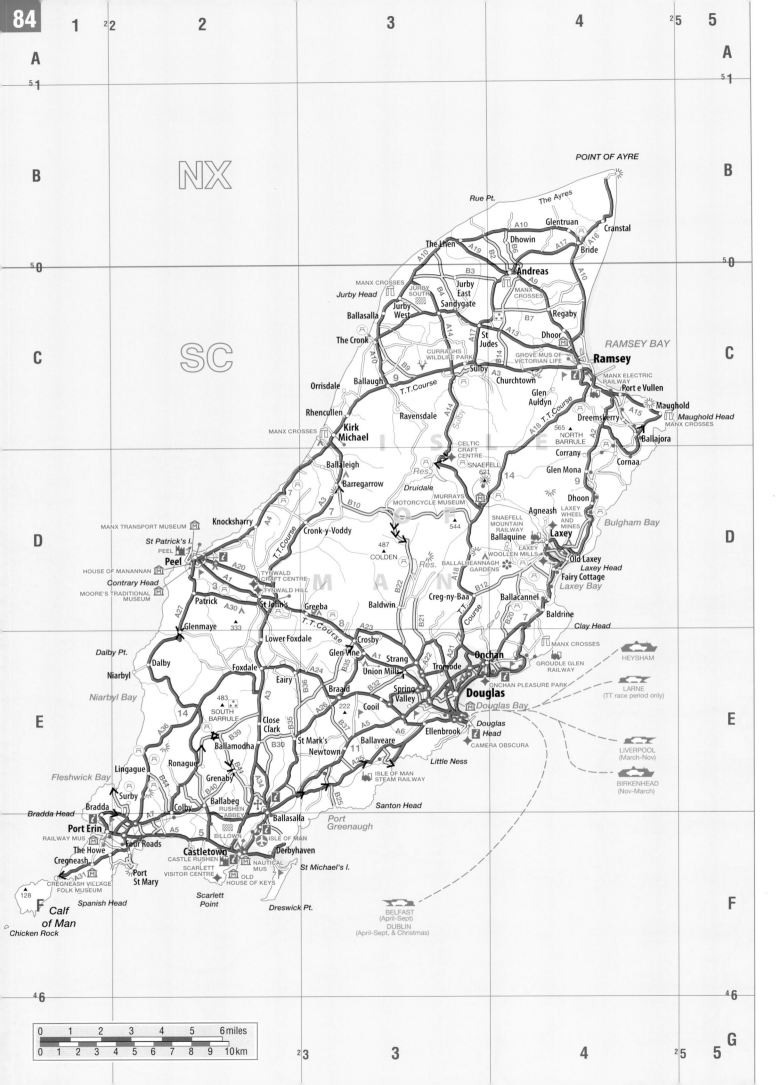

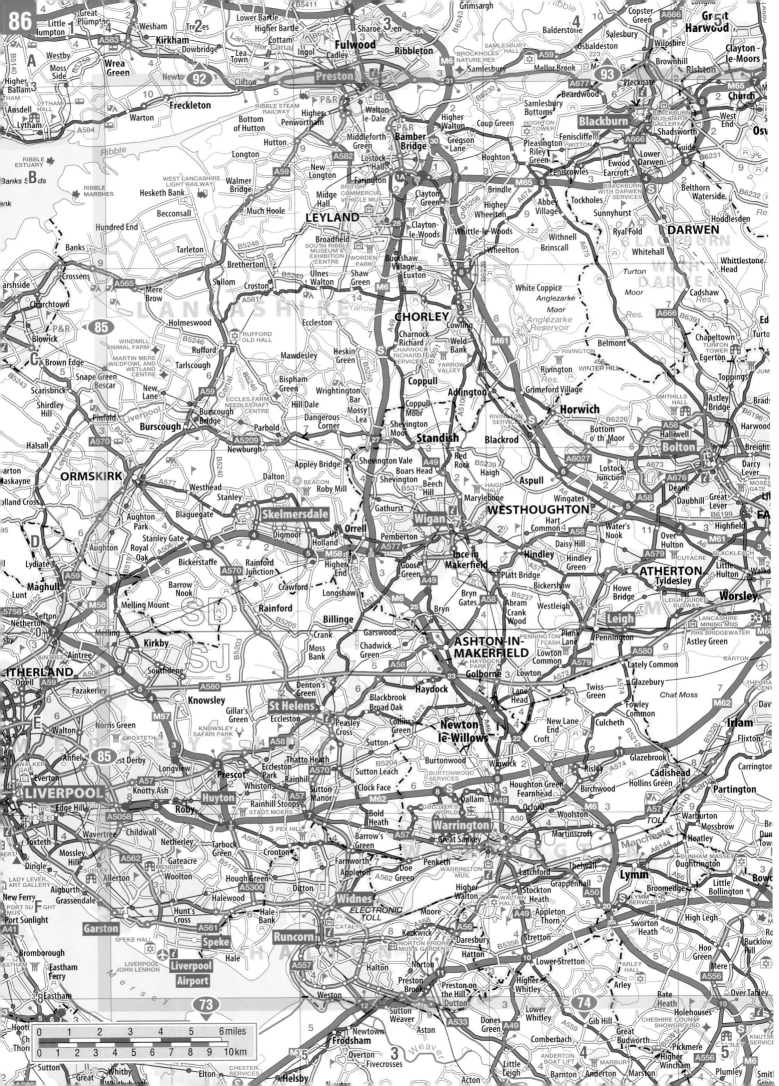

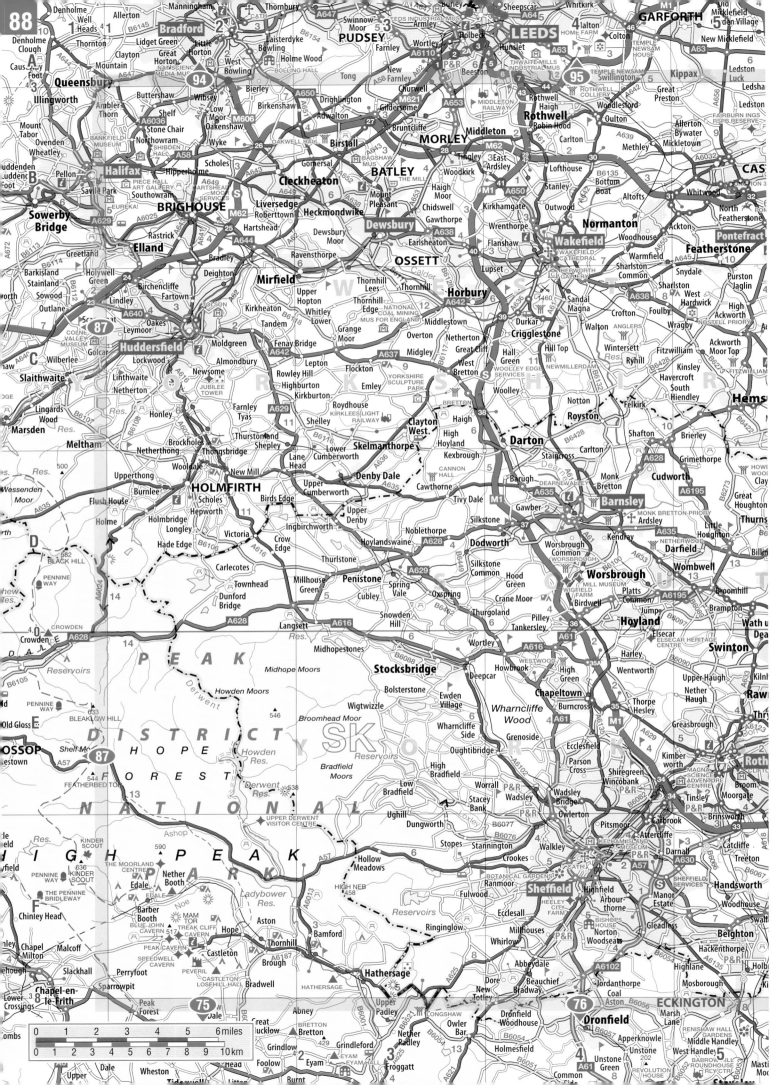

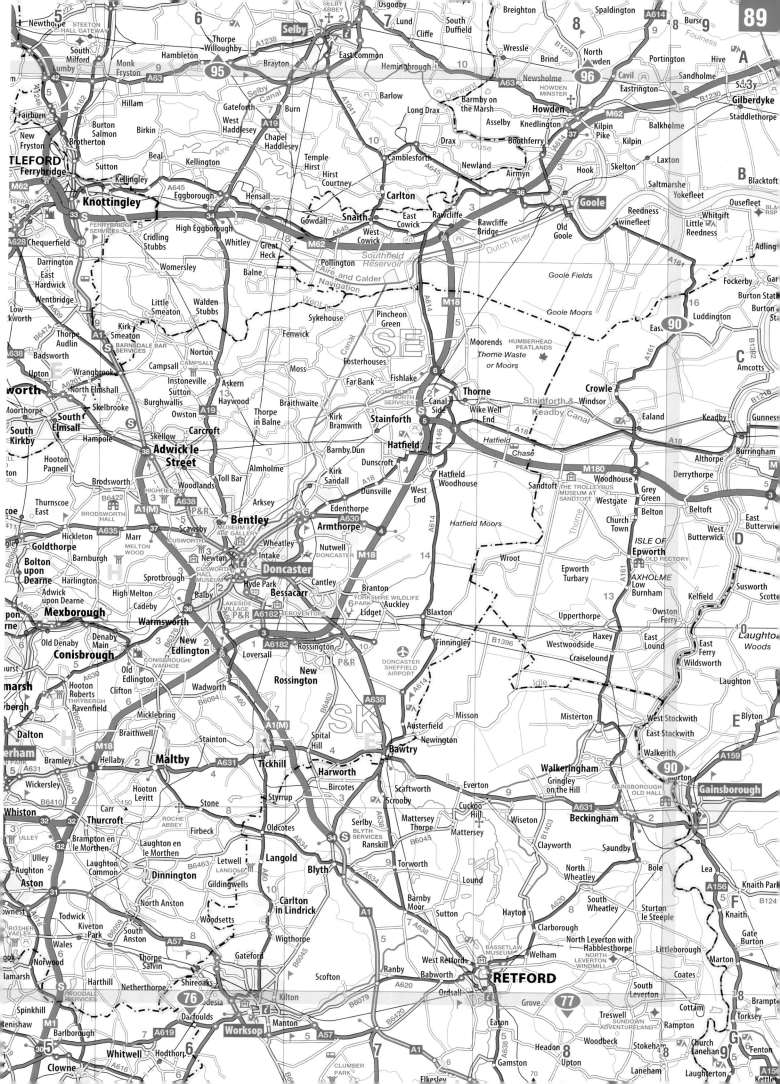

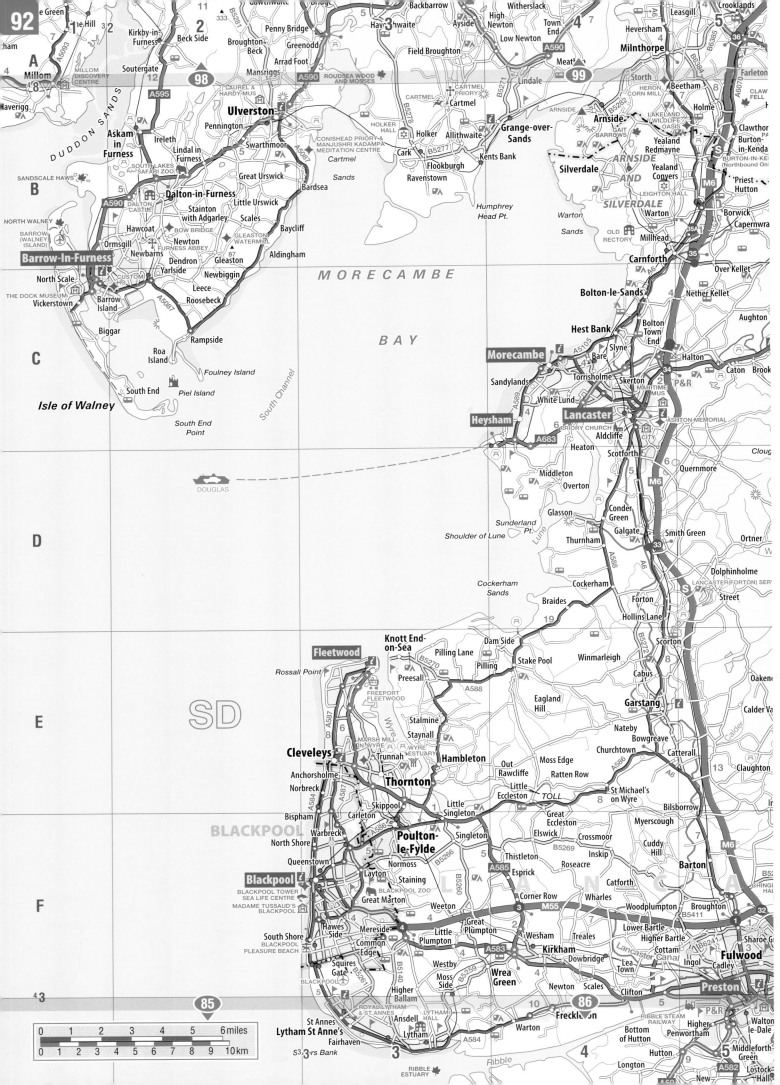

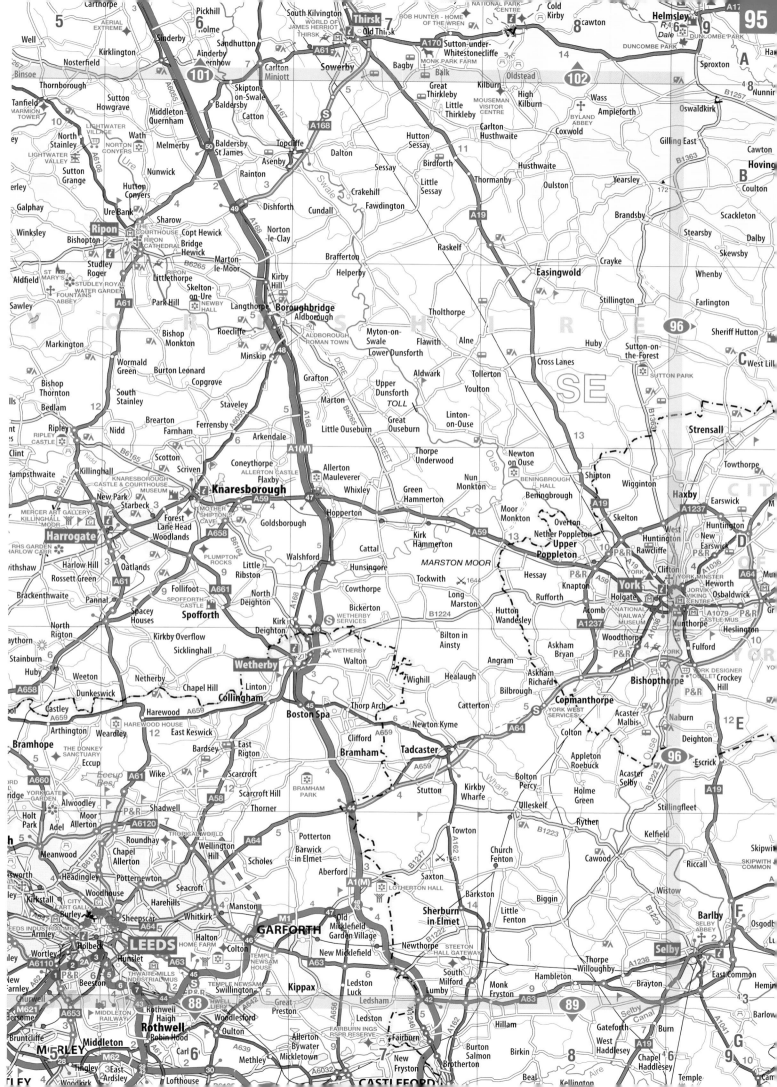

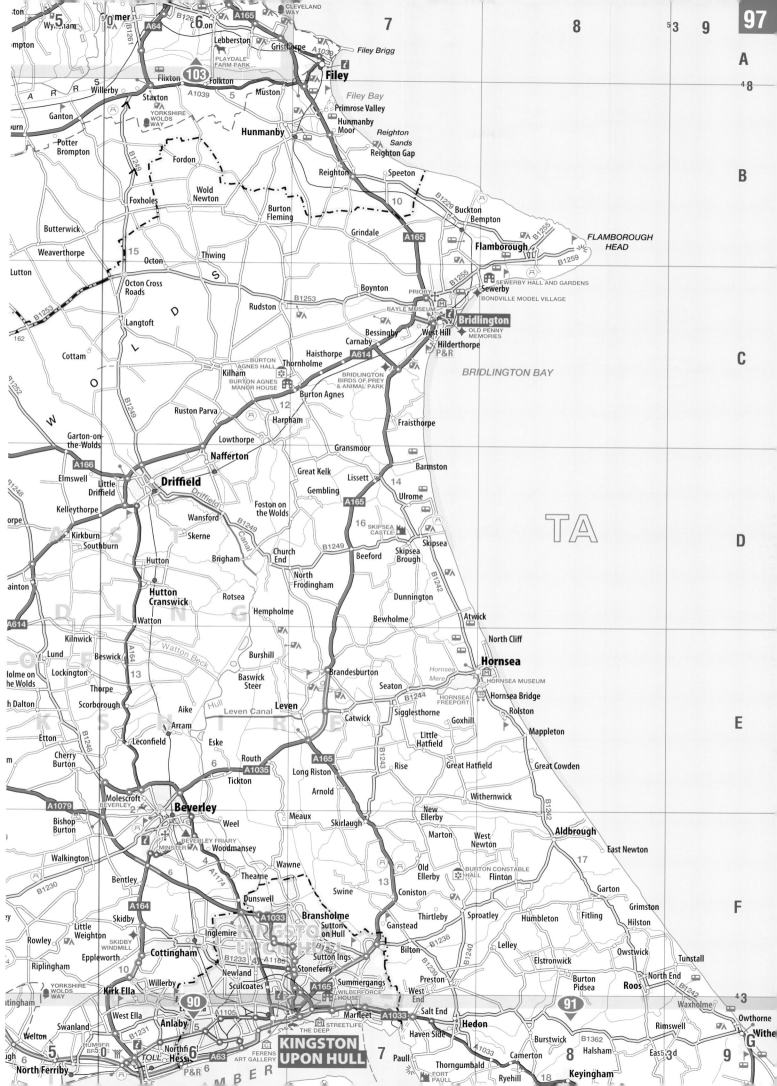

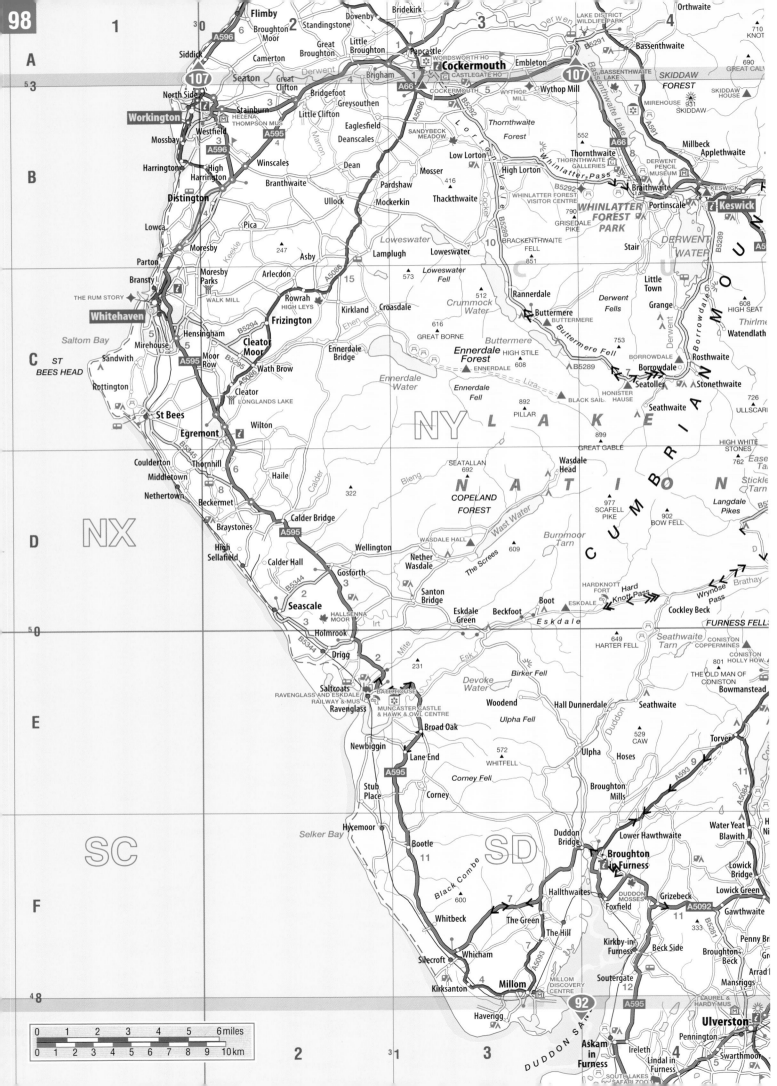

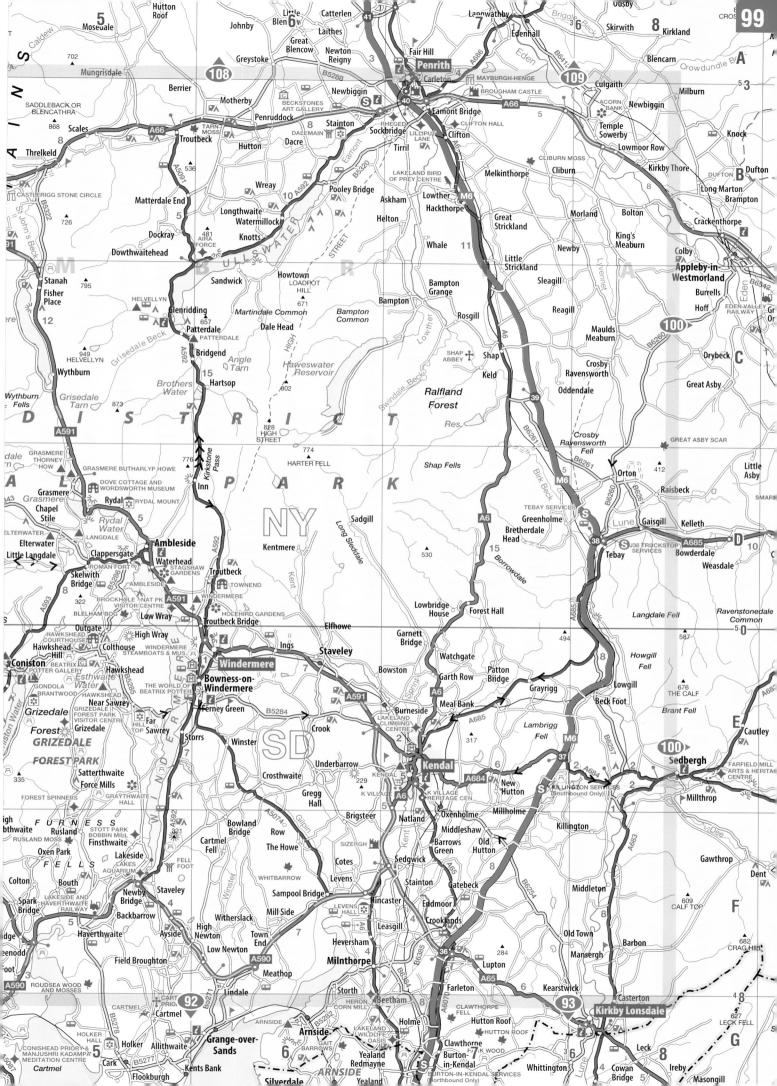

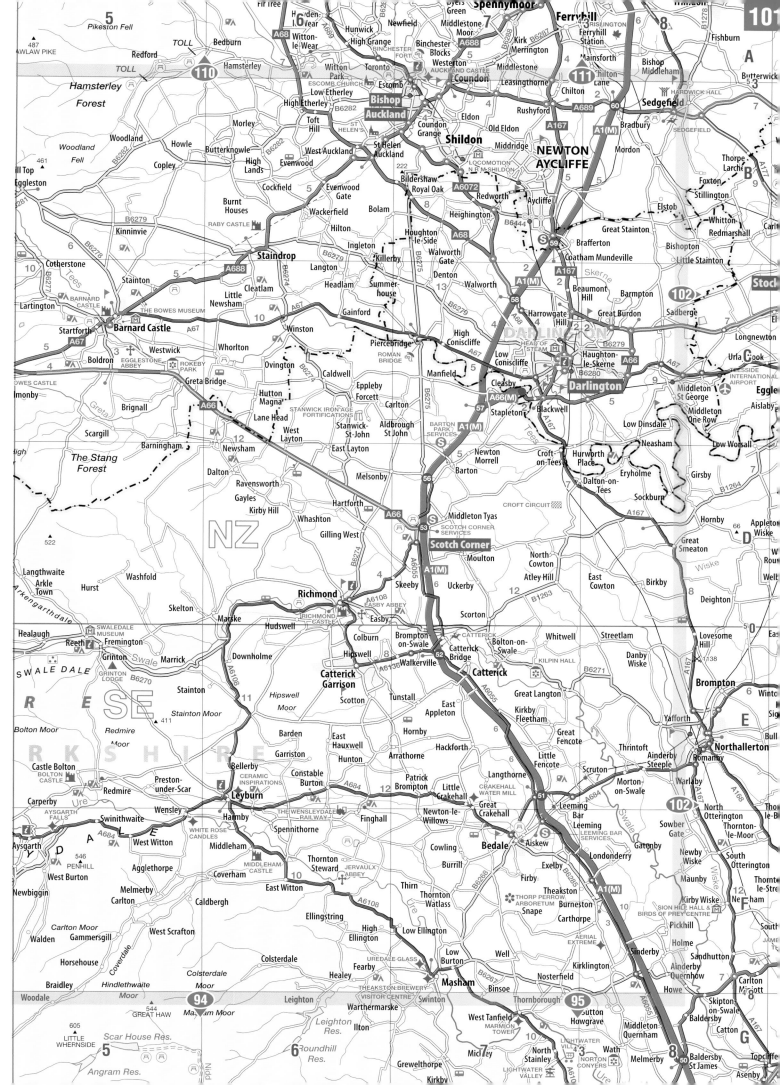

1   18   2   3   20   4   5

A

58

BELFAST
LARNE

B

Bennane Hd.

CARLETON
'STLE

112

Colmonell
B734   265   Knockdolian
Heronsford
Glen Tig
Balkiss

Ballantrae Bay
Ballantrae

Downan Pt.

Auchencrosh

439
BENERAIRD

A77
257

Mark

Glen App
17

Milleur Pt.

Corsewall Pt.

Barnhills   Portencalzie

North Cairn

South Cairn   B738   Corsewall
Loch Connell   Kirkcolm
Dounan Bay   Mains of Airies   Ervie
Low Salchrie
B798

Cairnryan

Braid Fell

Penwhirn Res.

Main Water of L...

C

Slouchnawen Bay   Knocknain   Leswalt
B738
B7043

The Wig
LOCH RYAN

6

Craigencross   A718

Innermessan

A77

Black Loch
CASTLE KENNEDY
GARDENS
White Loch

Auchmant...

Glenstockadale

NW

Broadsea Bay   T   H   E

Knockglass

Stranraer
STRANRAER
MUSEUM

CASTLE OF
ST.JOHN
VISITOR
CENTRE

Aird   Castle Kennedy

R   H   I   GL...
GA...

Soulseat Loch

A75

D

Black Hd.
Dunskey Ho.

B738

182

Lochans

Awhirk

A77
5   5

Mark

B7077
6

5   A716

B7084   6

Torrs War...

Luce Sa...

LITTLE
WHEELS
Portpatrick

Port of Spittal Bay

8
Stoneykirk
B7042

Cairngarroch

KIRKMADRINE
STONES

Sandhead
Sandhead Bay

E

Cairngarroch Bay
Money Hd.

Clachanmore

Hole Stone Bay

Ardwell
Mains

Ardwell   *Chapel Rossan...*

Ardwell Pt.   Logan
Mains

10

Balgowan Pt.

LOGAN
BOTANIC
GARDEN
Mull of Logan
LOGAN FISH POND
MARINE LIFE CENTRE
Port Nessock or Port Logan Bay   Port Logan

54

Cairnywellan Hd.

B7065   A716

Clanyard Bay

Low Clanyard

Laggantalluch Hd.   Kirkmaiden   Drumm...

F

164
Damnaglaur

B7041   Ma...

Crammag Hd.

Cairngaan

Port Kemin

0   1   2   3   4   5   6 miles
0 1 2 3 4 5 6 7 8 9 10km

19   3   20   4   5

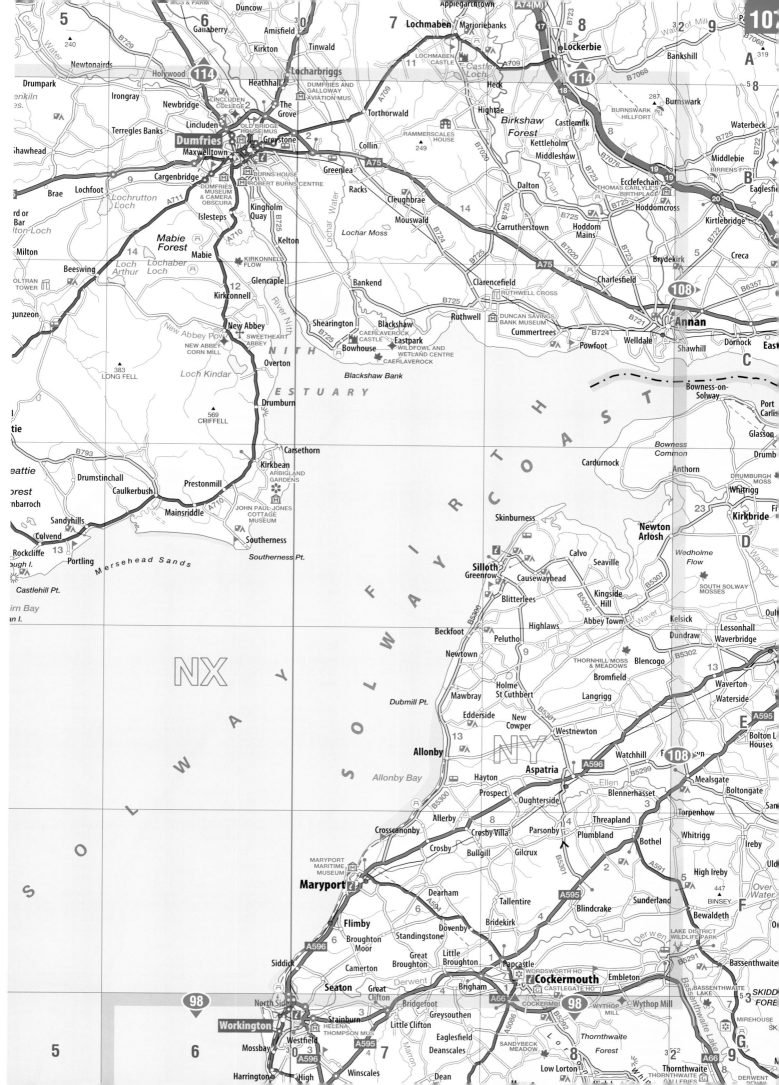

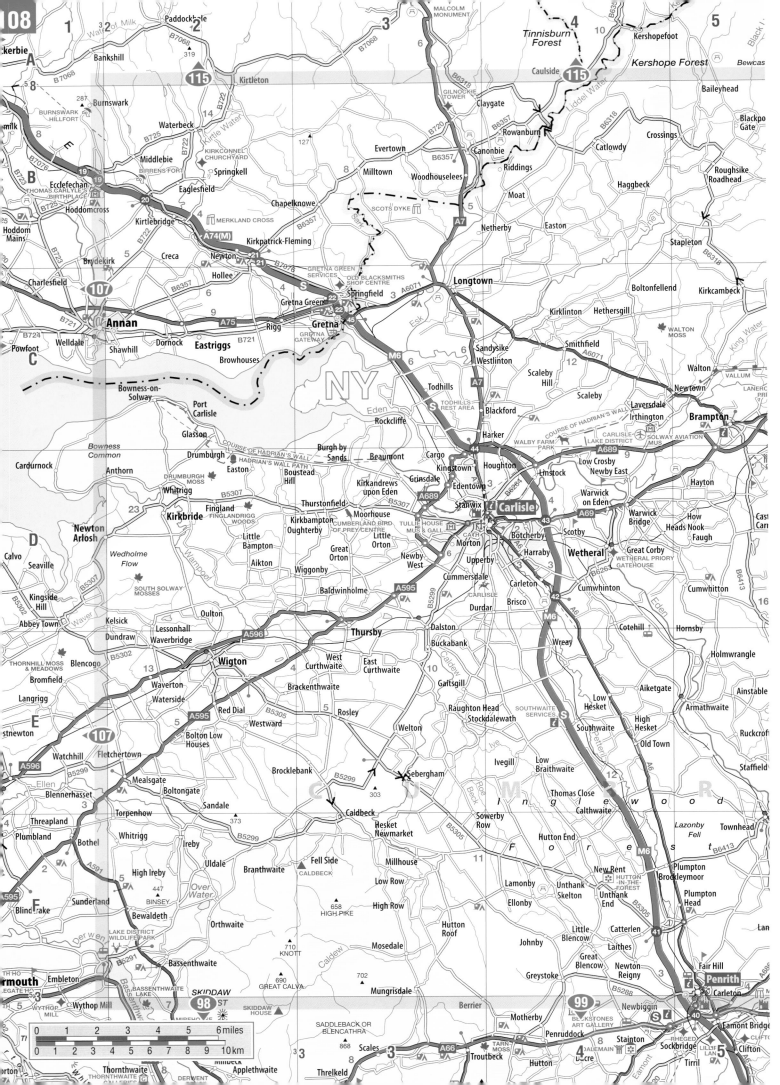

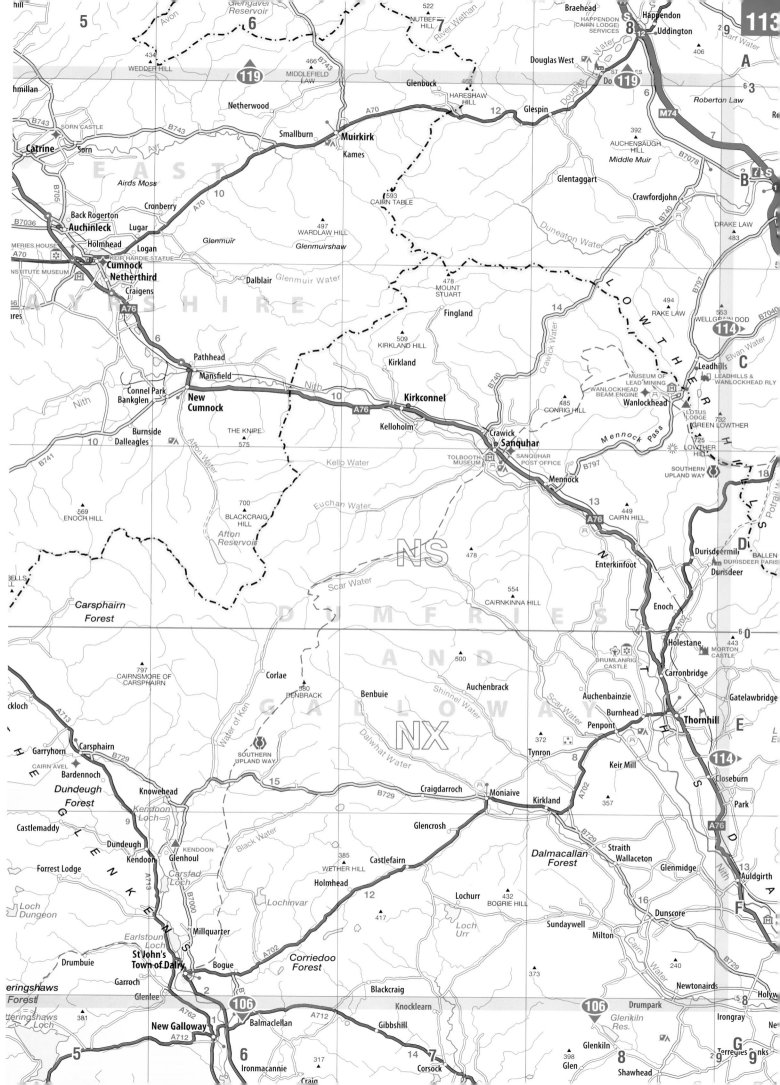

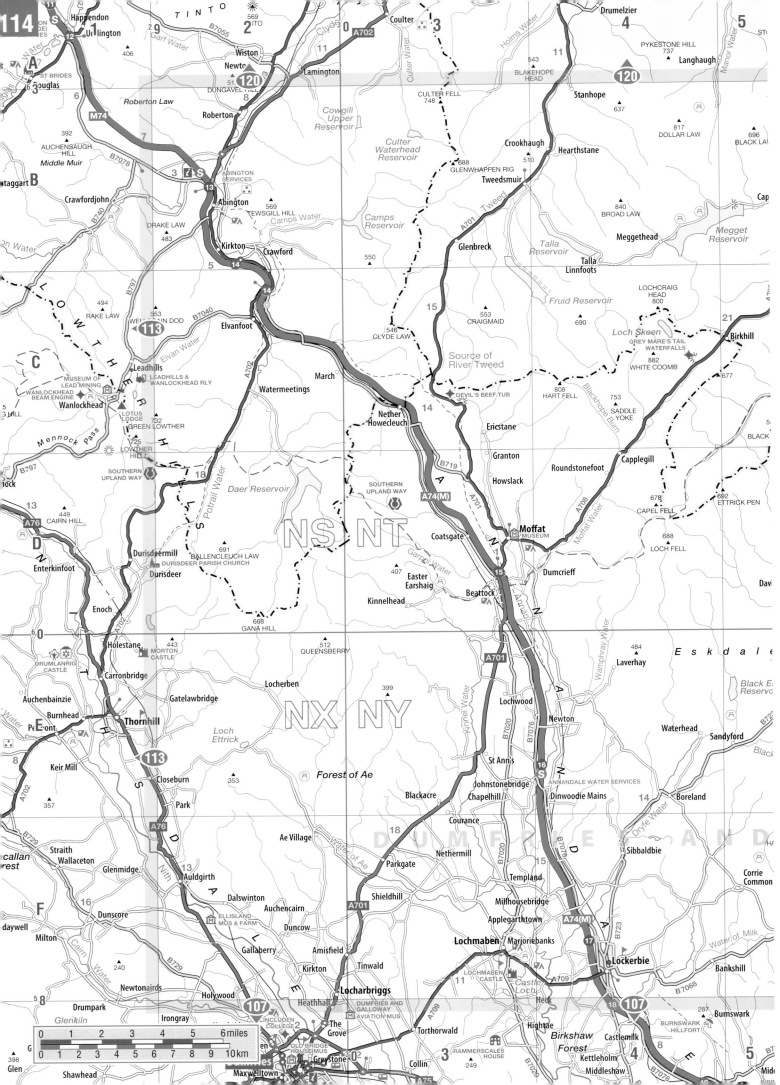

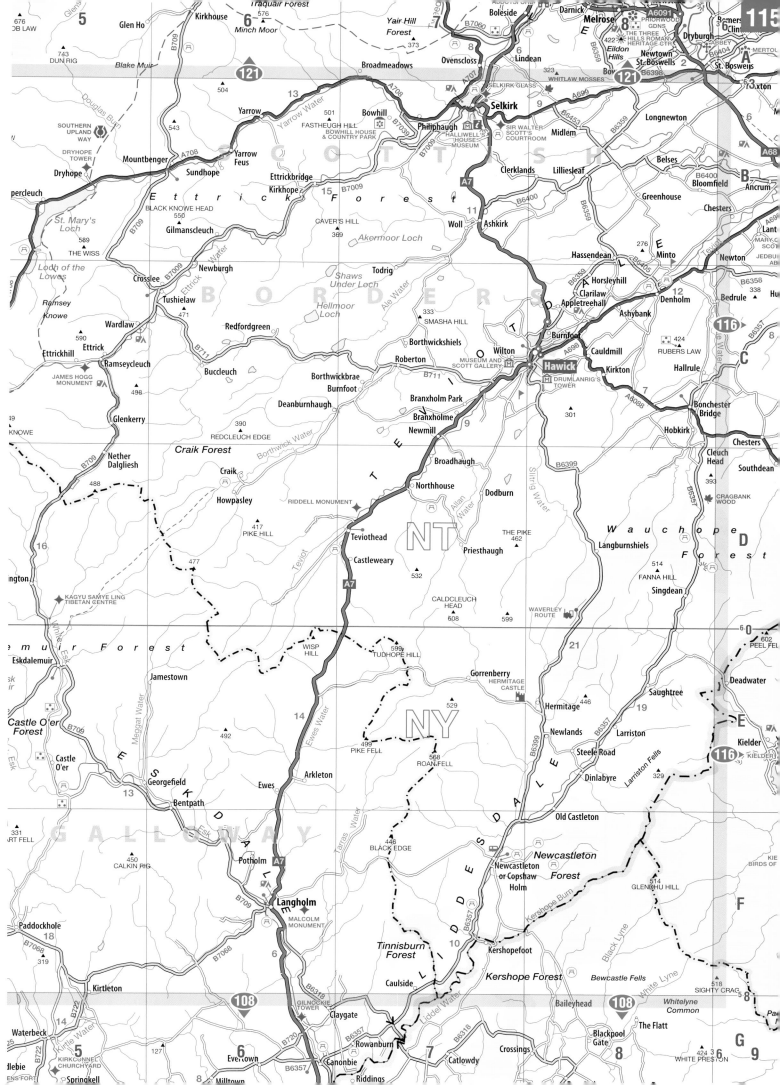

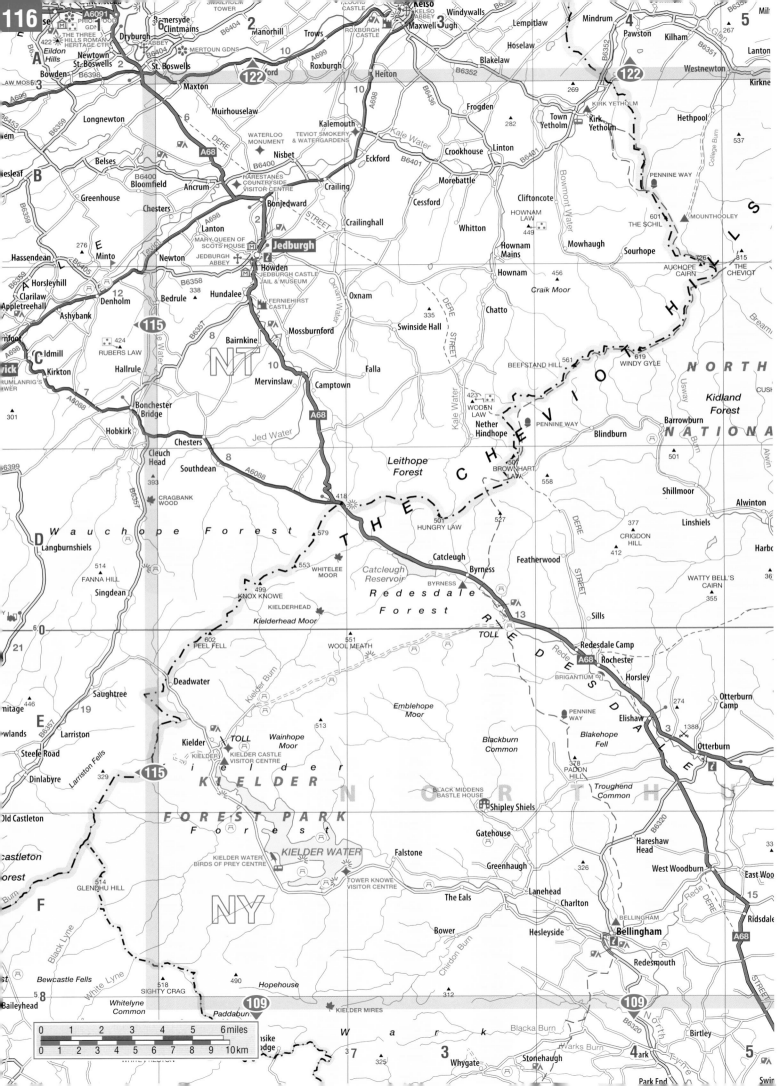

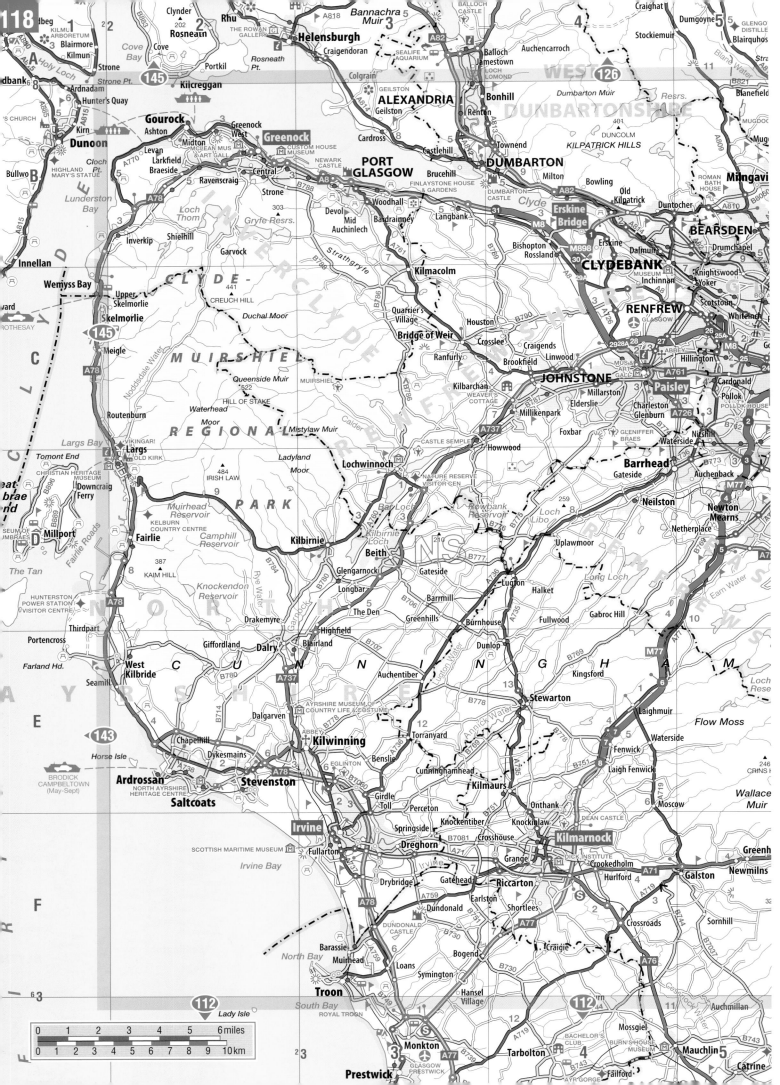

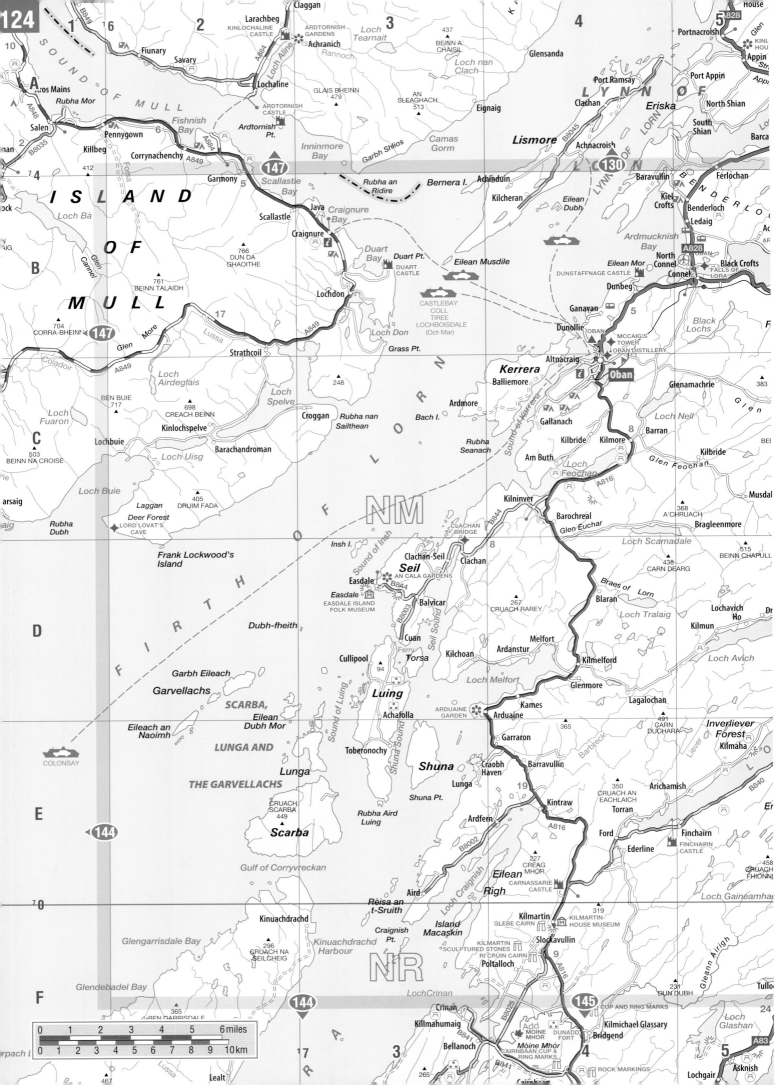

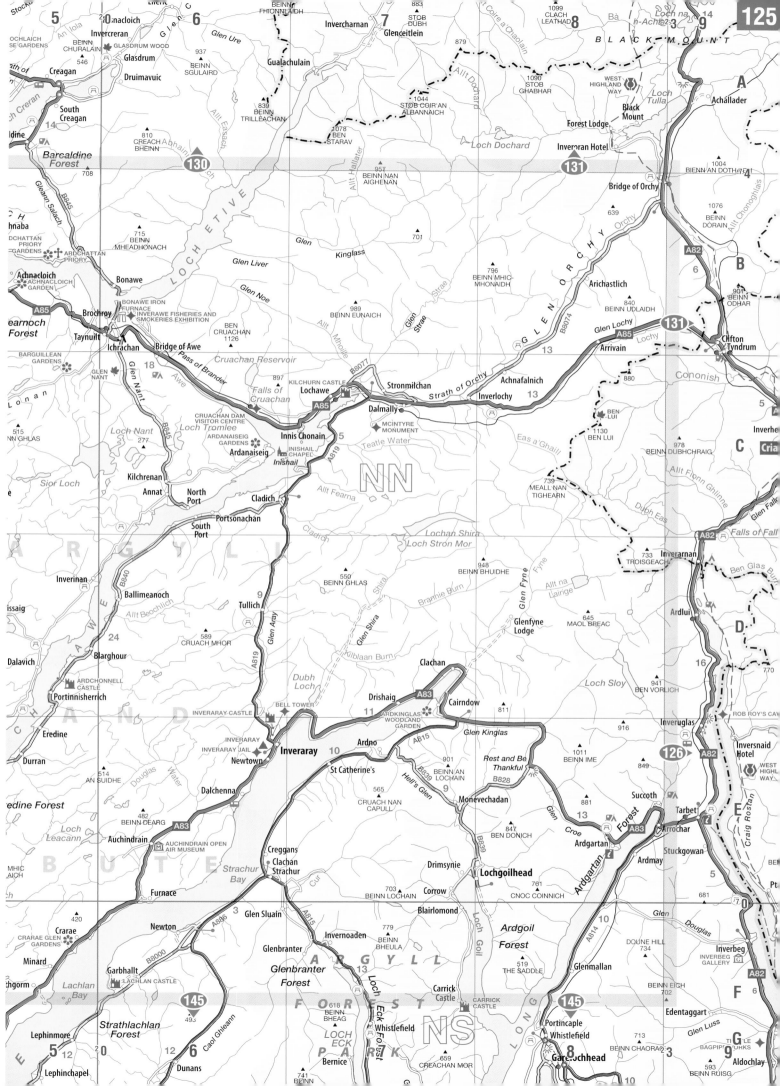

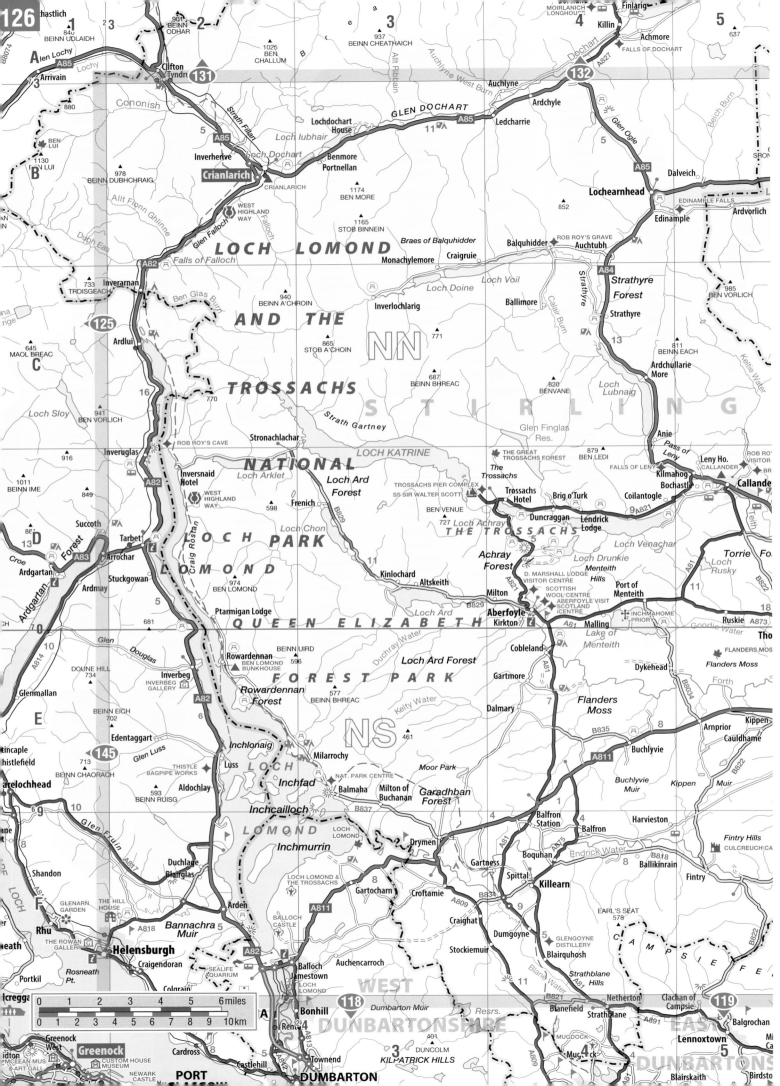

A map of the Fife and East Lothian coast region of Scotland, showing towns, roads and coastal features.

Top area (Dundee region, A row):
DUNDEE, Fintry, Downfield, Douglas & Angus, Baldovie, Mains of Ardestie, Carnoustie, CARNOUS, Barry Links, Craigie, West Ferry, Monifieth, Barnhill, Broughty Fe, Stannergate, BROUGHTY CASTLE MUSEUM, BROUGHTY CASTLE, Buddon Ness, Buddon Ness, Dundee, Tay Bridge, 134, 135

Row B:
Newport-on-Tay, Scotscraig, Tayport, Tentsmuir, Woodhaven, Tay Rail Bridge, Wormit, Kirkton Bottomcraig, Pickletillem, Tentsmuir Forest, Gauldry, Lucklawhill, Rhynd, Carrick, Kilmany, Balmullo, Logie, Rathillet, Leuchars, LEUCHARS NORMAN CHURCH, Guardbridge, EDEN ESTUARY CENTRE, Eden Mouth

Row C:
Cupar, Dairsie or Osnaburgh, Kincaple, St Andrews, ST ANDREWS AQUARIUM, ST ANDREWS BAY, BRITISH GOLF MUS, St Andrews, CATH & ST RULE'S TOWER, Cupar Muir, Kilmaron Castle, Strathkinness, Newpark, Brownhills, Buddo Ness, Boarhills, Babbet Ness, Kemback, Blebocraigs, Balone, ST ANDREWS BOTANIC GARDENS, Kingsbarns, Cambo Ness, CAMBO GARDENS, Carr Brigs, Pitscottie, Denhead, Prior Muir, Stravithie, Tullybothy Craigs, Craighead, Bridgend, HILL OF TARVIT MANSIONHOUSE, Baldinnie, Cameron Res, Cameron Burn, Dunino, Balcomie, Fife Ness, Ceres, Craigrothie, FIFE FOLK MUSEUM, SCOTSTARVIT TOWER

Row D:
Peat Inn, Kingsmuir, Lochty, CRAIL TOLBOOTH, Radernie, Kingshall, SCOTLAND'S SECRET BUNKER, Crail, CRAIL MUSEUM AND HERITAGE CENTRE, Woodside, Lathones, West Ness, New Gilston, Largoward, Carnbee, Pitcorthie, Montrave, KELLIE CASTLE AND GARDEN, Pitkierie, Wester Newburn, Arncroach, Kilrenny, FIFE COASTAL PATH, NO, Kirkton of Largo, Drumeldrie, Colinsburgh, Anstruther Easter, SCOTTISH FISHERIES MUSEUM, Lundin Links, Abercrombie, Pittenweem, Anstruther Wester, Bonnybank, Balchrystie, Kilconquhar, Scoonie, ROBINSON CRUSOE STATUE, Lower Largo, SILVERBURN ESTATE, ST FILLAN'S CAVE, ST MONAN'S WINDMILL, Balcurvie, Ardross, St Monans, ST MONAN'S CHURCH, Leven, Earlsferry, Elie, Sauchar Pt., ISLE OF MAY

Row E:
Methil, MUSEUM, Innerleven, Largo Bay, Ruddons Pt., Chapel Ness, Isle of May, Buckhaven, FIFE COASTAL PATH, Wemyss

Row F:
FORTH, Fidra, Craigleith, Bass Rock, Eyebroughy, SCOTTISH SEABIRD CENTRE MUSEUM, North Berwick, TANTALLON CASTLE, DIRLETON CASTLE & GARDENS, Auldhame, MUIRFIELD, Dirleton, Scoughall, Gullane Bay, NT, Gullane, West Fenton, Kingston, Whitekirk, St. Baldred's Cradle, Aberlady Bay, Fenton Barns, Tyne Mouth, JOHN MUIR BIRTHPLACE, Aberlady, MYRETON MOTOR MUSEUM, Drem

Row G (bottom):
121, Craigielaw, 122, JOHN MUIR, Dunbar, Gosford Bay, GOSFORD HOUSE, THE CHESTERS FORT, East Fortune, Tyninghame, Belhaven, West Barns, Cockenzie and Port Seton, SETON COLLEGIATE CHURCH, Ballencrieff, Spittal, NATIONAL MUS OF FLIGHT, Athelstaneford, Preston, East Linton, PRESTON MILL & PHANTASSIE DOOCOT, Broxburn, Barns Ness, Longniddry, Huntington, HOPETOUN MON, HAILES CASTLE, Traprain, Pitcox, Biel Water, Spott, Meikle, East Barns, Skateraw

Road numbers visible: A85, A92, A914, A919, A91, B945, B946, B940, B939, B9131, A917, B941, A915, B942, B9171, A916, B931, A198, B1347, B1345, B1377, A199, A1, B1343, B1407, A6137, B1337

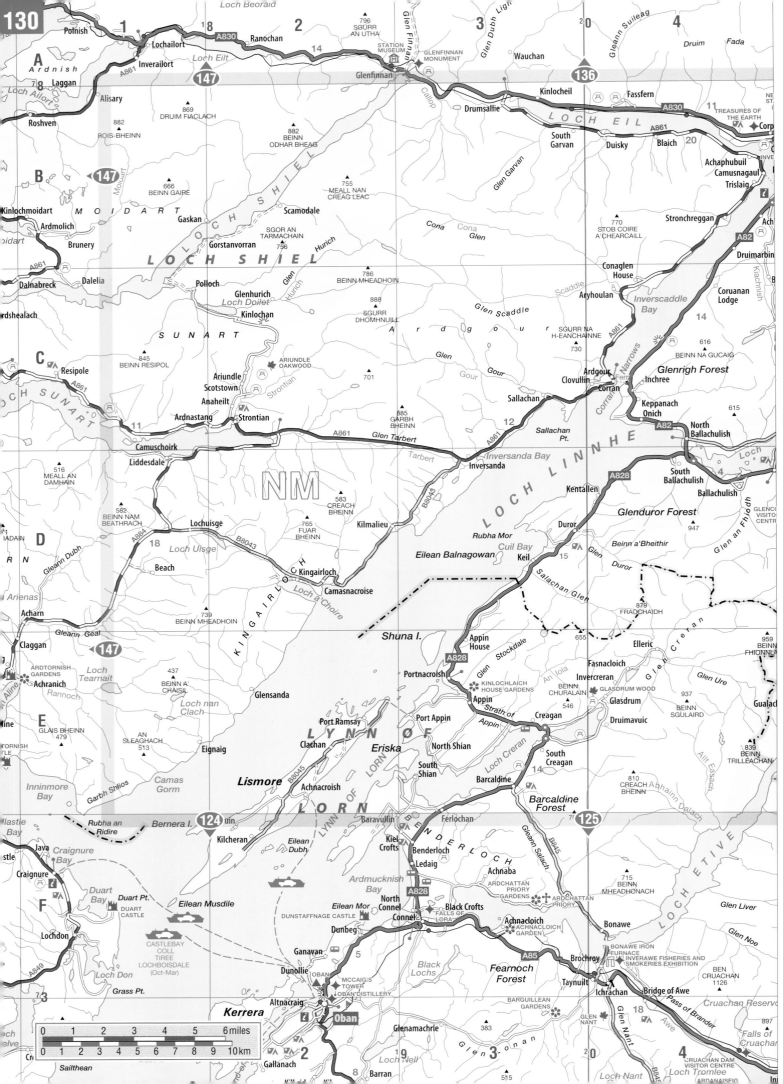

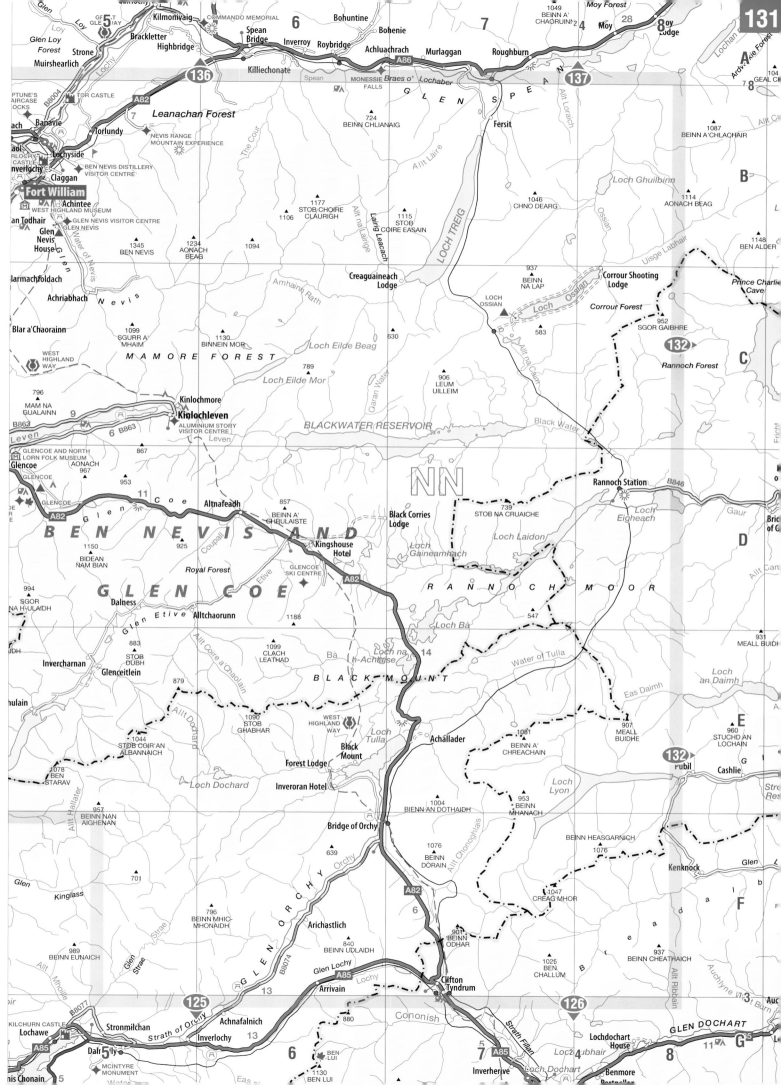

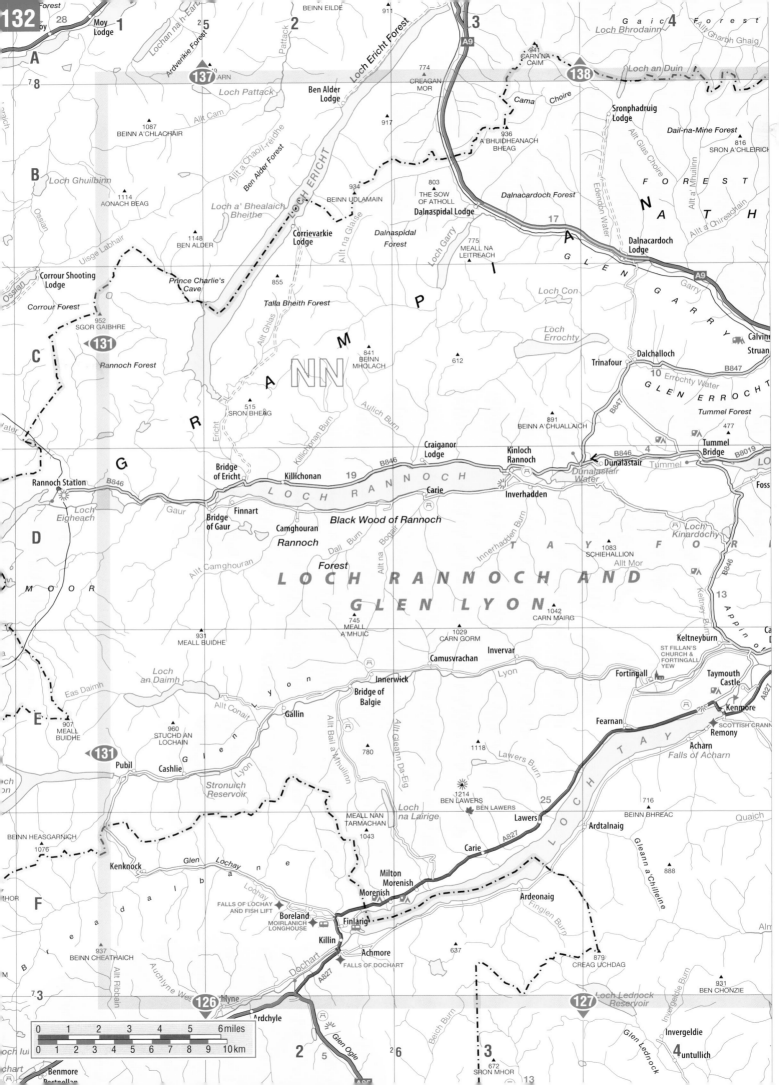

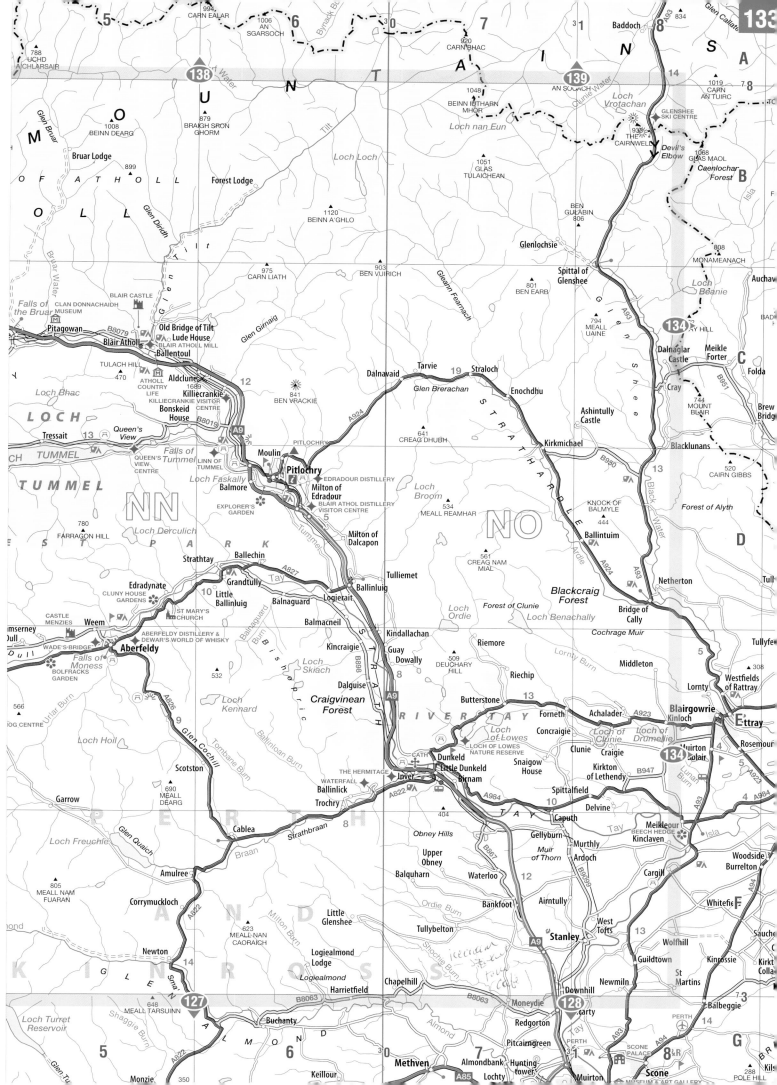

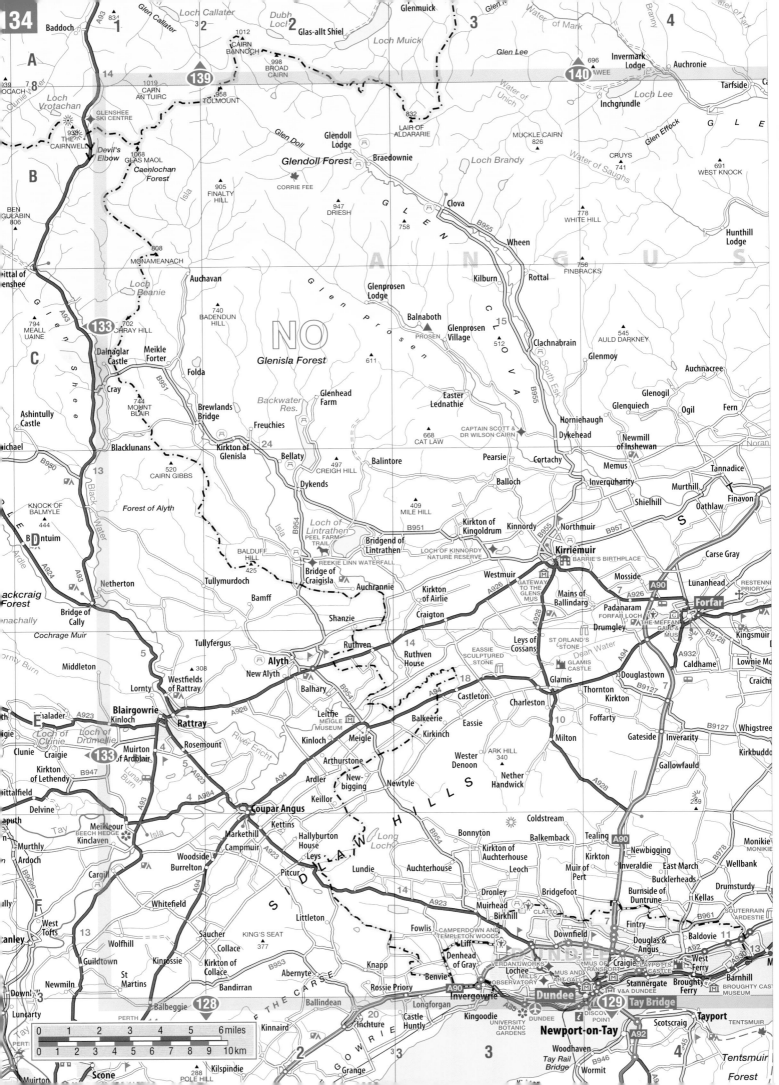

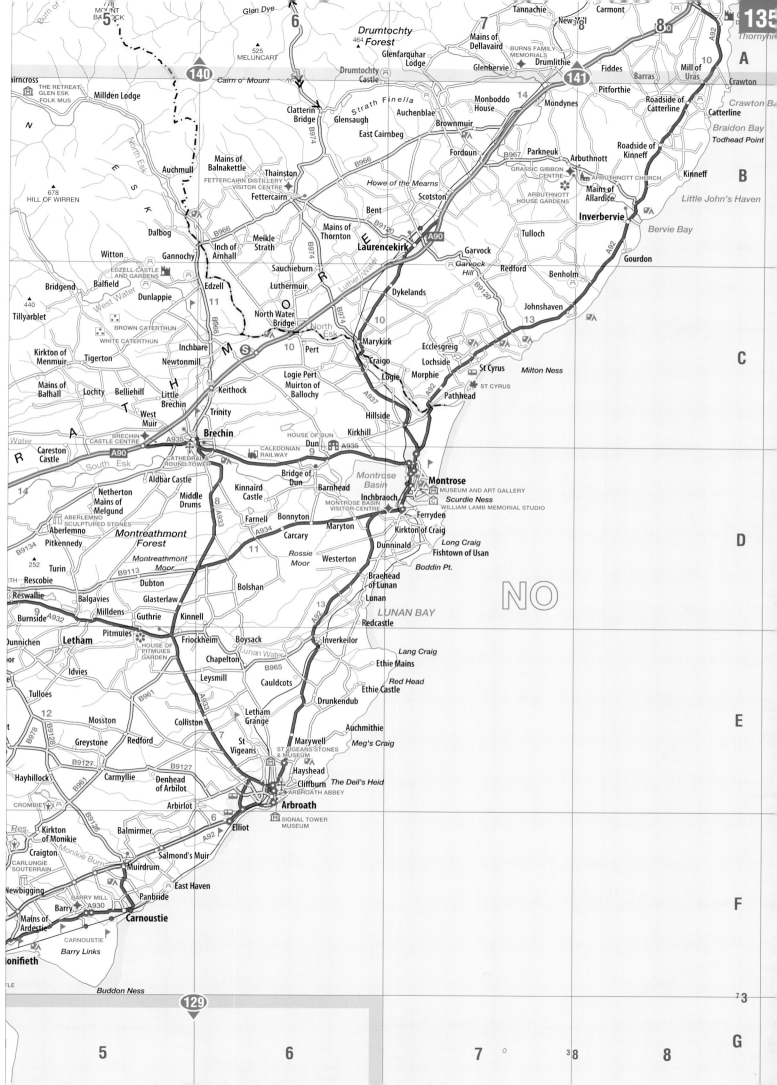

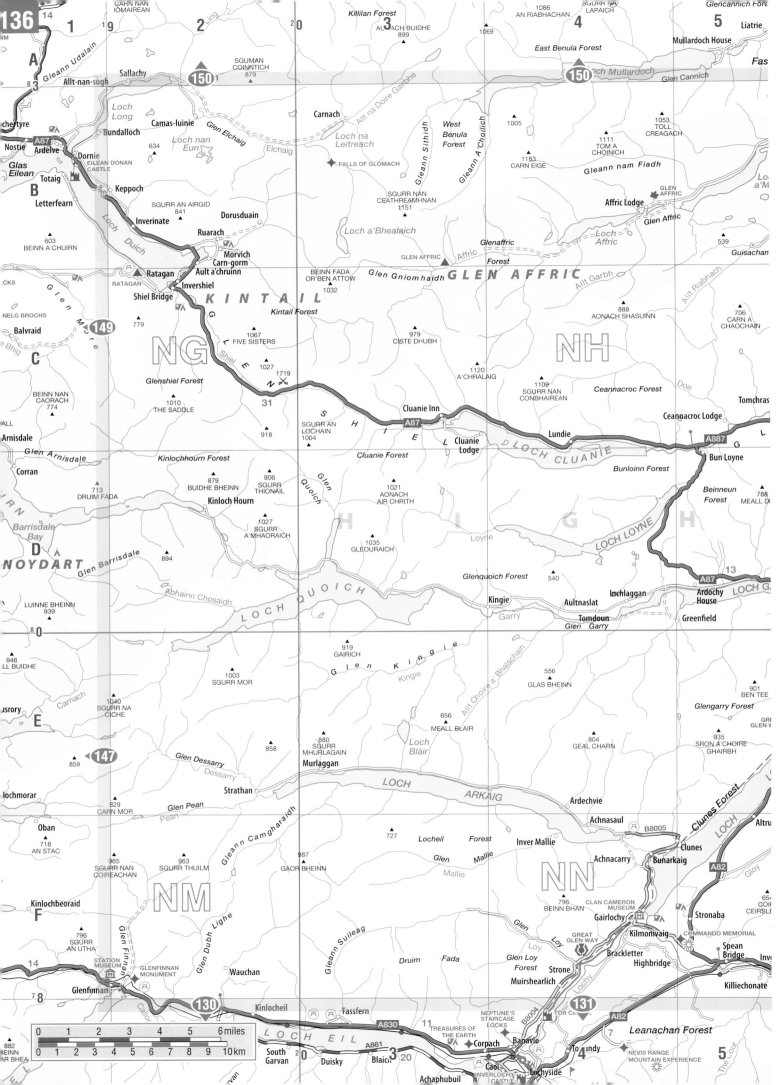

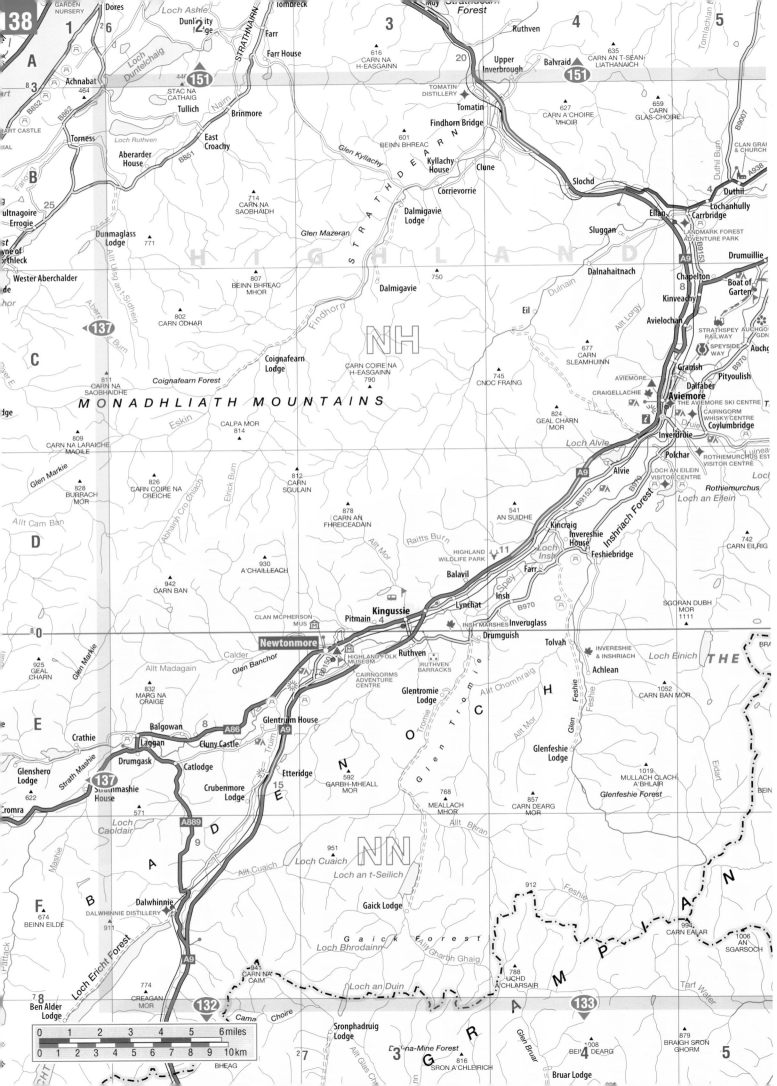

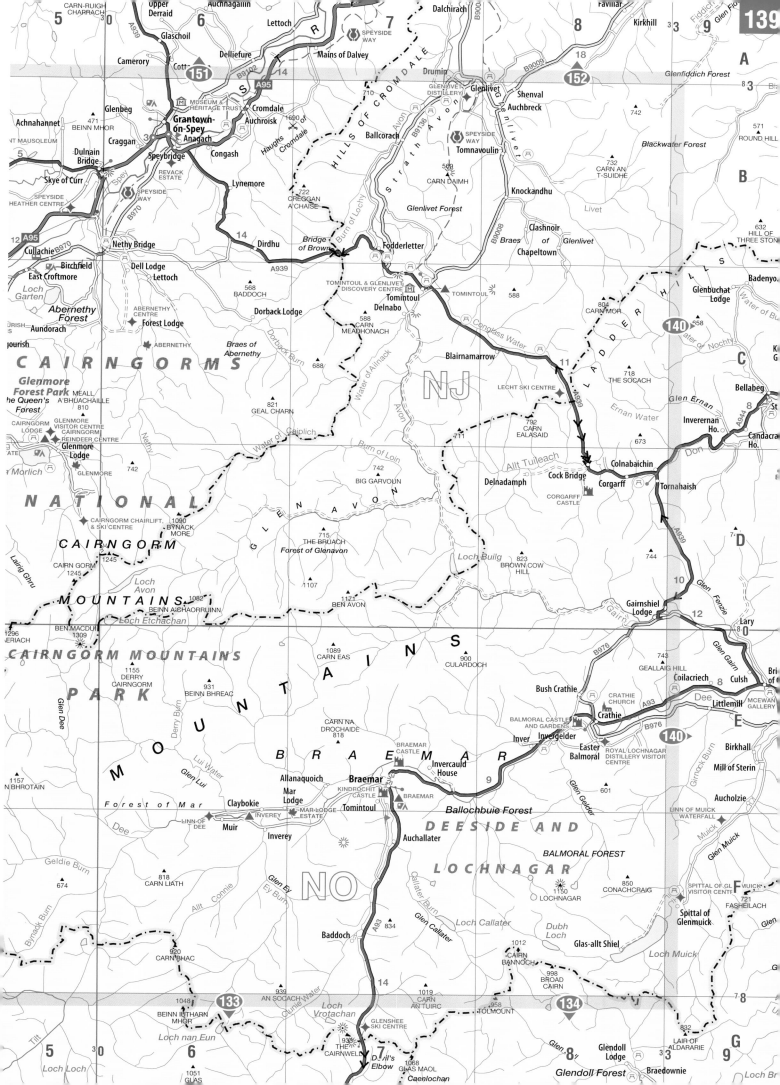

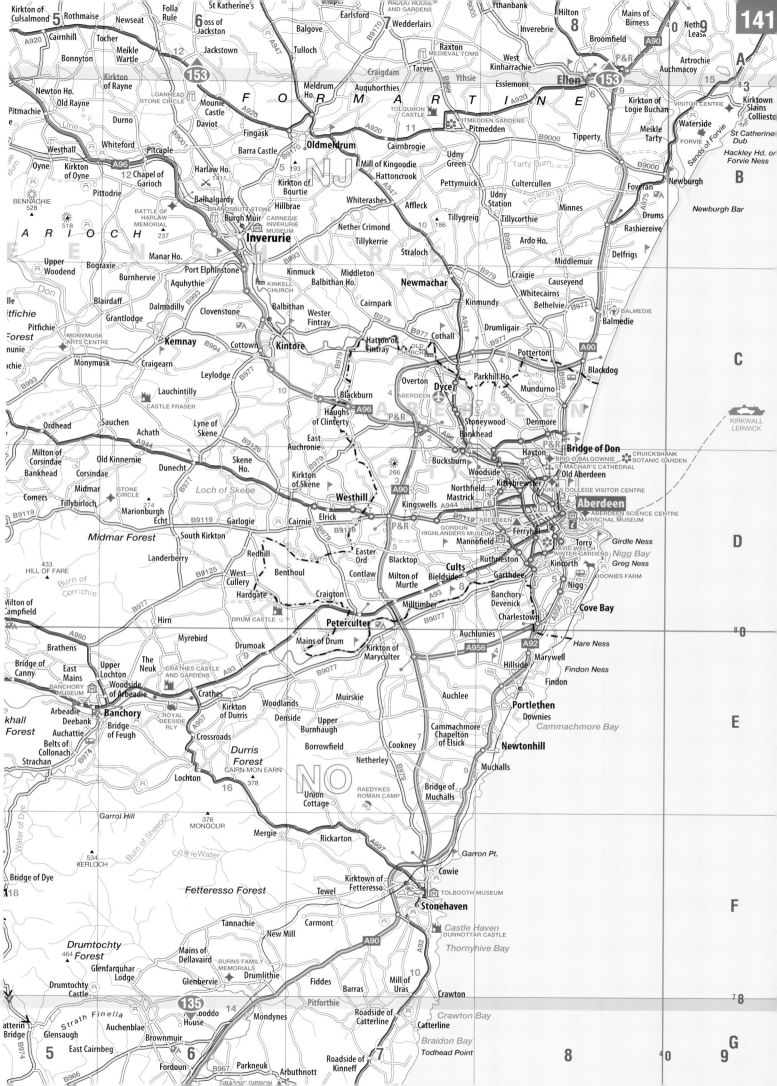

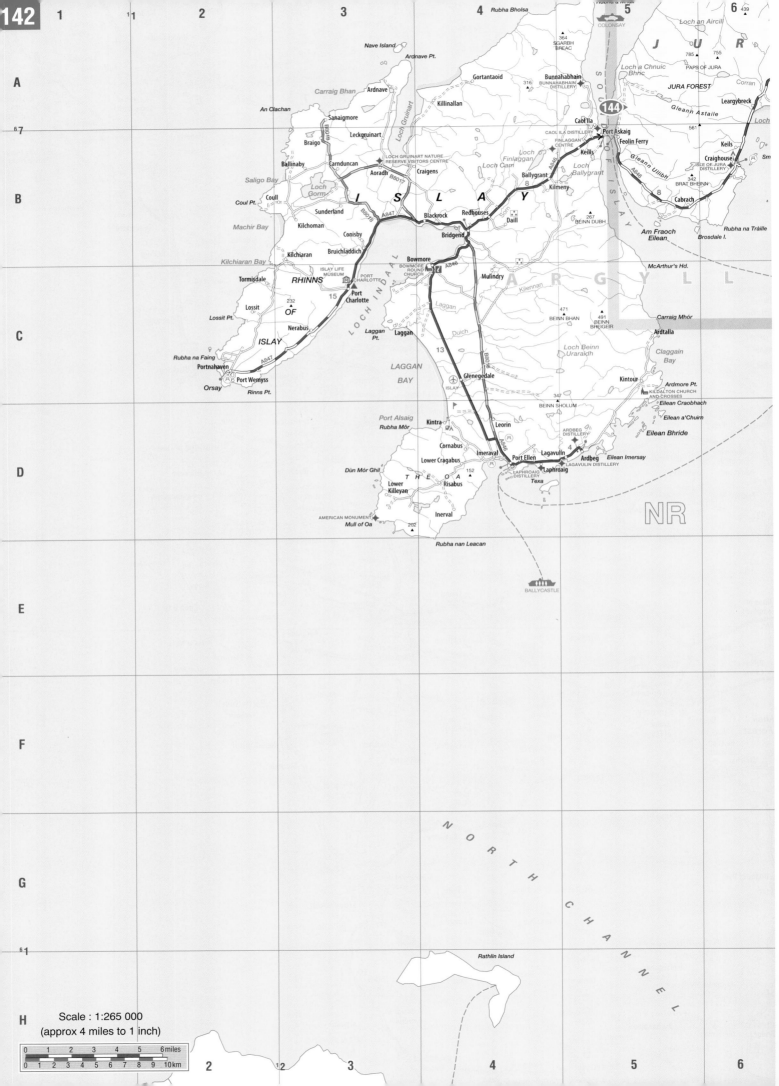

Scale : 1:265 000
(approx 4 miles to 1 inch)

0 1 2 3 4 5 6 miles
0 1 2 3 4 5 6 7 8 9 10km

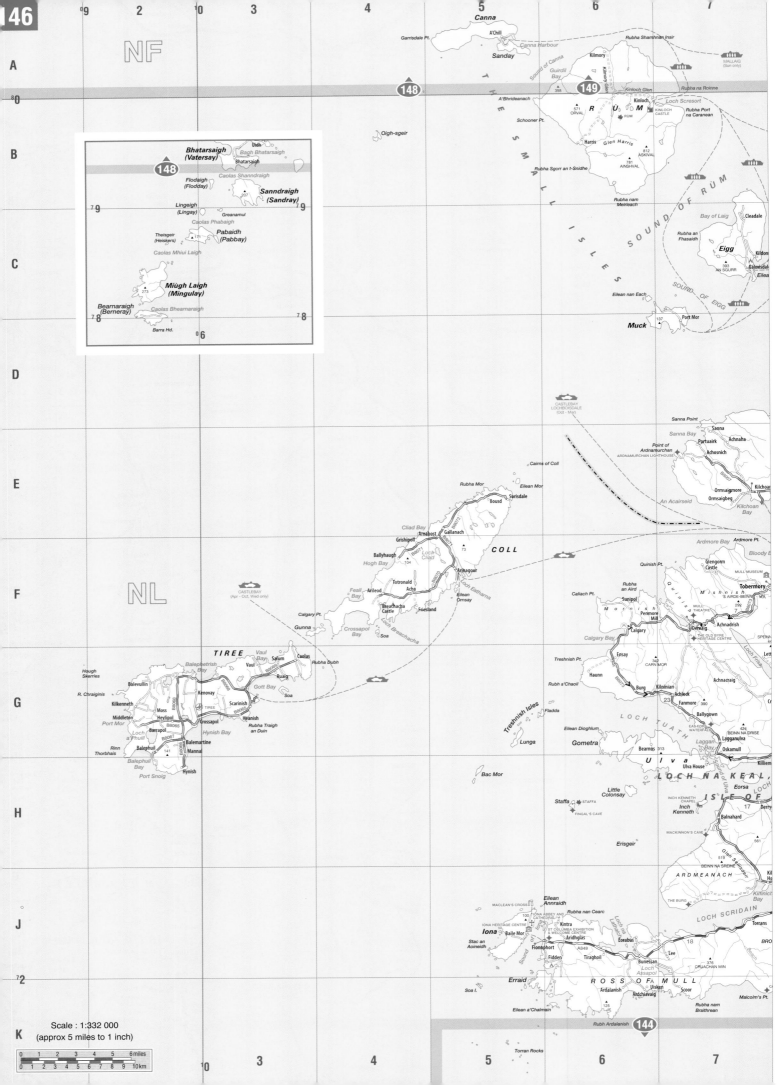

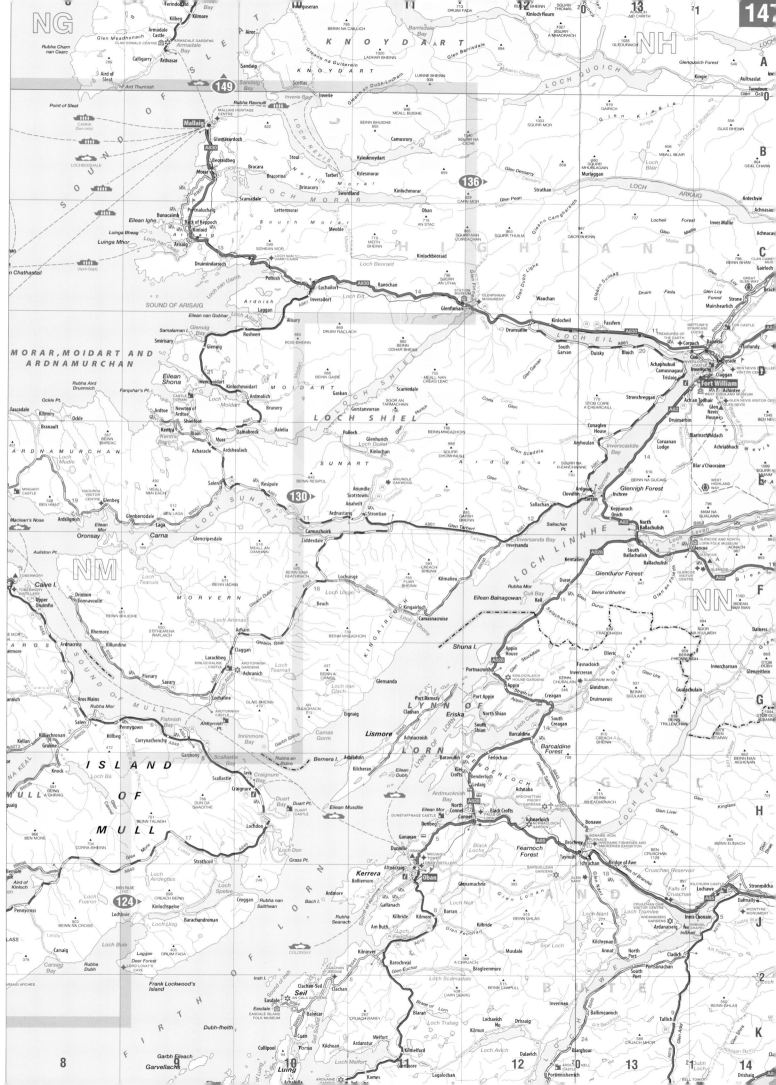

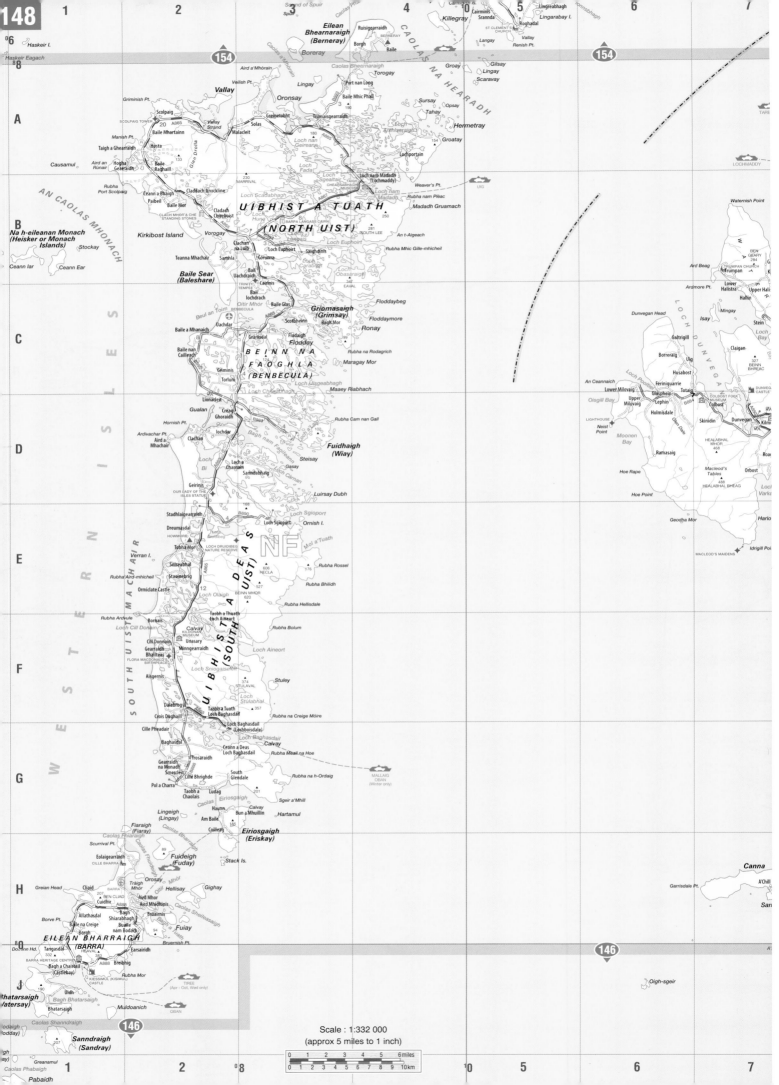

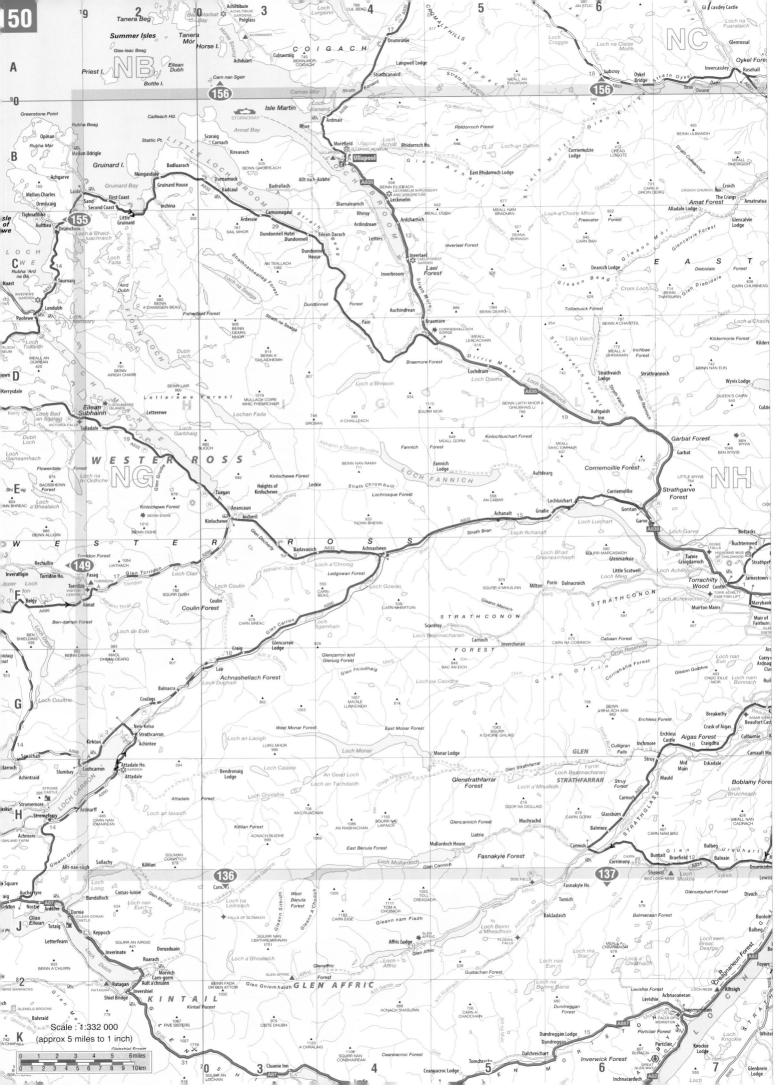

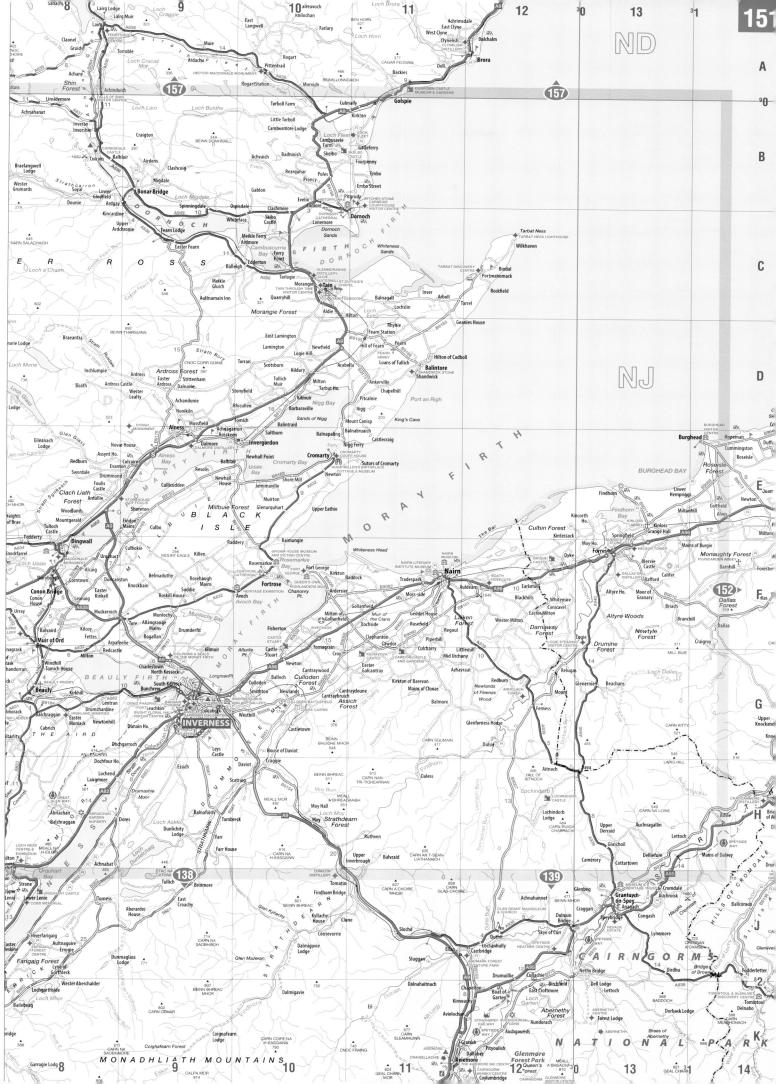

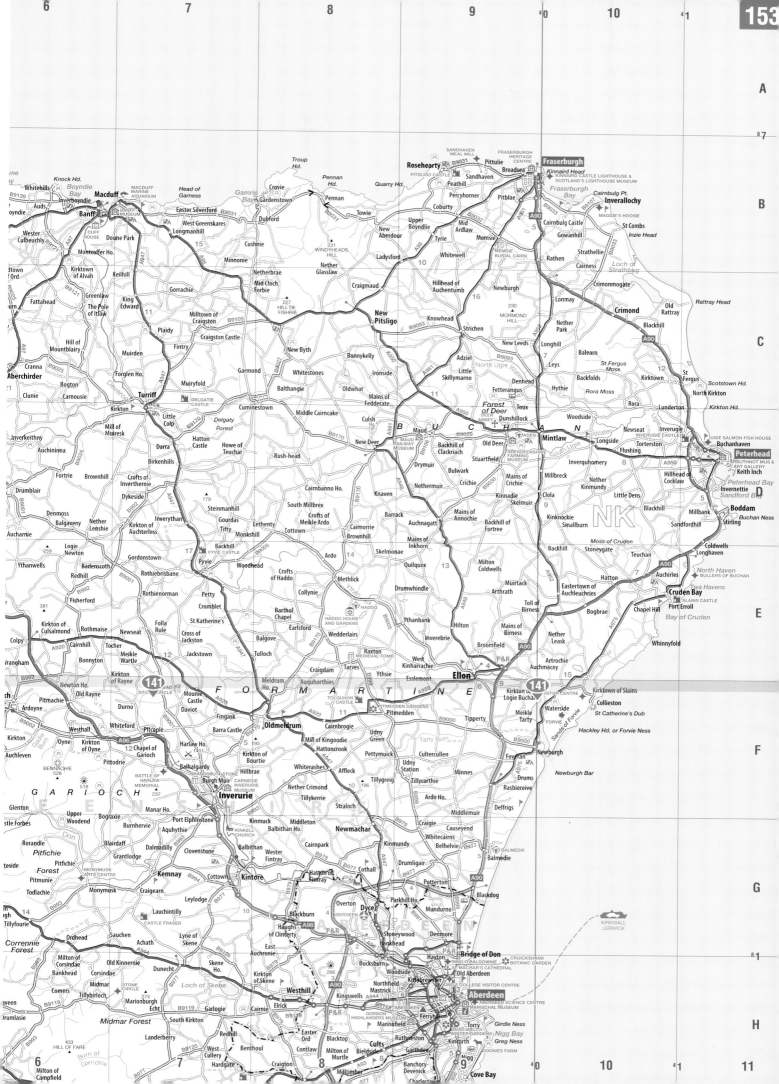

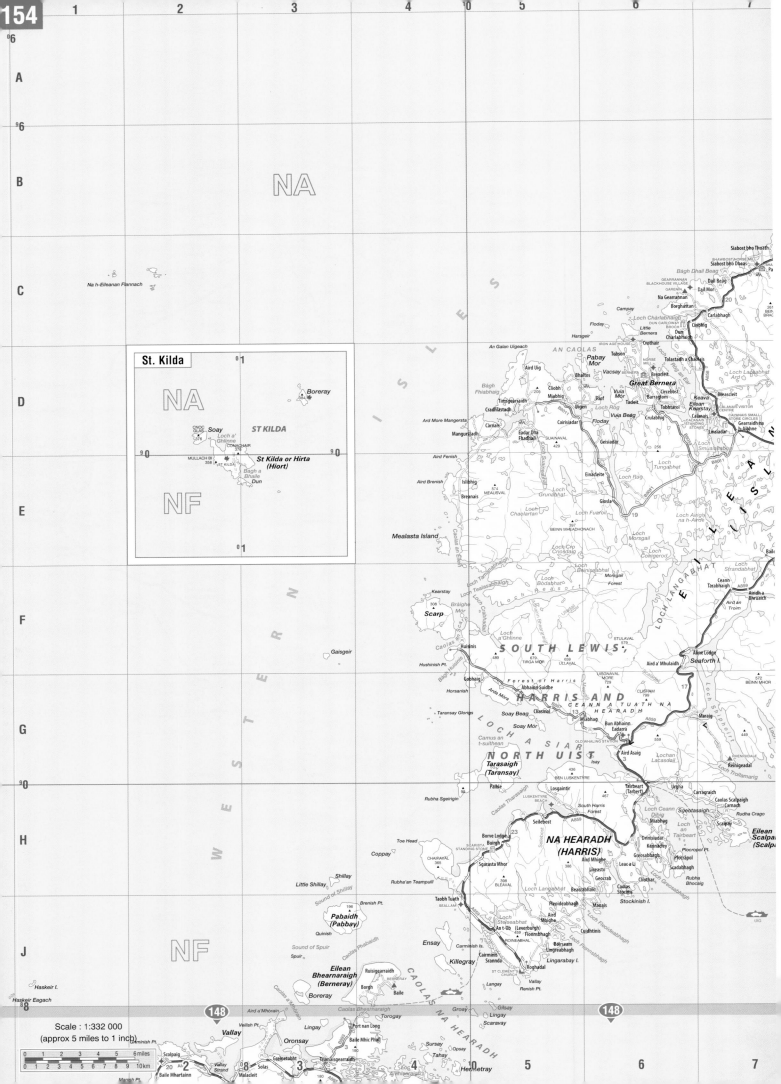

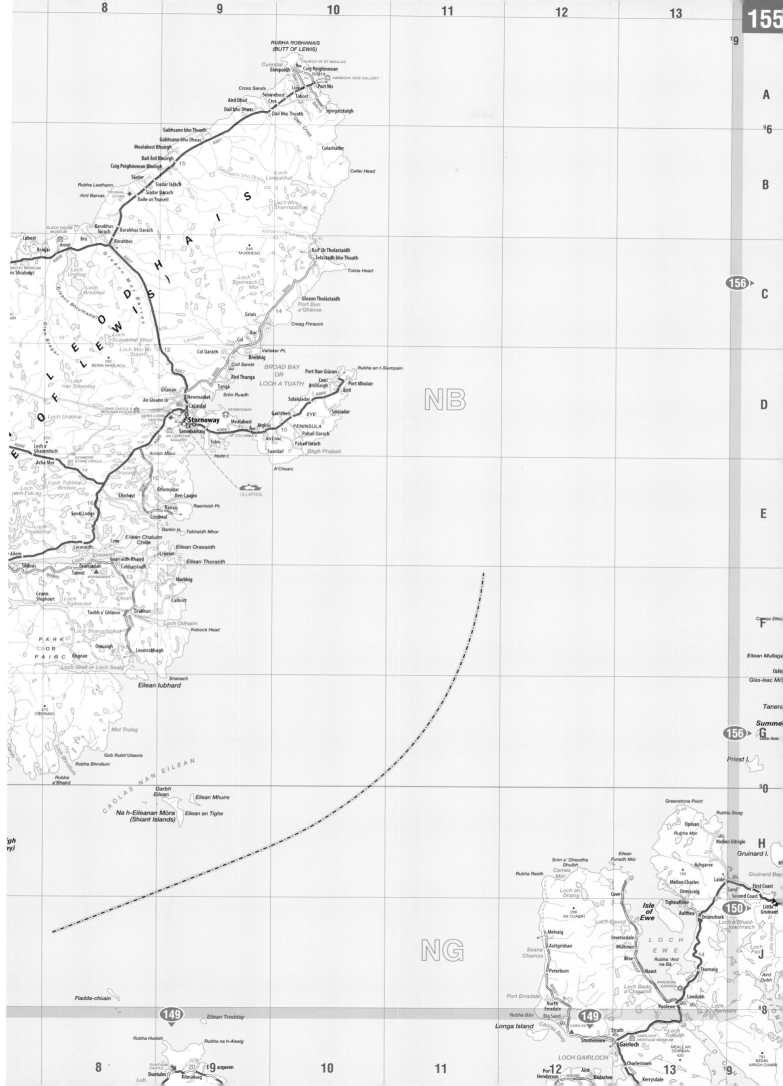

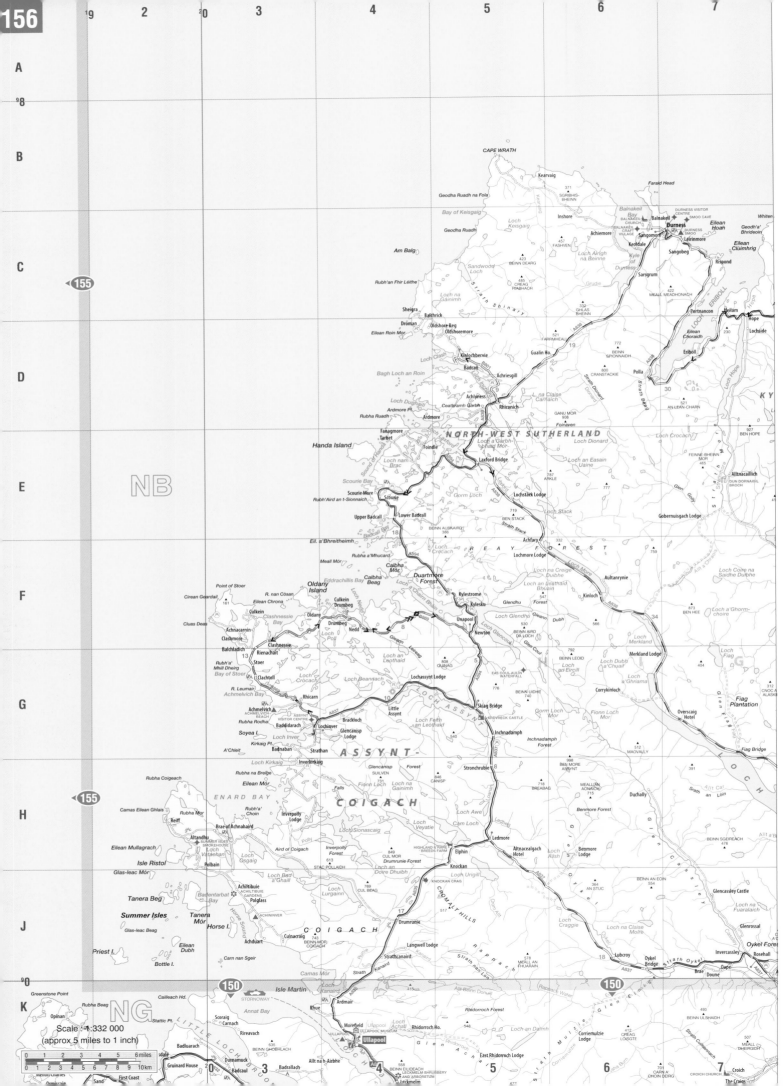

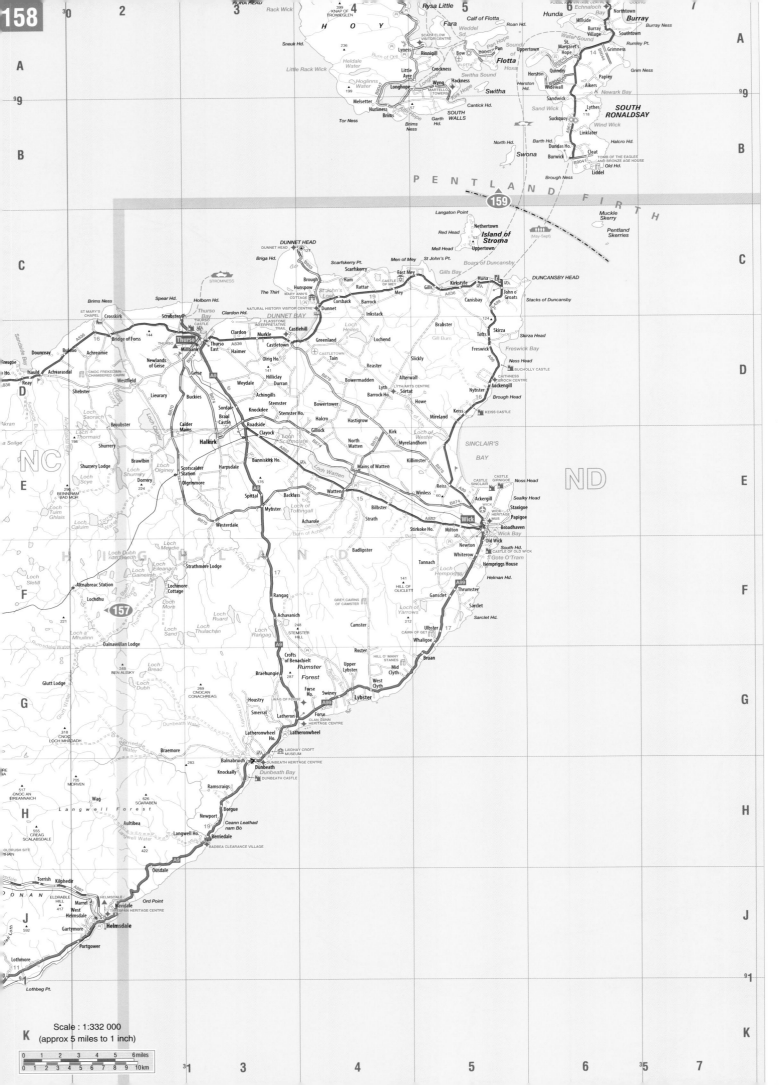

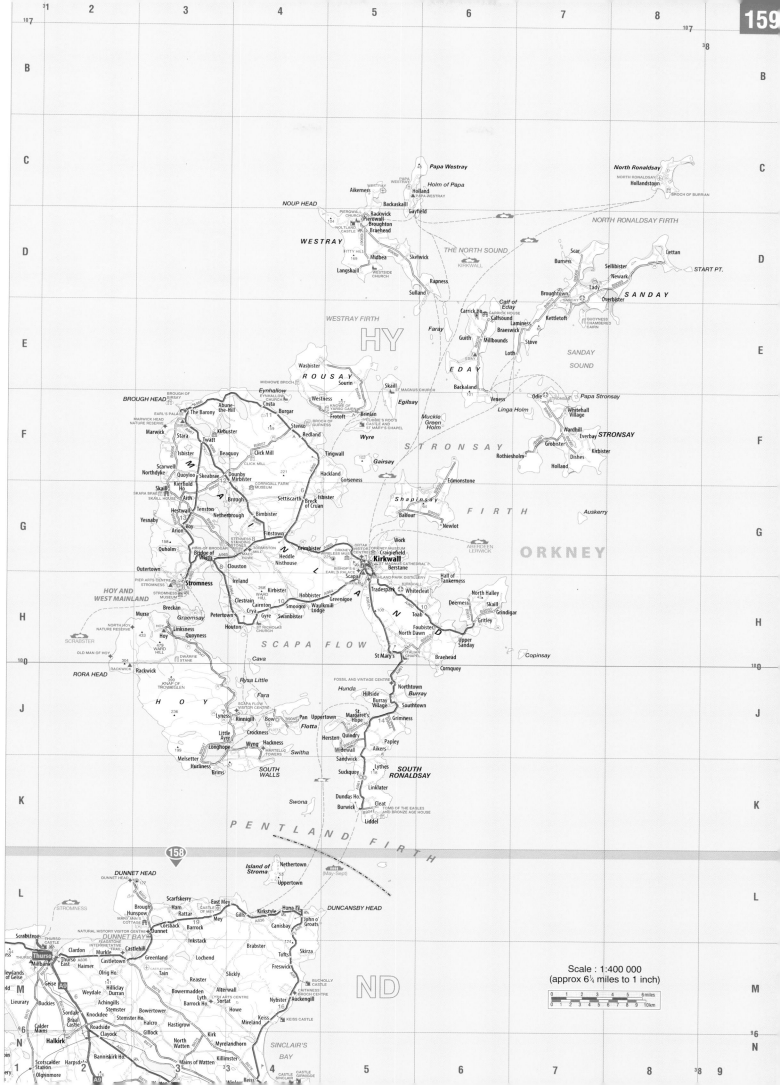

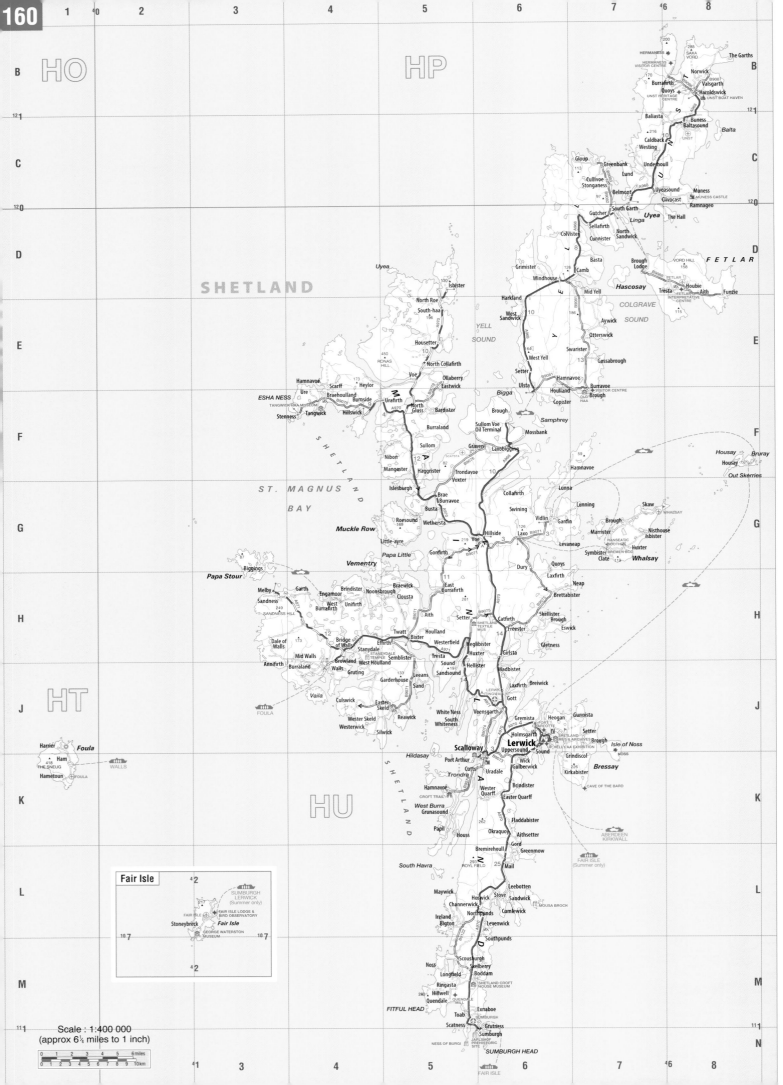

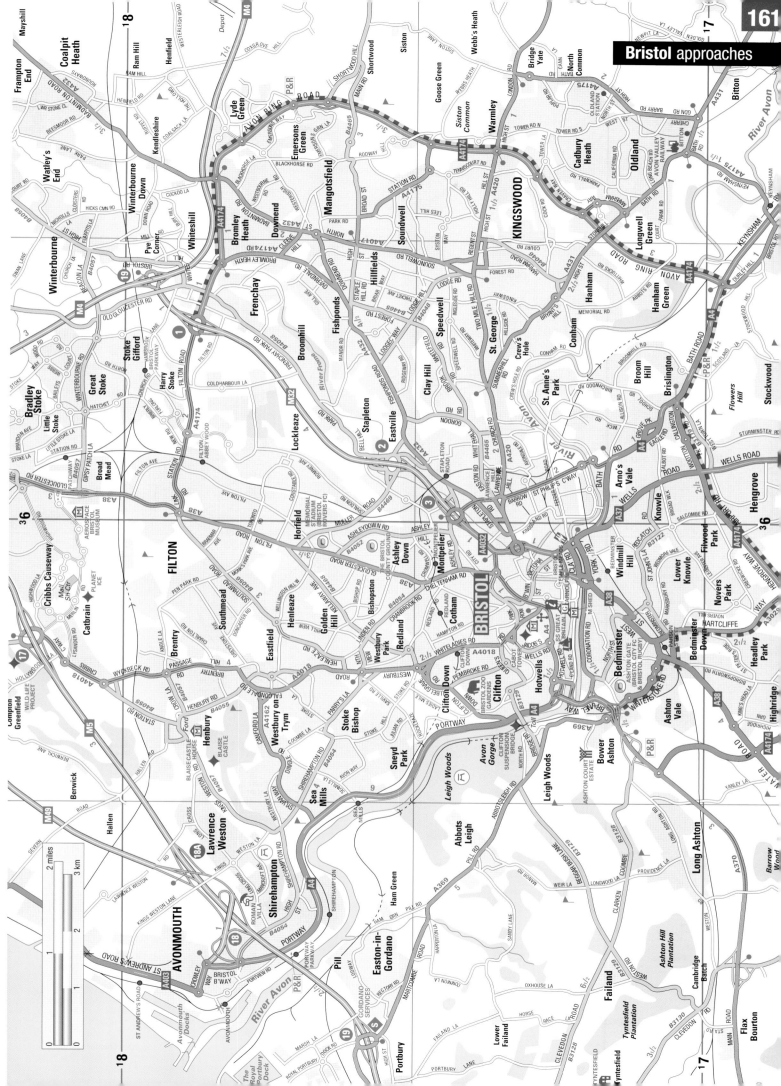

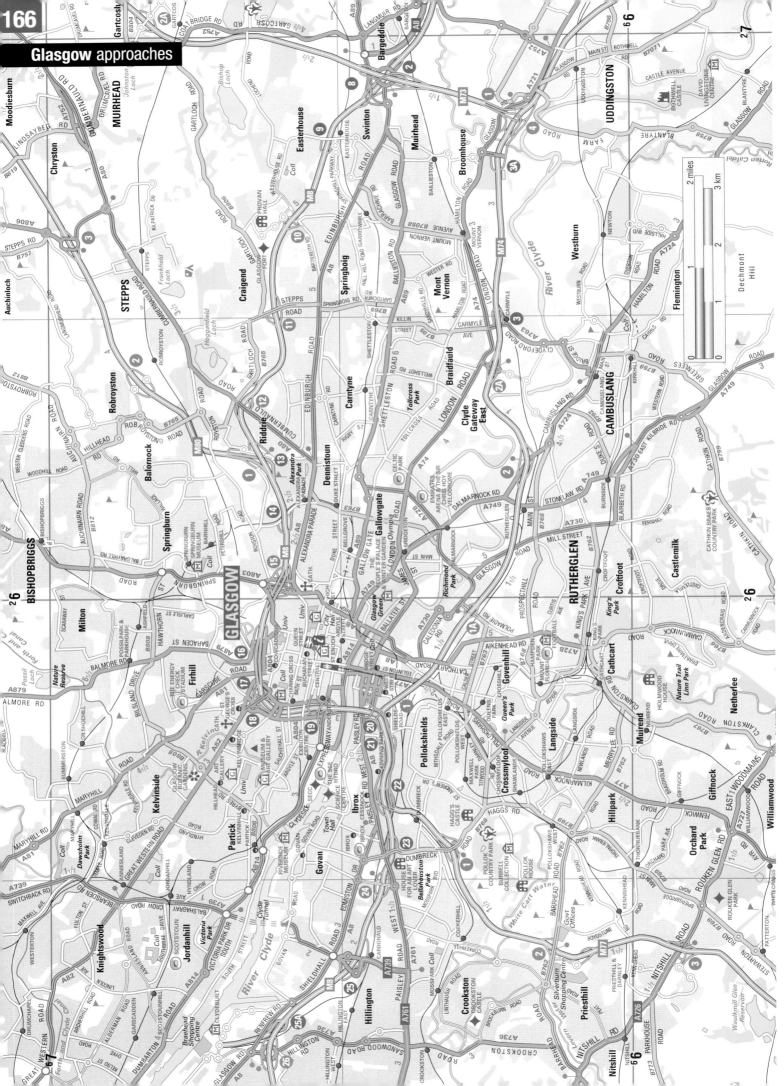

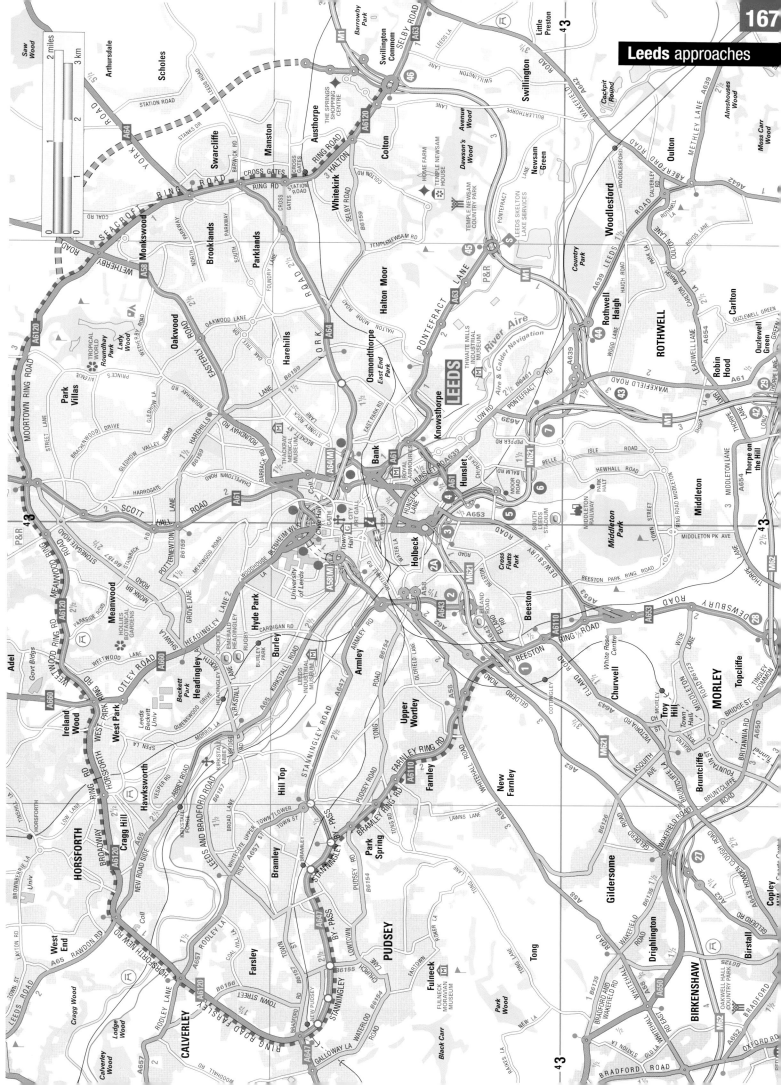

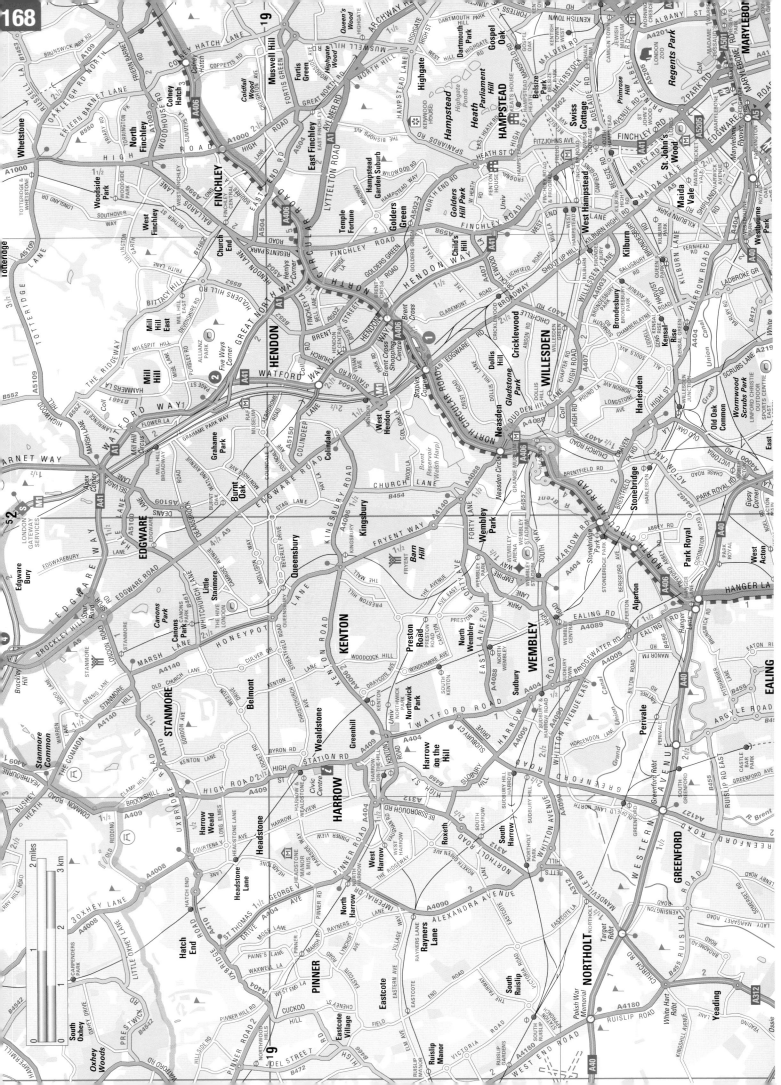

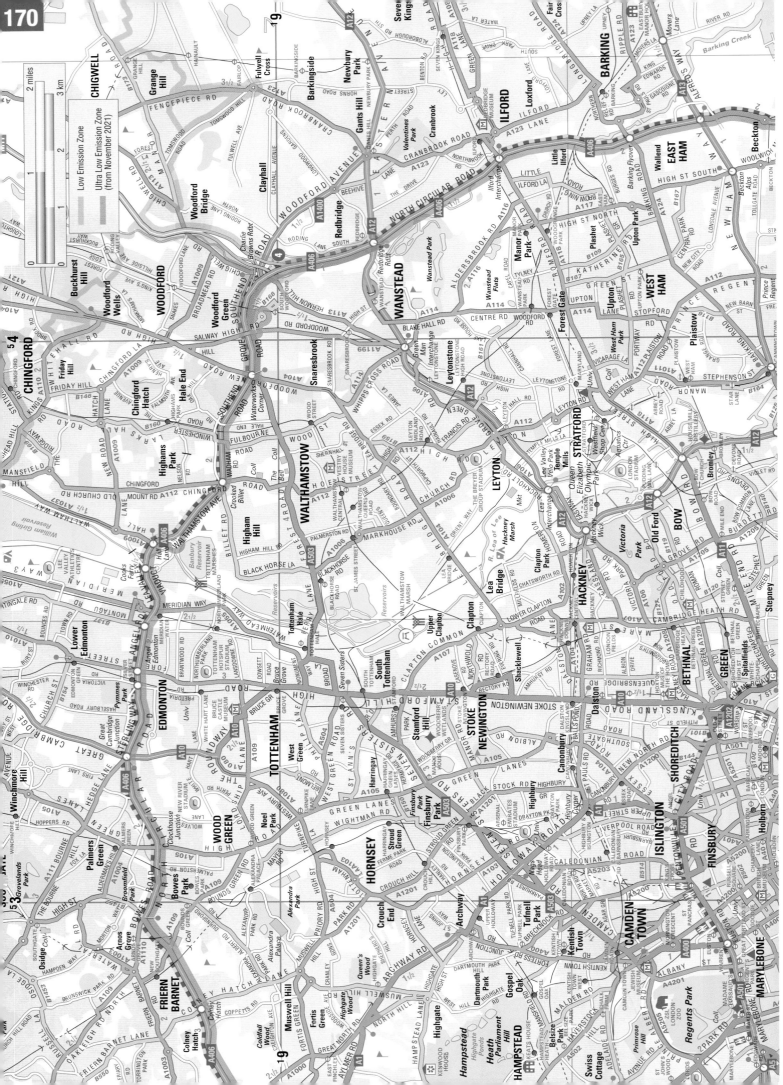

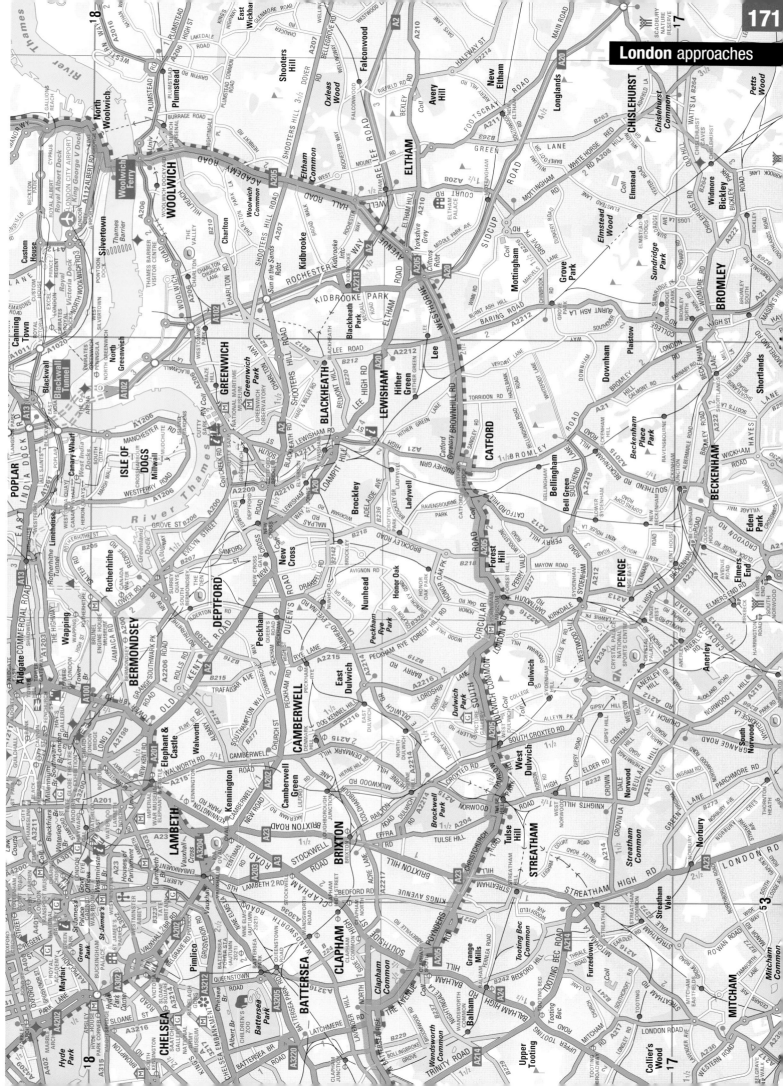

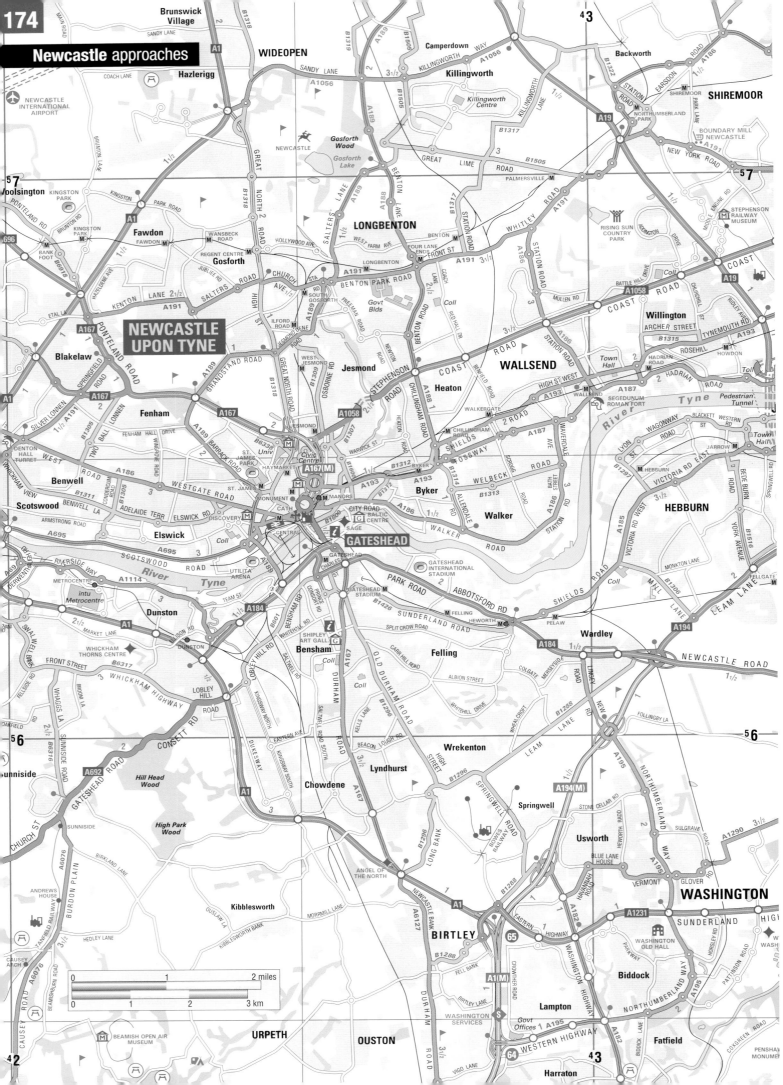

Town plan symbols

Motorway

Primary route – dual, single carriageway

A road – dual, single carriageway

B road – dual, single carriageway

Minor through road

One-way street

Pedestrian roads

Shopping streets

Railway with station

Tramway with station

Underground or Metro station

H Hospital

P Parking

Police

PO Post Office

Shopmobility

Youth hostel

Bus or railway station building

Shopping precinct or retail park

Park

Congestion charge zone

✝ Abbey or cathedral

Ancient monument

Aquarium

Art gallery

Bird collection or aviary

Building of interest

Castle

Church of interest

Cinema

Garden

Historic ship

House

House and garden

Museum

Preserved railway

Roman antiquity

Safari park

Theatre

ℹ Tourist information

Zoo

◆ Other place of interest

Aberdeen

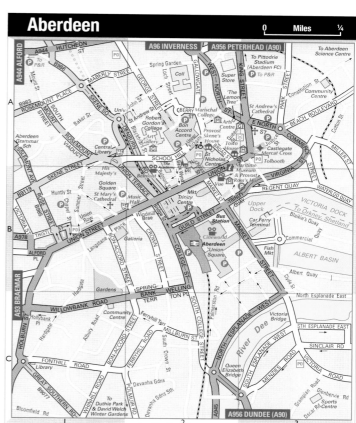

Ayr

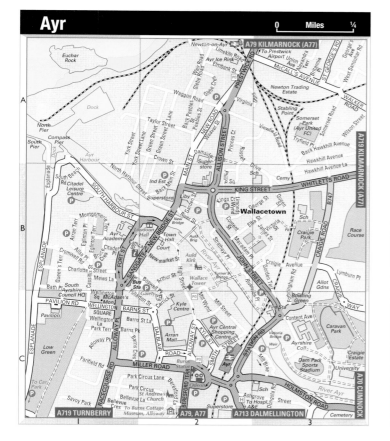

Bath

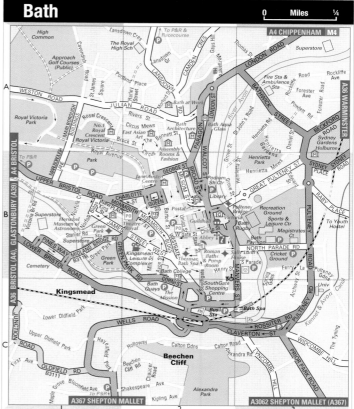

Birmingham

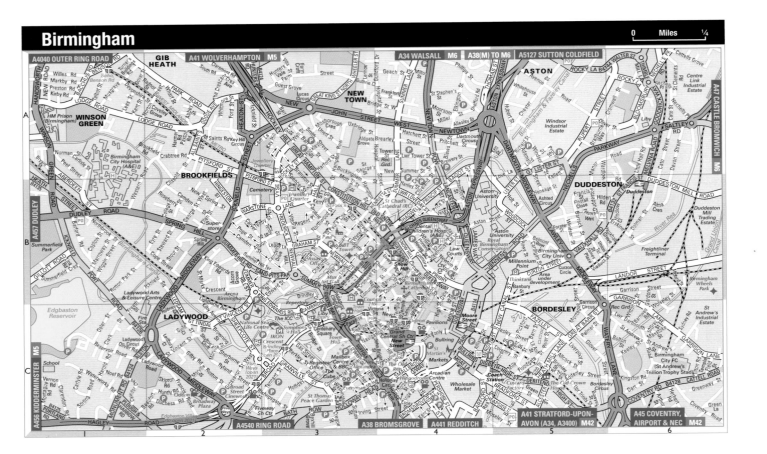

Blackpool

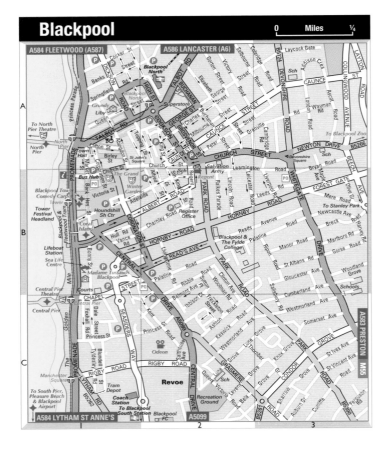

Bournemouth

Bradford

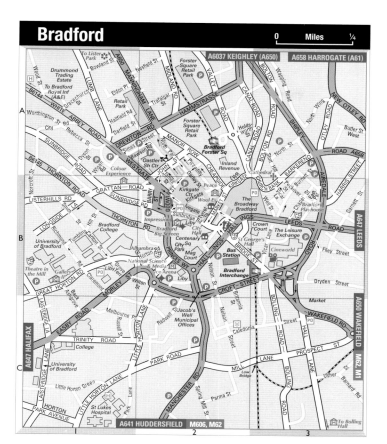

Brighton

Bristol

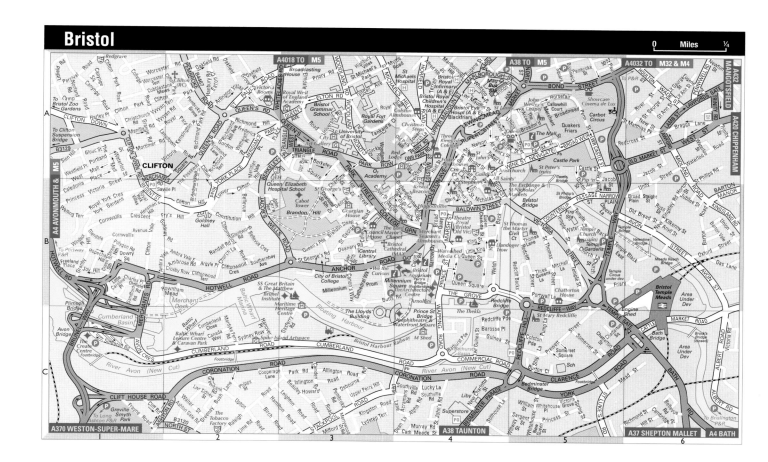

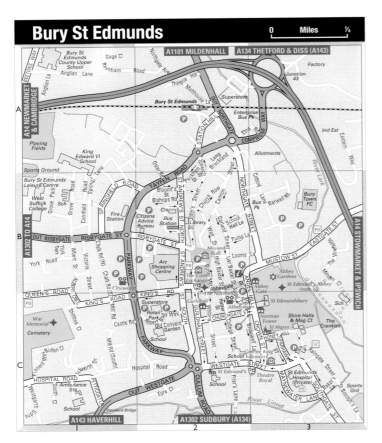

Bury St Edmunds

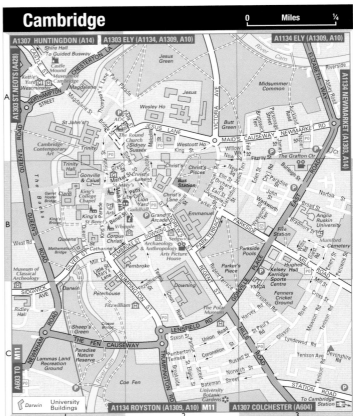

Cambridge

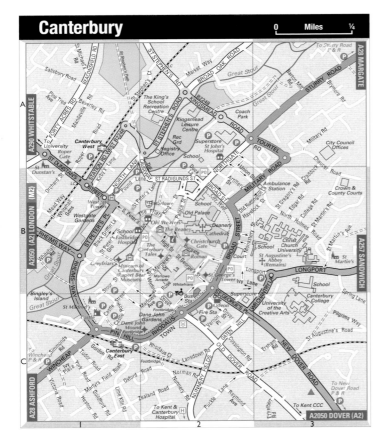

Canterbury

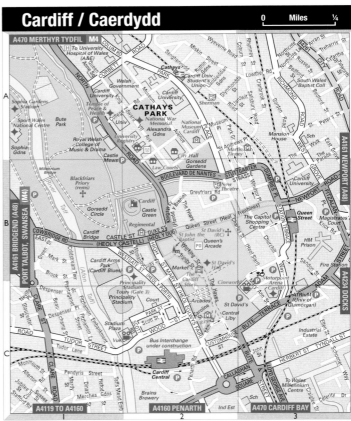

Cardiff / Caerdydd

Carlisle

0 Miles ¼

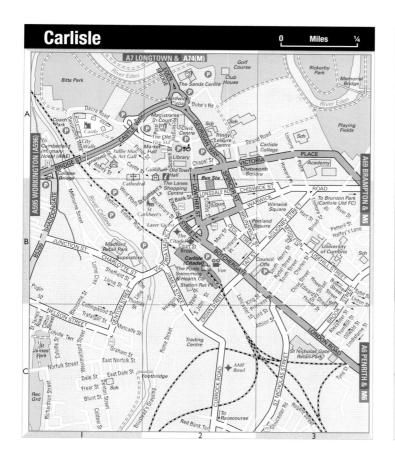

Chelmsford

0 Miles ¼

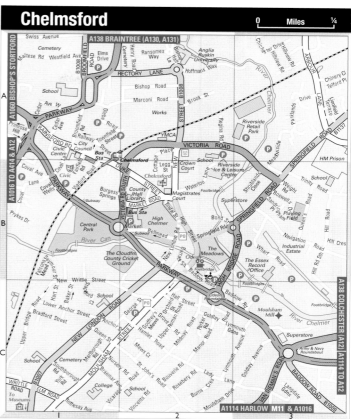

Cheltenham

0 Miles ¼

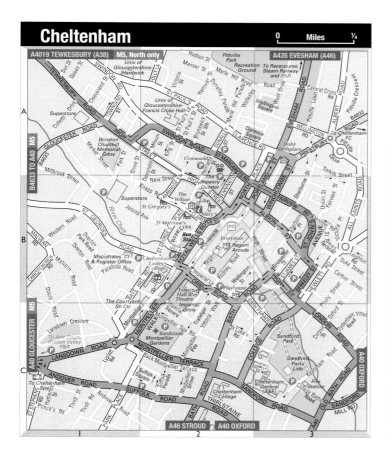

Chester

0 Miles ¼

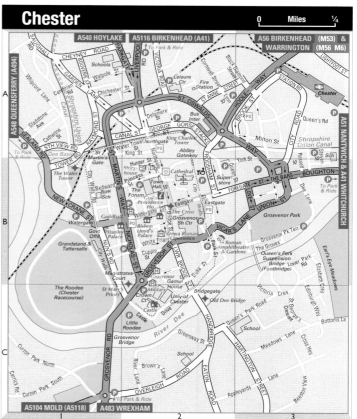

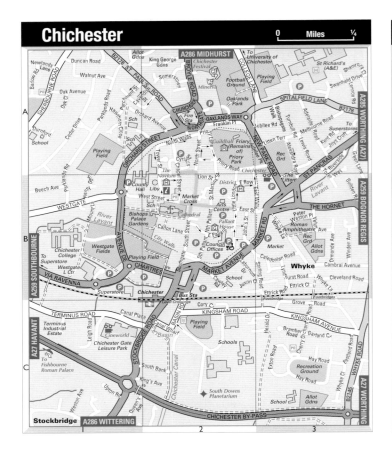

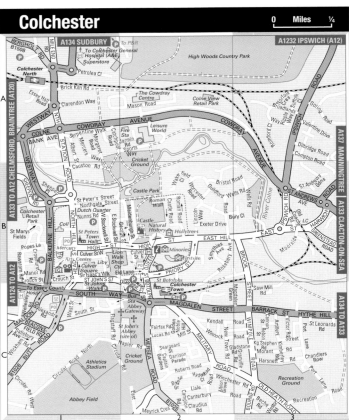

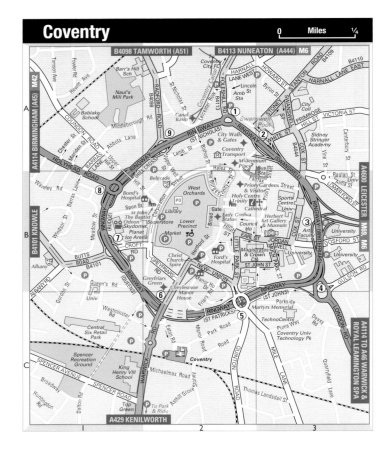

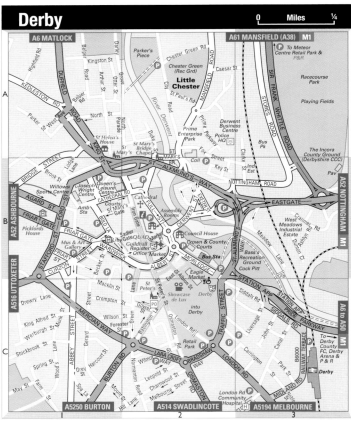

Dorchester

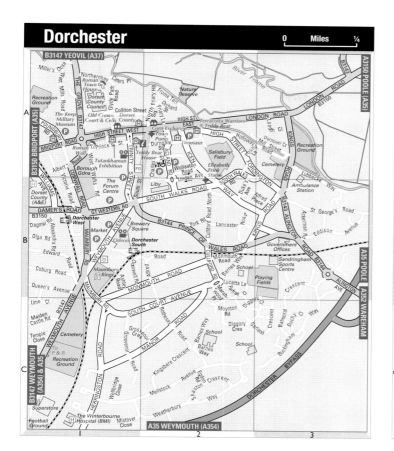

Dumfries

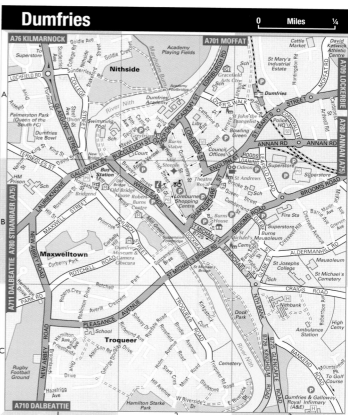

Dundee

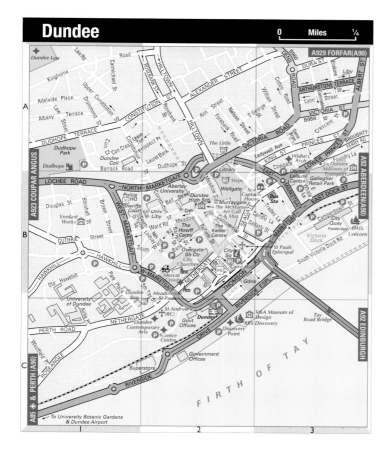

Durham

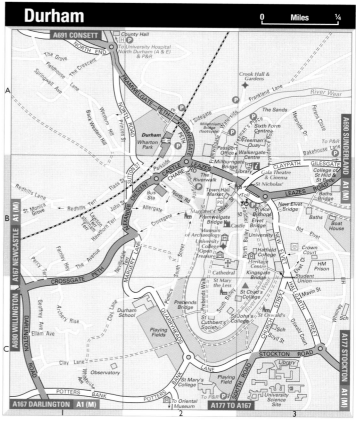

Edinburgh

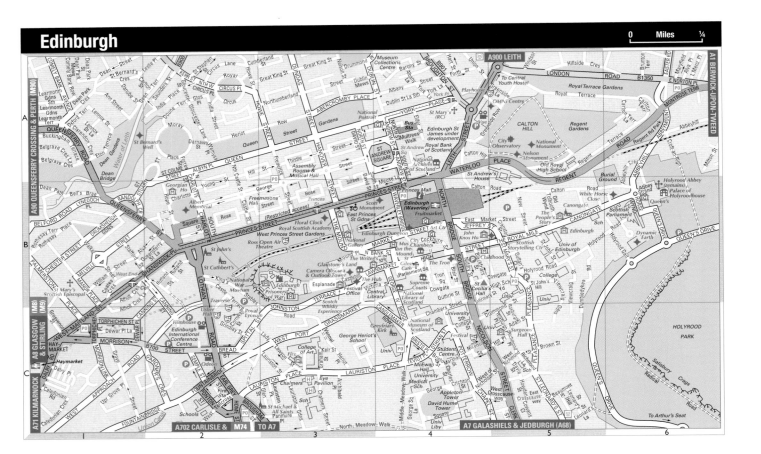

Exeter

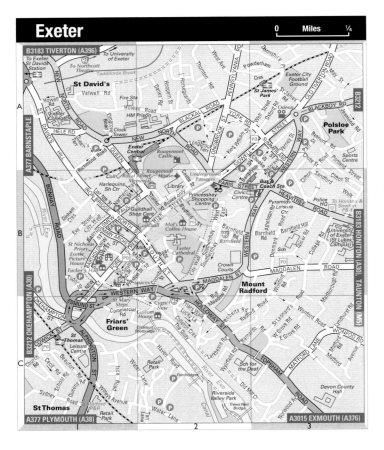

Gloucester

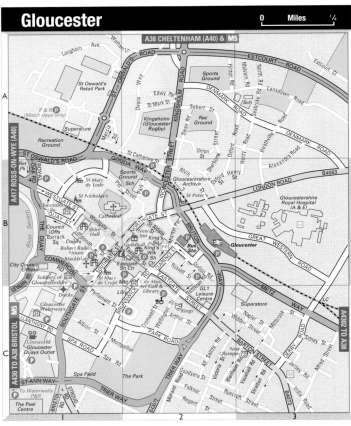

Glasgow

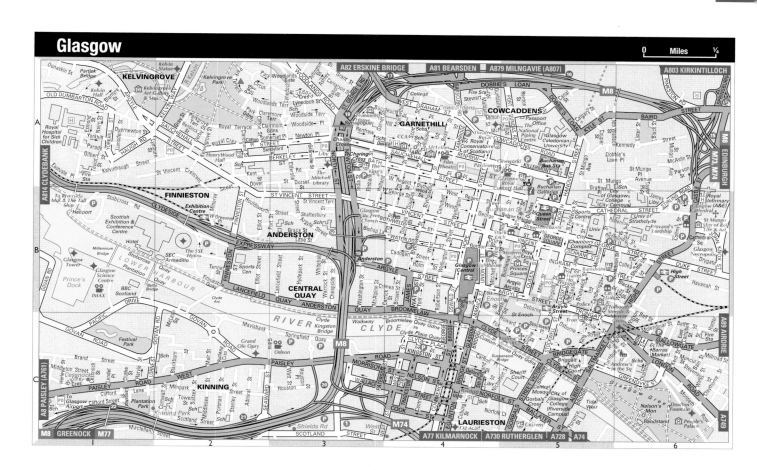

Grimsby

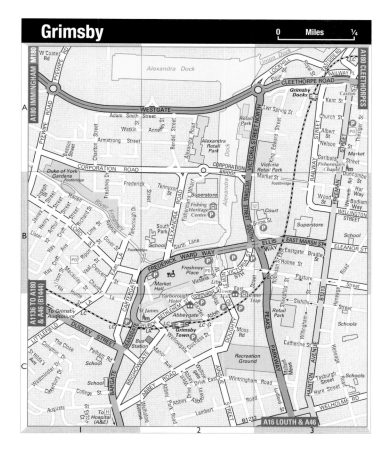

Harrogate

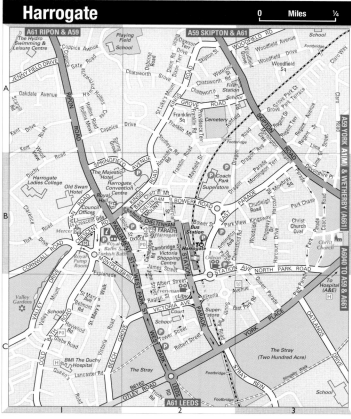

Hull

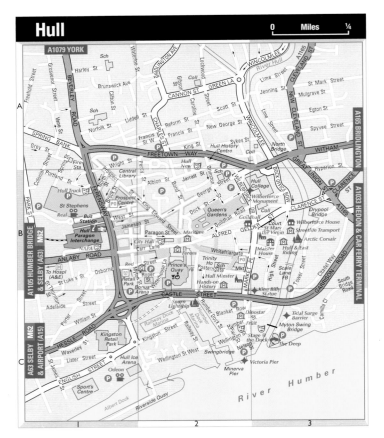

Inverness

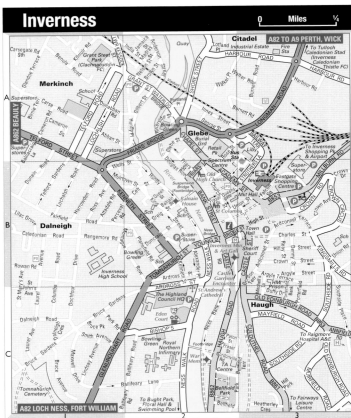

Ipswich

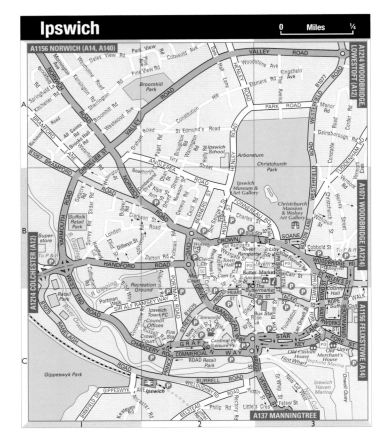

Kendal

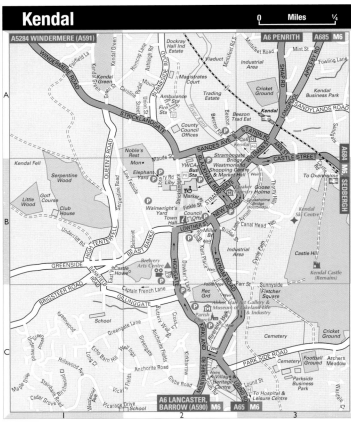

King's Lynn

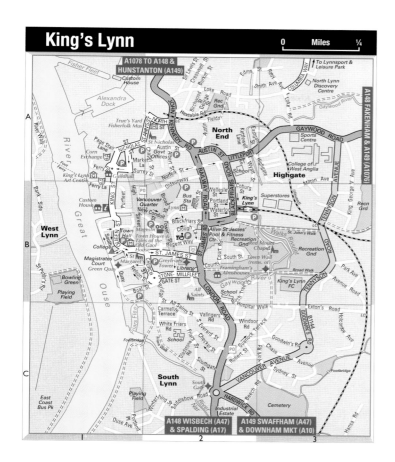

Lancaster

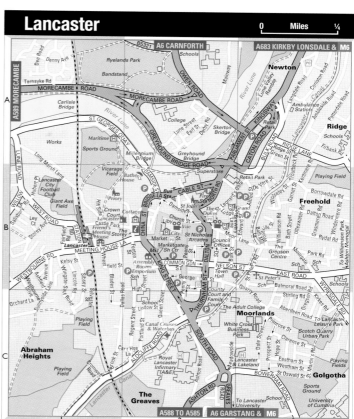

Leeds

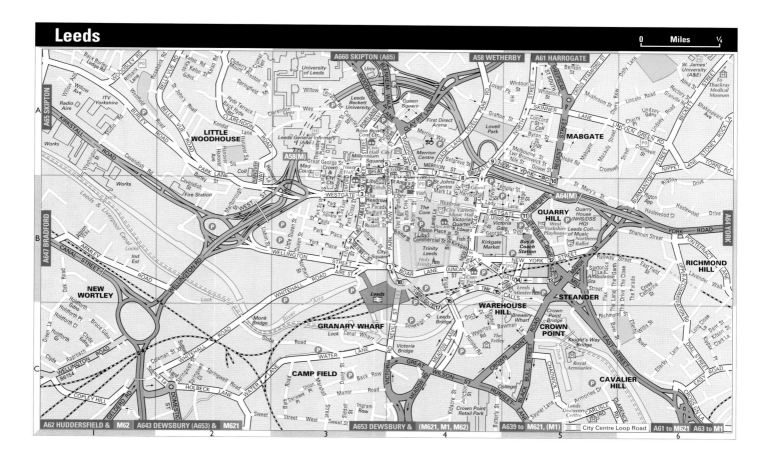

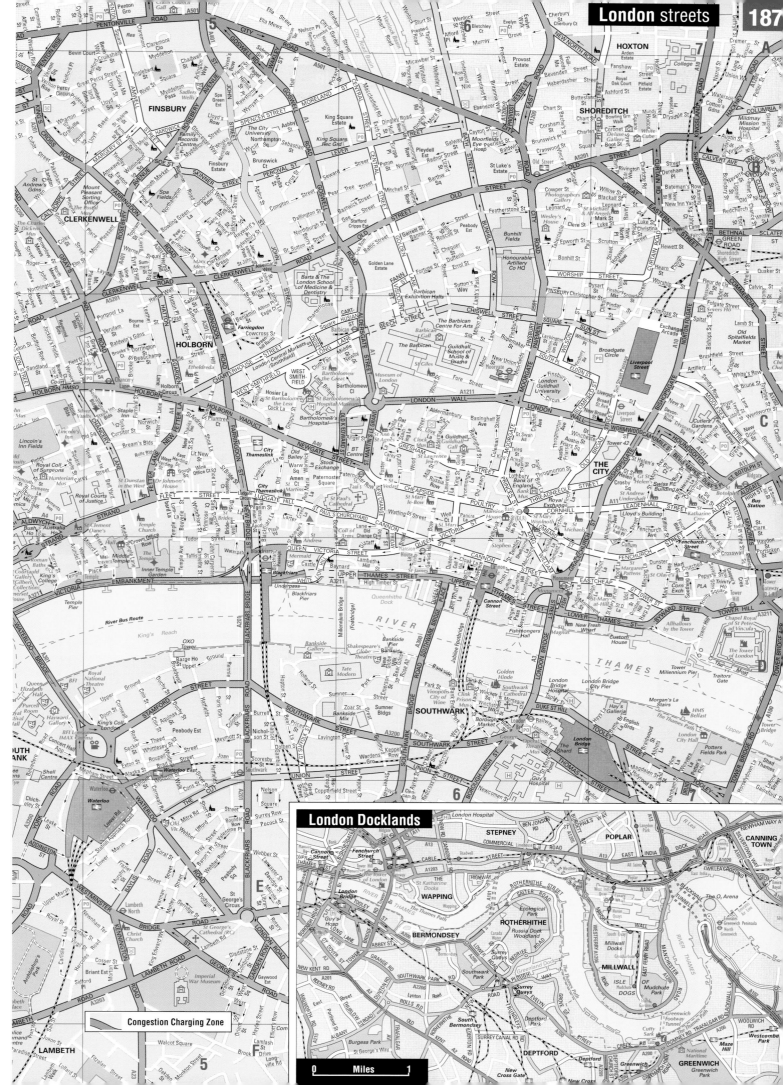

Congestion Charging Zone

London Docklands

0 — Miles — 1

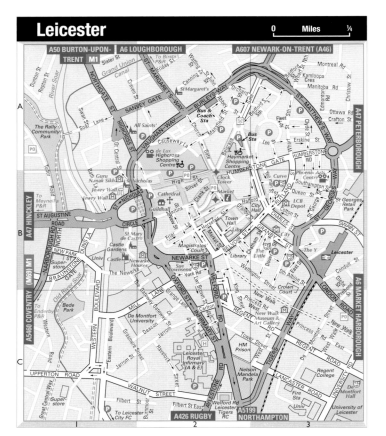

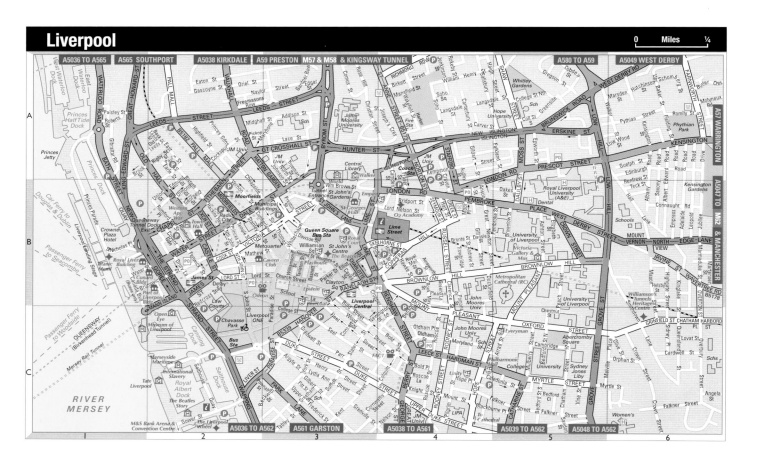

Llandudno

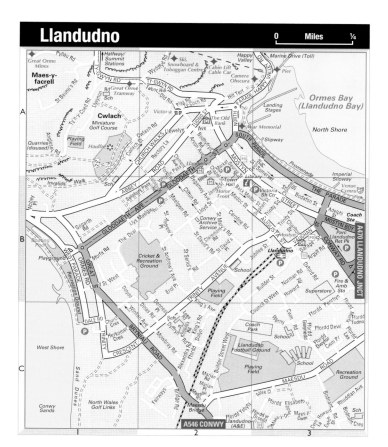

Llanelli

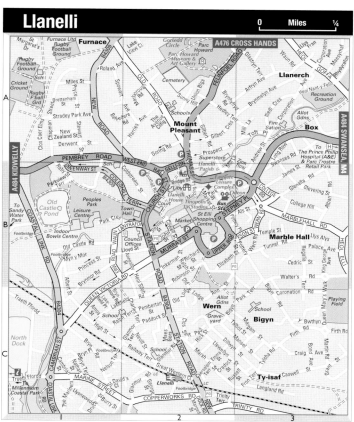

Luton

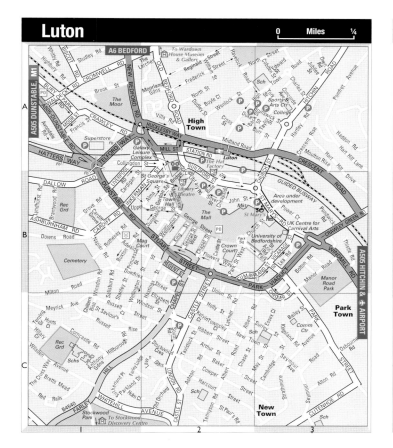

Macclesfield

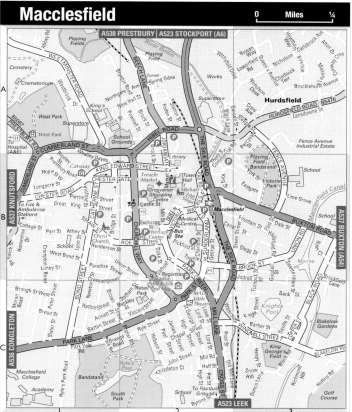

Manchester

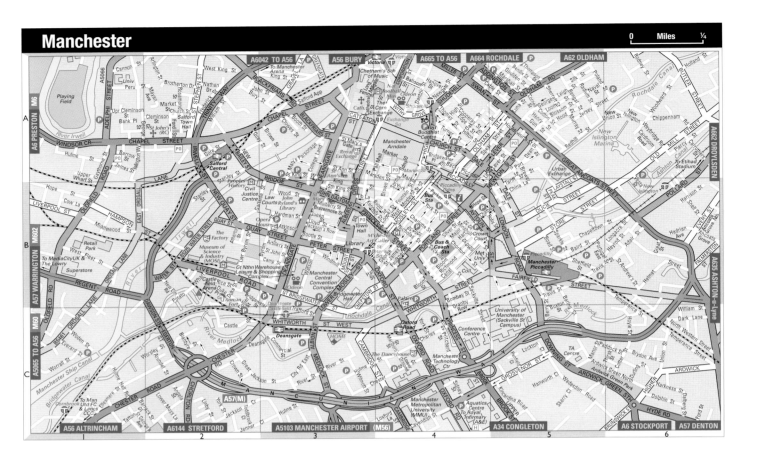

Maidstone

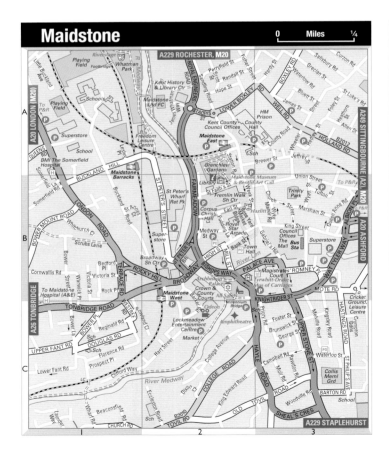

Merthyr Tydfil / Merthyr Tudful

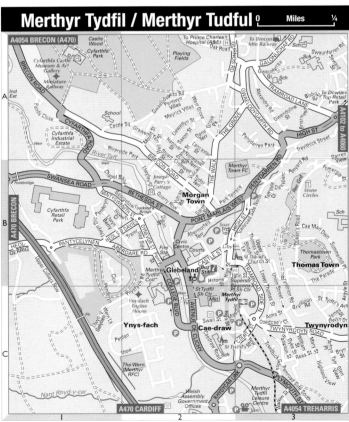

Middlesbrough

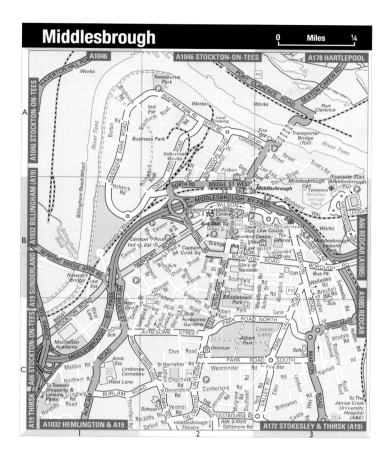

Milton Keynes

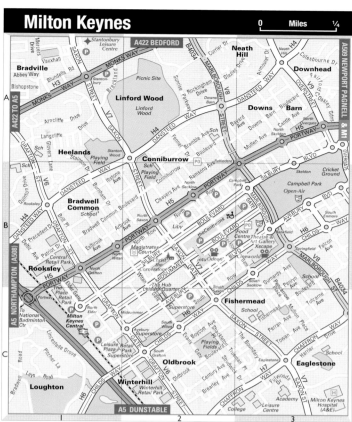

Newcastle upon Tyne

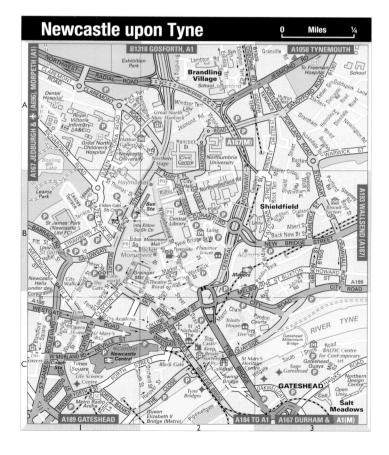

Newport / Casnewydd

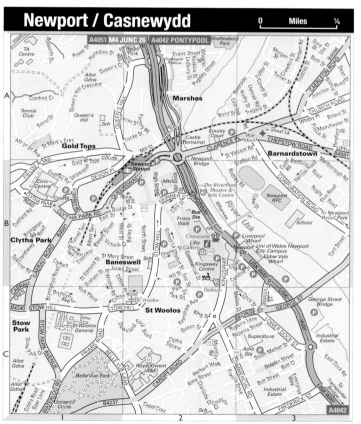

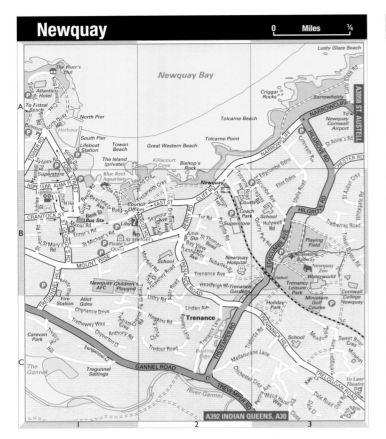

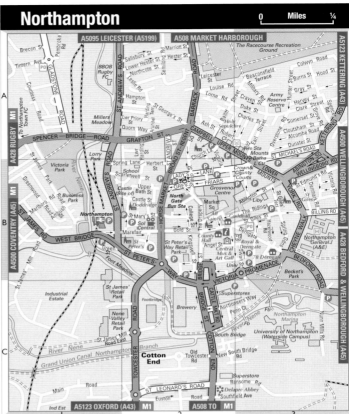

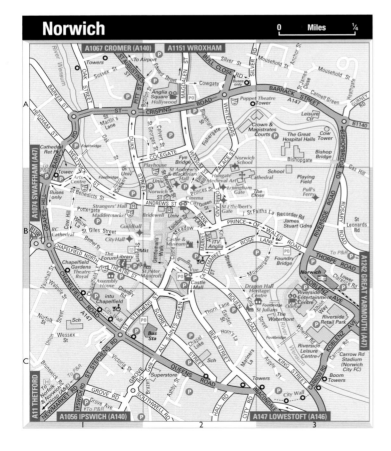

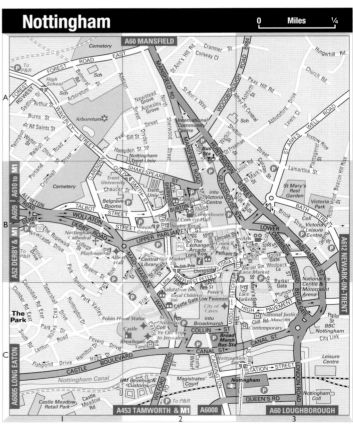

Oxford

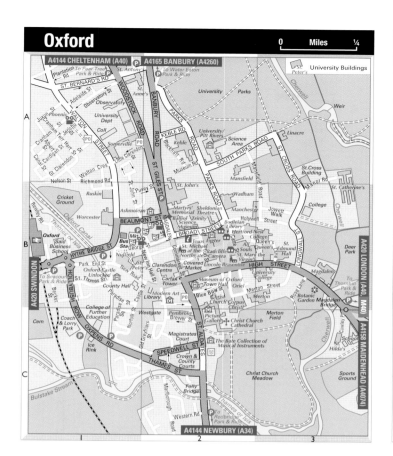

Perth

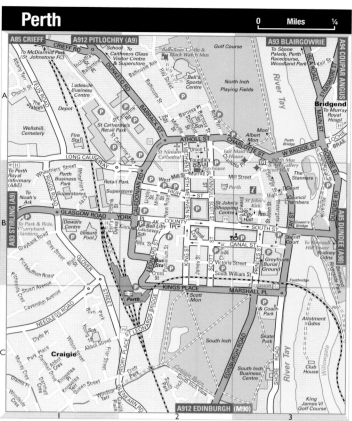

Peterborough

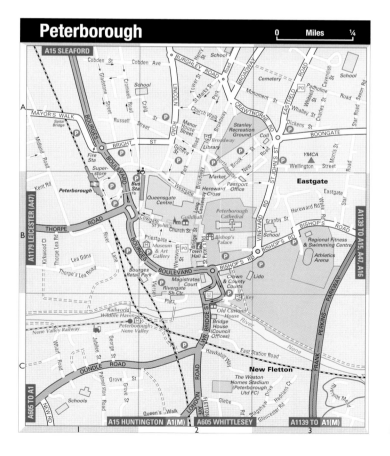

Plymouth

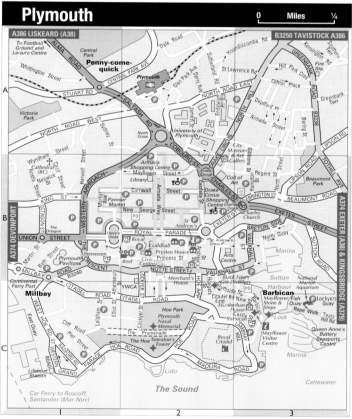

Poole

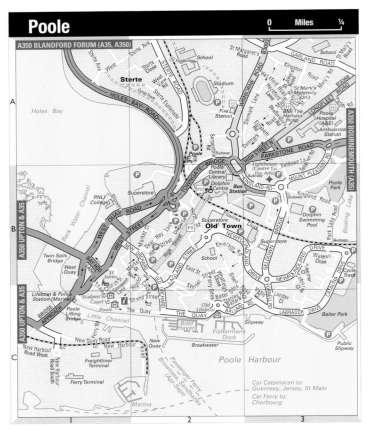

Portsmouth

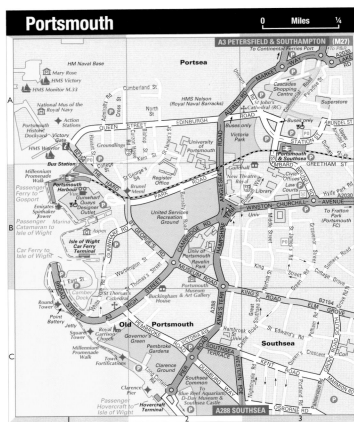

Preston

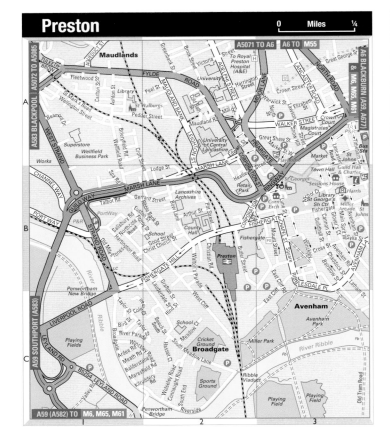

Reading

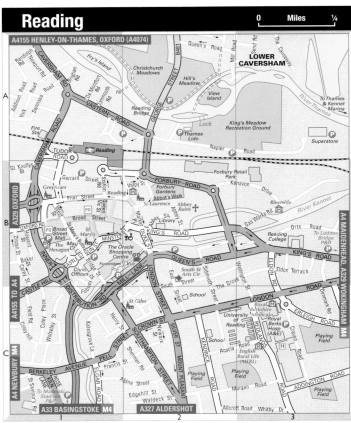

St Andrews

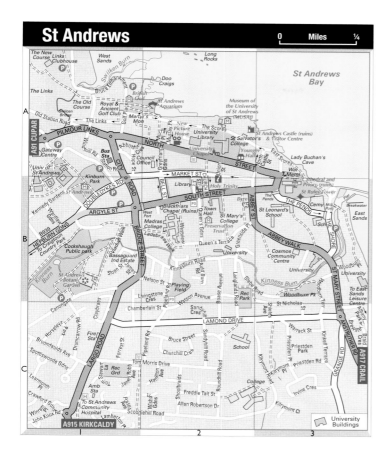

Salisbury

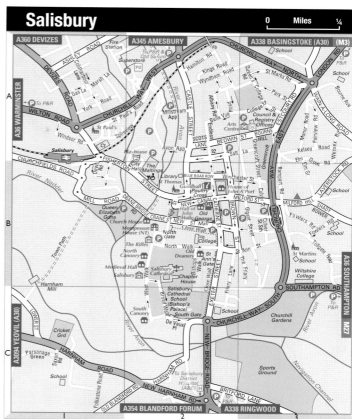

Scarborough

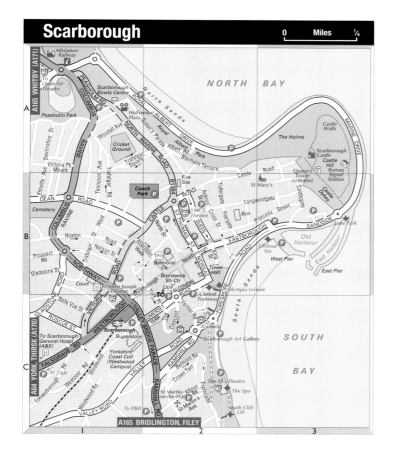

Shrewsbury

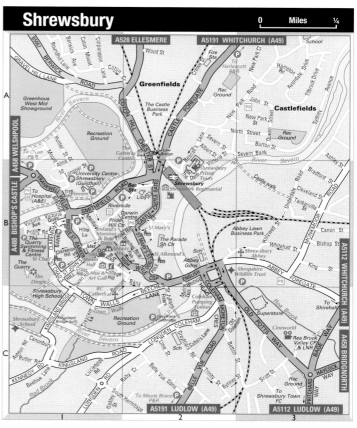

Sheffield

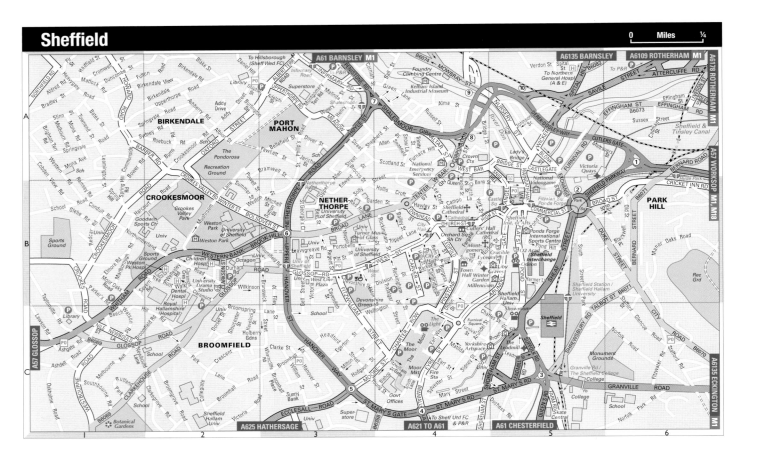

Stoke-on-Trent (Hanley)

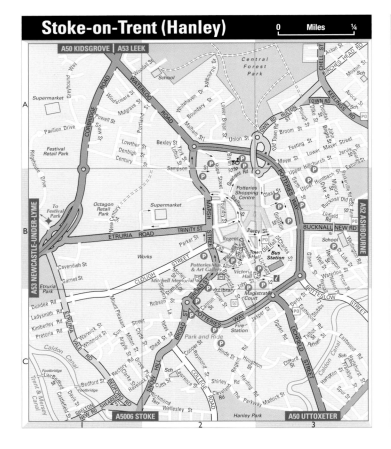

Southampton

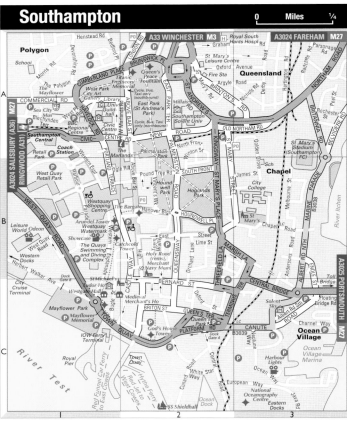

Southend-on-Sea

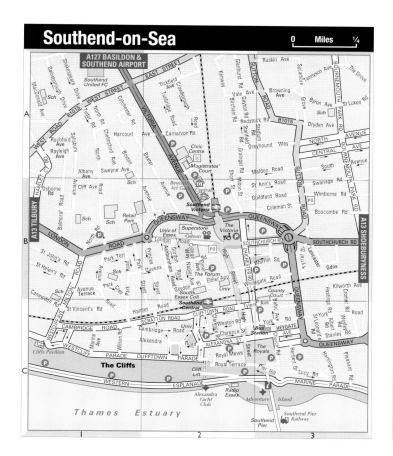

Stirling

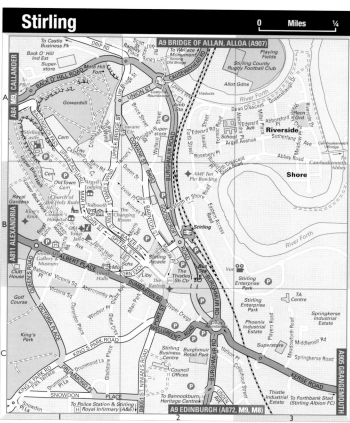

Stratford-upon-Avon

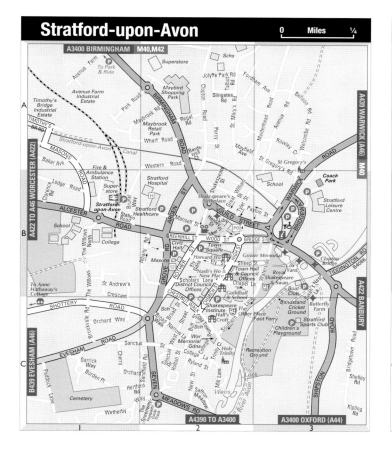

Sunderland

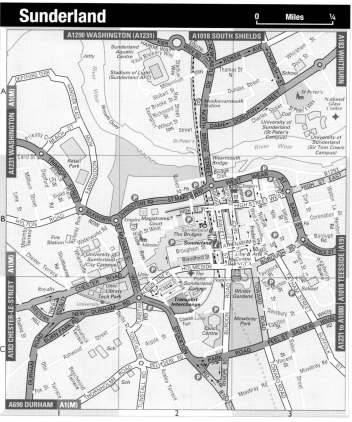

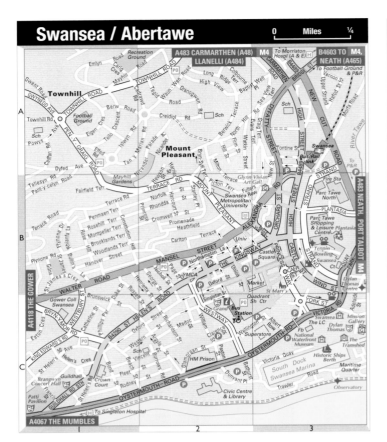

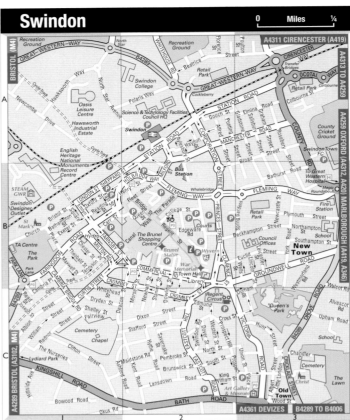

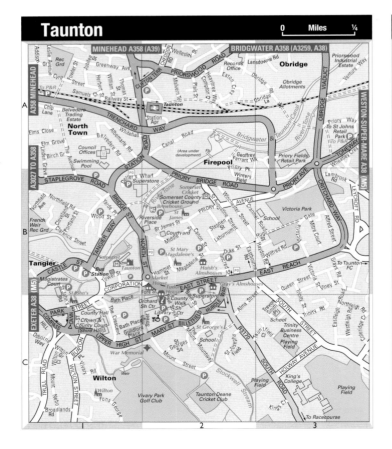

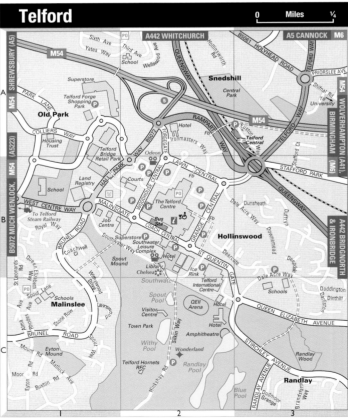

Torquay

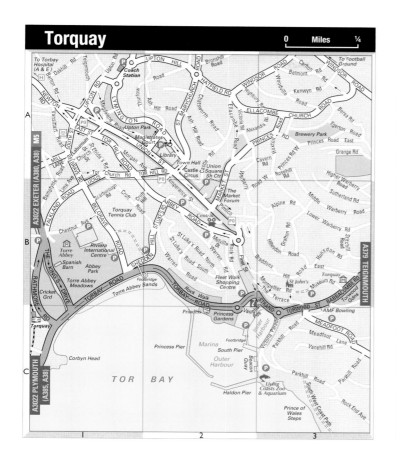

Truro

Winchester

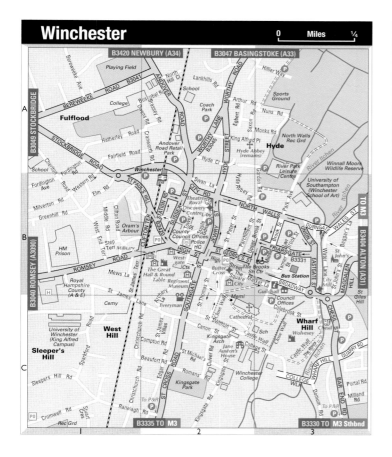

Windsor

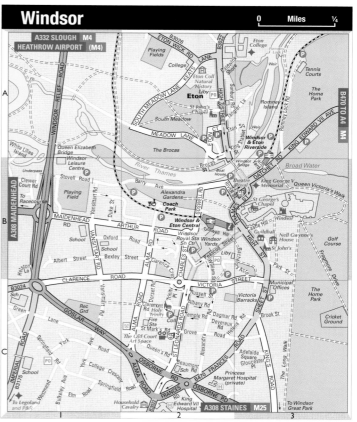

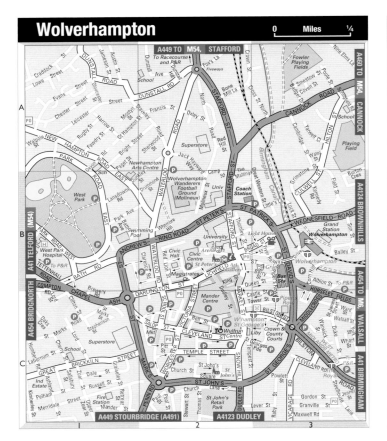

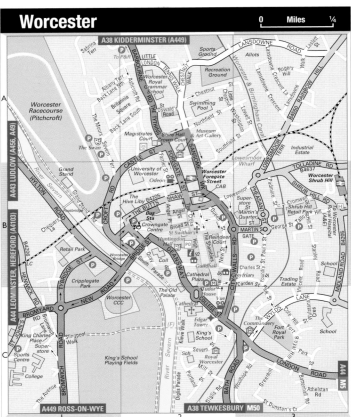

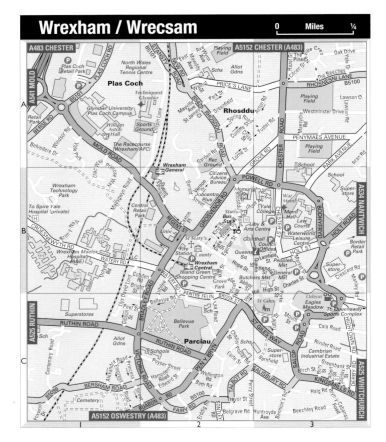

Aberdeen • Ayr • Bath • Birmingham • Blackpool • Bournemouth • Bradford 201

Town plan indexes

Aberdeen 175
Aberdeen B2
Aberdeen Grammar School A1
Academy,The B2
Albert Basin B3
Albert Quay B3
Albury Rd C1
Alford Place B1
Art Gallery A2
Arts Centre A2
Back Wynd A2
Baker St A1
Beach Blvd A3
Belmont B2
Belmont St B2
Berry St A2
Blackfriars St A2
Blaikie's Quay B3
Bloomfield Rd C1
Bon Accord Centre A2
Bon-Accord St B1/C1
Bridge St B2
Broad St A2
Bus Station B2
Car Ferry Terminal B3
Castlegate A3
Central Library A1
Chapel St B1
Cineworld B2
Clyde St B3
College A2
College St B2
Commerce St A3
Commercial Quay B3
Com Centre A3/C1
Constitution St A3
Cotton St A3
Crown St B2
Denburn Rd A2
Devanha Gdns C2
Devanha Gdns South C2
East North St A3
Esslemont Ave A1
Ferryhill Rd C2
Ferryhill Terr C2
Fish Market B3
Fonthill Rd C1
Galleria B1
Gallowgate A2
George St A2
Glenbervie Rd C3
Golden Sq B1
Grampian Rd C3
Great Southern Rd C1
Guild St B2
Hardgate B1/C1
His Majesty's Theatre A1
Holburn St C1
Hollybank Pl C1
Huntly St B1
Hutcheon St A1
Information Ctr B2
John St A2
Justice St A3
King St A2
Langstane Pl B1
Lemon Tree,The A2
Library C1
Loch St A2
Maberly St A1
Marischal Coll A2
Maritime Museum & Provost Ross's House B2
Market B2
Market St B2/B3
Menzies Rd C3
Mercat Cross A3
Millburn St C2
Miller St A3
Mount St A1
Music Hall B1
North Esp East C3
North Esp West C2
Oscar Rd C3
Palmerston Rd C2
Park St A3
Police Station A2
Polmuir Rd C2
Post Office A1/A2/A3/B1/C3
Provost Skene's House A2
Queen Elizabeth Br C2
Queen St A2
Regent Quay B3
Regent Road B3
Robert Gordon's College A2
Rose St B1
Rosemount Pl A1
Rosemount Viaduct A1
St Andrew St A2
St Andrew's Cath A3
St Mary's Cath B1
St Nicholas Centre A2
St Nicholas St A2
School Hill A2
Sinclair Rd C3
Skene Sq A1
Skene St B1
South College St C2
South Crown St C2
South Esp East C3
South Esp West C3
South Mount St A1
Sports Centre C3
Spring Garden A2
Springbank Terr C2
Summer St B1
Superstore A2
Thistle St B1
Tolbooth A3
Town House A2
Trinity Centre B2
Union Row B1
Union Square B2
Union St B1/B2
University A2
Upper Dock B3
Upper Kirkgate A2
Victoria Bridge C3
Victoria Dock B3
Victoria Rd C3
Victoria St B2
Virginia St A3
Vue B2
Waterloo Quay B3
Wellington Pl B2
West North St A2
Whinhill Rd C1
Willowbank Rd C1
Windmill Brae B2

Ayr 175
Ailsa Pl B1
Alexandra Terr A3
Allison St B2
Alloway Pk C1
Alloway Pl C1
Alloway St C2
Arran Mall C2
Arran Terrace B1
Arthur St B2
Ashgrove St C2
Auld Brig B2
Auld Kirk B2
Ayr C2
Ayr Academy B1
Ayr Central Shopping Centre C2
Ayr Harbour A1
Ayr Ice Rink A2
Ayrshire Coll C3
Back Hawkhill Ave A3
Back Main St B2
Back Peebles St A2
Barns Cres C1
Barns Pk C1
Barns St C1
Barns Street La C1
Bath Pl B1
Bellevue Cres C1
Bellevue La C1
Beresford La C2
Beresford Terr C2
Boswell Pk B2
Britannia Pl A3
Bruce Cres B1
Burns Statue C2
Bus Sta B1
Carrick St C2
Cassillis St B1
Cathcart St B1
Charlotte St B1
Citadel Leisure Ctr B1
Citadel Pl B1
Compass Pier A1
Content Ave C3
Content St B2
Craigie Ave B3
Craigie Rd B3
Craigie Way B3
Cromwell Rd B1
Crown St A2
Dalblair Rd C2
Dam Park Sports Stadium C3
Damside A2
Dongola Rd C3
Eglinton Pl B1
Eglinton Terr B1
Elba St B2
Elmbank St A2
Esplanade B1
Euchar Rock A1
Farifield Rd C1
Fort St B1
Fothringham Rd C3
Fullarton St C1
Gaiety C2
Garden St B2
George St B2
George's Ave A3
Glebe Cres A2
Glebe Rd A2
Gorden Terr B3
Green St A2
Green Street La A2
Hawkhill Ave A3
Hawkhill Avenue La B3
High St B2
Holmston Rd C3
Information Ctr B1
James St B3
John St B2
King St B2
Kings Ct B2
Kyle Centre C2
Kyle St C2
Library B2
Limekiln Rd A2
Limonds Wynd B2
Loudoun Hall B2
Lymburn Pl B3
Macadam Pl B2
Main St B2
Mcadam's Monument C1
Mccall's Ave A3
Mews La B1
Mill Brae C3
Mill St C2
Mill Wynd C2
Miller Rd C1
Montgomerie Terr B1
New Bridge B2
New Bridge St B2
New Rd A2
Newmarket St B2
Newton-on-Ayr Station A2
North Harbour St B1
North Pier A1
Odeon C2
Park Circus C1
Park Circus La C1
Park Terr C1
Pavilion Rd C1
Peebles St A2
Philip Sq B2
Police Station B2
Prestwick Rd B1
Princes Ct A2
Queen St B1
Queen's Terr B1
Racecourse Rd C1
River St B2
Riverside Pl B2
Russell Dr A2
St Andrews Church C2
St George's Rd A3
Sandgate B1
Savoy Park C1
Smith St C2
Somerset Park (Ayr United FC) A3
Somerset Rd A3
South Beach Rd B1
South Harbour St B1
South Pier A1
Station Rd C2
Strathayr Pl B2
Superstore A2/B2
Taylor St A2
Town Hall B2
Tryfield Pl A3
Turner's Bridge B2
Union Ave A3
Victoria Bridge C3
Victoria St B3
Viewfield Rd A3
Virginia Gdns A2
Waggon Rd A2
Walker Rd A3
Wallace Tower B2
Weaver St A2
Weir Rd A2
Wellington La C1
Wellington Sq C1
West Sanouhar Rd A3
Whitletts Rd B3
Wilson St A3
York St A1
York Street La B1

Bath 175
Alexandra Park C2
Alexandra Rd C2
Ambulance Station A3
Approach Golf Courses (Public) A1
Archway St C3
Assembly Rooms & Fashion Mus A2
Avon St B2
Barton St B2
Bath Abbey B2
Bath Aqua Glass A2
Bath at Work Museum A2
Bath College B2
Bath Rugby (The Rec) B3
Bath Spa Station C3
Bathwick St A3
Beckford Road A3
Beechen Cliff Rd C2
Bennett St A2
Bloomfield Ave C1
Broad Quay C2
Broad St B2
Brock St A1
Bus Station C2
Calton Gdns C2
Calton Rd C2
Camden Cr A2
Cavendish Rd A1
Cemetery B1
Charlotte St B2
Chaucer Rd C2
Cheap St B2
Circus Mews A2
Claverton St C2
Corn St C2
Cricket Ground B3
Daniel St A3
East Asian Art Museum A2
Edward St B3
Ferry La B3
Fire Station A3
First Ave C1
Forester Ave A3
Forester Rd A3
Gays Hill A2
George St B2
Great Pulteney St B3
Green Park B1
Green Park Rd B2
Green Park Sta B1
Grove St B2
Guildhall B2
Harley St A2
Hayesfield Park C1
Henrietta Gdns A3
Henrietta Mews B3
Henrietta Park B3
Henrietta Rd A3
Henrietta St B3
Henry St B2
Herschel Museum of Astronomy B1
High Common A1
Holburne Mus B3
Holloway C2
Information Ctr B2
James St West B1/B2
Jane Austen Ctr B2
Julian Rd A1
Junction Rd C1
Kingsmead Leisure Complex B2
Kipling Ave C2
Lansdown Cr A1
Lansdown Gr A2
Lansdown Rd A2
Library B2
London Rd A3
London St A2
Lower Bristol Rd B1
Lower Oldfield Park C1
Lyncombe Hill C3
Magistrates' Court B3
Manvers St B3
Maple Gr C1
Margaret's Hill A2
Marlborough Bldgs A1
Marlborough La B1
Midland Bridge Rd B1
Milk St B2
Milsom St B2
Mission The B2
Monmouth St B2
Morford St A2
Museum of Bath Architecture A2
New King St B1
No 1 Royal Cres A1
Norfolk Bldgs B1
Norfolk Cr B1
North Parade Rd B3
Oldfield Rd C1
Paragon A2
Pines Way B1
Podium Shopping Centre B2
Police Station B3
Portland Pl A2
Post Office B2/C2
Postal Museum B2
Powlett Rd A3
Prior Park Rd C3
Pulteney Bridge B2
Pulteney Gdns B3
Pulteney Rd B3/C3
Queen Sq B2
Raby Pl B3
Recreation Ground B3
Rivers St A2
Rockliffe Ave A3
Rockliffe Rd A3
Roman Baths & Pump Room B2
Rossiter Rd C3
Royal Ave A1
Royal Crescent A1
Royal High School,The A2
Royal Victoria Park A1
St James Sq A1
St John's Rd A3
Sally Lunn's House B2
Shakespeare Ave C2
Shopmobility B2
South Parade B3
SouthGate Shopping Centre C2
Sports & Leisure Centre B3
Spring Gdns C3
Stall St B2
Stanier Rd B1
Superstore A3/B1
Sydney Gdns A3
Sydney Pl B3
Sydney Rd B3
Theatre Royal B2
Thermae Bath Spa B2
Thomas St A3
Tyning,The C3
Union St B2
University C3
Upper Bristol Rd B1
Upper Oldfield Park C1
Victoria Art Gallery B2
Victoria Bridge Rd B1
Walcot St B2
Wells Rd C1
Westgate Buildings B2
Westgate St B2
Weston Rd A1
Widcombe Hill C3

Birmingham 176
Abbey St A2
Aberdeen St A1
Acorn Gr B2
Adams St A5
Adderley St C5
Albert St B4
Albion St B2
Alcester St C5
Aldgate Gr A3
All Saint's St A2
All Saints Rd A2
Allcock St C5
Allesley St A4
Allison St C4
Alma Cr B6
Alston Rd C1
Arcadian Centre C4
Arena Birmingham C2
Arthur St C6
Assay Office B3
Ashted Circus B5
Aston Expressway A5
Aston St B4
Aston University B4/B5
Avenue Rd A5
Bacchus Rd A1
Bagot St B4
Banbury St B5
Barford Rd B1
Barford St C4
Barn St C5
Barnwell Rd C6
Barr St A3
Barrack St B5
Barwick St B4
Bath Row C3
Beaufort Rd C1
Belmont Row B5
Benson Rd A1
Berkley St C3
Bexhill Gr C3
Birchall St C5
Birmingham City FC C6
Birmingham City Hospital (A&E) A1
Birmingham City University B3
Birmingham Wheels Park B6
Bishopsgate St C3
Blews St A4
Bloomsbury St A6
Blucher St C3
Bordesley St C4
Bowyer St C5
Bradburne Way A5
Bradford St C5
Branston St A3
Brearley St A4
Brewery St A4
Bridge St C3
Bridge St West A4
Brindley Dr B3
Brindley Place C3
Broad St C3
Broad Street Cineworld C2
Broadway Plaza C2
Bromley St C5
Bromsgrove St C4
Brookfield Rd A2
Browning St C2
Bryant St A1
BT Tower B3
Buckingham St A3
Bull St B4
Bull St B3
Bullring C4
Cambridge St C3
Camden Dr B3
Camden St B2
Cannon St C4
Cardigan St B5
Carlisle St A1
Carlyle Rd C1
Caroline St B3
Carver St B2
Cato St A6
Cattell Rd C6
Cattells Gr A6
Cawdor Cr C1
Cecil St B4
Cemetery A2/B2
Cemetery La A2
Centenary Square C3
Ctr Link Ind Est A6
Charlotte St B3
Cheapside C4
Chester St A5
Children's Hospital (A&E) B4
Church St B4
Claremont Rd A2
Clarendon Rd C1
Clark St C1
Clement St B3
Clissold St B2
Cliveland St B4
Coach Station C5
College St B2
Colmore Circus B4
Colmore Row B4
Commercial St C3
Constitution Hill B3
Convention Centre, The C3
Cope St B2
Coplow St B1
Corporation St C4
Council House B3
County Court B4
Coveley Gr A2
Coventry Rd C6
Coventry St C5
Cox St B3
Crabtree Rd A2
Cregoe St C3
Crescent Ave A2
Crescent Theatre C3
Crescent,The A2
Cromwell St A6
Cromwell St B3
Cube,The C3
Curzon Circle B5
Curzon St B5
Custard Factory C5
Cuthbert Rd B1
Dale End B4
Dart St C6
Dartmouth Circus A4
Dartmouth Middleway A5
Dental Hospital B4
Deritend C5
Devon St A6
Devonshire St A1
Digbeth High St C4
Dolman St B6
Dover St A1
Duchess Rd C2
Duddeston B6
Duddeston Manor Rd B5
Duddeston Mill Rd B6
Duddeston Mill Trading Estate B6
Dudley Rd B1
Edgbaston Village C2
Edmund St B3
Edward St B3
Elkington St A4
Ellen St B2
Ellis St C3
Erskine St B6
Essex St C4
Everyman C3
Eyre St B2
Farm Croft A3
Farm St A3
Fazeley St B4/C5
Felstead Way B5
Finstall Cl B5
Five Ways C2
Five Ways C2
Fiveway Shopping Centre C2
Fleet St B3
Floodgate St C5
Ford St A2
Fore St C4
Forster St B5
Francis Rd C2
Francis St B5
Frankfort St A4
Frederick St B3
Freeth St C1
Freightliner Terminal B6
Garrison Circus C5
Garrison La C6
Garrison St B6
Gas St C3
Geach St A4
George St B3
George St West B2
Gibb St C5
Gilby Rd C2
Gillott Rd B1
Glover St C5
Goode Ave A2
Goodrick Way A6
Gordon St B6
Graham St B3
Grand Central Shopping Centre C4
Granville St C3
Gray St C6
Great Barr St C5
Great Charles St Queensway B3
Great Francis St B6
Great Hampton Row A3
Great Hampton St A3
Great King St A3
Great King St North A3
Great Lister St A5
Great Tindal St C2
Green La C6
Green St C5
Greenway St C6
Grosvenor St West C2
Guest Gr A3
Guild Cl C2
Guildford Dr A4
Guthrie Cl A3
Hagley Rd C1
Hall St B3
Hampton St A3
Handsworth New Rd A1
Hanley St B4
Harford St A3
Harmer Rd A2
Harold Rd C1
Hatchett St A4
Heath Mill La C5
Heath St B1
Heaton St A2
Heneage St B5
Henrietta St B4
Herbert Rd C6
High St C4
High St C5
Hilden Rd B5
Hill St C3/C4
Hindlow Cl B6
Hingeston St B2
Hippodrome Theatre C4
HM Prison A1
Hockley Circus A2
Hockley Hill A3
Hockley St A3
Holliday St C3
Holloway Circus C4
Holloway Head C3
Holt St B5
Horse Fair C4
Hospital St A4
Howard St B3
Howe St B5
Hubert St A5
Hunters Rd A2
Hunters Vale A3
Huntly Rd C2
Hurst St C4
Icknield Port Rd B1
Icknield Sq B2
Icknield St A2/B2
IKON C3
Information Ctr C3
Inge St C4
Irving St C3
James Watt Queensway B4
Jennens Rd B5
Jewellery Quarter A3
Jewellery Quarter A3
Jewellery Quarter Museum B3
John Bright St C4
Keeley St C6
Kellett Rd B5
Kent St C4
Kenyon St B3
Key Hill A3
Key Hill Circus A2
Kilby Ave C2
King Edwards Rd B2
King Edwards Rd C3
Kingston Rd C6
Kirby Rd A1
Ladywood Arts & Leisure Centre B1
Ladywood Circus C1
Ladywood Middleway C2/C3
Ladywood Rd C1
Lancaster St B4
Landor St B6
Law Courts B4
Lawley Middleway B5
Ledbury Cl C2
Ledsam St B2
Lees St A1
Legge La B3
Lennox St A3
Library A6/C3
Library C3
Lighthorne Ave B2
Link Rd B1
Lionel St B3
Lister St B5
Little Ann St C5
Little Hall Rd A6
Liverpool St C5
Livery St B3/B4
Lodge Rd A1
Lord St A5
Love La A5
Loveday St B4
Lower Dartmouth St C6
Lower Loveday St B4
Lower Tower St A4
Lower Trinty St C5
Lucus Circus A3
Ludgate Hill B3
Mailbox Ctr & BBC C3
Margaret St B3
Markby Rd A1
Marroway St B1
Maxstoke St C6
Melvina Rd A6
Meriden St C4
Midland St B6
Milk St C5
Mill St A5
Millennium Point B5
Miller St A4
Milton St A4
Moat La C4
Montague Rd C1
Montague St C5
Monument Rd C1
Moor St Queensway C4
Moor Street C4
Moorsom St A4
Morville St C2
Mosborough Cr A3
Moseley St C4
Mott St B3
Museum & Art Gallery B3
Musgrave Rd A1
National Sea Life Centre C3
Navigation St C3
Nechell's Park Rd A6
Nechells Parkway B5
Nechells Pl A6
New Alexandra C3
New Bartholomew St C4
New Canal St C5
New John St West A3
New Spring St B2
New St C4
New Street C4
New Summer St A4
New Town Row A4
Newhall Hill B3
Newhall St B3
Newton St B4
Newtown A4
Noel Rd C1
Norman St A1
Northbrook St B1
Northwood St B3
Norton St A2
Odeon C2
Old Crown Ho C5
Old Rep Theatre, The C4
Old Snow Hill B4
Oliver Rd C1
Oliver St A5
Osler St C1
Oxford St C5
Palmer St C5
Paradise Circus Queensway C3
Paradise St C3
Park Rd A2
Park St C4
Pavilions C4
Paxton Rd A2
Peel St A1
Pershore St C4
Phillips St A4
Pickford St C5
Pinfold St C4
Pitsford St A2
Plough & Harrow Rd C1
Police Station A4/B4/C2/C4
Pope St B2
Portland Rd C1
Post Office A5/B1/B3/B5/C3/C5
Preston Rd A1
Price St B4
Princip St B4
Printing House St B4
Priory Queensway B4
Pritchett St A4
Proctor St A5
Radnor St A2
Rea St C4
Regent Pl B3
Register Office C3
Repertory Theatre C3
Reservoir Rd C1
Richard St A5
River St C5
Rocky La A5/A6
Rodney Cl C2
Roseberry St B2
Rotton Park St B1
Royal Birmingham Conservatoire B5
Rupert St A5
Ruston St C2
Ryland St C2
St Andrew's Ind Est C6
St Andrew's Rd C6
St Andrew's St C6
St Bolton St C6
St Chads B4
St Chad's Cathedral (RC) B4
St Chads Queensway B4
St Clements Rd A6
St George's St A3
St James Pl B5
St Marks Cr B2
St Martin's C4
St Paul's B3
St Paul's B3
St Paul's Sq B3
St Philip's B4
St Stephen's St A4
St Thomas' Peace Garden C3
St Vincent St C2
Saltley Rd A6
Sand Pits Pde B3
Severn St C3
Shadwell St B4
Sheepcote St C2
Shefford Rd A4
Sherborne St C2
Shylton's Croft C2
Skipton Rd C2
Smallbrook Queensway C4
Smith St A3
Snow Hill B4
Snow Hill Queensway B4
Soho, Benson Rd A1
South Rd A2
Spencer St B3
Spring Hill B2
Staniforth St B4
Station St C4
Steelhouse La B4
Stephenson St C4
Steward St B2
Stirling Rd C1
Stour St B2
Suffolk St Queensway C3
Summer Hill Rd B2
Summer Hill St B2
Summer Hill Terr B2
Summer La A4
Summer Row B3
Summerfield Cr B1
Summerfield Park B1
Superstore B2
Sutton St C3
Swallow St C3
Sydney Rd C6
Symphony Hall C3
Talbot St A1
Temple Row C4
Temple St C4
Templefield St C6
Tenby St B3
Tenby St North B2
Tennant St C2/C3
Thimble Mill La A6
Thinktank (Science & Discovery) B5
Thomas St A4
Thorpe St C4
Tilton Rd C6
Tower St A4
Town Hall C3
Town Hall C3
Trent St C5
Turner's Buildings A1
Unett St A3
Union Terr B5
Upper Trinity St C5
Uxbridge St A3
Vauxhall Gr B5
Vauxhall Rd B5
Vernon Rd C1
Vesey St B4
Viaduct St B5
Victoria Sq C3
Villa St A3
Vittoria St B3
Vyse St B3
Walter St A6
Wardlow Rd A5
Warstone La B2
Washington St C3
Water St B3
Waterworks Rd C1
Watery La C5
Western Rd B1
Wharf St A2
Wheeler St A3
Whitehouse St A5
Whitmore St A2
Whittall St B4
Wholesale Market C4
Wiggin St B1
Willes Rd A1
Windsor Ind Est A5
Windsor St A5
Windsor St B5
Winson Green Rd A1
Witton St C6
Wolseley St C6
Woodcock St B5

Blackpool 176
Abingdon St A1
Addison Cr A3
Adelaide St B1
Albert Rd B2
Alfred St B2
Ascot Rd A3
Ashton Rd C2
Auburn Gr C3
Bank Hey St B1
Banks St A1
Beech Ave A3
Bela Gr C2
Belmont Ave B2
Birley St A1
Blackpool & Fleetwood Tram B1
Blackpool & the Fylde College B2
Blackpool FC C2
Blackpool North A2
Blackpool North A2
Blackpool Tower B1
Blundell St C1
Bonny St B1
Breck Rd B3
Bryan Rd A3
Buchanan St A2
Bus Hub B1
Cambridge Rd A3
Caunce St A2/A3
Central Dr B1/C2
Central Pier C1
Central Pier C1
Central Pier Theatre C1
Chapel St C1
Charles St A2
Charnley Rd B2
Church St A1/A2
Clinton Ave B2
Coach Station A2/C1
Cocker St A1
Coleridge Rd A3
Collingwood Ave A3
Comedy Carpet B1
Condor Gr C3
Cookson St A2
Coronation St B1
Corporation St A1
Courts B1
Cumberland Ave B3
Cunliffe Rd C3
Dale St C1
Devonshire Rd A3
Devonshire Sq A3
Dickson Rd A1
Elizabeth St A2
Ferguson Rd C3
Forest Gate B3
Foxhall Rd C1
Freckleton St C2
George St A2
Gloucester Ave B3
Golden Mile,The C1
Gorse Rd B3
Gorton St A2
Grand Theatre, The B1
Granville Rd A2
Grasmere Rd C2
Grosvenor St A2
Grundy Art Gallery A1
Harvey Rd B3
Hornby Rd B2
Houndshill Shopping Centre B1
Hull Rd B1
Ibbison Ct C2
Kent Rd C2
Keswick Rd C2
King St A2
Knox Gr C3
Laycock Gate A3
Layton Rd A3
Leamington Rd B2
Leeds Rd B3
Leicester Rd B2
Levens Gr C2
Library A1
Lifeboat Station B1
Lincoln Rd B2
Liverpool Rd B3
Livingstone Rd B2
London Rd A3
Lune Gr C2
Lytham Rd C1
Madame Tussaud's Blackpool B1
Manchester Sq C1
Manor Rd B3
Maple Ave B3
Market St A1
Marlboro Rd B3
Mere Rd B3
Milbourne St A2
Newcastle Ave B3
Newton Dr A3
North Pier A1
North Pier A1
North Pier Theatre A1
Odeon C2
Olive Gr B3
Palatine Rd B2
Park Rd B2/C3
Peter St A2
Post Office B1/B2/B3
Princess Pde A1
Princess St C1/C2
Promenade A1/C1
Queen St A1
Queen Victoria Rd C2
Raikes Pde B2
Reads Ave B2
Regent Cinema B2
Regent Rd B2
Register Office B2
Ribble Rd B2
Rigby Rd C1/C2
Ripon Rd B3
St Albans Rd B3
St Ives Ave C3
St John's Square A1
St Vincent Ave C3
Salisbury Rd B3
Salthouse Ave C2
Salvation Army Ctr A2
Sands Way C2
Sea Life Centre B1
Seasiders Way C1
Selbourne Rd A2
Sharrow Gr C3
Somerset Ave C3
South King St B2
Springfield Rd A1
Sutton Pl B2
Talbot Rd A1/A2
Thornber Gr C2
Topping St A1
Tower B1
Town Hall A1
Tram Depot C1
Tyldesley Rd C1
Vance Rd B1
Victoria St B1
Victory Rd A2
Wayman Rd A3
Westmorland Ave C2/C3
Whitegate Dr B3
Winter Gardens Theatre B1
Woodland Gr B3
Woolman Rd B2

Bournemouth 176
Ascham Rd A3
Avenue Rd B1
Ave Shopping Ctr B1
Bath Rd C2
Beacon Rd C1
Beechey Rd A3
Bodorgan Rd B1
Bourne Ave B1
Bournemouth A3
Bournemouth & Poole College B3
Bournemouth International Ctr C1
Bournemouth Pier C2
Bournemouth Station B3
Braidley Rd A1
Cavendish Place A2
Cavendish Rd A2
Central Drive A1
Central Gdns B1
Christchurch Rd B3
Cliff Lift C1/C3
Coach House Pl A3
Coach Station A3
Commercial Rd B1
Cotlands Rd B3
Cranborne Rd C1
Cricket Ground A2
Cumnor Rd B2
Dean Park A2
Dean Park Cr B2
Dean Park Rd A2
Durrant Rd B1
East Overcliff Dr C3
Exeter Cr C1
Exeter La C2
Exeter Rd C1
Gervis Place B1
Gervis Rd B3
Glen Fern Rd B2
Golf Club B1
Grove Rd B3
Hinton Rd C2
Holdenhurst Rd B3
Horseshoe Common B2
Information Ctr C2
Lansdowne B3
Lansdowne Rd A2
Lorne Park Rd B2
Lower Gdns B1/C2
Madeira Rd B2
Methuen Rd A3
Meyrick Park A1
Meyrick Rd B3
Milton Rd A2
Nuffield Health Bournemouth Hosp (private) A2
Oceanarium C2
Odeon Cinema C1
Old Christchurch Rd B2
Ophir Rd A3
Oxford Rd B3
Park Rd A3
Parsonage Rd B2
Pavilion C2
Pier Approach C2
Pier Theatre C2
Police Sta A3/B3
Portchester Rd A3
Post Office B1/B3
Priory Rd C1
Quadrant,The B2
Recreation Ground A1
Richmond Gardens Shopping Centre B2
Richmond Hill Rd B1
Russell-Cotes Art Gallery & Mus C2
Russell Cotes Rd C2
St Anthony's Rd A1
St Michael's Rd C1
St Paul's A3
St Paul's La B3
St Paul's Rd A3
St Peter's B2
St Peter's B2
St Peter's Rd B2
St Stephen's Rd B1/B2
St Swithun's B3
St Swithun's Rd B3
St Swithun's Rd South B3
St Valerie Rd A2
St Winifred's Rd A2
Square,The B1
Stafford Rd B3
Terrace Rd B1
Town Hall B1
Tregonwell Rd C1
Triangle,The B1
Trinity Rd B2
Undercliff Drive C3
Upper Hinton Rd B2
Upper Terr Rd C1
Wellington Rd A2/A3
Wessex Way A3/B1/B2
West Cliff Prom C1
West Hill Rd C1
West Undercliff Promenade C1
Westover Rd B2
Wimborne Rd A2
Wootton Mount B2
Wychwood Dr A1
Yelverton Rd B2
York Rd B3
Zig-Zag Walks C1/C3

Bradford 177
Alhambra B2
Back Ashgrove B1
Barkerend Rd A3
Barnard Rd C3
Barry St B2
Bolling Rd C3
Bolton Rd A3
Bowland St A1
Bradford Big Screen B2
Bradford College B1
Bradford Forster Sq A2
Bradford Interchange B3
Bradford Playhouse B3
Bridge St B2
Britannia St B2
Broadway Bradford,The B2
Burnett St B3
Bus Station B2
Butler St West A3
Caledonia St C2
Canal Rd A2
Carlton St B1
Cathedral A3
Centenary Sq B2
Chapel St B3
Cheapside A2
Church Bank B3
Cineworld B3
City Hall B2
City Rd A1
Claremont B1
Colour Experience B1
Croft St B2
Crown Court B3
Darfield St A1
Darley St A2
Drewton Rd A1
Drummond Trading Estate A1
Dryden St B3
Dyson St A1
Easby Rd C1
East Parade B3
Eldon Pl A1
Filey St B3
Forster Square Retail Park A2
Gallery II B1
Garnett St B3
Godwin St B2
Gracechurch St A1
Grattan Rd B1
Great Horton Rd B1/B2
Grove Terr B1
Hall Ings B2
Hall La C3
Hallfield Rd A1
Hammstrasse A2
Harris St B3
Holdsworth St A2
Ice Arena B2
Impressions B2
Information Ctr B2
Inland Revenue A2
Ivegate B2
Jacob's Well Municipal Offices B2
James St A2
John St A2
Kirkgate B2
Kirkgate Centre B2
Laisteridge La C1
Leeds Rd B3
Leisure Exchange, The B3
Library B1/B2
Listerhills Rd B1
Little Horton Gn C1
Little Horton La C1
Longside La B1
Lower Kirkgate B2
Lumb La A1
Magistrates Court B2
Manchester Rd C2
Manningham La A1
Manor Row A2
Market C3
Market St B2
Melbourne Place C1
Midland Rd A2
Mill La C2
Morley St B1
National Science and Media Museum B2
Nelson St B2/C2
Nesfield St A2
New Otley Rd A3
Norcroft St B1
North Parade A2
North St A3
North Wing A3
Oastler Shopping Centre A2
Otley Rd A3
Park Ave C1
Park La C1
Park Rd C2
Parma St C2
Peace Museum B2
Peckover St B3
Piccadilly A2
Police Station C2
Post Office B1/B2/B3/C3

Princes Way ... B2
Prospect St ... C3
Radwell Drive ... A1
Rawson Rd ... A1
Rebecca St ... B1
Richmond Rd ... A1
Russell St ... C1
St George's Hall ... B2
St Lukes Hospital ... C1
Shipley Airedale Rd ... A3/B3
Shopmobility ... B2
Simes St ... B1
Smith St ... B1
Spring Mill St ... C2
Stott Hill ... B2
Sunbridge Rd ... A1/B1/B2
Theatre in the Mill ... B1
Thornton Rd ... A1/B1
Trafalgar St ... C1
Trinity Rd ... C1
Tumbling Hill St ... B1
Tyrrel St ... B2
University of Bradford ... B1/C1
Usher St ... C2
Valley Rd ... A2
Vicar La ... C3
Wakefield Rd ... B3
Wapping Rd ... A3
Well St ... B3
Westgate ... A1
White Abbey Rd ... A1
Wigan St ... B1
Wilton St ... B1
Wood St ... A1
Wool Exchange ... B2
Worthington St ... A1

Brighton 177
Addison Rd ... A1
Albert Rd ... A1
Albion Hill ... B3
Albion St ... B3
Ann St ... A3
Baker St ... A3
Black Lion St ... C2
Brighton ... B2
Brighton Centre ... C2
Brighton Fishing Museum ... C3
Brighton Pier (Palace Pier) ... C3
Brighton Wheel ... C3
British Airways i360 Tower ... C1
Broad St ... C3
Buckingham Pl ... A2
Buckingham Rd ... A2
Cannon Pl ... C1
Carlton Hill ... B3
Chatham Pl ... A3
Cheapside ... A3
Church St ... B2
Churchill Square Shopping Centre ... B2
Clifton Hill ... B1
Clifton Pl ... B1
Clifton Rd ... B1
Clifton St ... B2
Clifton Terr ... B1
Clyde Rd ... A3
Coach Station ... A2
Compton Ave ... A1
Davigdor Rd ... A1
Denmark Terr ... B1
Ditchling Rd ... A3
Dome ... B2
Duke St ... C2
Duke's La ... C2
Dyke Rd ... A1/B2
East St ... C2
Edward St ... B3
Elmore Rd ... B3
Fleet St ... A2
Frederick St ... B2
Gardner St ... B2
Gloucester Pl ... B2
Gloucester Rd ... B2
Goldsmid Rd ... A1
Grand Junction Rd ... C2
Grand Pde ... B3
Grove Hill ... B3
Guildford Rd ... B1
Hampton Pl ... B1
Hanover Terr ... B3
High St ... C3
Highdown Rd ... A1
Information Ctr ... C2
John St ... B3
Jubilee Clock Tower ... B2
Kemp St ... B2
Kensington Pl ... B2
Kings Rd ... C1
Lanes, The ... C2
Law Courts ... B2
Lewes Rd ... A3
Library ... A3
London Rd ... A3
Madeira Dr ... C3
Marine Pde ... C3
Middle St ... C2
Montpelier Pl ... B1
Montpelier Rd ... B1
Montpelier St ... B1
Museum & Art Gallery ... B3
New England Rd ... A2
New England St ... A2
New Rd ... B2
Nizells Ave ... A1
Norfolk Rd ... B1
Norfolk Terr ... B1
North Rd ... B2
North St ... B2
Odeon ... B2
Old Shoreham Rd ... A1
Old Steine ... C3
Osmond Rd ... A1
Over St ... B2
Oxford St ... A3
Park Crescent Terrace ... A3
Phoenix Brighton ... B3
Phoenix Rise ... A3
Police Station ... B3
Post Office ... A1/A3/C3
Preston Rd ... A3
Preston St ... C1
Prestonville Rd ... A1

Queen's Rd ... B2
Queen Sq ... B2
Regency Sq ... B2
Regent St ... B2
Richmond Pl ... B1
Richmond Rd ... B3
Richmond Terr ... B1
Rose Hill Terr ... B1
Royal Pavilion ... B2
St Bartholomew's
St James's St ... C3
St Nicholas Rd ... C2
St Nicholas' ... C2
St Peter's ... A3
Sea Life Brighton ... C3
Shaftesbury Rd ... A3
Ship St ... C2
Sillwood Rd ... B1
Sillwood St ... B1
Southover St ... A3
Spring Gdns ... B2
Stanford Rd ... A1
Stanley Rd ... A3
Surrey St ... B2
Sussex St ... B3
Swimming Pool ... B2
Sydney St ... B2
Temple Gdns ... B1
Terminus Rd ... B1
Theatre Royal ... B2
Tidy St ... B2
Town Hall ... C2
Toy & Model Museum ... B2
Trafalgar St ... B2
Union Rd ... A3
Univ of Brighton ... A3
Upper Lewes Rd ... A3
Upper North St ... B1
Viaduct Rd ... A3
Victoria Gdns ... B3
Victoria Rd ... B1
Volk's Electric Railway ... C3
West Pier (derelict) ... C1
West St ... C2
Western Rd ... B1
Whitecross St ... B2
YHA
London ... B1
York Pl ... B3
York Rd ... B1

Bristol 177
Acramans Rd ... C4
Albert Rd ... C6
Alfred Hill ... A4
All Saint's St ... B4
All Saints' ... B4
Allington Rd ... C3
Alpha Rd ... C3
AmbraVale ... B1
AmbraVale East ... B2
Ambrose Rd ... B1
Amphitheatre & Waterfront Sq ... B4
Anchor Rd ... B3
Anvil St ... B6
Arcade, The ... A5
Architecture Centre, The ... B4
Argyle Pl ... B2
Arlington Villas ... A2
Arnolfini ... B4
Art Gallery ... A3
Ashton Gate Rd ... C1
Ashton Rd ... C1
Avon Bridge ... C1
Avon Cr ... C1
Avon St ... B6
Baldwin St ... B4
Baltic Wharf ... C2
Baltic Wharf Leisure Centre & Caravan Park ... C2
Baltic Wharf Marina ... C2
Barossa Pl ... C4
Barton Manor ... B6
Barton Rd ... B6
Barton Vale ... B6
Bath Rd ... C6
Bathurst Basin ... C4
Bathurst Parade ... C4
Beauley Rd ... C2
Bedminster Bridge ... C4
Bedminster Parade ... C4
Bellevue ... B2
Bellevue Cr ... B2
Bellevue Rd ... C6
Berkeley Pl ... A2
Berkeley Sq ... A3
Birch Rd ... C2
Blackfriars ... A4
Bond St ... A5
Braggs La ... A6
Brandon Hill ... B3
Brandon Steep ... B3
Bristol Aquarium ... B4
Bristol Beacon ... B4
Bristol Bridge ... B5
Bristol Cath (CE) ... B3
Bristol Eye Hospital (A&E) ... A4
Bristol Grammar School ... A3
Bristol Harbour Railway ... C3
Bristol Royal Children's Hosp ... A4
Bristol Royal Infirmary (A&E) ... A4
Bristol Temple Meads Station ... B6
Broad Plain ... B5
Broad Quay ... B4
Broad St ... A4
Broad Weir ... A5
Broadcasting Ho ... A3
Broadmead ... A5
Brunel Institute ... B3
Brunel Sq ... C5
Brunswick Sq ... A5
Burton Cl ... C4
Bus Station ... A5
Butts Rd ... B3
Cabot Circus ... A5
Cabot Tower ... B3
Caledonia Pl ... B1
Callowhill Ct ... A5

Cambridge St ... C6
Camden Rd ... C6
Camp Rd ... A1
Canada Way ... C1
Cannon St ... A4
Canon's Way ... B3
Cantock's Cl ... A3
Canynge Rd ... A1
Canynge Sq ... A1
Castle Park ... A5
Castle St ... A5
Cathedral Walk ... B3
Catherine Meade St ... C5
Cattle Market Rd ... C6
Central Library ... B3
Charles Pl ... B1
Charlotte St ... B3
Charlotte St South ... B3
Chatterton Ho ... B5
Chatterton Sq ... C5
Chatterton St ... C5
Cheese La ... B5
Christchurch ... A4
Christchurch Rd ... A1
Christmas Steps ... A4
Church La ... B2/B5
Church St ... B5
City Museum ... A3
City of Bristol College ... C4
Civil and Family Justice Centre ... B5
Clare St ... B4
Clarence Rd ... C5
Cliff Rd ... C1
Clift House Rd ... C1
Clifton Cathedral (RC) ... A2
Clifton Down ... A1
Clifton Down Rd ... A1
Clifton Hill ... B2
Clifton Park ... A1/A2
Clifton Park Rd ... A2
Clifton Rd ... A2
Clifton Vale ... B2
Cliftonwood Cr ... B2
Cliftonwood Rd ... B2
Cliftonwood Terr ... B2
Cobblestone Mews ... A1
College Green ... B3
College Rd ... A1
College St ... B3
Colston Almshouses ... A4
Colston Ave ... A4
Colston Parade ... C5
Colston St ... A4
Commercial Rd ... C4
Constitution Hill ... B2
Cooperage La ... C1
Corn St ... B4
Cornwallis Ave ... B1
Cornwallis Cr ... B1
Coronation Rd ... C2/C4
Council House ... B3
Countership ... C5
Crosby Row ... B2
Crown Court ... A4
Culver St ... B3
Cumberland Basin ... C1
Cumberland Close ... C2
Cumberland Rd ... C2/C3
Dean La ... C4
Deanery Rd ... B3
Denmark St ... B4
Dowry Sq ... B1
Eaton Cr ... A2
Elmdale Rd ... A3
Elton Rd ... A3
Eugene St ... A4/A6
Exchange and St Nicholas' Mkts, The ... B4
Fairfax St ... B4
Fire Station ... B5
Floating Harbour ... B4
Fosseway, The ... A2
Foster Almshouses ... A4
Frayne Rd ... C1
Frederick Pl ... A2
Freeland Pl ... B1
Friary ... B5
Frogmore St ... B3
Fry's Hill ... B2
Gas La ... B6
Gasferry Rd ... C3
Georgian House ... B3
Glendale ... B1
Glenworth Rd ... C5
Gloucester St ... A1
Goldney Hall ... B2
Goldney Rd ... B2
Gordon Rd ... A2
Granby Hill ... B1
Grange Rd ... A1
Great Ann St ... A6
Great George Rd ... B3
Great George St ... A6/B3
Green St North ... C1
Green St South ... C1
Greenay Bush La ... C2
Greenbank Rd ... C1
Greville Smyth Park ... C1
Grove, The ... B4
Guinea St ... C4
Hamilton Rd ... C2
Hanbury Rd ... A2
Hanover Pl ... C2
Harley Pl ... A1
Haymarket ... A5
Hensman's Hill ... B1
High St ... B4
Highbury Villas ... A2
Hill St ... B3
Hinton La ... B1
Hippodrome ... B4
Hopechapel Hill ... B1
Horfield Rd ... A4
Horsefair, The ... A5
Horton St ... B6
Host St ... A4
Hotwell Rd ... B1/B2
Houlton St ... A6
Howard Rd ... C1
IMAX Cinema ... B4
Information Ctr ... B4
Islington Rd ... C3
Jacob St ... A5/A6

Jacob's Wells Rd ... B2
John Carr's Terr ... B1
John Wesley's Chapel ... A5
Joy Hill ... B1
Jubilee St ... B6
Kensington Pl ... A1
Kilkenny St ... B6
King St ... B4
Kingsland Rd ... B6
Kingston Rd ... C3
Lamb St ... A6
Lansdown Rd ... A2
Lawford St ... A6
Lawfords Gate ... A6
Leighton Rd ... C3
Lewins Mead ... A4
Lime Rd ... C1
Litfield Rd ... A1
Little Ann St ... A6
Little Caroline Pl ... B1
Little George St ... A6
Little King St ... B4
Llandoger Trow ... B4
Lloyds' Building, The ... B3
Lodge St ... A4
Lord Mayor's Chapel, The ... B4
Lower Castle St ... A5
Lower Church La ... A4
Lower Clifton Hill ... B2
Lower Guinea St ... C4
Lower Lamb St ... B3
Lower Maudlin St ... A4
Lower Park Rd ... A4
Lower Sidney St ... C2
Lucky La ... C4
Lydstep Terr ... C4
M Shed ... B4
Magistrates' Court ... B5
Mall (Galleries Shopping Centre), The ... A4
Mall, The ... A1
Manilla Rd ... A1
Mardyke Ferry Rd ... C2
Maritime Heritage Centre ... B3
Marlborough Hill ... A4
Marlborough St ... A4
Marsh St ... B4
Mead St ... C5
Merchant Dock ... C2
Merchant Seamen's Almshouses ... B4
Merchant St ... A5
Merchants Rd ... A1
Merchants Rd ... C1
Meridian Pl ... A2
Meridian Vale ... A2
Merrywood Rd ... C3
Midland Rd ... A6
Milford St ... C3
Millennium Promenade ... B3
Millennium Square ... B3
Mitchell La ... B5
Mortimer Rd ... A1
Murray Rd ... C1
Myrtle Rd ... A3
Narrow Plain ... B5
Narrow Quay ... B4
Nelson St ... B4
New Charlotte St ... C4
New Kingsley Rd ... B6
New Queen St ... C5
New St ... A6
Newgate ... A5
Newton St ... A6
Norland Rd ... A1
North St ... C2
O2 Academy ... B4
Oakfield Gr ... A2
Oakfield Pl ... A2
Oakfield Rd ... A2
Old Bread St ... B6
Old Market St ... A6
Old Park Hill ... A4
Oldfield Rd ... B1
Orchard Ave ... B4
Orchard La ... B4
Orchard St ... B4
Osbourne Rd ... C3
Oxford St ... B6
Park Pl ... A2
Park Rd ... C2
Park Row ... A3
Park St ... A3
Passage St ... B5
Pembroke Gr ... A2
Pembroke Rd ... A1
Pembroke St ... A5
Pembroke St ... A5
Penn St ... A5
Pennywell Rd ... A6
Percival Rd ... A1
Pero's Bridge ... B4
Perry Rd ... A4
Phipps St ... C2
Pip 'n' Jay ... A5
Plimsoll Bridge ... C1
Police Sta ... A5
Polygon Rd ... B1
Portland St ... A1
Portwall La ... B5
Post Office ... A1/A3/A5/B1/B4/C4/C5
Prewett St ... C5
Prince St ... B4
Prince St Bridge ... C4
Princess St ... C5
Princess Victoria St ... B1
Priory Rd ... A3
Pump La ... C5
QEH Theatre ... A3
Quakers Friars ... A5
Quay St ... A4
Queen Charlotte St ... B4
Queen Elizabeth Hospital School ... B3
Queen Sq ... B4
Queen St ... A5
Queen's Ave ... A3
Queen's Pde ... B3
Queen's Rd ... A2/A3
Raleigh Rd ... C2
Randall Rd ... B2
Red Lodge ... A4
Redcliffe Backs ... B5
Redcliffe Bridge ... B4
Redcliffe Hill ... C5
Redcliffe Parade ... C5
Redcliffe Way ... B5
Redcross St ... A6

Redgrave Theatre ... A1
Regent St ... B1
Richmond Hill ... A1
Richmond Hill Ave ... A1
Richmond La ... A1
Richmond Park Rd ... A1
Richmond Rd ... C6
Richmond Terrace ... A1
River St ... A6
Rownham Mead ... B2
Royal Fort Rd ... A3
Royal Park ... A2
Royal West of England Academy ... A3
Royal York Cr ... B1
Royal York Villas ... B1
Rupert St ... A4
Russ St ... A6
St Andrew's Walk ... B1
St George's Rd ... B3
St George's ... A4
St James ... A5
St John's ... B4
St John's Rd ... C4
St Luke's Rd ... C5
St Mary Redcliffe ... C5
St Matthias Park ... A6
St Michael's Hill ... A3
St Michael's Hospital ... A4
St Michael's Park ... A3
St Nicholas St ... B4
St Paul St ... A5
St Paul's Rd ... A2
St Peter's (ruin) ... A5
St Philip's Bridge ... B5
St Philips Rd ... A6
St Stephen's ... B4
St Stephen's St ... B4
St Thomas St ... B5
St Thomas the Martyr ... B5
Sandford Rd ... B1
Sargent St ... C5
Saville Pl ... B1
Ship La ... C5
Shopmobility ... A5
Showcase Cinema de Lux ... A5
Silver St ... A4
Sion Hill ... A1
Small St ... A4
Smeaton Rd ... C1
Somerset Sq ... C5
Somerset St ... C5
Southernhay Ave ... C4
Southville Rd ... C4
Spike Island Artspace ... C3
Spring St ... C5
SS Great Britain and the Matthew ... B3
Stackpool Rd ... C3
Straight St ... B6
Stillhouse La ... C4
Sydney Row ... C2
Tankard's Cl ... A3
Temple Back ... B5
Temple Back East ... B5
Temple Bridge ... B5
Temple Church ... B5
Temple Circus ... B5
Temple Gate ... C5
Temple St ... B5
Temple Way ... B5
Terrell St ... A4
Theatre Royal (Bristol Old Vic) ... B4
Thekla ... B4
Thomas La ... B5
Three Kings of Cologne ... B4
Three Queens La ... B5
Tobacco Factory, The ... C2
Tower Hill ... B5
Tower La ... A4
Trenchard St ... A4
Triangle South ... A3
Triangle West ... A3
Trinity Rd ... A6
Trinity St ... A4
Tyndall Ave ... A3
Union St ... A5
Union St ... B6
Unity St ... B3
Unity St ... A6
University of Bristol ... A3
University Rd ... A3
Upper Byron Pl ... A3
Upper Maudlin St ... A4
Upper Perry Hill ... C3
Upton Rd ... C1
Valentine Bridge ... B6
Victoria Gr ... C5
Victoria Rd ... A6
Victoria Rooms ... A2
Victoria Sq ... A2
Victoria St ... B5
Vyvyan Rd ... A1
Vyvyan Terr ... A1
Wade St ... A6
Walter St ... C2
Wapping Rd ... C4
Water La ... B5
Waterloo Rd ... A6
Waterloo St ... A6
Waterloo St ... B1
Watershed Media Centre ... B4
We the Curious ... B3
Welling Terr ... B1
Welsh Back ... B4
West Mall ... A1
West St ... A6
Westfield Pl ... A1
Wetherell Pl ... A2
Whitehouse Pl ... C5
Whitehouse St ... C5
Whiteladies Rd ... A2
Whitson St ... A5
William St ... C5
Willway St ... C5
Wine St ... B4
Woodland Rd ... A3
Woodland Rise ... A3
Worcester Rd ... A1
Worcester Terr ... A1
YHA ... B4
York Gdns ... B1
York Pl ... A2
York Rd ... C5
York Terr ... B1

Bury St Edmunds 178
Abbey Gardens ... B3
Abbey Gate ... B2
Abbeygate St ... B2
Albert Cr ... B1
Albert St ... B1
Ambulance Sta ... C1
Angel Hill ... B2
Angel La ... B2
Anglian Lane ... A2
Arc Shopping Ctr ... B2
Athenaeum ... B2
Barwell Rd ... A3
Beetons Way ... A1
Bishops Rd ... B2
Bloomfield St ... B2
Bridewell La ... C2
Bullen Cl ... C1
Bury St Edmunds County Upper Sch ... A3
Bury St Edmunds Leisure Centre ... A3
Bury Town FC ... B3
Bus Station ... B2
Business Park ... A1
Butter Mkt ... B2
Cannon St ... B2
Castle Rd ... C1
Cemetery ... C1
Chalk Rd (N) ... A1
Chalk Rd (S) ... A1
Church Row ... B2
Churchgate St ... C2
Cineworld ... B1
Citizens Advice Bureau ... B2
College St ... B2
Compiegne Way ... A3
Corn Exchange, The ... B2
Cornfield Rd ... B3
Cotton Lane ... B2
Courts ... B2
Covent Garden ... C2
Crown St ... C2
Cullum Rd ... C2
Eastern Way ... A3
Eastgate St ... B3
Enterprise Bsns Pk ... A2
Etna Rd ... B3
Eyre Cl ... C2
Fen Causeway, The ... C1
Fenner's Cricket Gd ... C3
Fire Station ... B3
Friar's Lane ... C2
Gage Cl ... A3
Garland St ... B2
Greene King Brewery ... C2
Grove Park ... B1
Grove Rd ... B1
Guildhall ... B2
Guildhall St ... B2
Hatter St ... B2
High Baxter St ... B2
Honey Hill ... C2
Hospital Rd ... C1/C2
Ickworth Dr ... C1
Industrial Estate ... B3
Ipswich St ... A2
King Edward VI Sch ... A1
King's Rd ... C1
Library ... B2
Long Brackland ... A2
Lwr Baxter St ... B2
Malthouse La ... A2
Maynewater La ... C2
Mill Rd ... B1
Mill Rd (South) ... C1
Minden Close ... A3
Moyses Hall ... B2
Mustow St ... B3
Norman Tower ... B2
Northgate Ave ... A3
Northgate St ... B2
Nutshell, The ... B2
Osier Rd ... A3
Out Northgate ... B1
Out Risbygate ... B1
Out Westgate ... C1
Parkway ... B1/C2
Peckham St ... B2
Petticoat La ... A3
Phoenix Day Hospital ... B1
Pinners Way ... A1
Police Station ... B2
Post Office ... B2/B3
Pump La ... B2
Queen's Rd ... C2
Raingate St ... C2
Raynham Rd ... A1
Retail Park ... A3
Risbygate St ... B1/B2
Robert Boby Way ... A2
St Andrew's St North ... B2
St Andrew's St South ... C2
St Botolph's La ... C3
St Edmund's Abbey (Remains) ... B3
St Edmunds Hospital (private) ... C2
St Edmundsbury ... B3
St John's St ... B2
St Marys ... C2
School Hall La ... C2
Shillitoe Cl ... A1
Shire Halls & Magistrates Ct ... B2
South Cl ... C3
Southgate St ... C2
Sparhawk St ... C2
Spring Lane ... B1
Springfield Rd ... B1
Station Hill ... A2
Swan La ... C3
Tayfen Rd ... A2
Theatre Royal ... C2
Thingoe Hill ... A2
Vinefields, The ... B3
War Memorial ... C2
Well St ... B2
West Suffolk Coll ... C1
Westgarth Gdns ... C1
Westgate St ... C2
Whiting St ... C2
York Rd ... B1
York Terr ... B1

Cambridge 178
Abbey Rd ... A3
ADC ... A2
Anglia Ruskin Univ. ... B3
Archaeology & Anthropology ... B2
Arts Picture Ho ... B2
Arts Theatre ... B2
Auckland Rd ... A3
Backs, The ... B1
Bateman St ... C2
Benet St ... B2
Bradmore St ... B3
Bridge St ... A1
Broad St ... B3
Brookside ... C2
Brunswick Terrace ... A3
Burleigh St ... B3
Bus Station ... B2
Butt Green ... A2
Cambridge Contemporary Art Gallery ... B2
Castle Mound ... A1
Castle St ... A1
Cemetery ... C1
Chesterton La ... A1
Christ's (Coll) ... B2
Christ's Lane ... B2
Christ's Pieces ... B2
City Rd ... B3
Clare (Coll) ... B1
Clarendon St ... B2
Coe Fen ... C2
Coronation St ... C2
Corpus Christi (Coll) ... B1
Court ... A3
Cross St ... C3
Crusoe Bridge ... C1
Darwin (Coll) ... C1
Devonshire Rd ... C3
Downing (Coll) ... B2
Downing St ... B2
Earl St ... B3
East Rd ... B3
Eden St ... B3
Elizabeth Way ... A3
Elm St ... B2
Emery St ... B3
Emmanuel (Coll) ... B2
Emmanuel Rd ... B2
Emmanuel St ... B2
Fair St ... A3
Fen Causeway, The ... C1
Fenner's Cricket Gd ... C3
Fire Station ... B3
Fitzroy St ... B3
Fitzwilliam Mus ... C2
Fitzwilliam St ... C2
Garret Hostel Bridge ... B1
Glisson Rd ... C3
Gonville & Caius (Coll) ... B1
Gonville Place ... C2
Grafton Centre, The ... B3
Grand Arcade ... B2
Green St ... B1
Gresham Rd ... C3
Guest Rd ... B3
Harvey Rd ... C3
Hills Rd ... C3
Hobson St ... B2
Hughes Hall (Coll) ... B3
Information Ctr ... B2
James St ... B3
Jesus (Coll) ... A2
Jesus Green ... A2
Jesus La ... A2
Jesus Terr ... B3
John St ... B3
Kelsey Kerridge Sports Centre ... B3
King St ... B2
King's (Coll) ... B1
King's College Chapel ... B1
King's Parade ... B1
Lammas Land Recreation Gd ... C1
Lensfield Rd ... C2
Library ... B2
Little St Mary's La ... B2
Lyndewod Rd ... C3
Magdalene (Coll) ... A1
Magdalene St ... A1
Maid's Causeway ... A3
Malcolm St ... B2
Market Hill ... B2
Market St ... B2
Mathematical Bridge ... B1
Mawson Rd ... C3
Midsummer Common ... A3
Mill La ... B2
Mill Rd ... B3
Mill St ... C3
Mumford Theatre ... B3
Museum of Cambridge ... A1
Museum of Classical Archeology ... B1
Napier St ... B3
New Square ... B2
Newmarket Rd ... A3
Newnham Rd ... C1
Norfolk St ... B3
Northampton St ... A1
Norwich St ... C2
Orchard St ... B2
Panton St ... C2
Paradise Nature Reserve ... C1
Paradise St ... B3
Park Parade ... A1
Park St ... A2
Park Terr ... B2
Parker St ... B2
Parker's Piece ... B3
Parkside ... B3
Parkside Pools ... B3
Parsonage St ... B3
Pembroke (Coll) ... B2
Pembroke St ... B2
Perowne St ... B3
Peterhouse (Coll) ... C1
Petty Cury ... B2
Polar Mus ... C2
Police Station ... B3

Post Office ... A1/A3/B2/B3/C1/C2/C3
Queen's La ... B1
Queen's Rd ... B1
Queens' (Coll) ... B1
Old Weavers ... A2
Riverside ... A3
Round Church, The ... A2
Russell St ... C3
St Andrew's St ... B2
St Benet's ... B2
Post Office ... B2
St Catharine's (Coll) ... B1
St Eligius St ... C2
St John's (Coll) ... A1
St Mary's ... B2
St Paul's Rd ... C3
Saxon St ... C2
Sedgwick Mus ... B2
Sheep's Green ... C1
Shire Hall ... A1
Sidgwick Ave ... C1
Sidney St ... B2
Sidney Sussex (Coll) ... A2
Silver St ... B1
Station Rd ... C3
Tenison Ave ... C3
Tenison Rd ... C3
Tennis Court Rd ... B2
Thompson's La ... A1
Trinity (Coll) ... A1
Trinity Hall (Coll) ... B1
Trinity St ... B2
Trumpington Rd ... C2
Trumpington St ... B2
Union Rd ... C2
University Botanic Gardens ... C3
Victoria Ave ... A2
Victoria St ... B2
Warkworth St ... B3
Warkworth Terr ... B3
Wesley House (Coll) ... A2
West Rd ... B1
Westcott Ho (Coll) ... A2
Westminster (Coll) ... A1
Whipple ... B2
Willis Rd ... B3
Willow Walk ... A2
YMCA ... C3

Canterbury 178
Artillery St ... A2
Barton Mill Rd ... A3
Beaconsfield Rd ... A1
Beaney, The ... B2
Beverley Rd ... A1
Bingley's Island ... B1
Black Griffin La ... B1
Broad Oak Rd ... A2
Broad St ... B2
Brymore Rd ... A3
Burgate ... B2
Bus Station ... B2
Canterbury College ... C3
Canterbury East ... C1
Canterbury Tales, The ... B2
Canterbury West ... A1
Castle ... C1
Castle Row ... C1
Castle St ... C1
Cathedral ... B2
Causeway, The ... A2
Chaucer Rd ... A3
Christ Church Univ. ... B3
Christchurch Gate ... B2
City Council Offices ... B2
City Wall ... B2
Coach Park ... B2
College Rd ... B3
Cossington Rd ... C2
Court ... B2
Craddock Rd ... A3
Crown & County Courts ... B2
Dane John Gdns ... C2
Dane John Mound ... C1
Deanery ... B2
Dover St ... C2
Duck La ... B2
Eastbridge Hosp ... B1
Edgar Rd ... C3
Ersham Rd ... C3
Ethelbert Rd ... C3
Fire Station ... C2
Forty Acres Rd ... A1
Friars, The ... B2
Gordon Rd ... C1
Greyfriars ... B2
Guildford Rd ... C1
Havelock St ... B3
Heaton Rd ... C2
High St ... B2
Information Ctr ... B2/B2
Ivy La ... B2
Ivy Pl ... C1
King St ... B2
King's School ... B2/B3
King's School Rec Ctr, The ... A2
Kingsmead Leisure Centre ... A2
Kingsmead Rd ... A2
Kirby's La ... B1
Lansdown Rd ... C2
Lime Kiln Rd ... C1
Longport ... B3
Lower Chantry La ... C3
Mandeville Rd ... A1
Market Way ... A2
Marlowe Arcade ... B2
Marlowe Theatre ... B2
Martyrs Field Rd ... C1
Mead Way ... B1
Military Rd ... B2
Monastery St ... B2
Museum of Canterbury (Rupert Bear Museum) ... B1
New Dover Rd ... C3
Norman Rd ... C2
North Holmes Rd ... B3
North La ... A1
Nunnery Fields ... C2
Nunnery Rd ... C2

Oaten Hill ... C2
Odeon Cinema ... C2
Old Dover Rd ... C2
Old Palace ... B2
Old Ruttington La ... B2
Orchard St ... B1
Oxford Rd ... C1
Palace St ... B2
Pilgrims Way ... C3
Pin Hill ... C1
Police Station ... B2
Post Office ... B2
Pound La ... B1
Puckle La ... C2
Raymond Ave ... C2
Recreation Ground ... A2
Registry Office ... B2
Rheims Way ... B1
Rhodaus Cl ... C2
Rhodaus Town ... C2
Roper Gateway ... A1
Roper Rd ... A1
Rose La ... B2
Shopmobility ... B2
St Augustine's Abbey (remains) ... B3
St Augustine's Rd ... C3
St Dunstan's St ... A1
St Dunstan's ... A1
St George's Pl ... C2
St George's St ... B2
St George's Tower ... B2
St Gregory's Rd ... B3
St John's Hosp ... B2
St Margaret's St ... B2
St Martin's Ave ... B3
St Martin's ... B3
St Martin's Rd ... B3
St Michael's Rd ... A1
St Mildred's ... C1
St Peter's Gr ... B1
St Peter's La ... B1
St Peter's Pl ... B1
St Peter's St ... B2
St Radigunds St ... B2
St Stephen's Ct ... A1
St Stephen's Path ... A1
St Stephen's Rd ... A2
Salisbury Rd ... A1
Simmonds Rd ... C2
Spring La ... C3
Station Rd West ... B1
Stour St ... B2
Sturry Rd ... A3
Tourtel Rd ... A2
Tudor Rd ... C1
Union St ... B2
University for the Creative Arts ... C3
Vernon Pl ... C2
Victoria Rd ... C1
Watling St ... B2
Westgate Gdns ... B1
Westgate Towers ... B1
Whitefriars ... B2
Whitehall Gdns ... B1
Whitehall Rd ... B1
Wincheap ... C1
York Rd ... C1
Zealand Rd ... C2

Cardiff Caerdydd 178
Adam St ... B3
Alexandra Gdns ... A2
Allerton St ... C1
Arran St ... A3
ATRiuM (Univ of Glamorgan) ... C3
Beauchamp St ... C1
Bedford St ... A3
Blackfriars Priory (rems) ... B1
Bvd de Nantes ... B2
Brains Brewery ... C2
Brook St ... B1
Bute Park ... A1
Bute St ... C2
Bute Terr ... C3
Callaghan Sq ... C2/C3
Capitol Shopping Centre, The ... B3
Cardiff Arms Park (Cardiff Blues) ... B2
Cardiff Bridge ... B1
Cardiff Castle ... B2
Cardiff Central Station ... C2
Cardiff Story, The ... B2
Cardiff University ... A1/A2/B2
Cardiff University Student's Union ... A2
Caroline St ... C2
Castle Green ... B2
Castle Mews ... A1
Castle (Heol y Castell) ... B1
Cathays Station ... A2
Celerity Dr ... C3
Central Library ... C2
Charles St ... B3
Churchill Way ... B3
City Hall ... A2
City Rd ... A3
Clare Rd ... C1
Clare St ... C1
Coburn St ... A3
Coldstream Terr ... B1
College Rd ... A1
Colum Rd ... A1
Court ... C1
Court Rd ... C1
Craiglee Drive ... C3
Cranbrook St ... A3
Customhouse St ... C2
Cyfartha St ... A3
David's ... B2/C2
Despenser Place ... C1
Despenser St ... C1
Dinas St ... C1
Duke St (Heol y Dug) ... B2
Dumfries Place ... B3
East Grove ... A3
Ellen St ... C3
Fire Station ... B3
Fitzalan Place ... B3
Fitzhamon Emb ... C1
Fitzhamon La ... C1

Friary, The ... B2
g39 ... B2
Gloucester St ... C1
Glynrhondda St ... A2
Gordon Rd ... A3
Gorsedd Gdns ... B2
Green St ... B1
Greyfriars Rd ... B2
Hafod St ... C1
Hayes, The ... B2
Herbert St ... C3
High St ... B2
HM Prison ... B3
Industrial Estate ... C3
John St ... C2
Jubilee St ... C1
King Edward VII Ave ... A2
Kingsway (Ffordd y Brenin) ... B2
Knox Rd ... B3
Law Courts ... B2
Llanbleddian Gdns ... A2
Llantwit St ... A2
Lloyd George Ave ... C3
Lower Cathedral Rd ... B1
Lowther Rd ... A3
Magistrates Court ... B2
Mansion House ... A3
Mardy St ... C1
Mark St ... B1
Market ... B2
Mary Ann St ... C3
Merches Gdns ... C1
Mill La ... C2
Millennium Bridge ... B1
Miskin St ... A2
Monmouth St ... C1
Motorpoint Arena Cardiff ... C3
Museum Ave ... A2
Museum Place ... A2
National Museum Cardiff ... A2
National War Memorial ... A2
Neville Place ... C1
New Theatre ... B2
Newport Rd ... B3
Northcote La ... A3
Northcote St ... A3
Parade, The ... A3
Park Grove ... A2
Park Place ... A2
Park St ... C2
Penarth Rd ... C2
Pendyris St ... C1
Plantagenet St ... C1
Post Office ... B2
Principality Stadium ... C1
Principality Stadium Tours (Gate 3) ... B2
Quay St ... B2
Queen's Arcade ... B2
Queen Anne Sq ... A1
Queen St (Heol y Frenhines) ... B2
Queen St Station ... B3
Regimental Museums ... B2
Rhymney St ... A3
Richmond Rd ... A3
Royal Welsh Coll of Music and Drama ... A1
Russell St ... A3
Ruthin Gdns ... A2
St Andrews Place ... A2
St David's ... B2
St David's Hall ... B2
St John the Baptist ... B2
St Mary St (Heol Eglwys Fair) ... C2
St Peter's St ... A3
Salisbury Rd ... A3
Sandon St ... C3
Schooner Way ... C3
Scott Rd ... C2
Scott St ... C2
Senghennydd Rd ... A2
Sherman Theatre ... A2
Sophia Gardens ... A1
Sophia Gardens Stadium ... A1
South Wales Baptist College ... A3
Sport Wales National Ctr ... A1
Stafford Rd ... C1
Stadium Plaza ... C1
Station Terr ... B3
Stuttgarter Strasse ... B2
Sussex St ... C1
Taffs Mead Emb ... C1
Talworth St ... A3
Temple of Peace & Health ... A1
Treharris St ... A3
Trinity St ... B2
Tudor La ... C1
Tudor St ... C1
Tyndall St ... C3
Vue ... B2

Walk, The ... A3
Welsh Government ... C3
West Grove ... A3
Westgate St (Heol y Porth) ... B2
Windsor Place ... B3
Womanby St ... B2
Wood St ... C2
Working St ... B2
Wyeverne Rd ... A2

Carlisle 179
Abbey St ... A1
Aglionby St ... B3
Albion St ... C3
Alexander St ... C3
AMF Bowl ... A2
Annetwell St ... A1
Bank St ... B2
Bitts Park ... A1
Blackfriars St ... B2
Blencome St ... C1
Blunt St ... C1
Botchergate ... C2
Boustead's Grassing ... C2
Bowman St ... B3
Bridge St ... A1
Broad St ... B3
Brook St ... C3
Brunswick St ... B2
Bus Station ... B2

Caldew Bridge A1
Caldew St C1
Carlisle (Citadel)
  Station B2
Carlisle College . . . A2
Castle A1
Castle St A1
Castle Way A1
Cathedral † A1
Cecil St B2
Chapel St A2
Charles St B3
Charlotte St B1
Chatsworth Square A2
Chiswick St B2
Citadel, The ♦ B2
City Walls A1
Civic Centre A2
Clifton St C1
Close St B3
Collingwood St. . . . C1
Colville St A1
Colville Terr A1
Council Offices . . . A2
Court B2
Court St Brow B2
Crosby St B2
Crown St C2
Currock Rd C2
Dacre Rd A1
Dale St C1
Denton St C1
Devonshire Walk . . A1
Duke's Rd A1
East Dale St C1
East Norfolk St C1
Eden Bridge B3
Edward St B3
Elm St B3
English St B2
Fire Station B2
Fisher St B2
Flower St B3
Freer St C1
Fusehill St C2
Georgian Way A2
Gloucester Rd C2
Golf Course. . . . . .
Graham St C1
Grey St B3
Guildhall
  Museum 🏛 A2
Halfey's La A2
Hardwicke Circus . . A2
Hart St. C2
Hewson St. C2
Howard Pl A1
Howe St. B3
Information Ctr 🅙 . . B2
James St. B2
Junction St. B1
King St B2
Lancaster St. A2
Lanes Shopping
  Centre, The B2
Laser Quest ♦ B2
Library A2
Lime St. C3
Lindisfarne St. C3
Linton St A3
Lismore Pl. C3
Lismore St. C3
London Rd C3
Lonsdale Rd C3
Lord St. C3
Lorne Cres B1
Lorne St B1
Lowther St B2
Madford Retail
  Park. B1
Magistrates' Ct. . . . A2
Market Hall B2
Mary St B2
Memorial Bridge . . C1
Metcalfe St. C1
Milbourne St B1
Myddelton St. C3
Nelson St C1
Norfolk St. C1
Old Fire Sta,The 🏛 A2
Old Town Hall A2
Oswald St C3
Peter St. B3
Petteril St C3
Pools A2
Portland Pl B2
Portland Sq B2
Post Office
  ▨ A2/B2/C1/C3
Princess St C2
Pugin St C1
Red Bank Terr C2
Regent St C1
Richardson St C1
Rickerby Park A3
Rickergate A2
River St B3
Rome St C2
Rydal St. C3
St Cuthbert's🏛 . . . B2
St Cuthbert's La . . . B2
St James' Park C1
St James' Rd C1
St Nicholas Gate
  Retail Park C3
St Nicholas St C3
Sands Centre, The . A2
Scotch St A2
Shaddongate B1
Sheffield St. C1
Shopmobility A2
South Henry St. . . . B3
South John St. C2
South St B3
Spencer St B2
Station Retail Park . B2
Strand Rd A2
Superstore B1
Sybil St B3
Tait St. C2
Thomas St. B1
Thomson St C1
Trafalgar St. C1
Trinity Leisure Ctr ♦ B1
Tullie Museum &
  Art Gallery 🏛 . . . A1
Tyne St C3
Univ of Cumbria . . A2
Viaduct Estate Rd . C1
Victoria Pl B1
VictoriaViaduct . . . B1
Vue 🎬 B1
Warwick Rd B2
Warwick Sq B2
Water St C2
West Walls B1
Westmorland St . . . C1

Chelmsford 179

Anchor St C1
Anglia Ruskin
  University A3
Arbour La A3
Baddow Rd B2/C3
Baker St C1
Barrack Sq B2
Bellmead B2
Bishop Hall La. . . . A2
Bishop Rd A2
Bond St B2
Boswells Dr B3
Bouverie Rd C1
Bradford St C1
Braemar Ave. C1
Brook St B2
Broomfield Rd A1
Burgess Springs . . . B1
Burns Cres C2
Bus Station B1/B2
Cedar Ave A1
Cedar Ave West . . . A1
Cemetery A1
Cemetery A2
Central Park B1
Central Cross Road A2
Cheltenham Coll . . C2
Cheltenham FC . . . B1
Cheltenham Dr. . . . A3
Chimery Cl A3
City Council B1
Civic Centre B2
CivicTheatre 🎭 . . . B1
Cloudfm County
  Cricket Gd,The. . . B2
College C1
Cottage Pl. B1
County Hall B2
Coval Ave B1
Coval La B1
Coval Wells B1
Crown Court B2
Duke St B2
Elm Rd. C1
Elms Dr A1
Essex Record
  Office,The B3
Fairfield Rd B2
Falcons Mead B1
George St C2
Glebe Rd A1
Godfrey's Mews . . . C3
Goldlay Ave. C3
Goldlay Rd C3
Grove Rd C2
Hall St C2
Hamlet Rd C2
Hart St. C1
Henry Rd A2
High Bridge Rd . . . B2
High Chelmer
  Shopping Centre . B2
High St B2
Hill Cres B3
Hill Rd B3
Hill Rd Sth B3
Hillview Rd A3
HM Prison A3
Hoffmans Way A2
Hospital 🏥 B2
Lady La C1
Langdale Gdns C3
Legg St B2
Library B2
Lionfield Terr A3
Lower Anchor St. . . C1
Lynmouth Ave C3
Lynmouth Gdns . . . C3
Magistrates Court . B2
Maltese Rd A1
Manor Rd C2
Marconi Rd A2
Market B2
Market Rd B2
Marlborough Rd . . C1
Meadows Shopping
  Centre,The B2
Meadowside A3
Mews Ct C3
Mildmay Rd C2
Moulsham Dr C2
Moulsham Mill ♦ . . C3
Moulsham St . . . C1/C2
Navigation Rd B3
New London Rd . B2/C1
New St. B2
New Writtle St C1
Nursery Rd C3
Orchard St C2
Odeon 🎬 B2
Parker Rd C2
Parklands Dr A3
Parkway A1/B1/B2
Police Station ▨ . . . B2
Post Office ▨ . . . B2/C2
Primrose Hill A1
Prykes Dr B1
Queen St B2
Queen's Rd C1
Railway St. B2
Rainsford Rd A1
Ransomes Way . . . A2
Rectory La B2
Regina Rd B2
Riverside Ice &
  Leisure Centre . . . A2
Riverside Retail Pk. A3
Rosebery Rd C3
Rothesay Ave C1
St John's Rd C2
Sandringham Pl . . . C3
Seymour St C1
Shopmobility B2
Shrublands Cl C3
Southborough Rd . . C1
Springfield
  Rd A3/B2/B3
Stapleford Cl C3
Superstore B2/C3
Swiss Ave B3
Telford Pl A3
Tindal St B2
Townfield St B2
Trinity Rd B3
University B1
Upper Bridge Rd. . . C1
Upper Roman Rd . . C2
Van Dieman's Rd . . C3
Viaduct Rd B1
Vicarage Rd C1
Victoria Rd B2
Victoria Rd South . . C2
Vincents Rd C3
Waterloo La B3
Weight Rd B3
Westfield Ave A1
Wharf Rd. B3
Writtle Rd C1
YMCA A2
York Rd C1

Cheltenham 179

Albert Rd. A3
Albion St. B3
All Saints Rd. B3
Ambrose St B2
Andover Rd. C1
Back Montpellier
  Terrace C2
Bandstand ♦ C2
Bath Pde. C2
Bath Rd. C2
Bays Hill Rd C1
Bennington St B2
Berkeley St. B3
Brewery Quarter,
  The. B2
Brunswick St South B2
Bus Station B2
Carlton St B3
Central Cross Road B3
Cheltenham Coll . . C2
Cheltenham FC . . . A2
Cheltenham General
  (A&E) 🏥 B3
Cheltenham Ladies'
  College B2
Christchurch Rd. . . B1
Clarence Rd A2
Clarence Sq A2
Clarence St. B2
Cleeveland St. A1
College Baths Road C2
College Rd C2
Colletts Dr A1
Corpus St C3
Devonshire St. A2
Douro Rd. C1
Duke St. B3
Dunalley Pde A2
Dunalley St A2
Evesham Rd. A3
Fairview Rd. B3
Folly La A3
Gloucester Rd A1
Grosvenor St. B3
Grove St A3
Hanover St A2
Hatherley St C1
Henrietta St A2
Hewlett Rd B3
High St B2/B3
Holst Birthplace
  Museum 🏛 A3
Hudson St A2
Imperial Gdns. C2
Imperial La B2
Imperial Sq C2
Information Ctr 🅙 . . B2
Keynsham Rd C3
King St A2
Knapp Rd B2
Lansdown Cr. C1
Lansdown Rd C1
Leighton Rd B3
Library B2
Lypiatt Rd C1
Magistrates' Court &
  Register Office . . . B2
Malvern Rd B1
Manser St A2
Market St. A1
Marle Hill Pde. A2
Marle Hill Rd. A2
Millbrook St A1
Milsom St A2
Montpellier Gdns . . C2
Montpellier Gr C2
Montpellier Pde. . . C2
Montpellier Spa Rd C2
Montpellier St. C2
Montpellier Terr . . . C2
Montpellier Walk . . C2
New St. B2
North Pl. B2
Old Bath Rd C3
Oriel Rd. C2
Overton Park Rd . . B1
Overton Rd B1
Oxford St C3
Parabola Rd B1
Park Pl. C1
Pittville Circus A3
Pittville Crescent . . A3
Pittville Lawn A3
Pittville Park. A2
Playhouse 🎭 B2
Portland St B3
Prestbury Rd A3
Prince's Rd C1
Priory St B3
Promenade B2
Queen St A1
Recreation Ground B3
Regent Arcade B2
Regent St B2
Rodney Rd B2
Royal Crescent B2
Royal Well Pl. B2
St George's Pl. B2
St George's Rd B1
St Gregory's 🏛 . . . B2
St James St. B3
St John's Ave B3
St Luke's Rd C3
St Margarets Rd. . . A2
St Mary's 🏛. B2
St Matthew's 🏛. . . B2
St Paul's La A2
St Paul's Rd A2
St Paul's St A2
St Stephen's Rd . . . C1
Sandford Parks
  Lido C3
Sandford Mill Road C3
Sandford Park C3
Sandford Rd C3
Selkirk St A3
Sherborne Pl B3
Sherborne St B3
Suffolk Pde. C2
Suffolk Sq C1
Sun St A1
Swindon Rd B2
Sydenham Villas Rd C3
Tewkesbury Rd A1
The Courtyard B1
Thirlstane Rd C2
Tivoli Rd C1
Tivoli St C1
Town Hall &
  Theatre ♦ B2
Townsend St. A1
Trafalgar St C2
Union St A3
University of
  Gloucestershire
  (Francis Close
  Hall). A1
University of
  Gloucestershire
  (Hardwick) A1
Victoria Pl B3
Victoria St. A2
Vittoria Walk. C2
Wellesley Rd A2
Wellington La. A2
Wellington Rd. A3
Wellington Sq. A3
Wellington St B3
West Drive A3
Western Rd B1
Whaddon Rd A3
Winchcombe St . . . B3
Winston Churchill
  Meml Gardens ❀ . A1

Chester 179

Abbey Gateway. . . . A2
Appleyards La C3
Bars,The B3
Bedward Row B1
Beeston View C3
Bishop Lloyd's
  Palace 🏛 B2
Black Diamond St . A2
Bottoms La C3
Boughton B3
Bouverie St A1
Bridge St B2
Bridgegate C2
Brook St A3
Brown's La C2
Cambrian Rd A1
Canal St A2
Carrick Rd. C1
Castle 🏰 C2
Castle Dr C2
Cathedral † B2
Catherine St C1
Chester 🏥 A3
Cheyney Rd. A1
Chichester St A1
City Rd. B3
City Walls B1/B2
City Walls Rd. B1
Cornwall St A1
Cross Hey C3
Cross,The ♦ B2
Crown Ct C2
Cuppin St C2
Curzon Park North . C1
Curzon Park South . C1
Dee Basin A1
Dee La. B3
Delamere St A2
Dewa Roman
  Experience 🏛 . . . B2
Duke St C2
Eastgate. B2
Eastgate St B2
Eaton Rd C2
Edinburgh Way . . . C3
Elizabeth Cr C3
Fire Station A3
Foregate St B3
Forum,The B2
Frodsham St B3
Gamul House C2
Garden La A1
George St A2
Gladstone Ave A1
God's Providence
  House 🏛 B2
Gorse Stacks A2
Greenway St C2
Grosvenor Bridge . C1
Grosvenor Mus 🏛 . C2
Grosvenor Park . . . B3
Grosvenor Park
  Terrace B3
Grosvenor
  Shopping Centre . B2
Grosvenor St C2
Groves Rd C3
Groves,The. C3
Guildhall Mus 🏛 . . B1
Handbridge C2
Hartington St C3
Hoole Way A3
Hunter St B2
Information Ctr 🅙 . . B2
King Charles'
  Tower ♦ A2
King St A2
Leisure Centre A3
Library B2
Lightfoot St A3
Little Roodee C2
Liverpool Rd A1
Love St B3
Lower Bridge St. . . . C2
Lower Park Rd C3
Lyon St A3
Magistrates Court . B2
Meadows La C3
Meadows,The C3
Milton St A3
New Crane St B1
Nicholas St B2
Northgate A2
Northgate St B2
Nun's Rd C1
Old Dee Bridge ♦ . C2
Overleigh Rd C2
Park St B2
Police Station ▨ . . . A2
Post Office
  ▨ A2/A3/B2
Princess St B2
Queen St B3
Queen's Park Rd . . C3
Queen's Rd B3
Race Course B1
Raymond St A1
River La C2
Roman Amphitheatre
  & Gardens 🏛 . . . B2
Roodee (Chester
  Racecourse),The . B1
Russell St A3
St Anne St A2
St George's Cr C3
St Martin's Gate . . A1
St Martin's Way . . . B1
St Oswalds Way . . . A2
St Werburgh St ♦ . . B2
Saughall Rd A1
Sealand Rd A1
South View Rd. A1
Stanley Palace 🏛 . . B1
Station Rd A3
Steven St A3
Storyhouse 🎭 B2
Superstore A3
Tower Rd B1
Town Hall B2
Union St B3
Univ of Chester. . . . C3
Victoria Cr. C3
Victoria Rd A3
Walpole St A1
Water Tower St A1
Water Tower,The ♦ . B1
Watergate B1
Watergate St B2
Whipcord La A1
White Friars. B2
York St B3

Chichester 180

Adelaide Rd A3
Alexandra Rd A3
Arts Centre B2
Ave de Chartres . B1/B2
Barlow Rd A1
Basin Rd C2
Beech Ave B1
Bishops Palace
  Gardens B1
Bishopsgate Walk . A3
Bramber Rd C3
Broyle Rd A2
Bus Station B2
Caledonian Rd B3
Cambrai Ave B3
Canal Pl. C1
Canal Wharf C2
Canon La B2
Cavendish St A1
Cawley Rd C2
Cedar Dr A1
Chapel St A2
Cherry Orchard Rd . C3
Chichester 🏥 B3
Chichester
  By-Pass C2/C3
Chichester Coll . . . C1
Chichester
  Cinema 🎬 B3
Chichester
  Festival 🎭. A2
Chichester Gate
  Leisure Pk. C1
Churchside A2
Cineworld 🎬 C1
City Walls B2
Cleveland Rd A2
College La B2
Cory Close. B3
Council Offices. . . . B2
County Hall B2
Cross,The ♦ B2
Duncan Rd A2
Durnford Cl. A1
East Pallant B2
East Row A2
East St B2
East Walls B3
Eastland Rd C3
Ettrick Cl C3
Ettrick Rd C3
Exton Rd A1
Fire Station. A3
Football Ground . . A1
Franklin Pl A2
Friary (Rems of) . . . A2
Garland Cl. C3
Green La A1
Grove Rd C2
Guilden Rd. C3
Guildhall 🏛 A2
Hawthorn Cl. A1
Hay Rd C3
Henty Gdns C1
Herald Dr C3
Hornet,The B3
Information Ctr 🅙 . . B2
John's St. B2
Joys Croft A3
Jubilee Rd A3
Juxon Cl B2
Kent Rd A3
King George Gdns . A2
King's Ave C2
Kingsham Ave C3
Kingsham Rd C2
Laburnum Gr A1
Leigh Rd C1
Lennox Rd A2
Lewis Rd. A3
Library B2
Lion St A2
LittenTerr A3
Litten,The. A3
Lyndhurst Rd A1
Market B2
Market Ave B2
Market Cross ♦ . . . B2
Market Rd B2
Melbourne Rd B3
Minerva 🎭 C2
Mount La B1
New Park Rd B3
Newlands La A1
North Pallant B2
North St A2
North Walls A2
Novium,The 🏛 . . . B2
Oak Ave. A1
Oak Close A1
Oaklands Park A2
Oaklands Way A2
Orchard Ave A1
Orchard St. A1
Ormonde Ave A1
Pallant House 🏛 . . B2
Parchment St A2
Parklands Rd A1/B1
Peter Weston Pl . . . B3
Police Station
Post Office
  ▨ A1/B2/C3
Priory La A2
Priory Park A2
Priory Rd. A2
Queen's Ave C1
Riverside B3
Roman
  Amphitheatre . . . B3
St Cyriacs A2
St Martins' St A2
St Pancras A3
St Paul's Rd A2
St Richard's Hospital
  (A&E) 🏥 A1
Shamrock Cl C3
Sherborne Rd A1
Somerstown. A2
South Bank C2
South Downs
  Planetarium ♦ . . . C2
South Pallant B2
South St B2
Southgate B2
Spitalfield La A3
Stirling Rd A3
Stockbridge Rd . C1/C2
Swanfield Dr A3
Terminus Ind Est . . C1
Tower St A2
Tozer Way A3
Turnbull Rd. A3
Upton Rd. A1
Velyn Ave B3
Via Ravenna. C2
Walnut La A1
West St B2
Westgate B1
Westgate Fields . . . B1
Westgate B1
Whyke Cl C3
Whyke La B3
Whyke Rd C3
Winden Ave B3

Colchester 180

Abbey Gateway † . . C2
Albert St B3
Albion Grove. C2
Alexandra Rd C1
Artillery St. C3
Balkerne Hill. B1
Barrack St C3
Beaconsfield Rd . . . C1
Beche Rd. C3
Bergholt Rd. A1
Bourne Rd C3
Brick Kiln Rd A1
Brigade Cr C2
Bristol Rd B3
Brook St B3
Bus Sta B2
Butt Rd C1
Campion Rd C2
Cannon St C3
Canterbury Rd C1
Captain Gardens . . C2
Castle 🏰 B2
Castle Park B2
Castle Rd. B2
Catchpool Rd A1
Causton Rd B1
Chandlers Row . . . C3
Circular Rd East . . . C2
Circular Rd North . . C1
Circular Rd West . . C1
Clarendon Way . . . A1
Claudius Rd. C2
Colchester ≥ A2
Colchester Camp
  Abbey Field C1
Colchester
  Retail Park B1
ColchesterTown ≥ . C2
Colne Bank Ave . . . A1
ColneView A2
Compton Rd A3
Cowdray Ave. . . A1/A2
Cowdray Ctr,The . . A2
Crouch St C1
Crowhurst Rd B3
Culver Square
  Shopping Centre . B2
Culver St East B2
Culver St West B1
Dilbridge Rd A3
East Hill B2
East St B3
East Stockwell St . . B2
Eld La B1
Essex Hall Rd A1
Exeter Dr C2
Fairfax Rd C2
Fire Station. A2
Firstsite 🏛 B2
Flagstaff Rd C1
Garrison Parade . . C2
George St B2
Gladstone Rd C2
Golden Noble Hill. . C2
Goring Rd. A3
Granville Rd C2
Greenstead Rd B3
Guildford Rd B3
Harsnett Rd C3
Harwich Rd B3
Head St B1
High St B1/B2
High Woods Cntry Pk A2
Hollytrees 🏛 B2
Hospital 🏥 C1
Hyderabad Cl C3
Hythe Hill C3
Information Ctr 🅙 . . B2
Jarmin Rd A2
Kendall Rd C2
Kimberley Rd C3
Leisure World B3
Library B1
Lincoln Way B3
Lion Walk
  Shopping Centre . B1
Lisle Rd C2
Lucas Rd C2
Magdalen Green . . C3
Magdalen St C2
Maidenburgh St . . . B2
Maldon Rd C1
Manor Rd B1
Margaret Rd A1
Mason Rd A2
Mercers Way A1
Mersea Rd C2
Meyrick Cr C2
Mile End Rd A1
Military Rd C2
Mill St C2
Minories 🏛 B2
Moorside B3
Morant Rd. C3
Napier Rd C2
New Town Rd C2
Norfolk Cr A3
North Hill B1
North Station Rd . . A1
Northgate St B2
Nunns Rd B1
Odeon 🎬 B1
Old Coach Rd B3
Old Heath Rd C3
Osborne St B2
Petrolea Cl A1
Popes La B1
Port La C3
Post Office
  ▨ B2/C1
Priory St B2
Queen St B2
Rawstorn Rd B1
Rebon St C3
Recreation Rd C2
Ripple Way A3
Roberts Rd C2
Roman Rd B2
Roman Wall B2
Romford Cl A3
Rosebery Ave C2
St Andrews Ave . . . C3
St Andrews Gdns . . C3
St Botolph St B2
St Botolph's 🏛 . . . B2
St John's Abbey
  (site of) † C2
St Johns Walk
  Shopping Centre . B1
St Leonards Rd . . . C3
St Marys Fields . . . B1
St Peter's St B1
St Peters 🏛 B1
Salisbury Ave C1
Saw Mill Rd C2
Sergeant St C2
Serpentine Walk . . C1
Sheepen Pl B1
Sheepen Rd B1
Sir Isaac's Walk . . . B1
Smythies Ave B3
South St C1
South Way C1
Sports Way A3
Suffolk Cl C3
Superstore. B3
Town Hall B2
Valentine Dr A3
Victor Rd. C2
Wakefield Cl A2
Wellesley Rd. C1
Wells Rd B2/B3
West Stockwell St . . B2
Weston Rd C3
Westway A1
Wickham Rd C1
Wimpole Rd C3
Winchester Rd C2
Winnock Rd C2
Worcester Rd C1

Coventry 180

Abbots La A1
Albany Rd B1
Alma St B3
Ambulance Sta. . . . A3
Art Faculty B3
Asthill Grove C2
Bablake School . . . A1
Barras La A1/B1
Barr's Hill School . . A1
Belgrade 🎭 B2
Bishop St. A2
Bond's Hospital 🏛 . B1
Broad Gate B2
Broadway. C1
Burges,The B2
Bus Station B3
Butts Radial B1
Byron St A3
Canal Basin ♦ A2
Canterbury St A3
Cathedral † B2
Central Six
  Retail Park C1
Chester St A1
Cheylesmore
  Manor House 🏛 . . B2
Christ Church
  Spire ♦ B2
City College C1
City Walls &
  Gates ♦ A2
Corporation St B2
Council House B2
Coundon Rd A1
Coventry Sta ≥ . . . C2
CoventryTransport
  Museum 🏛 A2
Coventry University
  Technology Park . . C3
Cox St A3
Croft Rd B1
Dalton Rd. C1
Deasy Rd C3
Earl St B2
Eaton Rd C2
Fairfax St B2
Foleshill Rd. A2
Ford's Hospital 🏛 . B2
Fowler Rd. A1
Friars Rd C2
Gordon St C1
Gosford St B3
Greyfriars Green ♦ . B2
Greyfriars Rd B2
Gulson Rd B3
Hales St A2
Harnall Lane East . . A3
Harnall Lane West . A2
Herbert Art Gallery
  & Museum 🏛 . . . B3
Hertford St B2
Hewitt Ave A1
High St B2
Hill St B1
Holy Trinity 🏛 B2
Holyhead Rd A1
Howard St. A3
Huntingdon Rd . . . C1
Information Ctr 🅙 . . B2
Jordan Well B2
King Henry VIII Sch . C1
Lady Godiva
  Statue ♦ B2
Lamb St A2
Leicester Row A2
Library B2
Lincoln St A2
Little Park St B2
London Rd C2
Lower Ford St B3
Lower Precinct
  Shopping Centre . B2
Magistrates &
  Crown Courts . . . A2
Manor House Drive B2
Manor Rd C2
Market B2
Martyrs Meml ♦ . . . C2
Meadow St B1
Meriden St A1
Michaelmas Rd . . . C2
Middleborough Rd . A1
Mile La C2
Millennium Pl ♦ . . . A2
Much Park St B2
Naul's Mill Park . . . A1
New Union B2
Odeon 🎬 B3
Park Rd C2
Parkside C3
Planet Ice Arena. . . C3
Post Office ▨. . . . . .
Primrose Hill St . . . A3
Priory Gardens &
  Visitor Centre . . . B2
Priory St B2
Puma Way C3
Quarryfield La C3
Queen's Rd B1
Radford Rd A2
Raglan St B3
Ringway (Hill
  Cross) A1
Ringway (Queens) . B1
Ringway (Rudge) . . B1
Ringway (St Johns) B3
Ringway
  (St Nicholas) A2
Ringway
  (St Patricks) C2
Ringway
  (Swanswell) A2
Ringway
  (Whitefriars) B3
St John St B2
St John the
  Baptist 🏛 B2
St Nicholas St A2
Sidney Stringer
  Academy A3
Skydome B1
Spencer Ave C1
Spencer Rec Gnd . . C1
Spencer Rd C1
Spon St B1
Sports Centre B3
Stoney Rd C2
Stoney Stanton Rd . A3
Superstore B2
Swanswell Pool . . . A3
Technocentre C3
Thomas
  Landsdail St C2
Tomson Ave A1
Top Green C1
Trinity St B2
University B3
Univ Sports Ctr . . . B3
Upper Hill St A1
Upper Well St A2
Victoria St A3
Vine St A3
Warwick Rd C2
Waveley Rd B1
West Orchards
  Shopping Ctr. . . . B2
Westminster Rd . . . C1
White St A3
Windsor St B1

Derby 180

Abbey St C1
Agard St B1
Albert St. B2
Albion St B2
Ambulance Station . B1
Arthur St A1
Ashlyn Rd A3
Assembly Rooms 🏛 B2
Babington La C2
Becket St B1
Belper Rd A1
Bold La B1
Bradshaw Way C2
Bradshaw Way
  Retail Park C2
Bridge St B1
Brook St B1
Burton Rd C1
Bus Station B3
Business Park A3
Caesar St A2
Canal St C3
Carrington St C3
Cathedral † B2
Cathedral Rd B1
Charnwood St. C2
City Rd A2
Clarke St A3
Cock Pitt B3
Cornmarket B2
Cornwall Rd A3
Courts B2
Cranmer Rd B3
Crompton St C1
Crown & County
  Courts B2
Curzon St B1
Darley Grove. A1
Derby 🏛 B2
Derwent Bsns Ctr . . A3
Derwent St B2
Drewry La C1
Duffield Rd A1
Duke St A2
Dunton Cl B3
Eagle Market C2
East St B2
Eastgate B3
Exeter St B3
Farm St C1
Ford St B1
Forester St C1
Fox St A3
Friar Gate B1
Friary St B1
Full St B2
Gerard St C1
Gower St C2
Green La C2
Grey St. C1
Guildhall ♦ B2
Harcourt St. C1
Highfield Rd A1
Hill La C1
Incora County Ground
  (Derbyshire CCC),
  The. B3
Information Ctr 🅙 . . B2
intu Derby C2
Iron Gate B2
John St C2
Joseph Wright Ctr . B1
Kedleston Rd A1
Key St B2
King Alfred St C1
King St A1
Kingston St A1
Lara Croft Way C2
Leopold St C2
Library B2
Liversage St C3
Lodge La A1
London Rd C2
London St C2
Macklin St C1
Mansfield Rd A2
Market B2
Market Pl B2
May St C1
Meadow La. B3
Melbourne St C2
Mercian Way C1
Midland Rd C3
Monk St C1
Mount St C1
Museum &
  Art Gallery 🏛 . . . B2
Noble St C1
North Parade A1
North St A1
Nottingham Rd . . . B3
Osmaston Rd C2
Otter St A1
Park St C3
Parker St A1
Pickfords House 🏛 . B1
Police HQ C2
Police Station ▨ . . . B2
Post Office
  ▨ A1/A2/B1/C2
Pride Parkway C3
Prime Enterprise
  Park A2
Prime Parkway A2
QUAD ♦ B2
Queens Leisure Ctr . B2
Racecourse Park . . A3
RailwayTerr C3
Register Office B2
Sadler Gate B1
St Alkmund's
  Way B1/B2
St Helens House ♦ . A1
St Mary's 🏛. B1
St Mary's Bridge . . B2
St Mary's
  Chapel ♦ B2
St Mary's Gate B1
St Paul's Rd A2
St Peter's St C2
Showcase De Lux ♦ C3
Siddals Rd C3
Sir Frank Whittle Rd A3
Spa La C3
Spring St C1
Stafford St B1
Station Approach . . C3
Stockbrook St C1
Stores Rd A3
Traffic St C2
Wardwick B2
Werburgh St C1
West Meadows
  Industrial Estate . . B3
Wharf Rd A2
Wilmot St C2
Wilson St C1
Wood's La. C1

Dorchester 181

Ackerman Rd B3
Acland Rd B2
Albert Rd A1
Alexandra Rd A1
Alfred Place B3
Alfred Rd B2
Alington Ave B3
Alington Rd A3
Ambulance Station . B2
Ashley Rd A3
Balmoral Cres C3
Barnes Way B3
Borough Gdns A1
Brewery Sq C2
Bridport Rd A1
Buckingham Way . . C3
Caters Place A1
Cemetery A3/C1
Charles St B2
City Rd B1
Clarence Rd B1
Colliton St A2
Cornwall Rd A2
Cromwell Rd B1
Culliford Rd B2
Culliford Rd North . B2
Dagmar Rd B1
Damer's Rd B1
Diggory Cres C3
Dinosaur Mus 🏛 . . A2
Dorchester Bypass . C2
Dorchester
  South Station ≥ . . C2
Dorchester
  West Station ≥ . . . B1
Dorset County
  (A&E) 🏥 B1
Dorset County
  Council Offices . . . A1
Dorset County
  Museum 🏛 A1
Duchy Close C3
Duke's Ave B1
Durngate St B2
Durnover Court . . . A3
Eddison Ave C2
Edward Rd B1
Egdon Rd C2
Elizabeth Frink
  Statue ♦ B2
Farfrae Cres B2
Forum Centre,The . B1
Friary Hill A2
Friary Lane A2
FromeTerr A2
Garland Cres C3
Glyde Path Rd A1
Government Offices B3
Grosvenor Cres . . . C1
Grosvenor Rd C1
Grove,The A1
Gt Western Rd B1
Herringston Rd . . . C1
High East St A2
High St Fordington . A2
High Street West . . A1
Holloway Rd A2
Icen Way A2
Keep Military
  Museum,The 🏛 . . A1
Kings Rd A3/B3
Kingsbere Cres . . . C2
Lancaster Rd B2
Library B1
Lime Cl C1
Linden Ave C1
London Cl A3
London Rd A2/A3
Lubbecke Way A3
Lucetta La C2
Maiden Castle Rd . . C1
Manor Rd B1
Market B2
Marshwood Pl B2
Maumbury Rings 🏛 B1
Maumbury Rd C1
Mellstock Ave C2
Mill St A3
Miller's Cl A1
Mistover Cl. C1
Monmouth Rd . . B1/B2
Moynton Rd C1
Nature Reserve . . . C2
North Sq A2
Northernhay A1
Odeon 🎬 B1
Old Crown Court
  & Cells 🏛 A1
Olga Rd C1
Orchard St A1
Police Station ▨ . . . B1
Post Office
  ▨ A1/A2
Pound Lane A1
Poundbury Rd A1
Prince of Wales Rd . B2
Prince's St B1
Queen's Ave C1
RomanTown Ho 🏛 . A1
Roman Wall † A1
Rothesay Rd C2
St George's Rd B3
Salisbury Field A2
Sandringham
  Sports Centre . . . B3
Shaston Cres C2
Smokey Hole La . . . C3
South Court Ave . . . C1
South St B1
South Walks Rd . . . B2
Superstore B2
Teddy Bear Ho 🏛 . B2
Temple Cl C1
Terracotta Warriors &
  Teddy Bear Mus 🏛 A2
Town Hall B2
Town Pump ♦ A2
Trinity St B1
Tutankhamun
  Exhibition 🏛 A1
Victoria Rd B1
Weatherbury Way . C2
Wellbridge Cl C3
West Mills Rd A1
West Walks Rd A1
Weymouth Ave . . . C1
Williams Ave B1
Winterbourne
  (BMI) 🏥 C1
Wollaston Rd B2
York Rd B2

Dumfries 181

Academy St A2
Aldermanhill Rd. . . B3
Ambulance Station C3
Annan Rd A3
Ardwall Rd A3
Ashfield Dr A1
Atkinson Rd C1
Averill Cres C1
Balliol Ave C1
Bank St B2
Bankend Rd C3
Barn Slaps B3
Barrie Ave C1
Beech Ave A1
Bowling Green. . . . A3
Brewery St B2
BridgendTheatre 🎭 B2
Brodie Ave C1
Brooke St C2
Broomlands Dr C1
Brooms Rd C2
Buccleuch St B2
Burns House 🏛 . . . B2
Burns Mausoleum . B3
Burns St B3
Burns Statue ♦ . . . B2
Bus Station B2
Cardoness St A3
Castle St B2
Catherine St A2
Cattle Market A3
Cemetery C3
Church Cres A2
Church St A2
College Rd A1
College St A1
Corbelly Hill B1
Corberry Park. C1
Cornwall Mt C2
Council Offices . . . A2

Court A2
Craigs Rd C3
Cresswell Ave. A3
Cresswell Hill B3
Cumberland St B2
David Keswick
 Athletic Centre . . . A3
David St. A1
Dock Park C3
Dockhead. A3
Dumfries B2
Dumfries Academy A2
Dumfries Ice Bowl . C1
Dumfries Museum
 & Camera
 Obscura A3
Dumfries & Galloway
 Royal Infirmary
 (A&E) C3
East Riverside Dr . . A2
Edinburgh Rd A2
English St B3
Fire Station B3
Friar's Vennel B2
Galloway St B1
George Douglas Dr . C1
George St A2
Gladstone Rd C2
Glasgow St A1
Glebe St A3
Glencaple Rd C3
Goldie Ave. A1
Goldie Cres. A1
Golf Course. C3
Gracefield
 Arts Centre A3
Greyfriars A3
Grierson Ave. B3
Hamilton Ave C1
Hamilton Starke Pk C3
Hazelrigg Ave B3
Henry St B3
Hermitage Dr C1
High Cemetery . . . C3
High St A2
Hill Ave C2
Hill St B1
HM Prison. A1
Holm Ave C3
Hoods Loaning . . . A3
Howgate St. A2
Huntingdon Rd. . . . A3
Information Ctr . . . B2
Irish St. B3
Irving St A1
King St A1
Kingholm Rd. C3
Kirkpatrick Ct. . . . C1
Laurieknowe B3
Leafield Rd B3
Library A2
Lochfield Rd A1
Loreburn Pk A2
Loreburn St. A2
Loreburne
 Shopping Centre . B2
Lover's Walk A2
Martin Ave B3
Mausoleum B3
Maxwell St B1
McKie Ave. A1
Mews La. A2
Mid Steeple B2
Mill Green. B1
Mill Rd. B1
Moat Rd A2
Moffat Rd A3
Mountainhall Pk. . . C3
Nelson St A1
New Abbey Rd . B1/C1
New Bridge B2
NewallTerr A2
Nith Ave C2
Nith Bank C2
Nithbank Hosp . . . C3
Nithside Ave A1
Odeon B2
Old Bridge B3
Old Bridge Ho . . . B3
Palmerston Pk (Queen
 of the South FC) . A1
Park Rd C1
Pleasance Ave C1
Police HQ A2
Police Sta A2/A3
Portland St A1
Post Office
 . . . . B1/B2/B3
Priestlands Dr C1
Primrose St A1
Queen St. B3
Queensberry St . . . A2
Rae St A2
Richmond Ave C2
Robert Burns Ctr . . B2
Roberts Cres. C1
Robertson Ave . . . C1
Robinson Dr C1
Rosefield Rd C2
Rosemount St. A1
Rotchell Park C1
Rotchell Rd. C2
Rugby Football Gd . C1
Ryedale Rd C1
St Andrews B3
St John the
 Evangelist A2
St Josephs College C3
St Mary's Ind Est. . A2
St Mary's St. A2
St Michael St. B3
St Michael's
 Bridge B2
St Michael's
 Bridge Rd B2
St Michael's
 Cemetery B3
Shakespeare St . . . B2
Solway St C1
Stakeford St A1
Stark Cres. A1
Station Rd A2
Steel Ave. A1
Sunderries Ave. . . . A1
Sunderries Rd. A1
Superstore B3
Suspension Brae . . B3
Swimming Pool . . . B1
Terregles St B1
Theatre Royal B2
Troqueer Rd C2
Union St A1
Wallace St A1
Welldale A1
West Riverside Dr. . B2
White Sands B2

Dundee 181
Abertay University . B2
Adelaide Pl A1
Airlie Pl C1
Albany Terr A1
Albert St A3
Alexander St A2
Ann St A2
Arthurstone Terr . . A3
Bank St B2
Barrack Rd A1
Barrack St B2
Bell St. B2
Blinshall St B1
Broughty Ferry Rd . B3
Brown St B1
Bus Station B3
Caird Hall B2
Camperdown St . . . B3
Candle La B2
Carmichael St A1
City Churches B2
City Quay. B3
City Sq. B2
Commercial St B2
Constable St A3
Constitution Cres . . A1
Constitution Ct . . . A1
Constitution St . A1/B2
Cotton Rd A3
Courthouse Sq B1
Cowgate. B3
Crescent St A3
Crichton St B2
Dens Brae A3
Dens Rd A3
Discovery Point . . . C2
Douglas St B1
Drummond St A1
Dudhope Castle . . . A1
Dudhope St A2
Dudhope Terr A1
Dundee C2
Dundee
 Contemporary
 Arts C2
Dundee High Sch . . B1
Dundee Law A1
Dundee Rep C2
Dunhope Park A1
Dura St A3
East Dock St B3
East Marketgait . . . B3
East Whale La B3
Erskine St A3
Euclid Cr. B2
Forebank Rd A2
Foundry La A3
Gallagher Retail Pk B3
Gellatly St B2
Government Offices C2
Guthrie St B1
Hawkhill B1
Hilltown A2
HMS Unicorn B3
Howff Cemetery,
 The. B1
Information Ctr . . . B2
Keiller Shopping Ctr B2
Keiller Ctr,The . . . B2
King St A3
Kinghorne Rd. A1
Ladywell Ave. A3
Laurel Bank A2
Law Rd A1
Law St A2
Library A2/A3
Library and Steps
 Theatre B1
LittleTheatre,
 The A1
Lochee Rd B1
Lower Princes St . . A3
Lyon St A3
McManus Art Gallery
 & Museum,The . . B2
Meadow Side B1
Meadowside
 St Pauls B2
Mercat Cross B2
Murraygate B2
Nelson St A2
Nethergate B2/C1
North Lindsay St. . . B2
North Marketgait . . A2
Old Hawkhill B1
Olympia Leisure Ctr B3
Overgate Shop Ctr . B2
Park Pl B1
Perth Rd C1
Police Station B2
Post Office . . . A1/B2
Post Office B2
Potters Bank . . . C1/C2
Princes St A3
Prospect Pl A2
Reform St B2
Riverside Dr C2
Riverside
 Esplanade C2
Roseangle C1
Rosebank St A2
RRS Discovery . . . C2
St Andrew's † C2
St Pauls
 Science Centre . . B2
Seagate. B2
Sheriffs Court. B2
Shopmobility B2
South George St . . B2
South Marketgait . . B3
South Tay St C1
South Victoria
 Dock Road. B3
South Ward Rd . . . B1
Tay Road Bridge . . C3
Thomson Ave A3
Trades La B3
Union St B2
Union Terr A2
University Library . . B1
Univ of Dundee. . . C1
Upper
 Constitution St . . A1
Verdant Works . . . B1
V&A Museum of
 Design C2
Victoria Dock B3
Victoria Rd B2
Victoria St. A3
Ward Rd B1
Wellgate B2
West Bell St. B1
West Marketgait B1/B2
Westfield Pl C1
William St A3
Wishart Arch A3

Durham 181
Alexander Cr. B2
Allergate. C1
Archery Rise C1
Avenue,The B1
Back Western Hill . . A1
Bakehouse La. A3
Baths. B3
Baths Bridge B3
Boat House B3
Bowling A2
Boyd St C3
Bus Station B2
Castle B2
Castle Chare. B2
Church St C3
Clay La. C1
Claypath B3
College of St Hild &
 St Bede B3
County Hall A1
County Hospital . . A1
Crescent,The A1
Crook Hall &
 Gardens A3
Crossgate B2
Crossgate Peth. . . . C2
Crown Court B2
Darlington Rd C1
Durham A2
Durham School . . . C2
Durham University
 Science Site C1
Ellam Ave C1
Elvet Bridge B3
Elvet Court B3
Farnley Hey. A1
Ferens Cl. B1
Fieldhouse La. B1
Flass St B1
Framwelgate
 Bridge B2
Framwelgate
 Peth A2
Framwelgate
 Waterside A3
Frankland La A3
Freeman's Pl A3
Freeman's Quay
 Leisure Centre . . A3
GalaTheatre &
 Cinema B2
Geoffrey Ave C1
Gilesgate B3
Grey College C2
Grove,The A1
Halgarth St C3
Hatfield College . . B3
Hawthorn Terr B1
Heritage Centre . . B2
HM Prison B3
Information Ctr . . . B2
John St B1
Kingsgate Bridge . . B3
LaburnumTerr A1
LawsonTerr B1
Leazes Rd B2/B3
Library B2
Library B3
Margery La B2
Market B2
Mavin St C3
Millburngate B2
Millburngate
 Bridge B2
Millennium Bridge
 (foot/cycle) A3
Mountjoy Research
 Centre C2
Museum of
 Archaeology . . . B2
NevilledaleTerr . . . B1
New Elvet B3
New Elvet Bridge . . B3
North Bailey B2
North End A1
North Rd A1/B2
Observatory C1
Old Elvet B3
OpenTreasure B2
Oriental Mus C2
Oswald Court C3
Parkside C3
Passport Office . . . B3
PercyTerr B1
Pimlico C2
Police Station B1
Post Office . . . A1/B2
Post Office B3
Potters Bank . . . C1/C2
Prebends Bridge . . C2
Prebends Walk . . . C2
Prince Bishops
 Shopping Centre . B3
Providence Row . . . A3
Quarryheads La . . . C2
Redhills La B1
RedhillsTerr B1
Riverwalk,The B2
Saddler St B3
St Chad's College . . C3
St Cuthbert's
 Society C2
St John's College . . C2
St Margaret's B2
St Mary the Less . . C2
St Mary's College . . C2
St Monica Grove . . C1
St Nicholas B3
St Oswald's C3
Sands,The A3
Shopmobility B3
Sidegate A2
Silver St B2
Sixth Form
 College A3
South Bailey C2
South Rd C2
South St. B2
Springwell Ave . . . A1
Stockton Rd C3
Student Union C3
Sutton St. B1
Town Hall B2
Univ Arts Block . . . B3
Walkergate
 Centre B3
Wearside Dr A1
Western Hill A1
Wharton Park A1
Whinney Hill C3
Whitehouse Ave . . . C1
YHA A3

Edinburgh 182
Abbey Strand B6
Abbeyhill A6
Abbeyhill Cr A6
Abbeymount. A6
Abercromby Pl A4
Adam St C5
Albany La A4
Albany Pl. A4
Albert Memorial . . B2
Albyn Pl. A3
Alva Pl A6
Alva St B2
Ann St A1
Appleton Tower . . . C4
Archibald Pl C3
Assembly Rooms &
 Musical Hall A3
Atholl Cr B2
Atholl Crescent La . C1
Bank St B4
Barony St A4
Beaumont Pl. C5
Belford Rd. B1
Belgrave Cr A1
Belgrave Cres La . . A1
Bell's Brae B1
Blackfriars St B5
Blair St B4
Bread St C2
Bristol Pl C4
Bristo St C4
Brougham St C2
Broughton St A4
Brown St C5
BruntonTerr A6
BuckinghamTerr . . A1
Burial Ground. A6
Bus Station A4
Caledonian Cr C1
Caledonian Rd. . . . C1
Calton Hill A5
Calton Hill A5
Calton Rd B5
Camera Obscura &
 OutlookTower . . . B3
Candlemaker Row . C4
Canning St C2
Canongate. B5
Canongate B5
Carlton St A1
CarltonTerr A6
CarltonTerrace La . A6
Castle St B2
CastleTerr. C2
Castlehill B3
Central Library . . . B4
Chalmers Hosp . . . C3
Chalmers St C3
Chambers St C4
Chapel St C4
Charles St C4
Charlotte Sq B2
Chester St B1
Circus La A2
Circus Pl A2
City Art Centre . . . B4
City Chambers . . . B4
City Observatory . . A5
Clarendon Cr A1
Clerk St C5
Coates Cr C1
Cockburn St B4
College of Art C3
Comely Bank Ave . A1
Comely Bank Row . A1
Cornwall St C2
Cowans Cl C5
Cowgate B4
Cranston St B5
Crichton St C4
Croft-An-Righ A6
Cumberland St . . . A3
Dalry Rd C1
Dalry Rd C1
Danube St A1
Darnaway St A2
David HumeTower . C4
Davie St C5
Dean Bridge A1
Dean Gdns A1
Dean Park Cr A1
Dean Park Mews . . A1
Dean Path B1
Dean St A1
DeanTerr A1
Dewar Pl C1
Dewar Place La . . . C1
DouneTerr A2
Drummond Pl A3
Drummond St C5
Drumsheugh Gdns . B1
Dublin Mews A3
Dublin St A4
Dublin St La South . A4
Dumbiedykes Rd . . B5
Dundas St A3
Dynamic Earth . . . B6
Earl Grey St C2
East
 Crosscauseway . . C5
East Market St . . . B4
East Norton Pl . . . A6
East Princes St
 Gdns B3
Easter Rd A6
Edinburgh
 (Waverley) B4
Edinburgh Castle . . B3
Edinburgh
 Dungeon B4
Edinburgh Int
 Conference Ctr . . C2
Elder St A4
Esplanade B3
EtonTerr A1
Eye Pavilion C4
Festival Office B4
FestivalTheatre
 Edinburgh C4
Filmhouse C2
Fire Station C2
Floral Clock B3
Forres St A2
Forth St A4
Fountainbridge . . . C2
Frederick St B3
Freemasons' Hall . . B3
Fruitmarket B4
Gardner's Cr C2
George Heriot's
 School C3
George IV Bridge . . B4
George Sq C4
George Sq La C4

George St B3
Georgian House . . . B2
Gladstone's
 Land B3
Glen St C3
Gloucester La A2
Gloucester Pl A2
Gloucester St A2
Graham St A1
Grassmarket B3
Great King St A3
Great Stuart B1
Greenside La A5
Greenside Row . . . A5
Greyfriars Kirk . . . C4
Grindlay St C2
Grosvenor St. C1
Grove St C1
Gullan's Cl B5
Guthrie St B4
Hanover St B3
Hart St A4
Haymarket C1
Haymarket Sta . . . C1
Heriot Pl C3
High School Yard . . B5
High St B4
Hill Pl C5
Hill St A2
Hillside Cr A5
Holyrood Abbey
 (Remains) † B6
Holyrood Gait B6
Holyrood Park C6
Holyrood Rd B5
Home St C2
Hope St B2
Horse Wynd B6
Howden St C5
Howe St A2
Hub,The B3
India Pl A2
India St A2
Infirmary St C4
Information Ctr . . . B4
Jeffrey St B4
John Knox Ho B5
Johnston Terr C3
Keir St C3
Kerr St A2
King's Stables Rd . . C3
Lady Lawson St . . . C3
Lauriston Gdns . . . C3
Lauriston Park C3
Lauriston Pl C3
Lauriston St C3
Lawnmarket B3
Learmonth Gdns . . A1
LearmonthTerr . . . A1
Leith St A4
Lennox St A1
Lennox St La A1
Leslie Pl A1
London Rd A6
Lothian Rd C2
Lothian St C4
Lower Menz Pl . . . A5
Lynedoch Pl B1
Manor Pl B1
Market Pl B4
Marshall St C4
Maryfield A6
McEwan Hall C4
Medical School . . . C4
Melville St B1
Meuse La. B4
Middle Meadow
 Walk C4
Milton St A6
MontroseTerr A6
Moray Place A2
Morrison Link C1
Morrison St C1
Mound Pl B3
Mound,The B3
Multrees Walk A4
Mus Collections Ctr A4
Museum of
 Childhood B5
Museum of
 Edinburgh B5
Museum of Fire . . . C3
Museum on the
 Mound B4
National Archives of
 Scotland A4
National Museum of
 Scotland C4
National Gallery . . B3
National Library of
 Scotland B4
National
 Monument A5
National Portrait
 Gallery A4
National War
 Museum B3
Nelson
 Monument A5
Nelson St A3
New St B5
Nicolson Sq C4
Nicolson St C4
Niddry St B4
North Bank St B3
North Bridge B4
North Castle St . . . A2
North Charlotte St . A2
North Mdw Walk . . C4
North St Andrew St A4
North St David St . A4
North West Cir Pl . . A2
NorthumberlandSt . A3
Odeon C2
Old Royal High
 School A5
OldTolbooth Wynd . B5
OMNi Centre A4
OxfordTerr A1
Palace of
 Holyroodhouse . . B6
Palmerston Pl B1
Panmure Pl C3
Parliament Sq B4
People's Story,
 The B5
Playhouse
 Theatre A4
Pleasance C5
Police Station B4
Post Office . . . A3/B4/
 . . . . B5/C1/C2/C4
Potterrow C4
Princes Mall B4
Princes St B3

Princes St B3
Prisoners of War . . B3
Queen's Gallery . . . B6
Queen St A3
Queen Street Gdns A3
Queen's Dr . . . B6/C6
Queensferry St . . . B1
Queensferry St La . B1
Radical Rd C6
Randolph Cr B1
Regent Gdns A5
Regent Rd B5
Regent Rd Park . . . A6
RegentTerr A5
Richmond La C5
Richmond Pl. C5
Rose St B2
Ross Open Air
 Theatre B3
Rothesay Pl B1
RothesayTerr B1
Roxburgh Pl C5
Roxburgh St A3
Royal Bank of
 Scotland A4
Royal Circus A2
Royal Lyceum C2
Royal Mile,The . . . B4
Royal Scottish
 Academy B3
RoyalTerr A5
RoyalTerrace Gdns A5
Rutland Sq B2
Rutland St B2
St Andrew Sq A4
St Andrew Sq A4
St Andrew's House . A4
St Bernard's Cr . . . A1
St Cecilia's Hall . . . B4
St Colme St B2
St Cuthbert's B2
St Giles' † B4
St John St B5
St John's † B2
St John's Hill C5
St Leonard's Hill . . C5
St Leonard's La . . . C5
St Leonard's St . . . C5
St Mary's A4
St Mary's Scottish
 Episcopal † B1
St Mary's St B5
St Michael &
 All Saints C3
St Stephen St A2
Salisbury Crags . . . C6
Saunders St A2
Scotch Whisky
 Experience B3
Scott Monument . . B4
Scottish Parliament B6
Scottish Storytelling
 Centre B5
Semple St C2
Shandwick Pl B2
South Bridge B4
South Charlotte St . B2
South College St . . C4
South Learmonth
 Gdns A1
South St Andrew St A4
South St David St . B3
Spittal St C2
Stafford St B1
Student Centre . . . C4
Surgeons' Hall . . . C5
Supreme Courts . . B4
Teviot Pl C4
Thistle St A3
Torphichen Pl C1
Torphichen St C1
Traverse Theatre . . C2
Tron,The B4
Union St A4
University C4
University Library . . C4
Univ of Edinburgh . B5
Upper Grove Pl . . . C1
Usher Hall C2
Vennel C3
Victoria St B4
Viewcraig Gdns . . . B5
Viewcraig St B5
Vue A4
Walker St B1
Waterloo Pl A4
Waverley Bridge . . B4
Wemyss Pl A2
West Approach Rd . C1
West
 Crosscauseway . . C5
West Maitland St . . C1
West of Nicholson
 St C4
West Port C3
West Princes Street
 Gdns B3
West Richmond St . C5
WestTollcross C2
White Horse Cl . . . B6
William St B1
Windsor St A5
Writer's Museum,
 The B4
York La A4
York Pl A4
Young St B2

Exeter 182
Alphington St C1
Athelstan Rd C3
Bampfylde St B2
Barnardo Rd C3
Barnfield Hill B3
Barnfield Rd . . . B2/B3
BarnfieldTheatre . . B2
Bartholomew St
 East B1
Bartholomew St
 West. B1
Bear St B2
Bedford St B2
Belgrave Rd A3
Belmont Rd A3
Blackall Rd A2
Blackboy Rd A3
Bonhay Rd B1
Verney St A3
Water La C1
Weirfield Rd C2

Cecil Rd C1
Cheeke St A3
Church Rd C1
Western
 Way A3/B1/B2
Willeys Ave C1
Wonford St C3
York Rd A2

Glasgow 183
Admiral St C3
Albert Bridge C5
Albion St B5
Anderston B3
Anderston Quay . . B3
Argyle Arcade C4
Argyle
 St . A1/A2/B3/B4/B5
Argyle Street C5
Arlington St A3
Arts Centre B3
Ashley St A3
Bain St C6
Baird St A5
Baliol St A3
BallaterSt. C5
Barras (Mkt),The . . C6
Bath St A3
BBC Scotland B1
Bell St C6
Bell's Bridge C1
Bentinck St A2
Berkeley St A3
Bishop La B3
Black St A5
Blackburn St C2
Blackfriars St C6
Blantyre St A1
Blythswood Sq . . . A3
Blythswood St B3
Bothwell St B3
Brand St C1
Breadalbane St. . . . A2
Bridgegate C5
Briggait C5
Broomielaw B3
Broomielaw
 Quay Gardens . . B3
Brown St B4
Brunswick St C5
Buccleuch St A3
Buchanan Bus Sta . A5
Buchanan Galleries A4
Buchanan St B4
Cadogan St B3
Caledonian Univ. . . A4
Calgary St A5
Cambridge St A4
Canal St. A4
Candleriggs C5
Carlton Pl C4
Carnarvon St A3
Carrick St B3
Castle St B6
Cathedral Sq B6
Cathedral St B5
Central Mosque . . . C6
Centre for
 Contemporary
 Arts A4
Centre St C4
Cessnock C1
Cessnock St C1
Charing Cross A3
Charlotte St C6
Cheapside St B3
Cineworld A4
Citizens'Theatre . . C5
City Chambers . . . B5
City Halls C5
City of Glasgow Coll
 (City Campus) . . . B5
City of Glasgow Coll
 (Riverside
 Campus) C5
Clairmont Gdns . . . A2
Claremont Pl A2
ClaremontTerr . . . A2
Claythorne St C6
Cleveland St A3
Clifford La C2
Clifford St C2
Clifton Pl A2
Clutha St C2
Clyde Arc C2
Clyde Pl C4
Clyde Place Quay . C3
Clyde St C4
Clyde Walkway . . . C4
Clydeside
 Expressway B2
Coburg St C4
Cochrane St B5
College St B6
Collins St B6
Commerce St C4
Cook St C4
Cornwall St C2
Couper St A5
Cowcaddens A4
Cowcaddens Rd . . A4
Crimea St B3
Custom House
 Quay Gardens . . C4
Dalhousie St A4
Danes'Rd A2
Dental Hospital . . . A3
Derby St A2
Dobbie's Loan A4/A5
Dobbie's Loan Pl . . A5
Dorset St A3
Douglas St B4
Doulton
 Fountain C6
Dover St A2
Drury St B4
Duke St B6
Dunaskin St A1
Dunblane St A4
Dunchattan St . . . B6
Dundas St B5
Dunlop St C5
East Campbell St . . C6
Eastvale Pl A1
Eglinton St C4
Elderslie St A2
Elliot St B2
Elmbank St A3
Esmond St A1
Exhibition Ctr B2

Finnieston Quay . . B2
Finnieston St B2
Fire Station C6
Florence St C5
Fox St C5
Gallowgate C6
Garnet St A3
Garnethill St A4
Garscube Rd A4
George Sq B5
George St B5
GeorgeV Bridge . . C4
Gilbert St A1
Glasgow Bridge . . C4
Glasgow Cath † . . . B6
Glasgow Central . . B4
Glasgow City
 Free Church A3
Glasgow
 Necropolis B6
Glasgow Royal
 Concert Hall A4
Glasgow Science
 Centre C1
Glasgow Tower . . . B1
Glassford St B5
Glebe St A6
Gorbals Cross C5
Gorbals St C5
Gordon St B4
Govan Rd . . . B1/C1/C2
Grace St B2
Grafton Pl A5
Grand Ole Opry . . . C3
Grant St A3
Granville St A2
Gray St A2
Greendyke St C6
Grey Eagle St B7
Harley St C1
Harvie St C1
Haugh Rd A1
Helen St C1
Henry Wood Hall . . A2
High Court C5
High St B6
High Street B6
Hill St A3
Holland St A3
Holm St B4
Hope St A5
Houldsworth St . . . A2
Houston St C2
Howard St C5
Hunter St C6
Hutcheson St B5
Hydepark St B3
Imax Cinema B1
India St A3
Information Ctr . . . B5
Ingram St B5
Jamaica St C4
James Watt St . . . B3
John Knox St. B6
John St B5
Kelvin Hall A1
Kelvin Statue A2
Kelvin Way A2
Kelvingrove Art
 Gallery & Mus . . . A1
Kelvingrove Park . . A2
Kelvingrove St . . . A2
Kelvinhaugh St . . . A1
Kennedy St A5
Kent Rd A2
Killermont St A5
King St C5
King's Dr,The C6
Kingston Bridge . . C3
Kinning Park C2
Kyle St A5
Lancefield Quay . . B2
Lancefield St B3
Langshot St C1
Lendel Pl C1
Lighthouse,The . . . B4
Lister St A6
Little St B3
London Rd C6
Lorne St C1
Lower Harbour . . . B2
Lumsden St A1
Lymburn St A1
Lyndoch Cr A2
Lynedoch Pl A2
Lynedoch St A2
Mair St C2
Maitland St A4
Mansell St A6
Mavisbank Gdns . . C2
Mcaslin St A6
McLean Sq C2
McLellan Gallery . . A4
McPhater St A4
Merchants' Ho . . . B5
Middlesex St C2
Middleton St C1
Midland St B4
Miller St B5
Millennium Bridge. B1
Millroad St C6
Milnpark St C2
Milton St A4
Minerva St A2
Mitchell St West . . B4
Mitchell Liby,The . . A3
Modern Art
 Gallery B5
Moir St C6
Molendinar St C6
Moncur St C6
Montieth Row C6
Montrose St B5
Morrison St C3
Nairn St A1
National Piping
 Centre,The A5
Nelson Mandela Sq B5
Nelson's
 Monument C6
Newton St A3
Newton Terr A3
Nile St B4
Norfolk Court C4
Norfolk St C5
North Frederick St . B5
North Hanover St . B5
North Portland St . B6
North St A3

North Wallace St . . A5
North St A4
O2 ABC A4
O2 Academy C4
Odeon B5/C5
Old Dumbarton Rd A1
Osborne St C5
Oswald St B4
Overnewton St . . . A1
Oxford St C4
Pacific Dr B1
Paisley Rd C3
Paisley Rd West . . C1
Park Circus A2
Park Gdns A2
Park St South A2
Park Terr A2
ParkgroveTerr A1
Parnie St C5
Parson St A6
Partick Bridge A1
Passport Office . . . C5
Pavilion Theatre . . A4
Pembroke St A2
People's Palace . . . C6
Pinkston Rd A6
Pitt St A4/B4
Plantation Park . . . C1
Plantation Quay . . C1
Police Mus B5
Police Station . . A4/A6
Port Dundas Rd . . A4
Port St B2
Portman St C2
Prince's Dock C1
Princes Sq B4
Provand's
 Lordship B6
Queen St B5
Queen Street B5
Ramshorn B5
Renfrew St . . . A3/A4
Renton St A5
Richmond St B5
Robertson St B4
Rose St A4
Rottenrow B5
Royal Concert
 Hall A4
Royal Conservatoire
 of Scotland A4
Royal Exchange Sq. B5
Royal Highland
 Fusiliers Mus . . . A3
West Glasgow
 Ambulatory
 Care A1
Royal Infirmary . . . B6
RoyalTerr A5
Rutland Cr C2
St Andrew's in the
 Square C6
St Andrew's (RC) † . C5
St Andrew's St . . . C5
St Enoch C5
St Enoch Shopping
 Centre B5
St George's Rd . . . A3
St James Rd B6
St Kent St A6
St Mungo Ave . A5/A6
St Mungo Museum
 of Religious Life &
 Art B6
St Mungo St A5
StVincent Cr A2
StVincent La B3
StVincent Pl B4
St Vincent St . . B3/B4
St Vincent Terr . . . A2
Saltmarket C5
Sandyford Pl A2
Sauchiehall St . . A2/A4
SEC Armadillo . . . B2
School of Art A4
Sclater St B7
Scotland St C2
Scott St A4
Scottish Exhibition &
 Conference Ctr. . . B2
Seaward St C2
Shaftesbury St . . . A2
Sheriff Court C5
Shields Rd C2
Shopmobility A5
Shuttle St B6
Somerset Pl A2
South Portland St . C4
Springburn Rd . . . A6
Springfield Quay . . C3
SSE HydroThe . . . B1
Stanley St C2
Stevenson St C6
Stewart St A4
Stirling Rd. B6
Stobcross Quay . . . B1
Stobcross Rd B2
Stock Exchange . . B5
Stockwell Pl C5
Stockwell St C5
Stow College A4
Sussex St C2
Synagogue A2
Taylor Pl A6
Tenement House . . A3
Teviot St A1
Theatre Royal A4
Tolbooth Steeple &
 Mercat Cross † . . C5
Tower St C2
Trades House B5
Tradeston St C4
Transport Mus . . . A1
Tron C5
Trongate C5
Tunnel St B2
Turnbull St C5
Union St B4
Univ of Strathclyde B5
Victoria Bridge . . . C5
Virginia St B5
Wallace St C3
Walls St B6
Walmer Cr C1
Warrock St B2
Washington St . . . B3
Waterloo St B3
Watt St C2
Wellington St B4
West Campbell St . B3
West George St . . . B4
West Graham St . . A3
West Greenhill Pl . . A1
West Nansen St . . . B4
West Regent St . . . B4
West St C4

- West St Ⓜ C4
- Whitehall St B3
- Wilkes St C7
- Wilson St B5
- Woodlands Gate A3
- Woodlands Rd A3
- Woodlands Terr A2
- Woodside Pl A3
- Woodside Terr A3
- York St B4
- Yorkhill Pde A1
- Yorkhill St A1

Gloucester 182
- Albion St C1
- Alexandra Rd B3
- Alfred St C3
- All Saints Rd C2
- Alvin St B2
- Arthur St C2
- Barrack Square B1
- Barton St C2
- Blackfriars ✝ B1
- Blenheim Rd C2
- Bristol Rd C1
- Brunswick Rd C2
- Bruton Way B2
- Bus Station B2
- Cineworld 🎦 C1
- City Council Offices B1
- City Mus, Art Gallery & Library 🏛 B2
- Clarence St B2
- Commercial Rd B1
- Council Offices B1
- Courts B1
- Cromwell St C2
- Deans Way A2
- Denmark Rd A3
- Derby Rd C3
- Docks ✦ C1
- Eastgate St B2
- Eastgate, The B1
- Edwy Pde A2
- Estcourt Cl A3
- Estcourt Rd A3
- Falkner St C2
- GL1 Leisure Centre C2
- Gloucester Cathedral ✝ B1
- Gloucester Life 🏛 B1
- Gloucester Quays Outlet C1
- Gloucester Sta ⇌ B2
- Gloucester Waterways 🏛 C1
- Gloucestershire Archive B2
- Gloucestershire Royal Hospital (A&E) Ⓗ B3
- Goodyere St C2
- Gouda Way A1
- Great Western Rd B3
- Guildhall 🏠 B2
- Heathville Rd A3
- Henry Rd B3
- Henry St B2
- Hinton Rd A2
- India Rd C3
- Information Ctr ℹ B1
- Jersey Rd C3
- King's 🎭 C2
- King's Walk Shopping Centre B2
- Kingsholm (Gloucester Rugby) A2
- Kingsholm Rd A2
- Lansdown Rd A3
- Library C2
- Llanthony Rd C1
- London Rd B3
- Longhorn Ave A1
- Longsmith St B1
- Malvern Rd A3
- Market B2
- Market Pde B2
- Mercia Rd A1
- Metz Way C3
- Midland Rd C2
- Millbrook St C3
- Montpellier C1
- Napier St C3
- Nettleton Rd C2
- New Inn 🏠 B2
- New Olympus 🎭 C3
- North Rd A3
- Northgate St B2
- Oxford Rd A2
- Oxford St B2
- Park & Ride Gloucester A1
- Park Rd C2
- Park St B2
- Park, The C2
- Parliament St C1
- Peel Centre, The C1
- Pitt St B1
- Police Station ▤ C3
- Post Office ✉ B2
- Quay St B1
- Quay, The B1
- Recreation Gd A1/A2
- Regent St C2
- Robert Raikes Ho 🏠 B1
- Royal Oak Rd B1
- Russell St B2
- Ryecroft St C2
- St Aldate St B2
- St Ann Way C1
- St Catherine St A2
- St Mark St A2
- St Mary de Crypt ⛪ B1
- St Mary de Lode ⛪ B1
- St Nicholas's ⛪ B1
- St Oswald's Rd A1
- St Oswald's Retail Park A1
- St Peter's ⛪ B2
- Seabroke Rd A3
- Sebert St A2
- Severn Rd C1
- Sherborne St B2
- Shire Hall 🏠 B1
- Sidney St C3
- Soldiers of Gloucestershire 🏛 B1
- Southgate St B1/C1
- Spa Field C1
- Spa Rd C1
- Sports Ground A2/B2
- Station Rd B2
- Stratton Rd C3
- Stroud Rd C1
- Superstore A1
- Swan Rd A2
- Trier Way C1/C2
- Union St A2
- Vauxhall Rd C3
- Victoria St C2
- Walham Lane A1
- Wellington St C2
- Westgate Retail Pk B1
- Westgate St B1
- Widden St C2
- Worcester St B2

Grimsby 183
- Abbey Drive East C2
- Abbey Drive West C2
- Abbey Park Rd C2
- Abbey Rd C2
- Abbey Walk C2
- Abbeygate Shopping Centre C2
- Abbotsway C2
- Adam Smith St A1/A2
- Ainslie St C2
- Albert St A3
- Alexandra Dock A2/B2
- Alexandra Rd A2/B2
- Alexandra Retail Pk A2
- Annesley St A2
- Armstrong St A1
- Arthur St B1
- Augusta St C1
- Bargate C1
- Beeson St A1
- Bethlehem St C2
- Bodiam Way B3
- Bradley St B3
- Brighowgate C1/C2
- Bus Station C2
- Canterbury Dr C1
- Cartergate B1/C1
- Catherine St C3
- Caxton 🎭 A3
- Chantry La B1
- Charlton St A1
- Church La C2
- Church St A3
- Cleethorpe Rd A3
- Close, The C1
- College St C1
- Compton Dr C1
- Corporation Bridge A2
- Corporation Rd A1
- Court B3
- Crescent St B1
- Deansgate C1
- Doughty Rd C2
- Dover St B1
- Duchess St C2
- Dudley St C1
- Duke of York Gardens B1
- Duncombe St B3
- Earl La B1
- East Marsh St B3
- East St B2
- Eastgate B3
- Eastside Rd A3
- Eaton Ct C1
- Eleanor St B3
- Ellis Way B3
- Fisherman's Chapel ⛪ A3
- Fisherman's Wharf B2
- Fishing Heritage Centre 🏛 B2
- Flour Sq A3
- Frederick St B1
- Frederick Ward Way B2
- Freeman St A3/B3
- Freshney Dr B1
- Freshney Pl B2
- Garden St C2
- Garibaldi St A3
- Garth La B2
- Grime St B3
- Grimsby Docks Station ⇌ A3
- Grimsby Town Station ⇌ C2
- Hainton Ave C3
- Har Way B3
- Hare St C3
- Harrison St B1
- Haven Ave B1
- Hay Croft Ave B1
- Hay Croft St B1
- Heneage Rd B3/C3
- Henry St B1
- Holme St B3
- Hume St C1
- James St B1
- Joseph St B1
- Kent St A3
- King Edward St A3
- Lambert Rd C2
- Library B2
- Lime St B1
- Lister St B1
- Littlefield La C1
- Lockhill A3
- Lord St B1
- Lower Spring St A3
- Ludford St C3
- Macaulay St B1
- Mallard Mews C3
- Manor Ave C2
- Market A3
- Market Hall B2
- Market St B3
- Moss Rd C2
- Nelson St A3
- New St B2
- Osbourne St B2
- Pasture St B3
- Peaks Parkway C3
- Pelham Rd C1
- Police Station ▤ B3
- Post Office ✉ B1/B2
- Pyewipe Rd A1
- Railway Pl A3
- Railway St A3
- Recreation Ground C2
- Rendel St A2
- Retail Park A2/B3
- Richard St B1
- Ripon St B1
- Robinson St East B3
- Royal St A3
- St Hilda's Ave C1
- St James ⛪ C2
- Sheepfold St B3/C3
- Shopmobility B2
- Sixhills St C3
- South Park B2
- Superstore B3/B2
- Tasburgh St C3
- Tennyson St B2
- Thesiger St A3
- Time Trap 🏛 C2
- Town Hall 🏠 B2
- Veal St B1
- Victoria Retail Park A3
- Victoria St North A2
- Victoria St South B2
- Victoria St West B2
- Watkin St A1
- Welholme Ave C2
- Welholme Rd C3
- Wellington St B3
- Wellowgate C2
- Werneth Rd B3
- West Coates Rd A1
- Westgate A2
- Westminster Dr C1
- Willingham St C3
- Wintringham Rd C2
- Wood St B3
- Yarborough Dr B1
- Yarborough Hotel 🏠 C2

Harrogate 183
- Albert St C2
- Alexandra Rd B2
- Arthington Ave B2
- Ashfield Rd A2
- Back Cheltenham Mount B2
- Beech Grove C1
- Belmont Rd C1
- Bilton Dr A2
- BMI The Duchy Hospital Ⓗ C1
- Bower Rd B2
- Bower St B2
- Bus Station B2
- Cambridge Rd B2
- Cambridge St B2
- Cemetery A2
- Chatsworth Grove A2
- Chatsworth Pl A2
- Chatsworth Rd A2
- Chelmsford Rd B3
- Cheltenham Cr B2
- Cheltenham Mt B2
- Cheltenham Pde B2
- Christ Church ⛪ B3
- Christ Church Oval B3
- Chudleigh Rd B3
- Clarence Dr B1
- Claro Rd A3
- Claro Way A3
- Coach Park B2
- Coach Rd B3
- Cold Bath Rd C1
- Commercial St B2
- Coppice Ave A1
- Coppice Dr A1
- Coppice Gate A1
- Cornwall Rd B1
- Council Offices B1
- Crescent Gdns B1
- Crescent Rd B1
- Dawson Terr A2
- Devonshire Pl B3
- Dixon Rd A2
- Dixon Terr A2
- Dragon Ave B3
- Dragon Parade B2
- Dragon Rd B2
- Duchy Rd B1
- East Parade B2
- East Park Rd C3
- Esplanade B1
- Everyman 🎦 B2
- Fire Station A2
- Franklin Mount A2
- Franklin Rd B2
- Franklin Square A2
- Glebe Rd C1
- Grove Park Ct A3
- Grove Park Terr A3
- Grove Rd A2
- Hampsthwaite Rd A1
- Harcourt Dr B3
- Harcourt Rd B3
- Harrogate ⇌ B2
- Harrogate Convention Ctr B1
- Harrogate Justice Ctr (Magistrates' and County Courts) C2
- Harrogate Ladies College B1
- Harrogate Theatre 🎭 B2
- Heywood Rd C1
- Hollins Cr A1
- Hollins Mews A1
- Hollins Rd A1
- Hydro Leisure Centre, The A1
- Information Ctr ℹ B1
- James St B2
- Jenny Field Dr A1
- John St B2
- Kent Dr A1
- Kent Rd A1
- Kings Rd A2
- Kingsway B3
- Kingsway Dr B3
- Lancaster Rd C1
- Leeds Rd C2
- Lime Grove B3
- Lime St A3
- Mayfield Grove B2
- Mercer 🖼 B1
- Montpellier Hill B1
- Mornington Cr A3
- Mornington Terr B3
- Mowbray Sq B3
- North Park Rd B3
- Oakdale Ave A1
- Oatlands Dr C3
- Odeon 🎦 B2
- Osborne Rd A2
- Otley Rd C2
- Oxford St B2
- Parade, The B2
- Park Chase B3
- Park Parade B3
- Park View B2
- Parliament St B1
- Police Station ▤ C3
- Post Office ✉ B2/C1
- Providence Terr A2
- Queen Parade C3
- Queen's Rd C1
- Raglan St C2
- Regent Ave A3
- Regent Grove A3
- Regent Parade A3
- Regent St A3
- Regent Terr A3
- Ripon Rd A1
- Robert St C2
- Royal Baths & Turkish Baths 🏠 B1
- Royal Pump Room 🏛 B1
- St Luke's Mount A2
- St Mary's Ave C1
- St Mary's Walk C1
- Scargill Rd A1
- Skipton Rd A3
- Skipton St A2
- Slingsby Walk C3
- South Park Rd C2
- Spring Grove A1
- Springfield Ave B1
- Station Ave B2
- Station Parade B2
- Stray Rein C3
- Stray, The C2/C3
- Studley Rd A2
- Superstore B2/C1
- Swan Rd B1
- Tower St C2
- Trinity Rd C2
- Union St B2
- Valley Dr C1
- Valley Gardens ✿ C1
- Valley Mount C1
- Victoria Ave C2
- Victoria Rd C1
- Victoria Shopping Centre B2
- Waterloo St A2
- West Park C2
- West Park St C2
- Wood View A1
- Woodfield Ave A3
- Woodfield Dr A3
- Woodfield Grove A3
- Woodfield Rd A3
- Woodfield Square A3
- Woodside B3
- York Pl C3
- York Rd B1

Hull 184
- Adelaide St C1
- Albert Dock C1
- Albion St B2
- Alfred Gelder St B2
- Anlaby Rd B1
- Arctic Corsair ✦ B3
- Beverley Rd A1
- Blanket Row C2
- Bond St B2
- Bonus Arena B2
- Bridlington Ave A2
- Brook St B1
- Brunswick Ave A1
- Bus Station B1
- Camilla Cl C3
- Cannon St A2
- Caroline St A2
- Carr La B2
- Castle St C2
- Central Library B1
- Charles St A2
- Citadel Way B3
- Clarence St B3
- Cleveland St A3
- Clifton St A1
- Colonial St B1
- Court B2
- Deep, The 🐟 C3
- Dinostar 🏛 C2
- Dock Office Row B3
- Dock St B2
- Drypool Bridge B3
- Egton St A3
- English St C1
- Ferens Gallery 🖼 B2
- Ferensway B1
- Fire Sta A1
- Francis St A2
- Francis St West A2
- Freehold St A1
- Freetown Way A2
- Früit Theatre 🎭 C2
- Garrison Rd B3
- George St B2
- Gibson St A2
- Great Thornton St B1
- Great Union St A3
- Green La A2
- Grey St A1
- Grimston St B2
- Grosvenor St A1
- Guildhall 🏠 B2
- Guildhall Rd B2
- Hands-on History 🏛 B2
- Harley St A1
- Hessle Rd C1
- High St B3
- Hull Minster ⛪ B2
- Hull Paragon Interchange Sta ⇌ B1
- Hull & East Riding Museum 🏛 B3
- Hull Ice Arena C1
- Hull City Hall 🎭 B2
- Hull College B3
- Hull History Centre A2
- Hull New Theatre 🎭 A2
- Hull Truck Theatre 🎭 B1
- Humber Dock Marina C2
- Humber Dock St C2
- Humber St C2
- Hyperion St A3
- Information Ctr ℹ B1
- Jameson St B1
- Jarratt St B2
- Jenning St A3
- King Billy Statue ✦ C2
- King Edward St B2
- King St A2
- Kingston Retail Pk C1
- Kingston St C2
- Liddell St A1
- Lime St A3
- Lister St C1
- Lockwood St A2
- Maister House 🏠 B3
- Maritime Mus 🏛 B2
- Market B2
- Market Place B2
- Minerva Pier C2
- Mulgrave St A3
- Myton Swing Bridge C3
- Myton St B1
- NAPA (Northern Academy of Performing Arts) 🎭 B1
- Nelson St C2
- New Cleveland St A3
- New George St A2
- Norfolk St A1
- North Bridge A3
- North St B1
- Odeon 🎦 C1
- Old Harbour C3
- Osborne St B1
- Paragon St B2
- Park St B1
- Percy St A2
- Pier St C2
- Police Station B1
- Porter St C1
- Portland St B1
- Post Office ✉ B1/B2
- Posterngate B2
- Prince's Quay B2
- Prospect Centre B1
- Prospect St B1
- Queen's Gdns B2
- Railway Dock Marina C2
- Railway St C2
- Real 🎦 B1
- Red Gallery 🖼 B1
- Reform St A2
- Retail Park B1
- Riverside Quay C2
- Roper St B2
- St James St C1
- St Luke's St B1
- St Mark St A3
- St Mary the Virgin ⛪ B3
- St Stephens Shopping Centre B1
- Scale La Footbridge B3
- Scott St A2
- South Bridge Rd B3
- Sport's Centre C1
- Spring Bank A1
- Spring St B1
- Spurn Lightship ⛵ C2
- Spyvee St A3
- Stage @TheDock 🎭 C3
- Streetlife Transport Museum 🏛 B3
- Sykes St A2
- Tidal Surge Barrier ✦ C3
- Tower St B3
- Trinity House B2
- Vane St A1
- Victoria Pier ✦ C2
- Waterhouse La B2
- Waterloo St A1
- Waverley St C1
- Wellington St C2
- Wellington St West C2
- West St B1
- Whitefriargate B2
- Wilberforce Dr B2
- Wilberforce Ho 🏠 B3
- Wilberforce Monument ✦ B3
- William St C1
- Wincolmlee A3
- Witham A3
- Wright St A1

Inverness 184
- Abban St A1
- Academy St B2
- Alexander Pl B2
- Anderson St A2
- Annfield Rd C3
- Ardconnel St B3
- Ardconnel Terr B3
- Ardross Pl B2
- Ardross St B2
- Argyle St B3
- Argyle Terr B3
- Attadale Rd B1
- Ballifeary La C2
- Ballifeary Rd C1/C2
- Balnacraig La A1
- Balnain House ✦ B2
- Balnain St B2
- Bank St B2
- Bellfield Park C2
- Bellfield Terr C3
- Benula Rd A1
- Birnie Terr A1
- Bishop's Rd C2
- Bowling Green B2
- Bridge St B2
- Brown St A2
- Bruce Ave C1
- Bruce Gdns C1
- Bruce Pk C1
- Burial Ground A2
- Burnett Rd A3
- Bus Station B3
- Caledonian Rd B1
- Cameron Rd A1
- Cameron Sq A1
- Carse Rd A1
- Carsegate Rd Sth A1
- Castle Garrison Encounter ✦ B2
- Castle Rd B2
- Castle St B3
- Celt St B2
- Chapel St A2
- Charles St B3
- Church St B2
- Columba Rd B1/C1
- Crown Ave B3
- Crown Circus B3
- Crown Dr B3
- Crown Rd B3
- Crown St B3
- Culduthel Rd C3
- Dalneigh Cres C1
- Dalneigh Rd C1
- Denny St B3
- Dochfour Dr B1/C1
- Douglas Row B2
- Duffy Dr C3
- Dunabban Rd A1
- Dunain Rd B1
- Duncraig St B2
- Eastgate Shopping Centre B3
- Eden Court 🎭🎦 C2
- Fairfield Rd B1
- Falcon Sq B3
- Fire Station A3
- Fraser St B2
- Fraser St C2
- Friars' Bridge A2
- Friars' La B2
- Friars' St A2
- George St A2
- Gilbert St A2
- Glebe St A2
- Glendoe Terr A1
- Glenurquhart Rd C1
- Gordon Terr B3
- Gordonville Rd C2
- Grant St A2
- Grant Street Park (Clachnacuddin FC) A1
- Greig St B2
- Harbour Rd A3
- Harrowden Rd B1
- Haugh Rd C2
- Heatherley Cres C3
- High St B3
- Highland Council HQ, The C2
- Hill Park C3
- Hill St B3
- HM Prison B3
- Huntly Pl A2
- Huntly St B2
- India St A2
- Industrial Estate A3
- Information Ctr ℹ B2
- Innes St A2
- Inverness ⇌ B3
- Inverness High Sch B1
- Inverness Museum & Art Gallery 🏛🖼 B2
- Jamaica St A2
- Kenneth St B2
- Kilmuir Rd A1
- King St B2
- Kingsmills Rd B3
- Laurel Ave B1/C1
- Library A3
- Lilac Gr B1
- Lindsay Ave C1
- Lochalsh Rd A1/B1
- Longman Rd A3
- Lotland Pl A2
- Lower Kessock St A1
- Madras St A2
- Maxwell Dr C1
- Mayfield Rd C3
- Millburn Rd B3
- Mitchell's La C3
- Montague Row B2
- Muirfield Rd C3
- Muirtown St B1
- Nelson St A2
- Ness Bank C2
- Ness Bridge B2
- Ness Walk B2/C2
- Old Edinburgh Rd C3
- Old High Church ⛪ B2
- Park Rd C1
- Paton St C2
- Perceval Rd B1
- Planefield Rd B2
- Police Station ▤ A3
- Porterfield Bank C3
- Porterfield Rd C3
- Portland Pl A2
- Post Office ✉ A2/B1/B2
- Queen St B2
- Queensgate B2
- Railway Terr A3
- Rangemore Rd B1
- Reay St B3
- Riverside St A2
- Rose St A2
- Ross Ave B1
- Rowan Rd B1
- Royal Northern Infirmary Ⓗ C2
- St Andrew's Cath ✝ C2
- St Columba ⛪ B2
- St John's Ave C1
- St Mary's Ave C1
- Sheriff Court B3
- Shore St A2
- Smith Ave C1
- Southside Pl C3
- Southside Rd C3
- Spectrum Centre B2
- Strothers La B3
- Superstore A1/B2
- TA Centre C2
- Telford Gdns B1
- Telford Rd A1
- Telford St A1
- Tomnahurich Cemetery C1
- Tomnahurich St B2
- Town Hall B3
- Union Rd B3
- Union St B3
- Victorian Market B3
- Walker Pl A2
- Walker Rd A3
- War Memorial ✦ C2
- Waterloo Bridge A2
- Wells St B1
- Young St B2

Ipswich 184
- Alderman Rd B2
- All Saints' Rd A1
- Alpe St B2
- Ancaster Rd C1
- Ancient House 🏠 B3
- Anglesea Rd B2
- Ann St B2
- Arboretum A2
- Austin St C2
- Avenue, The A3
- Belstead Rd C2
- Berners St B2
- Bibb Way B1
- Birkfield Dr C1
- Black Horse La B2
- Bolton La B3
- Bond St C3
- Bowthorpe Cl B2
- Bramford La A1
- Bramford Rd A1
- Bridge St C2
- Brookfield Rd A1
- Brooks Hall Rd A1
- Broomhill Park A2
- Broomhill Rd A1
- Broughton Rd A2
- Bulwer Rd B1
- Burrell Rd C2
- Bus Station B3
- Butter Market B2
- Buttermarket Shopping Ctr, The B3
- Cardinal Park Leisure Park C2
- Carr St B3
- Cecil Rd B2
- Cecilia St C2
- Chancery Rd C2
- Charles St B2
- Chevallier St A1
- Christchurch Mansion & Wolsey Art Gallery 🏠 B3
- Christchurch Park A3
- Christchurch St B3
- Cineworld 🎦 C2
- Civic Centre B2
- Civic Dr B2
- Clarkson St B1
- Cobbold St B3
- Commercial Rd C2
- Constable Rd A3
- Constantine Rd C1
- Constitution Hill A2
- Corder Rd A3
- Corn Exchange B2
- Cotswold Ave A2
- Council Offices C2
- County Hall B3
- Crown Court C2
- Crown St B2
- Cullingham Rd B1
- Cumberland St B2
- Curriers La B2
- Dale Hall La A2
- Dales View Rd A1
- Dalton Rd B2
- Dillwyn St B1
- Elliot St B1
- Elm St B2
- Elsmere Rd A3
- Falcon St C2
- Felaw St C3
- Fire Station C2
- Flint Wharf C3
- Fonnereau Rd B2
- Fore St C3
- Foundation St C3
- Franciscan Way C2
- Friars St C2
- Gainsborough Rd A3
- Gatacre Rd B1
- Geneva Rd B2
- Gippeswyk Ave C1
- Gippeswyk Park C1
- Grafton Way C2
- Graham Rd A1
- Great Whip St C3
- Grimwade St C3
- Handford Cut B1
- Handford Rd B1
- Henley Rd A2
- Hervey St B3
- High St B2
- Holly Rd A2
- Information Ctr ℹ B3
- Ipswich Haven Marina ✦ C3
- Ipswich Museum & Art Gallery 🏛 B2
- Ipswich School A2
- Ipswich Station ⇌ C2
- Ipswich Town FC (Portman Road) C2
- Ivry St A2
- Kensington Rd A1
- Kesteven Rd C1
- Key St C3
- Kingsfield Ave A3
- Kitchener Rd A1
- Little's Cr C2
- London Rd B1
- Low Brook St C3
- Lower Orwell St C3
- Luther Rd C2
- Magistrates Court B2
- Manor Rd A3
- Mornington Ave A1
- Museum St B2
- Neale St B3
- New Cardinal St C2
- New Cut East C3
- New Cut West C3
- New Wolsey 🎭 B2
- Newson St B2
- Norwich Rd A1/B1
- Oban St B2
- Old Custom House 🏠 C3
- Old Foundry Rd B3
- Old Merchant's House 🏠 C3
- Orford St B2
- Paget Rd A2
- Park Rd A3
- Park View Rd A2
- Peter's St C2
- Philip Rd C2
- Pine Ave A2
- Pine View Rd A2
- Police Station ▤ B2
- Portman Rd B2
- Portman Walk C1
- Post Office ✉ B2
- Princes St C2
- Prospect St B1
- Queen St B2
- Ranelagh Rd C1
- Recreation Ground B1
- Rectory Rd C2
- Regent Theatre 🎭 B3
- Retail Park C1
- Retail Park C2
- Richmond Rd A1
- Rope Walk C3
- Rose La C2
- Russell Rd C2
- St Edmund's Rd A2
- St George's St B2
- St Helen's St B3
- Sherrington Rd A1
- Shopmobility B2
- Silent St C2
- Sir Alf Ramsey Way C1
- Sirdar Rd B1
- Soane St B3
- Springfield La A1
- Star La C3
- Stevenson Rd B1
- Suffolk College C3
- Suffolk Retail Park B1
- Superstore B1
- Surrey Rd B1
- Tacket St C3
- Tavern St B3
- Tower Ramparts B2
- Tower Ramparts Shopping Centre B2
- Tower St B3
- Town Hall 🏠 B2
- Tuddenham Rd A3
- University C3
- Upper Brook St B3
- Upper Orwell St B3
- Valley Rd A2
- Vermont Cr B3
- Vermont Rd B3
- Vernon St C3
- Warrington Rd A2
- Waterloo Rd A1
- Waterworks St C3
- Wellington St B1
- West End Rd B1
- Westerfield Rd A3
- Westgate St B2
- Westholme Rd A1
- Westwood Ave A1
- Willoughby Rd C2
- Withipoll St B3
- Woodbridge Rd B3
- Woodstone Ave A3
- Yarmouth Rd B1

Kendal 184
- Abbot Hall Art Gallery & Mus of Lakeland Life & Industry 🖼 C2
- Ambulance Station A2
- Anchorite Fields C2
- Anchorite Rd C2
- Ann St A3
- Appleby Rd A3
- Archers Meadow C3
- Ashleigh Rd A2
- Aynam Rd B2
- Bankfield Rd B1
- Beast Banks B2
- Beezon Fields A2
- Beezon Rd A2
- Beezon Trad Est A3
- Belmont B2
- Birchwood Cl C1
- Blackhall Rd B2
- Brewery Arts Centre 🎭🎦 B2
- Bridge St B2
- Brigsteer Rd C1
- Burneside Rd A2
- Bus Station B2
- Buttery Well Rd C2
- Canal Head North B3
- Captain French La C2
- Caroline St A2
- Castle Hill B3
- Castle Howe B2
- Castle Rd B3
- Castle St A3/B3
- Cedar Gr C1
- Council Offices B2
- County Council Offices A2
- Cricket Ground A3
- Cricket Ground C3
- Cross La C2
- Dockray Hall Industrial Estate A2
- Dowker's La B2
- East View B1
- Echo Barn Hill C1
- Elephant Yard B2
- Fairfield La A1
- Finkle St B2
- Fire Station A2
- Fletcher Square C3
- Football Ground C3
- Fowling La A3
- Gillinggate C2
- Glebe Rd C2
- Golf Course B1
- Goose Holme B3
- Gooseholme Bridge B3
- Green St A1
- Greengate C2
- Greengate La C1/C2
- Greenside B1
- Greenwood C1
- Gulfs Rd B2
- High Tenterfell B1
- Highgate B2
- Hillswood Ave C1
- Horncop La A2
- Information Ctr ℹ B2
- Kendal 🏛 A3
- Kendal Bsns Park A3
- Kendal Castle (Remains) ♜ B3
- Kendal Fell B1
- Kendal Green A1
- Kendal Ski Ctr ✦ B3
- Kendal Station ⇌ A3
- Kent Pl B2
- Kirkbarrow C2
- Kirkland C2
- Library B2
- Library Rd B2
- Little Aynam B3
- Little Wood B1
- Long Cl C1
- Longpool A3
- Lound Rd C3
- Lound St C3
- Low Fellside B2
- Lowther St B2
- Magistrates Court A2
- Maple Dr C1
- Market Pl B2
- Maude St B2
- Miller Bridge B2
- Milnthorpe Rd C2
- Mint St A3
- Mintsfeet Rd A3
- Mintsfeet Rd South A2
- New Rd B2
- Noble's Rest B2
- Parish Church ⛪ C2
- Park Side Rd C3
- Parkside Bsns Park C3
- Parr St B3
- Police Station ▤ A2
- Post Office ✉ A3/B2
- Quaker Tapestry ✦ B2
- Queen's Rd B1
- Riverside Walk C2
- Rydal Mount A2
- Sandes Ave A2
- Sandgate A3
- Sandylands Rd A3
- Serpentine Rd B1
- Serpentine Wood B1
- Shap Rd A3
- South Rd C2
- Stainbank Rd C1
- Station Rd A3
- Stramongate B2
- Stramongate Bridge B2
- Stricklandgate A2/B2
- Sunnyside C3
- Thorny Hills B3
- Town Hall B2
- Undercliff Rd B1
- Underwood C1
- Union St A2
- Vicar's Fields C2
- Vicarage Dr C1/C2
- Wainwright's Yard B2
- Wasdale Cl C3
- Well Ings C2
- Westmorland Shopping Centre & Market Hall B2
- Westwood Ave C1
- Wildman St A3
- Windermere Rd A1
- YHA ▲ B2
- YWCA B2

King's Lynn 185
- Albert St A2
- Albion St B2
- Alive St James' Swimming Pool B2
- All Saints ⛪ B2
- All Saints St B2
- Austin Fields A2
- Austin St A2
- Avenue Rd B3
- Bank Side B1
- Beech Rd C2
- Birch Tree Cl B2
- Birchwood St A2
- Blackfriars Rd B2
- Blackfriars St B2
- Boal St B1
- Bridge St B2
- Broad St B2
- Broad Walk B3
- Burkitt St A2
- Bus Station B2
- Carmelite Terr C2
- Chapel St A2
- Chase Ave C3
- Checker St C2
- Church St B2
- Clough La B2
- Coburg St B2
- Coll of West Anglia A3
- Columbia Way A3
- Corn Exchange 🎭 A1
- County Court Rd B2
- Cresswell St A2
- Custom House 🏠 A1
- East Coast Bsns Pk C1
- Eastgate St A2
- Edma St A2
- Exton's Rd C3
- Ferry La B1
- Ferry St A1
- Framingham's Almshouses 🏠 B2
- Friars St C2
- Friars Walk C2
- Gaywood Rd A3
- George St A2
- Gladstone Rd C2
- Goodwin's Rd C3
- Green Quay ✦ B1
- Greyfriars' Tower ✦ B2
- Guanock Terr C2
- Guildhall 🏠 A1
- Hansa Rd C3
- Hardwick Rd C2
- Hextable Rd A2
- High St B1
- Holcombe Ave C3
- Hospital Walk C2
- Information Ctr ℹ B1
- John Kennedy Rd A2
- Kettlewell Lane A2
- King George V Ave B3
- King St B1
- King's Lynn Art Centre 🏛 A1
- King's Lynn FC B3
- King's Lynn Sta ⇌ B2
- Library B2
- Littleport St A2
- Loke Rd A2
- London Rd B2
- Lynn Museum B2
- Magistrates Court B1
- Majestic 🎦 B2
- Market La A1
- Millfleet B2
- Milton Ave A3
- Nar Valley Walk C2
- Nelson St B1
- New Conduit St B2
- Norfolk St A2
- North Lynn Discovery Ctr ✦ A3
- North St A2
- Oldsunway B2
- Ouse Ave C1
- Page Stair Lane A1
- Park Ave B3
- Police Station ▤ B2
- Portland Pl C1
- Portland St B2
- Purfleet B1
- Queen St B1
- Raby Ave A3
- Railway Rd A2
- Red Mount Chapel ⛪ B3
- Regent Way B2
- River Walk A1
- Robert St C2
- Saddlebow Rd C2
- Shopmobility B2
- St Ann's St A1
- St James St B2
- St James' Rd B2
- St John's Walk B3
- St Margaret's ⛪ B1
- St Nicholas ⛪ A2
- St Nicholas St A1
- St Peter's Rd B1
- Sir Lewis St A2
- Smith Ave A3
- South Everard St C2
- South Gate ✦ C2
- South Quay B1
- South St B2
- Southgate St C2
- Stonegate St B2
- Surrey St A1
- Sydney St C3
- Tennyson Ave B3
- Tennyson Rd B3
- Tower St B2
- Town Hall B1
- Town House & Tales of the Old Gaol House 🏛 B1
- Town Wall (Remains) ✦ B3
- True's Yard Fisherfolk Museum 🏛 A2
- Valingers Rd C2
- Vancouver Ave C2
- Vancouver Quarter B2
- Waterloo St B2
- Wellesley St B2
- White Friars Rd C2
- Windsor Rd C2
- Winfarthing St C2
- Wyatt St A2
- York Rd C3

Lancaster 185
- Aberdeen Rd C3
- Adult College, The C3
- Aldcliffe Rd C2
- Alfred St B3
- Ambleside Rd A3
- Ambulance Sta A3
- Ashfield Ave B1
- Ashton Rd C2
- Assembly Rooms Emporium 🏠 B2
- Balmoral Rd B3
- Bath House ♨ B2
- Bath Mill La B3
- Bath St B3
- Blades St B1
- Borrowdale Rd B3
- Bowerham Rd C3
- Brewery La B2
- Bridge La B2
- Brook St C1
- Bulk Rd A3
- Bulk St B2
- Bus Station B2
- Cable St B2
- Canal Cruises & Waterbus ✦ C2
- Carlisle Bridge A1
- Carr House La C2
- Castle ♜ B1
- Castle Park B1
- Caton Rd A3
- China St B2
- Church St B2
- City Museum 🏛 B2
- Clarence St C3
- Common Gdn St B2
- Coniston Rd A3
- Cottage Museum 🏛 B2
- Council Offices B2
- County Court & Family Court B2
- Cromwell Rd C1
- Crown Court B1
- Dale St C3
- Dallas Rd B1/C1
- Dalton Rd B3
- Dalton Sq B2
- Damside St B2
- De Vitre St B3
- Dee Rd A1
- Denny Ave A1
- Derby Rd A2
- Dukes, The B2
- Earl St A2
- East Rd B3
- Eastham St C3
- Edward St B3
- Fairfield Rd B1
- Fenton St B2
- Firbank Rd A3
- Fire Station B2
- Friend's Meeting House 🏠 B1
- Garnet St B3
- George St B2
- Giant Axe Field B1
- Grand 🎭 B2
- Grasmere Rd B3
- Greaves Rd C2
- Green St A3
- Gregson Ctr, The B3
- Gregson Rd C3
- Greyhound Bridge A2
- Greyhound Bridge Rd A2
- High St B2
- Hill Side B1
- Hope St C3
- Hubert Pl B1
- Information Ctr ℹ B2
- Kelsy St B1
- Kentmere Rd B3
- King St B2
- Kingsway A3
- Kirkes Rd C3
- Lancaster & Lakeland Ⓗ C3
- Lancaster City Football Club B1
- Lancaster Sta ⇌ B1
- Langdale Rd A3
- Ley Ct B1
- Library B2
- Lincoln Rd B1
- Lindow St C2
- Lodge St B2
- Long Marsh La B1
- Lune Rd A1
- Lune St A2
- Lune Valley Ramble A3
- Mainway A2
- Maritime Mus 🏛 A1
- Marketgate Shopping Centre B2
- Market St B2
- Meadowside C2
- Meeting House La B1
- Millennium Bridge A2
- Moor La B2
- Moorgate B3
- Morecambe Rd A1/A2
- Nelson St B2
- North Rd B2
- Orchard La C1
- Owen Rd A2
- Park Rd B3
- Parliament St A3
- Patterdale Rd A3
- Penny St B2
- Police Station ▤ B2
- Portland St C2
- Post Office ✉ B2
- Primrose St C3
- Priory ⛪ B1
- Prospect St C3

Quarry Rd B3
Queen St C2
Regent St A3
Ridge La A3
Ridge St A3
Royal Lancaster
  Infirmary (A&E) H . . B3
Rydal Rd B3
Rylands Park A1
St Georges Quay A1
St John's ♦ B2
St Leonard's Gate . . . B2
St Martin's Rd C3
St Nicholas Arcades
  Shopping Centre . . . C3
St Oswald St C3
St Peter's † C3
St Peter's Rd B3
Salisbury Rd B1
Scotch Quarry
  Urban Park C3
Sibsey St B3
Skerton Bridge A2
South Rd C2
Station Rd B1
Stirling Rd C3
Storey Ave B1
Sunnyside La C1
Sylvester St A1
Tarnsyke Rd A1
Thurnham St B2
Town Hall B2
Troutbeck Rd B3
Ulleswater Rd B3
Univ of Cumbria C3
Vicarage Field C3
Vue ♠ B2
West Rd B1
Westbourne Dr C1
Westbourne Rd C1
Westham St C2
Wheatfield St B1
White Cross
  Business Park C2
Williamson Rd B3
Willow La B3
Windermere Rd B3
Wingate-Saul Rd B3
Wolseley St B3
Woodville St C1
Wyresdale Rd B3

Leeds 185
Aire St B3
Albion Pl B3
Albion St B3
Albion Way B1
Alma St A6
Ambulance Sta C4
Arcades 🏛 B3
Armley Rd B1
Armouries Dr C5
Back Burley
  Lodge Rd A1
Back Hyde Terr A3
Back Row C3
Bath Rd C3
Beckett St A6
Bedford St B3
Belgrave St A4
Belle Vue Rd A2
Benson St A5
Black Bull St C5
Blenheim Walk A3
Boar La B4
Bond St B4
Bow St C5
Bowman La C4
Brewery ♦ B4
Brewery Wharf C4
Bridge St A5/B5
Briggate B4
Bruce Gdns C1
Burley Rd A1
Burley St B3
Burmantofts St B6
Bus & Coach Sta B5
Butterly St C4
Butts Ct B4
Byron St A5
Call La B4
Calls,The B4
Calverley St A3/B3
Canal St B1
Canal Wharf C3
Carlisle Rd C5
Cavendish Rd A1
Cavendish St A2
Chadwick St C4
Cherry Pl A5
Cherry Row A5
City Museum 🏛 A4
City Varieties
  Music Hall 🏛 B4
City Sq B3
Civic Hall 🏛 A3
Clarence Road C4
Clarendon Rd A2
Clarendon Way A3
Clark La C6
Clay Pit La A4
Cloberry St A2
Close,The A5
Clyde Approach C1
Clyde Gdns C1
Coleman St C2
Commercial St B4
Concord St A5
Cookridge St A4
Copley Hill C1
Core,The B4
Corn Exchange 🏛 B4
Cromer Terr A2
Cromwell St A5
Cross Catherine St . . . B6
Cross Green La C6
Cross Stamford St . . . A5
Crown & County
  Courts B4
Crown Point Bridge . . . C5
Crown Point Rd C4
Crown Point
  Retail Park C4
David St C3
Dent St C6
Derwent Pl C3
Dial St C6
Dock St C4
Dolly La A6
Domestic St C1
Drive,The B6
Duke St B4
Duncan St B4
Dyer St B4
East Field St B6
East Pde B3

East St C5
Eastgate B5
Easy Rd C6
Edward St B4
Ellerby La C6
Ellerby Rd C6
Fenton St A3
Fire Station B2
First Direct Arena . . . A4
Fish St B4
Flax Pl C5
Garth,The B5
Gelderd Rd C1
George St B4
Globe Rd C2
Gower St A5
Grafton St A5
Grand Theatre 🏛 B4
Granville Rd A6
Great George St A3
Great Wilson St C3
Greek St B3
Green La C1
Hanover Ave A2
Hanover La A2
Hanover Sq A2
Hanover Way A2
Harewood St B4
Harrison St B4
Haslewood Cl B6
Haslewood Drive B6
Headrow,The B3/B4
High Court B5
Holbeck La C2
Holdforth Cl C1
Holdforth Gdns C1
Holdforth Gr C1
Holdforth Pl C1
Holy Trinity 🏛 B4
Hope Rd A6
Hunslet La C4
Hunslet Rd C4
Hyde Terr A2
Infirmary St B3
Information Ctr 🏛 . . . B3
Ingram Row C3
ITV Yorkshire A1
Junction St C4
Kelso Gdns A2
Kelso Rd A2
Kelso St A2
Kendal La A2
Kendell St C4
Kidacre St C4
King Edward St B4
King St B3
Kippax Pl C6
Kirkgate B4
Kirkgate Market B4
Kirkstall Rd A1
Kitson St C6
Knight's Way
  Bridge C4
Lady La B4
Lands La B4
Lane,The B5
Lavender Walk B6
Leeds Art Gallery 🏛 . . A3
Leeds Beckett Univ . . . A3
Leeds Bridge C4
Leeds Coll of Music . . B5
Leeds Discovery
  Centre C5
Leeds General
  Infirmary (A&E) H . . A3
Leeds Minster ♦ B5
Leeds Station ≠ B3
Library B3/B4
Light,The A4
Lincoln Green Rd A6
Lincoln Rd A6
Lindsey Gdns A6
Lindsey Rd A6
Lisbon St B3
Little Queen St B3
Long Close La C6
Lord St C2
Lovell Park A4
Lovell Park Hill A4
Lovell Park Rd A4
Lower Brunswick St . . . A5
Mabgate A5
Macaulay St A5
Magistrates Court . . . A3
Manor Rd C3
Mark La B4
Marlborough St B2
Marsh La B5
Marshall St C2
Meadow La C4
Meadow Rd C3
Melbourne St A5
Merrion Centre A4
Merrion St A4
Merrion Way A4
Mill St B5
Millennium Sq A3
Monk Bridge A2
Mount Preston St A2
Mushroom St A5
Neville St C3
New Briggate A4/B4
New Market St B4
New York Rd A5
New York St B5
Nile St A5
Nippet La A6
North St A4
Northern Ballet 🏛 . . . B5
Northern St B3
Oak Rd B1
Oxford Pl B3
Oxford Row A3
Parade,The B6
Park Cross St B3
Park La B2
Park Pl B3
Park Row B4
Park Sq B3
Park Sq East B3
Park Sq West B3
Park St B3
Police Station A3
Pontefract La B6
Portland Cr A3
Portland Way A3
Post Office 🏤 B4/B5
Quarry House
  (NHS/DSS HQ) A5
Quebec St B3
Queen St B3
Radio Aire C4
Railway St B5
Rectory St A6
Regent St A5
Richmond St C5
Rigton Approach B6

Rigton Dr B6
Rillbank La A1
Rosebank Rd A1
Rose Bowl
  Conference Ctr A3
Royal Armouries 🏛 . . . C4
Russell St B3
St Anne's Cathedral
  (RC) † A4
St Anne's St B4
St John's Rd A2
St Johns Centre B4
St Mary's St B5
St Pauls St B3
Saxton La B5
Sayner La C4
Shakespeare Ave A6
Shannon St B6
Sheepscar St South . . . A5
Siddall St C3
Skinner La A5
South Pde B3
Sovereign St C4
Spence La C1
Springfield Mount . . . A2
Springwell Ct C2
Springwell Rd C2
Springwell St C2
Stoney Rock La A6
Studio Rd A1
Sutton St C2
Sweet St C3
Sweet St West C3
Swinegate B4
Templar St B5
Tetley,The 🏛 C4
Thoresby Pl A3
Torre Rd A6
Town Hall 🏛 B3
Trinity Leeds B4
Union Pl C3
Union St B5
University of Leeds . . A3
Upper Accom-
  modation Rd B6
Upper Basinghall St . . B4
Vicar La B4
Victoria Bridge C4
Victoria Gate B4
Victoria Quarter B4
Victoria Rd C4
Vue ♠ B4
Wade La A4
Washington St A1
Water La C3
Waterloo Rd C4
Wellington Rd B2/C1
Wellington St B3
West St B2
West Yorkshire
  Playhouse 🏛 B5
Westfield Rd A1
Westgate B3
Whitehall Rd B3/C2
Whitelock St A5
Willis St C6
Willow Approach A1
Willow Ave A1
Willow Terrace Rd . . . A3
Wintoun St A5
Woodhouse La A3/A4
Woodsley Rd A2
York Pl B3
York Rd B6

Leicester 188
Abbey St A2
All Saints' 🏛 A1
Aylestone Rd C2
Bath La A1
Bede Park C1
Bedford St A3
Bedford St South A3
Belgrave Gate A2
Belvoir St B2
Braunstone Gate B1
Burleys Way A2
Burnmoor St C2
Bus & Coach Sta A2
Canning St A2
Carlton St B2
Castle 🏛 B1
Castle Gardens B1
Cathedral † B2
Causeway La A2
Charles St B2
Chatham St B2
Christow St A3
Church Gate A2
City Gallery 🏛 B2
City Hall B2
Clank St B1
Clock Tower ♦ B2
Clyde St B3
Colton St B2
Conduit St B3
Crafton St B3
Craven St A1
Crown Courts B3
Curve 🏛 B3
De Lux ♠ A2
De Montfort Hall 🏛 . . C3
De Montfort St C2
De Montfort Univ C1
Deacon St C2
Dover St B2
Duns La B1
Dunton St A1
East St B3
Eastern Boulevard . . . C1
Edmonton Rd A3
Erskine St A3
Filbert St C1
Filbert St East C1
Fire Station B2
Fleet St A3
Friar La B2
Friday St A2
Gateway St C1
Gateway,The C1
Glebe St B3
Granby St B2
Grange La C2
Grasmere St C1
Great Central St A1
Guildhall 🏛 B2
Guru Nanak Sikh
  Museum 🏛 B1
Halford St B2
Havelock St C2
Haymarket
  Shopping Centre . . . A2
High St B2
Highcross
  Shopping Centre . . . A2

Highcross St A1
HM Prison C2
Horsefair St B2
Humberstone Gate . . . B2
Humberstone Rd A3
Infirmary St C2
Information Ctr 🏛 . . . B2
Jarrom St C1
Jewry Wall 🏛 B1
Kamloops Cr A3
King St B2
Lancaster Rd C2
Lee St A2
Leicester Royal
  Infirmary (A&E) H . . C2
Leicester Station ≠ . . B3
Library B2
London Rd B3
Lower Brown St B2
Magistrates' Court . . . B2
Manitoba Rd A3
Mansfield St A2
Market 🏛 B2
Market St B2
Mill La C1
Montreal Rd A3
Narborough Rd
  North B1
Nelson Mandela Pk . . . C2
New Park St B1
New St B2
New Walk C2
New Walk Museum
  & Art Gallery 🏛 . . . C3
Newarke Houses 🏛 . . . B1
Newarke St B2
Newarke,The B1
Northgate St A1
Orchard St A2
Ottawa Rd A3
Oxford St C2
Phoenix Arts Ctr 🏛 . . B3
Police Station A2
Post Office 🏤 . . . A1/B2/C3
Prebend St C3
Princess Rd East C3
Princess Rd West C2
Queen St B3
Rally Com Pk,The A1
Regent College C3
Regent Rd C2/C3
Repton St A1
Rutland St B3
St Augustine Rd B1
St Georges
  Retail Park B3
St George St B3
St Georges Way B3
St John St A2
St Margaret's 🏛 A2
St Margaret's Way . . . A2
St Martins B2
St Mary de Castro 🏛 . . B1
St Matthew's Way A3
St Nicholas 🏛 B1
St Nicholas Circle . . . B1
Sanvey Gate A2
Silver St B2
Slater St A1
South Albion St B3
Southampton St B3
Sue Townsend
  Theatre 🏛 B2
Swain St B3
Swan St A1
Tigers Way C3
Tower St C2
Town Hall B2
Tudor Rd B1
Univ of Leicester . . . C3
University Rd C3
Upperton Rd C1
Vaughan Way A1
Walnut St C1
Watling St A1
Welford Rd C2
Welford Rd Leicester
  Tigers RC C2
Wellington St B2
West St C2
West Walk C2
Western Boulevard . . . C1
Western Rd C1
Wharf St North A3
Wharf St South A3
Y Theatre,The 🏛 B3
Yeoman St B2
York Rd B2

Lincoln 188
Alexandra Terr B1
Anchor St C2
Arboretum B3
Arboretum Ave B3
Avenue,The B1
Baggholme Rd B3
Bailgate A2
Beaumont Fee B2
Brayford Way C1
Brayford Wharf East . . C1
Brayford Wharf
  North B1
Bruce Rd A2
Burton Rd A1
Bus Station (City) . . . B2
Canwick Rd C2
Cardinal's Hat ♦ B2
Carline Rd B1
Castle 🏛 B1
Castle St B1
Cathedral † B2
Cathedral St B2
Cecil St A2
Chapel La A2
Cheviot St B3
Church La A2
City Hall B1
Clasketgate B2
Clayton Sports Gd . . . A3
Coach Park C2
Collection,The 🏛 B2
County Hospital
  (A&E) H A3
County Office B2
Courts C1
Cross St C2
Crown Courts A1
Curle Ave A3
Danesgate B2
Drill Hall 🏛 B2
Drury La B1

East Bight A2
East Gate A2
Eastcliff Rd B3
Eastgate B2
Egerton Rd A3
Ellis Windmill ♦ A1
Engine Shed,
  The 🏛 C1
Environment
  Agency 🏛 A3
Exchequer Gate ♦ B2
Firth Rd C1
Flaxengate B2
Florence St B3
George St C2
Good La A2
Gray St A1
Great Northern Terr . . C3
Great Northern Terr
  Industrial Estate . . C3
Greetwell Rd B3
Greetwellgate B3
Grove,The A3
Haffenden Rd A3
High St B2/C1
HM Prison A3
Hungate B2
James St A2
Jews House & Ct 🏛 . . . B2
Kesteven St C2
Langworthgate A2
Lawn,The A1
Lee Rd A3
Library B2
Lincoln Central
  Station ≠ C2
Lincoln College B2
Lincolnshire Life/
  Royal Lincolnshire
  Regiment Mus 🏛 . . . A1
Lincoln Univ Technical
  College (UTC) C2
Lindum Rd B2
Lindum Sports Gd A3
Lindum Terr B3
Mainwaring Rd A3
Manor Rd A2
Market B2
Massey Rd A3
Medieval Bishop's
  Palace 🏛 B2
Mildmay St A1
Mill Rd A1
Millman Rd A3
Minster Yard B2
Monks Rd B3
Montague St B2
Mount St A1
Nettleham Rd A2
Newland B1
Newport A2
Newport Arch 🏛 A2
Newport Cemetery A2
Northgate A2
Odeon 🏛 C1
Orchard St B1
Oxford St C2
Park St B1
Pelham Bridge C2
Pelham St C2
Police Station B1
Portland St C2
Post Office 🏤 . . . A1/B3/C2
Potter Gate B2
Priory Gate B2
Queensway A3
Rasen La A1
Ropewalk C1
Rosemary La B2
St Anne's Rd B3
St Benedict's 🏛 B2
St Giles Ave A3
St Mark's
  Shopping Centre . . . C1
St Marks St C1
St Mary-le-
  Wigford 🏛 C1
St Mary's St C2
St Nicholas St A2
St Rumbold's St B2
St Swithin's 🏛 B2
Saltergate B2
Saxon St A1
Sewell Rd B3
Silver St B2
Sincil St C2
Spital St A2
Spring Hill B1
Stamp End C3
Steep Hill B2
Stonebow &
  Guildhall 🏛 C2
Stonefield Ave A2
Tentercroft St C2
Theatre Royal 🏛 B2
Tritton Rd C1
Tritton Retail Park . . C1
Union Rd B1
Univ of Lincoln C1
Upper Lindum St B3
Upper Long Leys Rd . . . A1
Usher 🏛 B2
Vere St A2
Victoria St B1
Victoria Terr B1
Vine St B3
Wake St A1
Waldeck St A1
Waterside North C2
Waterside
  Shopping Centre . . . C2
Waterside South C2
West Parade B1
Westgate A2
Wigford Way C1
Williamson St A2
Wilson St A1
Winn St B3
Wragby Rd A3
Yarborough Rd A1

Liverpool 188
Abercromby Sq C5
Addison St A3
Adelaide Rd B6
Ainsworth St B4
Albany Rd B6
Albert Edward Rd B6
Angela St C6
Argos St C5
Arrad St C5
Ashton St B5
Audley St A3
Back Leeds St A2

Basnett St B3
Bath St A1
Beacon,The ♦ B3
Beatles Story,
  The 🏛 C2
Beckwith St C3
Bedford Close C5
Bedford St North C5
Bedford St South C5
Benson St C4
Berry St C4
Birkett St A4
Bixteth St B2
Blackburne Place C4
Bluecoat 🏛 C3
Bold Place C4
Bold St C4
Bolton St B3
Bridport St B4
Bronte St B4
Brook St A1
Brownlow Hill B4/B5
Brownlow St B5
Brunswick Rd A5
Brunswick St B1
Bus Station B2
Butler Cr A6
Byrom St A3
Caledonia St C5
Cambridge St C5
Camden St A4
Canada Blvd B1
Canning Dock C2
Canterbury St A4
Cardwell St C6
Carver St A4
Cases St B3
Castle St B2
Catherine St C5
Cavern Club 🏛 B3
Central Library B3
Chapel St B2
Charlotte St B3
Chatham Place C6
Chatham St C5
Cheapside B2
Chavasse Park C2
Chestnut St C5
Christian St A3
Church St B3
Clarence St B4
Clayton Square
  Shopping Centre . . . B3
Coach Station A4
Cobden St A5
Cockspur St A2
College La C3
College St North A5
College St South A5
Colquitt St C4
Comus St A3
Concert St C4
Connaught Rd B6
Cook St B2
Copperas Hill B4
Cornwallis St C4
Covent Garden B2
Craven St A4
Cropper St B4
Crown St B5/C6
Cumberland St B2
Cunard Building 🏛 . . . B1
Dale St B2
Dansie St B4
Daulby St B5
Dawson St B3
Dental Hospital B5
Derby Sq B2
Drury La B2
Duckinfield St B4
Duke St C3
Earle St A2
East St A2
Eaton St A2
Edge La B6
Edinburgh Rd B6
Edmund St B2
Elizabeth St B5
Elliot St B3
Empire Theatre 🏛 B4
Empress Rd B6
Epstein Theatre 🏛 . . . B3
Epworth St A5
Erskine St A5
Everyman
  Theatre 🏛 C5
Exchange St East B2
FACT 🏛 C4
Falkland St A4
Falkner St C5/C6
Farnworth St A6
Fenwick St B2
Fielding St A6
Fire Sta A4
Fleet St C4
Fraser St A4
Freemasons Row A2
Gardner Row A3
Gascoyne St A2
George St B2
Gibraltar Road A1
Gilbert St C3
Gildart St B4
Gill St A4
Goree B1
Gower St C2
Gradwell St C3
Great Crosshall St . . . A3
Great George St C4
Great Howard St A1
Great Newton St B5
Greek St B4
Green La A5
Greenside A5
Greetham St C3
Gregson St A6
Grenville St S C3
Grinfield St C6
Grove St C5
Guelph St A6
Hackins Hey B2
Haigh St A4
Hall La B6
Hanover St C3
Harbord St C6
Hardman St C4
Harker St A4
Hatton Garden A2
Hawke St B4
Henry St C3
Highfield St A2
Highgate St B6
Hilbre St B4
Hope Place C4

Hope St C4
Hope University A5
Houghton St B3
Hunter St A3
Hutchinson St A6
Information
  Ctr 🏛 B4/C2
Institute for the
  Performing Arts
Int Slavery Mus 🏛 . . . C2
Irvine St B6
Irwell St B1
Islington A4
James St B2
James St Station ≠ . . . B2
Jenkinson St A4
John Moores
  Univ A2/A3/B4/C4
Johnson St A3
Jubilee Drive B6
Kempston St A4
Kensington B6
Kensington Gdns B6
Kensington St B6
Kent St C3
King Edward St A1
Kinglake St B6
Knight St C4
Lace St A3
Langsdale St A4
Law Courts C2
Leece St C4
Leeds St A2
Leopold Rd B6
Lime St B3
Lime St Station ≠ . . . B4
Liver St C2
Liverpool Central
  Station ≠ B3
Liverpool
  Landing Stage B1
Liverpool Institute
  for Performing
  Arts (LIPA) C4
Liverpool ONE C2
Liverpool Wheel,
  The C2
London Rd A4/B4
Lord Nelson St B4
Lord St B2
Lovat St C6
Low Hill A5
Low Wood St A6
Lydia Ann St C3
M&S Bank Arena ♦ C2
Mansfield St A4
Marmaduke St B6
Marsden St A6
Martensen St B6
Marybone A3
Maryland St C4
Mason St B6
Mathew St B3
May St B4
Melville Place C6
Merseyside Maritime
  Museum 🏛 C2
Metquarter B3
Metropolitan
  Cathedral (RC) † . . . B5
Midghall St A2
Molyneux Rd A6
Moor Place B4
Moorfields B2
Moorfields Sta ≠ B2
Moss St A5
Mount Pleasant . . . B4/B5
Mount St C4
Mount Vernon B6
Mulberry St C5
Municipal Buildings . . B2
Mus of Liverpool 🏛 . . . C2
Myrtle St C5
Naylor St A2
Nelson St C3
New Islington A4
New Quay B1
Newington St C3
North John St B2
North St A3
North View A6
Norton St A4
O2 Academy B5
Oakes St B5
Odeon 🏛 B4
Old Hall St A1
Old Leeds St A1
Oldham Place C4
Oldham St C4
Olive St C6
Open Eye Gallery 🏛 . . . C2
Oriel St A2
Ormond St B2
Orphan St C6
Overbury St C6
Overton St B6
Oxford St C5
Paisley St A1
Pall Mall A2
Paradise St C3
Park La C3
Parker St B3
Parr St C3
Peach St B5
Pembroke Place B4
Pembroke St B5
Philharmonic
  Hall 🏛 C5
Phythian Park A6
Pickop St A2
Pilgrim St C4
Pitt St C3
Playhouse
  Theatre 🏛 B3
Pleasant St B4
Police HQ 🏛 C3
Police Station 🏛 . . A4/A6/B4
Pomona St B4
Port of Liverpool
  Building 🏛 B1
Post Office 🏤 . . . A2/A4/
  A5/B2/B3/B4/C4
Pownall St C2
Prescot St A5
Preston St B3
Princes Dock A1
Princes Gdns A2
Princes Jetty A1
Princes Pde B1
Princes St B2
Pythian St A6
Queen Sq Bus Sta B3
Queensland St C6
Queensway Tunnel
  (Docks exit) A1
Queensway Tunnel
  (Entrance) B3

Radio City B2
Ranelagh St B3
Redcross St B2
Renfrew St B6
Renshaw St C4
Richmond Row A4
Richmond St B3
Rigby St A2
Roberts St A1
Rock St A6
Rodney St C4
Rokeby St A4
Roscoe La C4
Roscoe St C4
Rose Hill A3
Royal Albert Dock . . . C2
Royal Court
  Theatre 🏛 B3
Royal Liver
  Building 🏛 B1
Royal Liverpool
  Hospital (A&E) H . . . B5
Royal Mail St B4
Rumford Place B2
Rumford St B2
Russell St B4
St Andrew St B4
St Anne St A4
St Georges Hall 🏛 . . . B3
St John's Centre B3
St John's Gdns B3
St John's La B3
St Joseph's Cr A4
St Minishull St B5
St Nicholas Place . . . B1
St Paul's Sq A2
Salisbury St A4
Salthouse Dock C2
Salthouse Quay C2
Sandon St C5
Saxony Rd B6
Schomberg St A6
School La B3
Seel St C3
Seymour St B4
Shaw St A5
Shopmobility C3
Sidney Place C6
Sir Thomas St B3
Skelhorne St B4
Slater St C3
Smithdown La B6
Soho Sq A4
Soho St A4
South John St B2
Springfield A4
Stafford St A4
Standish St A3
Stanley St B2
Strand St C2
Strand,The B1
Suffolk St C3
Sydney Jones Liby . . . C5
Tabley St C3
Tarleton St B3
Tate Liverpool
  Gallery 🏛 C2
Teck St B6
Temple St B2
Titanic Memorial ♦ . . . B1
Tithebarn St B2
Town Hall 🏛 B2
Trowbridge St B4
Trueman St A3
Union St B2
Unity Theatre 🏛 C4
University B5
Univ of Liverpool . . . B5
Upper Baker St A6
Upper Duke St C4
Upper Frederick St . . . C3
Vauxhall Rd A2
Vernon St B2
Victoria Gallery &
  Museum 🏛 B5
Victoria St B2
Vine St C5
Wakefield St A4
Walker Art Gall 🏛 . . . B3
Walker St A6
Wapping C2
Water St B1/B2
Waterloo Rd A1
Wavertree Rd B6
West Derby Rd A6
West Derby St B5
Western Approaches
  War Museum 🏛 B2
Whitechapel B3
Whitley Gdns A5
William Brown St B3
William Henry St A4
Williamson St B3
Williamson's Tunnels
  Heritage Centre ♦ . . C6
Women's Hosp H C5
Wood St C3
World Museum,
  Liverpool 🏛 B3
York St C3

Llandudno 189
Abbey Pl B1
Abbey Rd B1
Adelphi St B2
Alexandra Rd C2
Anglesey Rd B3
Argyll Rd B3
Arvon Ave C2
Atlee Cl C3
Augusta St C2
Back Madoc St C2
Bodafon St C3
Bodhyfryd Rd B3
Bodnant Cr C3
Bodnant Rd C3
Bridge Rd C1
Bryniau Rd C1
Builder St C2
Builder St West C2
Cabin Lift A2
Cable Car ♦ A2
Camera Obscura ♦ A2
Caroline Rd B2
Chapel St B2
Charlton St B2
Church Cr C3
Church Walks A2
Claremont Rd C2
Clement Ave C2
Clifton Rd B2
Clonmel St B2
Coach Station B2
Conway Rd C1

Conwy Archive
  Service B2
Council St West C3
Cricket and Rec Gd . . . B3
Cwlach Rd A1
Cwlach St A1
Cwm Howard La C3
Cwm Pl C3
Dale Rd C1
Deganwy Ave B2
Denness Pl C2
Dinas Rd B1
Dolydd B1
Erol Pl B1
Ewloe Dr C3
Fairways C3
Ffordd Dewi C3
Ffordd Dulyn C3
Ffordd Dwyfor C3
Ffordd Elisabeth C3
Ffordd Gwynedd C3
Ffordd Las C3
Ffordd Morfa C3
Ffordd Penrhyn C3
Ffordd Tudno C3
Ffordd yr Orsedd C3
Ffordd Ysbyty C3
Fire & Ambulance
  Station B3
Garage St B3
George St A2
Gloddaeth Ave B1
Gloddaeth St B2
Gogarth Rd C1
Great Orme
  Mines ♦ A1
Great Ormes Rd A1
Great Orme
  Tramway ♦ A2
Happy Valley A2
Happy Valley Rd A3
Haulfre Gardens ❀ . . . C1
Herkomer Cr C3
Hill Terr A2
Home Front Mus 🏛 . . . B2
Hospice B1
Howard Rd B3
Information Ctr 🏛 . . . B2
Invalids' Walk C1
James St B2
Jubilee St B3
King's Ave C2
King's Rd C2
Knowles Rd C2
Lees Rd C3
Library B2
Llandudno (A&E) H . . . B3
Llandudno Sta ≠ B2
Llandudno Football
  Ground C3
Llewelyn Ave A2
Lloyd St B2
Lloyd St West C1
Llys Maelgwn C1
Madoc St B2
Maelgwn Rd C2
Maes-y-Orsedd C3
Maesdu Bridge C2
Maesdu Rd C2/C3
Marian Pl C2
Marian Rd C2
Marine Drive (Toll) . . A3
Market St B2
Miniature Golf
  Course A1
Morfa Rd B1
Mostyn 🏛 B2
Mostyn Broadway B3
Mostyn St B2
Mowbray Rd C2
New St B2
Norman Rd B3
North Parade A2
North Wales
  Golf Links C1
Old Bank,The B2
Old Rd A1
Oval,The B3
Oxford Rd B3
Parade,The A3
Parc Llandudno
  Retail Park B3
Pier ♦ A2
Plas Rd B2
Police Station 🏛 B2
Post Office 🏤 A2/B3
Promenade A3
Pyllau Rd A1
Rhuddlan Ave C3
St Andrew's Ave B2
St Andrew's Pl B2
St Beuno's Rd A1
St David's Pl B2
St David's Rd B2
St George's Pl A2
St Mary's Rd B2
St Seriol's Rd B2
Salisbury Pass B1
Salisbury Rd B2
Somerset St B3
South Parade A2
Stephen St B2
Tabor Hill B1
Town Hall B2
Trinity Ave B2
Trinity Cres C1
Trinity Sq B2
Tudno St A2
Ty-Coch Rd C3
Ty-Gwyn Rd A1/A2
Ty'n-y-Coed Rd A1
Vaughan St B2
Victoria
  Shopping Centre . . . B2
Victoria 🏛 B2
War Memorial ♦ A2
West Parade B1
Werny Wylan C3
Whiston Pass A2
Winllan Ave C2
Wyddfyd Rd A2
York Rd B2

Llanelli 189
Alban Rd B3
Albert St B2
Als St A2
Amos St A2
Andrew St A3
Ann St C2
Annesley St B2

Arfryn Ave A3
Avenue Cilfig,The . . . A2
Belvedere Rd B3
Bigyn Park Terr C3
Bigyn Rd C2
Bond Ave C3
Brettenham St A1
Bridge St B2
Bryn Pl B2
Bryn Rd B1
Bryn Terr B2
Bryn-More Rd C2
Brynhyfryd Rd A2
Brynmelyn Ave A3
Brynmor Rd B2
Burry St C2
Caersalem Terr B2
Cambrian St C1
Caswell St B2
Cedric St B1
Cemetery A2
Chapman St A1
Charles Terr A3
Church St B2
Clos Caer Elms A1
Clos Sant Paul C1
Coastal Link Rd . . . B1/C1
Coldstream St B2
Coleshill Terr B2
College Hill B2
College Sq B2
Copperworks Rd C2
Coronation Rd C2
Corporation Ave A3
Council Offices B3
Court B2
Cowell St B2
Cradock St B2
Craig Ave A3
Cricket Ground A1
Derwent St A1
Dillwyn St C2
Druce St C1
Eastgate Leisure
  Complex ♦ B2
Elizabeth St B2
Emma St C2
Erw Rd B2
Felinfoel Rd A2
Fire Station A2
Firth Rd C3
Fron Terr A2
Furnace Utd Rugby
  Football Ground . . . A1
Gelli-On B2
George St C2
Gilbert Cres A2
Gilbert Rd A2
Glanmor Rd C2
Glanmor Terr C2
Glasfryn Terr A3
Glenalla Rd C3
Glevering St B3
Goring Rd C3
Gorsedd Circle 🏛 A2
Grant St C1
Graveyard B2
Great Western Cl B1
Greenway St B1
Hall St B2
Harries Ave A2
Hedley Terr A1
Heol Elli C2
Heol Goffa A3
Heol Nant-y-Felin . . . A3
Heol Siloh B2
Hick St C2
High St B2
Indoor Bowls Ctr A1
Inkerman St B2
Island Pl B1
James St B3
John St B2
King George Ave A3
Lake View Cl C1
Lakefield Pl C1
Lakefield Rd C1
Langland Rd C2
Leisure Centre B3
Library B2
Llanelli House 🏛 B2
Llanelli Parish
  Church B2
Llanelli Station ≠ . . . C2
Llewellyn St B2
Lliedi Cres A3
Lloyd St B2
Llys Alys B3
Llys Fran A3
Llysnewedd C2
Long Row A2
Maes Gors C2
Maesyrhaf A3
Mansel St C2
Marblehall Rd A2
Marborough Rd A3
Margam St C2
Marine St C2
Mariners,The C1
Market B2
Market St B2
Marsh St C2
Martin Rd C2
Miles St A1
Mill La A3/B2
Mincing La B2
Murray St B2
Myn y Mor B1
Nathan St C1
Nelson Terr C2
Nevill St B2
New Dock Rd C2
New Rd A2
New Zealand St A1
Odeon 🏛 B2
Old Lodge A3
Old Rd A2
Paddock St C2
Palace Ave B2
Parc Howard A2
Parc Howard Museum
  & Art Gallery 🏛 . . . A2
Park Cres B2
Park St B2
Parkview Terr A1
Pemberton St C2
Pembrey Rd A1
Peoples Park B1
Pottery Pl C2
Pottery St C2
Princess St B2
Prospect Pl A1
Pryce St A1

Queen Mary's Walk . C3
QueenVictoria Rd . . V
Raby St B1
Railway Terr C2
Ralph St B2
Regalia Terr C1
Rhydyrafon A3
Richard St B2
Roland Ave A1
Russell St C3
St David's Cl C1
St Margaret's Dr . . . A1
Spowart Ave A1
Station St B2/C2
Stepney Pl B2
Stepney St B2
Stewart St A1
Stradey Park Ave . . A2
Sunny Hill A2
Superstore A2
Swansea Rd A3
Talbot St C3
Temple St B3
Thomas St C3
Tinopolos
 TV Studios ◆ B2
Toft Pl A3
Town Hall B2
Traeth Ffordd C1
Trinity Rd C3
Trinity Terr C2
Tunnel Rd B3
Tyisha Rd C3
Union Blgs B2
Upper Robinson St . B2
Vauxhall Rd B2
Walter's Rd B3
Waun Lanyrafon . . . B2
Waun Rd A2
Wern Rd B3
West End A2
Y Bwthyn C3
Zion Row B3

London 186

Abbey Orchard St . . E3
Abchurch La D6
Abingdon St E4
Achilles Way D2
Acton St B4
Addington St E4
Air St D3
Albany St B2
Albemarle St D3
Albert
 Embankment . . . F4
Aldenham St A3
Aldersgate St C6
Aldford St D2
Aldgate C7
Aldgate High St . . . C7
Aldwych C4
Allsop Pl B1
Amwell St B5
Angel A5
Appold St C7
Argyle Sq B4
Argyle St B4
Argyll St C3
Arnold Circus B7
Artillery La C7
Artillery Row E3
Association of
 Photographers
 Gallery 🖾 B6
Baker St ⊖ B1
Baker St B1
Baldwin's Gdns C5
Baltic St B6
Bank ⊖ C6
Bank Museum 🖾 . . . C6
Bank of England 🖾 . . C6
Bankside D6
Bankside Gallery 🖾 . D6
Banner St B6
Barbican ⊖ C6
Barbican Centre
 for Arts,The C6
Barbican
 Gallery 🖾 C6
Basil St E1
Bastwick St B6
Bateman's Row B7
Bath St B6
Bayley St C3
Baylis Rd E5
Beak St D3
Bedford Row C4
Bedford Sq C3
Bedford St D4
Bedford Way B3
Beech St C6
Belgrave Pl E2
Belgrave Sq E2
Bell La C7
Belvedere Rd D4
Berkeley Sq D3
Berkeley St D3
Bernard St B4
Berners Pl C3
Berners St C3
Berwick St C3
Bethnal Green Rd . . B7
Bevenden St B6
Bevis Marks C7
BFI (British Film
 Institute) 🎬 D4
BFI London IMAX
 Cinema 🎬 D5
Bidborough St B4
Binney St C2
Birdcage Walk E3
Bishopsgate C7
Blackfriars ⊖🚂 . . . D5
Blackfriars Bridge . . D5
Blackfriars Passage D5
Blackfriars St D5
Blandford St C2
Blomfield St C6
Bloomsbury St C3
Bloomsbury Way . . . C4
Bolton St D2
Bond St ⊖ C2
Borough High St . . . D6
Boswell St C4
Bow St C4
Bowling Green La . . B5
Brad St D5
Bressenden Pl E3
Brewer St D3
Brick St D2
Bridge St E4
Britannia Walk B6

British Film
 Institute (BFI) 🎬 . . D4
British Library 🏛 . . . B4
British Museum 🏛 . . C4
Britton St B5
Broad Sanctuary . . . E3
Broadway E3
Brook Dr F5
Brook St D2
Brunswick Shopping
 Centre,The B4
Brunswick Sq B4
Brushfield St C7
Bruton St D2
Bryanston St C1
BT Centre C6
Buckingham
 Palace 🏛 E3
Buckingham
 Palace Rd F2
Bunhill Row B6
Byward St D7
Cabinet War Rooms
 & Churchill Mus 🏛 E4
Cadogan La E2
Cadogan Pl E1
Cadogan Sq F1
Caledonian Rd A4
Calshot St A4
Calthorpe St B4
Calvert Ave B7
Cambridge Circus . . C3
Camomile St C7
Cannon St D6
Cannon St ⊖🚂 D6
Carey St C4
Carlisle La E4
Carlisle Pl E3
Carlton House Terr . E3
Carmelite St D5
Carnaby St C3
Carter La C5
Carthusian St C6
Cartwright Gdns . . . B4
Castle Baynard St . . D5
Cavendish Pl C2
Cavendish Sq C2
Caxton Hall E3
Caxton St E3
Central St B6
Chalton St A3
Chancery Lane ⊖ . . C5
Chapel St E2
Charing Cross ⊖🚂 . D4
Charing Cross Rd . . C3
Charles Dickens
 Museum,The B4
Charles II St D3
Charles Sq B6
Charles St D2
Charlotte Rd B7
Charlotte St C3
Chart St B6
Charterhouse Sq . . . C6
Charterhouse St . . . C5
Cheapside C6
Chenies St C3
Chesham St E2
Chester Sq F2
Chesterfield Hill . . . D2
Chiltern St C2
Chiswell St C6
City Garden Row . . . A5
City Rd B6
City Thameslink ⊖ . . C5
City University,The . B5
Claremont Sq A5
Clarges St D2
Clerkenwell Cl C5
Clerkenwell Green . . B5
Clerkenwell Rd B5
Cleveland St C3
Clifford St D3
Clink Prison Mus 🏛 . D6
Clock Museum 🏛 . . C6
Club Row B7
Cockspur St D3
Coleman St C6
Columbia Rd B7
Commercial St C7
Compton St B5
Conduit St D2
Constitution Hill . . . E2
Copperfield St E5
Coptic St C4
Cornhill C6
Cornwall Rd D5
Coronet St B7
Courtauld
 Gallery 🖾 D4
Covent Garden ⊖ . . D4
Covent Garden ◆ . . D4
Cowcross St C5
Cowper St B6
Cranbourn St D4
Craven St D4
Crawford St C1
Creechurch La C7
Cremer St A7
Cromer St B4
Cumberland Gate . . D1
CumberlandTerr . . . B2
Curtain Rd B7
Curzon St D2
Cut,The E5
D'arblay St C3
Davies St C2
Dean St C3
Deluxe Gallery 🖾 . . B7
Denmark St C3
Dering St C2
Devonshire St C2
Diana, Princess of
 Wales Meml Wlk . . E3
Dingley Rd B6
Dorset St C1
Doughty St B4
Dover St D3
Downing St E4
Druid St E7
Drummond St B3
Drury La C4
Drysdale St B7
Duchess St C2
Dufferin St B6
Duke of Wellington
 Place E2
Duke St C2
Duke St D1
Duke St Hill D6
Duke's Pl C7
Duncannon St D4
East Rd B6
Eastcastle St C3
Eastcheap D7

Eastman Dental
 Hospital 🏥 B4
Eaton Pl E2
Eaton Sq E2
Eccleston St E2
Edgware Rd C1
Eldon St C6
Embankment ⊖ . . . D4
Endell St C4
Endsleigh Pl B3
Euston ⊖🚂 B3
Euston Rd B3
Euston Square ⊖ . . B3
Evelina Children's
 Hospital E6
Eversholt St B3
Exmouth Market . . . B5
Fann St B6
Farringdon ⊖🚂 . . . C5
Farringdon Rd C5
Farringdon St C5
Featherstone St . . . B6
Fenchurch St D7
Fenchurch St ⊖🚂 . D7
Fetter La C5
Finsbury Circus C6
Finsbury Pavement . C6
Finsbury Sq B6
Fitzalan St F5
Fitzmaurice Pl D2
Fleet St C5
Floral St D4
Florence Nightingale
 Museum 🖾 E4
Folgate St C7
Foot Hospital 🏥 . . . B3
Fore St C6
Foster La C6
Foundling Museum,
 The 🖾 B4
Francis St F3
Frazier St E5
Freemason's Hall . . C4
Friday St C6
Furnival St C5
Gainsford St E7
Garden Row E5
Gee St B6
George St C1
Gerrard St D3
Giltspur St C5
Glasshouse St D3
Gloucester Pl C1
Golden Hinde ⚓ . . . D6
Golden La B6
Golden Sq D3
Goodge St ⊖ C3
Goodge St C3
Gordon Sq B3
Goswell Rd B6
Gough St B4
Goulston St C7
Gower St B3
Gracechurch St D6
Grafton Way B3
Gray's Inn Rd B4
Great Cumberland
 Pl C1
Great Eastern St . . . B7
Great Guildford St . . D6
Great Marlborough
 St C3
Great Ormond St . . . B4
Great Ormond St
 Children's Hosp 🏥 B4
Great Percy St A4
Great Peter St E3
Great Portland
 St ⊖ B2
Great Portland St . . C2
Great Queen St C4
Great Russell St . . . C3
Great Scotland Yd . . D4
Great Smith St E3
Great Suffolk St . . . D5
GreatTitchfield St . . C3
GreatTower St D7
Great Windmill St . . D3
Greek St C3
Green Park ⊖ D3
Green St D2
Greencoat Pl F3
Gresham St C6
Greville St B4/C5
Greycoat Hosp Sch . E3
Greycoat Pl E3
Grosvenor Gdns . . . E2
Grosvenor Pl E2
Grosvenor Sq D2
Grosvenor St D2
Guards Museum
 and Chapel 🖾 . . . E3
Guildhall
 Art Gallery 🖾 . . . C6
Guilford St B4
Guy's Hospital 🏥 . . D6
Haberdasher St B6
Hackney Rd B7
Half Moon St D2
Halkin St E2
Hall St B5
Hallam St C2
Hampstead Rd B3
Hanover Sq C2
Hans Cres E1
Hanway St C3
Hardwick St B5
Harley St C2
Harrison St B4
Hastings St B4
Hatfields D5
Hay's Galleria D7
Hay's Mews D2
Hayles St F5
Haymarket D3
Hayward Gallery 🖾 . D4
Helmet Row B6
Herbrand St B4
Hercules Rd E4
Hertford St D2
Hill St D2
Holborn ⊖ C4
Holborn C5
Holborn Viaduct . . . C5
Holland St D5
Holmes Mus 🖾 B1
Holywell La B7
Horse Guards' Rd . . D4
Houndsditch C7
Houses of
 Parliament 🏛 . . . E4
Howland St C3
Hoxton Sq B7

Hoxton St B7
Hunter St B4
Hunterian Mus 🖾 . . C4
Hyde Park D1
Hyde Park Cnr ⊖ . . . E2
Imperial War
 Museum 🖾 E5
Inner Circle B2
Inst of Archaeology
 (London Univ) . . . B3
Ironmonger Row . . . B6
James St C2
James St D4
Jermyn St D3
Jockey's Fields C4
John Carpenter St . . D5
John St B4
Judd St B4
Kennington Rd E5
King Charles St E4
King St D3
King St D4
King William St D6
King's Coll London . . D5
King's Cross ⊖ A4
King's Cross Rd B4
King's Cross St
 Pancras ⊖ A4
King's Rd F1
Kingley St C3
Kingsland Rd A7
Kingsway C4
Kinnerton St E1
Knightsbridge ⊖ . . . E1
Lamb's Conduit St . . C4
Lambeth Bridge F4
Lambeth High St . . . F4
Lambeth North ⊖ . . E5
Lambeth Palace 🏛 . . E4
Lambeth Palace Rd . E4
Lambeth Rd E5
Lambeth Walk F4
Lancaster Pl D4
Langham Pl C2
Leadenhall St C7
Leake St E4
Leather La C5
Leicester Sq ⊖ D3
Leicester St D3
Leonard St B6
Lever St B6
Lexington St D3
Lidlington Pl A3
Lime St D7
Lincoln's Inn Fields . C4
Lindsey St C5
Lisle St D3
Liverpool St C7
Liverpool St ⊖🚂 . . C7
Lloyd Baker St B5
Lloyd Sq B5
Lombard St C6
London
 Aquarium 🐠 E4
London Bridge ⊖🚂 . D6
London Bridge
 Hospital 🏥 D6
London City Hall 🏛 . D7
London Dungeon,
 The 🖾 E4
London Guildhall
 University C7
London Rd E5
London Transport
 Museum 🖾 D4
London Wall C6
London Eye ⊕ E4
Long Acre D4
Long La C5
Longford St B2
Lower Belgrave St . . E2
Lower Grosvenor Pl . E2
Lower Marsh E5
LowerThames St . . . D7
Lowndes St E2
Ludgate Circus C5
Ludgate Hill C5
Luxborough St C2
Lyall St E2
Macclesfield Rd . . . B6
Madame
 Tussaud's ◆ B2
Maddox St C3
Malet St C3
Mall,The E3
Manchester Sq C2
Manchester St C2
Mandeville Pl C2
Mansell St C7
Mansion House ⊖ . . C6
Mansion House 🏛 . . D6
Maple St C3
Marble Arch ⊖ C1
Marble Arch D1
Marchmont St B4
Margaret St C3
Margery St B5
Mark La D7
Marlborough Rd . . . D3
Marshall St C3
Marsham St E3
Marylebone High St . C2
Marylebone La C2
Marylebone Rd C1
Mecklenburgh Sq . . B4
MiddleTemple La . . . C5
Middlesex St
 (Petticoat La) . . . C7
Midland Rd A3
Minories C7
Monck St E3
Monmouth St C4
Montagu Pl C1
Montagu Sq C1
Montague Pl C3
Montague St C4
Monument ⊖ D6
Monument,The ◆ . . D6
Moor La C6
Moorfields C6
Moorfields Eye
 Hospital 🏥 B6
Moorgate ⊖🚂 C6
Moorgate C6
Moreland St B5
Morley St E5
Mortimer St C3
Mount Pleasant B5
Mount St D2
Murray Gr A6
Museum of Garden
 History 🖾 E4

Mus of London C6
Museum St C4
Myddelton Sq B5
Myddelton St B5
National Gallery 🖾 . . D3
National Hosp 🏥 . . . B4
National Portrait
 Gallery 🖾 D3
Neal St C4
Nelson's Column ◆ . D3
New Bond St C2/D2
New Bridge St C5
New Cavendish St . . C2
New Change C6
New Fetter La C5
New Inn Yard B7
New North Rd A6
New Oxford St C4
New Scotland Yard . . E3
New Sq C4
Newgate St C5
Newton St C4
Nile St B6
Noble St C6
Noel St C3
North Audley St . . . D2
North Cres C3
North Row C2
Northampton Sq . . . B5
Northington St B4
Northumberland
 Ave D4
Norton Folgate C7
Nottingham Pl C2
Obstetric Hosp 🏥 . . B4
Old Bailey C5
Old Broad St C6
Old Compton St C3
Old County Hall E4
Old Gloucester St . . C4
Old King Edward St . C6
Old Nichol St B7
Old Paradise St F4
Old Spitalfields Mkt C7
Old St ⊖🚂 B6
Old St B6
OldVic 🎭 E5
Open Air Theatre 🎭 B2
Operating Theatre
 Museum 🖾 D6
Orange St D3
Ossulston St A3
Outer Circle B1
Oxford Circus ⊖ . . . C3
Oxford St C2/C3
Paddington St C1
Palace St E3
Pall Mall D3
Pall Mall East D3
Pancras Rd A4
Paris Gdn D5
Park Cres B2
Park La D2
Park Rd B1
Park St D2
Park St D6
Parker St C4
Parliament Sq E4
Parliament St E4
Paternoster Sq C5
Paul St B6
Pear Tree St B5
Penton Rise B4
Penton St A5
Pentonville Rd A4/A5
Percival St B5
Petticoat La
 (Middlesex St) . . . C7
Petty France E3
Phoenix Pl B4
Phoenix Rd A3
Photo Gallery 🖾 . . . D3
Piccadilly D2
Piccadilly Circus ⊖ . D3
Pitfield St B7
Pollock's
 Toy Museum 🖾 . . C3
Polygon Rd A3
Pont St E1
Portland Pl C2
Portman Mews C2
Portman Sq C2
Portman St C2
Portugal St C4
Postal Museum,
 The 🖾 B4
Poultry C6
Primrose St C7
Princes St C6
Procter St C4
Provost St B6
Quaker St B7
Queen Anne St C2
Queen Sq B4
Queen St D6
Queen Street Pl . . . D6
Queen Victoria St . . D5
Radnor St B6
Rathbone Pl C3
Rawstorne St B5
Red Lion Sq C4
Red Lion St C4
Redchurch St B7
Redcross Way D6
Regency St F3
Regent Sq B4
Regent St C3
Regent's Park ⊖ . . . B2
Regent's Park B2
RichmondTerr E4
Ridgmount St C3
Rivington St B7
Robert St B2
Rochester Row F3
Ropemaker St C6
Rosebery Ave B5
Roupell St D5
Royal Academy
 of Arts 🖾 D3
Royal Academy of
 Dramatic Art B3
Royal Acad of Music 🖾 B2
Royal Artillery
 Memorial ◆ E2
Royal College of
 Nursing C3
Royal College of
 Surgeons C4
Royal Festival
 Hall 🎭 D4
Royal London Hospital
 for Integrated
 Medicine C4

Royal National
 Theatre 🎭 D5
Royal National
 Throat, Nose and Ear
 Hospital 🏥 B4
Royal Opera
 House 🎭 D4
Russell Square ⊖ . . B4
Russell Square B4
Sackville St D3
Sadlers Wells 🎭 . . . B5
Saffron Hill C5
St Alban's St D3
St Bartholomew's
 Hospital 🏥 C5
St Botolph St C7
St Bride St C5
St George's Circus . . E5
St George's Rd E5
St Giles High St C3
St James's Pal 🏛 . . D3
St James's Park ⊖ . . E3
St John St B5
St Margaret St E4
St Mark's Hosp 🏥 . . B5
St Martin's La D4
St Martin's Le
 Grand C6
St Mary Axe C7
St Pancras Int 🚂 . . . A4
St Paul's ⊖ C6
St Paul's Cath ✝ . . . C6
St Paul's
 Churchyard C5
St Peter's Hosp 🏥 . . D4
St Thomas St D6
St Thomas' Hosp 🏥 . E4
Savile Row D3
Savoy Pl D4
Savoy St D4
School of Hygiene &
 Tropical Medicine . C3
Scrutton St B7
Sekforde St B5
Serpentine Rd D1
Seven Dials C4
Seward St B5
Seymour St C1
Shad Thames D7
Shaftesbury Ave . . . D3
Shakespeare's Globe
 Theatre 🎭 D6
Shepherd Market . . . D2
Sherwood St D3
Shoe La C5
Shoreditch High St . B7
Shoreditch High
 St ⊖🚂 B7
Shorts Gdns C4
Shrek's
 Adventure ◆ E4
Sidmouth St B4
Silk St C6
Sir John Soane's
 Museum 🖾 C4
Skinner St B5
Sloane St E1
Snow Hill C5
Soho Sq C3
Somerset House 🏛 . D4
South Audley St . . . D2
South Carriage Dr . . E1
South Molton St . . . C2
South St D2
Southampton Row . . C4
Southampton St . . . D4
Southwark ⊖ D5
Southwark Bridge . . D6
Southwark Bridge
 Rd E6
Southwark Cath ✝ . . D6
Southwark St D6
Speakers' Corner . . . D1
Spencer St B5
Spital Sq C7
Stamford St D5
Stanhope St B3
Stephenson Way . . . B3
Stock Exchange . . . C5
Stoney St D6
Strand D4
Stratton St D2
Sumner St D6
Sutton's Way B6
Swanfield St B7
Swinton St B4
Tabernacle St B6
Tate Modern 🖾 D6
Tavistock Pl B4
Tavistock Sq B3
Tea & Coffee
 Museum 🖾 D6
Temple ⊖ D5
Temple Ave D5
Temple Pl D4
Terminus Pl E2
Thayer St C2
Theobald's Rd C4
Thorney St F4
Threadneedle St . . . C6
Throgmorton St C6
Tonbridge St B4
Tooley St D7
Torrington Pl B3
Tothill St E3
Tottenham
 Court Rd ⊖ C3
Tottenham Ct Rd ⊖ . C3
Tottenham St C3
Tower Bridge ◆ D7
Tower Bridge App . . D7
Tower Bridge Rd . . . E7
Tower Hill ⊖ D7
Tower Hill D7
Tower of London,
 The 🏰 D7
Toynbee St C7
Trafalgar Square . . . D4
Trinity Sq D7
Trocadero Centre ◆ . D3
Tudor St D5
Turnmill St B5
Ufford St E5
Union St D5
Univ of London B3
University of
 Westminster C3
Upper Belgrave St . . E2
Upper Berkeley St . . C1
Upper Brook St D2
Upper Ground D5

Upper Montague St . C1
Upper St Martin's
 La D4
UpperThames St . . . D6
Upper Wimpole St . . C2
Upper Woburn Pl . . B3
Vere St C2
Vernon Pl C4
Vestry St B6
Victoria ⊖🚂 E2
Victoria Emb D4
Victoria Place
 Shopping Centre . F2
Victoria St E2
Villiers St D4
Vincent Sq F3
Vinopolis
 City of Wine 🖾 . . D6
Virginia Rd B7
Wakley St B5
Walbrook C6
Wallace
 Collection 🖾 C2
Wardour St C3/D3
Warner St B5
Warren St ⊖ B3
Warren St B3
Waterloo ⊖🚂 E5
Waterloo Bridge . . . D4
Waterloo East 🚂 . . . D5
Waterloo Rd E5
Watling St C6
Webber St E5
Welbeck St C2
Wellington Arch ◆ . . E2
Wellington Mus 🖾 . . E2
Wells St C3
Wenlock St A6
Wentworth St C7
West Smithfield C5
West Sq E5
Westminster ⊖ E4
Westminster
 Abbey ✝ E4
Westminster
 Bridge E4
Westminster
 Bridge Rd E5
Westminster
 Cathedral (RC) ✝ . E3
Westminster
 City Hall E3
Westminster
 Hall 🏛 E4
Weymouth St C2
Wharf Rd A6
Wharton St B4
Whitcomb St D3
White Cube 🖾 B7
White Hart Hill D5
White Lion St A5
Whitecross St B6
Whitefriars St C5
Whitehall D4
Whitehall Pl D4
Wigmore Hall 🎭 . . . C2
Wigmore St C2
William IV St D4
Wilmington Sq B5
Wilson St C6
Wilton Cres E2
Wimpole St C2
Windmill Walk D5
Woburn Pl B4
Woburn Sq B3
Wood St C6
Woodbridge St B5
Wootton St D5
Wormwood St C7
Worship St B6
Wren St B4
Wynyatt St B5
York Rd E4
York St C1
YorkTerrace East . . B2
YorkTerrace West . . B2
York Way A4

Luton 189

Adelaide St B1
Albert Rd C2
Alma St B2
Alton Rd C2
Anthony Gdns A1
Arthur St C2
Ashburnham Rd . . . B1
Ashton Rd C2
Avondale Rd A1
Back St B2
Bailey St C3
Baker St C3
Biscot Rd A1
Bolton Rd C3
Boyle Cl A2
Brantwood Rd A1
Bretts Mead C1
Bridge St B2
Brook St A1
Brunswick St B3
Burr St B3
Bury Park Rd A1
Bute St B2
Buxton Rd B2
Cambridge St C3
Cardiff Grove B1
Cardiff Rd B1
Cardigan St B2
Castle St B2/C2
Chapel St C2
Charles St A3
Chase St C2
Cheapside B2
Chequer St C2
Chiltern Rise C1
Church St B2/B3
Cobden St A3
College A2
Collingdon St A1
Community Centre . . C2
Concorde Ave A3
Corncastle Rd C1
Cowper St C2
Crawley Green Rd . . C3
Crawley Rd A1
Crescent Rd A3
Crescent Rise A3
Cromwell Rd A1
Cross St A2
Cross Way,The C1
Crown Court B2
Cutenhoe Rd C3
Dallow Rd A1
Downs Rd A3
Dudley St A2
Duke St A2
Dumfries St C1
Dunstable Place . . . B2
Dunstable Rd A1/B1
Edward St A1
Elizabeth St C3
Essex Cl C3
Farley Hill C1
Farley Lodge C1
Flowers Way B2
Francis St A1
Frederick St B2
Galaxy Leisure
 Complex A2
George St B2
George St West B2
Gordon St B2
Grove Rd B1
Guildford St B2
Haddon Rd A3
Harcourt St C2
Hart Hill Drive A3
Hart Hill Lane A3
Hartley Rd A3
Hastings St B2
Hat Factory,The 🎭 . B2
Hatters Way A1
Havelock Rd A3
Hibbert St C2
High Town Rd A3
Highbury Rd A1
Hightown Com
 Sports & Arts Ctr . A3
Hillary Cres C1
Hillborough Rd C1
Hitchin Rd A3
Holly St C2
Holm C1
Hucklesby Way A2
Hunts Cl C1
Inkerman St B1
John St B2
Jubilee St A3
Kelvin Cl C1
King St B2
Kingsland Rd C2
Larches,The A3
Latimer Rd C2
Lawn Gdns C1
Lea Rd B3
Library B2
Liverpool Rd B1
London Rd C2
Luton Station 🚂 . . . B2
Lyndhurst Rd B1
Magistrates Court . . B2
Mall,The B2
Manchester St B1
Manor Rd B3
Manor Road Park . . . B3
May St B3
Meyrick Ave C1
Midland Rd B2
Mill St A2
Milton Rd C1
Moor St A1
Moor,The A1
Moorland Gdns A2
Moulton Rise A3
Napier Rd B1
New Bedford Rd . . . A1
NewTown St C2
Old Bedford Rd A2
Old Orchard C3
Osbourne Rd C3
Oxen Rd A3
Park Sq B2
Park St B2/C3
Park St West C2
Park Viaduct C2
Parkland Drive C1
Police Station 📮 . . . B1
Pomfret Ave A3
Pondwicks Rd B3
Post Office 📮 A1/B2
Power Court B3
Princess St B1
Red Rails C1
Regent St B2
Reginald St A2
Rothesay Rd B1
Russell Rise C1
Russell St C1
St Ann's Rd A3
St Mary's Square . . . B2
St Mary's Rd B3
St Paul's Rd C2
St Saviour's Cres . . . C1
Salisbury Rd B1
Seymour Ave C3
Seymour Rd C3
Silver St B2
Stanley St B1
Station Rd A2
Stockwood Cres . . . C1
Stockwood Park . . . C1
Strathmore Ave B3
Stuart St B2
Studley Rd A1
Surrey St C3
Sutherland Place . . . A1
Tavistock St C2
Taylor St A3
Telford Way A1
Tennyson Rd C2
Tenzing Grove C1
Thistle Rd B3
Town Hall B2
Townsley Cl C2
UK Centre for
 Carnival Arts 🎭 . . B3
Union St B3
University of
 Bedfordshire B3
Upper George St . . . B2
Vicarage St B3
Villa Rd A3
Waldeck Rd A1
Wardown House
 Museum & Gallery . A2
Wellington St B1/B2
Wenlock St C2
Whitby Rd A1
Whitehill Ave C1
William St A2
Wilsden Ave C1
Windmill Rd C3
Windsor St C2
York St A3

Macclesfield 189

108 Steps B2
Abbey Rd A1
Alton Dr A1
Armett St C2
Athey St B1
Bank St C2
Barber St C2
Barton St C1
Beech La C2
Beswick St B2
Black La A3
Black Rd C3
Blakelow Gardens . . A3
Blakelow Rd A3
Bond St B1/C1
Bread St C1
Bridge St B2
Brock St A2
Brocklehurst Ave . . . A3
Brook St B3
Brookfield La A3
Brough St West C1
Brown St C1
Brynton Rd A2
Buckley St C2
Bus Station B2
Buxton Rd C3
Byrons St C2
Canal St B2
Carlsbrook Ave A3
Castle St B2
Catherine St A1
Cemetery A1
Chadwick Terr A1
Chapel St C2
Charlotte St C2
Chester Rd A1
Chestergate B2
Christ Church 🏛 . . . B2
Churchill Way B2
Coare St A1
Commercial Rd B3
Conway Cres A3
Copper St C3
Cottage St B1
Crematorium A1
Crew Ave A3
Crompton Rd B1/C2
Cross St C2
Crossall St C1
Cumberland St . . . A1/B1
Dale St B2
Davenport St B3
Eastgate B2
Exchange St B2
Fence Ave A3
Fence Ave Ind Est . . A3
Flint St C3
Foden St C2
Fountain St B3
Garden St A2
Gas Rd B2
Gateway Gallery ◆ . . B2
George St B2
Glegg St B3
Golf Course A1
Goodall St A3
Grange Rd C1
Great King St B3
Green St B3
Grosvenor
 Shopping Centre . B2
Gunco La C3
Half St C2
Hallefield Rd B3
Hatton St C1
Hawthorn Way A3
Heapy St B3
Henderson St B1
Heritage Centre ◆ . . B2
Hibel Rd A2
High St B2
Hobson St C2
Hollins Rd C1
Hope St West B1
Horseshoe Dr A1
Hurdsfield Rd A3
Information Ctr ℹ . . . B2
James St B2
Jodrell St B3
John St C2
Jordangate B2
King Edward St C2
King George's Field . C3
King St B2
King's School A1
Knight Pool C3
Knight St C2
Lansdowne St A3
Library B2
Lime Gr A3
Loney St B1
Longacre St B1
Lord St C2
Lowe St C2
Lowerfield Rd A3
Lyon St B1
Macclesfield Coll . . . C1
Macclesfield Sta 🚂 . B2
MADS Little
 Theatre 🎭 A1
Marina B3
Market B2
Market Pl B2
Masons La B2
Mill La C2
Mill St B2
Moran Rd C1
New Hall St A3
Newton St B3
Nicholson Ave A3
Nicholson Cl A3
Northgate Ave A1
Old Mill La C2
Paradise Mill 🖾 C1
Paradise St C2
Park Green B2
Park La C1
Park Rd C1
Park Vale Rd B1
Parr St C2
Peel St C2
Percyvale St A2
Peter St C1
Pickford St B3
Pierce St C1
Pinfold St B3
Pitt St C2
Police Station 📮 . . . C2
Pool Bank Cl C2
Pool St B3
Poplar Rd C3
Post Office 📮 A2
Pownall St C2

Prestbury Rd A1/B1
Queen Victoria St . . B2
Registrar B2
Retail Park C1
Richmond Hill C3
Riseley St A1
Roan Ct A3
Roe St B2
Rowan Way A1
Ryle St C1
Ryle's Park Rd C1
St George's St C1
St Michael's 🏛 B2
Samuel St B1
Saville St C2
Shaw St B1
Silk Rd,The A2/B2
Slater St C1
Snow Hill C2
South Park C2
Spring Gdns A2
Statham St C2
Station St A2
Steeple St A3
Sunderland St B2
Superstore A1/A2/C2
Swettenham St B3
Thistleton Cl C2
Thorp St B2
Town Hall B2
Townley St C2
Treacle Market ◆ . . . B2
Turnock St C2
Union Rd B3
Union St C1
Victoria Park B1
Vincent St C2
Waters Green B2
Waterside B2
West Bond St B1
West Park A1
West Park Mus 🖾 . . A1
Westbrook Dr A1
Westminster Rd A1
Whalley Hayes B1
Windmill St C2
Withyfold Dr A2
York St B2

Maidstone 190

Albion Pl B3
All Saints 🏛 B2
Allen St A1
Amphitheatre ◆ . . . C2
Archbishop's
 Palace 🏛 B2
Bank St B2
Barker Rd C2
Barton Rd C3
Beaconsfield Rd . . . C1
Bedford Pl B1
Bishops Way B2
Bluett St A3
BMI The Somerfield
 Hospital 🏥 A1
Bower La C1
Bower Mount Rd . . . B1
Bower Pl C1
Bower St A2
Boxley Rd A3
Brenchley Gardens . A2
Brewer St A3
Broadway B2
Broadway Shopping
 Centre B2
Brunswick St C3
Buckland Hill A1
Buckland Rd B1
Bus Station B2
Campbell Rd C3
Church Rd C3
Church St A3
Cinema 🎬 B3
Clifford Way C1/C2
College Ave C2
College Rd C2
Collis Meml Gdn . . . C1
Cornwallis Rd B1
Corpus Christi Hall . B1
Council Offices B3
County Hall A2
County Rd A3
Crompton Gdns . . . B3
Crown & County
 Courts B2
Curzon Rd A3
Dixon Cl C1
Douglas Rd C1
Earl St B2
Eccleston Rd C2
Fairmeadow A2
Fisher St A3
Florence Rd C1
Foley St A3
Foster St C3
Freedom Leisure
 Centre A1/A2
Fremlin Walk
 Shopping Centre . B2
Gabriel's Hill B2
George St C3
Grecian St A3
Hardy St A3
Hart St B1
Hastings Rd C3
Hayle Rd C2
Hazlitt 🎭 B2
Heathorn St A3
Hedley St A3
High St B2
HM Prison A3
Holland Rd A3
Hope St A2
Information Ctr ℹ . . . B2
James Whatman
 Way A2
Jeffrey St A3
Kent County
 Council Offices . . . A2
Kent History &
 Library Centre . . . A2
King Edward Rd . . . C2
King St B2
Kingsley Rd C3
Knightrider St B2
Launder Way C1
Lesley Pl A1
Library B2
Little Buckland Ave . A1
Lockmeadow Leisure
 Complex B2
London Rd B1
Lower Boxley Rd . . . A2
Lower Fant Rd C1

Magistrates Court . B3
Maidstone Barracks
  Station ≥ A1
Maidstone
  East Station ≥ . . A2
Maidstone Museum &
  Bentlif Art Gall ☆ . A3
Maidstone Utd FC . . B2
Maidstone West
  Station ≥ B2
Mall, The B3
Market B3
Market Buildings . . B2
Marsham St B2
Medway Rd B2
Melville St B3
Mill St B3
Millennium Bridge . B3
Mote Rd B3
Muir St C2
Old Tovil Rd C2
Palace Ave B3
Perryfield St A2
Police Station ◼ . . . A2
Post Office ▣ . . B2/C3
Priory Rd C1
Prospect Pl C1
Pudding La B2
Queen Anne Rd . . . A3
Queens Rd A1
Randall St A2
Rawdon Rd C3
Reginald Rd C1
Riverstage ☆ A1
Rock Pl B1
Rocky Hill B2
Romney Pl B3
Rose Yard B2
Rowland Cl C1
Royal Engineers' Rd A2
Royal Star Arcade . B2
St Annes Ct B2
St Faith's St B2
St Luke's Rd A3
St Peter St B2
St Peter's Bridge . B2
St Peter's Wharf Retail
  Park A2
St Philip's Ave A3
Salisbury Rd A3
Sandling Rd A2
Scott St A2
Scrubs La C3
Sheal's Cres C3
Somerfield La B1
Somerfield Rd B1
Staceys St B2
Station Rd A2
Superstore . . . A1/B2/B3
Terrace Rd C2
Tonbridge Rd C1
Tovil Rd C2
Town Hall B3
Trinity Park B3
Tufton St B3
Tyrwhitt-Drake
  Museum of
  Carriages ☆ B2
Union St B3
Upper Fant Rd . . . C1
Upper Stone St . . . B3
Victoria St B1
Warwick Pl B1
Wat Tyler Way . . . C3
Waterloo St C3
Waterlow Rd A3
Week St B2
Well Rd A3
Westree Rd C1
Wharf Rd C1
Whatman Park . . . A1
Wheeler St A2
Whitchurch Cl A1
Woodville Rd C1
Wyatt St B3
Wyke Manor Rd . . . B3

Manchester 190

Adair St B6
Addington St A5
Adelphi St A3
Albert Sq C3
Albion St C3
Ancoats St ≥ A6
Ancoats Gr North . B6
Angela St C4
Aquatics Centre . . C4
Ardwick Gn North . . C5
Ardwick Green Park C5
Ardwick Gn South . C5
Arlington St A3
Artillery St C3
Arundel St B2
Atherton St B2
Atkinson St B3
Aytoun St C4
Back Piccadilly . . . B4
Baird St B5
Balloon St A4
Bank Pl A1
Baring St C5
Barrack St C1
Barrow St A5
Bendix St A5
Bengal St A5
Berry St C5
Blackfriars Rd . . . A3
Blackfriars St B3
Blantyre St C1
Bloom St B4
Blossom St A5
Boad St B5
Bombay St C4
Booth St B3
Booth St B4
Bootle St B3
Brazennose St . . . B3
Brewer St A5
Bridge St B3
Bridgewater Hall . B3
Bridgewater Pl . . . B4
Bridgewater St . . . B2
Brook St C4
Brotherton Dr . . . A1
Brown St B3
Brown St B4
Brunswick St . . . C6
Brydon Ave B5
Buddhist Centre . . A4
Bury St A2
Bus & Coach Sta . A5
Bus Station B4
Butler St A5
Buxton St C5
Byrom St B2
Cable St A5
Cambridge St . C3/C4
Camp St B3
Canal St B4
Cannon St A1
Cardroom Rd A6
Carruthers St A6
Castle St B2
Castlefield Arena . B2
Cateaton St A3
Cathedral † A3
Cathedral St A3
Cavendish St C3
Chapel St A1/A3
Chapeltown St . . . B5
Charles St C4
Charlotte St B4
Chatham St C4
Chepstow St B3
Chester Rd . . . C1/C2
Chester St C4
Chetham's School
  of Music A3
China La B5
Chippenham Rd . . A6
Chorlton Rd C1
Chorlton St B4
Church St A4
Church St B4
City Park A4
City Rd East C3
Civil Justice Centre B2
Cleminson St A2
Clowes St A3
College Land A3
Collier St B2
Commercial St . . . B3
Conference Centre C4
Cooper St C4
Copperas St A4
Corn Exchange,
  The A4
Cornbrook ≥ C1
Cornell St A5
Corporation St . . . A4
Cotter St C6
Cotton St A1
Cow La B1
Cross St A3
Crown Court B4
Crown St C2
Dalberg St A6
Dale St A4/B5
Dancehouse, The ☆ C4
Dantzic St A4
Dark La C6
Dawson St C2
Dean St A5
Deansgate . . . A3/B3/C2
Deansgate
  Castlefield ≥ . . . C2
Deansgate Sta ≥ . B3
Dolphin St C6
Downing St C5
Ducie St B5
Duke Pl B2
Duke St B2
Durling St C6
East Ordsall La . A2/B1
Edge St A4
Egerton St C2
Ellesmere St C1
Everard St C1
Every St A6
Exchange Sq ☆ . . . A4
Factory, The ☆ . . . B1
Fairfield St B5
Faulkner St A3
Fennel St A3
Ford St C6
Ford St C6
Fountain St B3
Frederick St A2
Gartside St B2
Gaythorne St A1
George Leigh St . . A5
George St B4
Gore St C1
Goulden St A5
Granby Row B4
Gravel La A3
Great St B6
Great Ancoats St . A5
Great Bridgewater
  St B3
Great George St . . A1
Great Jackson St . C2
Great Marlborough
  St C4
Great Northern
  Warehouse Leisure &
  Shopping Complex B3
Greengate A3
Grosvenor St C5
Gun St A5
Hadrian Ave B6
Hall St B3
Hampson St B1
Hanover St A4
Hanworth Cl C5
Hardman St B3
Harkness St C6
Harrison St B6
Hart St B4
Helmet St B5
Henry St A5
Heyrod St B6
High St A4
Higher Ardwick . . C6
Hilton St A4/B5
Holland St A6
HOME ◆ C2
Hood St A5
Hope St B4
Hope St B3
Houldsworth St . . A5
Hoyle St C6
Hulme Hall Rd . . . B1
Hulme St A1
Hulme St C3
Hyde Rd C6
Islington Way . . . A1
Irwell St B2
Jackson Cl C1
Jackson's Row . . . B3
James St A5
Jenner Cl C2
Jersey St A5
John Dalton St . . . B3
John Ryland's
  Library ☆ B3
John St A5
Kennedy St B3
Kincardine Rd . . . B5
King St B3
King St West A3
Law Courts B3
Laystall St B5
Lever St A5
Library A5
Linby St A4
Little Lever St . . . A5
Liverpool Rd B2
Liverpool St C1
Lloyd St B3
Lockton Cl C5
London Rd B5
Long Millgate . . . A3
Longacre St B6
Loom St A5
Lower Byrom St . . B2
Lower Mosley St . . B3
Lower Ormond St . C4
Loxford La C4
Luna St A5
Major St B4
Manchester
  Arndale A4
Manchester Art
  Gallery ☆ B3
Manchester Central
  Convention
  Complex B3
Manchester
  Metropolitan
  University
  (MMU) B4/C4
Manchester Piccadilly
  Station ≥ B5
Manchester
  Technology Centre C3
Mancunian Way . . C3
Manor St C5
Marble St A4
Market St A4
Market St ≥ A4
Marsden St A3
Marshall St A5
Mayan Ave A2
Medlock St C3
Middlewood St . . . B1
Miller St A4
Minshull St B4
Mosley St B3
Mount St B3
Mulberry St B3
Murray St A5
Museum of Science &
  Industry (MOSI) ☆ B2
Nathan Dr A2
National Football
  Museum ☆ A4
Naval St A5
New Bailey St . . . A2
New Elm Rd B2
New Islington A6
New Islington Sta ≥ B6
New Quay St B2
New Union St A5
Newgate St A4
Newton St B4
Nicholas St B4
North Western St . B6
Oak St A4
Odeon ☆ A4/B3
Old Mill St A6
Oldfield Rd . . . A1/C1
Oldham St A4
Oldham St B4
Opera House ☆ . . B3
Ordsall La C4
Oxford Rd C4
Oxford Rd ≥ C4
Oxford St B4
Paddock St C6
Pall Mall B3
Palmerston St . . . B6
Parker St B4
Peak St B5
Penfield Cl C5
Peoples' History
  Museum ☆ B2
Peru St A1
Peter St B3
Piccadilly A4
Piccadilly ≥ B5
Piccadilly Gdns ≥ . A4
Piercy St A6
Poland St A5
Police Sta ◼ . . B3/B5
Pollard St B6
Port St A5
Portland St B4
Portugal St East . B5
Post Office ▣ . . . .
  A1/A2/A4/A5/B3/B4
Potato Wharf B2
Princess St . . . B3/C4
Pritchard St B5
Quay St A2
Quay St B2
Queen St B3
Radium St A5
Redhill St A5
Regent Rd B1
Rice St B2
Richmond St B4
Roby St B5
Rodney St A6
Roman Fort ☆ . . . B2
Rosamond St B2
Royal Exchange ☆ . B3
Sackville St B4
St Andrew's St . . . B6
St Ann St A3
St Ann's ☆ B3
St George's Ave . C1
St James St B4
St John St B2
St John's Cathedral
  (RC) † A2
St Mary's ☆ B3
St Mary's Gate . . . A3
St Mary's
  Parsonage ☆ . . . A3
St Peter's Sq ☆ . . B3
St Stephen St . . . A2
Salford Approach . A2
Salford Central ≥ . A2
Sheffield St B5
Sherratt St A5
Shopmobility A4
Shudehill A4
Shudehill ☆ A4
Sidney St C4
Silk St A5
Silver St B4
Skerry Cl C5
Snell St B6
South King St B3
Sparkle St B4
Spear St A4
Spring Gdns B4
Stanley St A2/B2
Store St B5
Superstore B1
Swan St A4
Tariff St B5
Tatton St C1
Temperance St . B6/C6
Thirsk St C6
Thomas St A4
Thompson St A4
Tib La B3
Tib St A4
Town Hall
  (Manchester) . . . B3
Town Hall (Salford) A2
Trafford St C3
Travis St B5
Trinity Way A3
Turner St A4
Univ of Manchester
  (Sackville St
  Campus) C4
Univ of Salford . . . A1
Upper Brook St . . C5
Upper Cleminson St A1
Upper Wharf St . . A1
Urban Exchange . . A5
Vesta St B6
Victoria ≥ A3
Victoria Station ≥ . A4
Wadesdon St A5
Water St B2
Watson St B3
West Fleet St B5
West King St A2
West Mosley St . . B3
Weybridge St A6
Whitworth St B4
Whitworth St West . C3
William St A2
William St C6
Wilmott St C3
Windmill St B3
Windsor Cr A4
Withy Gr A4
Woden St C1
Wood St B3
Woodward St A6
Worrall St C1
Worsley St B2
York St A4
York St C4

Merthyr Tydfil
Merthyr Tudful 190

Aberdare Rd A3
Abermorlais Terr . A3
Alexandra Rd . . . A3
Alma St C3
Arfryn Pl C1
Argyle St C3
Avenue De Clichy . C2
Beacons Place
  Shopping Centre . B2
Bethesda St B1
Bishops Gr A3
Brecon Rd . . . A1/B2
Briarmead B2
Bryn St C3
Bryntirion Rd . . B3/C3
Bus Station B2
Cae Mari Dwn . . . C2
Caedraw Rd C2
Castle Sq B2
Castle St B1
Chapel B1
Chapel Bank B1
Church St B3
Civic Centre B2
Clos Penderyn . . . C1
Coedcae'r Ct C3
College Blvd C2
County and Crown
  Courts C3
Court St C3
Cromwell St B3
Cyfarthfa Castle,
  Museum and
  Art Gallery ☆ . . . A1
Cyfarthfa Ind Est . C1
Cyfarthfa Park . . . A1
Cyfarthfa Retail Pk . C1
Cyfarthfa St B2
Dane St A2
Dane Terr A2
Danyparc A3
DarrenView A3
Dixon St B2
Dyke St C2
Dynevor St B2
Elwyn Dr C2
Fire Station A2
Fothergill St A3
Galonuchaf Rd . . A3
Garth St C2
Georgetown B2
Grawen Terr A1
Grove Pk A2
Grove, The A2
Gurnos Rd A2
Gwaelodygarth
  Rd A2/A3
Gwaunfarren Gr . . A3
Gwaunfarren Rd . . A3
Gwendoline St . . . A3
Hampton St A3
Heol S O Davies . . B1
Heol-Gerrig A1
High St . . . A3/B2/B3/C2
Highland View . . . B1
Howell Cl B1
Information Ctr ℹ . B2
Jackson's Bridge . B2
James St C3
John St B3
Joseph Parry's
  Cottage ☆ A3
Lancaster St B2
Library B2
Llewellyn St B1
Llwyfen St A3
Llwyn Dic Penderyn B3
Llwyn-y-Gelynen . C1
Lower Thomas St . B3
Market C2
Mary St C3
Masonic St B1
Merthyr Tydfil Coll . B2
Merthyr Town FC . C3
Merthyr Tydfil Leisure
  Centre C3
Merthyr Tydfil
  Station ≥ C3
Meyrick Villas . . . A2
Miniature
  Railway ◆ A1
Mount St A1
Nantygwenith St . B1
Norman Terr B1
Oak Rd A2
Old Cemetery . . . B3
Pandy Cl A1
Pantycelynen . . . B1
Parade, The B1
Park Terr B1
Penlan View C2
Penry St B2
Pentwyn Villas . . A3
Penyard Rd A3
Penydarren Park . A3
Penydarren Rd . . . A3
Plymouth St C1
Police Station ◼ . . B2
Pont Marlais West . B2
Post Office ▣ B2
Quarry Row B2
Queen's St B3
Rees St C3
Rhydycar Link . . . B3
Riverside Park . . . A1
St David's B1
St Tydfil's ☆ C2
St Tydfil's Ave . . . C3
St Tydfil's Square
  Shopping Centre . C2
Saxon St B1
School of Nursing . B2
Seward St A1
Shiloh La B3
Stone Circles ☆ . . B1
Stuart St C2
Summerhill Pl . . . B3
Superstore B1
Swan St C2
Swansea Rd A3
Taff Glen View . . . C2
TaffVale Ct B3
Theatre Soar ☆ . . B2
Thomastown Park . B3
Tramroad La A3
Tramroad Side
  North B2
Tramroad Side
  South C3
Trevithick Gdns . . A3
Trevithick St A3
Tudor Terr B2
Twynyrodyn Rd . . C2
Union St B3
Upper Colliers Row B1
UpperThomas St . B3
Victoria St B2
Vue ☆ B2
Vulcan Rd B2
Walk,The C3
Warlow St C3
Well St C2
Welsh Assembly
  Government
  Offices C2
Wern La C1
Wern,The
  (Merthyr RFC) . . C1
West Gr C3
William St C3
Yew St C3
Ynysfach Engine
  House ◆ C2
Ynysfach Rd C2

Middlesbrough 191

Abingdon Rd C3
Acklam Rd C1
Albert Park C2
Albert Rd B2
Albert Terr C1
Ambulance Station C1
Aubrey St C3
Avenue,The C2
Ayresome Gdns . . C2
Ayresome Green La C1
Ayresome St C2
Barton Rd A1
Bilsdale Rd C3
Bishopton Rd C1
Borough Rd . . . B2/B3
Bowes Rd A2
Breckon Hill Rd . . B3
Bridge St West . . . B2
Brighouse Rd A2
Burlam Rd C1
Bus Station B2
Cannon Park B1
Cannon Park Way . B1
Cannon St B1
Captain Cook Sq . B2
Carlow St C1
Castle Way C1
Chipchase Rd C2
Cineworld ☆ A2
Cleveland Centre . B2
Clive Rd C2
Commercial St . . . B1
Corporation Rd . . B2
Costa St C2
Council Offices . . . B3
Crescent Rd C2
Crescent,The C2
Cumberland Rd . . C2
Depot Rd A2
Derwent St B2
Devonshire Rd . . . C2
Diamond Rd B2
Dock St B2
Dorman Mus ☆ . . C2
Douglas St B3
Eastbourne Rd . . . C2
Eden Rd C3
Fire Sta C3
Forty Foot Rd . . . A2
Gilkes St B2
Gosford St B1
Grange Rd B2
Gresham Rd B2
Harehills Rd C1
Harford St C2
Hartington Rd . . . B2
Haverton Hill Rd . . A1
Hey Wood St B1
Highfield Rd C3
Hillstreet Centre . B2
Holwick Rd B1
Hutton Rd C3
Ironmasters Way . B1
Lambton Rd C3
Lancaster Rd C2
Lansdowne Rd . . . C3
Latham Rd C3
Law Courts . . . B2/B3
Lees Rd C3
Leeway B3
Library B2/C2
Linthorpe
  Cemetery C1
Linthorpe Rd C2
Lloyd St B2
Longford St C2
Longlands Rd C3
Lower East St B3
Lower Lake C3
Macmillan Acad . . C1
Maldon Rd C1
Manor St B2
Marsh St B2
Marton Rd C3
Middlesbrough
  By-Pass B2/C1
Middlesbrough
  College C3
Middlesbrough
  Dock B3
Middlesbrough
  Leisure Park . . . C3
Middlesbrough
  Station ≥ B2
Middletown Park . C2
MIMA ☆ B2
Mulgrave Rd C1
Newport Bridge . . B1
Newport Bridge
  Approach Rd . . . B1
Newport Rd B2
North Ormesby Rd B3
North Rd B2
Northern Rd C1
Outram St B2
Oxford Rd C2
Park La C2
Park Rd North . . . B2
Park Rd South . . . C2
Park Vale Rd C3
Parliament Rd . . . B1
Police Station ◼ . . A3
Port Clarence Rd . A3
Portman St B2
Post Office ▣ . B3/C1/C2
Princes Rd B2
Python ◆ C2
Riverside Park Rd . A1
Riverside Stadium
  (Middlesbrough
  FC) B3
Rockliffe Rd C2
Romaldkirk Rd . . . B1
Roman Rd C2
Roseberry Rd C3
St Barnabas' Rd . . C2
St Paul's Rd B2
Saltwells Rd B3
Scott's Rd A3
Seaton Carew Rd . A3
Shepherdson Way . B3
Shopmobility C2
Snowdon Rd B2
South West
  Ironmasters Park . B1
Southfield Rd C2
Southwell Rd C2
Springfield Rd . . . C1
Startforth Rd A2
Stockton Rd C1
Stockton St B2
Stowe St C1
Suffield St C1
Surrey St C2
Sycamore Rd C2
Tax Offices B3
Tees Viaduct C1
Teessaurus Park . . A2
Teesside Tertiary
  College A3
Temenos ◆ B3
Thornfield Rd C1
Town Hall B3
Transporter Bridge
  (Toll) A3
Union St B2
Univ of Teesside . . B2
Upper Lake C3
Valley Rd C2
Ventnor Rd C2
Victoria Rd B2
Vulcan St A2
Warwick St C2
Wellesley Rd B3
West La C1
West Lane Hosp ℍ . C1
Westminster Rd . . C3
Wilson St B2
Windward Way . . . B3
Woodlands Rd . . . B2
York Rd C3

Milton Keynes 191

Abbey Way A1
Arbrook Ave B1
Armourer Dr C2
Arncliffe Dr A1
Avebury ◆ C2
Avebury Blvd C2
Bankfield B3
Bayard Ave A2
Belvedere ◆ C2
Bishopstone A1
Blundells Rd A1
Boundary,The . . . C3
Boycott Ave C2
Bradwell Common
  Boulevard B1
Bradwell Rd C1
Bramble Ave A2
Brearley Ave C2
Breckland A1
Brill Place B1
Burnham Dr A1
Campbell Park ◆ . B3
Cantle Ave A3
Central Retail Park B2
Century Ave C2
Chaffron Way . . . C3
Childs Way C1
Christ the
  Cornerstone ☆ . . B2
Cineworld ☆ B2
Civic Offices B2
Cleavers Ave B2
Colesbourne Dr . . A3
Conniburrow Blvd . B2
Currier Dr A3
Dansteed
  Way . . . A2/A3/B1
Deltic Ave B1
Downs Barn ◆ . . . A3
Downs Barn Blvd . A3
Eaglestone ◆ . . . C3
Eelbrook Ave B1
Elder Gate C2
Evans Gate C2
Fairford Cr A3
Falcon Ave B3
Fennel Dr A3
Fishermead Blvd . C3
Food Centre B2
Fulwoods Dr C3
Glazier Dr C2
Glovers La A1
Grafton Gate . . C1/C2
Grafton St . . . A1/C2
Gurnards Ave . . . B3
Harrier Dr C2
Hub Leisure
  Quarter,The . . B2/C2
Ibstone Ave C1
intu Milton Keynes B2
Langcliffe Dr A1
Leisure Centre . . . C3
Leisure Plaza B2
Leys Rd C2
Library B2
Lincslade Grove . . C1
Linford Wood . . . A2
Magistrates Court . B1
Marlborough Gate . B2
Marlborough St . A2/B3
Mercers Dr A1
Midsummer ◆ . . . C2
Midsummer Blvd . C2
Milton Keynes
  Central ≥ C1
Milton Keynes
  Hospital (A&E) ℍ . C3
Monks Way A1
Mullen Ave A3
Neath Hill A3
North Elder ◆ . . . C1
North Grafton . . . C1
North Overgate ◆ . A3
North Row B2
North Saxon ◆ . . . B2
North Secklow ◆ . B2
North Skeldon ◆ . A3
North Witan ◆ . . . A1
Oakley Gdns A3
Oldbrook Blvd . . . C2
Open-Air Theatre ☆ B3
Overgate A3
Overstreet A3
Patriot Dr B1
Pencarrow Pl B3
Penryn Ave C1
Perran Ave C2
Pitcher La C1
Place Retail Pk,The C1
Police Station ◼ . . A3
Portway ◆ C1
Post Office ▣ . A2/B2/B3
Precedent Dr B1
Quinton Dr B1
Ramsons Ave B2
Retail Park C2
Rockingham Dr . . C2
Rooksley C1
Saxon Gate B2
Saxon St A1/C3
Secklow Gate . . . B2
Shackleton Pl C2
Shopmobility B2
Silbury Blvd B2
Skeldon ◆ A3
South Enmore . . . B3
South Grafton . . . C2
South Row B2
South Saxon ◆ . . . C2
South Secklow ◆ . C2
South Witan ◆ . . . C2
Springfield ◆ C3
Stainton Dr A1
Stanton Wood ◆ . A2
Stantonbury ◆ . . . A1
Stantonbury
  Leisure Centre ◆ . A1
Strudwick Dr C3
Sunrise Parkway . . A2
Superstore . . . C1/C2
Theatre &
  Art Gallery ☆ . . . B3
theCentre:mk . . . B2
Tolcarne Ave C3
Towan Ave C3
Trueman Pl C3
Vauxhall A1
Winterhill Retail Pk C2
Witan Gate B2
Xscape ◆ B3

**Newcastle
upon Tyne 191**

Albert St B3
Argyle St B3
Back New Bridge St A3
BALTIC Centre for
  Contemporary
  Art ◆ C3
Barker St A3
Barrack Rd A1
Bath La B2
Bessie Surtees
  House ☆ C3
Bigg Market B2
Biscuit Factory ☆ . A3
Black Gate ☆ . . . C2
Blackett St B2
Blandford Sq C1
Boating Lake A1
Boyd St A3
Brandling Park . . . A2
Bus Station B3
Buxton St B3
Byron St A3
Camden St A3
Castle Keep ☆ . . . C2
Central ≥ C2
Central Library . . . B2
Central Motorway . A2
City Hall B3
City Rd B3/C3
City Walls ☆ C1
Civic Centre A2
Claremont Rd . . . A1
Clarence St B3
Clarence Walk . . . B3
Clayton St . . . C1/B1
Clayton St West . . C1
Close,The C2
Coach Station . . . C1
College St B2
Collingwood St . . C2
Copland Terr B3
Coppice Way A3
Corporation St . . . B1
Courts C2
Crawhall Rd B3
Dean St C2
Dental Hospital . . A1
Dinsdale Pl A3
Discovery ☆ C2
Doncaster Rd . . . A3
Durant Rd B2
Eldon Sq B2
Ellison Pl B2
Eskdale Terr A1
Eslington Terr . . . A1
Exhibition Park . . A1
Falconar St B3
Fenkle St C1
Forth Banks C1
Forth St C1
Gallowgate B1
Gate,The ◆ B1
Gateshead Millennium
  Bridge C3
Gateshead Quays ◆ C3
Gibson St B3
Goldspink La A3
Grainger Market . . B2
Grainger St B2
Grantham Rd A3
Granville Rd A2
Great North Children's
  Hospital ℍ A1
Great North
  Mus:Hancock ☆ . A2
Grey St C2
Great Market C2
Guildhall ☆ C2
Hancock St A2
Hanover St C2
Hatton Gallery ☆ . A1
Hawks Rd C3
Haymarket Ⓜ . . . B2
Heber St B1
Helmsley Rd A3
High Bridge B2
High Level Bridge . C2
Hillgate C2
Howard St B3
Hutton Terr A3
intu Eldon Sq
  Shopping Centre . B2
Jesmond Ⓜ A2
Jesmond Rd . . . A2/A3
John Dobson St . . B2
Jubilee Rd B3
Kelvin Gr A2
Kensington Terr . . A2
Laing Gallery ☆ . . B2
Lambton Rd A2
Leazes Cr B1
Leazes La B2
Leazes Park B1
Leazes Park Rd . . B1
Leazes Terr B1
Library B2
Life Science Ctr ◆ . C1
Low Friar St C1
Manor Chare C2
Manors ≥ C3
Manors Station ◆ . B3
Market St B2
Melbourne St B3
Mill Rd C3
Monument Ⓜ . . . B2
Monument Mall
  Shopping Centre . B2
Morpeth St A2
Mosley St C2
Napier St A3
New Bridge St
  West B2/B3
Newcastle Central
  Station ≥ C2
Newcastle Univ . . A1
Newgate St B2
Newington Rd . . . A3
Northern Design
  Centre C3
Northern Stage
  Theatre ☆ A2
Northumberland Rd B2
Northumberland St B2
Northumbria
  University B2
Northwest Radial
  Rd A1
O2 Academy ◆ . . C1
Oakwellgate C3
Open Univ C1
Orchard St C2
Osborne Rd A2
Osborne Terr A3
Pandon C3
Pandon Bank C3
Park Terr A1
Percy St B2
Pilgrim St B2
Pipewellgate C2
Pitt St B1
Plummer Tower ☆ . B2
Police Station ◼ . . A2
Portland Rd . . . A3/B3
Portland Terr A3
Post Office ▣ . . B1/B2
Pottery La C1
Prudhoe Pl B2
Prudhoe St B2
Quayside C3
Queen Elizabeth II
  Bridge C3
Queen Victoria Rd . A1
Richardson Rd . . . A1
Ridley Pl B2
Rock Terr B3
Rosedale Terr . . . A3
Royal Victoria
  Infirmary ℍ . . . A1
Sage Gateshead ◆ C3
St Andrew's St . . . B1
St James Ⓜ B1
St James' Blvd . . . C1
St James' Park
  (Newcastle Utd
  FC) B1
St Mary's Heritage
  Centre ◆ C3
St Mary's (RC) † . C1

**Newport
Casnewydd 191**

AlbertTerr B1
Allt-yr-Yn Ave . . . A1
Alma St C2
Ambulance Station C3
Bailey St A2
Barrack Hill A2
Bath St A3
Bedford Rd B3
Belle Vue La A1
Belle Vue Park . . . C1
Bishop St A3
Blewitt St B1
Bolt Cl C3
Bolt St C3
Bond St C3
Bosworth Dr A1
Bridge St B2
Bristol St A3
Bryngwyn Rd B1
Brynhyfryd Ave . . C1
Brynhyfryd Rd . . . C1
Bus Station B2
Caerau Cres C1
Caerau Rd B1
Caerleon Rd A3
Capel Cres C3
Cardiff Rd C2
Caroline St B3
Castle (Remains) . A2
Cedar Rd B3
Charles St B2
Charlotte Dr C2
Chepstow Rd A3
Church Rd A3
Cineworld ☆ B2
Civic Centre B1
Clarence Pl A2
Clifton Pl B1
Clifton Rd B1
Clyffard Cres B1
Clytha Park Rd . . B1
Clytha Sq C2
Coldra Rd C3
Collier St A3
Colne St B3
Comfrey Cl A1
Commercial Rd . . C3
Commercial St . . . B2
Corelli St A3
Corn St B2
Corporation Rd . . B3
Coulson Cl C3
County Court B2
Courts B2
Crawford St B3
Cyril St B2
Dean St B1
Devon Pl B1
Dewsland Park Rd . C2
Dolman ◆ C2
Dolphin St C3
East St B2
East Usk Rd A3
Ebbw Vale Wharf . A3
Emlyn St C2
Enterprise Way . . C3
Eton Rd A3
Evans St B1
Factory Rd A2
Fields Rd B1
Francis Dr C2
Frederick St C2
Friars Rd C2
Friars Walk C2
Gaer La C2
George St C1
George St Bridge . C1
Godfrey Rd B1
Gold Tops B1
Gore St A3
Gorsedd Circle ☆ . C1
Grafton Rd B3
Graham St B2
Granville St C3
Harlequin Dr C3
Harrow Rd B3
Herbert Rd A3
Herbert Walk C2
Hereford St A3
High St B2
Hill St B1
Hoskins St A2
Information Ctr ℹ . B2
Ivor St B3
Jones St B2
Junction Rd A3
Keynsham Ave . . . C2
King St C2
Kingsway B2
Kingsway Centre . B2
Ledbury Dr C3
Library B2
Library, Museum &
  Art Gallery ☆ . . . B2
Liverpool Wharf . . B3
Llanthewy Rd . . . A1
Llanvair Rd A3
Locke St A2
Lower Dock St . . . C3
Lucas St A2
Manchester St . . . B3
Market B3
Marlborough Rd . . B3
Mill St B1
Morgan St C3
Mountjoy Rd C2
Newport Bridge . . A2
Newport Ctr B2
Newport RFC A2
Newport Station ≥ B2
North St B2
Oakfield Rd B1
Park Sq C2
Police Sta ◼ . . A3/C2
Post Office ▣ . . A3/B2/C1
Power St A1
Prince St C3
Pugsley St A2
Queen St A1
Queen's Cl B1
Queen's Hill A1
Queen's Hill Cres . A1
Queensway B2
Railway St B2
Riverfront Theatre &
  Arts Centre,The ◆ A3
Riverside A3
Rodney Rd B2
Royal Gwent
  (A&E) ℍ C2
Rudry St A3
Rugby Rd A3
Ruperra La A3
Ruperra St A3
St Edmund St . . . A3
St Mark's Cres . . . A2
StVincent Rd A3
St Woolos ◆ C1
St Woolos General
  (no A&E) ℍ C1
St Woolos Rd B1
School La A3
Serpentine Rd . . . A3
Shaftesbury Park . A3
Sheaf La A2
Skinner St A2
Sorrel Dr A3
South Market St . . A3
Spencer Rd A1
Stow Hill . . . B2/C1/C2
Stow Park Ave . . . C2
Stow Park Dr C1
TA Centre A1
Talbot St A2
Tennis Club A1
Tregare St A3
Trostrey St A3
Tunnel Terr A1
Turner St A3
University of Wales
  Newport City
  Campus A3
Upper Dock St . . . B2
Usk St A3
Usk Way B3/C3
Victoria Cr B1
War Memorial . . . A3
Waterloo Rd C1
West St A1
Wharves A2
Wheeler St A2
Whitby Pl A3
Windsor Terr A1
York Pl C1

Newquay 192

Agar Rd B2
Alma Pl B1
Ambulance Station A2
Anthony Rd A2
Atlantic Hotel . . . A1
Bank St A1
Barrowfields A3
Bay View Terr . . . A2
Beach Rd A2
Beachfield Ave . . . B1
Beacon Rd A1
Belmont Pl A2
Berry Rd B2
Blue Reef
  Aquarium ◆ . . . B1
Boating Lake A3
Bus Station B1
Chapel Hill A1
Chester Rd A3
Cheviot Rd . . . C1/C2
Chichester Cres . . C2
Chynance Dr C2
Chyverton Cl A3
Cliff Rd B1
Coach Park A2
Colvreath Rd A3
Cornwall College
  Newquay B3
Council Offices . . . B1
Crantock St B1
Crescent,The A1
Criggar Rocks . . . A3
Dale Cl A3
Dale Rd A3
Dane Rd A2
East St B2
Edgcumbe Ave . . B2
Edgcumbe Gdns . B2
Eliot Gdns A3
Elm Cl A3
Ennor's Rd B2
Fernhill Rd B2
Fire Station A2
Fore St B1
Golf Driving Range A2
Gover La A2
Great Western
  Beach A1
Grosvenor Ave . . B3
Harbour A1
Headland Rd A1
Hilgrove Rd . . . A3/B3
Holywell Rd B2
Hope Terr A2
Huer's Hut,The ◆ . A1
Information Ctr ℹ . B1
Island Cres B2
Jubilee St B2
Kew Cl B2
Killacourt Cove . . A2

Northampton • Norwich • Nottingham • Oxford • Perth • Peterborough • Plymouth • Poole • Portsmouth 209

King Edward Cres A1
Lanhenvor Ave B2
Library B1
Lifeboat Station A1
Lighthouse B1
Linden Ave C2
Listry Rd C2
Lusty Glaze Beach A3
Lusty Glaze Rd A3
Manor Rd B1
Marcus Hill B2
Mayfield Rd B2
Meadowside C3
Mellanvrane La C2
Michell Ave B2
Miniature Golf Course C3
Miniature Railway ✦ B3
Mount Wise B1
Mowhay Cl C3
Narrowcliff A3
Newquay ≥ B2
Newquay Hosp H B2
Newquay Town Football Ground B1
Newquay Zoo B3
North Pier A1
North Quay Hill A1
Oakleigh Terr B2
Pargolla Rd B2
Pendragon Cres C3
Pengannel Cl C1
Penina Ave C3
Pirate's Quest B1
Police Station & Courts B2
Post Office B1/B2
Quarry Park Rd B3
Rawley La C2
Reeds Way B1
Robartes Rd B2
St Anne's Rd A3
St Aubyn Cres B3
St George's Rd B1
St John's Rd B1
St Mary's Rd B1
St Michael's B1
St Michael's Rd B1
St Thomas' Rd B2
Seymour Ave B2
South Pier A1
South Quay Hill A1
Superstore B2
Sweet Briar Cres C3
Sydney Rd A1
Tolcarne Beach A2
Tolcarne Point A2
Tolcarne Rd B2
Tor Rd B2
Towan Beach A1
Towan Blystra Rd B3
Tower Rd A1
Trebarwith Cres B2
Tredour Rd C2
Treforda Rd C3
Tregoss Rd B3
Tregunnel Hill B1/C1
Tregunnel Saltings C1
Trelawney Rd B2
Treloggan La C3
Treloggan Rd C3
Trembath Cres C1
Trenance Ave B2
Trenance Gardens B2
Trenance La C2
Trenance Leisure Park B3
Trenance Rd B2
Trenarth Rd B2
Treninnick Hill C3
Tretherras Rd B3
Trethewey Way C1
Trevemper Rd C2
Ulalia Rd B3
Vivian Cl B2
Waterworld B3
Whitegate Rd B3
Wych Hazel Way C3

Northampton 192
78 Derngate B3
Abington Sq B3
Abington St B3
Alcombe St A3
All Saints' B2
Ambush St B1
Angel St B2
Army Reserve Ctr A3
Arundel St A2
Ash St A2
Auctioneers Way C2
Bailiff St A2
Barrack Rd A2
BBOB Rugby FC A1
Beaconsfield Terr A3
Becket's Park C3
Bedford Rd B3
Billing Rd B3
Brecon St A1
Brewery C2
Bridge St C2
Broad St B2
Burns St A3
Bus Station A2
Campbell St A2
Castle (Site of) B2
Castle St B2
Cattle Market Rd C2
Central Museum & Art Gallery B2
Charles St A3
Cheyne Walk B3
Church La A2
Clare St A3
Cloutsham St A3
College St B2
Colwyn Rd A3
Cotton End C2
Countess Rd A1
County Hall B2
Court A2
Craven St A3
Crown & County Courts B3
Denmark Rd B3
Derngate B3
Doddridge Church B2
Drapery, The B2
Duke St A3
Dunster St A3
Earl St A3
Euston Rd C2
Fire Station A3
Foot Meadow B2
Gladstone Rd A1
Gold St B2
Grafton St A2
Gray St A3
Green St B1
Greenwood Rd B1
Greyfriars B2
Grosvenor Centre B2
Grove Rd A3
Guildhall B2
Hampton St A2
Harding Terr A2
Hazelwood Rd B3
Herbert St A2
Hervey St A3
Hester St A2
Holy Sepulchre A2
Hood St A3
Horse Market B2
Hunter St A3
Information Ctr B2
Kettering Rd A3
Kingswell St B2
Lady's La B2
Leicester St A2
Leslie Rd A2
Library B3
Lorne Rd A2
Lorry Park A1
Louise Rd A2
Lower Harding St A2
Lower Hester St A2
Lower Mounts B3
Lower Priory St A2
Main Rd C1
Marefair B2
Market Sq B2
Marlboro Rd B1
Marriott St A2
Military Rd A3
Mounts Baths Leisure Centre A3
Nene Valley Retail Park C1
New South Bridge Rd C2
Northampton General Hospital (A&E) H B3
Northampton Marina C3
Northampton Sta ≥ B1
Northcote St A2
Nunn Mills Rd C3
Old Towcester Rd C2
Overstone Rd A3
Pembroke Rd A1
Penn Court C2
Police Station B3
Post Office A1/B3
Quorn Way A2
Ransome Rd C3
Regent Sq A2
Ridings, The B3
Robert St A2
Royal & Derngate Theatres B3
St Andrew's Rd B1
St Andrew's St A2
St Edmund's Rd B3
St George's St A2
St Giles B3
St Giles St B3
St Giles' Terr B3
St James Park Rd B1
St James Rd B1
St James Retail Pk C1
St James' Mill Rd B1
St James' Mill Rd East C1
St Leonard's Rd C2
St Mary's St B2
St Michael's Rd A3
St Peter's B2
St Peter's Way Shopping Precinct B2
St Peter's Way B2
Salisbury St A2
Scarletwell St B2
Semilong Rd A2
Sheep St B2
Sol Central (Leisure Centre) B2
Somerset St A3
South Bridge C2
Southfield Ave C2
Spencer Bridge Rd A1
Spencer Rd A3
Spring Gdns B3
Spring La B2
Superstore C2
Swan St B3
Tintern Ave A1
Towcester Rd C2
Univ of Northampton (Waterside Campus) C3
Upper Bath St B2
Upper Mounts A2
Victoria Park A1
Victoria Prom B2
Victoria Rd B3
Victoria St A2
Wellingborough Rd B3
West Bridge B1
York Rd B3

Norwich 192
Albion Way C3
All Saints Green C2
Anchor St A3
Anglia Sq A2
Argyle St C3
Arts Centre B1
Ashby St C2
Assembly House B1
Bank Plain B2
Barker St A1
Barn Rd A1
Barrack St A3
Ber St C2
Bethel St B1
Bishop Bridge A3
Bishopbridge Rd A3
Bishopgate A3
Blackfriars St A2
Botolph St A2
Bracondale C3
Brazen Gate C2
Bridewell Mus B2
Brunswick Rd C1
Bull Close Rd A2
Bus Station C2
Calvert St A2
Cannell Green A3
Carrow Rd C3
Castle & Mus B2
Castle Mall B2
Castle Meadow B2
Cathedral ✝ B2
Cathedral (RC) ✝ B1
Cath Retail Park A1
Cattlemarket St B2
Chantry Rd C1
Chapel Loke C2
Chapelfield East B1
Chapelfield Gdns B1
Chapelfield North B1
Chapelfield Rd B1
Cinema City B2
City Hall ✦ B1
City Rd C2
City Wall C1/C3
Close, The B2/B3
Colegate A2
Coslany St B1
Cow Hill B1
Cow Tower A3
Cowgate A2
Crown & Magistrates' Courts A2
Dragon Hall Heritage Ctr C3
Duke St A1
Edward St A2
Elm Hill B2
Erpingham Gate ✦ B2
Fishergate A2
Forum, The B1
Foundry Bridge B3
Fye Bridge A2
Garden St C2
Gas Hill B3
Gentlemans Walk B2
Grapes Hill B1
Great Hospital Halls, The A3
Grove Ave C1
Grove Rd C1
Guildhall ✦ B1
Gurney Rd A3
Hall Rd C2
Heathgate A3
Heigham St A1
Hollywood A2
Horn's La C2
Hungate Medieval Art ✦ B2
Information Ctr B1
intu Chapelfield C1
Ipswich Rd C1
ITV Anglia C3
James Stuart Gdns B3
King St B2
King St C3
Koblenz Ave C3
Library B1
London St B2
Lower Clarence Rd B3
Maddermarket B1
Magdalen St A2
Mariners La C2
Market B2
Market Ave B2
Mountergate B3
Mousehold St A3
Newmarket Rd C1
Norfolk St C1
Norwich City FC C3
Norwich Gallery B2
Norwich School ✦ B2
Norwich Station ≥ B3
Oak St A1
Odeon C3
Palace St A2
Pitt St A1
Playhouse B2
Police Station B1
Post Office A2/B2/B3/C1
Pottergate B1
Prince of Wales Rd B2
Princes St B2
Pull's Ferry ✦ B3
Puppet Theatre A2
Queen St B2
Queens Rd C2
Recorder Rd B3
Riverside Entertainment Ctr C3
Riverside Leisure Centre C3
Riverside Rd B3
Riverside Retail Pk C3
Rosary Rd B3
Rose La B3
Rouen Rd C2
St Andrews St B2
St Augustines St A1
St Benedicts St B1
St Crispins Road A1
St Ethelbert's Gate ✦ B2
St Faiths La B3
St Georges St A2
St Giles St B1
St James Cl A3
St Julians C2
St Leonards Rd B3
St Martin's La A1
St Peter Mancroft B2
St Peters St B1
St Stephens Rd C1
St Stephens St C1
Shopmobility C1
Silver Rd A2
Silver St A2
Southwell Rd C2
St. Andrew's & Blackfriars' Hall ✦ B2
Strangers' Hall B1
Superstore C2
Surrey St C2
Sussex St A1
Theatre Royal B1
Theatre St B1
Thorn La C2
Thorpe Rd B3
Tombland B2
Union St C1
Vauxhall St B1
Victoria St C1
Vue C2
Walpole St B1
Waterfront, The C3
Wensum St A2
Wessex St C1
Westwick St A1
Wherry Rd C3
Whitefriars A2
Willow La B1

Nottingham 192
Abbotsford Dr A3
Addison St A1
Albert Hall ✦ B1
Alfred St Central A3
Alfreton Rd B1
All Saints St A1
Annesley Gr A2
Arboretum A1
Arboretum St A1
Arthur St A1
Arts Theatre B3
Ashforth St A3
Balmoral Rd A1
Barker Gate B3
Bath St B3
BBC Nottingham C3
Beacon Hill Rise B3
Belgrave Rooms B1
Bellar Gate B3
Belward St B3
Brewhouse Yard C2
Broad Marsh Bus Station C2
Broad St B3
Brook St B3
Burns St A1
Burton St B2
Bus Station A2
Canal St C2
Carlton St B3
Carrington St C2
Castle C2
Castle Blvd C1
Castle Gate C2
Castle Meadow Rd C1
Castle Meadow Retail Park C1
Castle Rd C2
Castle Wharf C2
Cavendish Rd East C1
Cemetery A1/B1
Chaucer St B1
Cheapside B2
Church Rd A3
City Link C3
City of Caves ✦ C2
Clarendon St B1
Cliff Rd C3
Clumber Rd East C1
Clumber St B2
College St B1
Collin St C2
Contemporary C3
Conway Cl A2
Cornerhouse, The B2
Council House B2
Cranbrook St B3
Cranmer St A2
Cromwell St B1
Curzon St B3
Derby Rd B1
Dryden St A2
Exchange Ctr, The B2
Fishpond Dr C1
Fletcher Gate B3
Forest Rd East A1
Forest Rd West A1
Friar La C2
Gedling Gr A1
Gedling St B3
George St B3
Gill St A2
Glasshouse St B2
Goldsmith St B2
Goose Gate B3
Great Freeman St A2
Guildhall B2
Hamilton Dr C1
Hampden St A1
Heathcote St B3
High Pavement C3
High School A1
HM Revenue & Customs C2
Holles Cr C1
Hope Dr C1
Hungerhill Rd A3
Huntingdon Dr C1
Huntingdon St A2
Information Ctr B2
Instow Rise A3
Int Com Ctr A2
intu Broadmarsh C2
intu Victoria Centre B2
Kent St B3
King St B2
Lace Market B3
Lace Mkt Theatre C3
Lamartine St B3
Leisure Ctr C3
Lenton Rd C1
Lewis Cl A3
Lincoln St B2
London Rd C3
Long Row B2
Low Pavement C2
Lower Parliament St B3
Magistrates' Court C2
Maid Marian Way B2
Mansfield Rd A2/B2
Middle Hill C2
Milton St B2
Mount St B2
National Ice Centre & Motorpoint Arena C3
National Justice Museum C3
Newcastle Dr B1
Newstead Gr A2
North Sherwood St A2
Nottingham Arena C3
Nottingham Cath ✝ B1
Nottingham Coll C3
Nottingham Station ≥ C3
Nottingham Trent University A2/B2
Old Mkt Square B2
Oliver St A1
Park Dr C1
Park Row C1
Park Terr B1
Park Valley C1
Park, The C1
Peas Hill Rd A3
Peel St A1
Pelham St B2
Peveril Dr C1
Plantagenet St A3
Playhouse Theatre B1
Plumptre St C3
Police Sta B1/B2
Poplar St C3
Portland Rd B1
Post Office B2
Queen's Rd C3
Raleigh St A1
Regent St B1
Rick St B3
Robin Hood St B3
Robin Hood Statue ✦ C2
Ropewalk, The B1
Royal Centre B2
Royal Children Inn C2
Royal Concert Hall B2
St Ann's Hill Rd A2
St Ann's Way A2
St Ann's Well Rd A3
St James' St B2
St Mark's St B3
St Mary's Rest Gdn B3
St Mary's Gate B3
St Nicholas C2
St Peter's C2
St Peter's Gate B2
Salutation Inn C2
Shakespeare St B2
Shelton St A2
Shopmobility A2
South Pde B2
South Rd C1
South Sherwood St B2
Station Street C3
Stoney St B3
Talbot St B1
Tattershall Dr C1
Tennis Dr B1
Tennyson St A1
Theatre Royal B2
Trent St C3
Trent University B2
Union Rd B3
Upper Parliament St B2
Victoria Leisure Ctr B3
Victoria Park B3
Victoria St B2
Walter St A1
Warser Gate B3
Watkin St A2
Waverley St A1
Wheeler Gate B2
Wilford Rd C2
Wilford St C2
Wollaton St B1
Woodborough Rd A2
Woolpack La B3
Ye Old Trip to Jerusalem ✦ C2
York St A2

Oxford 193
Adelaide St A1
Albert St A1
All Souls (Coll) B2
Ashmolean Mus B2
Balliol (Coll) B2
Banbury Rd A2
Bate Collection of Musical Instruments C2
Beaumont St B1
Becket St B1
Blackhall Rd A2
Blue Boar St B2
Bodleian Library B2
Botanic Garden B3
Brasenose (Coll) B2
Brewer St C2
Broad St B2
Burton-Taylor Theatre B2
Bus Station B1
Canal St A1
Cardigan St A1
Carfax Tower B2
Castle B1
Castle St B1
Catte St B2
Cemetery C1
Christ Church (Coll) B2
Christ Church Cathedral ✝ C2
Christ Church Mdw C2
Clarendon Centre B2
Coach & Lorry Park C1
College B3
Coll of Further Ed C1
Cornmarket St B2
Corpus Christi (Coll) B2
County Hall B1
Covered Market B2
Cowley Pl C3
Cranham St A1
Cranham Terr A1
Cricket Ground B1
Crown & County Courts C2
Deer Park B3
Exeter (Coll) B2
Folly Bridge C2
George St B1
Great Clarendon St A1
Hart St A1
Hertford (Coll) B2
High St B3
Hollybush Row B1
Holywell St B2
Hythe Bridge St B1
Ice Rink C1
Information Ctr B2
Jericho St A1
Jesus (Coll) B2
Jowett Walk B3
Juxon St A1
Keble (Coll) A2
Keble Rd A2
Library B2
Linacre (Coll) A3
Lincoln (Coll) B2
Little Clarendon St A1
Longwall St B3
Magdalen (Coll) B3
Magdalen Bridge B3
Magdalen St B2
Magistrate's Court C2
Manchester (Coll) B2
Manor Rd B3
Mansfield (Coll) A2
Mansfield Rd A3
Market B1
Marlborough Rd C2
Martyrs' Meml ✦ B2
Merton (Coll) B3
Merton Field B3
Merton St B2
Museum of Modern Art B2
Mus of Oxford B2
Museum Rd A2
New College (Coll) B3
New Inn Hall St B2
New Rd B1
New Theatre B2
Norfolk St C1
Nuffield (Coll) B1
Observatory A1
Observatory St A1
Odeon B1/B2
Old Fire Station B1
Old Greyfriars St C2
Oriel (Coll) B2
Oxford Station ≥ B1
Oxford University Research Centres A1
Oxpens Rd C1
Paradise Sq C1
Paradise St B1
Park End St B1
Parks Rd A2/B2
Pembroke (Coll) C2
Phoenix A1
Picture Gallery C2
Plantation Rd A1
Playhouse B2
Police Station C2
Post Office A1/B2
Pusey St B1
Queen's (Coll) B3
Queen's La B3
Radcliffe Camera B2
Rewley Rd B1
Richmond Rd A1
Rose La B3
Ruskin (Coll) B1
Said Bsns School B1
St Aldates C2
St Anne's (Coll) A1
St Antony's (Coll) A1
St Bernard's Rd A1
St Catherine's (Coll) B3
St Cross Building A3
St Cross Rd A3
St Edmund Hall (Coll) B3
St Giles St A2
St Hilda's (Coll) C3
St John St B2
St John's (Coll) B2
St Mary the Virgin B2
St Michael at the Northgate B2
St Peter's (Coll) B1
St Thomas St B1
Science Area A2
Science Museum B2
Sheldonian Theatre B2
Somerville (Coll) A1
South Parks Rd A2
Speedwell St C2
Sports Ground C3
Thames St C2
Town Hall B2
Trinity (Coll) B2
Turl St B2
University College (Coll) B3
University Museum & Pitt Rivers Mus A2
University Parks A2
Wadham (Coll) B2
Walton Cr A1
Walton St A1
Western Rd C2
Westgate C2
Woodstock Rd A1
Worcester (Coll) B1

Perth 193
AK Bell Library B2
Abbot Cres C1
Abbot St C1
Albany Terr A1
Albert Monument A3
Alexandra St B2
Atholl St A2
Balhousie Ave A2
Balhousie Castle & Black Watch Museum A2
Balhousie St A2
Ballantine Pl A1
Barossa Pl A2
Barossa St A2
Barrack St A2
Bell's Sports Ctr A2
Bellwood B3
Blair St B1
Burn Park C1
Bus Station B2
Caledonian Rd B2
Canal Cres B2
Canal St B3
Cavendish Ave C1
Charles St B2
Charlotte Pl A2
Charlotte St A3
Church St A1
City Hall B3
Club House C3
Clyde Pl C1
Coach Park C3
Commercial St A3
Concert Hall ✦ B3
Council Chambers B3
County Pl B2
Court B3
Craigie Pl C2
Crieff Rd A1
Croft Park C2
Cross St B2
Darnhall Cres C1
Darnhall Dr C1
Dewars Centre B1
Dundee Rd B3
Dunkeld Rd A1
Earl's Dykes B1
Edinburgh Rd C3
Elibank St B1
Fair Maid's Ho ✦ A3
Fergusson B3
Feus Rd A1
Fire Station A1
Foundary La A2
Friar St C1
George St B3
Glamis Pl C1
Glasgow Rd B1
Glenearn Rd C2
Glover St B1/C1
Golf Course A2
Gowrie St A3
Gray St B1
Graybank Rd B1
Greyfriars Burial Gd B3
Hay St A2
High St B2/B3
Inchaffray St A1
Ind/Retail Park B1
Information Ctr B2
Isla Rd A3
James St B2
Keir St A3
King Edward St B3
King James VI Golf Course C3
King St B2
Kings Pl C2
Kinnoull Causeway B2
Kinnoull St B2
Knowelea Pl C1
Knowelea Terr C1
Ladeside Bsns Ctr A1
Leisure Pool B1
Leonard St B2
Lickley St B2
Lochie Brae A3
Long Causeway A1
Low St A2
Main St A3
Marshall Pl C3
Melville St A2
Mill St B3
Milne St B2
Murray Cres C1
Murray St B2
Needless Rd C1
New Rd B2
North Inch A3
North Methven St A2
Park Pl C1
Perth B2
Perth Bridge A3
Perth Business Pk B1
Perth Museum & Art Gallery B3
Perth Station ≥ C2
Pickletulllum Rd B1
Pitheavlis Cres C1
Playhouse B2
Police Station A2
Pomarium St B2
Post Office B2/C2
Princes St B3
Priory Pl C2
Queen St C1
Queen's Bridge B3
Riggs Rd B1
Riverside B3
Riverside Park B3
Rodney Gdns B3
Rose Terr A2
St Catherine's Rd A1/A2
St Catherine's Retail Park A1
St John St B3
St John's Kirk B3
St John's Shopping Centre B2
St Leonards Bridge C2
St Ninians Cath ✝ A2
Scott Monument C2
Scott St B2
Sheriff Court B3
Shore Rd C3
Skate Park C3
South Inch C2
South Inch Bsns Ctr C3
South Inch Park C2
South Inch View C2
South Methven St B2
South St B3
South William St B2
Stables, The A1
Stanners, The B3
Stormont St A2
Strathmore St A3
Stuart Ave C1
Superstore B1/B2
Tay St B3
Union La A2
Victoria St B2
Watergate B3
Wellshill Cemetery A1
West Bridge St A3
West Mill St B2
Whitefriers Cres B1
Whitefriers St B1
Wilson St C1
Windsor Terr C1
Woodside Cres C1
York Pl B2
Young St C1

Peterborough 193
Athletics Arena B3
Bishop's Palace B2
Bishop's Rd B2/B3
Boongate A3
Bourges Boulevard A1
Bourges Retail Park B1/B2
Bridge House (Council Offices) C2
Bridge St B2
Bright St A1
Broadway A2
Broadway A2
Brook St A2
Burghley Rd A2
Bus Station B2
Cavendish St A3
Charles St A3
Church St B2
Church Walk A2
Cobden Ave A1
Cobden St A1
Cowgate B2
Craig St A2
Crawthorne Rd A2
Cromwell Rd A1
Dickens St A3
Eastfield Rd A3
Eastgate B3
East Station Road C2
Fire Station A1
Fletton Ave C2
Frank Perkins Parkway C3
Geneva St A2
George St C1
Gladstone St A1
Glebe Rd C2
Gloucester Rd C3
Granby St B3
Grove St C1
Guildhall B2
Hadrians Ct C3
Hawksbill Way C2
Henry St A2
Hereward Cross (shopping) B2
Hereward Rd B3
Information Ctr B2
Jubilee St C1
Kent Rd B1
Key Theatre C2
Kirkwood Cl B1
Lea Gdns B1
Library A2
Lincoln Rd A2
London Rd C2
Long Causeway B2
Lower Bridge St C2
Magistrates Court B2
Manor House St A2
Mayor's Walk A1
Midland Rd A1
Monument St A2
Morris St A3
Museum & Art Gallery B2
Nene Valley Railway C1
New Rd A2
New Rd C1
Northminster A2
Old Customs Ho C2
Oundle Rd C1
Padholme Rd A3
Palmerston Rd C1
Park Rd A2
Passport Office B2
Peterborough Cathedral ✝ B2
Peterborough Nene Valley C1
Peterborough Station ≥ B1
Police Station B2
Post Office A3/B2
Priestgate B2
Queen's Walk C2
Queensgate Centre B2
Railworld Wildlife Haven C1
Regional Fitness & Swimming Centre B3
River La B1
Rivergate Shopping Centre B2
Riverside Mead C3
Russell St A1
St John's B2
St John's St A3
St Marks St A2
St Peter's Rd B2
Saxon Rd A3
Spital Bridge A1
Stagshaw Dr C3
Star Rd B3
Superstore B1
Thorpe Lea Rd B1
Thorpe Rd B1
Thorpe's Lea Rd B1
Tower St A2
Town Hall B2
Viersen Platz B2
Vineyard Rd B3
Wake Rd B3
Wellington St A3
Wentworth St B2
Westgate B2
Weston Homes Stadium (Peterborough United FC) The C2
Whalley St A3
Wharf Rd C1
Whitsed St A3
YMCA A3

Plymouth 193
Alma Rd A1
Anstis St B1
Armada Shopping Centre B2
Armada St A3
Armada Way B2
Arts Centre B2
Athenaeum B1
Athenaeum St C1
Barbican C3
Barbican C3
Baring St A3
Bath St B1
Beaumont Park B3
Beaumont Rd B3
Black Friars Gin Distillery ✦ C2
Breton Side B3
Castle St C3
Cathedral (RC) ✝ B1
Cecil St B1
Central Park A1
Central Park Ave A2
Charles Church B3
Charles Cross B3
Charles St B2
Citadel Rd C2
Citadel Rd East C2
City Museum & Art Gallery B2
Civic Centre B2
Cliff Rd C1
Clifton Pl A3
Cobourg St A2
College of Art B2
Continental Ferry Port B1
Cornwall St B2
Crescent, The B1
Dale Rd A2
Deptford Pl A3
Derry Ave A2
Derry's Cross B1
Drake Circus B2
Drake Circus Shopping Centre B2
Eastlake St B2
Ebrington St B3
Elizabethan Ho C3
Elliot St C1
Endsleigh Pl A2
Exeter St B3
Fire Station A3
Fish Quay C3
Gibbons St A3
Glen Park Ave A2
Grand Parade C1
Great Western Rd C1
Greenbank Rd A3
Greenbank Terr A3
Guildhall B2
Hampton St B3
Harwell St B1
Hill Park Cr A3
Hoe Approach B2
Hoe Rd C2
Hoe, The C2
Hoegate St C2
Houndiscombe Rd A2
Information Ctr C3
James St A2
Kensington Rd A3
King St B1
Lambhay Hill C3
Leigham St C1
Library B2
Lipson Rd A3/B3
Lockyer St C2
Lockyers Quay C3
Madeira Rd C2
Marina B3
Market Ave B1
Martin St B1
Mayflower St B2
Mayflower Stone & Steps ✦ C3
Mayflower Visitor Centre ✦ C3
Merchant's Ho B2
Millbay Rd B1
National Marine Aquarium C3
Neswick St B1
New George St B2
New St C3
North Cross A2
North Hill A3
North Quay B2
North Rd East A2
North Rd West A1
North St B3
Notte St B2
Octagon, The B1
Octagon St B1
Pannier Market B1
Pennycomequick A1
Pier St C1
Plymouth Naval Memorial ✦ C2
Plymouth Pavilions B1
Plymouth Sta ≥ A2
Police Station B3
Post Office C2
Princess St B2
Promenade, The C2
Prysten House B2
Queen Anne's Battery Seasports Centre C3
Radford Rd C1
Reel B2
Regent St B3
Rope Walk C3
Royal Citadel C2
Royal Pde B2
Royal Theatre B2
St Andrew's B2
St Andrew's Cross B2
St Andrew's St B2
St Lawrence Rd A2
Saltash Rd A2
Shopmobility B2
Smeaton's Tower ✦ C2
Southern Terr A3
Southside St C2
Stuart Rd A1
Sutherland Rd A2
Sutton Rd B3
Sydney St A1
Teats Hill Rd C3
Tothill Ave B3
Union St B1
Univ of Plymouth A2
Vauxhall St B2/3
Victoria Park A1
West Hoe Rd C1
Western Approach B1
Whittington St A1
Wyndham St B1
YMCA B2
YWCA C2

Poole 194
Ambulance Station A3
Baiater Gdns C2
Baiter Park C3
Ballard Cl C2
Ballard Rd C2
Bay Hog La B1
BMI The Harbour Hospital H A3
Bridge Approach C1
Bus Station B2
Castle St B2
Catalina Dr B3
Chapel La B2
Church St B1
Cinnamon La B1
Colborne Cl B3
Dear Hay La B2
Denmark La A3
Denmark Rd A3
Dolphin Ctr B2
East St B2
Elizabeth Rd A3
Emerson Rd B2
Ferry Rd C1
Ferry Terminal C1
Fire Station A2
Freightliner Terminal C1
Furnell Rd B3
Garland Rd A3
Green Rd B2
Heckford La A3
Heckford Rd A3
High St B2
High St North A3
Hill St B2
Holes Bay Rd A1
Hospital (A&E) A3
Information Ctr C2
Kingland Rd B3
Kingston Rd A3
Labrador Dr C3
Lagland St B2
Lander Cl C3
Lighthouse, Poole Centre for the Arts ✦ B3
Longfleet Rd A3
Maple Rd A3
Market Cl B2
Market St B2
Mount Pleasant Rd B3
New Harbour Rd C1
New Harbour Rd South C1
New Harbour Rd West C1
New Orchard B1
New Quay Rd C1
New St B2
Newfoundland Dr B2
North St B2
Old Lifeboat C2
Old Orchard B2
Parish Rd A3
Park Lake Rd B3
Parkstone Rd A3
Perry Gdns B2
Pitwines Cl B2
Police Station A2
Poole Central Liby B2
Poole Lifting Bridge C1
Poole Park B2
Poole Station ≥ A2
Poole Museum C1
Post Office B2
Quay, The C2
RNLI College B1
St John's Rd A3
St Margaret's Rd A2
St Mary's Maternity Unit A3
St Mary's Rd A3
Seldown Bridge B3
Seldown La B3
Seldown Rd B3
Serpentine Rd A2
Scaplen's Court C1
Shaftesbury Rd A3
Skinner St B2
Slipway B1
Stanley Rd C2
Sterte Ave A2
Sterte Ave West A1
Sterte Cl A2
Sterte Esplanade A2
Sterte Rd A2
Strand St C2
Superstore B3
Swimming Pool B3
Taverner Cl B3
Thames St B1
Towngate Bridge B2
Twin Sails Bridge B1
Vallis Cl C3
Waldren Cl B3
West Quay B1
West Quay Rd B1
West St B1
West View Rd A2
Whatleigh Cl B2
Wimborne Rd A3

Portsmouth 194
Action Stations ✦ C1
Admiralty Rd A1
Alfred Rd A2
Anglesea Rd B2
Arundel St B3
Aspex B1
Bishop St A2
Broad St C1
Buckingham Ho C2
Burnaby Rd B2
Bus Station B1
Camber Dock C1
Cambridge Rd B2
Car Ferry to Isle of Wight B1
Cascades Shopping Centre A3
Castle Rd C3
Civic Offices B3
Clarence Pier C2
College St B1
Commercial Rd A3
Cottage Gr B3
Cross St A1
Cumberland St A2
Duisburg Way C2
Durham St A3
East St B1
Edinburgh Rd A2
Elm Gr C3
Emirates Spinnaker Tower ✦ B1
Governor's Grn C1
Great Southsea St C3
Green Rd B3
Greetham St B3
Grosvenor St B3
Groundlings A2
Grove Rd North C3
Grove Rd South C3
Guildhall B3
Guildhall Walk B3
Gunwharf Quays Designer Outlet B1
Gunwharf Rd B1
Hambrook St C2
Hampshire Terr B2
Hanover St A1
Hard, The B1
High St C2
HM Naval Base A1
HMS Nelson (Royal Naval Barracks) A2
HMS Monitor M. 33 A1
HMS Victory A1
HMS Warrior A1
Hovercraft Terminal C2
Hyde Park Rd B3
Information Ctr A1/B3
Isambard Brunel Rd B3
Isle of Wight Car Ferry Terminal B1
Kent Rd C3
Kent St A2
King St B3
King's Rd C3
King's Terr C2
Lake Rd A3
Law Courts B3
Library B3
Long Curtain Rd C2
Marina B1
Market Way A3
Marmion Rd C3
Mary Rose A1
Middle St B3

Millennium Promenade Walk B1/C1
Museum Rd B2
National Museum of the Royal Navy A1
Naval Rec Gd C2
Nightingale Rd C3
Norfolk St B3
North St A2
Osborne Rd C3
Paradise St A3
Park Rd B2
Passenger Catamaran to Isle of Wight B1
Passenger Ferry to Gosport B1
Pelham Rd C3
Pembroke Gdns C2
Pier Rd C2
Point Battery C1
Police Station B3
Portsmouth & Southsea Sta A3
Portsmouth Harbour Station B1
Portsmouth Historic Dockyard A1
Portsmouth Museum & Art Gallery B2
Post Office A1/A3/B3
Queen St A1
Queen's Cr C3
Ravelin Park B2
Register Office B2
Round Tower C1
Royal Garrison Church C1
St Edward's Rd C3
St George's Rd B2
St George's Sq B1
St George's Way B2
St James's Rd B3
St James's St A2
St John's Cathedral (RC) A3
St Thomas's Cathedral C1
St Thomas's St B2
Shopmobility A3/B1
Somers Rd B3
Southsea Common C2
Southsea Terr C2
Square Tower C1
Station St A3
Town Fortifications C1
Unicorn Rd A2
United Services Recreation Gd B2
University of Portsmouth A2/B2
Univ of Portsmouth B3
Upper Arundel St A3
Victoria Ave C2
Victoria Park A2
Victory Gate A1
Vue B1
Warblington St B1
Western Pde C2
White Hart Rd C1
Winston Churchill Ave B3

Preston 194

Adelphi St A2
Anchor Ct B3
Aqueduct St A1
Ardee Rd C1
Arthur St B2
Ashton St A1
Avenham La B3
Avenham Park C3
Avenham Rd B3
Avenham St B3
Bairstow St B3
Balderstone Rd C1
Beamont Dr A1
Beech St South C2
Bird St C1
Bow La B2
Brieryfield Rd A1
Broadgate C1
Brook St A2
Bus Station A3
Butler St B2
Cannon St B3
Carlton St A1
Chaddock St B3
Channel Way B1
Chapel St B3
Christ Church St B2
Christian Rd B2
Cold Bath St A2
Coleman Ct C1
Connaught Rd C2
Corn Exchange B3
Corporation St A2/B2
County Hall B2
Cricket Ground C2
Croft St A1
Cross St B3
Crown Court A3
Crown St A3
East Cliff C3
East Cliff Rd B3
Edward St A2
Elizabeth St A3
Euston St B1
Fishergate B2/B3
Fishergate Hill B2
Fishergate Shopping Centre B2
Fitzroy St B1
Fleetwood St A1
Friargate A3
Fylde Rd A1/A2
Gerrard St B2
Glover's Ct B3
Good St B2
Grafton St B2
Great George St A3
Great Shaw St A3
Greenbank St A2
Guild Way B1
Guild Hall & Charter B3
Guildhall St B3
Harrington St A2
Harris Museum B3
Hartington Rd B1
Hasset Cl C2
Heatley St B2
Hind St C2
Information Ctr B3
Kilruddery Rd C1
Lancashire Archives B2
Lancaster Rd A3/B3
Latham St B3
Lauderdale St C2
Lawson St A3
Leighton St A2
Leyland Rd C1
Library A1
Library B3
Liverpool Rd C1
Lodge St B2
Lune St B3
Magistrate's Court A3
Main Sprit West B3
Maresfield Rd C1
Market St West A3
Marsh La B1/B2
Maudland Bank A2
Maudland Rd A2
Meadow Ct C2
Meath Rd C1
Mill Hill A2
Miller Arcade B3
Miller Park C3
Moor La A3
Mount St B3
North Rd A3
North St A3
Northcote Rd B1
Old Milestones B1
Old Tram Rd C3
Pedder St A1/A2
Peel St A2
Penwortham Bridge C2
Penwortham New Bridge C1
Pitt St B2
Playhouse A3
Police Station A3
Port Way B1
Post Office B3
Preston Station B2
Retail Park B2
Ribble Bank St B2
Ribble Viaduct C2
Ribblesdale Pl B3
Ringway B3
River Parade C1
Riverside C2
St George's Shopping Centre B3
St Georges B3
St Johns B3
St Johns Shopping Centre A3
St Mark's Rd A1
St Walburges A1
Salisbury Rd B1
Sessions House B3
Snow Hill A3
South End C2
South Meadow La C2
Spa Rd B1
Sports Ground C2
Strand Rd B1
Syke St B3
Talbot Rd B1
Taylor St C1
Tithebarn St A3
Town Hall B3
Tulketh Brow A1
University of Central Lancashire A2
Valley Rd C1
Victoria St A2
Walker St A3
Walton's Parade B2
Warwick St A3
Wellfield Bsns Park A1
Wellfield Rd A1
Wellington St A1
West Cliff C2
West Strand A1
Winckley Rd C1
Winckley Square B3
Wolseley Rd C2

Reading 194

Abbey Ruins B2
Abbey Sq B2
Abbey St B2
Abbot's Walk B2
Acacia Rd C2
Addington Rd C3
Addison Rd A1
Allcroft Rd C3
Alpine St C2
Baker St B1
Berkeley Ave C1
Bridge St B1
Brigham Rd A1
Broad St B1
Broad Street Mall B1
Carey St B1
Castle Hill C1
Castle St B1
Causeway, The A3
Caversham Rd A1
Christchurch Meadows A2
Civic Offices B1
Coley Hill C1
Coley Pl C1
Craven Rd C3
Crown St C2
De Montfort Rd A1
Denmark Rd C3
Duke St B2
East St B2
Edgehill St C2
Eldon Rd B3
Eldon Terr B3
Elgar Rd C1
Erleigh Rd C3
Field Rd C1
Fire Station A1
Fobney St B1
Forbury Gdns B2
Forbury Rd B2
Forbury Retail Park B2
Francis St C1
Friar St B1
Garrard St B1
Gas Works Rd B3
George St A2
Great Knollys St B1
Greyfriars B1
Grove, The B2
Gun St B1
Henry St C1
Hexagon Theatre, The B1
Hill's Meadow A2
Howard St B1
Inner Distribution Rd B1
Katesgrove La C1
Kenavon Dr B2
Kendrick Rd C2
King's Mdw Rec Gd A2
King's Rd B2
Library B2
London Rd C3
London St B2
Lynmouth Rd A1
Magistrate's Court B1
Market Pl B2
Mill La B2
Mill Rd A2
Minster St B1
Morgan Rd C3
Mount Pleasant C2
Mus of English Rural Life (MERL) C3
Napier Rd A2
Newark St C2
Newport Rd A1
Oracle Shopping Centre, The B1
Orts Rd B3
Oxford Road B1
Pell St C1
Post Office B2
Queen Victoria St B1
Queen's Rd A2
Queen's Rd B2
Randolph Rd A1
Reading Bridge A2
Reading College B3
Reading Station A1
Redlands Rd C3
Riverside Mus B3
Rose Kiln La C1
Royal Berkshire Medical Mus C3
Royal Berks Hospital (A&E) C3
St Giles C2
St Laurence B2
St Mary's B1
St Mary's Butts B1
St Saviour's Rd C1
Send Rd A3
Sherman Rd C2
Sidmouth St B2
Silver St C2
South St B2
South St Arts Ctr B2
Southampton St C2
Station Rd B1
Superstore A3
Swansea Rd A1
Thames Lido A2
Tudor Road A1
Univ of Reading C3
Valpy St B2
Vastern Rd A1
Vue B2
Waldeck St C2
Watlington St B3
West St B1
Whitby Dr C3
Wolseley St C1
York Rd A1
Zinzan St B1

St Andrews 195

Abbey St B2
Abbey Walk B3
Abbotsford Cres A1
Albany Pk C3
Allan Robertson Dr C2
Ambulance Station C1
Anstruther Rd C3
Argyle St B1
Auld Burn Rd B2
Bassaguard Ind Est B1
Bell St B2
Blackfriars Chapel (Ruins) B2
Boase Ave B2
Braid Cres C3
Brewster Pl C3
Bridge St B1
British Golf Mus A1
Broomfaulds Ave C1
Bruce Embankment A1
Bruce St C2
Bus Station A1
Byre Theatre B2
Canongate C1
Cathedral and Priory (Ruins) B3
Cemetery B1
Chamberlain St C1
Church St B2
Churchill Cres C2
City Rd A1
Claybraes C1
Cockshaugh Public Park B1
Cosmos Com Ctr B3
Council Office A2
Crawford Gdns C1
Doubledykes Rd B1
Drumcarrow Rd C1
East Sands B3
East Scores A3
Fire Station C1
Forrest St C1
Fraser Ave C1
Freddie Tait St C2
Gateway Centre A1
Glebe Rd B2
Golf Pl A1
Grange Rd C3
Greenside Pl B2
Greyfriars Gdns A2
Hamilton Ave C2
Hepburn Gdns B1
Holy Trinity B2
Horseleys Park C1
Information Ctr B2
Irvine Cres C3
James Robb Ave C1
James St B1
John Knox Rd C1
Kennedy Gdns B1
Kilrymont Cl C3
Kilrymont Pl C3
Kilrymont Rd C3
Kinburn Park B1
Kinkell Terr C3
Kinnesburn Rd B2
Ladebraes Walk B2
Lady Buchan's Cave A3
Lamberton Pl C1
Lamond Dr C2
Langlands Rd B2
Largo Rd C1
Learmonth Pl C1
Library B2
Links Clubhouse A1
Links, The A1
Livingstone Cres B2
Long Rocks A2
Madras College B2
Market St A2
Martyr's Monument A1
Murray Pk A2
Murray Pl A2
Museum of the University of St Andrews (MUSA) A2
Nelson St B2
New Course, The A1
New Picture Ho A2
North Castle St A3
North St A2
Old Course, The A1
Old Station Rd A1
Pends, The B3
Pilmour Links A1
Pipeland Rd B2/C2
Police Sta A2/C1
Post Office B2
Preservation Trust B2
Priestden Pk C3
Priestden Pl C3
Priestden Rd C3
Queen's Gdns B2
Queen's Terr B2
Roundhill Rd C2
Royal & Ancient Golf Club A1
St Andrews B1
St Andrews Aquarium A2
St Andrews Botanic Garden B1
St Andrews Castle (Ruins) & Visitor Centre A2
St Leonard's School B3
St Mary St B3
St Mary's College B2
St Nicholas St C3
St Rules Tower B3
St Salvator's Coll A2
Sandyhill Cres C2
Sandyhill Rd C2
Scooniehill Rd C2
Scores, The A2
Shields Ave C3
Shoolbraids C2
Shore, The B3
Sloan St B1
South St B2
Spottiswoode Gdns C1
Station Rd A1
Swilcen Bridge A1
Tom Morris Dr C2
Tom Stewart La C1
Town Hall B2
Union St A2
Univ Chapel A2
University Library A2
University of St Andrews A1
Viaduct Walk B1
War Memorial A3
Wardlaw Gdns B1
Warrack St C3
Watson Ave B2
West Port B2
West Sands A1
Westview B2
Windmill Rd A1
Winram Pl C1
Wishart Gdns C2
Woodburn Pk B3
Woodburn Pl B3
Woodburn Terr B3
Younger Hall A2

Salisbury 195

Albany Rd A2
Arts Centre A3
Ashley Rd A1
Avon Approach A2
Ayleswade Rd C2
Bedwin St A2
Belle Vue A2
Bishops Walk B2
Blue Boar Row B2
Bourne Ave A3
Bourne Hill A3
Britford La C2
Broad Walk C2
Brown St B2
Castle St A2
Catherine St B2
Chapter House B2
Church House B2
Churchfields Rd B1
Churchill Gdns C3
Churchill Way East B3
Churchill Way North A3
Churchill Way South C2
Churchill Way West A1
City Hall B2
Close Wall B2
Coldharbour La A1
College St A3
Council and Registry Offices A3
Court A1
Crane Bridge Rd B2
Crane St B2
Cricket Ground C1
Culver St South B3
De Vaux Pl C2
Devizes Rd A1
Dews Rd B1
Elm Grove B3
Elm Grove Rd A3
Endless St A2
Estcourt Rd A3
Exeter St C2
Fairview Rd A3
Fire Station A1
Fisherton St A1
Folkestone Rd C1
Fowlers Hill B3
Fowlers Rd B3
Friary La B2
Friary, The B3
Gas La A1
Gigant St B3
Greencroft B3
Greencroft St A3
Guildhall B2
Hall of John Halle B2
Hamilton Rd A2
Harnham Mill B1
Harnham Rd C1/C2
High St B2
House of John A'Port B2
Information Ctr B2
Kelsey Rd A3
King's Rd A2
Laverstock Rd B3
Library A2
London Rd A3
Lower St C1
Maltings, The B2
Manor Rd A3
Marsh La A1
Medieval Hall B2
Milford Hill B3
Milford St B3
Mill Rd B1
Mill Stream App A2
Mompesson Ho B2
New Bridge Rd C2
New Canal B2
New Harnham Rd C2
New St B2
North Canonry B2
North Gate B2
North Walk B2
Old Blandford Rd C1
Old Deanery B2
Old George Hall B2
Park St A3
Parsonage Green C1
Playhouse Theatre A2
Police Station A3
Post Office A2/B2
Poultry Cross B2
Queen Elizabeth Gdns B1
Queen's Rd A3
Rampart Rd B3
Rifles, The B2
St Ann St B2
St Ann's Gate B2
St Marks Rd A3
St Martins B3
St Paul's A1
St Paul's Rd A1
St Thomas B2
Salisbury Cathedral B2
Salisbury Cathedral School (Bishop's Palace) C2
Salisbury Museum, The B2
Salisbury Station A1
Salt La A3
Saxon Rd C1
Scots La A2
Shady Bower B3
Shopmobility B2
South Canonry C2
South Gate C2
Southampton Rd B2
Spire View A1
Sports Ground C3
Tollgate Rd B3
Town Path B1
Wain-a-Long Rd A3
Wessex Rd A3
West Walk C2
Wilton Rd A1
Wiltshire College B3
Winchester St B3
Windsor Rd A1
Wyndham Rd A2
YHA B3
York Rd A1

Scarborough 195

Aberdeen Walk B2
Albert Rd A2
Albion Rd C2
Auborough St B2
Balmoral Ctr B2
Belle Vue St C1
Belmont Rd C2
Blenheim Terrace A2
Brunswick Shopping Ctr B2
Castle Dykes B3
Castle Hill A3
Castle Rd B2
Castle Walls A3
Castlegate B3
Cemetery C1
Central Tramway B2
Coach Park B1
Columbus Ravine A1
Court B1
Crescent, The C2
Cricket Ground A1
Cross St B2
Crown Terr C2
Dean Rd B1
Devonshire Dr A1
East Harbour B3
East Pier B3
Eastborough B2
Elmville Ave B1
Esplanade C2
Falconers Rd B2
Falsgrave Rd C1
Fire Station B2
Foreshore Rd B2
Friargate B2
Gladstone Rd B1
Gladstone St B1
Hollywood Plaza A1
Holms, The A3
Hoxton Rd B1
King St B2
Library B2
Lifeboat Station B3
Londesborough Rd C1
Longwestgate B3
Marine Dr A3
Luna Park B3
Miniature Railway A1
Nelson St B1
Newborough B2
Nicolas St B2
North Marine Rd A1
North St B2
Northway B1
Old Harbour B3
Olympia Leisure B2
Peasholm Park A1
Peasholm Rd A1
Police Station B1
Post Office B2/C1
Princess St B3
Prospect Rd B1
Queen St B2
Queen's Parade A2
Queen's Tower (Remains) A3
Ramshill Rd C2
Roman Signal Station A3
Roscoe St C1
Rotunda Mus C2
Royal Albert Dr A2
Royal Albert Park A2
St Martin-on-the-Hill C2
St Martin's Ave C2
St Mary's B3
St Thomas St B2
Sandside B3
Scarborough C1
Scarborough Art Gallery C2
Scarborough Bowls Centre A1
Scarborough Castle A3
Shopmobility C2
Somerset Terr C2
South Cliff Lift C2
Spa Theatre, The C2
Spa, The C2
Stephen Joseph Theatre C1
Tennyson Ave B1
Tollergate B2
Town Hall B2
Trafalgar Rd B1
Trafalgar Square A1
Trafalgar St West B1
Valley Bridge Par C2
Valley Rd C1
Vernon Rd C2
Victoria Park Mt A1
Victoria Rd B1
West Pier B3
Westborough C1
Westover Rd C1
Westwood C1
Woodall Ave A1
YMCA Theatre B2
York Pl B2
Yorkshire Coast College (Westwood Campus) C1

Sheffield 196

Addy Dr A2
Addy St A2
Adelphi St A3
Albert Terrace Rd A3
Albion St A2
Aldred Rd A1
Allen St A4
Alma St A4
Angel St B5
Arundel Gate B5
Arundel St C4
Ashberry Rd A2
Ashdell Rd C1
Ashgate Rd C1
Athletics Centre B2
Attercliffe Rd A6
Bailey St B4
Ball St A4
Balm Green B4
Bank St B4
Barber Rd A2
Bard St B5
Barker's Pool B4
Bates St A1
Beech Hill Rd C1
Beet St B3
Bellefield St A3
Bernard Rd A6
Bernard St B6
Birkendale A2
Birkendale Rd A2
Birkendale View A1
Bishop St C4
Blackwell Pl B6
Blake St A2
Blonk St A5
Bolsover St B2
Botanical Gdns C1
Bower Rd A1
Bradley St A1
Bramall La C4
Bramwell St A3
Bridge St A4/A5
Brighton Terrace Rd A1
Broad La B3
Broad St B6
Brocco St A3
Brook Hill B3
Broomfield Rd C1
Broomgrove Rd C2
Broomhall Pl C3
Broomhall Rd C2
Broomhall St C3
Broomspring La C2
Brown St C5
Brunswick St B3
Burgess St B4
Burlington St A2
Burns Rd A2
Cadman St A6
Cambridge St B4
Campo La B4
Carver St B4
Castle Square B5
Castlegate A5
Cathedral B4
Cathedral (RC) B4
Cavendish St B3
Charles St C4
Charter Row C4
Children's Hosp B2
Church St B4
City Hall B4
City Hall B4
City Rd C6
Claremont Cr B2
Claremont Pl B2
Clarke St C3
Clarkegrove Rd C2
Clarkehouse Rd C1
Clarkson St B2
Cobden View Rd A1
Collegiate Cr C2
Commercial St B5
Commonside A1
Conduit Rd B1
Cornish St A3
Corporation St A4
Cricket Inn Rd B6
Cromwell St A1
Crookes Rd B1
Crookes Valley Park B2
Crookes Valley Rd B2
Crookesmoor Rd A2
Crown Court A4
Crucible Theatre B5
Cutlers' Hall B4
Cutlers Gate A6
Daniel Hill A2
Dental Hospital B2
Derek Dooley Way A5
Devonshire Green B3
Devonshire St B3
Division St B4
Dorset St C2
Dover St A3
Duchess Rd C5
Duke St B5
Duncombe St A1
Durham Rd B2
Earl St C4
Earl Way C4
Ecclesall Rd C3
Edward St B3
Effingham Rd A6
Effingham St A6
Egerton St C3
Eldon St B3
Elmore Rd B1
Exchange St B5
Eyre St C4
Fargate B4
Farm Rd C5
Fawcett St A3
Filey St B3
Fir St A1
Fire Station C4
Fitzalan Sq/Ponds Forge B5
Fitzwater Rd C6
Fitzwilliam Gate C4
Fitzwilliam St B3
Flat St B5
Foley St A6
Foundry Climbing Centre A4
Fulton Rd A1
Furnace Hill A4
Furnival Rd A5
Furnival Sq C4
Furnival St C4
Garden St B3
Gell St B3
Gibraltar St A4
Glebe Rd B1
Glencoe Rd C6
Glossop Rd B2/B3/C1
Gloucester St C2
Government Offices C4
Granville Rd C6
Granville Rd / The Sheffield Coll C5
Graves Gallery B5
Green La A4
Hadfield St A1
Hanover St C3
Hanover Way C3
Harcourt Rd B1
Harmer La B5
Havelock St C2
Hawley St B4
Haymarket B5
Headford St C3
Heavygate Rd A1
Henry St A3
High St B4
Hodgson St C3
Holberry Gdns C2
Hollis Croft B4
Holly St B4
Hounsfield Rd B3
Howard Rd A1
Hoyle St A3
Hyde Park A6
Infirmary Rd A3
Infirmary Rd A3
Jericho St A3
Johnson St A5
Kelham Island Industrial Mus A4
Lawson Rd C1
Leadmill Rd C5
Leadmill St C5
Leadmill, The C5
Leamington St A1
Leavygreave Rd B3
Lee Croft B4
Leopold St B4
Leveson St A6
Library A2/B5/C1
Light, The C4
Lyceum Theatre B5
Malinda St A3
Maltravers St A5
Manor Oaks Rd B6
Mappin St B3
Marlborough Rd B1
Mary St C4
Matilda St C4
Matlock Rd A1
Meadow St A3
Melbourn Rd A1
Melbourne Ave C1
Millennium Galleries B5
Milton St C3
Mitchell St B3
Mona Ave A1
Mona Rd A1
Montgomery Terrace Rd A3
Montgomery Theatre B4
Monument Grounds C6
Moor Oaks Rd B1
Moor, The C4
Moor Market C4
Moore St C3
Mowbray St A4
Mushroom La B2
National Emergency Service A4
National Videogame B5
Netherthorpe Rd B3
Netherthorpe Rd B3
Newbould La C1
Nile St C1
Norfolk Park Rd C6
Norfolk Rd C6
Norfolk St B4
North Church St B4
Northfield Rd A1
Northumberland Rd B1
Nursery St A5
O2 Academy B5
Oakholme Rd C1
Octagon B2
Odeon B5
Old St B6
Orchard Square Shopping Centre B4
Oxford St A2
Paradise St B4
Park La C2
Park Sq B5
Parker's Rd B1
Pearson Building (University) C2
Penistone Rd A3
Pinstone St B4
Pitt St B3
Police Station B5
Pond Hill B5
Pondorosa, The A2
Pond St B5
Ponds Forge Int Sports Ctr B5
Portobello St B3
Post Office A2/B3/B5/C1/C3/C4/C6
Powell St A2
Queen St B4
Queen's Rd C5
Ramsey Rd B1
Red Hill B3
Redcar Rd B1
Regent St B3
Rockingham St B4
Roebuck Rd A2
Royal Hallamshire Hospital C2
Russell St A4
Rutland Park C1
St George's Cl B3
St Mary's Gate C3
St Mary's Rd C4/C5
St Philip's Rd A3
Savile St A5
School Rd B1
Scotland St A4
Severn Rd B1
Shalesmoor A4
Shalesmoor A3
Sheaf St B5
Sheffield Cath B4
Sheffield Hallam University B5
Sheffield Ice Sports Ctr – Skate Central C5
Sheffield Institute of Arts B5
Sheffield Interchange B5
Sheffield Parkway A6
Sheffield Station C5
Sheffield Station/ Sheffield Hallam University B5
Sheffield University B2
Shepherd St A3
Shipton St A2
Shopmobility B3
Shoreham St C4
Showroom C5
Shrewsbury Rd C5
Sidney St C4
Site Gallery C5
Slinn St A1
Smithfield A4
Snig Hill A5
Snow La A4
Solly St B3
South La C4
South Street Park B5
Southbourne Rd C1
Spital Hill A5
Spital St A5
Spring Hill B1
Spring Hill Rd B1
Springvale Rd A1
Stafford Rd C6
Stafford St B6
Suffolk Rd C5
Summer St B2
Sunny Bank C3
Superstore A3/C3
Surrey St B4
Sussex St A6
Sutton St B3
Sydney Rd A2
Sylvester St C4
Talbot St B5
Taptonville Rd B1
Tenter St B4
Town Hall B4
Townend St A1
Townhead St B4
Trafalgar St B4
Tree Root Walk B2
Trinity St A4
Trippet La B4
Turner Museum of Glass B3
Union St B4
University Drama Studio B2
Univ of Sheffield B3
Upper Allen St A3
Upper Hanover St B3
Upperthorpe Rd A2/A3
Verdon St A5
Victoria Rd C2
Victoria St B3
Waingate B5
Watery St A3
Watson Rd C1
Wellesley Rd B2
Wellington St C3
West Bar A4
West Bar Green A4
West One Plaza B3
West St B3
West St B4
Westbourne Rd C1
Western Bank B2
Western Rd A1
Weston Park B2
Weston Park Hospital B2
Weston Park Mus B2
Weston St B2
Wharncliffe Rd C3
Whitham Rd B1
Wicker A5
Wilkinson St B2
William St C3
Winter Garden B4
Winter St B2
York St B4
Yorkshire Artspace C5
Young St C4

Shrewsbury 195

Abbey Foregate B3
Abbey Gardens B2
Abbey Lawn Business Park B3
Abbots House B2
Albert St A2
Alma St B1
Ashley St A3
Ashton Rd C1
Avondale Dr A3
Bage Way C3
Barker St B1
Beacall's La A2
Beeches La C2
Beehive La C1
Belle Vue Gdns C2
Belle Vue Rd C2
Belmont Bank C1
Berwick Ave A1
Berwick Rd A1
Betton St C2
Bishop St B3
Bradford St B3
Bridge St B1
Burton St A3
Bus Station B2
Butcher Row B2
Butler Rd C1
Bynner St C2
Canon St B3
Canonbury C1
Castle Business Park, The A2
Castle Foregate A2
Castle Gates B2
Castle Walk B3
Castle St B2
Cathedral (RC) C1
Chester St A2
Cineworld C3
Claremont Bank B1
Claremont Hill B1
Cleveland St B3
Coleham Head B2
Coleham Pumping Station C2
College Hill B1
Corporation La A1
Coton Cres A1
Coton Hill A2
Coton Mount A1
Crescent La C1
Crewe St A2
Cross Hill B1
Dana, The B2
Darwin Centre B2
Dingle, The B1
Dogpole B2
English Bridge B2
Fish St B2
Frankwell B1
Gateway Ctr, The A2
Gravel Hill La A1
Greenhous West Mid Showground A1
Greyfriars Rd C2
Hampton Rd A3
Haycock Way C3
High St B1
Hills La B1
Holywell St B3
Hunter St A1
Information Ctr B1
Ireland's Mansion & Bear Steps B1
John St A3
Kennedy Rd C1
King St B3
Kingsland Bridge C1
Kingsland Bridge (toll) C1
Kingsland Rd C1
Library B2
Lime St C2
Longden Coleham C2
Longden Rd C1
Longner St B1
Luciefelde Rd C1
Mardol B1
Marine Terr C2
Market B1
Monkmoor Rd B3
Moreton Cr C2
Mount St A1
New Park Cl A3
New Park Rd A2
New Park St A3
North St A2
Oakley St C1
Old Coleham C2
Old Market Hall B1
Old Potts Way C3
Parade Shopping Centre, The B2
Police Station B1
Post Office B1/B2/B3
Pride Hill B1
Pride Hill Centre B1
Priory Rd B1
Pritchard Way C3
Quarry Swimming & Fitness Ctr, The B1
Queen St A3
Raby Cr C2
Rad Brook C1
Rea Brook C3
Rea Brook Valley Country Park & Local Nature Reserve C3
Riverside B1
Roundhill La A1
St Alkmund's B2
St Chad's B1
St Chad's Terr B1
St John's Hill B1
St Julians Friars C2
St Mary's B2
St Mary's St B2
Salters La C2
Scott St C3
Severn Theatre B1
Severn Bank A3
Severn St A2
Shrewsbury B2
Shrewsbury Abbey B3
Shrewsbury High School C1
Shrewsbury Museum & Art Gallery B1
Shrewsbury Prison Tours B2
Shrewsbury School C1
Shropshire Regimental Mus B2
Shropshire Wildlife Trust B3
Smithfield Rd B1
South Hermitage C1
Square, The B1
Superstore C3
Swan Hill B1
Sydney Ave A3
Tankerville St B3
Tilbrook Dr A3
Town Walls C1
Trinity St C2
Underdale Rd B3
University Centre Shrewsbury (Guildhall) B1
Victoria Ave B1
Victoria Quay B1
Victoria St B2
Welsh Bridge B1
Whitehall St B3
Wood St A2
Wyle Cop B2

Southampton 196

Above Bar St A2
Albert Rd North B3
Albert Rd South C3
Andersons Rd B3
Argyle Rd A2
Arundel Tower B1
Bargate, The B2
BBC Regional Ctr A1
Bedford Pl A1
Belvidere Rd A3
Bernard St C2
Blechynden Terr A1
Brinton's Rd A2
Britannia Rd A3
Briton St C2
Brunswick Pl A2
Bugle St C1
Canute Rd C3
Castle Way C2
Catchcold Tower B1
Central Bridge C3
Central Rd C2
Channel Way C3
Chapel Rd B3
City Art Gallery A1
City College B3
City Cruise Terminal C1
Civic Centre A1
Civic Centre Rd A1
Coach Station B1
Commercial Rd A1
Cumberland Pl A1
Cunard Rd C2
Derby Rd A3
Devonshire Rd A1
Dock Gate 4 C2
Dock Gate 8 B1
East Park (Andrew's Park) A2
East Park Terr A2
East St B2
Endle St B3
European Way C2
Fire Station A2
Floating Bridge Rd C3
God's House Tower C2
Golden Grove A3
Graham Rd A2
Guildhall A1
Hanover Bldgs B2
Harbour Lights C3
Harbour Pde B1
Hartington Rd A3
Havelock Rd A1
Henstead Rd A1
Herbert Walker Ave B1
High St B2
Hoglands Park B2
Holy Rood (Rems), Merchant Navy Memorial B2
Houndwell Park B2
Houndwell Pl B2
Hythe Ferry C2
Information Ctr A1
Isle of Wight Ferry Terminal C1
James St B3
Kingsway A2
Leisure World B1
Library A1
Lime St B2
London Rd A2
Marine Pde B3
Marlands Shopping Ctr, The A1
Marsh La B2
Mayflower Meml C1
Mayflower Park C1
Mayflower Theatre, The A1
Medieval Merchant's House C1
Melbourne St B3
Millais A2
Morris Rd A1
National Oceanography Centre C3
Neptune Way C3
New Rd A2
Nichols Rd A3
North Front A2
Northam Rd A3
Ocean Dock C2
Ocean Village Marina C3
Ocean Way C3
Odeon B1
Ogle Rd B1
Old Northam Rd A2
Orchard La B2
Oxford Ave A2
Oxford St C2
Palmerston Park A2
Palmerston Rd A2
Parsonage Rd A3
Peel St A3
Platform Rd C2
Polygon, The A1
Portland Terr B1
Post Office A2/A3/B2
Pound Tree Rd B2
Quays Swimming & Diving Complex, The B1
Queen's Park C2

Southend • Stirling • Stoke-on-Trent (Hanley) • Stratford-upon-Avon • Sunderland • Swansea • Swindon • Taunton 211

Queen's Peace Fountain ✦ A2
Queen's Terr C2
Queensway B2
Radcliffe Rd A3
Rochester St A3
Royal Pier C1
Royal South Hants Hospital A2
St Andrew's Rd A2
St Mary's B3
St Mary St A2
St Mary's Leisure Centre A2
St Mary's Pl B2
St Mary's Rd A2
St Mary's Stadium (Southampton FC) A3
St Michael's C1
Sea City Mus A1
Showcase Cinema de Lux B1
Solent Sky C3
South Front B2
Southampton Central Station A1
Southampton Solent University A2
SS Shieldhall C2
Terminus Terr C2
Threefield La B2
Titanic Engineers' Memorial ✦ A2
Town Quay C1
Town Walls B2
Tudor House C1
Vincent's Walk B2
Westgate Hall C1
West Marlands Rd A1
West Park A1
West Park Rd A1
West Quay Rd B1
West Quay Retail Pk B1
Western Esplanade B1
Westquay Shopping Centre B1
Westquay Watermark B1
White Star Way C2
Winton St A2

Southend-on-Sea 197
Adventure Island ✦ C3
Albany Ave A1
Albert Rd C3
Alexandra Rd C2
Alexandra St C2
Alexandra Yacht Club ✦ C2
Ashburnham Rd B2
Ave Rd B1
Avenue Terr B1
Balmoral Rd B1
Baltic Ave B3
Baxter Ave A2/B2
Beecroft Art Gallery B2
Bircham Rd A2
Boscombe Rd B3
Boston Ave A1/B2
Bournemouth Park Rd A3
Browning Ave A3
Bus Station C3
Byron Ave A3
Cambridge Rd C1/C2
Canewdon Rd B1
Carnarvon Rd A2
Central Ave A3
Central Museum B2
Chelmsford Ave A1
Chichester Rd B2
Church Rd C3
Civic Centre A2
Clarence Rd C2
Clarence St C2
Cliff Ave B1
Cliffs Pavilion C1
Clifftown Parade C2
Clifftown Rd C2
Colchester Rd A1
Coleman St B3
College Way B2
County Court B3
Cromer Rd B3
Crowborough Rd A2
Dryden Ave A3
East St A2
Elmer App B2
Elmer Ave B2
Forum,The B2
Gainsborough Dr A1
Gayton Rd A2
Glenhurst Rd A2
Gordon Pl B2
Gordon Rd B2
Grainger Rd A2
Greyhound Way A3
Grove,The A3
Guildford Rd B3
Hamlet Ct Rd B1
Hamlet Rd C1
Harcourt Ave A1
Hartington Rd C3
Hastings Rd B3
Herbert Gr C3
Heygate Ave C3
High St B2/C2
Information Ctr C3
Kenway A2
Kilworth Ave B3
Lancaster Gdns B3
London Rd B1
Lucy Rd C3
MacDonald Ave A1
Magistrates' Court A2
Maldon Rd A2
Marine Ave C1
Marine Parade C3
Marine Rd C1
Milton Rd B1
Milton St B2
Napier Ave B2
North Ave A3
North Rd A1/B1
Odeon B2
Osborne Rd B1
Park Cres B1
Park Rd B1
Park St B1
Park Terr B1
Pier Hill C3
Pleasant Rd C3
Police Station A2
Post Office B2/B3
Princes St B2
Queens Rd B2
Queensway B2/B3/C3
Radio Essex C2
Rayleigh Ave A1
Redstock Rd A2
Rochford Ave A1
Royal Mews C2
Royal Terr C2
Royals Shopping Centre,The C3
Ruskin Ave A3
St Ann's Rd B3
St Helen's Rd B1
St John's Rd B1
St Leonard's Rd C3
St Lukes Rd A3
St Vincent's Rd C1
Salisbury Ave A1/B1
Scratton Rd C2
Shakespeare Dr A1
Shopmobility B2
Short St A2
South Ave A3
Southchurch Rd B3
Southend Central B2
Southend Pier Railway C3
Southend Utd FC A1
Southend Victoria B2
Stanfield Rd A2
Stanley Rd C3
Sutton Rd A3/B3
Swanage Rd B3
Sweyne Ave A1
Sycamore Gr A3
Tennyson Ave A3
Tickfield Ave A2
Tudor Rd A1
Tunbridge Rd A2
Tylers Ave B3
Tyrrel Dr B3
Univ of Essex B2/C2
Vale Ave A2
Victoria Ave A2
Victoria Shopping Centre,The B2
Warrior Sq B3
Wesley Rd C3
West Rd A1
West St A1
Westcliff Ave C1
Westcliff Parade C1
Western Esplanade C1
Weston Rd C2
Whitegate Rd B3
Wilson Rd C1
Wimborne Rd B3
York Rd C3

Stirling 197
Abbey Rd A3
Abbotsford Pl A3
Abercromby Pl C1
Albert Halls B1
Albert Pl B1
Alexandra Pl A3
Allan Park C2
Ambulance Station A2
AMF Ten Pin Bowling ✦ B2
Argyll Ave A3
Argyll's Lodging ✦ B1
Back O' Hill Ind Est A1
Back O' Hill Rd A1
Baker St B2
Ballengeich Pass A1
Balmoral Pl B1
Barn Rd B1
Barnton St B2
Bastion,The ✦ C2
Bow St B1
Bruce St A2
Burghmuir Retail Park C2
Burghmuir Rd A2/B2/C2
Bus Station B2
Cambuskenneth Bridge A3
Castle Ct B1
Causewayhead Rd A2
Cemetery A1
Changing Room, The B1
Church of the Holy Rude B1
Clarendon Pl C1
Club House B1
Colquhoun St C3
Corn Exchange B2
Council Offices C2
Court B2
Cowane Ctr A2
Cowane St A2
Cowane's Hosp B1
Crofthead Rd A1
Dean Cres A3
Douglas St A2
Drip Rd A1
Drummond La C1
Drummond Pl C1
Drummond Pl La C1
Dumbarton Rd C2
Eastern Access Rd B2
Edward Ave A3
Edward Rd A2
Forrest Rd A2
Fort A1
Forth Cres B2
Forth St A2
Gladstone Pl C1
Glebe Ave C1
Glebe Cres C1
Golf Course C1
Goosecroft Rd B2
Gowanhill A1
Greenwood Ave B1
Harvey Wynd A1
Information Ctr B1
Irvine Pl B2
James St A2
John St B1
Kerse Rd C3
King's Knot ✦ B1
King's Park C1
King's Park Rd C1
Laurencecroft Rd A2
Leisure Pool B2
Library B2
Linden Ave C2
Lovers Wk A2
Lower Back Walk B1
Lower Bridge St A2
Lower Castlehill A1
Mar Pl B1
Meadow Pl A3
Meadowforth Rd C3
Middlemuir Rd C3
Millar Pl A3
Morris Terr B2
Mote Hill A1
Murray Pl B2
Nelson Pl C2
Old Town Cemetery B1
Old Town Jail ✦ B1
Park Terr C1
Phoenix Ind Est C3
Players Rd C3
Port St C2
Post Office B2
Princes St B2
Queen St B2
Queen's Rd B1
Queenshaugh Dr A3
Ramsay Pl A2
Riverside Dr A3
Ronald Pl A1
Rosebery Pl A2
Royal Gardens B1
Royal Gdns B1
St Mary's Wynd B1
St Ninian's Rd C2
Scott St A2
Seaforth Pl B2
Shore Rd B2
Smith Art Gallery & Museum B1
Snowdon Pl C1
Snowdon Pl La C1
Spittal St B2
Springkerse Ind Est C3
Springkerse Rd C3
Stirling Arcade B2
Stirling Bsns Centre C2
Stirling Castle A1
Stirling County Rugby Football Club A3
Stirling Enterprise Park B3
Stirling Old Bridge A2
Stirling Station B2
Superstore A1/A2
Sutherland Ave A3
TA Centre C3
Tannery La A2
Thistle Ind Est C3
Thistles Shopping Centre,The B2
Tolbooth ✦ B1
Town Wall B1
Union St A2
Upper Back Walk B1
Upper Bridge St A1
Upper Castlehill B1
Upper Craigs C2
Victoria Pl C1
Victoria Rd B1
Victoria Sq B1/C1
Vue B2
Wallace St A2
Waverley Cres A3
Wellgreen Rd C2
Windsor Pl C1
YHA B1

Stoke-on-Trent (Hanley) 196
Acton St A3
Albion St B2
Argyle St C1
Ashbourne Gr A2
Avoca St A3
Baskerville Rd B3
Bedford Rd C1
Bedford St C1
Bethesda St B2
Bexley St A2
Birches Head Rd A3
Botteslow St C3
Boundary St A2
Broad St C2
Broom St A3
Bryan St A2
Bucknall New Rd B3
Bucknall Old Rd B3
Bus Station C3
Cannon St C2
Castlefield St C1
Cavendish St B1
Central Forest Pk A2
Century Retail Park B1
Charles St B3
Cheapside B2
Chell St A3
Cinema B2
Clarke St C1
Cleveland Rd C2
Clifford St C3
Clough St B2
Clough St East B2
Clyde St C1
College Rd C2
Cooper St C2
Corbridge Rd A1
Cutts St C2
Davis St C1
Denbigh St A1
Derby St C3
Dilke St A3
Dudson Ctr,The A2
Dundas St A3
Dundee Rd C1
Dyke St B3
Eastwood Rd C3
Eaton St A3
Etruria Park B1
Etruria Rd B1
Etruria Vale Rd C1
Festing St A3
Festival Heights Retail Park A1
Festival Retail Park A1
Fire Station C2
Foundry St B2
Franklyn St C3
Garnet St B1
Garth St B3
George St A3
Gilman St B3
Glass St B3
Goodson St B3
Greyhound Way A1
Grove Pl C1
Hampton St C3
Hanley Park C2
Hanley Park C2
Harding Rd C2
Hassall St B3
Havelock Pl C1
Hazlehurst St C3
Hinde St C2
Hope St B2
Houghton St C2
Hulton St A3
Information Ctr B2
intu Potteries Shopping Centre B2
Jasper St C2
Jervis St A3
John Bright St A3
John St B2
Keelings Rd A3
Kimberley Rd C1
Ladysmith Rd C1
Lawrence St C2
Leek Rd C3
Library C2
Lichfield St C3
Linfield Rd B3
Loftus St A2
Lower Bedford St C1
Lower Bryan St A2
Lower Mayer St A3
Lowther St A1
Magistrates Court C2
Malham St A2
Marsh St B2
Matlock St C3
Mayer St A3
Milton St C1
Mitchell Arts Ctr B2
Moston St A3
Mount Pleasant C1
Mulgrave St A1
Mynors St B3
Nelson Pl B3
New Century St B1
Octagon Retail Park B1
Ogden Rd C3
Old Hall St B3
Old Town Rd A3
Pall Mall B2
Palmerston St C3
Park and Ride C2
Parkway,The C2
Pavilion Dr A1
Pelham St C3
Percy St B2
Piccadilly B2
Picton St B3
Plough St A3
Police Station C2
Portland St A1
Post Office A3/B2
Potteries Museum & Art Gallery B2
Potteries Way B2
Powell St A1
Pretoria Rd C1
Quadrant Rd B2
Ranelagh St C2
Raymond St C2
Rectory Rd C1
Regent Rd C2
Regent Theatre B2
Richmond Terr C2
Ridgehouse Dr A1
Robson St C2
St Ann St B3
St Luke St B3
Sampson St B2
Shaw St A1
Sheaf St C2
Shearer St C1
Shelton New Rd C1
Shirley Rd C2
Slippery La B2
Shopmobility B3
Snow Hill C2
Spur St C3
Stafford St B2
Stubbs La C3
Sun St C1
Supermarket A1/B2
Superstore B2
Talbot St C3
Town Hall B2
Town Rd A3
Trinity St B2
Union St A2
Upper Hillchurch St A3
Upper Huntbach St B3
Victoria Hall B3
Warner St C2
Warwick St C1
Waterloo Rd A1
Waterloo St B3
Well St B3
Wellesley St C2
Wellington Rd B3
Wellington St B3
Whitehaven Dr A2
Whitmore St C1
Windermere St A1
Woodall St A1
Yates St C2
York St A2

Stratford-upon-Avon 197
Albany Rd B1
Alcester Rd B1
Ambulance Station B1
Arden St B2
Avenue Farm A1
Ave Farm Ind Est A1
Avenue Rd A3
Baker Ave A1
Bandstand C3
Benson Rd A3
Birmingham Rd A2
Boat Club B3
Borden Pl C1
Bridge St B2
Bridgetown Rd C3
Bridgeway B3
Broad St C2
Broad Walk C2
Brookvale Rd C1
Brunel Way B1
Bull St C2
Butterfly Farm ✦ C3
Cemetery C1
Chapel La B2
Cherry Orchard C1
Chestnut Walk B2
Children's Playground C3
Church St C2
Civic Hall B2
Clarence Rd B1
Clopton Bridge ✦ B3
Clopton Rd A2
College B1
College La C2
College St C2
Com Sports Centre B1
Council Offices (District) B2
Courtyard,The C2
Cox's Yard ✦ B3
Cricket Ground C3
Ely Gdns B2
Ely St B2
Evesham Rd C1
Fire Station B1
Foot Ferry C3
Fordham Ave A2
Garrick Way C1
Gower Memorial ✦ B3
Great William St B2
Greenhill St B2
Greenway,The C2
Grove Rd B2
Guild St B2
Guildhall & School B2
Hall's Croft C2
Harvard House B2
Henley St B2
Hertford Rd C1
High St B2
Holton St C2
Holy Trinity C2
Information Ctr B3
Jolyffe Park Rd A2
Kipling Rd C3
Library B2
Lodge Rd B1
Maidenhead Rd A3
Mansell St B2
Masons Court B2
Masons Rd A1
Maybird Shopping Park A2
Maybrook Retail Pk A2
Maybrook Rd A1
Mayfield Ave A2
Meer St B2
Mill La C2
Moat House Hotel B3
Narrow La C2
Nash's House & New Place B2
New St C2
Old Town C2
Orchard Way C1
Other Place,The C2
Paddock La C1
Park Rd A1
Payton St B2
Percy St A2
Police Station B2
Post Office B2
Recreation Ground C2
Regal Road A2
Rother St B2
Rowley Cr A3
Royal Shakespeare Theatre B3
Ryland St C2
Saffron Meadow C2
St Andrew's Cr B1
St Gregory's A3
St Gregory's Rd A3
St Mary's Rd A2
Sanctus Dr C2
Sanctus St C1
Sandfield Rd C2
Scholars La B2
Seven Meadows Rd C2
Shakespeare Inst C2
Shakespeare St B2
Shakespeare's Birthplace ✦ B2
Sheep St B2
Shelley Rd C3
Shipston Rd C3
Shottery Rd C1
Slingates Rd A2
Southern La C2
Station Rd B1
Stratford Healthcare B2
Stratford Hosp B2
Stratford Leisure Centre B3
Stratford Sports Club B1
Stratford-upon-Avon Station B1
Swan Theatre B3
Swan's Nest La B3
Talbot Rd A2
Tiddington Rd B3
Timothy's Bridge Industrial Estate A1
Timothy's Bridge Rd A1
Town Hall & Council Offices B2
Town Sq B2
Trinity Cl C2
Tyler St B2
War Memorial Gardens B3
Warwick Rd B3
Waterside B3
Welcombe Rd A3
West St C2
Western Rd A2
Wharf Rd A2
Willows North,The B1
Willows,The B1
Wood St B2

Sunderland 197
Albion Pl C2
Alliance Pl B1
Argyle St C2
Ashwood St C1
Athenaeum St B2
Azalea Terr C2
Beach St A1
Bedford St B2
Beechwood Terr C1
Belvedere Rd C2
Blandford St B2
Borough Rd B3
Bridge Cr B2
Bridge St B2
Bridges,The B2
Brooke St A2
Brougham St B2
Burdon Rd C2
Burn Park C1
Burn Park Rd C1
Burn Park Tech Park C1
Carol St B1
Charles St A3
Chester Rd C1
Chester Terr B1
Church St A3
Civic Centre C2
Cork St B3
Coronation St B3
Cowan Terr C2
Dame Dorothy St A2
Deptford Rd B1
Deptford Terrace A1
Derby St C2
Derwent St C2
Dock St A3
Dundas St A2
Durham Rd C1
Easington St A2
Egerton St C3
Empire B3
Empire Theatre B2
Farringdon Row B1
Fawcett St B2
Fire Station B1
Fox St C1
Foyle St B3
Frederick St B3
Hanover Pl A1
Havelock Terr C1
Hay St A2
Headworth Sq B3
Hendon Rd B3
High St East B3
High St West B2/B3
Holmeside B2
Hylton Rd B1
Information Ctr B2
John St B3
Kier Hardie Way A2
Lambton St B3
Laura St C3
Lawrence St B3
Library & Arts Ctr B3
Lily St B1
Lime St B1
Livingstone Rd B2
Low Row B2
Magistrates' Court B2
Matamba Terr B1
Millburn St B1
Millennium Way A2
Minster B2
Monkwearmouth Station Mus A2
Mowbray Park C3
Mowbray Rd C3
Murton St C3
National Glass Centre ✦ A3
New Durham Rd C1
Newcastle Rd A2
Nile St B3
Norfolk St B3
North Bridge St A2
Northern Gallery for Contemporary Art (NGCA) B3
Otto Terr C1
Park La C2
Park Lane C2
Park Rd C2
Paul's Rd B3
Peel St C3
Point,The ✦ B2
Police Station B2
Priestly Cr A1
Queen St B2
Railway Row B1
Retail Park B1
Richmond St A2
Roker Ave A2
Royalty Theatre C1
Royalty,The C1
Ryhope Rd C2
St Mary's Way B2
St Michael's Way B2
St Peter's A3
St Peter's A2
St Peter's Way A3
St Vincent St C3
Salem Rd C3
Salem St C3
Salisbury St C3
Sans St B3
Shopmobility B2
Silkworth Row B1
Southwick Rd A2
Stadium of Light (Sunderland AFC) A2
Stadium Way A2
Stobart St A2
Stockton Rd C2
Suffolk St C3
Sunderland A2
Sunderland Aquatic Centre A2
Sunderland College C2
Sunderland Mus B3
Sunderland St B3
Sunderland Sta B2
Tatham St C3
Tavistock Pl B3
Thelma St C1
Thomas St North A2
Thornholme Rd C1
Toward Rd C3
Transport Interchange C2
Trimdon St Way B1
Tunstall Rd C2
University C1
University Library C1
Univ of Sunderland (City Campus) B1
Univ of Sunderland (St Peter's Campus) A3
University of Sunderland (Sir Tom Cowie Campus) A3
Vaux Brewery Way A2
Villiers St B3
Villiers St South B3
Vine Pl C2
Violet St B1
Walton La B3
Waterworks Rd B1
Wearmouth Bridge B2
West Sunniside B3
West Wear St B3
Westbourne Rd B1
Western Hill C1
Wharncliffe B1
Whickham St A3
White House Rd C3
Wilson St North A2
Winter Gdns C3
Wreath Quay A1

Swansea Abertawe 198
Adelaide St C3
Albert Row C3
Alexandra Rd B3
Argyle St C1
Baptist Well Pl A2
Beach St C1
Belle Vue Way B3
Berw Rd A1
Berwick Terr A2
Bond St C1
Brangwyn Concert Hall C1
Bridge St A3
Brooklands Terr B1
Brunswick St C1
Bryn-Syfi Terr A2
Bryn-y-Mor Rd C1
Bullins La B1
Burrows Rd C1
Bus Station C2
Bus/Rail link A3
Cadfan Rd A1
Cadrawd Rd A1
Caer St B3
Carig Cr A1
Carlton Terr B2
Carmarthen Rd A3
Castle Square B3
Castle St B3
Catherine St C1
Cinema C3
Civic Ctr & Library C2
Clarence St C2
Colbourne Terr A2
Constitution Hill B1
Court B3
Creidiol Rd A2
Cromwell St B2
Crown Courts C1
Duke St B1
Dunvant Pl C2
Dyfatty Park A3
Dyfatty St A3
Dyfed Ave A1
Dylan Thomas Centre ✦ B3
Dylan Thomas Theatre C3
Eaton Cr C1
Eigen Cr A1
Elfed Rd A1
Emlyn Rd A1
Evans Terr A3
Fairfield Terr B1
Ffynone Dr B1
Ffynone Rd B1
Fire Station B3
Firm St A2
Fleet St C1
Francis St C1
Fullers Row B2
George St B2
Glamorgan St C2
Glynn Vivian Art Gallery B3
Gower Coll Swansea C1
Graig Terr A3
Grand Theatre C2
Granogwen Rd A2
Guildhall C1
Guildhall Rd South C1
Gwent Rd A1
Gwynedd Ave A1
Hafod St A3
Hanover St B1
Harcourt St B2
Harries St A2
Heathfield B2
Henrietta St B1
Hewson St B2
High St A3/B3
High View A2
Hill St A2
Historic Ships Berth C3
HM Prison C2
Information Ctr C2
Islwyn Rd A1
King Edward's Rd C1
Kingsway,The B2
LC,The C3
Long Ridge A2
Madoc St C2
Mansel St B2
Maritime Quarter C3
Market B3
Mayhill Gdns B1
Mayhill Rd A1
Milton Terr A2
Mission Gallery C3
Montpelier Terr B1
Morfa Rd A3
Mount Pleasant B2
National Waterfront Museum C3
New Cut Rd A3
New St A3
Nicander Pde A2
Nicander Pl A2
Nicholl St B2
Norfolk St B2
North Hill Rd A2
Northampton La B2
Observatory ✦ C3
Orchard St B3
Oxford St B2
Oystermouth Rd C1
Page St B2
Pant-y-Celyn Rd B1
Parc Tawe North B3
Parc Tawe Shopping & Leisure Centre B3
Patti Pavilion C1
Paxton St C2
Pen-y-Graig Rd A1
Penmaen Terr B1
Phillips Pde C1
Picton Terr B2
Plantasia B3
Plantasia B3
Police Station B2
Post Office A1/A2/C1/C2
Powys Ave A1
Primrose St B2
Princess Way B3
Promenade B2
Pryder Gdns A1
Quadrant Shopping Centre C2
Quay Park B3
Rhianfa La B1
Rhondda St B2
Richardson St C2
Rodney St C1
Rose Hill B1
Rosehill Terr B1
Russell St B1
St Helen's Ave C1
St Helen's Cr C1
St Helen's Rd C1
St James Gdns B1
St James's Cr B1
St Mary's B3
Sea View Terr A3
Singleton St C2
South Dock C3
Stanley Pl B2
Strand B3
Swansea Castle B3
Swansea Metropolitan University B2
Swansea Mus C3
Swansea Sta A3
Taliesyn Rd B1
Tan y Marian Rd A1
Tegid Rd A2
Teilo Cr A1
Tenpin Bowling ✦ B3
Terrace Rd B1/B2
Tontine St A3
Townhill Rd A1
Tramshed,The C3
Trawler Rd C3
Union St B2
Upper Strand A3
Vernon St A3
Victoria Quay C3
Victoria Rd B3
Vincent St C1
Walter Rd B1
Watkin St A2
Waun-Wen Rd A2
Wellington St C2
Westbury St C1
Western St C1
Westway C2
William St C2
Wind St B3
Woodlands Terr B1
YMCA B2
York St C3

Swindon 198
Albert St C3
Albion St C1
Alfred St A2
Alvescot Rd C3
Art Gallery & Museum C3
Ashford Rd C1
Aylesbury St A2
Bath Rd C2
Bathampton St B1
Bathurst Rd B3
Beatrice St A2
Beckhampton St B3
Bowood Rd C1
Bristol St B1
Broad St A3
Brunel Shopping Centre,The B2
Brunel Statue B2
Brunswick St C2
Bus Station B2
Cambria Bridge Rd B1
Cambria Place B1
Canal Walk B2
Carr St B1
Cemetery C1/C3
Chandler Cl C3
Chapel C1
Chester St B1
Christ Church C3
Church Place B1
Cirencester Way A3
Clarence St B2
Clifton St C1
Cockleberry A2
Colbourne A3
Colbourne St A3
College St B2
Commercial Rd B2
Corporation St A2
Council Offices B3
County Cricket Gd A3
County Rd A3
Courts B2
Cricklade Street C3
Crombey St B1/C2
Cross St C2
Curtis St B1
Deacon St C1
Designer Outlet (Great Western) B1
Dixon St C2
Dover St C2
Dowling St C2
Drove Rd C3
Dryden St C1
Durham St C3
East St B1
Eastcott Hill C2
Eastcott Rd C2
Edgeware Rd B2
Edmund St C2
Elmina Rd A3
Emlyn Square B1
English Heritage National Monuments Record Centre B1
Euclid St B3
Exeter St B1
Fairview C1
Faringdon Rd B1
Farnsby St B1
Fire Station B3
Fleet St B2
Fleming Way B2/B3
Florence St A2
Gladstone St A3
Gooch St A2
Graham St A3
Great Western Way A1/A2
Groundwell Rd B3
Hawksworth Way A1
Haydon St A2
Henry St B2
Hillside Ave C1
Holbrook Way B2
Hunt St C3
Hydro B1
Hythe Rd C2
Information Ctr B2
Joseph St C1
Kent Rd C2
King William St C2
Kingshill Rd C1
Lansdown Rd C2
Lawn,The C3
Leicester St B3
Library B2
Lincoln St B3
Little London C3
London St B1
Magic B3
Maidstone Rd C2
Manchester Rd A3
Maxwell St B1
Milford St B2
Milton Rd B1
Morse St C2
Newcastle St B3
Newcombe Drive A1
Hawsworth Industrial Estate A1
Newhall St C2
North St C2
North Star A1
North Star Ave A1
Northampton St B3
Nurseries,The C1
Oasis Leisure Ctr A1
Ocotal Way A3
Okus Rd C1
Old Town C3
Oxford St B1
Parade,The B2
Park Lane B1
Park Lane B1
Park,The B1
Pembroke St C2
Plymouth St B3
Polaris Way A2
Police Station B2
Ponting St A2
Post Office B1/B2/C3
Poulton St A3
Princes St B2
Prospect Hill C2
Prospect Place C2
Queen St B2
Queen's Park C3
Radnor St C1
Read St C1
Reading St B1
Regent Circus C2
Regent St B2
Retail Park A2/A3/B3
Rosebery St A3
St Mark's B1
Salisbury St A3
Savernake St C2
Science & Technology Facilities Council HQ A2
Shelley St C1
Sheppard St B1
Shopmobility B2
South St C2
Southampton St B3
Spring Gardens B3
Stafford Street C2
Stanier St C2
Station Road A2
STEAM GWR B1
Swindon College A2
Swindon Rd C2
Swindon Station A2
Swindon Town Football Club A3
TA Centre B1
Tennyson St B1
Theobald St B1
Town Hall B2
Transfer Bridges A3
Union St C2
Upham Rd C3
Victoria Rd C3
Walcot Rd B3
War Memorial ✦ B2
Wells St B3
Western St C2
Westmorland Rd B3
Whalebridge B2
Whitehead St C1
Whitehouse Rd A2
William St C1
Wood St C3
Wyvern Theatre & Arts Centre B2
York Rd B3

Taunton 198
Addison Gr A1
Albemarle Rd A1
Alfred St B3
Alma St C2
Avenue,The A1
Bath Pl C1
Belvedere Rd A1
Billet St B2
Billetfield C2
Birch Gr A1
Brewhouse Theatre B2
Bridge St B1
Bridgwater & Taunton Canal A2
Broadlands Rd C1
Burton Pl C1
Bus Station B1
Canal Rd A2
Cann St C1
Canon St B2
Castle St B1
Cheddon Rd A2
Chip Lane A1
Clarence St B1
Cleveland St B1
Clifton Terr A2
Coleridge Cres C3
Compass Hill C1
Compton Cl A2
Corporation St B1
Council Offices A1
County Walk Shopping Centre C2
Courtyard B2
Cranmer Rd B2
Crescent,The C1
Critchard Way B3
Cyril St A1
Deller's Wharf B1
Duke St B2
East Reach B3
East St B3
Eastbourne Rd B2
Eastleigh Rd C3
Eaton Cres A2
Elm Gr A1
Elms Cl A1
Fons George C1
Fore St B2
Fowler St A1
French Weir Recreation Gd B1
Geoffrey Farrant Walk A2
Gray's Almshouses B2
Grays Rd B3
Greenway Ave A1
Guildford Pl C1
Hammet St B2
Haydon Rd B3
Heavitree Way A2
Herbert St A1
High St C2
Holway Ave C3
Hugo St B3
Huish's Almshouses B2
Hurdle Way C2
Information Ctr C2
Jubilee St A1
King's College C3
Kings Cl C3
Laburnum St B2
Lambrook Rd B3
Lansdowne Rd A3
Leslie Ave A1
Leycroft Rd B3
Library C2
Linden Gr A1
Magdalene St B2
Magistrates Court B1
Malvern Terr A2
Market House B2
Mary St C2
Middle St B2
Mitre Court B3
Mount Nebo C1
Mount St C2
Mount,The C2
Mountway C2
Museum of Somerset B1
North St B2
Northfield Ave B1
Northfield Rd B1
Northleigh Rd C3
Obridge Allotments A3
Obridge Lane A3
Obridge Rd A3
Obridge Viaduct A3
Orch Shopping Ctr C2
Osborne Way C1
Park St C1
Paul St C2
Plais St A2
Playing Field C3
Police Station A1
Portland St B1
Post Office B1/B2
Priorswood Industrial Estate A3
Priorswood Rd A2
Priory Ave B2
Priory Bridge Rd B2
Priory Fields Retail Park A3
Priory Park A2
Priory Way A3
Queen St B3
Railway St A1
Records Office A2
Recreation Grd A1
Riverside Place B2
St Augustine St B2
St George's C2
St Georges Sq C2
St James B2
St James St B2
St John's C1
St John's Rd B1
St Josephs Field C2
St Mary Magdalene's B2
Samuels Ct A1
Shire Hall & Law Courts C1
Somerset County Cricket Ground B2
Somerset County Hall C1
Somerset Cricket B2
South Rd C3
South St C3
Staplegrove Rd B1
Station Approach A2
Station Rd A1
Stephen St B2
Superstore C2
Swimming Pool A1
Tancred St B2
Tangier Way B1
Tauntfield Cl C3
Taunton Castle B1
Taunton Dean Cricket Club C2
Taunton Station A2
Thomas St A1
Toneway A3
Tower St B1
Trenchard Way A1
Trevor Smith Pl C3
Trinity Business Centre C3
Trinity Rd C3
Trinity St B3
Trull Rd C1
Tudor House B2
Upper High St C1
Venture Way A3
Victoria Gate B3
Victoria Park B3
Victoria St B3
Viney St B3
Vivary Park Golf Club C2
Vivary Rd C1
War Memorial ✦ C1
Wellesley St A2
Wheatley Cres A3
Whitehall A1
Wilfred Rd B3
William St A1
Wilton Church C1
Wilton Cl C1
Wilton Gr C1
Wilton St C1
Winchester St B2
Winters Field B2
Wood St B1
Yarde Pl B1

Telford 198

Alma Ave C1
Amphitheatre C2
Bowling Alley B2
Brandsfarm Way C3
Brunel Rd B1
Bus Station B2
Buxton Rd C1
Central Park A2
Chelsea Gardens ✿ B2
Coach Central B2
Coachwell Cl B1
Colliers Way A1
Courts B2
Dale Acre Way B3
Darliston C3
Deepdale B3
Deercote B2
Dinthill C3
Doddington C3
Dodmoor Grange C3
Downemead B3
Duffryn B3
Dunsheath B3
Euston Way A3
Eyton Mound C1
Eyton Rd C1
Forgegate A2
Grange Central B2
Hall Park Way B1
Hinkshay Rd C2
Hollinsworth Rd A2
Holyhead Rd A3
Housing Trust A1
Ice Rink B2
Information Ctr ℹ B2
Ironmasters Way A2
Job Centre B1
Land Registry B1
Lawn Central B2
Lawnswood C1
Library B2
Malinsgate B1
Matlock Ave C1
Moor Rd C1
Mount Rd C1
Odeon ▪ B2
Park Lane A1
Police Station ▤ B1
Post Office ✉ A2/B2/C1
Priorslee Ave A3
Queen Elizabeth Ave C3
Queen Elizabeth Way B1
Queensway A2/B3
QEII Arena C2
Rampart Way A2
Randlay Ave C3
Randlay Wood C3
Rhodes Ave C1
Royal Way B1
St Leonards Rd B1
St Quentin Gate B2
Shifnal Rd A3
Silkin Way C2
Sixth Ave A1
Southwater Leisure Complex ▪ B2
Southwater Way B1
Spout Lane C1
Spout Mound B1
Spout Way C1
Stafford Court B3
Stafford Park B3
Stirchley Ave C3
Stone Row C1
Superstoore B1
Telford Bridge Retail Park A1
Telford Central Station ≋ A3
Telford Centre, The B2
Telford Forge Shopping Park A1
Telford Hornets RFC C2
Telford Int Ctr C2
Telford Way A3
Third Ave A2
Town Park C2
Town Park Visitor Centre B2
Wellswood Ave A2
West Centre Way B1
Withywood Drive C1
Wonderland ✦ C2
Woodhouse Ctrl B2
Yates Way A1

Torquay 199

Abbey Rd B2
Alexandra Rd A2
Alpine Rd B3
AMF Bowling C3
Ash Hill Rd A2
Babbacombe Rd B3
Bampfylde Rd B1
Barton Rd A1
Beacon Quay C2
Belgrave Rd A1/B1
Belmont Rd A3
Berea Rd A3
Braddons Hill Rd East B3
Brewery Park A3
Bronshill Rd A2
Carlton Rd A3
Castle Circus A2
Castle Rd A2
Cavern Rd A3
Central ▪ B2
Chatsworth Rd A2
Chestnut Ave B1
Church St A1
Coach Station A1
Corbyn Head C1
Croft Hill B1
Croft Rd B1
East St A1
Egerton Rd A3
Ellacombe Church Rd A3
Ellacombe Rd A2
Falkland Rd B1
Fleet St B2
Fleet Walk Shopping Centre B2
Grafton Rd B3
Grange Rd A3
Haldon Pier C2
Hatfield Rd A2
Highbury Rd A2
Higher Warberry Rd A3
Hillesdon Rd B3
Hoxton Rd A3
Hunsdon Rd B3
Information Ctr ℹ B2
Inner Harbour C3
Kenwyn Rd A3
King's Drive, The B1
Laburnum St A1
Law Courts A2
Library A2
Lime Ave B1
Living Coasts ✦ C3
Lower Warberry Rd B3
Lucius St B1
Lymington Rd A1
Magdalene Rd A1
Marina C2
Market Forum, The B2
Market St B2
Meadfoot Lane C3
Meadfoot Rd C3
Melville St B2
Middle Warberry Rd B3
Mill Lane A1
Montpellier Rd B3
Morgan Ave A1
Museum Rd B3
Newton Rd A1
Oakhill Rd A1
Outer Harbour C2
Parkhill Rd C3
Pimlico B2
Police Station ▤ A1
Post Office ✉ A1/B2
Prince of Wales Steps C3
Princes Rd A3
Princes Rd East A3
Princes Rd West A3
Princess Gdns C2
Princess Pier C2
Princess Theatre ☺ C2
Rathmore Rd B1
Recreation Grd B1
Riviera Int Ctr B1
Rock End Ave C3
Rock Rd B2
Rock Walk B2
Rosehill Rd A3
South West Coast Path C3
St Efride's Rd A1
St John's ✝ B3
St Luke's Rd B2
St Luke's Rd North B2
St Luke's Rd South B2
St Marychurch Rd A2
Scarborough Rd B1
Shedden Hill B2
South Pier C2
South St A1
Spanish Barn B1
Stitchill Rd B3
Strand B3
Sutherland Rd B3
Teignmouth Rd A1
Temperance St B2
Terrace, The B3
Thurlow Rd A1
Tor Bay B1
Tor Church Rd A1
Tor Hill Rd A1
Torbay Rd B2
Torquay Museum ⌂ B3
Torquay Station ≋ C1
Torquay Tennis Club B1
Torre Abbey ⌂ B1
Torre Abbey Meadows B1
Torre Abbey Sands B1
Torwood Gdns B3
Torwood St C3
Town Hall A2
Union Square Shopping Centre A2
Union St A1
Upton Hill A2
Upton Park A1
Upton Rd A1
Vanehill Rd C3
Vansittart Rd A1
Vaughan Parade C2
Victoria Parade C3
Victoria Rd A2
Warberry Rd West B2
Warren Rd B2
Windsor Rd A2/A3
Woodville Rd A3

Truro 199

Adelaide Ter B1
Agar Rd B3
Arch Hill C2
Arundell Pl C2
Avenue, The A3
Avondale Rd B1
Back Quay B3
Barrack La C3
Barton Meadow A1
Benson Rd A2
Bishops Cl A2
Bosvean Gdns B1
Bosvigo Gardens ✿ B1
Bosvigo La A1
Bosvigo Rd B2
Broad St A3
Burley Cl C3
Bus Station B3
Calenick St B2
Campfield Hill B3
Carclew St B3
Carew Rd A2
Carey Park B2
Carlyon Rd A2
Carvoza Rd A3
Castle St B2
Cathedral View A2
Chainwalk Dr A2
Chapel Hill B1
Charles St B2
City Hall B3
City Rd B2
Coinage Hall ⌂ B3
Comprigney Hill A1
Coosebean La A1
Copes Gdns A2
County Hall B1
Courtney Rd A2
Crescent Rd B1
Crescent Rise B1
Crescent, The B1
Daniell Court C2
Daniell Rd C2
Daniell St C2
Daubuz Cl A2
Daubuz Moors Nature Reserve A3
Dobbs La B1
Edward St B2
Eliot Rd A2
Elm Court A3
Enys Cl A1
Enys Rd A1
Fairmantle St B3
Falmouth Rd C2
Ferris Town B2
Fire Station B1
Frances St B2
George St B2
Green Cl C2
Green La C1
Grenville Rd A2
Hall for Cornwall ☺ B3
Hendra Rd A2
Hendra Vean A1
High Cross B3
Higher Newham La C3
Higher Trehaverne A2
Hillcrest Ave B1
Hospital H B2
Hunkin Cl A2
Hurland Rd C3
Infirmary Hill B2
James Pl B3
Kenwyn Church Rd A1
Kenwyn Hill A1
Kenwyn Rd A2
Kenwyn St B2
Kerris Gdns A1
King St B3
Leats, The B2
Lemon Quay B3
Lemon St Gallery ⌂ B3
Library B1/B3
Malpas Rd B3
Magistrates Court A3
Market B3
Merrifield Close B1
Mitchell Hill A3
Moresk Cl A3
Moresk Rd A3
Morlaix Ave C3
Nancemere Rd A3
Newham Business Park C3
Newham Ind Est C3
Newham Rd C3
Northfield Dr C3
Oak Way A3
Pal's Terr A3
Park View C2
Pendarves Rd A2
Plaza Cinema ▪ B3
Police Sta ▤ A2/B3
Post Office ✉ B3
Prince's St B3
Pydar St A2
Quay St B3
Redannick Cres C2
Redannick La B2
Richard Lander Monument ✦ C2
Richmond Hill B1
River St B2
Rosedale Rd A2
Royal Cornwall Museum ⌂ B2
St Aubyn Rd C3
St Clement St B3
St George's Rd A1
Standing Cross ✦ B3
School La C2
Spires, The A2
Station Rd B1
Stokes Rd A2
Strangways Terr C3
Tabernacle St B3
Trehaverne La A2
Tremayne Rd A2
Treseder's Gdns A3
Treworder Rd B1
Treyew Rd B1
Truro Cathedral ✝ B3
Truro Harbour Office B3
Truro Station ≋ B3
Union St B3
Upper School La C2
Victoria Gdns B2
Waterfall Gdns B2

Winchester 199

Andover Rd A2
Andover Road Retail Park A2
Archery La C2
Arthur Rd A2
Bar End Rd C3
Beaufort Rd C2
Beggar's La B3
Bereweeke Ave A1
Bereweeke Rd A1
Boscobel Rd A2
Brassey Rd A2
Broadway B3
Brooks Shopping Centre, The B3
Bus Station B3
Butter Cross ✦ B2
Canon St C2
Castle Wall C2/C3
Cathedral ✝ C2
Cheriton Rd A1
Chesil St C3
Chesil Theatre ☺ C3
Christchurch Rd C1
City Mill ✦ B3
City Museum ⌂ B2
City Rd B2
Clifton Rd B1
Clifton Terr B2
Close Wall C2/C3
Coach Park A2
Colebrook St C3
College St C2
College Walk C3
Compton Rd C2
Council Offices C3
County Council Offices B2
Cranworth Rd A2
Cromwell Rd C1
Culver Rd C2
Discovery Centre ✦ B2
Domum Rd C3
Durngate Pl B3
Eastgate St B3
East Hill C3
Edgar Rd C2
Egbert Rd A2
Elm Rd B1
Everyman ▪ C2
Fairfield Rd A1
Fire Station B3
Fordington Ave B1
Fordington Rd A1
Friarsgate B3
Gordon Rd B3
Great Hall & Round Table, The ⌂ B2
Greenhill Rd B1
Guildhall ⌂ B3
Hatherley Rd A1
High St B2
Hillier Way A3
HM Prison B1
Hyde Abbey (Remains) ✝ A2
Hyde Abbey Rd B2
Hyde Cl A2
Hyde St A2
Information Ctr ℹ B3
Jane Austen's House ⌂ C2
Jewry St B2
King Alfred Pl A2
Kingsgate Arch C2
Kingsgate Park C2
Kingsgate Rd C2
Kingsgate St C2
Lankhills Rd A2
Law Courts B2
Library B2
Lower Brook St B3
Magdalen Hill B3
Market La B2
Mews La B1
Middle Brook St B3
Middle Rd B1
Military Museums ⌂ B2
Milland Rd C3
Milverton Rd B1
Monks Rd A3
North Hill Cl A2
North Walls B2
North Walls Recreation Gd A3
Nuns Rd A3
Oram's Arbour B1
Owens Rd A2
Parchment St B2
Park & Ride C3
Park Ave B3
Playing Field A1
Police HQ ▤ B1
Portal Rd C3
Post Office ✉ B2/C1
Ranelagh Rd C1
Regimental Museum ⌂ B2
River Park Leisure Centre B3
Romans' Rd C2
Romsey Rd B1
Royal Hampshire County Hospital (A&E) H B1
St Cross Rd C2
St George's St B2
St Giles Hill C3
St James Villas C2
St James' La B1
St James' Terr B1
St John's ✝ B3
St John's St B3
St Michael's Rd C2
St Paul's Hill B1
St Peter St B2
St Swithun St C2
St Thomas St C2
Saxon Rd A2
School of Art B3
Sleepers Hill Rd C1
Southgate St B2
Sparkford Rd C1
Square, The B2
Staple Gdns B2
Station Rd B2
Step Terr B1
Stockbridge Rd A1
Stuart Cres C1
Sussex St B2
Swan Lane B2
Tanner St B3
Theatre Royal ☺ B2
Tower St B2
Union St B3
University of Southampton (Winchester School of Art) B3
University of Winchester (King Alfred Campus) C1
Upper Brook St B2
Wales St B3
Water Lane B3
Weirs, The C3
West End Terr B1
Western Rd B1
Westgate ⌂ B2
Wharf Hill C3
Winchester Station ≋ A2
Winnall Moors Wildlife Reserve A3
Wolvesey Castle ♜ C3
Worthy Lane A2
Worthy Rd A2

Windsor 199

Adelaide Sq C3
Albany Rd C2
Albert St B1
Alexandra Gdns B2
Alexandra Rd C2
Alma Rd B2
Arthur Rd B2
Bachelors Acre B3
Barry Ave B2
Beaumont Rd C2
Bexley St B1
Boat House B2
Brocas St B2
Brocas, The A2
Brook St C3
Bulkeley Ave C1
Castle Hill B3
Charles St B2
Claremont Rd C2
Clarence Cr B2
Clarence Rd B1
Clewer Court Rd B1
Coach Park B2
College Cr C1
Cricket Ground C3
Dagmar Rd C2
Datchet Rd B3
Devereux Rd C2
Dorset Rd C2
Duke St B1
Elm Rd C1
Eton College ✦ A3
Eton College Natural History Mus ⌂ A2
Eton Ct A2
Eton Sq A2
Eton Wick Rd A2
Farm Yard B3
Fire Station C2
Frances Rd C2
Frogmore Dr B3
Gloucester Pl C3
Goslar Way C1
Goswell Hill B2
Goswell Rd B2
Green La C1
Grove Rd C2
Guildhall ⌂ B3
Helena Rd C2
Helston La B1
High St A2/B3
Holy Trinity ✝ C2
Home Park, The A3/C3
Household Cavalry ⌂ C2
Imperial Rd C1
Information Ctr ℹ B2
Keats La A2
King Edward VII Ave A3
King Edward VII Hospital H C2
King George V Memorial ✦ B3
King Stable St A2
King's Rd C3
Library A2/B2
Long Walk, The C3
Maidenhead Rd B1
Meadow La A2
Municipal Offices C3
Nell Gwynne's House ⌂ B3
Osborne Rd C2
Oxford Rd B1
Park St B3
Peascod St B2
Police Station ▤ C2
Post Office ✉ A2/C1
Princess Margaret Hosp (private) H C2
Old Court Art Space, The ☺ C2
Queen Elizabeth Bridge A1
Queen Victoria's Walk B3
Queen's Rd C2
River St B2
Romney Island A3
Romney Lock A3
Romney Lock Rd A3
Russell St C2
St George's Chapel ✝ B3
St John's ✝ B3
St John's Chapel ✝ A2
St Leonards Rd C2
St Mark's Rd C2
Sheet St C3
Shopmobility B2
South Meadow A2
South Meadow La A2
Springfield Rd C1
Stovell Rd B1
Sunbury Rd A3
Tangier La A2
Temple Rd C2
Thames St B3
Theatre Royal ☺ B3
Trinity Pl C2
Vansittart Rd B1/C1
Victoria Barracks C2
Victoria St C2
Westmead C1
White Lilies Island A1
William St B2
Windsor & Eton Central ≋ B2
Windsor & Eton Riverside ≋ A3
Windsor Bridge B3
Windsor Castle ♜ B3
Windsor Leisure Ctr B1
Windsor Relief Rd A1
Windsor Royal Station Shopping Centre B2
Windsor Yards B2
York Ave C1
York Rd C1

Wolverhampton 200

Albion St B3
Arena ☺ B2
Art Gallery ⌂ B2
Ashland St C1
Austin St A1
Badger Dr A3
Bailey St B3
Bath Ave B1
Bath Rd B1
Bell St C2
Berry St B3
Bilston Rd C3
Bilston St C3
Birmingham Canal A3
Bone Mill La A2
Brewery Rd B1
Bright St A1
Burton Cres B3
Bus Station B3
Cambridge St A3
Camp St B2
Cannock Rd A3
Castle St C2
Chapel Ash C1
Cherry St C1
Chester St A1
Church La C2
Church St C2
Civic Centre B2
Civic Hall B2
Clarence Rd B2
Cleveland St C2
Clifton St C1
Coach Station B2
Compton Rd B1
Corn Hill B3
Coven St A3
Craddock St A1
Cross St North A2
Crown & County Courts C3
Crown St A2
Culwell St B3
Dale St C1
Darlington St C1
Devon Rd A1
Drummond St B2
Dudley Rd C2
Dudley St B2
Duke St C3
Dunkley St B1
Dunstall Ave A2
Dunstall Hill A2
Dunstall Rd A1/A2
Evans St A1
Fawdry St A1
Field St B3
Fire Station C1
Fiveways ⟳ A2
Fowler Playing Fields A3
Fox's La A2
Francis St A2
Fryer St B3
Gloucester St A1
Gordon St C3
Graiseley St C1
Grand ☺ B3
Grand Station B3
Granville St C3
Great Brickkiln St C1
Great Hampton St A1
Great Western St A2
Grimstone St B3
Harrow St A1
Hilton St A3
Hive Liby The B2
Horseley Fields C3
Humber Rd C1
Information Ctr ℹ B3
Jack Hayward Way A2
Jameson St A1
Jenner St C3
Kennedy Rd B3
Kimberley St C1
King St B2
Laburnum St C1
Lansdowne Rd B1
Leicester St A1
Lever St C3
Library C3
Lichfield St B2
Light House ▪ B3
Little's La B3
Lock St B3
Lord St C1
Lowe St A1
Maltings, The B2
Mander Centre C2
Mander St C1
Market C2
Market St B2
Maxwell Rd C3
Merridale St C1
Middlecross C3
Molineux St B2
Mostyn St A1
Newhampton Arts Centre B1
New Hampton Rd East A1
Nine Elms La A3
North Rd A2
Oaks Cres C1
Oxley St A2
Paget St A1
Park Ave B1
Park Road East A1
Park Road West B1
Paul St C2
Pelham St C1
Penn Rd C2
Piper's Row B3
Piper's Row Ⓣ C3
Pitt St C2
Police Station ▤ C3
Pool St C2
Poole St A3
Post Office ✉ A1/B2/B2/C2/C3
Powlett St C3
Queen St B2
Raby St C3
Railway Dr B3
Red Hill St A2
Red Lion St B2
Retreat St C1
Ring Rd B2
Royal, The Ⓣ C3
Rugby St A1
Russell St C1
St Andrew's B1
St David's B3
St George's C3
St George's Pde C2
St James St C3
St John's C2
St John's ✝ C2
St John's Retail Pk C2
St John's Square C2
St Mark's C1
St Marks Rd C1
St Marks St C1
St Patrick's B2
St Peter's B2
St Peter's ✝ B2
Salisbury St C1
Salop St C2
School St C2
Sherwood St A2
Smestow St A3
Snow Hill C2
Springfield Rd A3
Stafford St A2/B2
Staveley Rd A1
Steelhouse La C3
Stephenson St C1
Stewart St C2
Sun St B3
Tempest St C2
Temple St C2
Tettenhall Rd B1
Thomas St C2
Thornley St B2
Tower St C2
University B2
Upper Zoar St C1
Vicarage Rd C3
Victoria St C2
Walpole St A1
Walsall St C3
Ward St C3
Warwick St C3
Water St A3
Waterloo Rd B2
Wednesfield Rd B3
West Park (not A&E) H B1
West Park Swimming Pool B1
Wharf St C3
Whitmore Hill B2
Wolverhampton ≋ B3
Wolverhampton Ⓣ B3
Wolverhampton St George's Ⓣ C2
Wolverhampton Wanderers Football Gnd (Molineux) B2
Worcester St C2
Wulfrun Centre C2
Yarwell Cl A3
York St C3
Zoar St C1

Worcester 200

Albany Terr A1
Angel Pl B2
Angel St B2
Ashcroft Rd A2
Athelstan Rd C3
Avenue, The C1
Back Lane North A1
Back Lane South A1
Barbourne Rd A2
Bath Rd C2
Battenhall Rd C3
Bridge St B2
Britannia Sq A1
Broad St B2
Bromwich La C1
Bromwich Rd C1
Bromyard Rd C1
Bus Station B2
Butts, The B2
Carden St B3
Castle St A2
Cathedral ✝ C2
Cathedral Plaza B2
Charles St B3
Chequers La B1
Chestnut St A2
Chestnut Walk A2
Citizens' Advice Bureau B2
City Walls Rd B2
Cole Hill C3
College St C2
Commandery, The ⌂ C3
Cripplegate Park B1
Croft Rd B1
Cromwell St B3
Cross, The B2
Crowngate Ctr B2
Deansway B2
Diglis Pde C2
Diglis Rd C2
Edgar Tower ✦ C2
Farrier St A2
Foregate St B2
Fort Royal Hill C3
Fort Royal Park C3
Foundry St B3
Friar St C2
George St B3
Grand Stand Rd B1
Greenhill C3
Greyfriars ⌂ B2
Guildhall ⌂ B2
Henwick Rd B1
High St B2
Hill St B3
Hive, The B2
Huntingdon Hall ☺ B2
Hylton Rd B1
Information Ctr ℹ B2
King Charles Place Shopping Centre C1
King's School C2
King's School Playing Field C2
Kleve Walk C2
Lansdowne Cr A3
Lansdowne Rd A3
Lansdowne Walk A3
Laslett St A3
Little Chestnut St A2
Little London A2
London Rd C3
Lowell St A3
Lowesmoor B2
Lowesmoor Terr A3
Lowesmoor Wharf A3
Magistrates Court A2
Midland Rd B3
Mill St C2
Moors Severn Terr, The A1
Museum & Art Gallery ⌂ A2
Museum of Royal Worcester ⌂ C2
New Rd C1
New St B2
Northfield St A2
Odeon ▪ B2
Old Palace The C2
Padmore St B3
Park St C3
Pheasant St B3
Pitchcroft Racecourse A1
Police Station ▤ A2
Portland St C2
Post Office ✉ B2
Quay St B2
Queen St B2
Rainbow Hill A3
Recreation Ground A2
Reindeer Court B2
Rogers Hill A3
Sabrina Terr A1
St Dunstan's Cr C3
St John's C1
St Martin's Gate B3
St Martin's Quarter B3
St Oswald's Rd A2
St Paul's St B3
St Swithin's Church ✝ B2
St Wulstans Cr C3
Sansome Walk A2
Severn St C2
Shambles, The B2
Shaw St B2
Shire Hall Crown Ct A2
Shrub Hill Rd B3
Shrub Hill Retail Pk B3
Slingpool Walk C1
South Parade B2
Southfield St A2
Sports Centre A3
Stanley Rd B3
Swan, The ☺ A1
Swimming Pool A2
Tallow Hill B3
Tennis Walk A2
Tolladine Rd B3
Tudor House ⌂ B2
Tybridge St B1
Tything, The A2
Univ of Worcester B2
Vincent Rd B3
Vue ▪ C2
Washington St A3
Woolhope Rd C3
Worcester Bridge B2
Worcester County Cricket Club C1
Worcester Foregate Street ≋ B2
Worcester Shrub Hill ≋ B3
Worcester Royal Grammar School A2
Wylds La C3

Wrexham
Wrecsam 200

Abbot St B2
Acton Rd A3
Albert St C3
Alexandra Rd C1
Aran Rd A3
Barnfield C3
Bath Rd C2
Beeches, The A3
Beechley Rd C3
Belgrave Rd C2
Bellevue Park C2
Bellevue Rd C2
Belvedere Dr A1
Bennion's Rd C3
Berse Rd A1
Bersham Rd C1
Birch St C3
Bodhyfryd B3
Border Retail Park B3
Bradley Rd C2
Bright St B1
Bron-y-Nant C1
Brook St C2
Bryn-y-Cabanau Rd C3
Bury St C3
Bus Station B2
Butchers Market B3
Caia Rd C3
Cambrian Ind Est C3
Caxton Pl B2
Cemetery C1
Centenary Rd C1
Central Retail Park B2
Chapel St C2
Charles St B3
Chester Rd A3
Chester St B3
Cilcen Gr A3
Citizens Advice Bureau B2
Cobden Rd B1
Council Offices B3
County ⌂ B2
Crescent Rd B3
Crispin La A2
Croesnewyth Rd B1
Cross St A2
Cunliffe St A2
Derby Rd C3
Dolydd Rd B1
Duke St B2
Eagles Meadow C3
Earle St C2
East Ave A2
Edward St C2
Egerton St B2
Empress Rd C1
Erddig Rd C2
Fairy Rd C2
Fire Station B2
Foster Rd A3
Foxwood Dr C1
Garden Rd A2
General Market B3
Gerald St B2
Gibson St C1
Glyndwr University Plas Coch Campus A1
Greenbank St C3
Greenfield A2
Grosvenor Rd B2
Grove Park ☺ B3
Grove Park Rd B3
Grove Rd A3
Guildhall B2
Haig Rd C3
Hampden Rd C2
Hazel Gr A3
Henblas St B3
High St B3
Hightown Rd C3
Hill St B2
Holt Rd B3
Holt St B3
Hope St B2
Huntroyde Ave C3
Information Ctr ℹ B3
Island Green Shopping Centre B2
Jobcentre Plus B2
Jubilee Rd B2
King St B2
Kingsmills Rd C3
Lambpit St B3
Law Courts B3
Lawson Cl A3
Lawson Rd A3
Lea Rd C2
Library & Arts Ctr B2
Lilac Way B1
Llys David Lord B1
Lorne St A2
Maesgwyn Rd B1
Maesydre Rd A3
Manley Rd B3
Market St B3
Mawddy Ave A2
Mayville Ave A2
Meml Gallery ⌂ B2
Memorial Hall B3
Mold Rd A1
Mount St C3
Neville Cres A3
New Rd A2
North Wales Regional Tennis Centre A1
Oak Dr A3
Odeon ▪ C3
Park Ave A3
Park St A2
Peel St C1
Pen y Bryn C2
Pentre Felin C2
Penymaes Ave A3
Peoples Market B3
Percy St C2
Pines, The A3
Plas Coch Rd A1
Plas Coch Retail Pk A1
Police Station ▤ B3
Poplar Rd C2
Post Office ✉ A2/B3/C3
Powell Rd B3
Poyser St C2
Price's La A2
Primose Way B1
Princess St C1
Queen St B3
Queens Sq B2
Regent St B2
Rhosddu Rd A2/B2
Rhosnesni La A3
Rivulet Rd C3
Ruabon Rd C2
Ruthin Rd C1/C2
St Giles ✝ C3
St Giles Way C3
St James Ct A2
St Mary's ✝ B2
Salisbury Rd C3
Salop Rd C3
Sontley Rd C2
Spring Rd A2
Stanley St C3
Stansty Rd A2
Station Approach B2
Studio ☺ B2
Superstore B3/C1
Talbot Rd C2
Techniquest Glyndwr ✦ A2
Town Hill C2
Trevor St C2
Trinity St B2
Tuttle St C3
Vale Park A1
Vernon St B2
Vicarage Hill B2
Victoria Rd C2
Walnut St A2
War Memorial ✦ B3
Waterworld Leisure Centre ✦ B3
Watery Rd B1/B2
Wellington Rd C2
Westminster Dr A3
William Aston Hall ☺ A1
Windsor Rd A1
Wrecsam
Wrexham AFC A1
Wrexham Central ≋ B2
Wrexham General ≋ B2
Wrexham Maelor Hospital (A&E) H B1
Wrexham Technology Park B1
Wynn Ave A2
Yale College B3
Yale Gr A3
Yorke St C3

York 200

Aldwark B2
Barbican Rd C3
Bar Convent Living Heritage Ctr ✦ C1
Barley Hall ⌂ B2
Bishopgate St C2
Bishopshill Senior C2
Bishopthorpe Rd C2
Blossom St C1
Bootham A1
Bootham Cr A1
Bootham Terr A1
Bridge St B2
Brook St A2
Brownlow St A2
Burton Stone La A1
Castle Museum ⌂ C2
Castlegate B2
Cemetery Rd C3
Cherry St C2
City Screen ▪ B2
City Wall A2/B1/C3
Clarence St A2
Clementhorpe C2
Clifford St B2
Clifford's Tower ♜ B2
Clifton A1
Coach park A2
Coney St B2
Coppergate Ctr B2
Cromwell Rd C2
Crown Court C2
Davygate B2
Deanery Gdns A2
DIG ✦ B2
Dodsworth Ave A3
Eboracum Way A3
Ebor Industrial Est B3
Eldon St A2
Everyman ▪ C1
Fairfax House ⌂ B2
Fire Station C2
Fishergate C3
Foss Islands Rd B3
Foss Islands Retail Park B3
Fossbank A3
Garden St A2
George St C3
Gillygate A2
Goodramgate B2
Grand Opera Ho ☺ B2
Grosvenor Terr A1
Guildhall B2
Hallfield Rd A3
Heslington Rd C3
Heworth Green A3
Holy Trinity ✝ B2
Hope St C3
Huntington Rd A3
Information Ctr ℹ B2
James St B3
Jorvik Viking Ctr ⌂ B2
Kent St C3
Lawrence St C3
Layerthorpe A3
Leeman Rd B1
Lendal B2
Lendal Bridge B1
Library A2/B1
Longfield Terr A1
Lord Mayor's Walk A2
Lowther St A2
Mansion House ⌂ B2
Margaret St C3
Marygate A1
Melbourne St C3
Merchant Adventurers' Hall ⌂ B2
Merchant Taylors' Hall ⌂ B2
Micklegate B1
Micklegate Bar ⌂ C1
Monkgate A2
Moss St C1
Museum Gdns ✿ B1
Museum St B1
National Railway Museum ⌂ B1
Navigation Rd B3
Newton Terr C2
North Pde A1
North St B2
Nunnery La C1
Nunthorpe Rd C1
Ouse Bridge B2
Paragon St C3
Park Gr A3
Park St C1
Parliament St B2
Peasholme Green B3
Penley's Grove St A2
Piccadilly B2
Police Station ▤ B2
Post Office ✉ B1/B2/C3
Priory St B1
Queen Anne's Rd A1
Regimental Museum ⌂ B2
Richard III Experience at Monk Bar ⌂ A2
Roman Bath ⌂ B2
Rowntree Park C2
St Andrewgate B2
St Benedict Rd C1
St John St A2
St Olave's Rd A1
St Peter's Gr A1
St Saviourgate B2
Scarcroft Hill C1
Scarcroft Rd C1
Shambles, The B2
Shopmobility B1
Skeldergate C2
Skeldergate Bridge C2
Station Rd B1
Stonebow, The B2
Stonegate B2
Superstore A3
Sycamore Terr A1
Terry Ave C2
Theatre Royal ☺ B2
Thorpe St C1
Toft Green B1
Tower St C2
Townend St A2
Treasurer's Ho ⌂ A2
Trinity La B1
Undercroft Mus ⌂ A2
Union Terr A2
Victor St C2
Vine St C2
Walmgate B3
War Memorial ✦ B1
Wellington St C3
York Art Gallery ⌂ A1
York Barbican ☺ C3
York Brewery ✦ B1
York Dungeon, The ⌂ B2
York Minster ✝ A2
York St John University A2
York Station ≋ B1

Index

Abbreviations used in the index

Abbrev	Full
Aberdeen	Aberdeen City
Aberds	Aberdeenshire
Ald	Alderney
Anglesey	Isle of Anglesey
Angus	Angus
Argyll	Argyll and Bute
Bath	Bath and North East Somerset
BCP	Bournemouth, Christchurch and Poole
Bedford	Bedford
Blackburn	Blackburn with Darwen
Blackpool	Blackpool
Bl Gwent	Blaenau Gwent
Borders	Scottish Borders
Brack	Bracknell
Bridgend	Bridgend
Brighton	City of Brighton and Hove
Bristol	City and County of Bristol
Bucks	Buckinghamshire
Caerph	Caerphilly
Cambs	Cambridgeshire
Cardiff	Cardiff
Carms	Carmarthenshire
C Beds	Central Bedfordshire
Ceredig	Ceredigion
Ches E	Cheshire East
Ches W	Cheshire West and Chester
Clack	Clackmannanshire
Conwy	Conwy
Corn	Cornwall
Cumb	Cumbria
Darl	Darlington
Denb	Denbighshire
Derby	City of Derby
Derbys	Derbyshire
Devon	Devon
Dorset	Dorset
Dumfries	Dumfries and Galloway
Dundee	Dundee City
Durham	Durham
E Ayrs	East Ayrshire
Edin	City of Edinburgh
E Dunb	East Dunbartonshire
E Loth	East Lothian
E Renf	East Renfrewshire
Essex	Essex
E Sus	East Sussex
E Yorks	East Riding of Yorkshire
Falk	Falkirk
Fife	Fife
Flint	Flintshire
Glasgow	City of Glasgow
Glos	Gloucestershire
Gtr Man	Greater Manchester
Guern	Guernsey
Gwyn	Gwynedd
Halton	Halton
Hants	Hampshire
Hereford	Herefordshire
Herts	Hertfordshire
Highld	Highland
Hrtlpl	Hartlepool
Hull	Hull
Invclyd	Inverclyde
IoM	Isle of Man
IoW	Isle of Wight
Jersey	Jersey
Kent	Kent
Lancs	Lancashire
Leicester	City of Leicester
Leics	Leicestershire
Lincs	Lincolnshire
London	Greater London
Luton	Luton
Mbro	Middlesbrough
Medway	Medway
Mers	Merseyside
Midloth	Midlothian
M Keynes	Milton Keynes
Mon	Monmouthshire
Moray	Moray
M Tydf	Merthyr Tydfil
N Ayrs	North Ayrshire
Neath	Neath Port Talbot
NE Lincs	North East Lincolnshire
Newport	City and County of Newport
N Lanark	North Lanarkshire
N Lincs	North Lincolnshire
N Nhants	North Northamptonshire
Norf	Norfolk
Northumb	Northumberland
Nottingham	City of Nottingham
Notts	Nottinghamshire
N Som	North Somerset
N Yorks	North Yorkshire
Orkney	Orkney
Oxon	Oxfordshire
Pboro	Peterborough
Pembs	Pembrokeshire
Perth	Perth and Kinross
Plym	Plymouth
Powys	Powys
Ptsmth	Portsmouth
Reading	Reading
Redcar	Redcar and Cleveland
Renfs	Renfrewshire
Rhondda	Rhondda Cynon Taff
Rutland	Rutland
S Ayrs	South Ayrshire
Scilly	Scilly
S Glos	South Gloucestershire
Shetland	Shetland
Shrops	Shropshire
S Lanark	South Lanarkshire
Slough	Slough
Som	Somerset
Soton	Southampton
Southend	Southend-on-Sea
Staffs	Staffordshire
Stirling	Stirling
Stockton	Stockton-on-Tees
Stoke	Stoke-on-Trent
Suff	Suffolk
Sur	Surrey
Swansea	Swansea
Swindon	Swindon
S Yorks	South Yorkshire
T&W	Tyne and Wear
Telford	Telford and Wrekin
Thurrock	Thurrock
Torbay	Torbay
Torf	Torfaen
V Glam	The Vale of Glamorgan
Warks	Warwickshire
Warr	Warrington
W Berks	West Berkshire
W Dunb	West Dunbartonshire
Wilts	Wiltshire
Windsor	Windsor and Maidenhead
W Isles	Western Isles
W Loth	West Lothian
W Mid	West Midlands
W Nhants	West Northamptonshire
Wokingham	Wokingham
Worcs	Worcestershire
Wrex	Wrexham
W Sus	West Sussex
W Yorks	West Yorkshire
York	City of York

How to use the index

Example

Trudoxhill Som   24 E2
- grid square
- page number
- county or unitary authority

A

Abbas Combe 12 B5
Abberley 50 C2
Abberton Essex ... 43 C6
  Worcs 50 D4
Abberwick 117 C7
Abbess Roding ... 42 C1
Abbey 11 C6
Abbey-cwm-hir ... 48 B2
Abbeydale 88 F4
Abbey Dore 49 F5
Abbey Field 43 B5
Abbey Hulton 75 E6
Abbey St Bathans 122 C3
Abbeystead 93 D5
Abbey Town 107 D8
Abbey Village 86 B4
Abbey Wood 29 B5
Abbots Bickington . 9 C5
Abbots Bromley .. 62 B4
Abbotsbury 12 F3
Abbotsham 9 B6
Abbotskerswell .. 7 C6
Abbots Langley ... 40 D3
Abbotsley 54 D3
Abbots Morton .. 50 D5
Abbots Ripton ... 54 B3
Abbots Salford .. 51 D5
Abbotswood 14 B4
Abbotts Ann 25 E8
Abcott 49 B5
Abdon 61 F5
Aber 46 E3
Aberaeron 46 C3
Aberaman 34 D4
Aberangell 58 C5
Aber-Arad 46 F2
Aberarder 137 F7
Aberarder House . 138 E2
Aberarder Lodge . 137 E8
Aberargie 128 C3
Aberarth 46 C3
Aberavon 33 E8
Aber-banc 46 E2
Aberbeeg 35 D6
Abercanaid 34 D4
Abercarn 35 E6
Abercastle 44 B3
Abercegir 58 D5
Aberchirder 152 C6
Aber Cowarth ... 59 C5
Abercraf 34 C2
Abercrombie 129 D7
Abercych 45 E4
Abercynafon 34 C4
Abercynon 34 E4
Aberdalgie 128 B2
Aberdâr
  = Aberdare 34 D3

Aberdare
  = Aberdâr 34 D3
Aberdaron 70 E2
Aberdaugleddau
  = Milford Haven .. 44 E4
Aberdeen 141 D8
Aberdesach 82 F4
Aberdour 128 F3
Aberdovey 58 E3
Aberdulais 34 D1
Aberedw 48 E2
Abererch 70 D4
Aberfan 34 D4
Aberfeldy 133 E5
Aberffraw 82 E3
Aberffrwd 47 B5
Aberford 95 F7
Aberfoyle 126 D4
Abergavenny
  = Y Fenni 35 C6
Abergele 72 B3
Aber-Giâr 46 E4
Abergorlech 46 F4
Abergwaun
  = Fishguard 44 B4
Abergwesyn 47 D7
Abergwili 33 B5
Abergwynant 58 C3
Aber-gwynfi 34 E2
Abergwyngregyn .. 83 D6
Abergynolwyn 58 D3
Aber-Hirnant 72 F3
Aberhonddu
  = Brecon 34 B4
Aberhosan 58 E5
Aberkenfig 34 F2
Aberlady 129 F6
Aberlemno 135 D5
Aberllefenni 58 D4
Abermagwr 47 B5
Abermaw
  = Barmouth 58 C3
Abermeurig 46 D4
Abermule 59 E8
Abernaint 59 B8
Abernant 32 B4
Aber-nant 34 D4
Abernethy 128 C3
Abernyte 134 F2
Aberpennar
  = Mountain Ash .. 34 E4
Aberporth 45 D4
Aber-Rhiwlech .. 59 B6
Abersoch 70 E4
Abersychan 35 D6
Abertawe
  = Swansea 33 E7
Aberteifi
  = Cardigan 45 E3
Aberthin 22 B2
Abertillery
  = Abertyleri 35 D6

Abertridwr Caerph. . 35 F5
  Powys 59 C7
Abertyleri
  = Abertillery 35 D6
Abertysswg 35 D5
Aberuthven 127 C8
Aber-Village 35 B5
Aberyscir 34 B3
Aberystwyth 58 F2
Abhainn Suidhe .. 154 G5
Abingdon-on-
  Thames 38 E4
Abinger Common . 28 E2
Abinger Hammer .. 27 E8
Abington 114 B2
Abington Pigotts .. 54 E4
Ab Kettleby 64 B4
Ab Lench 50 D5
Ablington Glos 37 D8
  Wilts 25 E6
Abney 75 B8
Aboyne 140 E4
Abram 86 D4
Abriachan 151 H8
Abridge 41 E7
Abronhill 119 B7
Abson 24 B2
Abthorpe 52 E4
Abune-the-Hill .. 159 F3
Aby 79 B7
Acaster Malbis .. 95 E8
Acaster Selby ... 95 E8
Accrington 87 B5
Acha 146 F4
Achabraid 145 E7
Achachork 149 D9
Achafolla 124 D3
Achagary 157 D10
Achahoish 144 F6
Achalader 133 E8
Achallader 131 E7
Acha Mor 155 E8
Achanalt 150 E5
Achanamara 144 E6
Achandunie 151 D9
Ach'an Todhair .. 130 B4
Achany 157 J8
Achaphubuil 130 B4
Acharacle 147 E9
Acharn Highld 147 F10
  Perth 132 E4
Acharole 158 E4
Achath 141 C6
Achavanich 158 F3
Achavraat 151 G12
Achddu 33 D5
Achduart 156 J3
Achentoul 157 F11
Achfary 156 F5
Achgarve 155 H13
Achiemore Highld .. 156 C6
  Highld 157 D11
A'Chill 148 H7

Achiltibuie 156 J3
Achina 157 C10
Achinduich 157 J8
Achinduin 124 B4
Achingills 158 D3
Achintee Highld .. 131 B5
  Highld 150 G2
Achintraid 149 E13
Achlean 138 E4
Achleck 146 G7
Achluachrach 137 F5
Achlyness 156 D5
Achmelvich 156 G3
Achmore Highld .. 149 E13
  Stirling 132 F2
Achnaba Argyll ... 124 B5
  Argyll 145 E8
Achnabat 151 H8
Achnacarnin 156 F3
Achnacarry 136 F4
Achnacloich Argyll 125 B5
  Highld 149 H10
Achnaconeran ... 137 C7
Achnacraig 146 G7
Achnacroish 130 E2
Achnadrish 146 F7
Achnafalnich 125 C8
Achnagarron 151 E9
Achnaha 146 E7
Achnahanat 151 B8
Achnahannet 139 B5
Achnairn 157 H8
Achnaluachrach .. 157 J9
Achnasaul 136 F4
Achnasheen 150 F4
Achosnich 146 E7
Achranich 147 G10
Achreamie 157 C13
Achriabhach 131 C5
Achriesgill 156 D5
Achrimsdale 157 J12
Achtoty 157 C9
Achurch 65 F7
Achuvoldrach ... 157 D8
Achvaich 151 B10
Achvarasdal 157 C12
Ackergill 158 E5
Acklam Mbro..... 102 C2
  N Yorks 96 C3
Ackleton 61 E7
Acklington 117 D8
Ackton 88 B5
Ackworth Moor
  Top 88 C5
Acle 69 C7
Acock's Green ... 62 F5
Acol 31 C7
Acomb Northumb .. 110 C2
  York 95 D8
Aconbury 49 F7
Acre 87 B5
Acrefair 73 E6
Acre Street 15 E8

Acton Ches E 74 D3
  Dorset 13 G7
  London 41 F5
  Shrops 60 F3
  Suff 56 E2
  Wrex 73 D7
Acton Beauchamp. 49 D8
Acton Bridge 74 B2
Acton Burnell ... 60 D5
Acton Green 49 D8
Acton Pigott 60 D5
Acton Round 61 E6
Acton Scott 60 F4
Acton Trussell .. 62 C3
Acton Turville .. 37 F5
Adbaston 61 B7
Adber 12 B3
Adderley 74 E3
Adderstone 123 F7
Addiewell 120 C2
Addingham 94 E3
Addington Bucks .. 39 B7
  Kent 29 D7
  London 28 C4
Addinston 121 D8
Addiscombe 28 C4
Addlestone 27 C8
Addlethorpe 79 C8
Adel 95 F5
Adeney 61 C7
Adfa 59 D7
Adforton 49 B6
Adisham 31 D6
Adlestrop 38 B2
Adlingfleet 90 B2
Adlington 86 C4
Admaston Staffs .. 62 B4
  Telford 61 C6
Admington 51 E7
Adstock 52 F5
Adstone 52 D3
Adversane 16 B4
Advie 152 E1
Adwalton 88 B3
Adwell 39 E6
Adwick le Street .. 89 D6
Adwick upon
  Dearne 89 D5
Adziel 153 C9
Ae Village 114 F2
Affleck 141 B7
Affpuddle 13 E6
Affric Lodge 136 B4
Afon-wen 72 B5
Afton 14 F4
Agglethorpe 101 F5
Agneash 84 D4
Aigburth 85 F4
Aiginis 155 D9
Aike 97 E6
Aikerness 159 C5
Aikers 159 J5
Aiketgate 108 E4

Aikton 108 D2
Ailey 48 E5
Ailstone 51 D7
Ailsworth 65 E8
Ainderby
  Quernhow 102 F1
Ainderby Steeple . 101 E8
Aingers Green 43 B7
Ainsdale 85 C4
Ainsdale-on-Sea .. 85 C4
Ainstable 108 E5
Ainsworth 87 C5
Ainthorpe 103 D5
Aintree 85 E4
Aird Argyll 124 E3
  Dumfries 104 C4
  Highld 149 A12
  W Isles 155 D10
Aird a' Mhachair .. 148 D2
Aird a' Mhulaidh .. 154 F6
Aird Asaig 154 G6
Aird Dhail 155 A9
Airdens 151 B9
Aird Mhidhinis .. 148 H2
Aird Mhighe
  W Isles 154 H6
  W Isles 154 J5
Aird Mhor 148 H2
Aird of Sleat ... 149 H10
Airdrie 119 C7
Airdtorrisdale .. 157 C9
Aird Uig 154 D5
Airidh a Bhruaich . 154 F7
Airieland 106 D4
Airmyn 89 B8
Airntully 133 F7
Airor 149 H12
Airth 127 F7
Airton 94 D2
Airyhassen 105 E7
Aisby Lincs 78 F3
  Lincs 90 E2
Aisgernis 148 F2
Aiskew 101 F7
Aislaby N Yorks .. 103 D6
  N Yorks 103 F5
  Stockton 102 C2
Aisthorpe 78 A2
Aith Orkney 159 G3
  Shetland 160 D8
  Shetland 160 H5
Aithsetter 160 K6
Aitkenhead 112 D3
Aitnoch 151 H12
Akeld 117 B5
Akeley 52 F5
Akenham 56 E5
Alaston 6 B2
Albaston 6 B2
Alberbury 60 C3
Albourne 17 C6
Albrighton Shrops .. 60 C4
  Shrops 62 D2

Alburgh 69 F5
Albury Herts 41 B7
  Sur 27 E8
Albury End 41 B7
Alby Hill 81 D7
Alcaig 151 F8
Alcaston 60 F4
Alcester 51 D5
Alciston 18 E2
Alcombe Som 21 E8
  Wilts 24 C3
Alconbury 54 B2
Alconbury Weston . 54 B2
Aldborough Norf .. 81 D7
  N Yorks 95 C7
Aldbourne 25 B7
Aldbrough 97 F8
Aldbrough St
  John 101 C7
Aldbury 40 C2
Aldcliffe 92 C4
Aldclune 133 C6
Aldeburgh 57 D8
Aldeby 69 E7
Aldenham 40 E4
Alderbury 14 B2
Aldercar 76 E4
Alderford 68 C4
Alderholt 14 C2
Alderley 36 E4
Alderley Edge ... 74 B5
Aldermaston 26 C3
Aldermaston
  Wharf 26 C4
Alderminster..... 51 E7
Alder's End 49 E8
Aldersey Green .. 73 D8
Aldershot 27 D6
Alderton Glos 50 F5
  Shrops 60 B4
  Suff 57 E7
  Wilts 37 F5
  W Nhants 52 E5
Alderwasley 76 D3
Aldfield 95 C5
Aldford 73 D8
Aldham Essex 43 B5
  Suff 56 E4
Aldie 151 C10
Aldingbourne 16 D3
Aldingham 92 B2
Aldington Kent .. 19 B7
  Worcs 51 E5
Aldington Frith .. 19 B7
Aldochlay 126 E2
Aldreth 54 B5
Aldridge 62 D4
Aldringham 57 C8
Aldsworth 38 C1
Aldunie 140 B2
Aldwark Derbys .. 76 D2
  N Yorks 95 C7

Aldwick 16 E3
Aldwincle 65 F7
Aldworth 26 B3
Alexandria 118 B3
Alfardisworthy .. 8 C4
Alfington 11 E6
Alfold 27 F8
Alfold Bars 27 F8
Alfold Crossways . 27 F8
Alford Aberds 140 C4
  Lincs 79 B7
  Som 23 F8
Alfreton 76 D4
Alfrick 50 D2
Alfrick Pound .. 50 D2
Alfriston 18 E2
Algaltraig 145 F9
Algarkirk 79 F5
Alhampton 23 F8
Aline Lodge 154 F6
Alisary 147 D10
Alkborough 90 B2
Alkerton 51 E8
Alkham 31 E6
Alkington 74 F2
Alkmonton 75 F8
Alladale Lodge .. 150 C7
Allaleigh 7 D6
Allanaquoich ... 139 E7
Allangrange
  Mains 151 F9
Allanton Borders . 122 D4
  N Lanark 119 D8
Allathasdal 148 H1
All Cannings 25 C5
Allendale Town .. 109 D8
Allenheads 109 E8
Allensford 110 D3
Allens Green 41 C7
Allensmore 49 F6
Allenton 76 F3
Aller 12 B2
Allerby 107 F7
Allerford 21 E8
Allerston 103 F6
Allerthorpe 96 E3
Allerton Mers ... 86 F2
  W Yorks 94 F4
Allerton Bywater . 88 B5
Allerton
  Mauleverer ... 95 D7
Allesley 63 F7
Allestree 76 F3
Allet 3 B6
Allexton 64 D5
Allgreave 75 C6
Allhallows 30 B2
Allhallows-on-Sea 30 B2
Alligin Shuas ... 149 C13
Allimore Green .. 62 C2
Allington Lincs .. 77 E8
  Wilts 25 C5
  Wilts 25 E7

Abb–Alt

Allithwaite 92 B3
Alloa 127 E7
Allonby 107 E7
Alloway 112 C3
All Saints South
  Elmham 69 F6
All Stretton 60 E4
Allt 33 D6
Alltchaorunn ... 131 D5
Alltforgan 59 B6
Alltmawr 48 E2
Alltnacaillich .. 156 E7
Allt na h-Airbhe . 150 B4
Allt-nan-sùgh .. 136 B2
Alltsigh 137 C7
Alltwalis 46 F3
Alltwen 33 D8
Alltyblaca 46 E4
Allwood Green .. 56 B4
Almeley 48 D5
Almer 13 E7
Almholme 89 D6
Almington 74 F4
Alminstone
  Cross 8 B5
Almondbank 128 B2
Almondbury 88 C2
Almondsbury ... 36 F3
Alne 95 C7
Alness 151 E9
Alnham 117 C5
Alnmouth 117 C8
Alnwick 117 C7
Alperton 40 F4
Alphamstone ... 56 F2
Alpheton 56 D2
Alphington 10 E4
Alport 76 C2
Alpraham 74 D2
Alresford 43 B6
Alrewas 63 C5
Alsager 74 D4
Alsagers Bank .. 74 E5
Alsop en le Dale . 75 D8
Alston Cumb 109 E7
  Devon 11 D8
Alstone 50 F4
Alstonefield 75 D8
Alswear 10 B2
Altandhu 156 H2
Altanduin 157 G11
Altarnun 8 F4
Altass 156 J7
Altham 93 F7
Althorne 43 E5
Althorpe 90 D2
Alticry 105 D6
Altnabreac
  Station 157 E13

Altnacealgach Hotel ... 156 H5
Altnacraig ... 124 C4
Altnafeadh ... 131 D6
Altnaharra ... 157 F8
Altofts ... 88 B4
Alton Derbys ... 76 C3
— Hants ... 26 F5
— Staffs ... 75 E7
Alton Pancras ... 12 D5
Alton Priors ... 25 C6
Altrincham ... 87 F5
Altrua ... 136 F5
Altskeith ... 126 D4
Altyre House ... 151 F13
Alva ... 127 E7
Alvanley ... 73 B8
Alvaston ... 76 F3
Alvechurch ... 50 B5
Alvecote ... 63 D6
Alvediston ... 13 B7
Alveley ... 61 F7
Alverdiscott ... 9 B7
Alverstoke ... 15 E7
Alverstone ... 15 F6
Alverton ... 77 E7
Alves ... 152 B1
Alvescot ... 38 D2
Alveston S Glos ... 36 F3
— Warks ... 51 D7
Alvie ... 138 D4
Alvingham ... 91 E7
Alvington ... 36 D3
Alwalton ... 65 E8
Alweston ... 12 C4
Alwinton ... 116 D5
Alwoodley ... 95 E5
Alyth ... 134 E2
Amatnatua ... 150 B7
Am Baile ... 148 G2
Ambergate ... 76 D3
Amber Hill ... 78 E5
Amberley Glos ... 37 D5
— W Sus ... 16 C4
Amble ... 117 D8
Amblecote ... 62 F2
Ambler Thorn ... 87 B8
Ambleside ... 99 D5
Ambleston ... 44 C5
Ambrosden ... 39 C6
Am Buth ... 124 C4
Amcotts ... 90 C2
Amersham ... 40 E2
Amesbury ... 25 E6
Amington ... 63 D6
Amisfield ... 114 F2
Amlwch ... 82 B4
Amlwch Port ... 82 B4
Ammanford = Rhydaman ... 33 C7
Amod ... 143 E8
Amotherby ... 96 B3
Ampfield ... 14 B5
Ampleforth ... 95 B8
Ampney Crucis ... 37 D7
Ampney St Mary ... 37 D7
Ampney St Peter ... 37 D7
Amport ... 25 E7
Ampthill ... 53 F8
Ampton ... 56 B2
Amroth ... 32 D2
Amulree ... 133 F5
Anagach ... 139 B6
Anaheilt ... 130 C2
Anancaun ... 150 E3
An Caol ... 149 C11
Ancaster ... 78 E2
Anchor ... 59 F8
Anchorsholme ... 92 E3
An Cnoc ... 155 D9
Ancroft ... 123 E5
Ancrum ... 116 B2
Anderby ... 79 B8
Anderson ... 13 E6
Anderton ... 74 B3
Andover ... 25 E8
Andover Down ... 25 E8
Andoversford ... 37 C7
Andreas ... 84 C4
Anfield ... 85 E4
Angersleigh ... 11 C6
Angle ... 44 E3
An Gleann Ur ... 155 D9
Angmering ... 16 D4
Angram N Yorks ... 95 E8
— N Yorks ... 100 E3
Anie ... 126 C4
Ankerville ... 151 D11
Anlaby ... 90 B4
Anmer ... 80 E3
Anmore ... 15 C7
Annan ... 107 C8
Annat Argyll ... 125 C6
— Highld ... 149 C13
Anna Valley ... 25 E8
Annbank ... 112 B4
Annesley ... 76 D5
Annesley Woodhouse ... 76 D4
Annfield Plain ... 110 D4
Annifirth ... 160 J3
Annitsford ... 111 B5
Annscroft ... 60 D4
Ansdell ... 85 B4
Ansford ... 23 F8
Ansley ... 63 E6
Anslow ... 63 B6
Anslow Gate ... 63 B5
Anstey Herts ... 54 F5
— Leics ... 64 D2
Anstruther Easter ... 129 D7
Anstruther Wester ... 129 D7
Ansty Hants ... 26 E5
— Warks ... 63 F7
— Wilts ... 13 B7
— W Sus ... 17 B6
Anthill Common ... 15 C7
Anthorn ... 107 D8
Antingham ... 81 D8
An t-Ob = Leverburgh ... 154 J5
Anton's Gowt ... 79 E5
Antonshill ... 127 F7
Antony ... 5 D8
Anwick ... 78 D4

Anwoth ... 106 D2
Aoradh ... 142 B3
Apes Hall ... 67 E5
Apethorpe ... 65 E7
Apeton ... 62 C2
Apley ... 78 B4
Apperknowle ... 76 B3
Apperley ... 37 B5
Apperley Bridge ... 94 F4
Appersett ... 100 E3
Appin ... 130 E3
Appin House ... 130 E3
Appleby ... 90 C3
Appleby-in-Westmorland ... 100 B1
Appleby Magna ... 63 D7
Appleby Parva ... 63 D7
Applecross ... 149 D12
Applecross House ... 149 D12
Appledore Devon ... 11 C5
— Devon ... 20 F3
— Kent ... 19 C6
Appledore Heath ... 19 B6
Appleford ... 39 E5
Appleshaw ... 25 E8
Appleshaw ... 25 E8
Applethwaite ... 98 B4
Appleton Halton ... 86 F3
— Oxon ... 38 D4
Appleton-le-Moors ... 103 E5
Appleton-le-Street ... 96 B3
Appleton Roebuck ... 95 E8
Appleton Thorn ... 86 F4
Appleton Wiske ... 102 D1
Appletreehall ... 115 C8
Appletreewick ... 94 C3
Appley ... 11 B5
Appley Bridge ... 86 D3
Apse Heath ... 15 F6
Apsley End ... 54 F2
Apuldram ... 16 D2
Aquhythie ... 141 C6
Arabella ... 151 D11
Arbeadie ... 141 E5
Arberth = Narberth ... 32 C2
Arbirlot ... 135 E6
Arboll ... 151 C11
Arborfield ... 27 C5
Arborfield Cross ... 27 C5
Arborfield Garrison ... 27 C5
Arbourthorne ... 88 F4
Arbroath ... 135 E6
Arbuthnott ... 135 B7
Archiestown ... 152 D2
Arclid ... 74 C4
Ardachu ... 157 J9
Ardalanish ... 146 K6
Ardanaiseig ... 125 C6
Ardaneaskan ... 149 E13
Ardanstur ... 124 D4
Ardargie House Hotel ... 128 C2
Ardarroch ... 149 E13
Ardbeg Argyll ... 142 D5
— Argyll ... 145 G10
Ardcharnich ... 150 C4
Ardchiavaig ... 146 K6
Ardchullarie More ... 126 C4
Ardchyle ... 126 B4
Ard-dhubh ... 149 D12
Arddleen ... 60 C2
Ardechvie ... 136 E4
Ardeley ... 41 B6
Ardelve ... 149 F13
Arden ... 126 F2
Ardens Grafton ... 51 D6
Ardentinny ... 145 E10
Ardentraive ... 145 F9
Ardeonaig ... 132 F3
Ardersier ... 151 F10
Ardessie ... 150 C3
Ardfern ... 124 E4
Ardgartan ... 125 E8
Ardgay ... 151 B8
Ardgour ... 130 C4
Ardheslaig ... 149 C12
Ardiecow ... 152 B5
Ardindrean ... 150 C4
Ardingly ... 17 B7
Ardington ... 38 F4
Ardlair ... 140 B4
Ardlamont House ... 145 G8
Ardleigh ... 43 B6
Ardler ... 134 E2
Ardley ... 39 B5
Ardlui ... 126 C2
Ardlussa ... 144 E5
Ardmair ... 150 B4
Ardmay ... 125 E8
Ardminish ... 143 D7
Ardmolich ... 147 D10
Ardmore Argyll ... 143 C7
— Highld ... 151 C10
— Highld ... 156 D5
Ardnacross ... 147 G8
Ardnadam ... 145 F10
Ardnagrask ... 151 G8
Ardnarff ... 149 E13
Ardnastang ... 130 C2
Ardnave ... 142 A3
Ardno ... 125 E7
Ardo ... 153 E8
Ardoch ... 133 F7
Ardochy House ... 136 D5
Ardo House ... 141 B8
Ardoyne ... 141 B5
Ardpatrick ... 144 G6
Ardpatrick House ... 144 H6
Ardpeaton ... 145 E11
Ardrishaig ... 145 E7
Ardross Fife ... 129 D7
— Highld ... 151 D9
Ardrossan ... 118 E2
Ardross Castle ... 151 D9
Ardshealach ... 147 E9
Ardsley ... 88 D4
Ardslignish ... 147 E8
Ardtalla ... 142 C5
Ardtalnaig ... 132 F4
Ardtoe ... 147 D9
Ardtrostan ... 127 B5
Arduaine ... 124 D3
Ardullie ... 151 E8

Ardvasar ... 149 H11
Ardvorlich ... 126 B5
Ardwell ... 104 E5
Ardwell Mains ... 104 E5
Ardwick ... 87 E6
Areley Kings ... 50 B3
Arford ... 27 F6
Argoed Caerph ... 35 E5
— Powys ... 47 C8
Arichamish ... 124 E5
Arichastlich ... 125 B8
Aridhglas ... 146 J6
Arileod ... 146 F4
Arinacrinachd ... 149 C12
Arinagour ... 146 F5
Arion ... 159 G3
Arisaig ... 147 C9
Ariundle ... 130 C2
Arkendale ... 95 C6
Arkesden ... 55 F5
Arkholme ... 93 B5
Arkle Town ... 101 D5
Arkley ... 41 E5
Arksey ... 89 D6
Arkwright Town ... 76 B4
Arle ... 37 B6
Arlecdon ... 98 C2
Arlesey ... 54 F2
Arleston ... 61 C6
Arley ... 86 F4
Arlingham ... 36 C4
Arlington Devon ... 20 E5
— E Sus ... 18 E2
— Glos ... 37 D8
Armadale Highld ... 157 C10
— W Loth ... 120 C2
Armadale Castle ... 149 H11
Armathwaite ... 108 E5
Arminghall ... 69 D5
Armitage ... 62 C4
Armley ... 95 F5
Armscote ... 51 E7
Armthorpe ... 89 D7
Arnabost ... 146 F5
Arncliffe ... 94 B2
Arncroach ... 129 D7
Arne ... 13 F7
Arnesby ... 64 E3
Arngask ... 128 C3
Arnisdale ... 149 G13
Arnish ... 149 D10
Arniston Engine ... 121 C6
Arnol ... 155 C8
Arnold E Yorks ... 97 E7
— Notts ... 77 E5
Arnprior ... 126 E5
Arnside ... 92 B4
Aros Mains ... 147 G8
Arowry ... 73 F8
Arpafeelie ... 151 F9
Arrad Foot ... 99 F5
Arram ... 97 E6
Arrathorne ... 101 E7
Arreton ... 15 F6
Arrington ... 54 D4
Arrivain ... 125 B8
Arrochar ... 125 E8
Arrow ... 51 D5
Arthington ... 95 E5
Arthingworth ... 64 F4
Arthog ... 58 C3
Arthrath ... 153 E9
Arthurstone ... 134 E2
Artrochie ... 153 E10
Arundel ... 16 D4
Aryhoulan ... 130 C4
Asby ... 98 B2
Ascog ... 145 G10
Ascot ... 27 C7
Ascott ... 51 F8
Ascott-under-Wychwood ... 38 C3
Asenby ... 95 B6
Asfordby ... 64 C4
Asfordby Hill ... 64 C4
Asgarby Lincs ... 78 E4
— Lincs ... 79 C6
Ash Kent ... 29 C6
— Kent ... 31 D6
— Som ... 12 B2
— Sur ... 27 D6
Ashampstead ... 26 B3
Ashbocking ... 57 D5
Ashbourne ... 75 E8
Ashbrittle ... 11 B5
Ash Bullayne ... 10 D2
Ashburton ... 7 C5
Ashbury Devon ... 9 E7
— Oxon ... 38 F2
Ashby ... 90 D3
Ashby by Partney ... 79 C7
Ashby cum Fenby ... 91 D6
Ashby de la Launde ... 78 D3
Ashby-de-la-Zouch ... 63 C7
Ashby Folville ... 64 C4
Ashby Magna ... 64 E2
Ashby Parva ... 64 F2
Ashby Puerorum ... 79 B6
Ashby St Ledgers ... 52 C3
Ashby St Mary ... 69 D6
Ashchurch ... 50 F4
Ashcombe ... 7 B7
Ashcott ... 23 F6
Ashdon ... 55 E6
Ashe ... 26 E3
Asheldham ... 43 D5
Ashen ... 55 E8
Ashendon ... 39 C7
Ashfield Carms ... 33 B7
— Stirling ... 127 D6
— Suff ... 57 C6
Ashfield Green ... 57 B6
Ashford Carms ... 17 B6
Ashford Devon ... 20 F4
— Hants ... 14 C2
— Kent ... 30 E4
— Sur ... 27 B8
Ashford Bowdler ... 49 B7
Ashford Carbonell ... 49 B7
Ashford Hill ... 26 C3
Ashford in the Water ... 75 C8
Ashgill ... 119 E7
Ash Green ... 63 F7
Ashill Devon ... 11 C5

Ashill continued
— Norf ... 67 D8
— Som ... 11 C8
Ashingdon ... 42 E4
Ashington Northumb ... 117 F8
— Som ... 12 B3
— W Sus ... 16 C5
Ashintully Castle ... 133 C8
Ashkirk ... 115 B7
Ashlett ... 15 D5
Ashleworth ... 37 B5
Ashley Cambs ... 55 C7
— Ches E ... 87 F5
— Devon ... 9 C8
— Dorset ... 14 D2
— Glos ... 37 E6
— Hants ... 14 E3
— Hants ... 25 F8
— N Nhants ... 64 E4
— Staffs ... 74 F4
Ashley Green ... 40 D2
Ashley Heath Dorset ... 14 D2
— Staffs ... 74 F4
Ash Magna ... 74 F2
Ashmanhaugh ... 69 B6
Ashmansworth ... 26 D2
Ashmansworthy ... 8 C5
Ash Mill ... 10 B2
Ashmore ... 13 C7
Ashorne ... 51 D8
Ashover ... 76 C3
Ashow ... 51 B8
Ashprington ... 7 D6
Ash Priors ... 11 B6
Ashreigney ... 9 C8
Ash Street ... 56 E4
Ashtead ... 28 D2
Ash Thomas ... 10 C5
Ashton Ches W ... 74 C2
— Corn ... 2 D5
— Hants ... 15 C6
— Hereford ... 49 C7
— Invclyd ... 118 B2
— N Nhants ... 65 F7
— W Nhants ... 53 E5
Ashton Common ... 24 D3
Ashton-in-Makerfield ... 86 E3
Ashton Keynes ... 37 E7
Ashton under Hill ... 50 F4
Ashton-under-Lyne ... 87 E7
Ashton upon Mersey ... 87 E5
Ashurst Hants ... 14 C4
— Kent ... 18 B2
— W Sus ... 17 C5
Ashurstwood ... 28 F5
Ash Vale ... 27 D6
Ashwater ... 9 E5
Ashwell Herts ... 54 F3
— Rutland ... 65 C5
— Som ... 11 C8
Ashwellthorpe ... 68 E4
Ashwick ... 23 E8
Ashwicken ... 67 C7
Ashybank ... 115 C8
Askam in Furness ... 92 B2
Askern ... 89 C6
Askerswell ... 12 E3
Askett ... 39 D8
Askham Cumb ... 99 B7
— Notts ... 77 B7
Askham Bryan ... 95 E8
Askham Richard ... 95 E8
Asknish ... 145 D8
Askrigg ... 100 E4
Askwith ... 94 E4
Aslackby ... 78 F3
Aslacton ... 68 E4
Aslockton ... 77 E7
Asloun ... 140 C4
Aspatria ... 107 E8
Aspenden ... 41 B6
Asperton ... 79 F5
Aspley Guise ... 53 F7
Aspley Heath ... 53 F7
Aspull ... 86 D4
Asselby ... 89 B8
Asserby ... 79 B7
Assington ... 56 F3
Assynt House ... 151 E8
Astbury ... 74 C5
Astcote ... 52 D4
Asterley ... 60 D3
Asterton ... 60 E3
Asthall ... 38 C2
Asthall Leigh ... 38 C3
Astley Shrops ... 60 C5
— Warks ... 63 F7
— Worcs ... 50 C2
Astley Abbotts ... 61 E7
Astley Bridge ... 86 C5
Astley Cross ... 50 C3
Astley Green ... 86 E5
Aston Ches E ... 74 E3
— Ches W ... 74 B2
— Derbys ... 88 F2
— Hereford ... 49 B6
— Herts ... 41 B5
— Oxon ... 38 D3
— Shrops ... 60 B5
— Staffs ... 74 E4
— S Yorks ... 89 F5
— Telford ... 61 D6
— W Mid ... 62 F4
— Wokingham ... 39 F7
Aston Abbotts ... 39 B8
Aston Botterell ... 61 F6
Aston-by-Stone ... 75 F6
Aston Cantlow ... 51 D6
Aston Clinton ... 40 C1
Aston Crews ... 36 B3
Aston Cross ... 50 F4
Aston End ... 41 B5
Aston Eyre ... 61 E6
Aston Fields ... 50 C4
Aston Flamville ... 63 E8
Aston Ingham ... 36 B3
Aston juxta Mondrum ... 74 D3
Aston le Walls ... 52 D2
Aston Magna ... 51 F6
Aston Munslow ... 60 F5
Aston on Clun ... 60 F3
Aston-on-Trent ... 63 B8
Aston Rogers ... 60 D3

Aston Rowant ... 39 E7
Aston Sandford ... 39 D7
Aston Somerville ... 50 F5
Aston Subedge ... 51 E6
Aston Tirrold ... 39 F5
Aston Upthorpe ... 39 F5
Astrop ... 52 F3
Astwick ... 54 F3
Astwood M Keynes ... 53 E7
— Worcs ... 50 D3
Astwood Bank ... 50 C5
Aswarby ... 78 F3
Aswardby ... 79 B6
Atcham ... 60 D5
Atch Lench ... 50 D5
Athelhampton ... 13 E5
Athelington ... 57 B6
Athelney ... 11 B8
Athelstaneford ... 121 B8
Atherington ... 9 B7
Atherstone ... 63 E7
Atherstone on Stour ... 51 D7
Atherton ... 86 D4
Atley Hill ... 101 D7
Atlow ... 76 E2
Attadale ... 150 H2
Attadale House ... 150 H2
Attenborough ... 76 F5
Atterby ... 90 E3
Attercliffe ... 88 F4
Attleborough Norf ... 68 E3
— Warks ... 63 E7
Attlebridge ... 68 C4
Atwick ... 97 D7
Atworth ... 24 C3
Auberrow ... 49 E6
Aubourn ... 78 C2
Auchagallon ... 143 E9
Auchallater ... 139 F7
Aucharnie ... 153 D6
Auchattie ... 141 E5
Auchavan ... 134 C1
Auchbreck ... 139 B8
Auchenback ... 118 D5
Auchenbainzie ... 113 E8
Auchenblae ... 135 B7
Auchenbrack ... 113 E7
Auchenbreck ... 145 E9
Auchencairn Dumfries ... 106 D4
— Dumfries ... 114 F2
— N Ayrs ... 143 F11
Auchencrosh ... 104 B5
Auchencrow ... 122 C4
Auchendinny ... 121 C5
Auchengray ... 120 D2
Auchenhalrig ... 152 B3
Auchenheath ... 119 E8
Auchenlochan ... 145 F8
Auchenmalg ... 105 D6
Auchensoul ... 112 E2
Auchentiber ... 118 E3
Auchertyre ... 149 F13
Auchgourish ... 138 C5
Auchincarroch ... 126 F3
Auchindrain ... 125 E6
Auchindrean ... 150 C4
Auchininna ... 153 D6
Auchinleck ... 113 B5
Auchinloch ... 119 B6
Auchinroath ... 152 C2
Auchintoul ... 140 C4
Auchiries ... 153 E10
Auchlee ... 141 E7
Auchleven ... 140 B5
Auchlochan ... 119 F8
Auchlossan ... 140 D4
Auchlunies ... 141 E7
Auchlyne ... 126 B4
Auchmacoy ... 153 E9
Auchmair ... 140 B2
Auchmantle ... 105 C5
Auchmithie ... 135 E6
Auchmuirbridge ... 128 D4
Auchmull ... 135 B5
Auchnacree ... 134 C4
Auchnagallin ... 151 H13
Auchnagatt ... 153 D9
Auchnaha ... 145 E8
Auchnashelloch ... 127 C6
Aucholzie ... 140 E2
Auchrannie ... 134 D2
Auchroisk ... 139 B6
Auchronie ... 140 F3
Auchterarder ... 127 C8
Auchteraw ... 137 D6
Auchterderran ... 128 E4
Auchterhouse ... 134 F3
Auchtermuchty ... 128 C4
Auchterneed ... 150 F7
Auchtertool ... 128 E4
Auchtertyre ... 152 C1
Auchtubh ... 126 B4
Auckengill ... 158 D5
Auckley ... 89 D7
Audenshaw ... 87 E7
Audlem ... 74 E3
Audley ... 74 D4
Audley End ... 55 F6
Auds ... 153 B6
Aughton E Yorks ... 96 F3
— Lancs ... 85 D4
— Lancs ... 93 C5
— S Yorks ... 89 F5
— Wilts ... 25 D7
Aughton Park ... 86 D2
Auldearn ... 151 F12
Aulden ... 49 D6
Auldgirth ... 114 F2
Auldhame ... 129 F7
Auldhouse ... 119 D6
Ault a'chruinn ... 136 B2
Aultanrynie ... 156 F6
Aultbea ... 155 J13
Aultdearg ... 150 E5
Aultgrishan ... 155 J12
Aultguish Inn ... 150 D6
Aultibea ... 157 G13
Aultiphurst ... 157 C11
Aultmore ... 152 C4
Aultnagoire ... 137 B8
Aultnamain Inn ... 151 C9
Aultnaslat ... 136 D4
Aulton ... 140 B5
Aundorach ... 139 C5
Aunsby ... 78 F3
Auquhorthies ... 141 B7
Aust ... 36 F2

Austendike ... 66 B2
Austerfield ... 89 E7
Austrey ... 63 D6
Austwick ... 93 C7
Authorpe ... 91 F8
Authorpe Row ... 79 B8
Avebury ... 25 C6
Aveley ... 42 F1
Avening ... 37 E5
Averham ... 77 D7
Aveton Gifford ... 6 E4
Avielochan ... 138 C5
Aviemore ... 138 C4
Avington Hants ... 26 F3
— W Berks ... 25 C8
Avoch ... 151 F10
Avon ... 14 E2
Avonbridge ... 120 B2
Avon Dassett ... 52 E2
Avonmouth ... 23 B7
Avonwick ... 6 D5
Awbridge ... 14 B4
Awhirk ... 104 D4
Awkley ... 36 F2
Awliscombe ... 11 D6
Awre ... 36 D4
Awsworth ... 76 E4
Axbridge ... 23 D6
Axford Hants ... 26 E4
— Wilts ... 25 B7
Axminster ... 11 E7
Axmouth ... 11 E7
Axton ... 85 F2
Aycliff ... 31 E7
Aycliffe ... 101 B7
Aydon ... 110 C3
Aylburton ... 36 D3
Ayle ... 109 E7
Aylesbeare ... 10 E5
Aylesbury ... 39 C8
Aylesby ... 91 D6
Aylesford ... 29 D8
Aylesham ... 31 D6
Aylestone ... 64 D2
Aylmerton ... 81 D7
Aylsham ... 81 E7
Aylton ... 49 F8
Aymestrey ... 49 C6
Aynho ... 52 F3
Ayot St Lawrence ... 40 C4
Ayot St Peter ... 41 C5
Ayr ... 112 B3
Aysgarth ... 101 F5
Ayside ... 99 F5
Ayston ... 65 D5
Aythorpe Roding ... 42 C1
Ayton ... 122 C5
Aywick ... 160 E7
Azerley ... 95 B5

B

Babbacombe ... 7 C7
Babbinswood ... 73 F7
Babcary ... 12 B3
Babel ... 47 F7
Babell ... 73 B5
Babraham ... 55 D6
Babworth ... 89 F7
Bac ... 155 C9
Bachau ... 82 C4
Backaland ... 159 E6
Backaskaill ... 159 C5
Backbarrow ... 99 F5
Backe ... 32 C3
Backfolds ... 153 C10
Backford ... 73 B8
Backford Cross ... 73 B7
Backhill Aberds ... 153 E10
Backhill of Clackriach ... 153 D9
Backhill of Fortree ... 153 D9
Backhill of Trustach ... 140 E5
Backies ... 157 J11
Backlass ... 158 E4
Back of Keppoch ... 147 C9
Back Rogerton ... 113 B5
Backwell ... 23 C6
Backworth ... 111 B6
Bacon End ... 42 C2
Baconsthorpe ... 81 D7
Bacton Hereford ... 49 F5
— Norf ... 81 D9
— Suff ... 56 C4
Bacton Green ... 56 C4
Bacup ... 87 B6
Badachro ... 149 A12
Badanloch Lodge ... 157 F10
Badavanich ... 150 F4
Badbury ... 38 F1
Badby ... 52 D3
Badcall ... 156 D5
Badcaul ... 150 B3
Baddeley Green ... 75 D6
Baddesley Clinton ... 51 B7
Baddesley Ensor ... 63 E6
Baddidarach ... 156 G3
Baddoch ... 139 F7
Baddock ... 151 F10
Badenscoth ... 153 E7
Badenyon ... 140 C2
Badger ... 61 E7
Badger's Mount ... 29 C5
Badgeworth ... 37 C6
Badgworth ... 23 D5
Badicaul ... 149 F12
Badingham ... 57 C7
Badlesmere ... 30 D4
Badlipster ... 158 F4
Badluarach ... 150 B2
Badminton ... 37 F5
Badnaban ... 156 G3
Badninish ... 151 B10
Badrallach ... 150 B3
Badsey ... 51 E5
Badshot Lea ... 27 E6
Badsworth ... 89 C5
Badwell Ash ... 56 C3
Bae Colwyn = Colwyn Bay ... 83 D8
Bag Enderby ... 79 B6
Bagendon ... 37 D7

Bagh a Chaisteil = Castlebay ... 148 J1
Baghasdal ... 148 G2
Bagh Mor ... 148 C3
Bagh Shiarabhagh ... 148 H2
Bagillt ... 73 B6
Baginton ... 51 B8
Baglan ... 33 E8
Bagley ... 60 B4
Bagnall ... 75 D6
Bagnor ... 26 C2
Bagshot Sur ... 27 C7
— Wilts ... 25 C8
Bagthorpe Norf ... 80 D3
— Notts ... 76 D4
Bagworth ... 63 D8
Bagwy Llydiart ... 35 B8
Bail Ard Bhuirgh ... 155 B9
Baildon ... 94 F4
Baile ... 154 J4
Baile Ailein ... 155 E7
Baile a Mhanaich ... 148 C2
Baile an Truiseil ... 155 B8
Bailebeag ... 137 C8
Baile Boidheach ... 144 F6
Baile Glas ... 148 C3
Baile Mhartainn ... 148 A2
Baile Mhic Phail ... 148 A3
Baile Mor Argyll ... 146 J5
— W Isles ... 148 B2
Baile na Creige ... 148 H1
Baile nan Cailleach ... 148 C2
Baile Raghaill ... 148 A2
Baileyhead ... 108 B5
Bailiesward ... 152 E4
Baillieston ... 119 C6
Bail'lochdrach ... 148 C3
Bail Uachdraich ... 148 B3
Bail'Ur Tholastaidh ... 155 C10
Bainbridge ... 100 E4
Bainsford ... 127 F7
Bainshole ... 152 E6
Bainton E Yorks ... 97 D5
— Pboro ... 65 D7
Bairnkine ... 116 C2
Baker's End ... 41 C6
Baker Street ... 42 F2
Bakewell ... 76 C2
Bala = Y Bala ... 72 F3
Balachuirn ... 149 D10
Balavil ... 138 D3
Balbeg Highld ... 137 B7
— Highld ... 150 H7
Balbeggie ... 128 B3
Balbithan ... 141 C6
Balbithan House ... 141 C6
Balblair Highld ... 151 B8
— Highld ... 151 E10
Balby ... 89 D6
Balchladich ... 156 F3
Balchraggan Highld ... 151 G8
— Highld ... 151 H8
Balchrick ... 156 D4
Balchrystie ... 129 D6
Balcladaich ... 137 B5
Balcombe ... 28 F4
Balcombe Lane ... 28 F4
Balcomie ... 129 C8
Balcurvie ... 128 D5
Baldersby ... 95 B6
Baldersby St James ... 95 B6
Balderstone ... 93 F6
Balderton Ches W ... 73 C7
— Notts ... 77 D8
Baldhu ... 3 B6
Baldinnie ... 129 C6
Baldock ... 54 F3
Baldovie ... 134 F4
Baldslow ... 18 D4
Baldwin ... 84 D3
Baldwinholme ... 108 D3
Baldwin's Gate ... 74 E4
Bale ... 81 D6
Balearn ... 153 C10
Balemartine ... 146 G2
Balephuil ... 146 G2
Balerno ... 120 C4
Balevullin ... 146 G2
Balfield ... 135 C5
Balfron ... 126 F4
Balfron Station ... 126 F4
Balgaveny ... 153 D6
Balgavies ... 135 D5
Balgonar ... 128 E2
Balgove ... 153 E8
Balgowan ... 138 E2
Balgown ... 149 B8
Balgrochan ... 119 B6
Balgy ... 149 C13
Balhaldie ... 127 D7
Balhalgardy ... 141 B6
Balham ... 28 B3
Balhary ... 134 E2
Baliasta ... 160 C8
Baligill ... 157 C11
Balintore Angus ... 134 D2
— Highld ... 151 D11
Balintraid ... 151 D10
Balk ... 102 F2
Balkeerie ... 134 E3
Balkemback ... 134 F3
Balkholme ... 89 B8
Balkissock ... 104 A5
Ball ... 60 B3
Ballabeg ... 84 E2
Ballacannell ... 84 D4
Ballachulish ... 130 C4
Ballajora ... 84 C4
Ballaleigh ... 84 D3
Ballamodha ... 84 E2
Ballantrae ... 104 A4
Ballaquine ... 84 D4
Ballards Gore ... 43 E5
Ballasalla IoM ... 84 C3
— IoM ... 84 E2
Ballater ... 140 E2
Ballaugh ... 84 C3
Ballaveare ... 84 E3
Ballcorach ... 139 B7
Ballechin ... 133 D6
Balleigh ... 151 C10
Ballencrieff ... 121 B7

Bapchild ... 30 C3
Barabhas ... 155 C8
Ball Haye Green ... 75 D6
Ball Hill ... 26 C2
Ballidon ... 76 D2
Balliemore Argyll ... 124 C4
— Argyll ... 145 E9
Ballikinrain ... 126 F4
Ballimeanoch ... 125 D6
Ballimore Argyll ... 145 E8
— Stirling ... 126 C4
Ballinaby ... 142 B3
Ballindean ... 128 B4
Ballingdon ... 56 E2
Ballinger Common ... 40 D2
Ballingham ... 49 F7
Ballingry ... 128 E3
Ballinlick ... 133 E6
Ballinluig ... 133 D6
Ballintuim ... 133 D8
Balloch Angus ... 134 D3
— Highld ... 151 G10
— N Lanark ... 119 B7
— W Dunb ... 126 F2
Ballochan ... 140 E4
Ballochford ... 152 E3
Ballochmorrie ... 112 F2
Ballochmyle ... 112 F4
Balls Cross ... 16 B3
Balls Green ... 43 B6
Ballygown ... 146 G7
Ballygrant ... 142 B4
Ballyhaugh ... 146 F4
Balmacara ... 149 F13
Balmacara Square ... 149 F13
Balmaclellan ... 106 B3
Balmacneil ... 133 D6
Balmacqueen ... 149 A9
Balmae ... 106 E3
Balmaha ... 126 E3
Balmalcolm ... 128 D5
Balmeanach ... 149 D10
Balmedie ... 141 C8
Balmer Heath ... 73 F8
Balmerino ... 129 B5
Balmerlawn ... 14 D4
Balmichael ... 143 E10
Balmirmer ... 135 F5
Balmore Highld ... 149 D7
— Highld ... 150 H6
— Highld ... 151 G11
— Perth ... 133 D6
Balmule ... 128 F4
Balmullo ... 129 B6
Balmungie ... 151 F10
Balnaboth ... 134 C3
Balnabruaich ... 151 E10
Balnabruich ... 158 H3
Balnacoil ... 157 H11
Balnacra ... 150 G2
Balnafoich ... 151 H9
Balnagall ... 151 C11
Balnaguard ... 133 D6
Balnahard Argyll ... 144 D3
— Argyll ... 146 H7
Balnain ... 150 H7
Balnakeil ... 156 C6
Balnaknock ... 149 B9
Balnapaling ... 151 E10
Balne ... 89 C6
Balochroy ... 143 C8
Balone ... 129 C6
Balornock ... 119 C6
Balquharn ... 133 F7
Balquhidder ... 126 B4
Balsall ... 51 B7
Balsall Common ... 51 B7
Balsall Heath ... 62 F4
Balscott ... 51 E8
Balsham ... 55 D6
Baltasound ... 160 C8
Balterley ... 74 D4
Baltersan ... 105 C8
Balthangie ... 153 C8
Baltonsborough ... 23 F7
Balvaird ... 151 F8
Balvicar ... 124 D3
Balvraid Highld ... 149 G13
— Highld ... 151 H11
Balwest ... 2 C4
Bamber Bridge ... 86 B3
Bambers Green ... 42 B1
Bamburgh ... 123 F7
Bamff ... 134 D2
Bamford Derbys ... 88 F3
— Gtr Man ... 87 C6
Bampton Cumb ... 99 C7
— Devon ... 10 B4
— Oxon ... 38 D3
Bampton Grange ... 99 C7
Banavie ... 131 B5
Banbury ... 52 E2
Bancffosfelen ... 33 C5
Banchory ... 141 E5
Banchory-Devenick ... 141 D8
Bancycapel ... 33 C5
Bancyfelin ... 32 C4
Bancyffordd ... 46 F3
Bandirran ... 134 F2
Banff ... 153 B6
Bangor ... 83 D5
Bangor-is-y-coed = Bangor-on-Dee ... 73 E7
Bangor-on-Dee = Bangor-is-y-coed ... 73 E7
Banham ... 68 F3
Bank ... 14 D3
Bankend ... 107 C7
Bankfoot ... 133 F7
Bankglen ... 113 C5
Bankhead Aberdeen ... 141 C7
— Aberds ... 141 D5
Banknock ... 119 B7
Banks Cumb ... 109 C5
— Lancs ... 85 B4
Bankshill ... 114 F4
Bank Street ... 49 C8
Banningham ... 81 E8
Banniskirk House ... 158 E3
Bannister Green ... 42 B2
Bannockburn ... 127 E7
Banstead ... 28 D3
Bantham ... 6 E4
Banton ... 119 B7
Banwell ... 23 D5
Banyard's Green ... 57 B6
Bapton ... 24 F4

Baptist End ... 62 F3
Barabhas ... 155 C8
Barabhas Iarach ... 155 C8
Barabhas Uarach ... 155 B8
Barachandroman ... 124 C2
Barassie ... 118 F3
Baravullin ... 124 E4
Barbaraville ... 151 D10
Barber Booth ... 88 F2
Barbieston ... 112 C4
Barbon ... 99 F8
Barbridge ... 74 D3
Barbrook ... 21 E6
Barby ... 52 B3
Barcaldine ... 130 E3
Barcheston ... 51 F7
Barcombe ... 17 C8
Barcombe Cross ... 17 C8
Barden ... 101 E6
Bardennoch ... 113 E5
Barden Scale ... 94 D3
Bardfield Saling ... 42 B2
Bardister ... 160 F5
Bardney ... 78 C4
Bardon ... 63 C8
Bardon Mill ... 109 C7
Bardowie ... 119 B5
Bardrainney ... 118 B3
Bardsea ... 92 B3
Bardsey ... 95 E6
Bardwell ... 56 B3
Bare ... 92 C4
Barfad ... 145 G7
Barford Norf ... 68 D4
— Warks ... 51 C7
Barford St John ... 52 F2
Barford St Martin ... 25 F5
Barford St Michael ... 52 F2
Barfrestone ... 31 D6
Bargoed = Bargod ... 35 E5
Bargod = Bargoed ... 35 E5
Bargrennan ... 105 B7
Barham Cambs ... 54 B2
— Kent ... 31 D6
— Suff ... 56 D5
Barharrow ... 106 D3
Barhill ... 106 C5
Bar Hill ... 54 C4
Barholm ... 65 C7
Barkby ... 64 D3
Barkestone-le-Vale ... 77 F7
Barkham ... 27 C5
Barking London ... 41 F7
— Suff ... 56 D4
Barkingside ... 41 F7
Barking Tye ... 56 D4
Barkisland ... 87 C8
Barkston Lincs ... 78 E2
— N Yorks ... 95 F7
Barkway ... 54 F4
Barlaston ... 75 F5
Barlavington ... 16 C3
Barlborough ... 76 B4
Barlby ... 96 F2
Barlestone ... 63 D8
Barley Herts ... 54 F4
— Lancs ... 93 E8
Barley Mow ... 111 D5
Barleythorpe ... 64 D5
Barling ... 43 F5
Barlow Derbys ... 76 B3
— N Yorks ... 89 B7
— T&W ... 110 C4
Barmby Moor ... 96 E3
Barmby on the Marsh ... 89 B7
Barmer ... 80 D4
Barmoor Castle ... 123 F5
Barmoor Lane End ... 123 F6
Barmouth = Abermaw ... 58 C3
Barmpton ... 101 C8
Barmston ... 97 D7
Barnack ... 65 D7
Barnacle ... 63 F7
Barnard Castle ... 101 C5
Barnard Gate ... 38 C4
Barnardiston ... 55 E8
Barnbarroch ... 106 D5
Barnburgh ... 89 D5
Barnby ... 69 F7
Barnby Dun ... 89 D7
Barnby in the Willows ... 77 D8
Barnby Moor ... 89 F7
Barnes Street ... 29 E7
Barnet ... 41 E5
Barnetby le Wold ... 90 D4
Barney ... 81 D5
Barnham Suff ... 56 B2
— W Sus ... 16 D3
Barnham Broom ... 68 D3
Barnhead ... 135 D6
Barnhill Ches W ... 73 D8
— Dundee ... 134 F4
— Moray ... 152 C1
Barnhills ... 104 B3
Barningham Durham ... 101 C5
— Suff ... 56 B3
Barnoldby le Beck ... 91 D6
Barnoldswick ... 93 E8
Barns Green ... 16 B5
Barnsley Glos ... 37 D7
— S Yorks ... 88 D4
Barnstaple ... 20 F4
Barnston Essex ... 42 C2
— Mers ... 85 F3
Barnstone ... 77 F7
Barnt Green ... 50 B5
Barnton Ches W ... 74 B3
— Edin ... 120 B4
Barnwell All Saints ... 65 F7
Barnwell St Andrew ... 65 F7
Barnwood ... 37 C5
Barochreal ... 124 C4
Barons Cross ... 49 D6
Barr ... 112 E2
Barra Castle ... 141 B6
Barrachan ... 105 E7
Barrack ... 153 D8
Barraglom ... 154 D6
Barrahormid ... 144 E6
Barran ... 124 C4
Barrapol ... 146 G2
Barras Aberds ... 141 F7

Barras continued
 Cumb . . . 100 C3
Barrasford . . . 110 B2
Barravullin . . . 124 E4
Barregarrow . . . 84 D3
Barrhead . . . 118 D4
Barrhill . . . 112 F2
Barrington Cambs . . . 54 E4
 Som . . . 11 C8
Barripper . . . 2 C5
Barrmill . . . 118 D3
Barrock . . . 158 C4
Barrock House . . . 158 D4
Barrow Lancs . . . 93 F7
 Rutland . . . 65 C5
 Suff . . . 55 C8
Barroway Drove . . . 67 D5
Barrowburn . . . 116 C4
Barrowby . . . 77 F8
Barrowcliff . . . 103 F8
Barrowden . . . 65 D6
Barrowford . . . 93 F8
Barrow Green . . . 30 C3
Barrow Gurney . . . 23 C7
Barrow Haven . . . 90 B4
Barrow-in-Furness . . . 92 C2
Barrow Island . . . 92 C1
Barrow Nook . . . 86 D2
Barrows Green
 Ches E . . . 74 D3
 Cumb . . . 99 F7
Barrow's Green . . . 86 F3
Barrow Street . . . 24 F3
Barrow upon Humber . . . 90 B4
Barrow upon Soar . . . 64 C2
Barrow upon Trent . . . 63 B7
Barry . . . 135 F5
Barry = Y Barri . . . 22 C3
Barry Island . . . 22 C3
Barsby . . . 64 C3
Barsham . . . 69 F6
Barston . . . 51 B7
Bartestree . . . 49 E7
Barthol Chapel . . . 153 E8
Barthomley . . . 74 D4
Bartley . . . 14 C4
Bartley Green . . . 62 F4
Bartlow . . . 55 E6
Barton Cambs . . . 54 D5
 Ches W. . . . 73 D8
 Glos . . . 37 B8
 Lancs . . . 85 D4
 Lancs . . . 92 F5
 N Yorks . . . 101 D7
 Oxon . . . 39 D5
 Torbay . . . 7 C7
 Warks . . . 51 D6
Barton Bendish . . . 67 D7
Barton Hartshorn . . . 52 F4
Barton in Fabis . . . 76 F5
Barton in the Beans . . . 63 D7
Barton-le-Clay . . . 53 F8
Barton-le-Street . . . 96 B3
Barton-le-Willows . . . 96 C3
Barton Mills . . . 55 B8
Barton on Sea . . . 14 E3
Barton on the Heath . . . 51 F7
Barton St David . . . 23 F7
Barton Seagrave . . . 53 B6
Barton Stacey . . . 26 E2
Barton Turf . . . 69 B6
Barton-under-Needwood . . . 63 C5
Barton-upon-Humber . . . 90 B4
Barton Waterside . . . 90 B4
Barugh . . . 88 D4
Barway . . . 55 B6
Barwell . . . 63 E8
Barwick Herts . . . 41 C6
 Som . . . 12 C3
Barwick in Elmet . . . 95 F6
Baschurch . . . 60 B4
Bascote . . . 52 C2
Basford Green . . . 75 D6
Bashall Eaves . . . 93 E6
Bashley . . . 14 E3
Basildon . . . 42 F3
Basingstoke . . . 26 D4
Baslow . . . 76 B2
Bason Bridge . . . 22 E5
Bassaleg . . . 35 F6
Bassenthwaite . . . 108 F2
Bassett . . . 14 C5
Bassingbourn . . . 54 E4
Bassingfield . . . 77 F6
Bassingham . . . 78 C2
Bassingthorpe . . . 65 B6
Basta . . . 160 D7
Baston . . . 65 C8
Bastwick . . . 69 C7
Baswick Steer . . . 97 E6
Batchworth Heath . . . 40 E3
Batcombe Dorset . . . 12 D4
 Som . . . 23 F8
Bate Heath . . . 74 B3
Batford . . . 40 C4
Bath . . . 24 C2
Bathampton . . . 24 C2
Bathealton . . . 11 B5
Batheaston . . . 24 C2
Bathford . . . 24 C2
Bathgate . . . 120 C2
Bathley . . . 77 D7
Bathpool Corn . . . 5 B7
 Som . . . 11 B7
Bathville . . . 120 C2
Batley . . . 88 B3
Batsford . . . 51 F6
Battersby . . . 102 D3
Battersea . . . 28 B3
Battisborough Cross . . . 6 E3
Battisford . . . 56 D4
Battisford Tye . . . 56 D4
Battle E Sus . . . 18 D4
 Powys . . . 48 F2
Battledown . . . 37 B6
Battlefield . . . 60 C5
Battlesbridge . . . 42 E3
Battlesden . . . 40 B2
Battleton . . . 10 B4
Battram . . . 63 D8
Battramsley . . . 14 E4

Baughton . . . 50 E3
Baughurst . . . 26 D3
Baulking . . . 38 E3
Baumber . . . 78 B5
Baunton . . . 37 D7
Baverstock . . . 24 F5
Bawburgh . . . 68 D4
Bawdeswell . . . 81 E6
Bawdrip . . . 22 F5
Bawdsey . . . 57 E7
Bawtry . . . 89 E7
Baxenden . . . 87 B5
Baxterley . . . 63 E6
Baybridge . . . 15 B6
Baycliff . . . 92 B2
Baydon . . . 25 B7
Bayford Herts . . . 41 D6
 Som . . . 12 B5
Bayles . . . 109 E7
Baylham . . . 56 D5
Baynard's Green . . . 39 B5
Bayston Hill . . . 60 D4
Baythorn End . . . 55 F8
Bayton . . . 49 B8
Beach . . . 130 D1
Beachampton . . . 53 F5
Beachamwell . . . 67 D7
Beachans . . . 151 G13
Beacharr . . . 143 D7
Beachborough . . . 19 B8
Beachley . . . 36 E2
Beacon . . . 11 D6
Beacon End . . . 43 B5
Beacon Hill . . . 27 F6
Beacon's Bottom . . . 39 E7
Beaconsfield . . . 40 F2
Beacrabhaic . . . 154 H6
Beadlam . . . 102 F4
Beadlow . . . 54 F2
Beadnell . . . 117 B8
Beaford . . . 9 C7
Beal Northumb . . . 123 E6
 N Yorks. . . . 89 B6
Beamhurst . . . 75 F7
Beaminster . . . 12 D2
Beamish . . . 110 D5
Beamsley . . . 94 D3
Bean . . . 29 B6
Beanacre . . . 24 C4
Beanley . . . 117 C6
Beaquoy . . . 159 F4
Bear Cross . . . 13 E8
Beardwood . . . 86 B4
Beare Green . . . 28 E2
Bearley . . . 51 C6
Bearnus . . . 146 G6
Bearpark . . . 110 E5
Bearsbridge . . . 109 D7
Bearsden . . . 118 B5
Bearsted . . . 29 D8
Bearstone . . . 74 F4
Bearwood BCP . . . 13 E8
 Hereford . . . 49 D5
 W Mid . . . 62 F4
Beattock . . . 114 D3
Beauchamp Roding . . . 42 C1
Beauchief . . . 88 F4
Beaufort . . . 35 C5
Beaufort Castle . . . 151 G8
Beaulieu . . . 14 D4
Beauly . . . 151 G8
Beaumaris . . . 83 D6
Beaumont Cumb . . . 108 D3
 Essex . . . 43 B7
Beaumont Hill . . . 101 C7
Beausale . . . 51 B7
Beauworth . . . 15 B6
Beazley End . . . 42 B3
Bebington . . . 85 F4
Bebside . . . 117 F8
Beccles . . . 69 F7
Becconsall . . . 86 B2
Beckbury . . . 61 D7
Beckenham . . . 28 C4
Beckermet . . . 98 D2
Beckfoot Cumb . . . 98 D3
 Cumb . . . 107 E7
Beck Foot . . . 99 E8
Beckford . . . 50 F4
Beckhampton . . . 25 C5
Beck Hole . . . 103 D6
Beckingham Lincs . . . 77 D8
 Notts. . . . 89 F8
Beckington . . . 24 D3
Beckley E Sus . . . 19 C5
 Hants. . . . 14 E3
 Oxon . . . 39 C5
Beck Row . . . 55 B7
Beck Side . . . 98 F4
Beckton . . . 41 F7
Beckwithshaw . . . 95 D5
Becontree . . . 41 F7
Bedale . . . 101 F7
Bedburn . . . 110 F4
Bedchester . . . 13 C6
Beddau . . . 34 F4
Beddgelert . . . 71 C6
Beddingham . . . 17 D8
Beddington . . . 28 C4
Bedfield . . . 57 C6
Bedford . . . 53 D8
Bedham . . . 16 B4
Bedhampton . . . 15 D8
Bedingfield . . . 57 C5
Bedlam . . . 95 C5
Bedlington . . . 117 F8
Bedlington Station . . . 117 F8
Bedlinog . . . 34 D4
Bedminster . . . 23 B7
Bedmond . . . 40 D3
Bednall . . . 62 C3
Bedrule . . . 116 C2
Bedstone . . . 49 B5
Bedwas . . . 35 F5
Bedworth . . . 63 F7
Bedworth Heath . . . 63 F7
Bed-y-coedwr . . . 71 E8
Beeby . . . 64 D3
Beech Hants . . . 26 F4
 Staffs. . . . 75 F5
Beech Hill Gtr Man. . . . 86 D4
 W Berks . . . 26 C4
Beechingstoke . . . 25 D5
Beedon . . . 26 B2
Beeford . . . 97 D7
Beeley . . . 76 C2

Beelsby . . . 91 D6
Beenham . . . 26 C3
Beeny . . . 8 E3
Beer . . . 11 F7
Beercrocombe . . . 11 B8
Beer Hackett . . . 12 C3
Beesands . . . 7 E6
Beesby . . . 91 F8
Beeson . . . 7 E6
Beeston C Beds . . . 54 E2
 Ches W. . . . 74 D2
 Norf . . . 68 C2
 Notts. . . . 76 F5
 W Yorks. . . . 95 F5
Beeston Regis . . . 81 C7
Beeswing . . . 107 C5
Beetham . . . 92 B4
Beetley . . . 68 C2
Begbroke . . . 38 C4
Begelly . . . 32 D2
Beggar's Bush . . . 48 C5
Beguildy . . . 48 B3
Beighton Norf. . . . 69 D6
 S Yorks. . . . 88 F5
Beighton Hill . . . 76 D2
Beith . . . 118 D3
Bekesbourne . . . 31 D5
Belaugh . . . 69 C5
Belbroughton . . . 50 B4
Belchamp Otten . . . 56 E2
Belchamp St Paul . . . 55 E8
Belchamp Walter . . . 56 E2
Belchford . . . 79 B5
Belford . . . 123 F7
Belhaven . . . 122 B2
Belhelvie . . . 141 C8
Belhinnie . . . 140 B3
Bellabeg . . . 140 C2
Bellamore . . . 112 F2
Bellanoch . . . 144 D6
Bellaty . . . 134 D2
Bell Bar . . . 41 D5
Bell Busk . . . 94 D2
Belleau . . . 79 B7
Bellehiglash . . . 152 E1
Bell End . . . 50 B4
Bellerby . . . 101 E6
Bellever . . . 6 B4
Belliehill . . . 135 C5
Bellingdon . . . 40 D2
Bellingham . . . 116 F4
Belloch . . . 143 E7
Bellochantuy . . . 143 E7
Bell o'th'Hill . . . 74 E2
Bellsbank . . . 112 D4
Bellshill N Lanark . . . 119 C7
 Northumb . . . 123 F7
Bellspool . . . 120 F4
Bellsquarry . . . 120 C3
Bells Yew Green . . . 18 B3
Belmaduthy . . . 151 F9
Belmesthorpe . . . 65 C7
Belmont Blackburn. . . . 86 C4
 London. . . . 28 C3
 S Ayrs. . . . 112 B3
 Shetland. . . . 160 C7
Belnacraig . . . 140 C2
Belowda . . . 4 C4
Belper . . . 76 E3
Belper Lane End . . . 76 E3
Belsay . . . 110 B4
Belses . . . 115 B8
Belsford . . . 7 D5
Belstead . . . 56 E5
Belston . . . 112 B3
Belstone . . . 9 E8
Belthorn . . . 86 B5
Beltinge . . . 31 C5
Beltoft . . . 90 D2
Belton Leics. . . . 63 B8
 Lincs. . . . 78 F2
 N Lincs. . . . 89 D8
 Norf. . . . 69 D7
Belton in Rutland. . . . 64 D5
Beltring . . . 29 E7
Belts of Collonach . . . 141 E5
Belvedere . . . 29 B5
Belvoir . . . 77 F8
Bembridge . . . 15 F7
Bemersyde . . . 121 F8
Bemerton . . . 25 F6
Bempton . . . 97 B7
Ben Alder Lodge . . . 132 B2
Ben Armine Lodge . . . 157 H10
Benbecula . . . 148 D2
Benbuie . . . 113 E7
Ben Casgro . . . 155 E9
Benderloch . . . 124 B5
Bendronaig Lodge . . . 150 H3
Benenden . . . 18 B5
Benfield . . . 105 C7
Bengate . . . 69 B6
Bengeworth . . . 50 E5
Benhall Green . . . 57 C7
Benhall Street . . . 57 C7
Benholm . . . 135 C8
Beningbrough . . . 95 D8
Benington Herts . . . 41 B5
 Lincs . . . 79 E6
Benllech . . . 82 C5
Benmore Argyll . . . 145 E10
 Stirling . . . 126 B3
Benmore Lodge . . . 156 H6
Bennacott . . . 8 E4
Bennan . . . 143 F10
Benniworth . . . 91 F6
Benover . . . 29 E8
Bensham . . . 110 C5
Benslie . . . 118 E3
Benson . . . 39 E6
Bent . . . 135 B6
Bent Gate . . . 87 B5
Benthall Northumb. . . . 117 B8
 Shrops. . . . 61 D6
Bentham . . . 37 C6
Benthoul . . . 141 D7
Bentlawnt . . . 60 D3
Bentley E Yorks . . . 97 F6
 Hants. . . . 27 E5
 Suff. . . . 56 F5
 S Yorks. . . . 89 D6
 Warks. . . . 63 E6
 Worcs . . . 50 C4
Bentley Heath . . . 51 B6
Benton . . . 21 F6
Bentpath . . . 115 E6

Bents . . . 120 C2
Bentworth . . . 26 E4
Benvie . . . 134 F3
Benwick . . . 66 E3
Beoley . . . 51 C5
Beoraidbeg . . . 147 B9
Bepton . . . 16 C2
Berden . . . 41 B7
Bere Alston . . . 6 C2
Bere Ferrers . . . 6 C2
Berepper . . . 3 D5
Bere Regis . . . 13 E6
Bergh Apton . . . 69 D6
Berinsfield . . . 39 E5
Berkeley . . . 36 E3
Berkhamsted . . . 40 D2
Berkley . . . 24 E3
Berkswell . . . 51 B7
Bermondsey . . . 28 B4
Bernera . . . 149 F13
Bernice . . . 145 D10
Bernisdale . . . 149 C9
Berrick Salome . . . 39 E6
Berriedale . . . 158 H3
Berrier . . . 99 B5
Berriew . . . 59 D8
Berrington Northumb . . . 123 E6
 Shrops. . . . 60 D5
Berrow . . . 22 D5
Berrow Green . . . 50 D2
Berry Down Cross . . . 20 E4
Berryfield . . . 24 C3
Berry Hill Glos . . . 36 C2
 Pembs . . . 45 E2
Berryhillock . . . 152 B5
Berrynarbor . . . 20 E4
Berry Pomeroy . . . 7 C6
Bersham . . . 73 E7
Berstane . . . 159 G5
Berwick . . . 18 E2
Berwick Bassett . . . 25 B5
Berwick Hill . . . 110 B4
Berwick St James . . . 25 F5
Berwick St John . . . 13 B7
Berwick St Leonard . . . 24 F4
Berwick-upon-Tweed . . . 123 D5
Bescar . . . 85 C4
Besford . . . 50 E4
Bessacarr . . . 89 D7
Bessels Leigh . . . 38 D4
Bessingby . . . 97 C7
Bessingham . . . 81 D7
Bestbeech Hill . . . 18 B3
Besthorpe Norf . . . 68 E3
 Notts. . . . 77 C8
Bestwood . . . 77 E5
Bestwood Village . . . 77 E5
Beswick . . . 97 E6
Betchworth . . . 28 E3
Bethania Ceredig . . . 46 C4
 Gwyn. . . . 71 C8
 Gwyn. . . . 83 F6
Bethel Anglesey . . . 82 D3
 Gwyn. . . . 82 E5
 Gwyn. . . . 83 E5
Bethersden . . . 30 E3
Bethesda Gwyn . . . 83 E6
 Pembs. . . . 32 C1
Bethlehem . . . 33 B7
Bethnal Green . . . 41 F6
Betley . . . 74 E4
Betsham . . . 29 B7
Betteshanger . . . 31 D7
Bettiscombe . . . 11 E8
Bettisfield . . . 73 F8
Betton Shrops . . . 60 D3
 Shrops. . . . 74 F3
Bettws Bridgend . . . 34 F3
 Mon. . . . 35 C6
 Newport. . . . 35 E6
Bettws Cedewain . . . 59 E8
Bettws Gwerfil Goch . . . 72 E4
Bettws Ifan . . . 46 E2
Bettws Newydd . . . 35 D7
Bettws-y-crwyn . . . 60 F2
Bettyhill . . . 157 C10
Betws . . . 33 C7
Betws Bledrws . . . 46 D4
Betws-Garmon . . . 82 E5
Betws-y-Coed . . . 83 F7
Betws-yn-Rhos . . . 72 B3
Beulah Ceredig . . . 45 E4
 Powys. . . . 47 D8
Bevendean . . . 17 D7
Bevercotes . . . 77 B6
Beverley . . . 97 F6
Beverston . . . 37 E5
Bevington . . . 36 E3
Bewaldeth . . . 108 F2
Bewcastle . . . 109 B5
Bewdley . . . 50 B2
Bewerley . . . 94 C4
Bewholme . . . 97 D7
Bexhill . . . 18 E4
Bexley . . . 29 B5
Bexleyheath . . . 29 B5
Bexwell . . . 67 D6
Beyton . . . 56 C3
Bhaltos . . . 154 D5
Bhatarsaigh . . . 148 J1
Bibury . . . 37 D8
Bicester . . . 39 B5
Bickenhall . . . 11 C7
Bickenhill . . . 63 F5
Bicker . . . 78 F5
Bickershaw . . . 86 D4
Bickerstaffe . . . 86 D2
Bickerton Ches E . . . 74 D2
 N Yorks. . . . 95 D7
Bickington Devon . . . 7 B5
 Devon. . . . 20 F4
Bickleigh Devon . . . 6 C3
 Devon. . . . 10 D4
Bickleton . . . 20 F4
Bickley . . . 28 C5
Bickley Moss . . . 74 E2
Bicknacre . . . 42 D3
Bicknoller . . . 22 F3
Bicknor . . . 30 D2
Bickton . . . 14 C2
Bicton Shrops . . . 60 C4
 Shrops. . . . 60 F2
Bidborough . . . 29 E6
Biddenden . . . 19 B5
Biddenham . . . 53 D8
Biddestone . . . 24 B3

Biddisham . . . 23 D5
Biddlesden . . . 52 E4
Biddlestone . . . 117 D5
Biddulph . . . 75 D5
Biddulph Moor . . . 75 D6
Bideford . . . 9 B6
Bidford-on-Avon . . . 51 D6
Bidston . . . 85 E3
Bielby . . . 96 E3
Bieldside . . . 141 D7
Bierley IoW . . . 15 G6
 W Yorks. . . . 94 F4
Bierton . . . 39 C8
Big Sand . . . 149 A12
Bigbury . . . 6 E4
Bigbury on Sea . . . 6 E4
Bigby . . . 90 D4
Biggar Cumb . . . 92 C1
 S Lanark. . . . 120 F3
Biggin Derbys . . . 75 D8
 Derbys. . . . 76 E2
 N Yorks. . . . 95 F8
Biggings . . . 160 G3
Biggin Hill . . . 28 D5
Biggleswade . . . 54 E2
Bighouse . . . 157 C11
Bighton . . . 26 F4
Bignor . . . 16 C3
Bigton . . . 160 L5
Bilberry . . . 4 C5
Bilborough . . . 76 E5
Bilbrook . . . 22 E2
Bilbrough . . . 95 E8
Bilbster . . . 158 E4
Bildershaw . . . 101 B7
Bildeston . . . 56 E3
Billericay . . . 42 E2
Billesdon . . . 64 D4
Billesley . . . 51 D6
Billingborough . . . 78 F4
Billinge . . . 86 D3
Billingford . . . 81 E6
Billingham . . . 102 B2
Billinghay . . . 78 D4
Billingley . . . 88 D5
Billingshurst . . . 16 B4
Billingsley . . . 61 F7
Billington C Beds . . . 40 B2
 Lancs. . . . 93 F7
Billockby . . . 69 C7
Billy Row . . . 110 F4
Bilsborrow . . . 92 F5
Bilsby . . . 79 B7
Bilsham . . . 16 D3
Bilsington . . . 19 B7
Bilson Green . . . 36 C3
Bilsthorpe . . . 77 C6
Bilsthorpe Moor . . . 77 D6
Bilston Midloth . . . 121 C5
 W Mid. . . . 62 E3
Bilstone . . . 63 D7
Bilting . . . 30 E4
Bilton E Yorks . . . 97 F7
 Northumb . . . 117 C8
 Warks. . . . 52 B2
Bilton in Ainsty . . . 95 E7
Bimbister . . . 159 G4
Binbrook . . . 91 E6
Binchester Blocks . . . 110 F5
Bincombe . . . 12 F4
Bindal . . . 151 C12
Binegar . . . 23 D8
Binfield . . . 27 B6
Binfield Heath . . . 26 B5
Bingfield . . . 110 B2
Bingham . . . 77 F7
Bingley . . . 94 F4
Bings Heath . . . 60 C5
Binham . . . 81 D5
Binley Hants . . . 26 D2
 W Mid. . . . 51 B8
Binley Woods . . . 51 B8
Binniehill . . . 119 B8
Binsoe . . . 94 B5
Binstead . . . 15 E6
Binsted . . . 27 E5
Binton . . . 51 D6
Bintree . . . 81 E6
Binweston . . . 60 D3
Birch Essex . . . 43 C5
 Gtr Man. . . . 87 D6
Bircham Newton . . . 80 D3
Bircham Tofts . . . 80 D3
Birchanger . . . 41 B8
Bircher . . . 49 C6
Birch Green . . . 43 C5
Birchgrove Cardiff . . . 35 F5
 Swansea. . . . 33 E7
Birch Heath . . . 74 C2
Birch Hill . . . 74 B2
Birchington . . . 31 C6
Birchmoor . . . 63 D6
Birchover . . . 76 C2
Birch Vale . . . 87 F8
Birchwood Lincs . . . 78 C2
 Warr. . . . 86 E4
Bircotes . . . 89 E7
Birdbrook . . . 55 E8
Birdforth . . . 95 B7
Birdham . . . 16 E2
Birdholme . . . 76 C4
Birdingbury . . . 52 C2
Birdlip . . . 37 C6
Birds Edge . . . 88 D3
Birdsall . . . 96 C4
Birdsgreen . . . 61 F7
Birdsmoor Gate . . . 11 D8
Birdston . . . 119 B6
Birdwell . . . 88 D4
Birdwood . . . 36 C4
Birgham . . . 122 F3
Birkby . . . 101 D8
Birkdale . . . 85 C4
Birkenhead . . . 85 F4
Birkenhills . . . 153 D7
Birkenshaw
 N Lanark . . . 119 C6
 W Yorks. . . . 88 B3
Birkhall . . . 140 E2
Birkhill Angus . . . 134 F3
 Borders. . . . 114 C5
Birkholme . . . 65 B6
Birkin . . . 89 B6
Birley . . . 49 D6
Birling Kent . . . 29 C7
 Northumb . . . 117 D8

Birling Gap . . . 18 F2
Birlingham . . . 50 E4
Birmingham . . . 62 F4
Birnam . . . 133 E7
Birse . . . 140 E4
Birsemore . . . 140 E4
Birstall Leics . . . 64 D2
 W Yorks. . . . 88 B3
Birstwith . . . 94 D5
Birthorpe . . . 78 F4
Birtley Hereford . . . 49 C5
 Northumb . . . 109 B8
 T&W. . . . 111 D5
Birts Street . . . 50 F2
Bisbrooke . . . 65 E5
Biscathorpe . . . 91 F6
Bish Mill . . . 10 B2
Bisham . . . 39 F8
Bishampton . . . 50 D4
Bishop Auckland . . . 101 B7
Bishopbridge . . . 90 E4
Bishopbriggs . . . 119 C6
Bishop Burton . . . 97 F5
Bishop Middleham . . . 111 F6
Bishopmill . . . 152 B2
Bishop Monkton . . . 95 C6
Bishop Norton . . . 90 E3
Bishopsbourne . . . 31 D5
Bishops Cannings . . . 24 C5
Bishop's Castle . . . 60 F3
Bishop's Caundle . . . 12 C4
Bishop's Cleeve . . . 37 B6
Bishops Frome . . . 49 E8
Bishop's Green . . . 42 C2
Bishop's Hull . . . 11 B7
Bishop's Itchington . . . 51 D8
Bishops Lydeard . . . 11 B6
Bishops Nympton . . . 10 B2
Bishop's Offley . . . 61 B7
Bishop's Stortford . . . 41 B7
Bishop's Sutton . . . 26 F4
Bishop's Tachbrook . . . 51 C8
Bishopsteignton . . . 7 B7
Bishopstoke . . . 15 C5
Bishopston . . . 33 F6
Bishopstone Bucks . . . 39 C8
 E Sus. . . . 17 D8
 Hereford. . . . 49 E6
 Swindon. . . . 38 F2
 Wilts. . . . 13 B8
Bishopstrow . . . 24 E3
Bishop Sutton . . . 23 D7
Bishop's Waltham . . . 15 C6
Bishopswood . . . 11 C7
Bishop's Wood . . . 62 D2
Bishopsworth . . . 23 C7
Bishop Thornton . . . 95 C5
Bishopthorpe . . . 95 E8
Bishopton Darl . . . 102 B1
 Dumfries. . . . 105 E8
 N Yorks. . . . 95 B6
 Renfs. . . . 118 B4
 Warks. . . . 51 D6
Bishop Wilton . . . 96 D3
Bishton . . . 35 F7
Bisley Glos . . . 37 D6
 Sur. . . . 27 D7
Bispham . . . 92 E3
Bispham Green . . . 86 C2
Bissoe . . . 3 B6
Bisterne Close . . . 14 D3
Bitchfield . . . 65 B6
Bittadon . . . 20 E4
Bittaford . . . 6 D4
Bittering . . . 68 C2
Bitterley . . . 49 B7
Bitterne . . . 15 C5
Bitteswell . . . 64 F2
Bitton . . . 23 C8
Bix . . . 39 F7
Bixter . . . 160 H5
Blaby . . . 64 E2
Blackacre . . . 114 E3
Blackadder West . . . 122 D4
Blackawton . . . 7 D6
Blackborough . . . 11 D5
Blackborough End . . . 67 C6
Black Bourton . . . 38 D2
Blackboys . . . 18 C2
Blackbrook Derbys . . . 76 E3
 Mers. . . . 86 E3
 Staffs. . . . 74 F4
Blackburn Aberds . . . 141 C7
 Aberds. . . . 152 E5
 Blackburn. . . . 86 B4
 W Loth. . . . 120 C2
Black Callerton . . . 110 C4
Black Clauchrie . . . 112 F2
Black Corries Lodge . . . 131 D6
Blackcraig . . . 113 F7
Black Crofts . . . 124 B5
Blackden Heath . . . 74 B4
Black Dog . . . 10 D3
Blackdog . . . 141 C8
Blackfell . . . 111 D5
Blackfield . . . 14 D5
Blackford Cumb . . . 108 C3
 Perth. . . . 127 D7
 Som. . . . 12 B4
 Som. . . . 23 E6
Blackfordby . . . 63 C7
Blackgang . . . 15 G5
Blackhall Colliery . . . 111 F7
Blackhall Mill . . . 110 D4
Blackhall Rocks . . . 111 F7
Blackham . . . 29 F5
Blackheath Essex . . . 43 B6
 Suff. . . . 57 B8
 Sur. . . . 27 E8
 W Mid. . . . 62 F3
Black Heddon . . . 110 B3
Blackhill Aberds . . . 153 C10
 Aberds. . . . 153 D10
 Highld. . . . 149 C8
Blackhills Highld . . . 151 F12
Blackhorse . . . 23 B8
Blackland . . . 24 C5
Black Lane . . . 87 D5
Blacklaw . . . 153 D6
Blackley . . . 87 D6
Blacklunans . . . 134 C1

Black Marsh . . . 60 E3
Blackmill . . . 34 F3
Blackmoor . . . 27 F5
Blackmoor Gate . . . 21 E5
Blackmore . . . 42 D2
Blackmore End Essex . . . 55 F8
 Herts . . . 40 C4
Black Mount . . . 131 E6
Blackness . . . 120 B3
Blacknest . . . 27 E5
Black Notley . . . 42 B3
Blacko . . . 93 E8
Black Pill . . . 33 E7
Blackpool Blackpool . . . 92 F3
 Devon. . . . 7 E6
 Pembs. . . . 32 C1
Blackpool Gate . . . 108 B5
Blackridge . . . 119 C8
Blackrock Argyll . . . 142 B4
 Mon. . . . 35 C6
Blackrod . . . 86 C4
Blackshaw . . . 107 C7
Blackshaw Head . . . 87 B7
Black Tar . . . 44 E4
Blackthorn . . . 39 C6
Blackthorpe . . . 56 C3
Blacktoft . . . 90 B2
Blacktop . . . 141 D7
Black Torrington . . . 9 D6
Blacktown . . . 35 F6
Blackwall Tunnel . . . 41 F6
Blackwater Corn . . . 3 B6
 Hants. . . . 27 D6
 IoW. . . . 15 F6
Blackwaterfoot . . . 143 F9
Blackwell Darl . . . 101 C7
 Derbys. . . . 75 B8
 Derbys. . . . 76 D4
 Warks. . . . 51 E7
 Worcs . . . 50 B4
 W Sus. . . . 28 F4
Blackwood . . . 119 E7
Blackwood = Coed Duon . . . 35 E5
Blackwood Hill . . . 75 D6
Blacon . . . 73 C7
Bladnoch . . . 105 D8
Bladon . . . 38 C4
Blaenannerch . . . 45 E4
Blaenau Ffestiniog . . . 71 C8
Blaenavon . . . 35 D6
Blaencelyn . . . 46 D2
Blaendyryn . . . 47 F8
Blaenffos . . . 45 F3
Blaengarw . . . 34 E3
Blaengwrach . . . 34 D2
Blaen-gwynfi . . . 34 E2
Blaenpennal . . . 46 C5
Blaenplwyf . . . 46 B4
Blaenporth . . . 45 E4
Blaenrhondda . . . 34 D3
Blaen-waun . . . 32 B3
Blaen-y-coed . . . 32 B4
Blaen-y-Cwm Denb . . . 72 F4
 Powys. . . . 59 B7
Blagdon N Som . . . 23 D7
 Torbay. . . . 7 C6
Blagdon Hill . . . 11 C7
Blagill . . . 109 E7
Blaguegate . . . 86 D2
Blaich . . . 130 B4
Blain . . . 147 E9
Blaina . . . 35 D6
Blair Atholl . . . 133 C5
Blairbeg . . . 143 E11
Blairdaff . . . 141 C5
Blair Drummond . . . 127 E6
Blairglas . . . 126 F2
Blairgowrie . . . 134 E1
Blairhall . . . 128 F2
Blairingone . . . 128 E2
Blairland . . . 118 E3
Blairlogie . . . 127 E7
Blairlomond . . . 145 E10
Blairmore . . . 145 E10
Blairnamarrow . . . 139 C8
Blairquhosh . . . 126 F4
Blair's Ferry . . . 145 G8
Blairskaith . . . 119 B5
Blaisdon . . . 36 C4
Blakebrook . . . 50 B3
Blakedown . . . 50 B3
Blakelaw . . . 122 F3
Blakeley . . . 62 E2
Blakeley Lane . . . 75 E6
Blakemere . . . 49 E5
Blakeney Glos . . . 36 D3
 Norf. . . . 81 C6
Blakenhall Ches E . . . 74 E4
 W Mid. . . . 62 E3
Blakeshall . . . 62 F2
Blakesley . . . 52 D4
Blanchland . . . 110 D2
Blandford Forum . . . 13 D6
Blandford St Mary . . . 13 D6
Bland Hill . . . 94 D5
Blanefield . . . 119 B5
Blankney . . . 78 C3
Blantyre . . . 119 D6
Blar a'Chaorainn . . . 131 C5
Blaran . . . 124 D4
Blarghour . . . 125 D5
Blarmachfoldach . . . 130 C4
Blarnalearoch . . . 150 B4
Blashford . . . 14 D2
Blaston . . . 64 E5
Blatherwycke . . . 65 E6
Blawith . . . 98 F4
Blaxhall . . . 57 D7
Blaxton . . . 89 D7
Blaydon . . . 110 C4
Bleadon . . . 22 D5
Bleak Hey Nook . . . 87 D8
Blean . . . 30 C5
Bleasby Lincs . . . 90 F5
 Notts. . . . 77 E7
Bleasdale . . . 93 E5
Bleatarn . . . 100 C2
Blebocraigs . . . 129 C6
Bleddfa . . . 48 C4
Bledington . . . 38 B2
Bledlow . . . 39 D7
Bledlow Ridge . . . 39 E7

Blegbie . . . 121 C7
Blencarn . . . 109 F6
Blencogo . . . 107 E8
Blendworth . . . 15 C8
Blennerhasset . . . 107 E8
Blervie Castle . . . 151 F13
Bletchingdon . . . 39 C5
Bletchingley . . . 28 D4
Bletchley M Keynes . . . 53 F6
 Shrops. . . . 74 F3
Bletherston . . . 32 B1
Bletsoe . . . 53 D8
Blewbury . . . 39 F5
Blickling . . . 81 E7
Blidworth . . . 77 D5
Blindcrake . . . 107 F8
Blindley Heath . . . 28 E4
Blisland . . . 5 B6
Blissford . . . 14 C2
Bliss Gate . . . 50 B2
Blisworth . . . 52 D5
Blithbury . . . 62 B4
Blitterlees . . . 107 D8
Blockley . . . 51 F6
Blofield . . . 69 D6
Blofield Heath . . . 69 C6
Blo' Norton . . . 56 B4
Bloomfield . . . 115 B8
Blore . . . 75 E8
Blount's Green . . . 75 F7
Blowick . . . 85 C4
Bloxham . . . 52 F2
Bloxholm . . . 78 D3
Bloxwich . . . 62 D3
Bloxworth . . . 13 E6
Blubberhouses . . . 94 D4
Blue Anchor Som . . . 22 E2
 Swansea. . . . 33 E6
Blue Row . . . 43 C6
Blundeston . . . 69 E8
Blunham . . . 54 D2
Blunsdon St Andrew . . . 37 F8
Bluntington . . . 50 B3
Bluntisham . . . 54 B4
Blunts . . . 5 C8
Blyborough . . . 90 E3
Blyford . . . 57 B8
Blymhill . . . 62 C2
Blyth Northumb . . . 117 F9
 Notts. . . . 89 F7
Blyth Bridge . . . 120 E4
Blythburgh . . . 57 B8
Blythe . . . 121 E8
Blythe Bridge . . . 75 E6
Blyton . . . 90 E2
Boarhills . . . 129 C7
Boarhunt . . . 15 D7
Boars Head . . . 86 D3
Boarshead . . . 18 B2
Boars Hill . . . 38 D4
Boarstall . . . 39 C6
Boasley Cross . . . 9 E6
Boath . . . 151 D8
Boat of Garten . . . 138 C5
Bobbing . . . 30 C2
Bobbington . . . 62 E2
Bobbingworth . . . 41 D8
Bocaddon . . . 5 D6
Bochastle . . . 126 D5
Bocking . . . 42 B3
Bocking Churchstreet . . . 42 B3
Boddam Aberds . . . 153 D11
 Shetland. . . . 160 M5
Boddington . . . 37 B5
Bodedern . . . 82 C3
Bodelwyddan . . . 72 B4
Bodenham Hereford . . . 49 D7
 Wilts . . . 14 B2
Bodenham Moor . . . 49 D7
Bodermid . . . 70 E2
Bodewryd . . . 82 B3
Bodfari . . . 72 B4
Bodffordd . . . 82 D4
Bodham . . . 81 C7
Bodiam . . . 18 C4
Bodicote . . . 52 F2
Bodieve . . . 4 B4
Bodinnick . . . 5 D6
Bodle Street Green . . . 18 D3
Bodmin . . . 5 C5
Bodney . . . 67 E8
Bodorgan . . . 82 E3
Bodsham . . . 30 E5
Boduan . . . 70 D4
Bodymoor Heath . . . 63 E5
Bogallan . . . 151 F9
Bogbrae . . . 153 E10
Bogend Borders . . . 122 E3
 S Ayrs. . . . 118 F3
Boghall . . . 120 C2
Boghead . . . 119 E7
Bogmoor . . . 152 B3
Bogniebrae . . . 152 D5
Bognor Regis . . . 16 E3
Bograxie . . . 141 C6
Bogside . . . 119 D8
Bogton . . . 153 C6
Bogue . . . 113 F6
Bohenie . . . 137 F5
Bohortha . . . 3 C7
Bohuntine . . . 137 F5
Boirseam . . . 154 J5
Bojewyan . . . 2 F2
Bolam Durham . . . 101 B6
 Northumb . . . 117 F6
Bolberry . . . 6 F4
Bold Heath . . . 86 F3
Boldon . . . 111 C6
Boldon Colliery . . . 111 C6
Boldre . . . 14 E4
Boldron . . . 101 C5
Bole . . . 89 F8
Bolehill . . . 76 D2
Boleside . . . 121 F7
Bolham . . . 10 C4
Bolham Water . . . 11 C6
Bolingey . . . 4 D2
Bollington . . . 75 B6
Bollington Cross . . . 75 B6
Bolney . . . 17 B6
Bolnhurst . . . 54 D2
Bolshan . . . 135 D6
Bolsover . . . 76 B4

Bolsterstone . . . 88 E3
Bolstone . . . 49 F7
Boltby . . . 102 F2
Bolter End . . . 39 E7
Bolton Cumb . . . 99 B8
 E Loth. . . . 121 B8
 E Yorks. . . . 96 D3
 Gtr Man. . . . 86 D5
 Northumb . . . 117 C7
Bolton Abbey . . . 94 D3
Bolton Bridge . . . 94 D3
Bolton-by-Bowland . . . 93 E7
Boltonfellend . . . 108 C4
Boltongate . . . 108 E2
Bolton-le-Sands . . . 92 C4
Bolton Low Houses . . . 108 E2
Bolton-on-Swale . . . 101 E7
Bolton Percy . . . 95 E8
Bolton Town End . . . 92 C4
Bolton upon Dearne . . . 89 D5
Bolventor . . . 5 B6
Bomere Heath . . . 60 C4
Bonar Bridge . . . 151 B9
Bonawe . . . 125 B6
Bonby . . . 90 C4
Boncath . . . 45 F4
Bonchester Bridge . . . 115 C8
Bonchurch . . . 15 G6
Bondleigh . . . 9 D8
Bonehill Devon . . . 6 B5
 Staffs. . . . 63 D5
Bo'ness . . . 127 F8
Bonhill . . . 118 B3
Boningale . . . 62 D2
Bonjedward . . . 116 B2
Bonkle . . . 119 D8
Bonnavoulin . . . 147 F8
Bonnington Edin . . . 120 C4
 Kent. . . . 19 B7
Bonnybank . . . 129 D5
Bonnybridge . . . 127 F7
Bonnykelly . . . 153 C9
Bonnyrigg and Lasswade . . . 121 C6
Bonnyton Aberds . . . 153 E6
 Angus. . . . 134 F3
 Angus. . . . 135 D6
Bonsall . . . 76 D2
Bonskeid House . . . 133 C5
Bont . . . 35 C7
Bontddu . . . 58 C3
Bont-Dolgadfan . . . 59 D5
Bont-goch . . . 58 F3
Bonthorpe . . . 79 B7
Bontnewydd Ceredig . . . 46 C5
 Gwyn. . . . 82 E4
Bont-newydd . . . 72 B4
Bont Newydd Gwyn. . . . 71 C8
 Gwyn. . . . 71 E8
Bontuchel . . . 72 D4
Bonvilston . . . 22 B2
Bon-y-maen . . . 33 E7
Booker . . . 39 E8
Boon . . . 121 E8
Boosbeck . . . 102 C4
Boot . . . 98 D3
Booth . . . 87 B8
Boothby Graffoe . . . 78 D2
Boothby Pagnell . . . 78 F2
Boothen . . . 75 E5
Boothferry . . . 89 B8
Boothville . . . 53 C5
Booth Wood . . . 87 C8
Bootle Cumb . . . 98 F3
 Mers. . . . 85 E4
Booton . . . 81 E7
Boot Street . . . 57 E6
Boquhan . . . 126 F4
Boraston . . . 49 B8
Borden Kent . . . 30 C2
 W Sus. . . . 16 B2
Bordley . . . 94 C2
Bordon . . . 27 F6
Bordon Camp . . . 27 F5
Boreham Essex . . . 42 D3
 Wilts. . . . 24 E3
Boreham Street . . . 18 D3
Borehamwood . . . 40 E4
Boreland Dumfries . . . 114 E4
 Stirling. . . . 132 F2
Borgh W Isles . . . 148 H1
 W Isles. . . . 154 J4
Borghastan . . . 154 C7
Borgie . . . 157 D9
Borgue Dumfries . . . 106 E3
 Highld. . . . 158 H3
Borley . . . 56 E2
Bornais . . . 148 F2
Bornesketaig . . . 149 A8
Borness . . . 106 E3
Boroughbridge . . . 95 C6
Borough Green . . . 29 D7
Borras Head . . . 73 D7
Borreraig . . . 148 C6
Borrobol Lodge . . . 157 G11
Borrowash . . . 76 F4
Borrowby . . . 102 F2
Borrowdale . . . 98 C4
Borrowfield . . . 141 E7
Borth . . . 58 E3
Borthwickbrae . . . 115 C7
Borthwickshiels . . . 115 C7
Borth-y-Gest . . . 71 D6
Borve . . . 149 D9
Borve Lodge . . . 154 H5
Borwick . . . 92 B5
Bosavern . . . 2 C2
Bosbury . . . 49 E8
Boscastle . . . 8 E3
Boscombe BCP . . . 14 E2
 Wilts. . . . 25 F7
Boscoppa . . . 4 D5
Bosham . . . 16 D2
Bosherston . . . 44 F4
Boskenna . . . 2 D3
Bosley . . . 75 C6
Bossall . . . 96 C3
Bossiney . . . 8 F2
Bossingham . . . 31 E5
Bossington . . . 21 E7
Bostock Green . . . 74 C3

Boston . . . 79 E6
Boston Long Hedges . . . 79 E6
Boston Spa . . . 95 E7
Boston West . . . 79 E5
Boswinger . . . 3 B8
Botallack . . . 2 C2
Botany Bay . . . 41 E5
Botcherby . . . 108 D4
Botcheston . . . 63 D8
Botesdale . . . 56 B4
Bothal . . . 117 F8
Bothamsall . . . 77 B6
Bothel . . . 107 F8
Bothenhampton . . . 12 E2
Bothwell . . . 119 D7
Botley Bucks . . . 40 D2
Hants . . . 15 C6
Oxon . . . 38 D4
Botolph Claydon . . . 39 B7
Botolphs . . . 17 D5
Bottacks . . . 150 E7
Bottesford Leics . . . 77 F8
N Lincs . . . 90 D2
Bottisham . . . 55 C6
Bottlesford . . . 25 D6
Bottom Boat . . . 88 B4
Bottomcraig . . . 129 B5
Bottom House . . . 75 D7
Bottom of Hutton . . 86 B2
Bottom o'th'Moor . 86 C4
Botusfleming . . . 6 C2
Botwnnog . . . 70 D3
Bough Beech . . . 29 E5
Boughrood . . . 48 F3
Boughspring . . . 36 E2
Boughton Norf . . . 67 D6
Notts . . . 77 C6
W Nhants . . . 53 C5
Boughton Aluph . . . 30 E4
Boughton Lees . . . 30 E4
Boughton Malherbe . . . 30 E2
Boughton Monchelsea . . . 29 D8
Boughton Street . . 30 D4
Boulby . . . 103 C5
Boulden . . . 60 F5
Boulmer . . . 117 C8
Boulston . . . 44 D4
Boultenstone . . . 140 C3
Boultham . . . 78 C2
Bourn . . . 54 D4
Bourne . . . 65 B7
Bourne End Bucks . . 40 F1
C Beds . . . 53 E7
Herts . . . 40 D3
Bournemouth . . . 13 E8
Bournes Green Glos . . . 37 D6
Southend . . . 43 F5
Bournheath . . . 50 B4
Bournmoor . . . 111 D6
Bournville . . . 62 F4
Bourton Dorset . . . 24 F2
N Som . . . 23 C5
Oxon . . . 38 F2
Shrops . . . 61 E5
Bourton on Dunsmore . . . 52 B2
Bourton on the Hill . . . 51 F6
Bourton-on-the-Water . . . 38 B1
Bousd . . . 146 E5
Boustead Hill . . . 108 D2
Bouth . . . 99 F5
Bouthwaite . . . 94 B4
Boveney . . . 27 B7
Boverton . . . 21 C8
Bovey Tracey . . . 7 B6
Bovingdon . . . 40 D3
Bovingdon Green Bucks . . . 39 F8
Herts . . . 40 D3
Bovinger . . . 41 D8
Bovington Camp . . . 13 F6
Bow Borders . . . 121 E7
Devon . . . 10 D2
Orkney . . . 159 J4
Bowbank . . . 100 B4
Bow Brickhill . . . 53 F7
Bowburn . . . 111 F6
Bowcombe . . . 15 F5
Bowd . . . 11 E6
Bowden Borders . . . 121 F8
Devon . . . 7 E6
Bowden Hill . . . 24 C4
Bowderdale . . . 100 D1
Bowdon . . . 87 F5
Bower . . . 116 F3
Bowerchalke . . . 13 B8
Bowerhill . . . 24 C4
Bower Hinton . . . 12 C2
Bowermadden . . . 158 D4
Bowers Gifford . . . 42 F3
Bowershall . . . 128 E2
Bowertower . . . 158 D4
Bowes . . . 100 C4
Bowgreave . . . 92 E4
Bowgreen . . . 87 F5
Bowhill . . . 115 B7
Bowhouse . . . 107 C7
Bowland Bridge . . . 99 F6
Bowley . . . 49 D7
Bowlhead Green . . 27 F7
Bowling W Dunb . . . 118 B4
W Yorks . . . 94 F4
Bowling Bank . . . 73 E7
Bowling Green . . . 50 D3
Bowmanstead . . . 99 E5
Bowmore . . . 142 C4
Bowness-on-Solway . . . 108 C2
Bowness-on-Windermere . . . 99 E6
Bow of Fife . . . 128 C5
Bowsden . . . 123 E5
Bowside Lodge . . 157 C11
Bowston . . . 99 E6
Bow Street . . . 58 F3
Bowthorpe . . . 68 D4
Box Glos . . . 37 D5
Wilts . . . 24 C3
Boxbush . . . 36 C4
Box End . . . 53 E8
Boxford Suff . . . 56 E3
W Berks . . . 26 B2
Boxgrove . . . 16 D3
Boxley . . . 29 D8
Boxmoor . . . 40 D3
Boxted Essex . . . 56 F4
Suff . . . 56 D2
Boxted Cross . . . 56 F4
Boxted Heath . . . 56 F4
Boxworth . . . 54 C4
Boxworth End . . . 54 C4
Boyden Gate . . . 31 C6
Boylestone . . . 75 F8
Boyndie . . . 153 B6
Boynton . . . 97 C7
Boysack . . . 135 E6
Boyton Corn . . . 8 E5
Suff . . . 57 E7
Wilts . . . 24 F4
Boyton Cross . . . 42 D2
Boyton End . . . 55 E8
Bozeat . . . 53 D7
Braaid . . . 84 E3
Braal Castle . . . 158 D3
Brabling Green . . . 57 C6
Brabourne . . . 30 E4
Brabourne Lees . . . 30 E4
Brabster . . . 158 D5
Bracadale . . . 149 E8
Bracara . . . 147 B10
Braceborough . . . 65 C7
Bracebridge . . . 78 C2
Bracebridge Heath 78 C2
Bracebridge Low Fields . . . 78 C2
Braceby . . . 78 F3
Bracewell . . . 93 E8
Brackenfield . . . 76 D3
Brackenthwaite Cumb . . . 108 E2
N Yorks . . . 95 D5
Bracklesham . . . 16 E2
Brackletter . . . 136 F4
Brackley Argyll . . . 143 D8
W Nhants . . . 52 F3
Brackloch . . . 156 G4
Bracknell . . . 27 C6
Braco . . . 127 D7
Bracobrae . . . 152 C5
Bracon Ash . . . 68 E4
Bracorina . . . 147 B10
Bradbourne . . . 76 D2
Bradbury . . . 101 B8
Bradda . . . 84 F1
Bradden . . . 52 E4
Braddock . . . 5 C6
Bradeley . . . 75 D5
Bradenham Bucks . . 39 E8
Norf . . . 68 D2
Bradenstoke . . . 24 B5
Bradfield Essex . . . 56 F5
Norf . . . 81 D8
W Berks . . . 26 B4
Bradfield Combust 56 D2
Bradfield Green . . . 74 D3
Bradfield Heath . . . 43 B7
Bradfield St Clare . 56 D3
Bradfield St George . . . 56 C3
Bradford Corn . . . 5 B6
Derbys . . . 76 C2
Devon . . . 9 D6
Northumb . . . 123 F7
W Yorks . . . 94 F4
Bradford Abbas . . . 12 C3
Bradford Leigh . . . 24 C3
Bradford-on-Avon 24 C3
Bradford-on-Tone 11 B6
Bradford Peverell . 12 E4
Brading . . . 15 F7
Bradley Derbys . . . 76 E2
Hants . . . 26 E4
NE Lincs . . . 91 D6
Staffs . . . 62 C2
W Mid . . . 62 E3
W Yorks . . . 88 B2
Bradley Green . . . 50 C4
Bradley in the Moors . . . 75 E7
Bradley Stoke . . . 36 F3
Bradlow . . . 50 F2
Bradmore Notts . . . 77 F5
W Mid . . . 62 E2
Bradninch . . . 10 D5
Bradnop . . . 75 D7
Bradpole . . . 12 E2
Bradshaw Gtr Man . . 86 C5
W Yorks . . . 87 C8
Bradstone . . . 9 F5
Bradwall Green . . . 74 C4
Bradway . . . 88 F4
Bradwell Derbys . . . 88 F2
Essex . . . 42 B4
M Keynes . . . 53 F6
Norf . . . 69 D8
Staffs . . . 74 E5
Bradwell Grove . . . 38 D2
Bradwell on Sea . . 43 D6
Bradwell Waterside . . . 43 D5
Bradworthy . . . 8 C5
Bradworthy Cross . . 8 C5
Brae Dumfries . . . 107 B5
Highld . . . 155 J13
Highld . . . 156 J7
Shetland . . . 160 G5
Braeantra . . . 151 D8
Braedownie . . . 134 B2
Braefield . . . 150 H7
Braegrum . . . 128 B2
Braehead Dumfries . . . 105 D8
Orkney . . . 159 D5
Orkney . . . 159 H6
S Lanark . . . 119 F8
S Lanark . . . 120 D2
Braehead of Lunan . . . 135 D6
Braehoulland . . . 160 F4
Braehungie . . . 158 G3
Braelangwell Lodge . . . 151 B8
Braemar . . . 139 E7
Braemore Highld . . 150 D4
Highld . . . 158 G2
Brae of Achnahaird . . . 156 H3
Brae Roy Lodge . . 137 E6
Braeside . . . 118 B2
Braes of Enzie . . . 152 C3
Braeswick . . . 159 E7
Braewick . . . 160 H5
Brafferton Darl . . . 101 B7
N Yorks . . . 95 B7
Brafield-on-the-Green . . . 53 D6
Bragar . . . 155 C7
Bragbury End . . . 41 B5
Bragleenmore . . . 124 C5
Braichmelyn . . . 83 E6
Braid . . . 120 C5
Braides . . . 92 D4
Braidley . . . 101 F5
Braidwood . . . 119 E8
Braigo . . . 142 B3
Brailsford . . . 76 E2
Brainshaugh . . . 117 D8
Braintree . . . 42 B3
Braiseworth . . . 56 B5
Braishfield . . . 14 B4
Braithwaite Cumb . . 98 B4
S Yorks . . . 89 C7
W Yorks . . . 94 E3
Braithwell . . . 89 E6
Bramber . . . 17 C5
Bramcote Notts . . . 76 F5
Warks . . . 63 F8
Bramdean . . . 15 B7
Bramerton . . . 69 D5
Bramfield Herts . . . 41 C5
Suff . . . 57 B7
Bramford . . . 56 E5
Bramhall . . . 87 F6
Bramham . . . 95 E7
Bramhope . . . 95 E5
Bramley Hants . . . 26 D4
Sur . . . 27 E8
S Yorks . . . 89 E5
W Yorks . . . 94 F5
Bramling . . . 31 D6
Brampford Speke . . 10 E4
Brampton Cambs . . . 54 B3
Cumb . . . 100 B1
Cumb . . . 108 C5
Derbys . . . 76 B3
Hereford . . . 49 F6
Lincs . . . 77 B8
Norf . . . 81 E8
Suff . . . 69 F7
S Yorks . . . 88 D5
Brampton Abbotts . 36 B3
Brampton Ash . . . 64 F4
Brampton Bryan . . 49 B5
Brampton en le Morthen . . . 89 F5
Bramshall . . . 75 F7
Bramshaw . . . 14 C3
Bramshill . . . 26 C5
Bramshott . . . 27 F6
Branault . . . 147 E8
Brancaster . . . 80 C3
Brancaster Staithe 80 C3
Brancepeth . . . 110 F5
Branch End . . . 110 C3
Branchill . . . 151 F13
Branderburgh . . . 152 A2
Brandesburton . . . 97 E7
Brandeston . . . 57 C6
Brand Green . . . 36 B4
Brandhill . . . 49 B6
Brandis Corner . . . 9 D6
Brandiston . . . 81 E7
Brandon Durham . . 110 F5
Lincs . . . 78 E2
Northumb . . . 117 C6
Suff . . . 67 F7
Warks . . . 52 B2
Brandon Bank . . . 67 F6
Brandon Creek . . . 67 E6
Brandon Parva . . . 68 D3
Brandsby . . . 95 B8
Brandy Wharf . . . 90 E4
Brane . . . 2 D3
Bran End . . . 42 B2
Branksome . . . 13 E8
Branksome Park . . 13 E8
Bransby . . . 77 B8
Branscombe . . . 11 F6
Bransford . . . 50 D2
Bransgore . . . 14 E2
Branshill . . . 127 E7
Bransholme . . . 97 F7
Branson's Cross . . 51 B5
Branston Leics . . . 64 B5
Lincs . . . 78 C3
Staffs . . . 63 B6
Branston Booths . . 78 C3
Branstone . . . 15 F6
Bransty . . . 98 C1
Brant Broughton . . 78 D2
Brantham . . . 56 F5
Branthwaite Cumb . . 98 B2
Cumb . . . 108 F2
Brantingham . . . 90 B3
Branton Northumb . . 117 C6
S Yorks . . . 89 D7
Branxholme . . . 115 C7
Branxholm Park . . 115 C7
Branxton . . . 122 F4
Brassey Green . . . 74 C2
Brassington . . . 76 D2
Brasted . . . 29 D5
Brasted Chart . . . 29 D5
Brathens . . . 141 E5
Bratoft . . . 79 C7
Brattleby . . . 90 F3
Bratton Telford . . . 61 C6
Wilts . . . 24 D4
Bratton Clovelly . . . 9 E6
Bratton Fleming . . . 20 F5
Bratton Seymour . . 12 B4
Braughing . . . 41 B6
Braunston . . . 52 C3
Braunstone Town . . 64 D2
Braunston-in-Rutland . . . 64 D5
Braunton . . . 20 F3
Brawby . . . 96 B3
Brawl . . . 157 C11
Brawlbin . . . 158 E2
Bray . . . 27 B7
Braybrooke . . . 64 F4
Braye . . . 16 I1
Brayford . . . 21 F5
Bray Shop . . . 5 B8
Braystones . . . 98 D2
Braythorn . . . 94 E5
Brayton . . . 95 F9
Bray Wick . . . 27 B6
Brazacott . . . 8 E4
Breach . . . 30 C2
Breachacha Castle . . . 146 F4
Breachwood Green . . . 40 B4
Breacleit . . . 154 D6
Breaden Heath . . . 73 F8
Breadsall . . . 76 F3
Breadstone . . . 36 D4
Breage . . . 2 D5
Breakachy . . . 150 G7
Bream . . . 36 D3
Breamore . . . 14 C2
Brean . . . 22 D4
Breanais . . . 154 E4
Brearton . . . 95 C6
Breascleit . . . 154 D7
Breaston . . . 76 F4
Brechfa . . . 46 F4
Brechin . . . 135 C5
Breckan . . . 159 H3
Breck of Cruan . . . 159 G4
Breckrey . . . 149 B10
Brecon = Aberhonddu . . . 34 B4
Bredbury . . . 87 E7
Brede . . . 18 D5
Bredenbury . . . 49 D8
Bredfield . . . 57 D6
Bredgar . . . 30 C2
Bredhurst . . . 29 C8
Bredicot . . . 50 D4
Bredon . . . 50 F4
Bredon's Norton . . . 50 F4
Bredwardine . . . 48 E5
Breedon on the Hill . . . 63 B8
Breibhig W Isles . . . 148 J1
W Isles . . . 155 D9
Breich . . . 120 C2
Breightmet . . . 86 D5
Breighton . . . 96 F3
Breinton . . . 49 F6
Breinton Common . 49 E6
Breiwick . . . 160 J6
Bremhill . . . 24 B4
Bremirehoull . . . 160 L6
Brenchley . . . 29 E7
Brendon . . . 21 E6
Brenkley . . . 110 B5
Brent Eleigh . . . 56 E3
Brentford . . . 28 B2
Brentingby . . . 64 C4
Brent Knoll . . . 22 D5
Brent Pelham . . . 54 F5
Brentwood . . . 42 E1
Brenzett . . . 19 C7
Brereton . . . 62 C4
Brereton Green . . . 74 C4
Brereton Heath . . . 74 C5
Bressingham . . . 68 F3
Bretby . . . 63 B6
Bretford . . . 52 B2
Bretforton . . . 51 E5
Bretherdale Head . . 99 D7
Bretherton . . . 86 B2
Brettabister . . . 160 H6
Brettenham Norf . . . 68 F2
Suff . . . 56 D3
Bretton Derbys . . . 76 B2
Flint . . . 73 C7
Brewer Street . . . 28 D4
Brewlands Bridge . . . 134 C1
Brewood . . . 62 D2
Briach . . . 151 F13
Briants Puddle . . . 13 E6
Brick End . . . 42 B1
Brickendon . . . 41 D6
Bricket Wood . . . 40 D4
Bricklehampton . . . 50 E4
Bride . . . 84 B4
Bridekirk . . . 107 F8
Bridell . . . 45 E3
Bridestowe . . . 9 F7
Brideswell . . . 152 E5
Bridford . . . 10 F3
Bridfordmills . . . 10 F3
Bridge . . . 31 D5
Bridge End . . . 78 F4
Bridgefoot Angus . . 134 F3
Cumb . . . 98 B2
Bridge Green . . . 55 F5
Bridgehampton . . . 12 B3
Bridge Hewick . . . 95 B6
Bridgehill . . . 110 D3
Bridgemary . . . 15 D6
Bridgemont . . . 87 F8
Bridgend Aberds . . . 140 C4
Aberds . . . 152 E5
Angus . . . 135 C5
Argyll . . . 142 B4
Argyll . . . 143 E8
Argyll . . . 145 D7
Cumb . . . 99 C5
Fife . . . 129 C5
Moray . . . 152 E3
N Lanark . . . 119 B6
Pembs . . . 45 E3
W Loth . . . 120 B3
Bridgend = Pen-y-Bont Ar Ogwr . . . 21 B8
Bridgend of Lintrathen . . . 134 D2
Bridge of Alford . . 140 C4
Bridge of Allan . . . 127 E6
Bridge of Avon . . . 152 E1
Bridge of Awe . . . 125 C6
Bridge of Balgie . . 132 E2
Bridge of Cally . . . 133 D8
Bridge of Canny . . 141 E5
Bridge of Craigisla . . . 134 D2
Bridge of Dee . . . 106 D4
Bridge of Don . . . 141 C8
Bridge of Dun . . . 135 D6
Bridge of Dye . . . 141 F5
Bridge of Earn . . . 128 C3
Bridge of Ericht . . 132 D2
Bridge of Feugh . . 141 E6
Bridge of Forss . . 157 C13
Bridge of Gairn . . . 140 E2
Bridge of Gaur . . . 132 D2
Bridge of Muchalls . . . 141 E7
Bridge of Oich . . . 137 D6
Bridge of Orchy . . 125 B8
Bridge of Waith . . 159 G3
Bridge of Walls . . 160 H4
Bridge of Weir . . . 118 C3
Bridgerule . . . 8 D4
Bridges . . . 60 E3
Bridge Sollers . . . 49 E6
Bridge Street . . . 56 E2
Bridgeton . . . 119 C6
Bridgetown Corn . . . 8 F5
Som . . . 21 F8
Bridge Trafford . . . 73 B8
Bridge Yate . . . 23 B8
Bridgham . . . 68 F2
Bridgnorth . . . 61 E7
Bridgtown . . . 62 D3
Bridgwater . . . 22 F5
Bridlington . . . 97 C7
Bridport . . . 12 E2
Bridstow . . . 36 B2
Brierfield . . . 93 F8
Brierley Glos . . . 36 C3
Hereford . . . 49 D6
S Yorks . . . 88 C5
Brierley Hill . . . 62 F3
Briery Hill . . . 35 D5
Brigg . . . 90 D4
Briggswath . . . 103 D6
Brigham Cumb . . . 107 F7
E Yorks . . . 97 D6
Brighouse . . . 88 B2
Brighstone . . . 14 F5
Brightgate . . . 76 D2
Brighthampton . . . 38 D3
Brightling . . . 18 C3
Brightlingsea . . . 43 C6
Brighton Brighton . . 17 D7
Corn . . . 4 D4
Brighton Hill . . . 26 E4
Brightons . . . 120 B2
Brightwalton . . . 26 B2
Brightwell . . . 57 E6
Brightwell Baldwin . . . 39 E6
Brightwell cum Sotwell . . . 39 E5
Brignall . . . 101 C5
Brig o'Turk . . . 126 D4
Brigsley . . . 91 D6
Brigsteer . . . 99 F6
Brigstock . . . 65 F6
Brill . . . 39 C6
Brilley . . . 48 E4
Brimaston . . . 44 C4
Brimfield . . . 49 C7
Brimington . . . 76 B4
Brimley . . . 7 B5
Brimpsfield . . . 37 C6
Brimpton . . . 26 C3
Brims . . . 159 K3
Brimscombe . . . 37 D5
Brimstage . . . 85 F4
Brinacory . . . 147 B10
Brind . . . 96 F3
Brindister Shetland . . . 160 H4
Shetland . . . 160 K6
Brindle . . . 86 B4
Brindley Ford . . . 75 D5
Brineton . . . 62 C2
Bringhurst . . . 64 E5
Brington . . . 53 B8
Brinian . . . 159 F5
Briningham . . . 81 D6
Brinkhill . . . 79 B6
Brinkley . . . 55 D7
Brinklow . . . 52 B2
Brinkworth . . . 37 F7
Brinmore . . . 138 B2
Brinscall . . . 86 B4
Brinsea . . . 23 C6
Brinsley . . . 76 E4
Brinsop . . . 49 E6
Brinsworth . . . 88 F5
Brinton . . . 81 D6
Brisco . . . 108 D4
Brisley . . . 81 E5
Brislington . . . 23 B8
Bristol . . . 23 B7
Briston . . . 81 D6
Britannia . . . 87 B6
Britford . . . 14 B2
Brithdir . . . 58 C4
British Legion Village . . . 29 D8
Briton Ferry . . . 33 E8
Britwell Salome . . . 39 E6
Brixham . . . 7 D7
Brixton Devon . . . 6 D3
London . . . 28 B4
Brixton Deverill . . . 24 F3
Brixworth . . . 52 B5
Brize Norton . . . 38 D3
Broad Blunsdon . . . 38 E1
Broadbottom . . . 87 E7
Broadbridge . . . 16 D2
Broadbridge Heath 28 F2
Broad Campden . . . 51 F6
Broad Chalke . . . 13 B8
Broadclyst . . . 10 E4
Broadfield Gtr Man . 87 C6
Lancs . . . 86 B3
Pembs . . . 32 D2
W Sus . . . 28 F3
Broadford . . . 149 F11
Broadford Bridge . . 16 B4
Broad Green C Beds . . . 53 E7
Essex . . . 42 B4
Worcs . . . 50 D2
Broadhaugh . . . 115 D7
Broadhaven . . . 158 E5
Broad Haven . . . 44 D3
Broadheath . . . 87 F5
Broad Heath . . . 49 C8
Broadhembury . . . 11 D6
Broadhempston . . . 7 C6
Broad Hill . . . 55 B6
Broad Hinton . . . 25 B6
Broadholme Derbys . 76 E3
Lincs . . . 77 B8
Broadland Row . . . 18 D5
Broadlay . . . 32 D4
Broad Laying . . . 26 C2
Broadley Lancs . . . 87 C6
Moray . . . 152 B3
Broadley Common . 41 D7
Broad Marston . . . 51 E6
Broadmayne . . . 12 F5
Broadmeadows . . . 121 F7
Broadmere . . . 26 E4
Broadmoor . . . 32 D1
Broadoak . . . 31 C5
Broad Oak Carms . . . 33 B6
Cumb . . . 98 E3
Dorset . . . 12 E2
Dorset . . . 13 C5
E Sus . . . 18 C3
E Sus . . . 18 D5
Hereford . . . 36 B1
Mers . . . 86 E3
Broadrashes . . . 152 C4
Broadsea . . . 153 B9
Broadstairs . . . 31 C7
Broadstone BCP . . . 13 E8
Shrops . . . 60 F5
Broad Street . . . 30 D2
Broad Street Green . . . 42 D4
Broad Town . . . 25 B5
Broadtown Lane . . . 25 B5
Broadwas . . . 50 D2
Broadwater Herts . . 41 B5
W Sus . . . 17 D5
Broadway Carms . . . 32 D3
Pembs . . . 44 D3
Som . . . 11 C8
Suff . . . 57 B7
Worcs . . . 51 F5
Broadwell Glos . . . 36 C2
Glos . . . 38 B2
Oxon . . . 38 D2
Warks . . . 52 C2
Broadwell House . . 110 D2
Broadwey . . . 12 F4
Broadwindsor . . . 12 D2
Broadwood Kelly . . 9 D8
Broadwoodwidger . . 9 F6
Brobury . . . 48 E5
Brochel . . . 149 D10
Brochloch . . . 113 E5
Brochroy . . . 125 B6
Brockamin . . . 50 D2
Brockbridge . . . 15 C7
Brockdam . . . 117 B7
Brockdish . . . 57 B6
Brockenhurst . . . 14 D4
Brocketsbrae . . . 119 F8
Brockford Street . . 56 C5
Brockhall . . . 52 C4
Brockham . . . 28 E2
Brockhampton Glos . . . 37 B7
Hereford . . . 49 F7
Brockholes . . . 88 C2
Brockhurst Derbys . . 76 C3
Hants . . . 15 D7
Brocklebank . . . 108 E3
Brocklesby . . . 90 C5
Brockley . . . 23 C6
Brockley Green . . . 56 D2
Brockleymoor . . . 108 F4
Brockton Shrops . . . 60 D3
Shrops . . . 60 F3
Shrops . . . 61 D7
Shrops . . . 61 E5
Telford . . . 61 C7
Brockweir . . . 36 D2
Brockwood . . . 15 B7
Brockworth . . . 37 C5
Brocton . . . 62 C3
Brodick . . . 143 E11
Brodsworth . . . 89 D6
Brogaig . . . 149 B9
Brogborough . . . 53 F7
Brokenborough . . . 37 F6
Broken Cross Ches E . . . 75 B5
Ches W . . . 74 B3
Bromborough . . . 85 F4
Brome . . . 56 B5
Brome Street . . . 57 B5
Bromeswell . . . 57 D7
Bromfield Cumb . . . 107 E8
Shrops . . . 49 B6
Bromham Bedford . . . 53 D8
Wilts . . . 24 C4
Bromley London . . . 28 C5
W Mid . . . 62 F3
Bromley Common . . 28 C5
Bromley Green . . . 19 B6
Brompton Medway . . 29 C8
N Yorks . . . 102 E1
N Yorks . . . 103 F7
Brompton-on-Swale . . . 101 E7
Brompton Ralph . . 22 F2
Brompton Regis . . . 21 F8
Bromsash . . . 36 B3
Bromsberrow Heath . . . 50 F2
Bromsgrove . . . 50 B4
Bromyard . . . 49 D8
Bromyard Downs . . 49 D8
Bronaber . . . 71 D8
Brongest . . . 46 E2
Bronington . . . 73 F8
Bronllys . . . 48 F3
Bronnant . . . 46 C5
Bronwydd Arms . . . 33 B5
Bronydd . . . 48 E4
Bronygarth . . . 73 F6
Brook Carms . . . 32 D3
Hants . . . 14 B4
Hants . . . 14 C3
IoW . . . 14 F4
Kent . . . 30 E4
Sur . . . 27 E8
Sur . . . 27 F7
Brooke Norf . . . 69 E5
Rutland . . . 64 D5
Brookenby . . . 91 E6
Brookend . . . 36 E2
Brook End . . . 53 C8
Brookfield . . . 118 C4
Brook Hill . . . 14 C3
Brookhouse . . . 92 C5
Brookhouse Green 74 C5
Brookland . . . 19 C6
Brooklands Dumfries . . . 106 B5
Gtr Man . . . 87 E5
Shrops . . . 74 E2
Brookmans Park . . 41 D5
Brooks . . . 59 E8
Brooks Green . . . 16 B5
Brook Street Kent . . 19 B6
Kent . . . 29 E6
W Sus . . . 17 B7
Brookthorpe . . . 37 C5
Brookville . . . 67 E7
Brookwood . . . 27 D7
Broom C Beds . . . 54 E2
S Yorks . . . 88 E5
Warks . . . 51 D5
Worcs . . . 50 B4
Broome Norf . . . 69 E6
Shrops . . . 60 F4
Broomedge . . . 86 F5
Broome Park . . . 117 C7
Broomer's Corner . 16 B5
Broomfield Aberds . 153 E9
Essex . . . 42 C3
Kent . . . 30 D2
Kent . . . 31 C5
Som . . . 22 F4
Broomfleet . . . 90 B2
Broom Green . . . 81 E5
Broomhall Ches E . . . 74 E3
Windsor . . . 27 C7
Broomhaugh . . . 110 C3
Broomhill Norf . . . 67 D6
Northumb . . . 117 D8
S Yorks . . . 88 D5
Broom Hill . . . 13 D8
Broomholm . . . 81 D9
Broomley . . . 110 C3
Broompark . . . 110 E5
Broom's Green . . . 50 F2
Broomy Lodge . . . 14 C3
Brora . . . 157 J12
Broseley . . . 61 D6
Brotherhouse Bar . 66 C2
Brotherstone . . . 122 F2
Brothertoft . . . 79 E5
Brotherton . . . 89 B5
Brotton . . . 102 C4
Broubster . . . 157 C13
Brough Cumb . . . 100 C2
Derbys . . . 88 F2
E Yorks . . . 90 B3
Highld . . . 158 C4
Notts . . . 77 D8
Orkney . . . 159 G4
Shetland . . . 160 F6
Shetland . . . 160 F7
Shetland . . . 160 G7
Shetland . . . 160 H6
Shetland . . . 160 J7
Broughall . . . 74 E2
Brough Lodge . . . 160 D7
Brough Sowerby . 100 C2
Broughton Borders . . . 120 F4
Cambs . . . 54 B3
Flint . . . 73 C7
Hants . . . 25 F8
Lancs . . . 92 F5
M Keynes . . . 53 E6
N Lincs . . . 90 D3
N Nhants . . . 53 B6
N Yorks . . . 94 D2
N Yorks . . . 96 B3
Orkney . . . 159 D5
Oxon . . . 52 F2
V Glam . . . 21 B8
Broughton Astley . . 64 E2
Broughton Beck . . . 98 F4
Broughton Common . . . 24 C3
Broughton Gifford . 24 C3
Broughton Hackett . . . 50 D4
Broughton in Furness . . . 98 F4
Broughton Mills . . . 98 E4
Broughton Moor . . 107 F7
Broughton Park . . . 87 D6
Broughton Poggs . . 38 D2
Broughtown . . . 159 D7
Broughty Ferry . . . 134 F4
Browhouses . . . 108 C2
Browland . . . 160 H4
Brown Candover . . 26 F3
Brown Edge Lancs . . 85 C4
Staffs . . . 75 D6
Brown Heath . . . 73 C8
Brownhill Aberds . . 153 D6
Aberds . . . 153 D8
Blackburn . . . 93 F6
Shrops . . . 60 B4
Brownhills Fife . . . 129 C7
W Mid . . . 62 D4
Brownlow . . . 74 C5
Brownlow Heath . . 74 C5
Brownmuir . . . 135 B7
Brown's End . . . 50 F2
Brownshill . . . 37 D5
Brownston . . . 6 D4
Brownyside . . . 117 B7
Broxa . . . 103 E7
Broxbourne . . . 41 D6
Broxburn E Loth . . . 122 B2
W Loth . . . 120 B3
Broxholme . . . 78 B2
Broxted . . . 42 B1
Broxton . . . 73 D8
Broxwood . . . 49 D5
Broyle Side . . . 17 C8
Brù . . . 155 C8
Bruairnis . . . 148 H2
Bruan . . . 158 G5
Bruar Lodge . . . 133 B5
Brucehill . . . 118 B3
Bruera . . . 73 C8
Bruern Abbey . . . 38 B2
Bruichladdich . . . 142 B3
Bruisyard . . . 57 C7
Brumby . . . 90 D2
Brund . . . 75 C8
Brundall . . . 69 D6
Brundish . . . 57 C6
Brundish Street . . . 57 B6
Brunery . . . 147 D10
Brunshaw . . . 93 F8
Brunswick Village . . . 110 B5
Bruntcliffe . . . 88 B3
Bruntingthorpe . . . 64 E3
Brunton Fife . . . 128 B5
Northumb . . . 117 B8
Wilts . . . 25 D7
Brushford Devon . . . 9 D8
Som . . . 10 B4
Bruton . . . 23 F8
Bryanston . . . 13 D6
Brydekirk . . . 107 B8
Bryher . . . 2 E3
Brymbo . . . 73 D6
Brympton . . . 12 C3
Bryn Carms . . . 33 D6
Gtr Man . . . 86 D3
Neath . . . 34 E2
Shrops . . . 60 F2
Brynamman . . . 33 C8
Brynberian . . . 45 F3
Brynbryddan . . . 34 E1
Brynbuga = Usk . . . 35 D7
Bryncae . . . 34 F3
Bryncethin . . . 34 F3
Bryncir . . . 71 C5
Bryn-coch . . . 33 E8
Bryncroes . . . 70 D3
Bryncrug . . . 58 D3
Bryn Du . . . 82 D3
Bryneglwys . . . 72 E5
Brynford . . . 73 B5
Bryn Gates . . . 86 D3
Bryn-glas . . . 83 E8
Bryn Golau . . . 34 F3
Bryngwran . . . 82 D3
Bryngwyn Ceredig . . 45 E4
Mon . . . 35 D7
Powys . . . 48 E3
Brynhenllan . . . 45 F2
Brynhoffnant . . . 46 D2
Brynithel . . . 35 D6
Bryn-Iwan . . . 46 F2
Brynmawr . . . 35 C5
Bryn-mawr . . . 70 D3
Brynmenyn . . . 34 F3
Brynmill . . . 33 E7
Brynna . . . 34 F3
Bryn-nantllech . . . 72 C3
Bryn-penarth . . . 59 D8
Brynrefail Anglesey . 82 C4
Gwyn . . . 83 E5
Bryn Rhyd-yr-Arian . . . 72 C3
Brynsadler . . . 34 F4
Bryn Saith Marchog . . . 72 D4
Brynsiencyn . . . 82 E4
Bryn Sion . . . 59 C5
Brynteg Anglesey . . . 82 C4
Ceredig . . . 46 E3
Bryn-y-gwenin . . . 35 C7
Bryn-y-maen . . . 83 D8
Bryn-yr-eryr . . . 70 C4
Buaile nam Bodach . . . 148 H2
Bualintur . . . 149 F9
Buarthmeini . . . 72 F2
Bubbenhall . . . 51 B8
Bubwith . . . 96 F3
Buccleuch . . . 115 C6
Buchanhaven . . . 153 D11
Buchanty . . . 127 B8
Buchlyvie . . . 126 E4
Buckabank . . . 108 E3
Buckden Cambs . . . 54 C2
N Yorks . . . 94 B2
Buckenham . . . 69 D6
Buckerell . . . 11 D6
Buckfast . . . 6 C5
Buckfastleigh . . . 6 C5
Buckhaven . . . 129 E5
Buckholm . . . 121 F7
Buckholt . . . 36 C2
Buckhorn Weston . . 13 B5
Buckhurst Hill . . . 41 E7
Buckie . . . 152 B4
Buckies . . . 158 D3
Buckingham . . . 52 F4
Buckland Bucks . . . 40 C1
Devon . . . 6 E4
Glos . . . 51 F5
Hants . . . 14 E4
Herts . . . 54 F4
Kent . . . 31 E7
Oxon . . . 38 E3
Sur . . . 28 D3
Buckland Brewer . . . 9 B6
Buckland Common . . . 40 D2
Buckland Dinham . . 24 D2
Buckland Filleigh . . 9 D6
Buckland in the Moor . . . 6 B5
Buckland Monachorum . . . 6 C2
Buckland Newton . . 12 D4
Buckland St Mary . . 11 C7
Bucklebury . . . 26 B3
Bucklegate . . . 79 F6
Bucklerheads . . . 134 F4
Bucklers Hard . . . 14 E5
Bucklesham . . . 57 E6
Buckley = Bwcle . . . 73 C6
Bucklow Hill . . . 86 F5
Buckminster . . . 65 B5
Bucknall Lincs . . . 78 C4
Stoke . . . 75 E6
Bucknell Oxon . . . 39 B5
Shrops . . . 49 B5
Buckpool . . . 152 B4
Bucksburn . . . 141 D7
Buck's Cross . . . 8 B5
Bucks Green . . . 27 F8
Buckshaw Village . 86 B3
Bucks Horn Oak . . . 27 E6
Buckskin . . . 26 D4
Buck's Mills . . . 9 B5
Buckton E Yorks . . . 97 B7
Hereford . . . 49 B5
Northumb . . . 123 F6
Buckworth . . . 54 B2
Budbrooke . . . 51 C7
Budby . . . 77 C6
Budd's Titson . . . 8 D4
Bude . . . 8 D4
Budlake . . . 10 E4
Budle . . . 123 F7
Budleigh Salterton 11 F5
Budock Water . . . 3 C6
Buerton . . . 74 E3
Buffler's Holt . . . 52 F4
Bugbrooke . . . 52 D4
Buglawton . . . 75 C5
Bugle . . . 4 D5
Bugley . . . 24 E3
Bugthorpe . . . 96 D3
Buildwas . . . 61 D6
Builth Road . . . 48 D2
Builth Wells = Llanfair-ym-Muallt . . . 48 D2
Buirgh . . . 154 H5
Bulby . . . 65 B7
Bulcote . . . 77 E6
Buldoo . . . 157 C12
Bulford . . . 25 E6
Bulford Camp . . . 25 E6
Bulkeley . . . 74 D2
Bulkington Warks . . 63 F7
Wilts . . . 24 D4
Bulkworthy . . . 9 C5
Bullamoor . . . 102 E1
Bullbridge . . . 76 D3
Bullbrook . . . 27 C6
Bulley . . . 36 C4
Bullgill . . . 107 F7
Bull Hill . . . 14 E4
Bullington Hants . . . 26 E2
Lincs . . . 78 B3
Bull's Green . . . 41 C5
Bullwood . . . 145 F10
Bulmer Essex . . . 56 E2
N Yorks . . . 96 C2
Bulmer Tye . . . 56 F2
Bulphan . . . 42 F2
Bulverhythe . . . 18 E4
Bulwark . . . 153 D9
Bulwell . . . 76 E5
Bulwick . . . 65 E6
Bumble's Green . . . 41 D7
Bun Abhainn Eadarra . . . 154 G6
Bunacaimb . . . 147 C9
Bun a'Mhuillin . . . 148 G2
Bunarkaig . . . 136 F4
Bunbury . . . 74 D2
Bunbury Heath . . . 74 D2
Bunchrew . . . 151 G9
Bundalloch . . . 149 F13
Buness . . . 160 C8
Bunessan . . . 146 J6
Bungay . . . 69 F6
Bunkers Hill . . . 38 C4
Bunker's Hill Lincs . . 78 B2
Lincs . . . 79 D5
Bunloit . . . 137 B8
Bun Loyne . . . 136 D5
Bunnahabhain . . . 142 A5
Bunny . . . 64 B2
Buntait . . . 150 H6
Buntingford . . . 41 B6
Bunwell . . . 68 E4
Burbage Derbys . . . 75 B7
Leics . . . 63 E8
Wilts . . . 25 C7
Burchett's Green . . 39 F8
Burcombe . . . 25 F5
Burcot . . . 39 E5
Burcott . . . 40 B1
Burdon . . . 111 D6
Bures . . . 56 F3
Bures Green . . . 56 F3
Burford Ches E . . . 74 D3
Oxon . . . 38 C2
Shrops . . . 49 C7
Burg . . . 146 G6
Burgar . . . 159 F4
Burgate Hants . . . 14 C2
Suff . . . 56 B4
Burgess Hill . . . 17 C7
Burgh . . . 57 D6
Burgh by Sands . . 108 D3
Burgh Castle . . . 69 D7
Burghclere . . . 26 C2
Burghead . . . 151 E14
Burghfield . . . 26 C4
Burghfield Common . . . 26 C4
Burghfield Hill . . . 26 C4
Burgh Heath . . . 28 D3
Burghill . . . 49 E6
Burgh le Marsh . . . 79 C8
Burgh Muir . . . 141 B6
Burgh next Aylsham . . . 81 E8
Burgh on Bain . . . 91 F6
Burgh St Margaret . 69 C7
Burgh St Peter . . . 69 E7
Burghwallis . . . 89 C6
Burham . . . 29 C8
Buriton . . . 15 B8
Burland . . . 74 D3
Burlawn . . . 4 B4
Burleigh . . . 27 C6
Burlescombe . . . 11 C5
Burleston . . . 13 E5
Burley Hants . . . 14 D3
Rutland . . . 65 C5
W Yorks . . . 95 F5
Burleydam . . . 74 E3
Burley Gate . . . 49 E7
Burley in Wharfedale . . . 94 E4
Burley Lodge . . . 14 D3
Burley Street . . . 14 D3
Burlingjobb . . . 48 D4
Burlow . . . 18 D2
Burlton . . . 60 B4
Burmarsh . . . 19 B7
Burmington . . . 51 F7
Burn . . . 89 B6
Burnaston . . . 76 F2
Burnbank . . . 119 D7
Burnby . . . 96 E4
Burncross . . . 88 E4
Burneside . . . 99 E7
Burness . . . 159 D7
Burneston . . . 101 F8
Burnett . . . 23 C8
Burnfoot Borders . . . 115 C7
Borders . . . 115 C8
E Ayrs . . . 112 D4
Perth . . . 127 D8
Burnham Bucks . . . 40 F2
N Lincs . . . 90 C4
Burnham Deepdale . . . 80 C4
Burnham Green . . . 41 C5
Burnham Market . . 80 C4
Burnham Norton . . 80 C4
Burnham-on-Crouch . . . 43 E5
Burnham-on-Sea . . 22 E5
Burnham Overy Staithe . . . 80 C4
Burnham Overy Town . . . 80 C4
Burnham Thorpe . . 80 C4
Burnhead Dumfries . . . 113 E8
S Ayrs . . . 112 D2

Burnhervie 141 C6
Burnhill Green 61 D7
Burnhope 110 E4
Burnhouse 118 D3
Burniston 103 E8
Burnlee 88 D2
Burnley 93 F8
Burnley Lane 93 F8
Burnmouth 123 C5
Burn of Cambus 127 D6
Burnopfield 110 D4
Burnsall 94 C3
Burnside Angus 135 D5
E Ayrs 113 C5
Fife 128 D3
Shetland 160 F4
S Lanark 119 C6
W Loth 120 B3
Burnside of Duntrune 134 F4
Burnswark 107 B8
Burntcommon 27 D8
Burnt Heath 76 B2
Burnthouse 3 C6
Burnt Houses 101 B6
Burntisland 128 F4
Burnton 112 D4
Burntwood 62 D4
Burnt Yates 95 C5
Burnwynd 120 C4
Burpham Sur 27 D8
W Sus 16 D4
Burradon
Northumb 117 D5
T&W 111 B5
Burrafirth 160 B8
Burraland Shetland 160 F5
Shetland 160 J4
Burras 3 C5
Burravoe Shetland 160 F7
Shetland 160 G5
Burray Village 159 J5
Burrells 100 C1
Burrelton 134 F2
Burridge Devon 20 F4
Hants 15 C6
Burrill 101 F7
Burringham 90 D2
Burrington Devon 9 C8
Hereford 49 B6
N Som 23 D6
Burrough Green 55 D7
Burrough on the Hill 64 C4
Burrow-bridge 11 B8
Burrowhill 27 C7
Burry 33 E5
Burry Green 33 E5
Burry Port = Porth Tywyn 33 D5
Burscough 86 C2
Burscough Bridge 86 C2
Bursea 96 F4
Burshill 97 E6
Bursledon 15 D5
Burslem 75 E5
Burstall 56 E4
Burstock 12 D2
Burston Norf 68 F4
Staffs 75 F6
Burstow 28 E4
Burstwick 91 B6
Burtersett 100 F3
Burtle 23 E5
Burton BCP 14 E2
Ches W 73 B7
Ches W 74 C2
Lincs 78 B2
Northumb 123 F7
Pembs 44 E4
Som 22 E3
Wilts 24 B3
Burton Agnes 97 C7
Burton Bradstock 12 F2
Burton Dassett 51 D8
Burton Fleming 97 B6
Burton Green
W Mid 51 B7
Wrex 73 D7
Burton Hastings 63 E8
Burton-in-Kendal 92 B5
Burton in Lonsdale 93 B6
Burton Joyce 77 E6
Burton Latimer 53 B7
Burton Lazars 64 C4
Burton-le-Coggles 65 B6
Burton Leonard 95 C6
Burton on the Wolds 64 B2
Burton Overy 64 E3
Burton Pedwardine 78 E4
Burton Pidsea 97 F8
Burton Salmon 89 B5
Burton Stather 90 C2
Burton upon Stather 90 C2
Burton upon Trent 63 B6
Burtonwood 86 E3
Burwardsley 74 D2
Burwarton 61 F6
Burwash 18 C3
Burwash Common 18 C3
Burwash Weald 18 C3
Burwell Cambs 55 C6
Lincs 79 B6
Burwen 82 B4
Burwick 159 K5
Bury Cambs 66 F2
Gtr Man 87 C6
Som 10 B4
W Sus 16 C4
Bury Green 41 B7
Bury St Edmunds 56 C2
Burythorpe 96 C3
Busby 119 D5
Buscot 38 E2
Bush Bank 49 D6
Bushbury 62 D3
Bushby 64 D3
Bush Crathie 139 E8
Bushey 40 E4
Bushey Heath 40 E4
Bush Green 68 F5
Bushley 50 F3
Bushton 25 B5
Buslingthorpe 90 F4
Busta 160 G5
Butcher's Cross 18 C2
Butcombe 23 C7
Butetown 22 B3
Butleigh 23 F7
Butleigh Wootton 23 F7
Butler's Cross 39 D8
Butler's End 63 F6
Butlers Marston 51 E8
Butley 57 D7
Butley High Corner 57 E7
Butterburn 109 B6
Buttercrambe 96 D3
Butterknowle 101 B6
Butterleigh 10 D4
Buttermere Cumb 98 C3
Wilts 25 C8
Buttershaw 88 B2
Butterstone 133 E7
Butterton 75 D7
Butterwick
Durham 102 B1
Lincs 79 E6
N Yorks 96 B3
N Yorks 97 B5
Butt Green 74 D3
Buttington 60 D2
Buttonoak 50 B2
Buttsash 14 D5
Butt's Green 14 B4
Buxhall 56 D4
Buxhall Fen Street 56 D4
Buxley 122 D4
Buxted 17 B8
Buxton Derbys 75 B7
Norf 81 E8
Buxworth 87 F8
Bwcle = Buckley 73 C6
Bwlch 35 B5
Bwlchgwyn 73 D6
Bwlch-Llan 46 D4
Bwlchnewydd 32 B4
Bwlchtocyn 70 E4
Bwlch-y-cibau 59 C8
Bwlchyddar 59 B8
Bwlch-y-fadfa 46 E3
Bwlch-y-ffridd 59 E7
Bwlchygroes 45 F4
Bwlch-y-sarnau 48 B2
Byermoor 110 D4
Byers Green 110 F5
Byfield 52 D3
Byfleet 27 C8
Byford 49 E5
Bygrave 54 F3
Byker 111 C5
Bylchau 72 C3
Byley 74 C4
Bynea 33 E6
Byrness 116 D3
Bythorn 53 B8
Byton 49 C5
Byworth 16 B3

C

Cabharstadh 155 E8
Cablea 133 F6
Cabourne 90 D5
Cabrach Argyll 144 G3
Moray 140 B2
Cabrich 151 G8
Cabus 92 E4
Cackle Street 17 B8
Cadbury 10 D4
Cadbury Barton 9 C8
Cadder 119 B6
Caddington 40 C3
Caddonfoot 121 F7
Cadeby Leics 63 D8
S Yorks 89 D6
Cadeleigh 10 D4
Cade Street 18 C3
Cadgwith 3 E6
Cadham 128 D4
Cadishead 86 E5
Cadle 33 E7
Cadley Lancs 92 F5
Wilts 25 C7
Wilts 25 D7
Cadmore End 39 E7
Cadnam 14 C3
Cadney 90 D4
Cadole 73 C6
Cadoxton 22 C3
Cadoxton-Juxta-Neath 34 E1
Cadshaw 86 C5
Cadzow 119 D7
Caeathro 82 E4
Caehopkin 34 C2
Caenby 90 F4
Caenby Corner 90 F3
Caerau Bridgend 34 E2
Cardiff 22 B3
Caér-bryn 33 C6
Caerdeon 58 C3
Caerdydd = Cardiff 22 B3
Caerfarchell 44 C2
Caerffili = Caerphilly 35 F5
Caerfyrddin = Carmarthen 33 B5
Caergeiliog 82 D3
Caergwrle 73 D7
Caergybi = Holyhead 82 C2
Caerleon = Caerllion 35 E7
Caer Llan 36 D1
Caerllion = Caerleon 35 E7
Caernarfon 82 E4
Caerphilly = Caerffili 35 F5
Caersws 59 E7
Caerwedros 46 D2
Caerwent 36 E1
Caerwych 71 D7
Caerwys 72 B5
Caethle 58 E3
Caim 83 C6
Caio 47 F5
Cairinis 148 B3
Cairisiadar 154 D5
Cairminis 154 J5
Cairnbaan 145 D7
Cairnbanno House 153 D8
Cairnborrow 152 D4
Cairnbrogie 141 B7
Cairnbulg Castle 153 B10
Cairncross Angus 134 B4
Borders 122 C4
Cairndow 125 D7
Cairness 153 B10
Cairneyhill 128 F2
Cairnfield House 152 B4
Cairngaan 104 F5
Cairngarroch 104 E4
Cairnhill 153 E6
Cairnie Aberds 141 D7
Aberds 152 D4
Cairnorrie 153 D8
Cairnpark 141 C7
Cairnryan 104 C4
Cairnton 159 H4
Caister-on-Sea 69 C8
Caistor 90 D5
Caistor St Edmund 68 D5
Caistron 117 D5
Caitha Bowland 121 E7
Calais Street 56 F3
Calanais 154 D7
Calbost 155 F9
Calbourne 14 F5
Calceby 79 B6
Calcot Row 26 B4
Calcott 31 C5
Caldback 160 C8
Caldbeck 108 F3
Caldbergh 101 F5
Caldecote Cambs 54 D4
Cambs 65 F8
Herts 54 F3
Northants 52 D4
Caldecott N Nhants 53 C7
Oxon 38 E4
Rutland 65 E5
Calderbank 119 C7
Calder Bridge 98 D2
Calderbrook 87 C7
Caldercruix 119 C8
Calder Hall 98 D2
Calder Mains 158 E2
Caldermill 119 E6
Calder Vale 92 E5
Calderwood 119 D6
Caldhame 134 E4
Caldicot 36 F1
Caldwell Derbys 63 C6
N Yorks 101 C6
Caldy 85 F3
Caledrhydiau 46 D3
Calfsound 159 E6
Calgary 146 F6
Califer 151 F13
California Falk 120 B2
Norf 69 C8
Calke 63 B7
Callakille 149 C11
Callaly 117 D6
Callander 126 D5
Callaughton 61 E6
Callestick 4 D2
Calligarry 149 H11
Callington 5 C8
Callow 49 F6
Callow End 50 E3
Callow Hill Wilts 37 F7
Worcs 50 B2
Callows Grave 49 C7
Calmore 14 C4
Calmsden 37 D7
Calne 24 B5
Calow 76 B4
Calshot 15 D5
Calstock 6 C2
Calstone Wellington 24 C5
Calthorpe 81 D7
Calthwaite 108 E4
Calton N Yorks 94 D2
Staffs 75 D8
Calveley 74 D2
Calver 76 B2
Calverhall 74 F3
Calver Hill 49 E5
Calverleigh 10 C4
Calverley 94 F5
Calvert 39 B6
Calverton M Keynes 53 F5
Notts 77 E6
Calvine 133 C5
Calvo 107 D8
Cam 36 E4
Camas-luinie 136 B2
Camasnacroise 130 D2
Camastianavaig 149 E10
Camasunary 149 G10
Camault Muir 151 G8
Camb 160 D7
Camber 19 D6
Camberley 27 C6
Camberwell 28 B4
Camblesforth 89 B7
Cambo 117 F6
Cambois 117 F9
Camborne 3 B5
Cambourne 54 D4
Cambridge Cambs 55 D5
Glos 36 D4
Cambridge Town 43 F5
Cambus 127 E7
Cambusavie Farm 151 B10
Cambusbarron 127 E6
Cambuskenneth 127 E7
Cambuslang 119 C6
Cambusmore Lodge 151 B10
Camden 41 F5
Camelford 8 F3
Camelsdale 27 F6
Camerory 151 H13
Camer's Green 50 F2
Camerton Bath 23 D8
Cumb 107 F7
E Yorks 91 B6
Camghouran 132 D2
Cammachmore 141 E8
Cammeringham 90 F3
Camore 151 B10
Campbeltown 143 F8
Camperdown 111 B5
Camp Hill 63 E7
Campmuir 134 F2
Campsall 89 C6
Campsey Ash 57 D7
Campton 54 F2
Camptown 116 C2
Camrose 44 C4
Camserney 133 E5
Camster 158 F4
Camuschoirk 130 C1
Camuscross 149 G11
Camusnagaul Highld 130 B4
Highld 150 C3
Camusrory 147 B11
Camusteel 149 D12
Camusterrach 149 D12
Camusvrachan 132 E3
Canada 14 C3
Canadia 18 D4
Canal Side 89 C7
Candacraig House 140 C2
Candlesby 79 C7
Candy Mill 120 E3
Cane End 26 B4
Canewdon 42 E4
Canford Bottom 13 D8
Canford Cliffs 13 F8
Canford Magna 13 E8
Canham's Green 56 C4
Canholes 75 B7
Canisbay 158 C5
Cann 13 B6
Cannard's Grave 23 E8
Cann Common 13 B6
Cannich 150 H6
Cannington 22 F4
Cannock 62 D3
Cannock Wood 62 C4
Canonbie 108 B3
Canon Bridge 49 E6
Canon Frome 49 E8
Canon Pyon 49 E6
Canons Ashby 52 D3
Canonstown 2 C4
Canterbury 30 D5
Cantley Norf 69 D6
S Yorks 89 D7
Cantlop 60 D5
Canton 22 B3
Cantraybruich 151 G10
Cantraydoune 151 G10
Cantraywood 151 G10
Cantsfield 93 B6
Canvey Island 42 F3
Canwick 78 C2
Canworthy Water 8 E4
Caol 131 B5
Caolas 146 G3
Caolas Scalpaigh 154 H7
Caolas Stocinis 154 H6
Caol Ila 142 A5
Capel 28 E2
Capel Bangor 58 F3
Capel Betws Lleucu 46 D5
Capel Carmel 70 E2
Capel Coch 82 C4
Capel Curig 83 F7
Capel Cynon 46 E2
Capel Dewi Carms 33 B5
Ceredig 46 E3
Ceredig 58 F3
Capel Garmon 83 F8
Capel-gwyn 82 D3
Capel Gwyn 33 B5
Capel Gwynfe 33 B8
Capel Hendre 33 C6
Capel Hermon 71 E8
Capel Isaac 33 B6
Capel Iwan 45 F4
Capel le Ferne 31 F6
Capel Llanilltern 34 F4
Capel Mawr 82 D4
Capel St Andrew 57 E7
Capel St Mary 56 F4
Capel Seion 46 B5
Capel Tygwydd 45 E4
Capel Uchaf 70 C5
Capelulo 83 D7
Capel-y-graig 82 E5
Capenhurst 73 B7
Capernwray 92 B5
Capheaton 117 F6
Cappercleuch 115 B5
Capplegill 114 D4
Capton 7 D6
Caputh 133 F7
Carbis Bay 2 C4
Carbost Highld 149 D9
Highld 149 E8
Carbrook 88 F4
Carbrooke 68 D2
Carburton 77 B6
Carcant 121 D6
Carcary 135 D6
Carclaze 4 D5
Car Colston 77 E7
Carcroft 89 C6
Cardenden 128 E4
Cardeston 60 C3
Cardiff = Caerdydd 22 B3
Cardigan = Aberteifi 45 E3
Cardington Bedford 53 E8
Shrops 60 E5
Cardinham 5 C6
Cardonald 118 C5
Cardow 152 D1
Cardrona 121 F6
Cardross 118 B3
Cardurnock 107 D8
Careby 65 C7
Careston Castle 135 D5
Carew 32 D1
Carew Cheriton 32 D1
Carew Newton 32 D1
Carey 49 F7
Carfrae 121 C8
Cargenbridge 107 B6
Cargill 134 F1
Cargo 108 D3
Cargreen 6 C2
Carham 122 F4
Carhampton 22 E2
Carharrack 3 B6
Carie Perth 132 D3
Perth 132 F3
Carines 4 D2
Carisbrooke 15 F5
Cark 92 B3
Carlabhagh 154 C7
Carland Cross 4 D3
Carlby 65 C7
Carlecotes 88 D2
Carlesmoor 94 B4
Carleton Cumb 99 B7
Cumb 108 D4
Lancs 92 F3
N Yorks 94 E2
Carleton Forehoe 68 D3
Carleton Rode 68 E4
Carlingcott 23 D8
Carlin How 103 C5
Carlisle 108 D4
Carlops 120 D4
Carlton Bedford 53 D7
Cambs 55 D7
Leics 63 D7
Notts 77 E6
N Yorks 89 B7
N Yorks 101 C6
N Yorks 101 F5
N Yorks 102 F4
Stockton 102 B1
Suff 57 C7
S Yorks 88 C4
W Yorks 88 B4
Carlton Colville 69 F8
Carlton Curlieu 64 E3
Carlton Husthwaite 95 B7
Carlton in Cleveland 102 D3
Carlton in Lindrick 89 F6
Carlton le Moorland 78 D2
Carlton Miniott 102 F1
Carlton on Trent 77 C7
Carlton Scroop 78 E2
Carluke 119 D8
Carmarthen = Caerfyrddin 33 B5
Carmel Anglesey 82 C3
Carms 33 C6
Flint 73 B5
Guern 16 I2
Gwyn 82 F4
Carmont 141 F7
Carmunnock 119 D6
Carmyle 119 C6
Carmyllie 135 E5
Carnaby 97 C7
Carnach Highld 136 B3
Highld 150 B3
W Isles 154 H7
Carnachy 157 D10
Càrnais 154 D5
Carnbee 129 D7
Carnbo 128 D2
Carnbrea 3 B5
Carnduff 119 E6
Carnduncan 142 B3
Carne 3 C8
Carnforth 92 B4
Carn-gorm 136 B2
Carnhedryn 44 C3
Carnhell Green 2 C5
Carnkie Corn 3 C5
Corn 3 C6
Carno 59 E6
Carnoch Highld 150 F5
Highld 150 H6
Carnock 128 F2
Carnon Downs 3 B6
Carnousie 153 C6
Carnoustie 135 F5
Carnwath 120 E2
Carnyorth 2 C2
Carperby 101 F5
Carpley Green 100 F4
Carr 89 E6
Carradale 143 E9
Carragraich 154 H6
Carrbridge 138 B5
Carrefour Selous 17 I3
Carreglefn 82 C3
Carreg-wen 45 E4
Carr Hill 111 C5
Carrick Argyll 145 E8
Fife 129 B6
Carrick Castle 145 D10
Carrick House 159 E6
Carriden 128 F2
Carrington Gtr Man 86 E5
Lincs 79 D6
Midloth 121 C6
Carrog Conwy 71 C8
Denb 72 E5
Carron Falk 127 F7
Moray 152 D2
Carronbridge 113 E8
Carron Bridge 127 F6
Carronshore 127 F7
Carrshield 109 E8
Carrutherstown 107 B8
Carrville 111 E6
Carsaig Argyll 144 E6
Argyll 147 J8
Carscreugh 105 D6
Carsegowan 105 D8
Carse Gray 134 D4
Carse House 144 G6
Carseriggan 105 C7
Carsethorn 107 D6
Carshalton 28 C3
Carsington 76 D2
Carskiey 143 H7
Carsluith 105 D8
Carsphairn 113 E5
Carstairs 120 E2
Carstairs Junction 120 E2
Carswell Marsh 38 E3
Carter's Clay 14 B4
Carterton 38 D2
Carterway Heads 110 D3
Carthew 4 D5
Carthorpe 101 F8
Cartington 117 D6
Cartland 119 E8
Cartmel 92 B3
Cartmel Fell 99 F6
Carway 33 D5
Cary Fitzpaine 12 B3
Cascob 48 C4
Cas-gwent = Chepstow 36 E2
Cashlie 132 E1
Cashmoor 13 C7
Casnewydd = Newport 35 F7
Cassey Compton 37 C7
Cassington 38 C4
Cassop 111 F6
Castell 72 C5
Castellau 34 F4
Castell-Howell 46 E3
Castell-Nedd = Neath 33 E8
Castell Newydd Emlyn = Newcastle Emlyn 46 E2
Castell-y-bwch 35 E6
Casterton 93 B6
Castle Acre 67 C8
Castle Ashby 53 D6
Castlebay = Bagh a Chaisteil 148 J1
Castle Bolton 101 E5
Castle Bromwich 62 F5
Castle Bytham 65 C6
Castlebythe 32 B1
Castle Caereinion 59 D8
Castle Camps 55 E7
Castle Carrock 108 D5
Castlecary 119 B7
Castle Cary 23 F8
Castle Combe 24 B3
Castlecraig 151 E11
Castle Donington 63 B8
Castle Douglas 106 C4
Castle Eaton 37 E8
Castle Eden 111 F7
Castlefairn 113 F7
Castle Forbes 140 C5
Castleford 88 B5
Castle Frome 49 E8
Castle Green 27 C7
Castle Gresley 63 C6
Castle Heaton 122 E5
Castle Hedingham 55 F8
Castlehill Borders 120 F5
Highld 158 D3
W Dunb 118 B3
Castle Hill 29 E7
Castle Huntly 128 B5
Castle Kennedy 104 D5
Castlemaddy 113 F5
Castlemartin 44 F4
Castlemilk Dumfries 107 B8
Glasgow 119 D6
Castlemorris 44 B4
Castlemorton 50 F2
Castle O'er 115 E5
Castle Pulverbatch 60 D4
Castle Rising 67 B6
Castleside 110 E3
Castle Stuart 151 G10
Castlethorpe 53 E6
Castleton Angus 134 E3
Argyll 145 E7
Derbys 88 F2
Gtr Man 87 C6
Newport 35 F6
N Yorks 102 D4
Castletown Ches W 73 D8
Highld 151 G10
Highld 158 D3
IoM 84 F2
T&W 111 D6
Castleweary 115 D7
Castley 95 E5
Caston 68 E2
Castor 65 E8
Catacol 143 D10
Catbrain 36 F2
Catbrook 36 D2
Catchall 2 D3
Catchems Corner 51 B7
Catchgate 110 D4
Catcleugh 116 D3
Catcliffe 88 F5
Catcott 23 F5
Caterham 28 D4
Catfield 69 B6
Catfirth 160 H6
Catford 28 B4
Catforth 92 F4
Cathays 22 B3
Cathcart 119 C5
Cathedine 35 B5
Catherington 15 C7
Catherton 49 B8
Catlodge 138 E2
Catlowdy 108 B4
Catmore 38 F4
Caton 92 C5
Caton Green 92 C5
Catrine 113 B5
Cat's Ash 35 E7
Catsfield 18 D4
Catshill 50 B4
Cattal 95 D7
Cattawade 56 F5
Catterall 92 E4
Catterick 101 E7
Catterick Bridge 101 E7
Catterick Garrison 101 E6
Catterlen 108 F4
Catterline 135 B8
Catterton 95 E8
Catthorpe 52 B3
Cattistock 12 E3
Catton Northumb 109 D8
N Yorks 95 B6
Catwick 97 E7
Catworth 53 B8
Caudlesprings 68 D2
Caulcott 39 B5
Cauldcots 135 E6
Cauldhame 126 E5
Cauldmill 115 C8
Cauldon 75 E7
Caulkerbush 107 D6
Caulside 115 F7
Caunsall 62 F2
Caunton 77 D7
Causewayend 120 F3
Causeway End 105 C8
Causeway Foot 94 F3
Causewayhead Cumb 107 D8
Stirling 127 E6
Causeyend 141 C8
Causey Park Bridge 117 E7
Cautley 100 E1
Cavendish 56 E2
Cavendish Bridge 63 B8
Cavenham 55 C8
Caversfield 39 B5
Caversham 26 B5
Caverswall 75 E6
Cavil 96 F3
Cawdor 151 F11
Cawkwell 79 B5
Cawood 95 F8
Cawsand 6 D2
Cawston 81 E7
Cawthorne 88 D3
Cawthorpe 65 B7
Cawton 96 B2
Caxton 54 D4
Caynham 49 B7
Caythorpe Lincs 78 E2
Notts 77 E6
Cayton 103 F8
Ceann a Bhaigh 148 B2
Ceannacroc Lodge 136 C5
Ceann a Deas Loch Baghasdail 148 G2
Ceann Shiphoirt 155 F7
Ceann Tarabhaigh 154 F7
Cearsiadair 155 E8
Cefn Berain 72 C3
Cefn-brith 72 D3
Cefn Canol 73 F6
Cefn-coch 83 E8
Cefn Coch 59 B8
Cefn-coed-y-cymmer 34 D4
Cefn Cribbwr 34 F2
Cefn Cross 34 F2
Cefn-ddwysarn 72 F3
Cefn Einion 60 F2
Cefneithin 33 C6
Cefn-gorwydd 47 E8
Cefn-mawr 73 E6
Cefn-y-bedd 73 D7
Cefn-y-pant 32 B2
Cei-bach 46 D3
Ceinewydd = New Quay 46 D2
Ceint 82 D4
Cellan 46 E5
Cellarhead 75 E6
Cemaes 82 B3
Cemmaes 58 D5
Cemmaes Road 58 D5
Cenarth 45 E4
Cenin 71 C5
Central 118 B2
Ceos 155 E8
Ceres 129 C6
Cerne Abbas 12 D4
Cerney Wick 37 E7
Cerrigceinwen 82 D4
Cerrigydrudion 72 E3
Cessford 116 B3
Ceunant 82 E5
Chaceley 50 F3
Chacewater 3 B6
Chackmore 52 F4
Chacombe 52 E2
Chadderton 87 D7
Chadderton Fold 87 D6
Chaddesden 76 F3
Chaddesley Corbett 50 B3
Chaddleworth 26 B2
Chadlington 38 B3
Chadshunt 51 D8
Chad Valley 62 F4
Chadwell 64 B4
Chadwell St Mary 29 B7
Chadwick End 51 B7
Chadwick Green 86 E3
Chaffcombe 11 C8
Chagford 10 F2
Chailey 17 C7
Chainbridge 66 D4
Chain Bridge 79 E6
Chainhurst 29 E8
Chalbury 13 D8
Chalbury Common 13 D8
Chaldon 28 D4
Chaldon Herring 13 F5
Chale 15 G5
Chale Green 15 G5
Chalfont Common 40 E3
Chalfont St Giles 40 E2
Chalfont St Peter 40 E3
Chalford 37 D5
Chalgrove 39 E6
Chalk 29 B7
Challacombe 21 E5
Challoch 105 C7
Challock 30 D4
Chalton C Beds 40 B3
Hants 15 C8
Chalvington 18 E2
Chancery 46 B4
Chandler's Ford 14 B5
Channel Tunnel 19 B8
Channerwick 160 L6
Chantry Som 24 E2
Suff 56 E5
Chapel 128 E4
Chapel Allerton Som 23 D6
W Yorks 95 F6
Chapel Amble 4 B4
Chapel Brampton 52 C5
Chapel Chorlton 74 F5
Chapel End 63 E7
Chapel-en-le-Frith 87 F8
Chapelgate 66 B4
Chapel Green Warks 52 C2
Warks 63 F6
Chapel Haddlesey 89 B6
Chapelhall 119 C7
Chapel Head 66 F3
Chapelhill Dumfries 114 E3
Highld 151 D11
N Ayrs 118 E2
Perth 128 B4
Perth 133 F7
Chapel Hill Aberds 153 E10
Lincs 78 D5
Mon 36 E2
N Yorks 95 E6
Chapelknowe 108 B3
Chapel Lawn 48 B5
Chapel-le-Dale 93 B7
Chapel Milton 87 F8
Chapel of Garioch 141 B6
Chapel Row 26 C3
Chapel St Leonards 79 B8
Chapel Stile 99 D5
Chapelton Angus 135 E6
Devon 9 B7
Highld 138 C5
S Lanark 119 E6
Chapeltown Blackburn 86 C5
Moray 139 B8
S Yorks 88 E4
Chapmanslade 24 E3
Chapmans Well 9 E5
Chapmore End 41 C6
Chappel 42 B4
Chard 11 D8
Chardstock 11 D8
Charfield 36 E4
Charford 50 C4
Charing 30 E3
Charing Cross 14 C2
Charing Heath 30 E3
Charingworth 51 F7
Charlbury 38 C3
Charlcombe 24 C2
Charlecote 51 D7
Charles 21 F5
Charlesfield 107 C8
Charleston Angus 134 E3
Renfs 118 C4
Charlestown Aberdeen 141 D8
Corn 4 D5
Derbys 87 E8
Dorset 12 G4
Fife 128 F2
Gtr Man 87 D6
Highld 149 A13
Highld 151 G9
W Yorks 87 B7
Charlestown of Aberlour 152 D2
Charles Tye 56 D4
Charlesworth 87 E8
Charleton 7 E5
Charlton Hants 25 E8
Herts 40 B4
London 28 B5
Northumb 116 F4
Som 23 D8
Telford 61 C5
Wilts 13 B7
Wilts 25 D6
Wilts 37 F6
W Nhants 52 F3
Worcs 50 E5
W Sus 16 C2
Charlton Abbots 37 B7
Charlton Adam 12 B3
Charlton-All-Saints 14 B2
Charlton Down 12 E4
Charlton Horethorne 12 B4
Charlton Kings 37 B6
Charlton Mackerell 12 B3
Charlton Marshall 13 D6
Charlton Musgrove 12 B5
Charlton on Otmoor 39 C5
Charltons 102 C4
Charlwood 28 E3
Charlynch 22 F4
Charminster 12 E4
Charmouth 11 E8
Charndon 39 B6
Charney Bassett 38 E3
Charnock Richard 86 C3
Charsfield 57 D6
Chart Corner 29 D8
Charter Alley 26 D3
Charterhouse 23 D6
Charterville Allotments 38 C3
Chartham 30 D5
Chartham Hatch 30 D5
Chartridge 40 D2
Chart Sutton 30 E2
Charvil 27 B5
Charwelton 52 D3
Chasetown 62 D4
Chastleton 38 B2
Chasty 8 D5
Chatburn 93 E7
Chatcull 74 F4
Chatham 29 C8
Chathill 117 B7
Chattenden 29 B8
Chatteris 66 F3
Chattisham 56 E4
Chatto 116 C3
Chatton 117 B6
Chawleigh 10 C2
Chawley 38 D4
Chawston 54 D2
Chawton 26 F5
Cheadle Gtr Man 87 F6
Staffs 75 E7
Cheadle Heath 87 F6
Cheadle Hulme 87 F6
Cheam 28 C3
Cheapside 27 D8
Chearsley 39 C7
Chebsey 62 B2
Checkendon 39 F6
Checkley Ches E 74 E4
Hereford 49 F7
Staffs 75 F7
Chedburgh 55 D8
Cheddar 23 D6
Cheddington 40 C2
Cheddleton 75 D6
Cheddon Fitzpaine 11 B7
Chedglow 37 E6
Chedgrave 69 E6
Chedington 12 D2
Chediston 57 B7
Chedworth 37 C7
Chedzoy 22 F5
Cheeklaw 122 D3
Cheeseman's Green 19 B7
Cheglinch 20 E4
Cheldon 10 C2
Chelford 74 B5
Chellaston 76 F3
Chell Heath 75 D5
Chellington 53 D7
Chelmarsh 61 F7
Chelmer Village 42 D3
Chelmondiston 57 F6
Chelmorton 75 C8
Chelmsford 42 D3
Chelsea 28 B3
Chelsfield 29 C5
Chelsworth 56 E3
Cheltenham 37 B6
Chelveston 53 C7
Chelvey 23 C6
Chelwood 23 C8
Chelwood Common 17 B8
Chelwood Gate 17 B8
Chelworth 37 E6
Chelworth Green 37 E7
Chemistry 74 E2
Chenies 40 E3
Cheny Longville 60 F4
Chepstow = Cas-gwent 36 E2
Chequerfield 89 B5
Cherhill 24 B5
Cherington Glos 37 E6
Warks 51 F7
Cheriton Devon 21 E6
Hants 15 B6
Kent 19 B8
Swansea 33 E5
Cheriton Bishop 10 E2
Cheriton Fitzpaine 10 D3
Cheriton or Stackpole Elidor 44 F4
Cherrington 61 B6
Cherrybank 128 B3
Cherry Burton 97 E5
Cherry Hinton 55 D5
Cherry Orchard 50 D3
Cherry Willingham 78 B3
Chertsey 27 C8
Cheselbourne 13 E5
Chesham 40 D2
Chesham Bois 40 E2
Cheshunt 41 D6
Cheslyn Hay 62 D3
Chessington 28 C2
Chester 73 C8
Chesterblade 23 E8
Chesterfield 76 B3
Chester-le-Street 111 D5
Chester Moor 111 E5
Chesters Borders 116 B2
Borders 116 C2
Chesterton Cambs 55 C5
Cambs 65 E8
Glos 37 D7
Oxon 39 B5
Shrops 61 E7
Staffs 74 E5
Warks 51 D8
Chesterwood 109 C8
Chestfield 30 C5
Cheston 6 D4
Cheswardine 61 B7
Cheswick 123 E6
Chetnole 12 D4
Chettiscombe 10 C4
Chettisham 66 F5
Chettle 13 C7
Chetton 61 E6
Chetwode 39 B6
Chetwynd Aston 61 C7
Cheveley 55 C7
Chevening 29 D5
Chevington 55 D8
Chevithorne 10 C4
Chew Magna 23 C7
Chew Stoke 23 C7
Chewton Keynsham 23 C8
Chewton Mendip 23 D7
Chicheley 53 E7
Chichester 16 D2
Chickerell 12 F4
Chicklade 24 F4
Chicksgrove 24 F4
Chidden 15 C7
Chiddingfold 27 F7
Chiddingly 18 D2
Chiddingstone 29 E5
Chiddingstone Causeway 29 E6
Chiddingstone Hoath 29 E5
Chideock 12 E2
Chidham 15 D8
Chidswell 88 B3
Chieveley 26 B2
Chignall St James 42 D2
Chignall Smealy 42 C2
Chigwell 41 E7
Chigwell Row 41 E7
Chilbolton 25 F8
Chilcomb 15 B6
Chilcombe 12 E3
Chilcompton 23 D8
Chilcote 63 C6
Childer Thornton 73 B7
Child Okeford 13 C6
Childrey 38 F3
Child's Ercall 61 B6
Childswickham 51 F5
Childwall 86 F2
Childwick Green 40 C4
Chilfrome 12 E3
Chilgrove 16 C2
Chilham 30 D4
Chilhampton 25 F5
Chilla 9 D6
Chillaton 9 F6
Chillenden 31 D6

Chillerton 15 F5
Chillesford 57 D7
Chillingham 117 B6
Chillington Devon 7 E5
  Som 11 C8
Chilmark 24 F4
Chilson 38 C3
Chilsworthy Corn. 6 B2
  Devon 8 D5
Chilthorne Domer . 12 C3
Chiltington 17 C7
Chilton Bucks 39 C6
  Durham 101 B7
  Oxon 38 F4
Chilton Cantelo . 12 B3
Chilton Foliat 25 B8
Chilton Lane 111 F6
Chilton Polden . . . 23 F5
Chilton Street 55 E8
Chilton Trinity . . . 22 F4
Chilvers Coton . . . 63 E7
Chilwell 76 F5
Chilworth Hants. . . 14 C5
  Sur. 27 E8
Chimney 38 D3
Chineham 26 D4
Chingford 41 E6
Chinley 87 F8
Chinley Head 87 F8
Chinnor 39 D7
Chipnall 74 F4
Chippenhall Green 57 B6
Chippenham Cambs 55 C7
  Wilts 24 B4
Chipperfield 40 D3
Chipping Herts. . . . 54 F4
  Lancs. 93 E6
Chipping Campden 51 F6
Chipping Hill 42 C4
Chipping Norton . 38 B3
Chipping Ongar . . 42 D1
Chipping Sodbury . 36 F4
Chipping Warden . 52 E2
Chipstable 10 B5
Chipstead Kent. . . . 29 D5
  Sur. 28 D3
Chirbury 60 E2
Chirk = Y Waun . 73 F6
Chirk Bank 73 F6
Chirmorrie 105 B6
Chirnside 122 D4
Chirnsidebridge . 122 D4
Chirton 25 D5
Chisbury 25 C7
Chiselborough 12 C2
Chiseldon 25 B6
Chiserley 87 B8
Chislehampton . . 39 E5
Chislehurst 28 B5
Chislet 31 C6
Chiswell Green . . 40 D4
Chiswick 28 B3
Chiswick End 54 E4
Chisworth 87 E7
Chithurst 16 B2
Chittering 55 B5
Chitterne 24 E4
Chittlehamholt 9 B8
Chittlehampton . . .9 B8
Chittoe 24 C4
Chivenor 20 F4
Chobham 27 C7
Choicelee 122 D3
Cholderton 25 E7
Cholesbury 40 D2
Chollerford 110 B2
Chollerton 110 B2
Cholmondeston . 74 C3
Cholsey 39 F5
Cholstrey 49 D6
Chop Gate 102 E3
Choppington 117 F8
Chopwell 110 D4
Chorley Ches E . . . 74 D2
  Lancs. 86 C3
  Shrops. 61 F6
  Staffs. 62 C4
Chorleywood 40 E3
Chorlton cum
  Hardy 87 E6
Chorlton Lane . . . 73 E8
Choulton 60 F3
Chowdene 111 D5
Chowley 73 D8
Chrishall 54 F5
Christchurch BCP . 14 E2
  Cambs 66 E4
  Glos 36 C2
  Newport 35 F7
Christian Malford . 24 B4
Christleton 73 C8
Christmas
  Common 39 E7
Christon 23 D5
Christon Bank . . 117 B8
Christow 10 F3
Chryston 119 B6
Chudleigh 7 B6
Chudleigh Knighton .7 B6
Chulmleigh 9 C8
Chunal 87 E8
Church 86 B5
Churcham 36 C4
Church Aston . . . 61 C7
Churchbank 48 B4
Church Brampton . 52 C5
Churchbridge 62 D3
Church Broughton 76 F2
Church Crookham . 27 D6
Churchdown 37 C5
Church Eaton . . . 62 C2
Churchend Essex. . 42 E2
  Essex. 43 E6
  S Glos. 36 F3
Church End Cambs . 66 D3
  Cambs 66 E1
  C Beds. 40 B2
  C Beds. 53 E5
  C Beds. 54 F2
  Essex. 42 B3
  Essex. 55 E6
  E Yorks. 97 D6
  Hants. 26 D4
  Lincs 78 B3
  Warks 63 E6
  Warks 63 E6

Church End continued
  Wilts 24 B5
Church Enstone . . 38 B3
Church Fenton . . . 95 F8
Churchfield 62 E4
Church Green 41 C7
Church Green
  Devon 11 E6
  Norf 68 E3
Church Gresley . . 63 C6
Church
  Hanborough . . . 38 C4
Church Hill 74 C3
Church Houses . . 102 E4
Churchill Devon . . . 11 D8
  Devon 20 E4
  N Som 23 D6
  Oxon 38 B2
  Worcs 50 B3
  Worcs 50 D4
Churchinford 11 C7
Church Knowle . . 13 F7
Church Laneham . 77 B8
Church Langton . . 64 E4
Church Lawford . . 52 B2
Church Lawton . . 74 D5
Church Leigh 75 F7
Church Lench 50 D5
Church Mayfield . 75 E8
Church Minshull . . 74 C3
Church Norton . . 16 E2
Churchover 64 F2
Church Preen 60 E5
Church
  Pulverbatch . . . 60 D4
Churchstanton . . . 11 C6
Church Stoke 60 E2
Churchstow 6 E5
Church Stowe 52 D4
Church Street 29 B8
Church Stretton . . 60 E4
Churchtown Derbys 76 C2
  IoM 84 C4
  Lancs. 92 E4
  Mers 85 C4
Church Town
  N Lincs. 89 D8
  Sur. 28 D4
Church Village . . 34 F4
Church Warsop . . 77 C5
Churnsike Lodge 109 B6
Churston Ferrers . .7 D7
Churt 27 F6
Churton 73 D8
Churwell 88 B3
Chute Standen . . . 25 D8
Chwilog 70 D5
Chyandour 2 C3
Cilan Uchaf 70 E3
Cilcain 73 C5
Cilcennin 46 C4
Cilfor 71 D7
Cilfrew 34 D1
Cilfynydd 34 E4
Cilgerran 45 E3
Cilgwyn Carms . . . 33 B8
  Gwyn 82 F4
  Pembs 45 F2
Ciliau Aeron 46 D3
Cill Donnain . . . 148 F2
Cille Bhrighde . . 148 G2
Cille Pheadair . . 148 G2
Cilmery 48 D2
Cilsan 33 B6
Ciltalgarth 72 E2
Cilwendeg 45 F4
Cilybebyll 33 D8
Cilycwm 47 F6
Cimla 34 E1
Cinderford 36 C3
Cippyn 45 E3
Circebost 154 D6
Cirencester 37 D7
Ciribhig 154 C6
City London 41 F6
  Powys 60 F2
City Dulas 82 C4
Clachaig 145 E10
Clachan Argyll. . . 124 D3
  Argyll 125 D7
  Argyll 130 E2
  Argyll 144 H6
  Highld 149 E10
  W Isles 148 D2
Clachaneasy 105 B7
Clachan na Luib 148 B3
Clachan of
  Campsie. 119 B6
Clachan of
  Glendaruel . . . 145 E8
Clachan-Seil 124 D3
Clachan Strachur . 125 E6
Clachbreck 144 F6
Clachnabrain . . . 134 C3
Clachtoll 156 G3
Clackmannan . . . 127 E8
Clacton-on-Sea. . 43 C7
Cladach
  Chireboist 148 B2
Claddach-
  knockline. 148 B2
Cladich 125 C6
Claggan Highld . . 131 B5
  Highld 147 G9
Claigan 148 C7
Claines 50 D3
Clandown 23 D8
Clanfield Hants. . . 15 C7
  Oxon 38 D2
Clanville 25 E8
Claonaig 145 H7
Claonel 157 J8
Clapgate Dorset. . 13 D8
  Herts. 41 B7
Clapham Bedford . 53 D8
  London. 28 B3
  N Yorks. 93 C7
  W Sus 16 D4
Clap Hill 19 B7
Clappers 122 D5
Clappersgate 99 D5
Clapton 12 D2
Clapton-in-
  Gordano 23 B6
Clapton-on-the-
  Hill. 38 C1
Clapworthy 9 B8
Clarach 58 F3

Clara Vale 110 C4
Clarbeston 32 B1
Clarbeston Road . 32 B1
Clarborough 89 F8
Clardon 158 D3
Clare 55 E8
Clarebrand 106 C4
Clarencefield . . . 107 C7
Clarilaw 115 C8
Clark's Green . . . 28 F2
Clarkston 119 D5
Clashandorran . . 151 G8
Clashcoig 151 B9
Clashindarroch . 152 E4
Clashmore
  Highld 151 C10
  Highld 156 F3
Clashnessie 156 F3
Clashnoir 139 B8
Clate 160 G2
Clathy 127 C8
Clatt 140 B4
Clatter 59 E6
Clatterford 15 F5
Clatterin Bridge . 135 B6
Clatworthy 22 F2
Claughton Lancs . 92 E5
  Lancs. 93 C5
  Mers 85 F4
Claverdon 51 C6
Claverham 23 C6
Clavering 55 F5
Claverley 61 E7
Claverton 24 C2
Clawdd-newydd . 72 D4
Clawthorpe 92 B5
Clawton 9 E5
Claxby Lincs. 79 B7
  Lincs 90 E5
Claxton Norf 69 D6
  N Yorks. 96 C2
Claybokie 139 E6
Claybrooke Magna 63 F8
Claybrooke Parva . 63 F8
Clay Common . . . 69 F7
Clay Coton 52 B3
Clay Cross 76 C3
Claydon Oxon . . . 52 D2
  Suff 56 D5
Claygate Dumfries 108 B3
  Kent. 29 E8
  Sur. 28 C2
Claygate Cross . . 29 D7
Clayhanger Devon . 16 B3
  W Mid 62 D4
Clayhidon 11 C6
Clayhill E Sus. . . . 18 C5
  Hants. 14 D4
Clay Hill 26 B3
Clay Lake 66 B2
Clayock 158 E3
Claypole 77 E8
Clayton Staffs . . . 75 E5
  S Yorks. 89 D5
  W Sus 17 C6
  W Yorks. 94 F4
Clayton Green . . . 86 B3
Clayton-le-Moors . 93 F7
Clayton-le-Woods 86 B3
Clayton West . . . 88 C3
Clayworth 89 F8
Cleadale 146 C7
Cleadon 111 C6
Clearbrook 6 C3
Clearwell 36 D2
Cleasby 101 C7
Cleat 159 K5
Cleatlam 101 C6
Cleator 98 C2
Cleator Moor . . . 98 C2
Clebrig 157 F8
Cleckheaton 88 B2
Cleedownton 61 F5
Cleehill 49 B7
Clee St Margaret . 61 F5
Cleethorpes 91 D7
Cleeton St Mary . 49 B8
Cleeve 23 C6
Cleeve Hill 37 B6
Cleeve Prior 51 E5
Clegyrnant 59 D6
Clehonger 49 F6
Cleish 128 E2
Cleland 119 D8
Clench Common . 25 C6
Clenchwarton . . 67 B5
Clent 50 B4
Cleobury
  Mortimer 49 B8
Cleobury North. . 61 F6
Cleongart 143 E7
Clephanton 151 F11
Clerklands 115 B8
Clestrain 159 H4
Cleuch Head . . . 115 C8
Cleughbrae 107 B7
Clevancy 25 B5
Clevedon 23 B6
Cleveley 38 B3
Cleveleys 92 E3
Cleverton 37 F6
Clevis 21 B6
Clewer 23 D6
Cley next the Sea . 81 C6
Cliaid 148 H1
Cliasmol 154 G5
Cliburn 99 B7
Click Mill 159 F4
Cliddesden 26 E4
Cliffburn 135 E6
Cliffe Medway . . 29 B8
  N Yorks. 96 F2
Cliff End 19 D5
Cliffe Woods 29 B8
Clifford Hereford . 48 E4
  W Yorks. 95 E7
Clifford Chambers 51 D6
Clifford's Mesne . 36 B4
Cliffsend 31 C7
Clifton Bristol . . . 23 B7
  C Beds. 54 F2
  Cumb 99 B7
  Derbys. 75 E8
  Lancs. 92 F4
  Northumb 117 F8
  Nottingham 77 F5
  N Yorks. 94 D4
  Oxon 52 F2
  Stirling 131 D7

Clifton continued
  S Yorks. 89 E6
  Worcs 50 E3
  York 95 D8
Clifton Campville . 63 C6
Cliftoncote 116 B4
Clifton Green . . . 87 D5
Clifton Hampden . 39 E5
Clifton Reynes . . 53 D7
Clifton upon
  Dunsmore 52 B3
Clifton upon Teme . 50 C2
Cliftonville 31 B7
Climaen gwyn . . 33 D8
Climping 16 D4
Climpy 120 D2
Clink 24 E2
Clint 95 D5
Clint Green 68 C3
Clintmains 122 F2
Cliobh 154 D5
Clippesby 69 C7
Clipsham 65 C6
Clipston 64 F4
  Notts 77 F5
Clipstone 77 C5
Clitheroe 93 E7
Cliuthar 154 H6
Clive 60 B5
Clivocast 160 C8
Clixby 90 D5
Clocaenog 72 D4
Clochan 152 B4
Clock Face 86 E3
Clockmill 122 D3
Cloddiau 60 D2
Clodock 35 B7
Clola 153 D10
Clophill 53 F8
Clopton N Nhants . 65 F7
  Suff 57 D6
Clopton Corner . . 57 D6
Clopton Green . . 55 D8
Closeburn 113 E8
Close Clark 84 E2
Closworth 12 C3
Clothall 54 F3
Clotton 74 C2
Clough Foot 87 B7
Cloughton 103 E8
Cloughton
  Newlands 103 E8
Clousta 160 H5
Clouston 159 G3
Clova Aberds . . . 140 B3
  Angus 134 B3
Clovelly 8 B5
Clove Lodge . . . 100 C4
Clovenfords 121 F7
Clovenstone . . . 141 C6
Clovullin 130 C4
Clow Bridge 87 B6
Clowne 76 B4
Clows Top 50 B2
Cloy 73 E7
Cluanie Inn 136 C3
Cluanie Lodge . . 136 C3
Clun 60 F3
Clunbury 60 F3
Clunderwen 32 C2
Clune 138 B3
Clunes 136 F5
Clungunford 49 B5
Clunie Aberds . . 153 C6
  Perth 133 E8
Clunton 60 F3
Cluny 128 E4
Cluny Castle . . . 138 E2
Clutton Bath 23 D8
  Ches W. 73 D8
Clwt-grugoer . . . 72 C3
Clwt-y-bont 83 E5
Clydach Mon 35 C6
  Swansea 33 D7
Clydach Vale . . . 34 E3
Clydebank 118 B4
Clydey 45 F4
Clyffe Pypard . . . 25 B5
Clynder 145 E11
Clyne 34 D2
Clynelish 157 J11
Clynnog-fawr . . . 82 F4
Clyro 48 E4
Clyst Honiton . . . 10 E5
Clyst Hydon 10 D5
Clyst St George . 10 F4
Clyst St Lawrence . 10 D5
Clyst St Mary . . . 10 E4
Cnoc Amhlaigh . 155 D10
Cnwch-coch 47 B5
Coachford 152 D4
Coad's Green 5 B7
Coal Aston 76 B3
Coalbrookdale . . 61 D6
Coalbrookvale . . 35 D5
Coalburn 119 F8
Coalburns 110 C4
Coalcleugh 109 E8
Coaley 36 D4
Coalhall 112 C4
Coalhill 42 E3
Coalpit Heath . . . 36 F3
Coalport 61 D6
Coalsnaughton . 127 E8
Coaltown of
  Balgonie 128 E4
Coaltown of
  Wemyss 128 E5
Coalville 63 C8
Coalway 36 C2
Coat 12 B2
Coatbridge 119 C7
Coatdyke 119 C7
Coate Swindon . . 38 F1
  Wilts 24 C5
Coates Cambs . . . 66 E3
  Glos 37 D6
  Lancs. 93 E8
  Notts 90 F2
  W Sus 16 C3
Coatham 102 B3
Coatham
  Mundeville . . . 101 B7
Coatsgate 114 D3
Cobbaton 9 B8
Cobbler's Green . 69 E5
Coberley 37 C6
Cobham Kent . . . 29 C7
  Sur. 28 C2
Cobholm Island . 69 D8

Cobleland 126 E4
Cobnash 49 C6
Coburty 153 B9
Cockayne 102 E4
Cockayne Hatley . 54 E3
Cock Bank 73 E7
Cock Bridge . . . 139 D8
Cockburnspath . 122 B3
Cock Clarks 42 D4
Cockenzie and Port
  Seton 121 B7
Cockerham 92 D4
Cockermouth . . 107 F8
Cockernhoe Green 40 B4
Cockfield Durham . 101 B6
  Suff 56 D3
Cockfosters 41 E5
Cocking 16 C2
Cockington 7 C6
Cocklake 23 E6
Cockley Beck . . . 98 D4
Cockley Cley . . . 67 D7
Cockshutt 60 B4
Cockthorpe 81 C5
Cockwood 10 F4
Cockyard 49 F6
Codda 5 B6
Coddenham 56 D5
Coddington
  Ches W. 73 D8
  Hereford 50 E2
  Notts 77 D8
Codford St Mary . 24 F4
Codford St Peter . 24 F4
Codicote 41 C5
Codmore Hill . . . 16 B4
Codnor 76 E4
Codrington 24 B2
Codsall 62 D2
Codsall Wood . . . 62 D2
Coed Duon
  = Blackwood . . 35 E5
Coedely 34 F4
Coedkernew 35 F6
Coed Mawr 83 D5
Coed Morgan . . . 35 C7
Coedpoeth 73 D6
Coed-Talon 73 D6
Coedway 60 C3
Coed-y-bryn 46 E2
Coed-y-paen . . . 35 E7
Coed-yr-ynys . . . 35 B5
Coed Ystumgwern 71 E6
Coelbren 34 C2
Coffinswell 7 C6
Cofton Hackett . . 50 B5
Cogan 22 B3
Cogenhoe 53 C6
Cogges 38 D3
Coggeshall 42 B4
Coggeshall Hamlet 42 B4
Coggins Mill . . . 18 C2
Coignafearn
  Lodge 138 C2
Coig
  Peighinnean . . 155 A10
Coig Peighinnean
  Bhuirgh 155 B9
Coilacriech 140 E2
Coilantogle 126 D4
Coilleag 148 G2
Coillore 149 E8
Coity 34 F3
Col 155 C9
Colaboll 157 H8
Colan 4 C3
Colaton Raleigh . 11 F5
Colbost 148 D7
Colburn 101 E6
Colby Cumb 100 B1
  IoM 84 E2
  Norf 81 D8
Colchester 43 B6
Colcot 22 C3
Cold Ash 26 C3
Cold Ashby 52 B4
Cold Ashton 24 B2
Cold Aston 37 C8
Coldbackie 157 D9
Coldblow 29 B6
Cold Blow 32 C2
Cold Brayfield . . 53 D7
Coldean 17 D7
Coldeast 7 B6
Colden 87 B7
Colden Common . 15 B5
Coldfair Green . . 57 C8
Coldham 66 D4
Cold Hanworth . . 90 F4
Coldharbour Glos . 36 D2
  Kent 29 D6
  Sur. 28 E2
Cold Harbour . . . 78 F2
Cold Hatton 61 B6
Cold Hesledon . . 111 E7
Cold Higham . . . 52 D4
Coldingham 122 C5
Cold Kirby 102 F3
Cold Newton . . . 64 D4
Cold Northcott . . .8 F4
Cold Norton 42 D4
Cold Overton . . . 64 C5
Coldrain 128 D2
Coldred 31 E6
Coldridge 9 D8
Coldstream Angus . 134 F3
  Borders 122 F4
Coldwaltham . . . 16 C4
Coldwells 153 D11
Coldwells Croft . 140 B4
Coldyeld 60 E3
Cole 23 F8
Colebatch 60 F3
Colebrooke 10 D5
Colebrooke 10 E2
Coleby Lincs 78 C2
  N Lincs 90 C2
Coleford Devon . . 10 D2
  Glos 36 C2
  Som 23 E8
Cole Green 41 C5
Cole Henley 26 D2
Colehill 13 D8
Coleman's Hatch . 29 F5
Colemere 73 F8
Colemore 26 F5
Coleorton 63 C8
Colerne 24 B3

Colesbourne 37 C6
Colesden 54 D2
Coles Green 56 E4
Cole's Green 57 C6
Coleshill Bucks. . . .40 E2
  Oxon 38 E2
  Warks 63 F6
Colestocks 11 D5
Colgate 28 F3
Colgrain 126 F2
Colinsburgh . . . 129 D6
Colinton 120 C5
Colintraive 145 F9
Colkirk 80 E5
Collace 134 F2
Collafirth 160 G6
Collaton St Mary . .7 D6
College Milton . . 119 D6
Collessie 128 C4
Collier Row 41 E8
Collier's End 41 B6
Collier's Green . . 18 B4
Collier Street . . . 29 E8
Colliery Row . . . 111 E6
Collieston 141 B9
Collin 107 B7
Collingbourne
  Ducis 25 D7
Collingbourne
  Kingston 25 D7
Collingham Notts . 77 C8
  W Yorks. 95 E6
Collington 49 C8
Collingtree 53 D5
Collins Green . . . 86 E3
Colliston 135 E6
Collycroft 63 F7
Collynie 153 E8
Collyweston 65 D6
Colmonell 104 A5
Colmworth 54 D2
Colnabaichin . . 139 D8
Colnbrook 27 B8
Colne Cambs . . . 54 B4
  Lancs 93 E8
Colne Edge 93 E8
Colne Engaine . . 56 F2
Colney 68 D4
Colney Heath . . . 41 D5
Colney Street . . . 40 D4
Coln Rogers 37 D7
Coln St Aldwyn's . 37 D8
Coln St Dennis . . 37 C7
Colpy 153 E6
Colquhar 121 E6
Colsterdale 101 F6
Colsterworth . . . 65 B6
Colston Bassett . . 77 F6
Coltfield 151 E14
Colthouse 99 E5
Coltishall 69 C5
Coltness 119 D8
Colton Cumb 99 F5
  Norf 68 D4
  N Yorks. 95 E8
  Staffs. 62 B4
  W Yorks. 95 F6
Col Uarach 155 D9
Colva 48 D4
Colvend 107 D5
Colvister 160 D7
Colwall Green . . 50 E2
Colwall Stone . . 50 E2
Colwell 110 B2
Colwich 62 B4
Colwick 77 E6
Colwinston 21 B8
Colworth 16 D3
Colwyn Bay
  = Bae Colwyn . 83 D8
Colyford 11 E7
Colyton 11 E7
Combe Hereford . 48 C5
  Oxon 38 C4
  W Berks 25 C8
Combe Common . 27 F7
Combe Down . . . 24 C2
Combe Florey . . . 22 F3
Combe Hay 24 D2
Combeinteignhead . .7 B7
Combe Martin 20 E4
Combe Moor . . . 49 C5
Combe Raleigh . . 11 D6
Comberbach 74 B3
Comberton Cambs. 54 D4
  Hereford 49 C6
Combe St
  Nicholas 11 C8
Combpyne 11 E7
Combridge 75 F7
Combrook 51 D8
Combs Derbys. . . 75 B7
  Suff 56 D4
Combs Ford 56 D4
Combwich 22 E4
Comers 141 D5
Commercial End . 55 C6
Commins Capel
  Betws 46 D5
Commins Coch . . 58 D5
Commondale . . . 102 C4
Common Edge . . 92 F3
Commonmoor 5 C7
Commonside . . . 74 B2
Common Side . . . 76 B3
Compstall 87 E7
Compton Devon . . .7 C6
  Hants. 15 B5
  Sur. 27 E6
  Sur. 27 E7
  W Berks 26 B3
  Wilts 25 D6
  W Sus 15 C8
Compton Abbas . 13 C6
Compton Abdale . 37 C7
Compton Bassett . 24 B5
Compton
  Beauchamp . . . 38 F2
Compton Bishop . 23 D5
Compton
  Chamberlayne . 13 B8
Compton Dando . 23 C8
Compton Dundon . 23 F6
Compton Martin . 23 D7
Compton
  Pauncefoot . . . 12 B4
Compton Valence . 12 E3
Comrie Fife 128 F2

Comrie continued
  Perth 127 B6
Conaglen House . 130 C4
Conchra 145 E9
Concraigie 133 E8
Conder Green . . . 92 D4
Conderton 50 F4
Condicote 38 B1
Condorrat 119 B7
Condover 60 D4
Coneyhurst 16 B5
Coneysthorpe . . . 96 B3
Coneythorpe . . . 95 D6
Conford 27 F6
Congash 139 B6
Congdon's Shop. . .5 B7
Congerstone . . . 63 D7
Congham 80 E3
Congleton 75 C5
Congl-y-wal 71 C8
Congresbury . . . 23 C6
Congreve 62 C3
Conicavel 151 F12
Coningsby 78 D5
Conington Cambs . 54 C4
  Cambs 65 F8
Conisbrough . . . 89 E6
Conisby 142 B3
Conisholme 91 E8
Coniston Cumb . . 99 E5
  E Yorks 97 F7
Coniston Cold . . 94 D2
Conistone 94 C2
Connah's Quay . . 73 C6
Connel 124 B5
Connel Park . . . 113 C6
Connor Downs . . .2 C4
Conon Bridge . . 151 F8
Conon House . . . 151 F8
Cononley 94 E2
Conordan 149 E10
Consall 75 E6
Consett 110 D4
Constable Burton 101 E6
Constantine 3 D6
Constantine Bay . .4 B3
Contin 150 F7
Contlaw 141 D7
Conwy 83 D7
Conyer 30 C3
Conyers Green . . 56 C2
Cooden 18 E4
Cooil 84 E3
Cookbury 9 D6
Cookham 40 F1
Cookham Dean . . 40 F1
Cookham Rise . . 40 F1
Cookhill 51 D5
Cookley Suff 57 B7
  Worcs 62 F2
Cookley Green . . 39 E6
Cookney 141 E7
Cooksbridge . . . 17 C8
Cooksmill Green . 42 D2
Coolham 16 B5
Cooling 29 B8
Coombe Corn 4 D4
  Corn. 8 C4
  Hants. 15 B7
  Wilts 25 D6
Coombe Bissett . 14 B2
Coombe Hill 37 B5
Coombe Keynes . 13 F6
Coombes 17 D5
Coopersale
  Common 41 D7
Cootham 16 C4
Copdock 56 E5
Copford Green . . 43 B5
Copgrove 95 C6
Copister 160 F6
Cople 54 E2
Copley 101 B5
Coplow Dale . . . 75 B8
Copmanthorpe . . 95 E8
Coppathorne 8 D4
Coppenhall 62 C3
Coppenhall Moss 74 D4
Copperhouse 2 C4
Coppingford . . . 65 F8
Copplestone . . . 10 D2
Coppull 86 C3
Coppull Moor . . . 86 C3
Copsale 17 B5
Copster Green . . 93 F6
Copston Magna . 63 F8
Copt Heath 51 B6
Copt Hewick . . . 95 B6
Copthorne Shrops. 60 C4
  Sur. 28 F4
Copt Oak 63 C8
Copy's Green . . . 80 D5
Copythorne 14 C4
Corbets Tey 42 F1
Corbridge 110 C2
Corby 65 F5
Corby Glen 65 B6
Cordon 143 E11
Coreley 49 B8
Cores End 40 F2
Corfe 11 C7
Corfe Castle 13 F7
Corfe Mullen . . . 13 E7
Corfton 60 F4
Corgarff 139 D8
Corhampton 15 B7
Corlae 113 E6
Corley 63 F7
Corley Ash 63 F7
Corley Moor 63 F6
Cornaa 84 D4
Cornabus 142 D4
Cornel 83 E7
Corner Row 92 F4
Corney 98 E3
Cornforth 111 F6
Cornhill 152 C5
Cornhill-on-
  Tweed 122 F4
Cornholme 87 B7
Cornish Hall End . 55 F7
Cornquoy 159 J6
Cornsay 110 E4
Cornsay Colliery . 110 E4
Corntown Highld . 151 F8
  V Glam. 21 B8
Cornwell 38 B2

Cornwood 6 D4
Cornworthy 7 D6
Corpach 130 B4
Corpusty 81 D7
Corran Highld . . . 130 C4
  Highld 149 H13
Corranbuie 145 G7
Corrany 84 D4
Corrie 143 D11
Corrie Common . 114 F5
Corriecravie . . . 143 F10
Corriemoillie . . . 150 E6
Corriemulzie
  Lodge 150 B6
Corrievarkie
  Lodge 132 B2
Corrievorrie . . . 138 B3
Corrimony 150 H6
Corringham Lincs . 90 E2
  Thurrock 42 F3
Corris 58 D4
Corris Uchaf . . . 58 D4
Corrour Shooting
  Lodge 131 C8
Corrow 125 E7
Corry 149 F11
Corrykinloch . . . 156 G6
Corrymuckloch . 133 F5
Corrynachenchy .147 G9
Corry of
  Ardnagrask . . . 151 G8
Corsback 158 C4
Corscombe 12 D3
Corse Aberds. . . 152 D6
  Glos 36 B4
Corse Lawn 50 F3
Corse of Kinnoir . 152 D5
Corsewall 104 C4
Corsham 24 B3
Corsindae 141 D5
Corsley 24 E3
Corsley Heath . . 24 E3
Corsock 106 B4
Corston Bath. . . . 23 C8
  Wilts 37 F6
Corstorphine . . . 120 B4
Cors-y-Gedol . . . 71 E6
Cortachy 134 D3
Corton Suff 69 E8
  Wilts 24 E4
Corton Denham . 12 B4
Coruanan Lodge . 130 C4
Corunna 148 B3
Corwen 72 E4
Coryton Devon . . .9 F6
  Thurrock 42 F3
Cosby 64 E2
Coseley 62 E3
Cosgrove 53 E5
Cosham 15 D7
Cosheston 32 D1
Cossall 76 E4
Cossington Leics . 64 C3
  Som 23 E5
Costa 159 F4
Costessey 68 C4
Costock 64 B2
Coston 64 C5
Cote 38 D3
Cotebrook 74 C2
Cotehill 108 D4
Cotes Cumb 99 F6
  Leics 64 B2
  Staffs. 74 F5
Cotesbach 64 F2
Cotgrave 77 F6
Cothall 141 C7
Cotham 77 E7
Cothelstone 22 F3
Cotherstone . . . 101 C5
Cothill 38 E4
Cotleigh 11 D7
Cotmanhay 76 E4
Cotmaton 11 F6
Coton Cambs . . . 54 D5
  Staffs. 62 B2
  Staffs. 75 F6
  W Nhants. 52 B4
Coton Clanford . 62 B2
Coton Hill Shrops. 60 C4
  Staffs. 75 F6
Coton in the Elms . 63 C6
Cott 7 C5
Cottam E Yorks . . 97 C5
  Lancs. 92 F5
  Notts 77 B8
Cottartown 151 H13
Cottenham 54 C5
Cotterdale 100 E3
Cottered 41 B6
Cotteridge 50 B5
Cotterstock 65 E7
Cottesbrooke . . . 52 B5
Cottesmore 65 C6
Cotteylands 10 C4
Cottingham
  E Yorks. 97 F6
  N Nhants. 64 E5
Cottingley 94 F4
Cottisford 52 F3
Cotton Staffs . . . 75 E7
  Suff 56 C4
Cotton End 53 E8
Cottown Aberds . 140 B4
  Aberds. 141 C6
  Aberds. 153 D8
Cotwalton 75 F6
Couch's Mill 5 D6
Coughton Hereford . 36 B2
  Warks 51 C5
Coulaghailtro . . 144 G6
Coulags 150 G2
Coulby Newham . 102 C3
Coulderton 98 D1
Coulin 150 F3
Coull Aberds. . . . 140 D4
  Argyll 142 B3
Coulport 145 E11
Coulsdon 28 D3
Coulston 24 D4
Coulter 120 F3
Coulton 96 B2
Cound 61 D5
Coundon Durham . 101 B7
  W Mid 63 F7
Coundon Grange . 101 B7
Countersett 100 F4
Countess 25 E6
Countess Wear . . 10 F4

Countesthorpe . . 64 E2
Countisbury 21 E6
County Oak 28 F3
Coupar Angus . . 134 E2
Coup Green 86 B3
Coupland 122 F5
Cour 143 D9
Courance 114 E3
Court-at-Street . . 19 B7
Courteenhall . . . 53 D5
Court Henry 33 B6
Courtsend 43 E6
Courtway 22 F4
Cousland 121 C6
Cousley Wood . . 18 B3
Cove Argyll. 145 E11
  Borders 122 B3
  Devon 10 C4
  Hants. 27 D6
  Highld 155 H13
Cove Bay 141 D8
Cove Bottom . . . 57 B8
Covehithe 69 F8
Coven 62 D3
Coveney 66 F4
Covenham St
  Bartholomew . . 91 E7
Covenham St Mary 91 E7
Coventry 51 B8
Coverack 3 E6
Coverham 101 F6
Covesea 152 A1
Covington Cambs. 53 B8
  S Lanark. 120 F2
Cow Ark 93 E6
Cowan Bridge . . 93 B6
Cow Ark 93 E6
Cowbeech 18 D3
Cowbit 66 C2
Cowbridge Lincs . 79 E6
  Som 21 E8
Cowbridge
  = Y Bont-Faen . 21 B8
Cowdale 75 B7
Cowden 29 E5
Cowdenbeath . . 128 E3
Cowdenburn . . . 120 D5
Cowers Lane . . . 76 E3
Cowes 15 E5
Cowesby 102 F2
Cowfold 17 B6
Cowgill 100 F2
Cowie Aberds. . . 141 F7
  Stirling 127 F7
Cowley Devon . . . 10 E4
  Glos 37 C6
  London. 40 F3
  Oxon 39 D5
Cowleymoor . . . 10 C4
Cowling Lancs . . 86 C3
  N Yorks. 94 E2
  N Yorks. 101 F7
Cowlinge 55 D8
Cowpe 87 B6
Cowpen 117 F8
Cowpen Bewley . 102 B2
Cowplain 15 C7
Cowshill 109 E8
Cowslip Green . . 23 C6
Cowstrandburn . 128 E2
Cowthorpe 95 D7
Coxbank 74 E3
Coxbench 76 E3
Cox Common . . . 69 F6
Coxford Norf . . . 80 E4
  Soton 14 C4
Cox Green 27 B6
Coxheath 29 D8
Coxhill 31 E6
Coxhoe 111 F6
Coxley 23 E7
Cox Moor 76 D5
Coxwold 95 B8
Coychurch 21 B8
Coylton 112 B4
Coylumbridge . . 138 C5
Coynach 140 D3
Coynachie 152 E4
Coytrahen 34 F2
Crabadon 7 D5
Crabbs Cross . . . 50 C5
Crabtree 17 B6
Crackenthorpe . 100 B1
Crackington Haven .8 E3
Crackley 51 B7
Crackleybank . . . 61 C7
Crackpot 100 E4
Cracoe 94 C2
Craddock 11 C5
Cradhlastadh . . . 154 D5
Cradley 50 E2
Cradley Heath . . 62 F3
Crafthole 5 D8
Cragg Hill 94 F5
Craggan Highld . 151 H10
  Highld 157 H11
Cragg Vale 87 B8
Craghead 110 D5
Crai. 34 B2
Craibstone 152 C4
Craichie 135 E5
Craig Dumfries . . 106 B3
  Dumfries. 106 C3
  Highld 150 G3
Craiganor Lodge . 132 D3
Craig Castle . . . 140 B3
Craig-cefn-parc . 33 D7
Craigdam 153 E8
Craigdarroch
  Dumfries 113 E7
  Highld 150 F7
Craigdhu 150 G7
Craigearn 141 C6
Craigellachie . . 152 D2
Craigencross . . 104 C4
Craigend Perth. . 128 B3
  Stirling 127 F6
Craigendive . . . 145 E9
Craigendoran . . 126 F2
Craigends 118 C4
Craigens Argyll . 142 B3
  E Ayrs. 113 C5
Craighat 126 F3
Craighead 129 D8
Craighlaw Mains 105 C7

Craigie continued
S Ayrs......118 F4
Craigiefield....159 G5
Craigielaw.....121 B7
Craiglockhart...120 B5
Craigmalloch....112 E4
Craigmaud.....153 C8
Craigmillar....121 B5
Craigmore....145 G10
Craignant......73 F6
Craigneuk
  N Lanark.....119 C7
  N Lanark.....119 D7
Craignure.....124 B3
Craigo........135 C6
Craigow.......128 D2
Craig Penllyn...21 B8
Craigrothie....129 C5
Craigroy.....151 F14
Craigston Castle.153 C7
Craigton Aberdeen.141 D7
  Angus........134 D3
  Angus........135 F5
  Highld.......151 B9
Craigtown.....157 D11
Craig-y-don.....83 C7
Craig-y-nos.....34 C2
Craik.........115 D6
Crail.........129 D8
Crailing......116 B2
Crailinghall....116 B2
Craiselound....89 E8
Crakehill......95 B7
Crakemarsh.....75 F7
Crambe........96 C3
Cramlington....111 B5
Cramond......120 B4
Cramond Bridge..120 B4
Cranage........74 C4
Cranberry......74 F5
Cranborne......13 C8
Cranbourne.....27 B7
Cranbrook Devon..10 E5
  Kent.........18 B4
Cranbrook
  Common......18 B4
Crane Moor......88 D4
Crane's Corner...68 C2
Cranfield......53 E7
Cranford......28 B2
Cranford St
  Andrew........53 B7
Cranford St John.53 B7
Cranham Glos....37 C5
  London........42 F1
Crank.........86 E3
Crank Wood......86 D4
Cranleigh......27 F8
Cranley........57 B5
Cranmer Green...56 B4
Cranmore......14 F4
Cranna.......153 C6
Crannich......147 G8
Crannoch......152 C4
Cranoe........64 E4
Cransford......57 C7
Cranshaws.....122 C2
Cranstal.......84 B4
Crantock.......4 C2
Cranwell......78 E3
Cranwich......67 E7
Cranworth.....68 D2
Craobh Haven...124 E3
Crapstone.......6 C3
Crarae.......125 F5
Crask Inn.....157 G8
Craskins......140 D4
Crask of Aigas..150 G7
Craster......117 C8
Craswall......48 F4
Cratfield......57 B7
Crathes......141 E6
Crathie Aberds..139 E8
  Highld.......137 E8
Crathorne.....102 D2
Craven Arms....60 F4
Crawcrook.....110 C4
Crawford Lancs..86 D2
  S Lanark.....114 B2
Crawfordjohn..113 B8
Crawick......113 C7
Crawley Hants...26 F3
  Oxon.........38 C3
  W Sus........28 F3
Crawley Down....28 F4
Crawleyside....110 E2
Crawshawbooth...87 B6
Crawton......135 B8
Cray N Yorks....94 B2
  Perth.......133 C8
Crayford......29 B6
Crayke........95 B8
Crays Hill......42 E3
Cray's Pond.....39 F6
Creacombe......10 C2
Creagan......130 E3
Creag Ghoraidh..148 D2
Creaguaineach
  Lodge.......131 C7
Creaksea......43 E5
Creaton.......52 B5
Creca........108 B2
Credenhill.....49 E6
Crediton......10 D3
Creebridge....105 C8
Creech Heathfield.11 B7
Creech St Michael.11 B7
Creed.........3 B8
Creekmouth.....41 F7
Creeting Bottoms.56 D5
Creeting St Mary..56 D4
Creeton.......65 B7
Creetown.....105 D8
Creggans.....125 E6
Cregneash.....84 F1
Creg-ny-Baa....84 D3
Cregrina......48 D3
Creich.......128 B5
Creigiau......34 F4
Cremyll.......6 D2
Creslow.......39 B7
Cressage......61 D5
Cressbrook.....75 B8
Cresselly......32 D1
Cressing......42 B3
Cresswell
  Northumb.....117 E8
  Staffs.......75 F6

Cresswell Quay...32 D1
Creswell......76 B5
Cretingham.....57 C6
Cretshengan...144 G6
Crewe Ches E....74 D4
  Ches W........73 D8
Crewgreen......60 C3
Crewkerne......12 D2
Crianlarich...126 B2
Cribyn.........46 D4
Criccieth......71 D5
Crich.........76 D3
Crichie.......153 D9
Crichton......121 C6
Crick Mon......36 E1
  W Nhants......52 B3
Crickadarn.....48 E2
Cricket Malherbie.11 C8
Cricket St Thomas.11 D8
Crickheath......60 B2
Crickhowell.....35 C6
Cricklade......37 E8
Cricklewood.....41 F5
Cridling Stubbs..89 B6
Crieff........127 B7
Criggion......60 C2
Crigglestone....88 C4
Crimond......153 C10
Crimonmogate..153 C10
Crimplesham....67 D6
Crinan.......144 D6
Cringleford.....68 D4
Cringles.......94 E3
Crinow........32 C2
Cripplesease.....2 C4
Cripple's Corner..18 C4
Croasdale......98 C2
Crockenhill.....29 C6
Crockernwell....10 E2
Crockerton.....24 E3
Crocketford or
  Ninemile Bar..106 B5
Crockey Hill.....96 E2
Crockham Hill...28 D5
Crockleford Heath.43 B6
Crockness.....159 J4
Crock Street....11 C8
Croes-goch.....44 B3
Croes-lan......46 E2
Croesor.......71 C7
Croesyceiliog
  Carms........33 C5
  Torf.........35 E7
Croes-y-mwyalch.35 E7
Croeswaun.....82 F5
Croft Leics.....64 E2
  Lincs........79 C8
  Pembs........45 E3
  Warr.........86 E4
Croftamie.....126 F3
Croftmalloch...120 C2
Crofton Wilts...25 C7
  W Yorks......88 C4
Croft-on-Tees..101 D7
Crofts of
  Benachielt...158 G3
Crofts of Haddo.153 E8
Crofts of
  Inverthernie..153 D7
Crofts of Meikle
  Ardo........153 D8
Crofty.........33 E6
Croggan......124 C3
Croglin......109 E5
Croich.......150 B7
Crois Dughaill..148 F2
Cromarty.....151 E10
Cromblet.....153 E7
Cromdale.....139 B6
Cromer Herts...41 B5
  Norf.........81 C8
Cromford......76 D2
Cromhall......36 E3
Cromhall Common.36 F3
Cromor.......155 E9
Cromra.......137 E8
Cromwell......77 C7
Cronberry.....113 B6
Crondall......27 E5
Cronk-y-Voddy..84 D3
Cronton......110 F4
Crook Cumb.....99 E6
  Durham.......110 F4
Crookedholm...118 F4
Crookes.......88 F4
Crookham
  Northumb.....122 F5
  W Berks......26 C3
Crookham Village.27 D5
Crookhaugh....114 B4
Crookhouse....116 B3
Crooklands.....99 F7
Crook of Devon.128 D2
Cropredy......52 E2
Cropston......64 C2
Cropthorne.....50 E5
Cropton......103 F5
Cropwell Bishop..77 F6
Cropwell Butler..77 F6
Cros........155 A10
Crosbost.....155 E8
Crosby Cumb...107 F7
  IoM..........84 E3
  N Lincs.......90 C2
Crosby Garrett..100 D2
Crosby
  Ravensworth..99 C8
Crosby Villa...107 F7
Croscombe.....23 E7
Cross........23 D6
Crossaig.....143 C9
Crossal......149 E9
Crossapol.....146 G2
Cross Ash......35 C8
Cross-at-Hand..29 E8
Crossburn.....119 B8
Crossbush.....16 D4
Crosscanonby...81 D8
Crossdale Street.81 D8
Crossens......85 C4
Crossflatts....94 E4
Crossford Fife.128 F2
  S Lanark.....119 E8
Crossgate......66 B2
Crossgatehall..121 C6
Crossgates Fife.128 F3
  Powys........48 C2

Cross Green Devon..9 C5
  Suff.........56 D2
  Suff.........56 D3
  Warks........51 D8
Cross-hands.....32 B2
Cross Hands Carms.33 C6
  Pembs........32 C1
Crosshill E Ayrs.112 B4
  Fife........128 E3
  S Ayrs......112 D3
Cross Hill......76 E4
Crosshouse....118 F3
Cross Houses....60 D5
Crossings....108 B5
Cross in Hand
  E Sus.........18 C2
  Leics........64 F2
Cross Inn Ceredig..46 C4
  Ceredig......46 D2
  Rhondda......34 F4
Crosskeys......35 E6
Cross Keys......29 D6
Crosskirk....157 B13
Cross Lane Head..61 E7
Crosslanes.....60 C3
Cross Lanes Corn..3 D5
  N Yorks.......95 C8
  Wrex.........73 E7
Crossle.......118 C4
Crosslee.....115 C6
Crossmichael..106 C4
Crossmoor.....92 F4
Cross Oak......35 B5
Cross of
  Jackston....153 E7
Cross o'th'hands.76 E2
Crossroads Aberds.141 E6
  E Ayrs.......118 F4
Cross Street.....57 B5
Crossway Hereford.49 F8
  Mon..........35 C8
  Powys........48 D2
Crossway Green..50 C3
Crossways......13 F5
Crosswell......45 F3
Crosswood.....47 B5
Crosthwaite....99 E6
Croston.......86 C2
Crostwick......69 C5
Crostwight.....69 B6
Crothair.....154 D6
Crouch........29 D7
Croucheston....13 B8
Crouch Hill.....12 C5
Crouch House
  Green........28 E5
Croughton......52 F3
Crovie.......153 B8
Crowan.........2 C5
Crowborough....18 B2
Crowcombe......22 F3
Crowdecote.....75 C8
Crowden......87 E8
Crowell........39 E7
Crowfield Suff..56 D5
  W Nhants......52 E4
Crow Hill......36 B3
Crowhurst E Sus..18 D4
  Sur..........28 E4
Crowhurst Lane
  End.........28 E4
Crowland......66 C2
Crowlas........2 C4
Crowle N Lincs...89 C8
  Worcs........50 D4
Crowmarsh
  Gifford......39 F6
Crown Corner...57 B6
Crownhill.......6 D2
Crownland.....56 C4
Crownthorpe....68 D3
Crowntown......2 C5
Crows-an-wra....2 D2
Crowshill......68 D2
Crowsnest......60 D3
Crowthorne.....27 C6
Crowton......74 B2
Croxall........63 C5
Croxby........91 E5
Croxdale......111 F5
Croxden.......75 F7
Croxley Green..40 E3
Croxton Cambs..54 C3
  N Lincs.......90 C4
  Norf.........67 F8
  Staffs.......74 F4
Croxtonbank....74 F4
Croxton Kerrial..64 B5
Croy Highld..151 G10
  N Lanark.....119 B7
Croyde.........20 F3
Croydon Cambs..54 E4
  London........28 C4
Crubenmore
  Lodge.......138 E2
Cruckmeole.....60 D4
Cruckton......60 C4
Cruden Bay...153 E10
Crudgington....61 C6
Crudwell......37 E6
Crug..........48 B3
Crugmeer.......4 B4
Crugybar......47 F5
Crulabhig.....154 D6
Crumlin = Crymlyn.35 E6
Crumpsall......87 D6
Crundale Kent..30 E4
  Pembs........44 D4
Cruwys Morchard.10 C3
Crux Easton....26 D2
Crwbin........33 C5
Crya........159 H4
Cryers Hill.....40 E1
Crymlyn.......83 D6
Crymlyn = Crumlin.35 E6
Crymych.......45 F3
Crynant.......34 D1
Crynfryn.......46 C4
Cuaig......149 C12
Cuan........124 D3
Cubbington.....51 C8
Cubeck........100 F4
Cubert.........4 D2
Cubley........88 D3
Cubley Common..75 F8
Cublington Bucks.39 B8
  Hereford......49 F6

Cuckfield......17 B7
Cucklington....13 B5
Cuckney.......77 B5
Cuckoo Hill.....89 E8
Cuddesdon......39 C7
Cuddington Bucks..39 C7
  Ches W........74 B3
Cuddington Heath.73 E8
Cuddy Hill......92 F4
Cudham........28 D5
Cudliptown......9 F7
Cudworth Som....11 C8
  S Yorks.......88 D4
Cuffley........41 D6
Cuiashader....155 B10
Cuidhir......148 H1
Cuidhtinis....154 J5
Culbo........151 E9
Culbokie......151 F9
Culburnie.....150 G7
Culcabock.....151 G9
Culcairn.....151 E9
Culcharry....151 F11
Culcheth......86 E4
Culdrain......152 E5
Culduie......149 D12
Culford.......56 B2
Culgaith......99 B8
Culham........39 E5
Culkein......156 F3
Culkein Drumbeg.156 F3
Culkerton......37 E6
Cullachie.....139 B5
Cullen.......152 B5
Cullercoats...111 B6
Cullicudden...151 E9
Cullingworth...94 F3
Cullipool.....124 D3
Cullivoe......160 C7
Culloch......127 C6
Culloden....151 G10
Cullompton.....10 D5
Culmaily.....157 J11
Culmazie.....105 D7
Culmington.....60 F4
Culmstock......11 C6
Culnacraig....156 J3
Culnaknock...149 B10
Culpho........57 E6
Culrain......151 B8
Culross......127 F8
Culroy.......112 C3
Culsh Aberds...140 E2
  Aberds......153 D8
Culshabbin...105 D7
Culswick.....160 J4
Cultercullen..141 B8
Cults Aberdeen..141 D7
  Aberds......152 E5
  Dumfries.....105 E8
Culverstone Green.29 C7
Culverthorpe...78 E3
Culworth......52 E3
Culzie Lodge..151 D8
Cumbernauld..119 B7
Cumbernauld
  Village.....119 B7
Cumberworth...79 B8
Cuminestown..153 C8
Cumlewick....160 L6
Cummersdale..108 D3
Cummertrees..107 C8
Cummingston..152 B1
Cumnock......113 B5
Cumnor........38 D4
Cumrew......108 D5
Cumwhitton...108 D5
Cundall........95 B7
Cunninghamhead.118 E3
Cunnister....160 D7
Cupar.......129 C5
Cupar Muir....129 C5
Cupernham.....14 B4
Curbar........76 B2
Curbridge Hants..15 C6
  Oxon.........38 D3
Curdridge......15 C6
Curdworth......63 E5
Curland.......11 C7
Curlew Green...57 C7
Curridge......26 B2
Currie.......120 C4
Curry Mallet...11 B8
Curry Rivel....11 B8
Curtisden Green.29 E8
Curtisknowle....6 D5
Cury..........3 D5
Cushnie......153 B7
Cushuish......22 F3
Cusop........48 E4
Cutcloy......105 F8
Cutcombe......21 F8
Cutgate.......87 C6
Cutiau........58 C3
Cutlers Green...55 F6
Cutnall Green...50 C3
Cutsdean......51 F5
Cutthorpe......76 B3
Cutts........160 K6
Cuxham........39 E6
Cuxton........29 C8
Cuxwold.......91 D5
Cwm Bl Gwent...35 D5
  Denb.........72 B4
  Swansea......33 E7
Cwmafan......34 E1
Cwmaman......34 E4
Cwmann........46 E4
Cwmavon......35 D6
  W Nhants......52 C5
Cwmbach Carms..32 B3
  Carms........33 D5
  Powys........48 D2
  Powys........48 F3
Cwmbâch......34 D4
Cwmbelan......59 F6
Cwmbrân
  = Cwmbrân....35 E6
Cwmbran
  = Cwmbrân....35 E6
Cwmbrwyno....58 F4
Cwm-byr.......46 F5
Cwmcarn......35 E6
Cwmcarvan.....36 D1
Cwm-Cewydd....59 C5
Cwm-cou......45 E4
Cwmcych.......45 F3
Cwmdare.......34 D3

Cwmderwen.....59 D6
Cwmdu Carms....46 F5
  Powys........35 B5
  Swansea......33 E7
Cwmduad.......46 F2
Cwm-Dulais.....33 D7
Cwmdwr........47 F6
Cwmfelin Bridgend.34 F2
  M Tydf.......34 D4
Cwmfelin Boeth..32 C2
Cwm-felin-fach..35 E5
Cwmfelin Mynach.32 B3
Cwmffrwd......33 C5
Cwm Ffrwd-oer..35 D6
Cwmgiedd......34 C1
Cwmgwili......33 C6
Cwmgwrach......34 D2
Cwm-hesgen....46 F2
Cwm-hwnt......34 D3
Cwmifor.......33 B7
Cwm Irfon......47 E7
Cwmisfael......33 C5
Cwm-Llinau.....58 D5
Cwmllynfell....33 C8
Cwm-mawr......33 C6
Cwm-morgan....45 F4
Cwm-parc......34 E3
Cwmpengraig....46 F2
Cwm Penmachno..71 C8
Cwmrhos......35 B5
Cwmsychpant....46 E3
Cwmtillery.....35 D6
Cwm-twrch Isaf..34 C1
Cwm-twrch Uchaf.34 C1
Cwmwysg......34 B2
Cwm-y-glo Carms..33 C6
  Gwyn........82 E5
Cwmyoy........35 B6
Cwmystwyth.....47 B6
Cwrt..........58 D3
Cwrt-newydd....46 E3
Cwrt-y-cadno...47 E5
Cwrt-y-gollen..35 C6
Cydweli
  = Kidwelly....33 D5
Cyffordd Llandudno
  = Llandudno
  Junction.....83 D7
Cyffylliog.....72 D4
Cyfronydd......59 D8
Cymer.........34 E2
Cyncoed.......35 F5
Cynghordy.....47 E7
Cynheidre......33 D5
Cynwyd........72 E4
Cynwyl Elfed...32 B4
Cywarch.......59 C5

D

Dacre Cumb.....99 B6
  N Yorks.......94 C4
Dacre Banks....94 C4
Daddry Shield..109 F8
Dadford.......52 F4
Dadlington.....63 E8
Dafarn Faig....71 C5
Dafen.........33 D6
Daffy Green....68 D2
Dagenham......41 F7
Daglingworth...37 D6
Dagnall.......40 C2
Dail Beag.....154 C7
Dail bho Dheas.155 A9
Dail bho Thuath.155 A9
Daill........142 B4
Dailly.......112 D2
Dail Mor......154 C7
Dairsie or
  Osnaburgh....129 C6
Daisy Hill......86 D4
Dalabrog.....148 F2
Dalavich.....125 D5
Dalbeattie....106 C5
Dalblair......113 C6
Dalbog.......135 B5
Dalbury.......76 F2
Dalby IoM......84 E2
  N Yorks.......96 B2
Dalchalloch...132 C4
Dalchenna....125 E6
Dalchirach...152 E1
Dalchork.....157 H8
Dalchreichart..137 C5
Dalchruin....127 C6
Dalderby......78 C5
Dale.........44 E3
Dale Abbey.....76 F4
Dale Head......99 C6
Dalelia.....147 E10
Dale of Walls.160 H3
Daless......151 H11
Dalfaber.....138 C5
Dalgarven....118 E2
Dalgety Bay...128 F3
Dalginross....127 B6
Dalguise.....133 E6
Dalhalvaig...157 D11
Dalham........55 C8
Dalinlongart..145 E10
Dalkeith.....121 C6
Dallam........86 E3
Dallas......151 F14
Dalleagles....113 C5
Dallinghoo....57 D6
Dallington E Sus..18 D3
  W Nhants......52 C5
Dallow........94 B4
Dalmadilly....141 C6
Dalmally.....125 C7
Dalmarnock...119 C6
Dalmary......126 E4
Dalmellington..112 D4
Dalmeny.....120 B4
Dalmigavie...138 C3
Dalmigavie
  Lodge.......138 B3
Dalmore.....151 E9
Dalmuir......118 B4
Dalnabreck...147 E9
Dalnacardoch
  Lodge.......132 B4
Dalnaglar Castle.133 C8
Dalnahaitnach..138 B4

Dalnaspidal
  Lodge.......132 B3
Dalnavaid....133 C7
Dalnavie.....151 D9
Dalnawillan
  Lodge......157 E13
Dalness......131 D5
Dalnessie....157 H9
Dalqueich....128 D2
Dalreavoch...157 J10
Dalry.......118 E2
Dalrymple....112 C3
Dalserf......119 D8
Dalston.....108 D3
Dalswinton...114 F2
Dalton Dumfries.107 B8
  Lancs........86 D2
  Northumb.....110 B4
  Northumb.....110 D2
  N Yorks.......95 B7
  N Yorks.......101 D6
  S Yorks.......89 E5
Dalton-in-Furness.92 B2
Dalton-le-Dale.111 E7
Dalton-on-Tees.101 D7
Dalton Piercy..111 F7
Dalveich.....126 B5
Dalvina Lodge.157 E9
Dalwhinnie...138 F2
Dalwood.......11 D7
Dalwyne.....112 E3
Damerham......14 C2
Damgate......69 D7
Dam Green.....68 F3
Damnaglaur...104 F5
Damside......120 E4
Dam Side......92 E4
Danaby........42 D3
Danby.......103 D5
Danby Wiske...101 E8
Dandaleith...152 D2
Danderhall...121 C6
Danebridge....75 C6
Dane End......41 B6
Danehill......17 B8
Danemoor Green.68 D3
Danesford.....61 E7
Daneshill.....26 D4
Dangerous Corner.86 C3
Danskine....121 C8
Darcy Lever...86 D5
Darenth.......29 B6
Daresbury.....86 F3
Darfield......88 D5
Darfoulds.....77 B5
Dargate.......30 C4
Darite.........5 C7
Darlaston.....62 E3
Darley........94 D5
Darley Bridge..76 C2
Darley Head....94 D4
Darlingscott...51 E7
Darlington...101 C7
Darliston.....74 F2
Darlton.......77 B7
Darnall.......88 F4
Darnick......121 F8
Darowen.......58 D5
Darra........153 D6
Darracott......20 F3
Darras Hall...110 B4
Darrington....89 B5
Darsham.......57 C8
Dartford......29 B6
Dartford Crossing.29 B6
Dartington.....7 C5
Dartmeet......6 B4
Dartmouth......7 D6
Darton........88 D4
Darvel.......119 F5
Darwell Hole...18 D3
Darwen........86 B4
Datchet.......27 B7
Datchworth....41 C5
Datchworth Green.41 C5
Daubhill......86 D5
Daugh of
  Kinnermony..152 D2
Dauntsey......37 F6
Davenham......74 B3
Davenport Green.74 B5
Daventry......52 C3
Davidson's Mains 120 B5
Davidstow......8 F3
David's Well...48 B2
Davington.....115 D5
Daviot Aberds..141 B6
  Highld......151 H10
Davoch of
  Grange......152 C4
Davyhulme.....87 E5
Dawley........61 D6
Dawlish........7 B7
Dawlish Warren..7 B7
Dawn..........83 D8
Daws Heath.....42 F4
Daw's House Corn..8 F5
  Corn..........8 F5
Dawsmere......79 F7
Dayhills.......75 F6
Daylesford....38 B2
Ddôl-Cownwy...59 C7
Ddrydwr.......82 D3
Deadwater....116 E2
Deaf Hill.....111 F6
Deal..........31 D7
Deal Hall......43 E6
Dean Cumb......98 B2
  Devon.........20 E4
  Devon.........7 C7
  Dorset........13 C7
  Hants.........15 C6
  Hants.........26 B3
Deanburnhaugh..115 C6
Deane Gtr Man..86 D4
  Hants........26 D3
Deanich Lodge.150 C6
Deanland......13 C7
Dean Prior......6 C5
Dean Row......87 F6
Deans.......120 C3
Deanscales....98 B2
Deanshanger...53 F5
Deanston.....127 D6
Dearham.....107 F7
Debach........57 D6
Debden Essex...41 E7
  Essex........55 F6

Debden Cross...55 F6
Debenham......57 C5
Dechmont....120 B3
Deddington....52 F2
Dedham........56 F4
Dedham Heath...56 F4
Deebank......141 E5
Deene.........65 E6
Deenethorpe...65 E6
Deepcar.......88 E3
Deepcut.......27 D7
Deepdale.....100 F2
Deeping Gate...65 D8
Deeping St James.65 D8
Deeping St
  Nicholas......66 C2
Deerhill......152 C4
Deerhurst......37 B5
Deerness.....159 H6
Defford.......50 E4
Defynnog......34 B3
Deganwy.......83 D7
Deighton N Yorks.102 D1
  W Yorks.......88 C2
  York.........96 E2
Deiniolen......83 E5
Delabole.......8 F2
Delamere......74 C2
Delfrigs.....141 B8
Delliefure...151 H13
Dell Lodge...139 C6
Delnabo......139 C7
Delnadamph...139 D8
Delph.........87 D7
Delves.......110 E4
Delvine......133 E8
Dembleby......78 F3
Denaby Main....89 E5
Denbigh
  = Dinbych....72 C4
Denbury.......7 C6
Denby.........76 E3
Denby Dale.....88 D3
Denchworth....38 E3
Dendron.......92 B2
Denel End......53 F8
Denend.......152 E6
Denford.......53 B7
Dengie........43 D5
Denham Bucks...40 F3
  Suff.........55 C8
  Suff.........57 B5
Denham Street..57 B5
Denhead Aberds.153 C9
  Fife........129 C6
Denholm......115 C8
Denholme......94 F3
Denholme Clough.94 F3
Denio.........70 D4
Denmead......15 C7
Denmore......141 C8
Denmoss.....153 D6
Dennington....57 C6
Denny.......127 F7
Dennyloanhead.127 F7
Denny Lodge....14 D4
Denshaw.......87 C7
Denside......141 E7
Denston.......55 D8
Denstone......75 E8
Dent.........100 F2
Denton Cambs...65 F8
  Darl.........101 C7
  E Sus.........17 D8
  Gtr Man.......87 E7
  Kent.........31 E6
  Lincs........77 F8
  Norf.........69 F5
  N Yorks.......94 E4
  Oxon.........39 D5
  W Nhants......53 D6
Denton's Green..86 E2
Denver........67 D6
Denwick......117 C8
Deopham......68 D3
Deopham Green..68 E3
Depden.......55 D8
Depden Green...55 D8
Deptford London.28 B4
  Wilts........24 F5
Derby.........76 F3
Derbyhaven....84 F2
Dereham......68 C2
Deri..........35 D5
Derril.........8 D5
Derringstone...31 E6
Derrington.....62 B2
Derriton.......8 D5
Derryguaig...146 H7
Derry Hill.....24 B4
Derrythorpe....90 D2
Dersingham....80 D2
Dervaig.....146 F7
Derwen........72 D4
Derwenlas.....58 E4
Desborough....64 F5
Desford.......63 D8
Detchant.....123 F6
Detling.......29 D8
Deuddwr.......60 C2
Devauden......36 E1
Devil's Bridge..47 B6
Devizes.......24 C5
Devol........118 B3
Devonport......6 D2
Devonside....127 E8
Devoran.......3 C6
Dewar........121 E6
Dewlish.......13 E5
Dewsall Court..49 F6
Dewsbury......88 B3
Dewsbury Moor..88 B3
Dhoon........84 D4
Dhoor........84 C4
Dhowin.......84 B4
Dial Post......17 C5
Dibden........14 D5
Dibden Purlieu..14 D5
Dickleburgh....68 F4
Didbrook......51 F5
Didcot........39 F5
Diddington....54 C2
Diddlebury....60 F5
Didley........49 F6
Didling.......16 C2
Didmarton.....37 F5
Didsbury......87 E6

Didworthy......6 C4
Digby.........78 D3
Digg.........149 B9
Diggle........87 D8
Digmoor.......86 D2
Digswell Park..41 C5
Dihewyd.......46 D3
Dilham........69 B6
Dilhorne......75 E6
Dillarburn...119 E8
Dillington.....54 C2
Dilston......110 C2
Dilton Marsh...24 E3
Dilwyn........49 D6
Dinas Carms....45 F4
  Gwyn........70 D3
Dinas Cross....45 F2
Dinas Dinlle...82 F4
Dinas-Mawddwy..59 C5
Dinas Powys....22 B3
Dinbych
  = Denbigh....72 C4
Dinbych-y-Pysgod
  = Tenby......32 D2
Dinder........23 E7
Dinedor.......49 F7
Dingestow......36 C1
Dingle........85 F4
Dingleden.....18 B5
Dingley.......64 F4
Dingwall.....151 F8
Dinlabyre....115 E8
Dinmael.......72 E4
Dinnet.......140 E3
Dinnington Som..12 C2
  S Yorks.......89 F6
  T&W.........110 B5
Dinorwic......83 E5
Dinton Bucks...39 C7
  Wilts........24 F5
Dinwoodie
  Mains......114 E4
Dinworthy......8 C5
Dippen.......143 F11
Dippenhall.....27 E6
Dipple Moray..152 C3
  S Ayrs......112 D2
Diptford.......6 D5
Dipton......110 D4
Dirdhu......139 B6
Dirleton.....129 F7
Dirt Pot.....109 E8
Discoed.......48 C4
Diseworth......63 B8
Dishes.......159 F7
Dishforth.....95 B6
Disley........87 F7
Diss..........56 B5
Disserth......48 D2
Distington.....98 B2
Ditchampton....25 F5
Ditcheat.......23 F8
Ditchingham....69 E6
Ditchling......17 C7
Ditherington...60 C5
Dittisham......7 D6
Ditton Halton..86 F2
  Kent.........29 D8
Ditton Green...55 D7
Ditton Priors..61 F6
Divach......137 B7
Divlyn........47 F6
Dixton Glos....50 F4
  Mon..........36 C2
Dobcross......87 D7
Dobwalls.......5 C7
Doccombe......10 F2
Dochfour House.151 H9
Dochgarroch...151 G9
Docking.......80 D3
Docklow.......49 D7
Dockray.......99 B5
Dockroyd......94 F3
Doc Penfro
  = Pembroke Dock.44 E4
Dodburn......115 D7
Doddinghurst...42 E1
Doddington Cambs.66 E3
  Kent.........30 D3
  Lincs........78 B2
  Northumb.....123 F5
  Shrops.......61 F6
Doddiscombsleigh.10 F3
Dodford W Nhants.52 C4
  Worcs........50 B4
Dodington......24 A2
Dodleston.....73 C7
Dods Leigh.....75 F7
Dodworth......88 D4
Doe Green......86 F3
Doe Lea.......76 C4
Dogdyke.......78 D5
Dogmersfield...27 D5
Dogridge......37 F7
Dogsthorpe....65 D8
Dog Village....10 E4
Dolanog.......59 C7
Dolau Powys....48 C3
  Rhondda......34 F3
Dolbenmaen....71 C6
Dolfach.......59 D6
Dolfor........59 F8
Dol-fôr.......58 D5
Dolgarrog.....83 E7
Dolgellau.....58 C4
Dolgran.......46 F3
Dolhendre.....72 F2
Doll........157 J11
Dollar.......127 E8
Dolley Green...48 C4
Dollwen.......58 F3
Dolphin.......73 B5
Dolphinholme..92 D5
Dolphinton...120 E4
Dolton........9 C7
Dolwen Conwy...83 D8
  Powys........59 D6
Dolwyd........83 D8
Dolwyddelan....83 F7
Dôl-y-Bont....58 F3
Dol-y-cannau..48 E4
Dolyhir.......48 D4
Doncaster......89 D6
Dones Green....74 B3

Donibristle...128 F3
Donington.....78 F5
Donington on Bain 91 F6
Donington South
  Ing..........78 F5
Donisthorpe....63 C7
Donkey Town....27 C7
Donnington Glos.38 B1
  Hereford......50 F2
  Shrops.......61 D5
  Telford.......61 C7
  W Berks......26 C2
  W Sus........16 D2
Donnington Wood.61 C7
Donyatt........11 C8
Doonfoot.....112 C3
Dorback Lodge.139 C6
Dorchester Dorset.12 E4
  Oxon.........39 E5
Dordon........63 D6
Dore..........88 F4
Dores........151 H8
Dorking.......28 E2
Dormansland....28 E5
Dormanstown..102 B3
Dormington....49 E7
Dormston......50 D4
Dornal.......105 B6
Dorney........27 B7
Dornie......149 F13
Dornoch.....151 C10
Dornock......108 C2
Dorrery.......158 E2
Dorridge......51 B6
Dorrington Lincs.78 D3
  Shrops.......60 D4
Dorsington.....51 E6
Dorstone......48 E5
Dorton........39 C6
Dorusduain...136 B2
Dosthill......63 E6
Dottery.......12 E2
Doublebois.....5 C6
Dougarie.....143 E9
Doughton......37 E5
Douglas IoM....84 E3
  S Lanark.....119 F8
Douglas & Angus.134 E4
Douglastown..134 E4
Douglas Water.119 F8
Douglas West..119 F8
Doulting......23 E8
Dounby......159 F3
Doune Highld..156 J7
  Stirling.....127 D6
Doune Park...153 B7
Douneside....140 D3
Dounie......151 B8
Dounreay...157 C12
Dousland......6 C3
Dovaston......60 B3
Dove Holes....75 B7
Dovenby......107 F7
Dover.........31 E7
Dovercourt....57 F6
Doverdale.....50 C3
Doveridge.....75 F8
Doversgreen...28 E3
Dowally......133 E7
Dowbridge.....92 F4
Dowdeswell....37 C6
Dowlais.......34 D4
Dowland.......9 C7
Dowlish Wake...11 C8
Down Ampney...37 E8
Downcraig
  Ferry.......145 H10
Downderry......5 D8
Downe........28 C5
Downend IoW....15 F6
  S Glos.......23 B8
  W Berks......26 B2
Downfield....134 F3
Downgate......5 B8
Downham Essex..42 E3
  Lancs........93 E7
  Northumb.....122 F4
Downham Market..67 D6
Down Hatherley..37 B5
Downhead......23 E8
Downhill Perth.133 F7
  T&W.........111 D6
Downholland
  Cross........85 D4
Downholme....101 E6
Downies......141 E8
Downley.......39 E8
Down St Mary...10 D2
Downside Som...23 E8
  Sur..........28 D2
Down Thomas....6 D2
Downton Hants..14 E3
  Wilts........14 B2
Downton on the
  Rock.........49 B6
Dowsby........65 B8
Dowsdale......66 C2
Dowthwaitehead.99 B5
Doxey.........62 B3
Doxford......117 B7
Doxford Park..111 D6
Doynton.......24 B2
Draffan......119 E7
Dragonby......90 C3
Drakeland Corner.6 D3
Drakemyre....118 D2
Drake's Broughton.50 E4
Drakes Cross...51 B5
Drakewalls......6 B2
Draughton N Yorks.94 D3
  W Nhants......53 B5
Drax..........89 B7
Draycote......52 B2
Draycott Derbys.76 F4
  Glos.........51 F6
  Som.........23 D6
Draycott in the
  Clay.........63 B6
Draycott in the
  Moors........75 E6
Drayford......10 C2
Drayton Leics..64 E5
  Lincs........78 F5
  Norf.........68 C4
  Oxon.........38 E4
  Oxon.........52 E2

Drayton continued
Ptsmth....15 D7
Som....12 B2
Worcs....50 B4
Drayton Bassett..63 D5
Drayton Beauchamp..40 C2
Drayton Parslow..39 B8
Drayton St Leonard....39 E5
Drebley....94 D3
Dreemskerry....84 C4
Dreenhill....44 D4
Drefach Carms....33 C6
  Carms....46 F2
Dre-fach Carms....33 C7
  Ceredig....46 E4
Drefelin....46 F2
Dreghorn....118 F3
Drellingore....31 E6
Drem....121 B8
Dresden....75 E6
Dreumasdal....148 E2
Drewsteignton....10 E2
Driby....79 B6
Driffield E Yorks..97 D6
  Glos....37 E7
Drigg....98 E2
Drighlington....88 B3
Drimnin....147 F8
Drimpton....12 D2
Drimsynie....125 E7
Drinisiadar....154 H6
Drinkstone....56 C3
Drinkstone Green..56 C3
Drishaig....125 D7
Drissaig....124 D5
Drochil....120 E4
Drointon....62 B4
Droitwich Spa..50 C3
Droman....156 D4
Dron....128 C3
Dronfield....76 B3
Dronfield Woodhouse..76 B3
Drongan....112 C4
Dronley....134 F3
Droxford....15 C7
Droylsden....87 E7
Druid....72 E4
Druidston....44 D3
Druimarbin....130 B4
Druimavuic....130 E4
Druimdrishaig..144 F6
Druimindarroch..147 C9
Druimyeon More.143 C7
Drum Argyll....145 F8
  Perth....128 D2
Drumbeg....156 F4
Drumblade....152 D5
Drumblair....153 D6
Drumbuie Dumfries..113 F5
  Highld....149 E12
Drumburgh....108 D2
Drumburn....107 C6
Drumchapel....118 B5
Drumchardine..151 G8
Drumchork....155 J13
Drumclog....119 F6
Drumderfit....151 F9
Drumeldrie....129 D6
Drumelzier....120 F4
Drumfearn....149 G11
Drumgask....138 E2
Drumgley....134 D4
Drumguish....138 E3
Drumin....152 E1
Drumlasie....140 D5
Drumlemble....143 G7
Drumligair....141 C8
Drumlithie....141 F6
Drummoddie....105 E7
Drummond....151 E9
Drummore....104 F5
Drummuir....152 D3
Drummuir Castle.152 D3
Drumnadrochit..137 B8
Drumnagorrach.152 C5
Drumoak....141 E6
Drumpark....107 A5
Drumphail....105 C6
Drumrash....106 B3
Drumrunie....156 J4
Drums....141 B8
Drumsallie....130 B3
Drumstinchall..107 D5
Drumsturdy....134 F4
Drumtochty Castle....135 B6
Drumtroddan..105 E7
Drumuie....149 D9
Drumuillie....138 B5
Drumvaich....127 D5
Drumwhindle..153 E9
Drunkendub..135 E6
Drury....73 C6
Drury Square..68 C2
Drybeck....100 C1
Drybridge Moray..152 B4
  N Ayrs....118 F3
Drybrook....36 C3
Dryburgh....121 F8
Dry Doddington..77 E8
Dry Drayton....54 C4
Dryhope....115 B5
Drylaw....120 B5
Drym....2 C5
Drymen....126 F3
Drymuir....153 D9
Drynoch....149 E9
Dryslwyn....33 B6
Dryton....61 D5
Dubford....153 B8
Dubton....135 D5
Duchally....156 H2
Duck Corner....57 E7
Duckington....73 D8
Ducklington....38 D3
Duckmanton....76 B4
Duck's Cross....54 D2
Duddenhoe End..55 F5
Duddingston..121 B5
Duddington....65 D6
Duddleswell....17 B8

Duddo....122 E5
Duddon....74 C2
Duddon Bridge..98 F4
Dudleston....73 F7
Dudleston Heath..73 F7
Dudley W Mid....62 E3
  T&W....111 B5
Dudley Port....62 E3
Duffield....76 E3
Duffryn Neath....34 E2
  Newport....35 F6
Dufftown....152 E3
Duffus....152 B1
Dufton....100 B1
Duggleby....96 C4
Duirinish....149 E12
Duisdalemore..149 G12
Duisky....130 B4
Dukestown....35 C5
Dukinfield....87 E7
Dulas....82 C4
Dulcote....23 E7
Dulford....11 D5
Dull....133 E5
Dullatur....119 B7
Dullingham....55 D7
Dulnain Bridge.139 B5
Duloe Bedford....54 C2
  Corn....5 D7
Dulsie....151 G12
Dulverton....10 B4
Dulwich....28 B4
Dumbarton....118 B3
Dumbleton....50 F5
Dumcrieff....114 D4
Dumfries....107 B6
Dumgoyne....126 F4
Dummer....26 E3
Dumpford....16 B2
Dumpton....31 C7
Dun....135 D6
Dunain House..151 G9
Dunalastair....132 D4
Dunan....149 F10
Dunball....22 E5
Dunbar....122 B2
Dunbeath....158 H3
Dunbeg....124 B4
Dunblane....127 D6
Dunbog....128 C4
Duncanston....151 F8
Duncanstone..140 B4
Dun Charlabhaigh..154 C6
Dunchurch....52 B2
Duncote....52 D4
Duncow....114 F2
Duncraggan....126 D4
Duncrievie....128 D3
Duncton....16 C3
Dundas House..159 K5
Dundee....134 F4
Dundeugh....113 F5
Dundon....23 F6
Dundonald....118 F3
Dundonnell....150 C3
Dundonnell Hotel 150 C3
Dundonnell House....150 C4
Dundraw....108 E2
Dundreggan....137 C6
Dundreggan Lodge....137 C6
Dundrennan..106 E4
Dundry....23 C7
Dunecht....141 D6
Dunfermline..128 F2
Dunfield....37 E8
Dunford Bridge..88 D2
Dungworth....88 F3
Dunham....77 B8
Dunham-on-the-Hill....73 B8
Dunhampton....50 C3
Dunham Town..86 F5
Dunholme....78 B3
Dunino....129 C7
Dunipace....127 F7
Dunira....127 B6
Dunkeld....133 E7
Dunkerton....24 D2
Dunkeswell....11 D6
Dunkeswick....95 E6
Dunkirk Kent....30 D4
  Norf....81 E8
Dunk's Green..29 D7
Dunlappie....135 C5
Dunley Hants....26 D2
  Worcs....50 C2
Dunlichity Lodge.151 H9
Dunlop....118 E4
Dunmaglass Lodge....137 H8
Dunmore Argyll..144 G6
  Falk....127 F7
Dunnet....158 C4
Dunnichen....135 E5
Dunninald....135 D7
Dunning....128 C2
Dunnington E Yorks....97 D7
  Warks....51 D5
  York....96 D2
Dunnockshaw....87 B6
Dunollie....124 B4
Dunoon....145 F10
Dunragit....105 D5
Dunrostan....144 E6
Duns....122 D3
Dunsby....65 B8
Dunscore....113 F8
Dunscroft....89 D7
Dunsdale....102 C4
Dunsden Green..26 B5
Dunsfold....27 F8
Dunsford....10 F3
Dunshalt....128 C4
Dunshillock....153 D9
Dunskey House.104 D4
Dunsley....103 C6
Dunsmore....40 D1
Dunsop Bridge..93 D6
Dunstable....40 B3
Dunstall....63 B5
Dunstall Common..50 E3
Dunstall Green..55 C8
Dunstan....117 C8
Dunstan Steads..117 B8

Dunster....21 E8
Duns Tew....38 B4
Dunston Lincs....78 C3
  Norf....68 D5
  Staffs....62 C3
  T&W....110 C5
Dunsville....89 D7
Dunswell....97 F6
Dunsyre....120 E3
Dunterton....5 B8
Duntisbourne Abbots....37 D6
Duntisbourne Leer 37 D6
Duntisbourne Rouse....37 D6
Duntish....12 D4
Duntocher....118 B4
Dunton C Beds....54 E3
  Bucks....39 B8
  Norf....80 D4
Dunton Bassett..64 E2
Dunton Green..29 D6
Dunton Wayletts..42 E2
Duntulm....149 A9
Dunure....112 C2
Dunvant....33 E6
Dunvegan....148 D7
Dunwich....57 B8
Dunwood....75 D6
Dupplin Castle..128 C2
Durdar....108 D4
Durgates....18 B3
Durham....111 E5
Durisdeer....113 D8
Durisdeermill..113 D8
Durkar....88 C4
Durleigh....22 F4
Durley Hants....15 C6
  Wilts....25 C7
Durnamuck....150 B3
Durness....156 C7
Durno....141 B6
Duror....130 D3
Durran Argyll....125 E5
  Highld....158 D3
Durrington Wilts..25 E6
  W Sus....16 D5
Dursley....36 E4
Durston....11 B7
Durweston....13 D6
Dury....160 G6
Duston....52 C5
Duthil....138 B5
Dutlas....48 B4
Duton Hill....42 B2
Dutson....5 C8
Dutton....74 B2
Duxford Cambs....55 E5
  Oxon....38 E3
Dwygyfylchi....83 D7
Dwyran....82 E4
Dyce....141 C7
Dye House....110 D2
Dyffryn Bridgend..34 E2
  Carms....32 B4
  Pembs....44 B4
Dyffryn Ardudwy..71 E6
Dyffryn Castell..58 F4
Dyffryn Ceidrych..33 B8
Dyffryn Cellwen..34 D2
Dyke Lincs....65 B8
  Moray....151 F12
Dykehead Angus..134 C3
  N Lanark....119 D8
  Stirling....126 E4
Dykelands....135 C7
Dykends....134 D2
Dykeside....153 D7
Dykesmains....118 E2
Dylife....59 E5
Dymchurch....19 C7
Dymock....50 F2
Dyrham....24 B2
Dysart....128 E5
Dyserth....72 B4

E
Eadar Dha Fhadhail....154 D5
Eagland Hill....92 E4
Eagle....77 C8
Eagle Barnsdale..77 C8
Eagle Moor....77 C8
Eaglescliffe....102 C2
Eaglesfield Cumb..98 B2
  Dumfries....108 B2
Eaglesham....119 D5
Eaglethorpe....65 E7
Eairy....84 E2
Eakley Lanes....53 E6
Eakring....77 C6
Ealand....89 C8
Ealing....40 F4
Eals....109 D6
Eamont Bridge..99 B7
Earby....94 E2
Earcroft....86 B4
Eardington....61 E7
Eardisland....49 D6
Eardisley....48 E5
Eardiston Shrops..60 B3
  Worcs....49 C8
Earith....54 B4
Earl Barton....53 C6
Earls Colne....42 B4
Earl's Croome..50 E3
Earlsdon....51 B8
Earlsferry....129 E6
Earlsfield....78 F2
Earl's Green....56 C4
Earlsheaton....88 B3
Earl Shilton....63 E8
Earlsmill....151 F12
Earl Soham....57 C6
Earl Sterndale..75 C7
Earlston Borders.121 F8
  E Ayrs....118 F4
Earl Stonham....56 D5
Earlswood Mon....36 E1
  Sur....28 E3
  Warks....51 B6
Earnley....16 E2

Earsairidh....148 J2
Earsdon....111 B6
Earsham....69 F6
Earswick....96 D2
Eartham....16 D3
Easby N Yorks....101 D6
  N Yorks....102 D3
Easdale....124 D3
Easebourne....16 B2
Easenhall....52 B2
Eashing....27 E7
Easington Bucks..39 C6
  Durham....111 E7
  E Yorks....91 C7
  Northumb....123 F7
  Oxon....39 E6
  Oxon....52 F2
  Redcar....103 C5
Easington Colliery....111 E7
Easington Lane..111 E6
Easingwold....95 C8
Easole Street....31 D6
Eassie....134 E3
East Aberthaw..22 C2
East Adderbury..52 F2
East Allington....7 E5
East Anstey....10 B3
East Appleton..101 E7
East Ardsley....88 B4
East Ashling....16 D2
East Auchronie..141 D7
East Ayton....35 D6
East Bank....91 F5
East Barkwith..91 F5
East Barming....29 D8
East Barnby....103 C6
East Barnet....41 E5
East Barns....122 B3
East Barsham....80 D5
East Beckham..81 D7
East Bedfont....27 B8
East Bergholt..56 F4
East Bilney....68 C2
East Blatchington..17 D8
East Boldre....14 D4
Eastbourne....18 F3
East Brent....22 D5
Eastbridge....57 C8
East Bridgford..77 E6
East Buckland..21 F5
East Budleigh..11 F5
Eastburn....94 E3
East Burrafirth..160 H5
East Burton....13 F6
Eastbury London..40 E3
  W Berks....25 B8
East Butsfield..110 E4
East Butterwick..90 D2
Eastby....94 D3
East Cairnbeg..135 B7
East Calder....120 C3
East Carleton..68 D4
East Carlton N Nhants..64 F5
  W Yorks....94 E5
East Chaldon..13 F5
East Challow....38 F3
East Chiltington..17 C7
East Chinnock..12 C2
East Chisenbury..25 D6
Eastchurch....30 B3
East Clandon..27 D8
East Claydon..39 B7
East Clyne....157 J12
East Coker....12 C3
Eastcombe....37 D5
East Combe....22 F3
East Common..96 F2
East Compton..23 E8
Eastcote London..40 F4
  W Mid....51 B6
  W Nhants....52 D4
Eastcott Corn....8 C4
  Wilts....24 D5
East Cottingwith..96 E3
Eastcourt Wilts....25 C7
  Wilts....37 E6
East Cowes....15 E6
East Cowick....89 B7
East Cowton....101 D8
East Cramlington.111 B5
East Cranmore..23 E8
East Creech....13 F7
East Croachy..138 B2
East Croftmore..139 C5
East Curthwaite..108 E3
East Dean E Sus..18 F2
  Hants....14 B3
  W Sus....16 C3
East Down....20 E5
East Drayton..77 B7
East Ella....90 B4
East End Dorset..13 E7
  E Yorks....91 B6
  Hants....14 E4
  Hants....15 B7
  Herts....41 B7
  Kent....18 B5
  N Som....23 B6
  Oxon....38 C3

Eastertown of Auchleuchries.153 E10
Easter Whyntie..152 B6
East Farleigh....29 D8
East Farndon....64 F4
East Ferry....90 E2
Eastfield N Lanark.119 C8
  N Yorks....103 F8
Eastfield Hall....117 D8
East Fortune....121 B8
East Garston....25 B8
East Ginge....38 F4
East Goscote....64 C3
East Grafton....25 C7
East Grimstead..14 B3
East Grinstead..28 F4
East Guldeford..19 C6
East Haddon....52 C4
East Hagbourne..39 F5
East Halton....90 C5
East Ham....41 F7
Eastham....85 F4
Eastham Ferry..85 F4
Easthampstead..27 C6
East Hanney....38 E4
East Hanningfield..42 D3
East Hardwick..89 C5
East Harling....68 F2
East Harlsey....102 E2
East Harnham..14 B2
East Harptree..23 D7
East Hartford..111 B5
East Harting....15 C8
East Hatley....54 D3
East Hauxwell..101 E6
East Haven....135 F5
East Heckington..78 E4
East Hedleyhope..110 E4
East Hendred..38 F4
East Herrington.111 D6
East Heslerton..96 B5
East Hoathly....18 D2
Easthope....61 E5
Easthorpe Essex..43 B5
  Leics....77 F8
  Notts....77 D7
East Horrington..23 E7
East Horsley....27 D8
East Horton....123 F6
East Huntington..123 B6
Easthouses....121 C6
East Huntspill..22 E5
East Hyde....40 C4
East Ilkerton..21 E6
East Ilsley....38 F4
Easting....160 C8
Eastington Devon..10 D2
  Glos....36 D4
  Glos....37 D8
East Keal....79 C6
East Kennett....25 C6
East Keswick....95 E6
East Kilbride....119 D6
East Kirkby....79 C6
East Knapton..96 B4
East Knighton..13 F6
East Knoyle....24 F3
East Kyloe....123 F6
East Lambrook..12 C2
East Lamington.151 D10
East Langdon..31 E7
East Langton..64 E4
East Langwell..157 J10
East Lavant....16 D2
East Lavington..16 C3
East Layton....101 D6
Eastleach Martin..38 D1
Eastleach Turville..38 D1
East Leake....64 B2
East Learmouth.122 F4
Eastleigh Devon....9 B6
  Hants....14 C5
East Leigh....10 D2
East Lexham....67 C8
East Lilburn....117 B6
Eastling....30 D3
East Linton....121 B8
East Liss....15 B8
East Looe....5 D7
East Lound....89 E8
East Lulworth..13 F6
East Lutton....96 C5
East Lydford....23 F7
East Mains....141 E5
East Malling....29 D8
East March....134 F4
East Marden....16 C2
East Markham..77 B7
East Marton....94 D2
East Meon....15 B7
East Mere....10 C4
East Mersea....43 C6
East Mey....158 C5
East Molesey....28 C2
Eastmoor Derbys..76 B3
  Norf....67 D7
East Morden....13 E7
East Morton....94 E3
East Ness....96 B2
East Newton....97 F8
Eastney....15 E7
Eastnor....50 F2
East Norton....64 D4
East Nynehead..11 B6
East Oakley....26 D3
Eastoft....90 C2
East Ogwell....7 B6
Eastoke....15 E8
Easton Cambs....54 B2
  Cumb....108 B4
  Cumb....108 D2
  Devon....10 F2
  Dorset....12 G4
  Hants....15 B6
  Lincs....65 B6
  Norf....68 C4
  Som....23 E7
  Suff....57 C6
  Wilts....24 B3

Eastpark....107 C7
East Peckham..29 E7
East Pennard....23 F7
East Perry....54 C2
East Portlemouth..6 F5
East Prawle....7 F5
East Preston....16 D4
East Putford....9 C5
East Quantoxhead..22 E3
East Rainton....111 E6
East Ravendale..91 E6
East Raynham..80 E4
Eastrea....66 E2
East Rhidorroch Lodge....150 B5
Eastriggs....108 C2
East Rigton....95 E6
Eastrington....89 B8
East Rounton..102 D2
East Row....103 C6
East Rudham....80 E4
East Runton....81 C7
East Ruston....69 B6
Eastry....31 D7
East Saltoun....121 C7
East Sleekburn..117 F8
East Somerton..69 C7
East Stockwith..89 E8
East Stoke Dorset..13 F6
  Notts....77 E7
East Stour....13 B6
East Stourmouth..31 C6
East Stowford....9 B8
East Stratton....26 F3
East Studdal....31 E7
East Suisnish..149 E10
East Taphouse....5 C6
East-the-Water..9 B6
East Thirston....117 E7
East Tilbury....29 B7
East Tisted....26 F5
East Torrington..90 F5
East Tuddenham..68 C3
East Tytherley..14 B3
East Tytherton..24 B4
East Village....10 D3
Eastville Bristol..23 B8
  Lincs....79 D7
East Wall....60 E5
East Walton....67 C7
Eastwell....64 B4
East Wellow....14 B4
East Wemyss....128 E5
East Whitburn..120 C2
Eastwick Herts....41 C7
  Shetland....160 F5
East Williamston..32 D1
East Winch....67 C6
East Winterslow..25 F7
East Wittering..15 E8
East Witton....101 F6
Eastwood Notts....76 E4
  Southend....42 F4
  W Yorks....87 B7
East Woodburn..116 F5
East Woodhay..26 C2
East Worldham..26 F5
East Worlington..10 C2
East Worthing..17 D5
Eathorpe....51 C8
Eaton Ches E....75 C5
  Ches W....74 C2
  Leics....64 B4
  Norf....68 D5
  Notts....77 B7
  Oxon....38 D4
  Shrops....60 F3
  Shrops....60 F5
Eaton Bishop....49 F6
Eaton Bray....40 B2
Eaton Constantine 61 D5
Eaton Green....40 B2
Eaton Hastings..38 E2
Eaton on Tern..61 B6
Eaton Socon....54 D2
Eavestone....94 C5
Ebberston....103 F6
Ebbesbourne Wake....13 B7
Ebbw Vale = Glyn Ebwy..35 D5
Ebchester....110 D4
Ebford....10 F4
Ebley....37 D5
Ebnal....73 E8
Ebrington....51 E6
Ecchinswell....26 D2
Ecclaw....122 C3
Ecclefechan....107 B8
Eccles Borders..122 E3
  Gtr Man....87 E5
  Kent....29 C8
Ecclesall....88 F4
Ecclesfield....88 E4
Ecclesgreig....135 C7
Eccleshall....62 B2
Eccleshill....94 F4
Ecclesmachan..120 B3
Eccles on Sea..69 B7
Eccles Road....68 E3
Eccleston Ches W..73 C8
  Lancs....86 C3
  Mers....86 E2
Eccleston Park..86 E2
Eccup....95 E5
Echt....141 D6
Eckford....116 B3
Eckington Derbys..76 B4
  Worcs....50 E4
Ecton....53 C6
Edale....88 F2
Edburton....17 C6
Edderside....107 E7
Edderton....151 C10
Eddistone....8 B4
Eddleston....120 E5
Edenbridge....28 E5
Edenfield....87 C5
Edenhall....109 F5
Edenham....65 B7
Eden Park....28 C4
Edensor....76 C2
Edentaggart....126 E2
Edenthorpe....89 D7
Edentown....108 D3
Ederline....124 E4
Edern....70 D3
Edgarley....23 F7

Edgcott Bucks....39 B6
  Som....21 F7
Edge....60 D3
Edgebolton....61 B5
Edge End....36 C2
Edgefield....81 D6
Edgefield Street..81 D6
Edge Green....73 D8
Edge Hill....85 F4
Edgeside....87 B6
Edgeworth....37 D6
Edgmond....61 C7
Edgmond Marsh..61 B7
Edgton....60 F3
Edgware....40 E4
Edgworth....86 C5
Edinample....126 B4
Edinbane....149 C8
Edinburgh....121 B5
Edingale....63 C6
Edingight House..152 C5
Edingley....77 D6
Edingthorpe....69 A6
Edingthorpe Green....69 A6
Edington Som....23 F5
  Wilts....24 D4
Edintore....152 D3
Edith Weston....65 D6
Edithmead....22 E5
Edingham....28 C3
Edmondsham....13 C8
Edmondsley....110 E5
Edmondthorpe..65 C5
Edmonstone....159 F6
Edmonton....41 E6
Edmundbyers....110 D3
Ednam....122 F3
Ednaston....76 E2
Edradynate....133 D5
Edrom....122 D4
Edstaston....74 F2
Edstone....51 C6
Edvin Loach....49 D8
Edwalton....77 F5
Edwardstone....56 E3
Edwinsford....46 F5
Edwinstowe....77 C6
Edworth....54 E3
Edwyn Ralph....49 D8
Edzell....135 C5
Efail Isaf....34 F4
Efailnewydd....70 D4
Efailwen....32 B2
Efenechtyd....72 D5
Effingham....28 D2
Effirth....160 H5
Efford....10 D4
Egdon....50 D4
Egerton Gtr Man..86 C5
  Kent....30 E3
Egerton Forstal..30 E2
Eggborough....89 B6
Eggbuckland....6 D3
Eggington....40 B2
Egginton....63 B6
Egglescliffe....102 C2
Eggleston....100 B4
Egham....27 B8
Egleton....65 D5
Eglingham....117 C7
Egloshayle....4 B5
Egloskerry....8 F4
Eglwys-Brewis..22 C2
Eglwys Cross....73 E8
Eglwys Fach....58 E3
Eglwyswen....45 F3
Eglwyswrw....45 F3
Egmanton....77 C7
Egremont Cumb....98 C2
  Mers....85 E4
Egton....103 D6
Egton Bridge....103 D6
Eight Ash Green..43 B5
Eignaig....130 E1
Eil....138 C4
Eilanreach....149 G13
Eileanach Lodge.151 E8
Eilean Darach..150 C4
Einacleite....154 E6
Eisgean....155 F8
Eisingrug....71 D7
Elan Village....47 C8
Elberton....36 F3
Elburton....6 D3
Elcho....128 B3
Elcombe....37 F8
Eldernell....66 E3
Eldersfield....50 F3
Elderslie....118 C4
Eldon....101 B7
Eldrick....112 F2
Eldroth....93 C7
Eldwick....94 E4
Elfhowe....99 E6
Elford Northumb..123 F7
  Staffs....63 C5
Elgin....152 B2
Elgol....149 G10
Elham....31 E5
Elie....129 D6
Elim....82 C3
Eling....14 C4
Elishader....149 B10
Elishaw....116 E4
Elkesley....77 B6
Elkstone....37 C6
Ellan....138 B4
Elland....88 B2
Ellary....144 F6
Ellastone....75 E8
Ellemford....122 C3
Ellenbrook....84 E3
Ellenhall....62 B2
Ellen's Green....27 F8
Ellerbeck....102 E2
Ellerburn....103 F6
Ellerby....103 C5
Ellerdine Heath..61 B6
Ellerhayes....10 D4
Elleric....130 E4
Ellerker....90 B3
Ellerton E Yorks....96 F3
  Shrops....61 B7
Ellesborough....39 D8

Ellesmere....73 F8
Ellesmere Port..73 B8
Ellingham Norf....69 E6
  Northumb....117 B7
Ellingstring....101 F6
Ellington Cambs..54 B2
  Northumb....117 E8
Elliot....135 F6
Ellisfield....26 E4
Ellistown....63 C8
Ellon....153 E9
Ellonby....108 F4
Ellough....69 F7
Elloughton....90 B3
Ellwood....36 D2
Elm....66 D4
Elmbridge....50 C4
Elmdon Essex....55 F5
  W Mid....63 F5
Elmdon Heath....63 F5
Elmers End....28 C4
Elmesthorpe....63 E8
Elmfield....15 E7
Elm Hill....13 B6
Elmhurst....62 C5
Elmley Castle....50 E4
Elmley Lovett....50 C3
Elmore....36 C4
Elmore Back....36 C4
Elm Park....41 F8
Elmscott....8 B4
Elmsett....56 E4
Elmstead Market..43 B6
Elmsted....30 E5
Elmstone....31 C6
Elmstone Hardwicke....37 B6
Elmswell E Yorks..97 D5
  Suff....56 C3
Elmton....76 B5
Elphin....156 H5
Elphinstone....121 B6
Elrick....141 D7
Elrig....105 E7
Elsdon....117 E5
Elsecar....88 E4
Elsenham....41 B8
Elsfield....39 C5
Elsham....90 C4
Elsing....68 C3
Elslack....94 E2
Elson....73 F7
Elsrickle....120 E3
Elstead....27 E7
Elsted....16 C2
Elsthorpe....65 B7
Elstob....101 B8
Elston Notts....77 E7
  Wilts....25 E5
Elstone....9 C8
Elstow....53 E8
Elstree....40 E4
Elstronwick....97 F8
Elswick....92 F4
Elsworth....54 C4
Elterwater....99 D5
Eltham....28 B5
Eltisley....54 D3
Elton Cambs....65 E7
  Ches W....73 B8
  Derbys....76 C2
  Glos....36 C4
  Hereford....49 B6
  Notts....77 F7
  Stockton....102 C2
Elton Green....73 B8
Elvanfoot....114 C2
Elvaston....76 F4
Elveden....56 B2
Elvingston....121 B7
Elvington Kent....31 D6
  York....96 E2
Elwick Hrtlpl....111 F7
  Northumb....123 F7
Elworth....74 C4
Elworthy....22 F2
Ely Cambs....66 F5
  Cardiff....22 B3
Emberton....53 E6
Embleton Cumb..107 F8
  Northumb....117 B8
Embo....151 B11
Emborough....23 D8
Embo Street....151 B11
Embsay....94 D3
Emery Down....14 D3
Emley....88 C3
Emmbrook....27 C5
Emmer Green....26 B5
Emmington....39 D7
Emneth....66 D4
Emneth Hungate..66 D5
Empingham....65 D6
Empshott....27 F5
Emstrey....60 C5
Emsworth....15 D8
Enborne....26 C2
Enchmarsh....60 E5
Enderby....64 E2
Endmoor....99 F7
Endon....75 D6
Endon Bank....75 D6
Enfield....41 E6
Enfield Wash....41 E6
Enford....25 D6
Engamoor....160 H4
Engine Common..36 F3
Englefield....26 B4
Englefield Green..27 B7
Englesea-brook..74 D4
English Bicknor..36 C2
Englishcombe....24 C2
English Frankton..60 B4
Enham Alamein..25 E8
Enmore....22 F4
Ennerdale Bridge..98 C2
Enoch....113 D8
Enochdhu....133 C7
Ensay....146 G6
Ensbury....13 E8
Ensdon....60 C4
Ensis....9 B7
Enstone....38 B3
Enterkinfoot....113 D8
Enterpen....102 D2
Enville....62 F2
Eolaigearraidh..148 H2
Eorabus....146 J6

Eòropaidh....155 A10
Epperstone....77 E6
Epping....41 D7
Epping Green Essex..41 D7
  Herts....41 D5
Epping Upland....41 D7
Eppleby....101 C6
Eppleworth....97 F6
Epsom....28 C3
Epwell....51 E8
Epworth....89 D8
Epworth Turbary..89 D8
Erbistock....73 E7
Erbusaig....149 F12
Erchless Castle..150 G7
Erdington....62 E5
Eredine....125 E5
Eriboll....156 D7
Ericstane....114 C3
Eridge Green....18 B2
Erines....145 F7
Eriswell....55 B8
Erith....29 B6
Erlestoke....24 D4
Ermine....78 B2
Ermington....6 D4
Erpingham....81 D7
Errogie....137 B8
Errol....128 B4
Erskine....118 B4
Erskine Bridg....118 B4
Ervie....104 C4
Erwarton....57 F6
Erwood....48 E2
Eryholme....101 D8
Eryrys....73 D6
Escomb....101 B6
Escrick....96 E2
Esgairdawe....46 E5
Esgairgeiliog....58 D4
Esh....110 E4
Esher....28 C2
Esholt....94 E4
Eshott....117 E8
Eshton....94 D2
Esh Winning....110 E4
Eskadale....150 H7
Eskbank....121 C6
Eskdale Green....98 D3
Eskdalemuir....115 E5
Eske....97 E6
Eskham....91 E7
Esk Valley....103 D6
Esprick....92 F4
Essendine....65 C7
Essendon....41 D5
Essich....151 H9
Essington....62 D3
Esslemont....141 B8
Eston....102 C3
Estover....6 D3
Eswick....160 H6
Etal....122 F5
Etchilhampton..24 C5
Etchingham....18 C4
Etchinghill Kent..19 B8
  Staffs....62 C4
Ethie Castle....135 E6
Ethie Mains....135 E6
Etling Green....68 C3
Eton....27 B7
Eton Wick....27 B7
Etteridge....138 E2
Ettersgill....100 B3
Ettingshall....62 E3
Ettington....51 E7
Etton E Yorks....97 E5
  Pboro....65 D8
Ettrick....115 C5
Ettrickbridge....115 B6
Ettrickhill....115 C5
Etwall....76 F2
Euston....56 B2
Euximoor Drove..66 E4
Euxton....86 C3
Evanstown....34 F3
Evanton....151 E9
Evedon....78 E3
Evelix....151 B10
Evenjobb....48 C4
Evenley....52 F3
Evenlode....38 B2
Evenwood....101 B6
Evenwood Gate..101 B6
Everbay....159 F7
Evercreech....23 F8
Everdon....52 D3
Everingham....96 E4
Everleigh....25 D7
Everley....103 F7
Eversholt....53 F7
Evershot....12 D3
Eversley....27 C5
Eversley Cross....27 C5
Everthorpe....96 F5
Everton C Beds....54 D3
  Hants....14 E3
  Mers....85 E4
  Notts....89 E7
Evertown....108 B3
Evesbatch....49 E8
Evesham....50 E5
Evington....64 D3
Ewden Village....88 E3
Ewell....28 C3
Ewell Minnis....31 E6
Ewelme....39 E6
Ewen....37 E7
Ewenny....21 B8
Ewerby....78 E4
Ewerby Thorpe..78 E4
Ewes....115 E6
Ewesley....117 E7
Ewhurst....27 E8
Ewhurst Green E Sus..18 C4
  Sur....27 F8
Ewloe....73 C7
Ewloe Green....73 C6
Ewood....86 B4
Eworthy....9 E6
Ewshot....27 E6
Ewyas Harold....35 B7
Exbourne....9 D8
Exbury....14 E5
Exebridge....10 B4
Exelby....101 F7
Exeter....10 E4
Exford....21 F7

Exhall.....51 D6
Exley Head.....94 F3
Exminster.....10 F4
Exmouth.....10 F5
Exnaboe.....160 M5
Exning.....55 C7
Exton Devon.....10 F4
Hants.....15 B7
Rutland.....65 C6
Som.....21 F8
Exwick.....10 E4
Eyam.....76 B2
Eydon.....52 D3
Eye Hereford.....49 C6
Pboro.....66 D2
Suff.....56 B5
Eye Green.....66 D2
Eyemouth.....122 C5
Eyeworth.....54 E3
Eyhorne Street.....30 D2
Eyke.....57 D7
Eynesbury.....54 D2
Eynort.....149 F8
Eynsford.....29 C6
Eynsham.....38 D4
Eype.....12 E2
Eyre Highld......149 C9
Highld.....149 E10
Eythorne.....31 E6
Eyton Hereford.....49 C6
Shrops.....60 F3
Wrex.....73 E7
Eyton upon the Weald Moors.....61 C6

F

Faceby.....102 D2
Facit.....87 C6
Faddiley.....74 D2
Fadmoor.....102 F4
Faerdre.....33 D7
Failand.....23 B7
Failford.....112 B4
Failsworth.....87 D6
Fain.....150 D4
Fairbourne.....58 C3
Fairburn.....89 B5
Fairfield Derbys.....75 B7
Stockton.....102 C2
Worcs.....50 B4
Worcs.....50 E5
Fairford.....38 D1
Fair Green.....67 C6
Fairhaven.....85 B4
Fair Hill.....108 F5
Fairlie.....118 D2
Fairlight.....19 D5
Fairlight Cove.....19 D5
Fairmile.....11 E5
Fairmilehead.....120 C5
Fairoak.....74 F4
Fair Oak.....15 C5
Fair Oak Green.....26 C4
Fairseat.....29 C7
Fairstead Essex.....42 C3
Norf.....67 C6
Fairwarp.....17 B8
Fairy Cottage.....84 D4
Fairy Cross.....9 B6
Fakenham.....80 E5
Fakenham Magna.....56 B3
Fala.....121 C7
Fala Dam.....121 C7
Falahill.....121 D6
Falcon.....49 F8
Faldingworth.....90 F4
Falfield.....36 E3
Falkenham.....57 F6
Falkirk.....119 B8
Falkland.....128 D4
Falla.....116 C3
Fallgate.....76 C3
Fallin.....127 E7
Fallowfield.....87 E6
Fallsidehill.....122 E2
Falmer.....17 D7
Falmouth.....3 C7
Falsgrave.....103 F8
Falstone.....116 F3
Fanagmore.....156 E4
Fangdale Beck.....102 E3
Fangfoss.....96 D3
Fankerton.....127 F6
Fanmore.....146 G7
Fannich Lodge.....150 E5
Fans.....122 E2
Far Bank.....89 C7
Far Bletchley.....53 F6
Farcet.....66 E2
Far Cotton.....52 D5
Farden.....49 B7
Fareham.....15 D6
Farewell.....62 C4
Far Forest.....50 B2
Farforth.....79 B6
Faringdon.....38 E2
Farington.....86 B3
Farlam.....109 D5
Farlary.....157 J10
Far Laund.....76 E3
Farleigh N Som.....23 C6
Sur.....28 C4
Farleigh Hungerford.....24 D3
Farleigh Wallop.....26 E4
Farleton Cumb.....99 F7
Lancs.....93 C5
Farley Shrops.....60 D3
Staffs.....75 E7
Wilts.....14 B3
Farley Green.....27 E8
Farley Hill Luton.....40 B3
Wokingham.....26 C5
Farleys End.....36 C4
Farlington.....96 C2
Farlow.....61 F6
Farmborough.....23 C8
Farmcote Glos.....37 B7
Shrops.....61 E7
Farmington.....37 C8
Farmoor.....38 D4
Farmtown.....152 C5
Farnborough Hants.....27 D6
London.....28 C5
Warks.....52 E2
W Berks.....38 F4

Farnborough Green.....27 D6
Farncombe.....27 E7
Farndish.....53 C7
Farndon ChesW.....73 D8
Notts.....77 D7
Farnell.....135 D6
Farnham Dorset.....13 C7
Essex.....41 B7
N Yorks.....95 C6
Suff.....57 C7
Sur.....27 E7
Farnham Common.....40 F2
Farnham Green.....41 B7
Farnham Royal.....40 F2
Farnhill.....94 E3
Farningham.....29 C6
Farnley N Yorks.....94 E5
W Yorks.....95 F5
Farnley Tyas.....88 C2
Farnsfield.....77 D6
Farnworth Gtr Man.....86 D5
Halton.....86 F3
Farr Highld.....138 D4
Highld.....151 H9
Highld.....157 C10
Farr House.....151 H9
Farringdon.....10 E5
Farrington Gurney.....23 D8
Far Sawrey.....99 E5
Farsley.....94 F5
Farthinghoe.....52 F3
Farthinghoe.....31 E6
Farthingstone.....52 D4
Fartown.....88 C2
Farway.....11 E6
Fasag.....149 C13
Fascadale.....147 D8
Faslane Port.....145 E11
Fasnacloich.....130 E4
Fasnakyle Ho.....137 B6
Fassfern.....130 B4
Fatfield.....111 D6
Fattahead.....153 C6
Faugh.....108 D5
Fauldhouse.....120 C2
Faulkbourne.....42 C3
Faulkland.....24 D2
Fauls.....74 F2
Faversham.....30 C4
Favillar.....152 E2
Fawdington.....95 B7
Fawfieldhead.....75 C7
Fawkham Green.....29 C6
Fawler.....38 C3
Fawley Bucks.....39 F7
Hants.....15 D5
W Berks.....38 F3
Fawley Chapel.....36 B2
Faxfleet.....90 B2
Faygate.....28 F3
Fazakerley.....85 E4
Fazeley.....63 D6
Fearby.....101 F6
Fearn.....151 D11
Fearnan.....132 E4
Fearnbeg.....149 C12
Fearnhead.....86 E4
Fearn Lodge.....151 C9
Fearnmore.....149 B12
Fearn Station.....151 D11
Featherwood.....116 D4
Feckenham.....50 C5
Feering.....42 B4
Feetham.....100 E4
Feizor.....93 C7
Felbridge.....28 F4
Felbrigg.....81 D8
Felcourt.....28 E4
Felden.....40 D3
Felin-Crai.....34 B2
Felindre Carms.....33 B6
Carms.....33 B8
Carms.....46 F2
Carms.....47 F5
Ceredig.....46 E3
Powys.....59 F8
Swansea.....33 D7
Felindre Farchog.....45 F3
Felinfach Ceredig.....46 D4
Powys.....48 F2
Felinfoel.....33 D6
Felingwmisaf.....33 B6
Felingwmuchaf.....33 B6
Felinwynt.....45 D4
Felixkirk.....102 F2
Felixstowe.....57 F6
Felixstowe Ferry.....57 F6
Felkington.....122 E5
Felkirk.....88 C4
Felling.....111 C5
Fell Side.....108 F3
Felmersham.....53 D7
Felmingham.....81 E8
Felpham.....16 E3
Felsham.....56 D3
Felsted.....42 B2
Feltham.....28 B2
Felthorpe.....68 C4
Felton Hereford.....49 E7
Northumb.....117 D7
N Som.....23 C7
Felton Butler.....60 C3
Feltwell.....67 E7
Fenay Bridge.....88 C2
Fence.....93 F8
Fence Houses.....111 D6
Fen Ditton.....55 C5
Fen Drayton.....54 C4
Fen End.....51 B7
Fengate Norf.....81 E7
Pboro.....66 E2
Fenham.....123 E6
Feniscliffe.....86 B4
Feniscowles.....86 B4
Feniton.....11 E6
Fenlake.....53 E8
Fenny Bentley.....75 D8
Fenny Bridges.....11 E6
Fenny Compton.....52 D2
Fenny Drayton.....63 E7
Fenny Stratford.....53 F6
Fenrother.....117 E7
Fen Side.....79 D6
Fenstanton.....54 C4
Fenton Cambs.....54 B4

Fenton *continued*
Lincs.....77 D8
Lincs.....77 D8
Stoke.....75 E5
Fenton Barns.....129 F7
Fenton Town.....123 F5
Fenwick E Ayrs.....118 E4
Northumb.....110 B3
Northumb.....123 E6
S Yorks.....89 C6
Feochaig.....143 G8
Feock.....3 C7
Feolin Ferry.....144 G3
Ferindonald.....149 H11
Feriniquarrie.....148 C6
Ferlochan.....130 E3
Fern.....134 C4
Ferndale.....34 E4
Ferndown.....13 D8
Ferness.....151 G12
Ferney Green.....99 E6
Fernham.....38 E2
Fernhill Heath.....50 D3
Fernhurst.....16 B2
Fernie.....128 C5
Ferniegair.....119 D7
Fernilea.....149 E8
Fernilee.....75 B7
Ferrensby.....95 C6
Ferring.....16 D4
Ferrybridge.....89 B5
Ferryden.....135 D7
Ferryhill Aberdeen.....141 D8
Durham.....111 F5
Ferry Hill.....66 F2
Ferryhill Station.....111 F6
Ferry Point.....151 C10
Ferryside.....32 C4
Fersfield.....68 F3
Fersit.....131 B7
Ferwig.....45 E3
Feshiebridge.....138 D4
Fetcham.....28 D2
Fetterangus.....153 C9
Fettercairn.....135 B6
Fettes.....151 F8
Fewcott.....39 B5
Fewston.....94 D4
F Faccombe.....25 D8
Ffairfach.....33 B7
Ffair-Rhos.....47 C6
Ffaldybrenin.....46 E5
Ffarmers.....47 E5
Ffawyddog.....35 C6
Fforest.....33 D6
Fforest-fâch.....33 E7
Ffostrasol.....46 E2
Ffos-y-ffin.....46 C3
Ffridd-Uchaf.....83 F5
Ffrith.....73 D6
Ffrwd.....82 F4
Ffynnon ddrain.....33 B5
Ffynnongroyw.....85 F2
Ffynnon-oer.....46 D4
Fidden.....146 J6
Fiddes.....141 F7
Fiddington Glos.....50 F5
Som.....22 E4
Fiddleford.....13 C6
Fiddlers Hamlet.....41 D7
Field.....75 F7
Field Broughton.....99 F5
Field Dalling.....81 D6
Field Head.....63 D8
Fifehead Magdalen.....13 B5
Fifehead Neville.....13 C5
Fifield Oxon.....38 C2
Wilts.....25 D6
Windsor.....27 B7
Fifield Bavant.....13 B8
Figheldean.....25 E6
Filands.....37 F6
Filby.....69 C7
Filey.....97 A7
Filgrave.....53 E6
Filkins.....38 D2
Filleigh Devon.....9 B8
Devon.....10 C2
Fillingham.....90 F3
Fillongley.....63 F6
Filton.....23 B8
Fimber.....96 C4
Finavon.....134 D4
Fincham.....67 D6
Finchampstead.....27 C5
Finchdean.....15 C8
Finchingfield.....55 F7
Finchley.....41 E5
Findern.....76 F3
Findhorn.....151 E13
Findhorn Bridge.....138 B4
Findochty.....152 B4
Findo Gask.....128 B2
Findon Aberds.....141 E8
W Sus.....16 D5
Findon Mains.....151 E9
Findrack House.....140 D5
Finedon.....53 B7
Fingal Street.....57 C6
Fingask.....141 B6
Fingerpost.....50 B2
Fingest.....39 E7
Finghall.....101 F6
Fingland Cumb.....108 D2
Dumfries.....113 C7
Finglesham.....31 D7
Fingringhoe.....43 B6
Finlarig.....132 F2
Finmere.....52 F4
Finnart.....132 D2
Finningham.....56 C4
Finningley.....89 E7
Finnygaud.....152 C5
Finsbury.....41 F6
Finstall.....50 C4
Finsthwaite.....99 F5
Finstock.....38 C3
Finstown.....159 G4
Fintry Aberds.....153 C7
Dundee.....134 F4
Stirling.....126 F5
Finzean.....140 E5
Fionnphort.....146 J6
Fionnsbhagh.....154 J5
Firbeck.....89 F6
Firby N Yorks.....96 C3
N Yorks.....101 F7

Firgrove.....87 C7
Firsby.....79 C7
Firsdown.....25 F7
First Coast.....150 B2
Fir Tree.....110 F4
Fishbourne IoW.....15 E6
W Sus.....16 D2
Fishburn.....111 F6
Fishcross.....127 E7
Fisherford.....153 E6
Fisher Place.....99 C5
Fisher's Pond.....15 B5
Fisherstreet.....27 F7
Fisherton Highld.....151 F10
S Ayrs.....112 C2
Fishguard = Abergwaun.....44 B4
Fishlake.....89 C7
Fishleigh Barton.....9 B7
Fishponds.....23 B8
Fishpool.....36 B3
Fishtoft.....79 E6
Fishtoft Drove.....79 E6
Fishtown of Usan.....135 D7
Fishwick.....122 D5
Fiskavaig.....149 E8
Fiskerton Lincs.....78 B3
Notts.....77 D7
Fitling.....97 F8
Fittleton.....25 E6
Fittleworth.....16 C4
Fitton End.....66 C4
Fitz.....60 C4
Fitzhead.....11 B6
Fitzwilliam.....88 C5
Fiunary.....147 G9
Five Acres.....36 C2
Five Ashes.....18 C2
Fivecrosses.....74 B2
Fivehead.....11 B8
Five Oak Green.....29 E7
Five Oaks Jersey.....17 I3
W Sus.....16 B4
Five Roads.....33 D5
Flack's Green.....42 C3
Flackwell Heath.....40 F1
Fladbury.....50 E4
Fladdabister.....160 K6
Flagg.....75 C8
Flamborough.....97 B8
Flamstead.....40 C3
Flamstead End.....41 D6
Flansham.....16 D3
Flanshaw.....88 B4
Flasby.....94 D2
Flash.....75 C7
Flashader.....149 C8
Flask Inn.....103 D7
Flaunden.....40 D3
Flawith.....95 C7
Flax Bourton.....23 C7
Flaxby.....95 D6
Flaxholme.....76 E3
Flaxley.....36 C3
Flaxpool.....22 F3
Flaxton.....96 C2
Fleckney.....64 E3
Flecknoe.....52 C3
Fledborough.....77 B8
Fleet Hants.....15 D8
Hants.....27 D6
Lincs.....66 B3
Fleetham.....117 B7
Fleet Hargate.....66 B3
Fleetlands.....15 D6
Fleetville.....40 D4
Fleetwood.....92 E3
Flemingston.....22 B2
Flemington.....119 D6
Flempton.....56 C2
Fleoideabhagh.....154 J5
Fletchertown.....108 E2
Fletching.....17 B8
Flexbury.....8 D4
Flexford.....27 E7
Flimby.....107 F7
Flimwell.....18 B4
Flint = Y Fflint.....73 B6
Flintham.....77 E7
Flint Mountain.....73 B6
Flinton.....97 F8
Flitcham.....80 E3
Flitton.....53 F8
Flitwick.....53 F8
Flixborough.....90 C2
Flixborough Stather.....90 C2
Flixton Gtr Man.....86 E5
N Yorks.....97 B6
Suff.....69 F6
Flockton.....88 C3
Flodaigh.....148 C3
Flodden.....122 F5
Flodigarry.....149 A9
Flood's Ferry.....66 E3
Flookburgh.....92 B3
Florden.....68 E4
Flore.....52 C4
Flotterton.....117 D5
Flowton.....56 E4
Flush House.....88 D2
Flushing Aberds.....153 D10
Corn.....3 C7
Flyford Flavell.....50 D4
Foals Green.....57 B6
Fobbing.....42 F3
Fochabers.....152 C3
Fochriw.....35 D5
Fockerby.....90 C2
Fodderletter.....139 B7
Fodderty.....151 F8
Foel.....59 C6
Foel-gastell.....33 C6
Foffarty.....134 E4
Foggathorpe.....96 F3
Fogo.....122 E3
Fogorig.....122 E3
Foindle.....156 E4
Folda.....134 C1
Foleshill.....63 F7
Folke.....12 C4
Folkestone.....31 F6
Folkingham.....78 F3
Folkington.....18 E2
Folksworth.....65 F8
Folkton.....97 B6

Folla Rule.....153 E7
Follifoot.....95 D6
Folly Gate.....9 E7
Fonthill Bishop.....24 F4
Fonthill Gifford.....24 F4
Fontmell Magna.....13 C6
Fontwell.....16 D3
Foolow.....75 B8
Foots Cray.....29 B5
Forbestown.....140 C2
Force Mills.....99 E5
Forcett.....101 C6
Ford Argyll.....124 E4
Bucks.....39 D7
Devon.....9 B6
Glos.....37 B7
Northumb.....122 F5
Shrops.....60 C4
Staffs.....75 D7
Wilts.....24 B3
W Sus.....16 D3
Fordcombe.....29 E6
Fordell.....128 F3
Forden.....60 D2
Ford End.....42 C2
Forder Green.....7 C5
Fordham Cambs.....55 B7
Essex.....43 B5
Norf.....67 E6
Fordhouses.....62 D3
Fordingbridge.....14 C2
Fordon.....97 B6
Ford's Green.....56 C4
Fordstreet.....43 B5
Ford Street.....11 C6
Fordwells.....38 C3
Fordwich.....31 D5
Fordyce.....152 B5
Forebridge.....62 B3
Forest.....109 F8
Forest Becks.....93 D7
Forestburn Gate.....117 E6
Foresterseat.....152 C1
Forest Gate.....41 F7
Forest Green.....28 E2
Forest Hall.....99 D7
Forest Head.....109 D5
Forest Hill.....39 D5
Forest Lane Head.....95 D6
Forest Lodge Argyll.....131 D6
Highld.....139 C6
Perth.....133 B6
Forest Mill.....127 E8
Forest Row.....28 F5
Forestside.....15 C8
Forest Town.....77 C5
Forfar.....134 D4
Forgandenny.....128 C2
Forge.....58 E4
Forge Side.....35 D6
Forgewood.....119 D7
Forgie.....152 C3
Forglen House.....153 C6
Formby.....85 D4
Forncett End.....68 E4
Forncett St Mary.....68 E4
Forncett St Peter.....68 E4
Forneth.....133 E7
Fornham All Saints.....56 C2
Fornham St Martin.....56 C2
Forres.....151 F13
Forrestfield.....119 C8
Forrest Lodge.....113 F5
Forsbrook.....75 E6
Forse.....158 G4
Forse House.....158 G4
Forsinain.....157 E12
Forsinard.....157 E11
Forsinard Station.....157 E11
Forston.....12 E4
Fort Augustus.....137 D6
Forteviot.....128 C2
Fort George Guern.....16 I2
Highld.....151 F10
Forth.....120 D2
Forthampton.....50 F3
Forth Road Bridge.....120 B4
Fortingall.....132 E4
Forton Hants.....26 E2
Lancs.....92 D4
Shrops.....60 C4
Staffs.....61 B7
Forton Heath.....60 C4
Fortrie.....153 D6
Fortrose.....151 F10
Fortuneswell.....12 G4
Fort William.....131 B5
Forty Green.....40 E2
Forty Hill.....41 E6
Forward Green.....56 D4
Fosbury.....25 D8
Fosdyke.....79 F6
Foss.....132 D4
Foss Cross.....37 D7
Fossebridge.....37 C7
Fosterhouses.....89 C7
Foster Street.....41 D7
Foston Derbys.....75 F8
Lincs.....77 E8
N Yorks.....96 C2
Foston on the Wolds.....97 D7
Fotherby.....91 E7
Fotheringhay.....65 E7
Foubister.....159 H6
Foulby.....88 C4
Foulden Borders.....122 D5
Norf.....67 E7
Foulis Castle.....151 E8
Foul Mile.....18 D3
Foulridge.....93 E8
Foulsham.....81 E6
Fountainhall.....121 E7
Four Ashes Staffs.....62 F2
Suff.....56 B4
Four Crosses Powys.....59 D7
Powys.....60 C2
Wrex.....73 D6
Four Elms.....29 E5
Four Forks.....22 F4
Four Gotes.....66 C4

Fourlane Ends.....76 D3
Four Lane Ends.....74 C2
Fourlanes End.....74 D5
Four Lanes.....3 C5
Four Marks.....26 F4
Four Mile Bridge.....82 D2
Four Oaks E Sus.....19 C5
W Mid.....62 E5
W Mid.....63 F6
Fourpenny.....151 B11
Four Roads Carms.....33 D5
IoM.....84 F2
Fourstones.....109 C8
Four Throws.....18 C4
Fovant.....13 B8
Foveran.....141 B8
Fowey.....5 D6
Fowley Common.....86 E4
Fowlis.....134 F3
Fowlis Wester.....127 B8
Fowlmere.....54 E5
Fownhope.....49 F7
Foxbar.....118 C4
Foxcombe Hill.....38 D4
Foxdale.....84 E2
Foxearth.....56 E2
Foxfield.....98 F4
Foxham.....24 B4
Foxhole Corn.....4 D4
Swansea.....33 E7
Foxholes.....97 B6
Foxhunt Green.....18 D2
Fox Lane.....27 D6
Foxley Norf.....81 E6
Wilts.....37 F5
Fox Street.....43 B6
Foxt.....75 E7
Foxton Cambs.....54 E5
Durham.....102 B1
Leics.....64 E4
Foxup.....93 B8
Foxwist Green.....74 C3
Foxwood.....49 B8
Foy.....36 B2
Foyers.....137 B7
Fraddam.....2 C4
Fraddon.....4 D4
Fradley.....63 C5
Fradswell.....75 F6
Fraisthorpe.....97 C7
Framfield.....17 B8
Framingham Earl.....69 D5
Framingham Pigot.....69 D5
Framlingham.....57 C6
Frampton Dorset.....12 E4
Lincs.....79 F6
Frampton Cotterell.....36 F3
Frampton Mansell.....37 D6
Frampton on Severn.....36 D4
Frampton West End.....79 E6
Framsden.....57 D5
Framwellgate Moor.....111 E5
Franche.....50 B3
Frankby.....85 F3
Frankley.....62 F3
Frank's Bridge.....48 D3
Frankton.....52 B2
Fraserburgh.....153 B9
Frating Green.....43 B6
Fratton.....15 E7
Freathy.....5 D8
Freckenham.....55 B7
Freckleton.....86 B2
Freeby.....64 B5
Freehay.....75 E7
Freeland.....38 C4
Freester.....160 H6
Freethorpe.....69 D7
Freiston.....79 E6
Fremington Devon.....20 F4
N Yorks.....101 E5
Frenchay.....23 B8
Frenchbeer.....9 F8
French.....126 D3
Frensham.....27 E6
Fresgoe.....157 C12
Freshfield.....85 D3
Freshford.....24 C2
Freshwater.....14 F4
Freshwater Bay.....14 F4
Freshwater East.....32 E1
Fressingfield.....57 B6
Freston.....57 F5
Freswick.....158 D5
Fretherne.....36 D4
Frettenham.....68 C5
Freuchie.....128 D4
Freuchies.....134 C2
Freystrop.....44 D4
Friar's Gate.....29 F5
Friarton.....128 B3
Friday Bridge.....66 D4
Friday Street.....18 E3
Fridaythorpe.....96 D4
Friern Barnet.....41 E5
Friesland.....146 F4
Friesthorpe.....90 F4
Frieth.....39 E7
Frilford.....38 E4
Frilsham.....26 B3
Frimley.....27 D6
Frimley Green.....27 D6
Frindsbury.....29 B8
Fring.....80 D3
Fringford.....39 B6
Frinsted.....30 D2
Frinton-on-Sea.....43 B8
Friockheim.....135 E5
Friog.....58 C3
Frisby on the Wreake.....64 C3
Friskney.....79 D7
Friskney Eaudike.....79 D7
Friskney Tofts.....79 D7
Friston E Sus.....18 F2
Suff.....57 C8
Fritchley.....76 D3
Fritham.....14 C3
Frith Bank.....79 E6
Frith Common.....49 C8
Frithelstock.....9 C6
Frithelstock Stone.....9 C6

Frithville.....79 D6
Frittenden.....30 E2
Frittiscombe.....7 E6
Fritton Norf.....68 E5
Norf.....69 D7
Fritwell.....39 B5
Frizinghall.....94 F4
Frizington.....98 C2
Frocester.....36 D4
Frodesley.....60 D5
Frodingham.....90 C2
Frodsham.....74 B2
Frogden.....116 B3
Froggatt.....76 B2
Froghall.....75 E7
Frogmore Devon.....7 E5
Hants.....27 D6
Frognall.....65 C8
Frogshail.....81 D8
Frolesworth.....64 E2
Frome.....24 E2
Frome St Quintin.....12 D3
Fromes Hill.....49 E8
Fron Denb.....72 C4
Gwyn.....70 D4
Gwyn.....82 F5
Powys.....48 C2
Powys.....59 E8
Powys.....60 D2
Froncysyllte.....73 E6
Frongoch.....72 F3
Frostenden.....69 F7
Frosterley.....110 F3
Frotoft.....159 F5
Froxfield.....25 C7
Froxfield Green.....15 B8
Froyle.....27 E5
Fryerning.....42 D2
Fryton.....96 B2
Fulbeck.....78 D2
Fulbourn.....55 D6
Fulbrook.....38 C2
Fulford Som.....11 B7
Staffs.....75 F6
York.....96 E2
Fulham.....28 B3
Fulking.....17 C6
Fullarton Glasgow.....119 C6
N Ayrs.....118 F3
Fuller's Moor.....73 D8
Fuller Street.....42 C3
Fullerton.....25 F8
Fulletby.....79 B5
Full Sutton.....96 D3
Fullwood.....118 D4
Fulmer.....40 F2
Fulmodestone.....81 D5
Fulnetby.....78 B3
Fulstow.....91 E7
Fulwell.....111 D6
Fulwood Lancs.....92 F5
S Yorks.....88 F4
Fundenhall.....68 E4
Fundenhall Street.....68 E4
Funtington.....15 D8
Funtley.....15 D6
Funtullich.....127 B6
Funzie.....160 D8
Furley.....11 D7
Furnace Argyll.....125 E6
Carms.....33 D6
Furnace End.....63 E6
Furneaux Pelham.....41 B7
Furness Vale.....87 F8
Furzehill.....21 E6
Furze Platt.....40 F1
Fyfett.....11 C7
Fyfield Essex.....42 D1
Glos.....38 D2
Hants.....25 E7
Oxon.....38 E4
Wilts.....25 C6
Fylingthorpe.....103 D7
Fyvie.....153 E7

G

Gabhsann bho Dheas.....155 B9
Gabhsann bho Thuath.....155 B9
Gablon.....151 B10
Gabroc Hill.....118 D4
Gaddesby.....64 C3
Gadebridge.....40 D3
Gaer.....35 B5
Gaerllwyd.....36 E1
Gaerwen.....82 D4
Gagingwell.....38 B4
Gaick Lodge.....138 F3
Gailey.....62 C3
Gainford.....101 C6
Gainsborough Lincs.....90 E2
Suff.....57 E5
Gainsford End.....55 F8
Gairloch.....149 A13
Gairlochy.....136 F4
Gairney Bank.....128 E3
Gairnshiel Lodge.....139 D8
Gaisgill.....99 D8
Gaitsgill.....108 E3
Galashiels.....121 F7
Galgate.....92 D4
Galhampton.....12 B4
Gallaberry.....114 F2
Gallachoille.....144 E6
Gallanach Argyll.....124 C4
Argyll.....146 E5
Gallantry Bank.....74 D2
Gallatown.....128 E4
Galley Common.....63 E7
Galleyend.....42 D3
Galley Hill.....54 B4
Galleywood.....42 D3
Gallin.....132 E2
Gallowfauld.....134 E4
Gallows Green.....75 E7
Galltair.....149 F13
Galmisdale.....146 C7
Galmpton Devon.....6 E4
Torbay.....7 D6
Galphay.....95 B5
Galston.....118 F5
Galtrigill.....148 C6
Gamblesby.....109 F6
Gamesley.....87 E8
Gamlingay.....54 D3
Gammersgill.....101 F5
Gamston.....77 B7

Gawthwaite.....98 F4
Gaydon.....51 D8
Gayfield.....159 C5
Gayhurst.....53 E6
Gayle.....100 F3
Gayles.....101 D6
Gay Street.....16 B4
Gayton Mers.....85 F3
Norf.....67 C7
Staffs.....62 B3
W Nhants.....52 D5
Gayton le Marsh.....91 F8
Gayton le Wold.....91 F6
Gayton Thorpe.....67 C7
Gaywood.....67 B6
Gazeley.....55 C8
Geanies House.....151 D11
Gearraidh Bhailteas.....148 F2
Gearraidh Bhaird.....155 E8
Gearraidh na h-Aibhne.....154 D7
Gearraidh na Monadh.....148 G2
Geary.....148 B7
Geddes House.....151 F11
Gedding.....56 D3
Geddington.....65 F5
Gedintailor.....149 E10
Gedling.....77 E6
Gedney.....66 B4
Gedney Broadgate.....66 B4
Gedney Drove End.....66 B4
Gedney Dyke.....66 B4
Gedney Hill.....66 C3
Gee Cross.....87 E7
Geilston.....118 B3
Geirinis.....148 D2
Geise.....158 D3
Geisiadar.....154 D6
Geldeston.....69 E6
Gell.....83 E8
Gelli Pembs.....32 C1
Rhondda.....34 E4
Gellideg.....34 D4
Gellifor.....72 C5
Gelligaer.....35 E5
Gellilydan.....71 D7
Gellinudd.....33 D8
Gellyburn.....133 F7
Gellywen.....32 B3
Gelston Dumfries.....106 D4
Lincs.....78 E2
Gembling.....97 D7
Gentleshaw.....62 C4
Geocrab.....154 H6
Georgefield.....115 E5
George Green.....40 F3
Georgeham.....20 F3
George Nympton.....10 B2
Georgetown.....35 D5
Gerlan.....83 E6
Germansweek.....9 E6
Germoe.....2 D4
Gerrans.....3 C7
Gerrards Cross.....40 F3
Gestingthorpe.....56 F2
Geuffordd.....60 C2
Gibbet Hill.....64 F2
Gibbshill.....106 B4
Gib Hill.....74 B3
Gidea Park.....41 F8
Gidleigh.....9 F8
Giffnock.....119 D5
Gifford.....121 C8
Giffordland.....118 E2
Giffordtown.....128 C4
Giggleswick.....93 C8
Gilberdyke.....90 B2
Gilchriston.....121 C7
Gilcrux.....107 F8
Gildersome.....88 B3
Gildingwells.....89 F6
Gileston.....22 C2
Gilfach.....35 E5
Gilfach Goch.....34 F3
Gilfachrheda.....46 D3
Gillamoor.....102 F4
Gillar's Green.....86 E2
Gillen.....148 C7
Gilling East.....96 B2
Gillingham Dorset.....13 B6
Medway.....29 C8
Norf.....69 E7
Gilling West.....101 D6
Gillock.....158 E4
Gillow Heath.....75 D5
Gills.....158 C5
Gill's Green.....18 B4
Gilmanscleuch.....115 B6
Gilmerton Edin.....121 C5
Perth.....127 B7
Gilmonby.....100 C4
Gilmorton.....64 F2
Gilmourton.....119 E6
Gilsland.....109 C6
Gilsland Spa.....109 C6
Gilston Borders.....121 D7
Herts.....41 C7
Gilwern.....35 C6
Gimingham.....81 D8
Giosla.....154 E6
Gipping.....56 C4
Gipsey Bridge.....79 E5
Girdle Toll.....118 E3
Girlsta.....160 H6
Girsby.....102 D1
Girtford.....54 D2
Girthon.....106 D3
Girton Cambs.....54 C5
Notts.....77 C8
Girvan.....112 E1
Gisburn.....93 E8
Gisleham.....69 F8
Gislingham.....56 B4
Gissing.....68 F4
Gittisham.....11 E6
Gladestry.....48 D4
Gladsmuir.....121 B7
Glais.....33 D8
Glaisdale.....103 D5
Glame.....149 D10
Glamis.....134 E3
Glan Adda.....83 D5
Glanaman.....33 C7
Glan Conwy Conwy.....83 D8

Glan Conwy continued
Conwy ...83 F8
Glandford ...81 C6
Glan-Duar ...46 E4
Glandwr ...32 B2
Glan-Dwyfach ...71 C5
Glandy Cross ...32 B2
Glandyfi ...58 E3
Glan Gors ...82 D4
Glangrwyney ...35 C6
Glanmule ...59 E8
Glanrafon ...58 F3
Glanrhyd Gwyn ...70 D3
Pembs ...45 E3
Glanton ...117 C6
Glanton Pike ...117 C6
Glan-traeth ...82 D2
Glanvilles
Wootton ...12 D4
Glan-y-don ...73 B5
Glan-y-nant ...59 F6
Glan-yr-afon
Anglesey ...83 C6
Gwyn ...72 E3
Gwyn ...72 E4
Glan-y-wern ...71 D7
Glapthorn ...65 E7
Glapwell ...76 C4
Glas-allt Shiel ...139 F8
Glasbury ...48 F3
Glaschoil ...151 H13
Glascoed Denb ...35 D7
Mon ...35 D7
Powys ...59 C8
Glascorrie ...140 E2
Glascote ...63 D6
Glascwm ...48 D3
Glasdrum ...130 E4
Glasfryn ...72 D3
Glasgow ...119 C5
Glashvin ...149 B9
Glasinfryn ...83 E5
Glasnacardoch ...149 G10
Glasnakille ...149 G10
Glasphein ...148 D6
Glaspwll ...58 E4
Glassburn ...150 H6
Glasserton ...105 F8
Glassford ...119 E7
Glasshouse Hill ...36 B4
Glasshouses ...94 C4
Glasslie ...128 D4
Glasson Cumb ...108 C2
Lancs ...92 D4
Glassonby ...109 F5
Glasterlaw ...135 D5
Glaston ...65 D5
Glastonbury ...23 F7
Glatton ...65 F8
Glazebrook ...86 E4
Glazebury ...86 E4
Glazeley ...61 F7
Gleadless ...88 F4
Gleadsmoss ...74 C5
Gleann
Tholàstaidh ...155 C10
Gleaston ...92 B2
Gleiniant ...59 E6
Glemsford ...56 E2
Glen Dumfries ...106 B5
Dumfries ...106 C2
Glenamachrie ...124 C5
Glen Auldyn ...84 C4
Glenbarr ...143 E7
Glenbeg Highld ...139 B6
Highld ...147 E8
Glen Bernisdale ...149 D9
Glenbervie ...141 F6
Glenboig ...119 C7
Glenborrodale ...147 E9
Glenbranter ...125 F7
Glenbreck ...114 B3
Glenbrein Lodge ...137 C7
Glenbrittle House 149 F9
Glenbuchat
Lodge ...140 C2
Glenbuck ...113 B7
Glenburn ...118 C4
Glencalvie Lodge 150 C7
Glencanisp
Lodge ...156 G4
Glencaple ...107 C6
Glencarron
Lodge ...150 F3
Glencarse ...128 B3
Glencassley
Castle ...156 J7
Glenceitlein ...131 E5
Glencoe ...130 D4
Glencraig ...128 E3
Glencripesdale ...147 F9
Glencrosh ...113 F7
Glendavan House 140 D3
Glendevon ...127 D8
Glendoebeg ...137 D7
Glendoe Lodge ...137 D7
Glendoick ...128 B3
Glendoll Lodge ...134 B2
Glendoune ...112 E1
Glenduckie ...128 C4
Glendye Lodge ...140 F5
Gleneagles Hotel 127 C8
Gleneagles
House ...127 D8
Glenegedale ...142 C4
Glenelg ...149 G13
Glenernie ...151 G13
Glenfarg ...128 C3
Glenfarquhar
Lodge ...141 F6
Glenferness
House ...151 G13
Glenfeshie Lodge 138 E4
Glenfield ...64 D2
Glenfinnan ...147 C11
Glenfoot ...128 C3
Glenfyne Lodge ...125 D8
Glengap ...106 D3
Glengarnock ...118 D3
Glengorm Castle ...146 F7
Glengrasco ...149 D9
Glen Ho ...121 F5
Glenhoul ...113 F6
Glenhurich ...130 C2

Glenkerry ...115 C5
Glenkiln ...106 B5
Glenkindie ...140 C3
Glenlatterach ...152 C1
Glenlee ...113 F6
Glenlichorn ...127 C6
Glenlivet ...139 B7
Glenlochsie ...133 B7
Glenloig ...143 E10
Glenluce ...105 D6
Glenmallan ...125 F8
Glenmarksie ...150 F6
Glenmassan ...145 E10
Glenmavis ...119 C7
Glenmaye ...84 E2
Glenmidge ...113 F8
Glen Mona ...84 D4
Glenmore Argyll ...124 D4
Highld ...149 D9
Glenmore Lodge ...139 D5
Glenmoy ...134 C4
Glen Nevis House 131 B5
Glenogil ...134 C4
Glenprosen
Lodge ...134 C3
Glenprosen
Village ...134 C3
Glenreasdell
Mains ...145 H7
Glenree ...143 F10
Glenridding ...99 C5
Glenrossal ...156 J7
Glenrothes ...128 D4
Glensanda ...130 E2
Glensaugh ...135 B6
Glenshero Lodge ...137 E8
Glen Sluain ...125 F6
Glenstockadale ...104 C4
Glenstriven ...145 F9
Glentaggart ...113 B8
Glen Tanar
House ...140 E3
Glentham ...90 E4
Glentirranmuir ...127 E5
Glenton ...140 B5
Glentress ...121 F5
Glentromie
Lodge ...138 E3
Glen Trool Lodge ...112 F4
Glentrool Village ...105 B7
Glentruan ...84 B4
Glentruim House 138 E2
Glentworth ...90 F3
Glenuig ...147 D9
Glen Village ...119 B8
Glen Vine ...84 E3
Glespin ...113 B8
Gletness ...160 H6
Glewstone ...36 B2
Glinton ...65 D8
Glooston ...64 E4
Glororum ...123 F7
Glossop ...87 E8
Gloster Hill ...117 D8
Gloucester ...37 C5
Gloup ...160 C7
Glusburn ...94 E3
Glutt Lodge ...157 F12
Glutton Bridge ...75 C7
Glympton ...38 B4
Glynarthen ...46 E2
Glynbrochan ...59 F6
Glyn-Ceiriog ...73 F6
Glyncoch ...34 E4
Glyncorrwg ...34 E2
Glyn-cywarch ...71 D7
Glynde ...17 D8
Glyndebourne ...17 C8
Glyndyfrdwy ...72 E5
Glyn Ebwy
= Ebbw Vale ...35 D5
Glynedd
= Glynneath ...34 D2
Glynneath
= Glynedd ...34 D2
Glynogwr ...34 F3
Glyntaff ...34 F4
Glyntawe ...34 C2
Gnosall ...62 B2
Gnosall Heath ...62 B2
Goadby ...64 E4
Goadby Marwood ...64 B4
Goatacre ...24 B5
Goathill ...12 C4
Goathland ...103 D6
Goathurst ...22 F4
Goat Lees ...30 E4
Gobernuisgach
Lodge ...156 E7
Gobhaig ...154 G5
Gobowen ...73 F7
Godalming ...27 E7
Godley ...87 E7
Godmanchester ...54 B3
Godmanstone ...12 E4
Godmersham ...30 D4
Godney ...23 E6
Godolphin Cross ...2 C5
Godre'r-graig ...34 D1
Godshill Hants ...14 C2
IoW ...15 F6
Godstone ...28 D4
Godwinscroft ...14 E2
Goetre ...35 D7
Goferydd ...82 C2
Goff's Oak ...41 D6
Gogar ...120 B4
Goginan ...58 F3
Golan ...71 C6
Golant ...5 D6
Golberdon ...5 B8
Golborne ...86 E4
Golcar ...88 C2
Goldcliff ...35 F7
Golden Cross ...18 D2
Golden Green ...29 E7
Golden Grove ...33 C6
Goldenhill ...75 D5
Golden Hill ...14 E3
Golden Pot ...26 E5
Golden Valley ...37 B6
Golders Green ...41 F5
Goldhanger ...43 D5
Gold Hill ...66 E5
Golding ...60 D5
Goldington ...53 D8

Goldsborough
N Yorks ...95 D6
N Yorks ...103 C6
Goldsithney ...2 C4
Goldsworthy ...9 B5
Goldthorpe ...89 D5
Gollanfield ...151 F11
Golspie ...157 J11
Golval ...157 C11
Gomeldon ...25 F6
Gomersal ...88 B3
Gomshall ...27 E8
Gonalston ...77 E6
Gonfirth ...160 G5
Good Easter ...42 C2
Gooderstone ...67 D7
Goodleigh ...20 F5
Goodmanham ...96 E4
Goodnestone Kent ...30 C4
Kent ...31 D6
Goodrich ...36 C2
Goodrington ...7 D6
Goodshaw ...87 B6
Goodwick = Wdig. ...44 B4
Goodworth
Clatford ...25 E8
Goole ...89 B8
Goonbell ...3 D6
Goonhavern ...4 D2
Goose Eye ...94 E3
Goose Green
Gtr Man ...86 D3
Norf ...68 F4
W Sus ...16 C5
Gooseham ...8 C4
Goosey ...38 E3
Goosnargh ...93 F5
Goostrey ...74 B4
Gorcott Hill ...51 C5
Gord ...160 L6
Gordon ...122 E2
Gordonbush ...157 J11
Gordonsburgh ...152 B4
Gordonstoun ...152 B1
Gordonstown
Aberds ...152 C5
Aberds ...153 E7
Gore ...31 D7
Gorebridge ...121 C6
Gore Cross ...24 D5
Gorefield ...66 C4
Gore Pit ...42 C4
Gorey ...17 I3
Gorgie ...120 B5
Goring ...39 F6
Goring-by-Sea ...16 D5
Goring Heath ...26 B4
Gorleston-on-Sea 69 D8
Gornalwood ...62 E3
Gorrachie ...153 C7
Gorran Churchtown .3 B9
Gorran Haven ...3 B9
Gorrenberry ...115 E7
Gors ...46 B5
Gorsedd ...73 B5
Gorse Hill ...38 F1
Gorseinon ...33 E6
Gorseness ...159 G5
Gorsgoch ...46 D3
Gorslas ...33 C6
Gorsley ...36 B3
Gorstan ...150 E6
Gorstanvorran ...130 B2
Gorsty Hill ...62 B5
Gortantaoid ...142 A4
Gorton ...87 E6
Gosbeck ...57 D5
Gosberton ...78 F5
Gosberton Clough .65 B8
Gosfield ...42 B3
Gosford ...49 C7
Gosforth Cumb ...98 D2
T&W ...110 C5
Gosmore ...40 B4
Gosport ...15 E7
Gossabrough ...160 E7
Gossington ...36 D4
Goswick ...123 E6
Gotham ...76 F5
Gotherington ...37 B6
Gott ...160 J6
Goudhurst ...18 B4
Goulceby ...79 B5
Gourdas ...153 D7
Gourdon ...135 B8
Gourock ...118 B2
Govan ...119 C5
Govanhill ...119 C5
Goveton ...7 E5
Govilon ...35 C6
Gowanhill ...153 B10
Gowdall ...89 B7
Gowerton ...33 E6
Gowkhall ...128 F2
Gowthorpe ...96 D3
Goxhill E Yorks ...97 F7
N Lincs ...90 B5
Goxhill Haven ...90 B5
Goytre ...34 F1
Grabhair ...155 F8
Graby ...65 B7
Grade ...3 E6
Graffham ...16 C3
Grafham Cambs ...54 C2
Sur ...27 E8
Grafton Hereford ...49 F6
N Yorks ...95 C7
Oxon ...38 D2
Shrops ...60 C4
Worcs ...49 C7
Grafton Flyford ...50 D4
Grafton Regis ...53 E5
Grafton
Underwood ...65 F6
Grafty Green ...30 E2
Graianrhyd ...73 D6
Graig Conwy ...83 D8
Denb ...72 B4
Graig-fechan ...72 D5
Grain ...30 B2
Grainsby ...91 E6
Grainthorpe ...91 E7
Grampound ...3 B8
Grampound Road ...4 D4
Gramsdal ...148 C3
Granborough ...39 B7
Granby ...77 F7
Grandborough ...52 C2
Great Ellingham ...68 E3

Grandtully ...133 D5
Grange Cumb ...98 C4
E Ayrs ...118 F4
Medway ...29 C8
Mers ...85 F3
Perth ...128 B4
Grange
Crossroads ...152 C4
Grange Hall ...151 E13
Grange Hill ...41 E7
Grangemill ...76 D2
Grange Moor ...88 C3
Grangemouth ...127 F8
Grange of
Lindores ...128 C4
Grange-over-
Sands ...92 B4
Grangepans ...128 F2
Grangetown Cardiff 22 B3
Redcar ...102 B3
Grange Villa ...110 D5
Granish ...138 C5
Gransmoor ...97 D7
Granston ...44 B3
Grantchester ...54 D5
Grantham ...78 F2
Grantley ...94 C5
Grantlodge ...141 C6
Granton Dumfries ...114 D3
Edin ...120 B5
Grantown-on-
Spey ...139 B6
Grantshouse ...122 C4
Grappenhall ...86 F4
Grasby ...90 D4
Grasmere ...99 D5
Grasscroft ...87 D7
Grassendale ...85 F4
Grassholme ...100 B4
Grassington ...94 C3
Grassmoor ...76 C4
Grassthorpe ...77 C7
Grateley ...25 E7
Gratwich ...75 F7
Graveley Cambs ...54 C3
Herts ...41 B5
Gravelly Hill ...62 E5
Gravels ...60 D3
Graven ...160 F6
Graveney ...30 C4
Gravesend Herts ...41 B7
Kent ...29 B7
Grayingham ...90 E3
Grayrigg ...99 E7
Grays ...29 B7
Grayshott ...27 F6
Grayswood ...27 F7
Graythorp ...102 B3
Grazeley ...26 C4
Greasbrough ...88 E5
Greasby ...85 F3
Great Abington ...55 E6
Great Addington ...53 B7
Great Alne ...51 D6
Great Altcar ...85 D4
Great Amwell ...41 C6
Great Asby ...100 C1
Great Ashfield ...56 C3
Great Ayton ...102 C3
Great Baddow ...42 D3
Great Bardfield ...55 F7
Great Barford ...54 D2
Great Barr ...62 E4
Great Barrington ...38 C2
Great Barrow ...73 C8
Great Barton ...56 C2
Great Barugh ...96 B3
Great Bavington ...117 F5
Great Bealings ...57 E6
Great Bedwyn ...25 C7
Great Bentley ...43 B7
Great Billing ...53 C6
Great Bircham ...80 D3
Great Blakenham ...56 D5
Great Blencow ...108 F4
Great Bolas ...61 B6
Great Bookham ...28 D2
Great Bourton ...52 E2
Great Bowden ...64 F4
Great Bradley ...55 D7
Great Braxted ...42 C4
Great Bricett ...56 D4
Great Brickhill ...53 F7
Great Bridge ...62 E3
Great Bridgeford ...62 B2
Great Brington ...52 C4
Great Bromley ...43 B6
Great Broughton
Cumb ...107 F7
N Yorks ...102 D3
Great Budworth ...74 B3
Great Burdon ...101 C8
Great Burgh ...28 D3
Great Burstead ...42 E2
Great Busby ...102 D3
Great Canfield ...42 C1
Great Carlton ...91 F8
Great Casterton ...65 D7
Great Chart ...30 E3
Great Chatwell ...61 C7
Great Chesterford .55 E6
Great Cheverell ...24 D4
Great Chishill ...54 F5
Great Clacton ...43 C7
Great Cliff ...88 C4
Great Clifton ...98 B2
Great Coates ...91 D6
Great Comberton ...50 E4
Great Corby ...108 D4
Great Cornard ...56 E2
Great Cowden ...97 E8
Great Coxwell ...38 E2
Great Crakehall ...101 E7
Great Cransley ...53 B6
Great
Cressingham ...67 D8
Great Crosby ...85 E4
Great Cubley ...75 F8
Great Dalby ...64 C4
Great Denham ...53 E8
Great Doddington .53 C6
Great Dunham ...67 C8
Great Dunmow ...42 B2
Great Durnford ...25 F6
Great Easton Essex 42 B2
Leics ...64 E5
Great Eccleston ...92 E4
Great Edstone ...103 F5
Great Ellingham ...68 E3

Great Elm ...24 E2
Greater Doward ...36 C2
Greater Everseden .54 D4
Great Fencote ...101 E7
Great Finborough ...56 D4
Greatford ...65 C7
Great Fransham ...67 C8
Great Gaddesden ...40 C3
Greatgate ...75 E7
Great Gidding ...65 F8
Great Givendale ...96 D4
Great Glemham ...57 C7
Great Glen ...64 E3
Great Gonerby ...77 F8
Great Green Norf ...69 F5
Suff ...56 D3
Great Habton ...96 B3
Great Hale ...78 E4
Great Hallingbury ...41 C8
Greatham Hants ...27 F5
Hrtlpl ...102 B2
W Sus ...16 C4
Great Hampden ...39 D8
Great Harrowden ...53 B6
Great Harwood ...93 F7
Great Haseley ...39 D6
Great Hatfield ...97 E7
Great Haywood ...62 B4
Great Heath ...63 F7
Great Heck ...89 B6
Great Henny ...56 F2
Great Hinton ...24 D4
Great Hockham ...68 E2
Great Holland ...43 C8
Great Horkesley ...56 F3
Great Hormead ...41 B6
Great Horton ...94 F4
Great Horwood ...53 F5
Great Houghton
S Yorks ...88 D5
W Nhants ...53 D5
Great Hucklow ...75 B8
Great Kelk ...97 D7
Great Kimble ...39 D8
Great Kingshill ...40 E1
Great Langton ...101 E7
Great Leighs ...42 C3
Great Lever ...86 D5
Great Limber ...90 D5
Great Linford ...53 E6
Great Livermere ...56 B2
Great Longstone ...76 B2
Great Lumley ...111 E5
Great Lyth ...60 D4
Great Malvern ...50 E2
Great Maplestead ...56 F2
Great Marton ...92 F3
Great Massingham ...80 E3
Great Melton ...68 D4
Great Milton ...39 D6
Great Missenden ...40 D1
Great Mitton ...93 F7
Great Mongeham ...31 D7
Great Moulton ...68 E4
Great Munden ...41 B6
Great Musgrave ...100 C2
Great Ness ...60 C3
Great Notley ...42 B3
Great Oakley Essex 43 B7
N Nhants ...65 F5
Great Offley ...40 B4
Great Ormside ...100 C2
Great Orton ...108 D3
Great Ouseburn ...95 C7
Great Oxendon ...64 F4
Great Oxney
Green ...42 D2
Great Palgrave ...67 C8
Great Parndon ...41 D7
Great Paxton ...54 C3
Great Plumpton ...92 F3
Great Plumstead ...69 C6
Great Ponton ...78 F2
Great Preston ...88 B5
Great Raveley ...66 F2
Great Rissington ...38 C1
Great Rollright ...51 F8
Great Ryburgh ...81 E5
Great Ryle ...117 C6
Great Ryton ...60 D4
Great Saling ...42 B3
Great Salkeld ...109 F5
Great Sampford ...55 F7
Great Sankey ...86 F3
Great Saxham ...55 C8
Great Shefford ...25 B8
Great Shelford ...55 D5
Great Smeaton ...101 D8
Great Snoring ...80 D5
Great Somerford ...37 F6
Great Stainton ...101 B8
Great Stambridge .42 E4
Great Staughton ...54 C2
Great Steeping ...79 C7
Great Stonar ...31 D7
Greatstone on Sea 19 C7
Great Strickland ...99 B7
Great Stukeley ...54 B3
Great Sturton ...78 B5
Great Sutton
Ches W ...73 B7
Shrops ...60 F5
Great Swinburne 110 B2
Great Tew ...38 B3
Great Tey ...42 B4
Great Thurkleby ...95 B7
Great Thurlow ...55 D7
Great Torrington ...9 C6
Great Tosson ...117 D6
Great Totham
Essex ...42 C4
Essex ...42 C4
Great Tows ...91 E6
Great Urswick ...92 B2
Great Wakering ...43 F5
Great Waldingfield 56 E3
Great Walsingham .80 D5
Great Waltham ...42 C2
Great Warley ...42 E1
Great
Washbourne ...50 F4
Great Weldon ...65 F6
Great Welnetham ...56 D2
Great Wenham ...56 F4
Great
Whittington ...110 B3
Great Wigborough 43 C5
Great Wilbraham ...55 D6
Great Wishford ...25 F5

Great Witcombe ...37 C6
Great Witley ...50 C2
Great Wolford ...51 F7
Greatworth ...52 E3
Great Wratting ...55 E7
Great Wymondley ...41 B5
Great Wyrley ...62 D3
Great Wytheford ...61 C5
Great Yarmouth ...69 D8
Great Yeldham ...55 F8
Greave ...87 B6
Greeba ...84 D3
Green ...72 C4
Greenbank ...160 C7
Greenburn ...120 C2
Greendikes ...117 B6
Green End ...54 D2
Greenfield C Beds ...53 F8
Flint ...73 B5
Gtr Man ...87 D7
Highld ...136 D5
Oxon ...39 E7
Greenford ...40 F4
Greengairs ...119 B7
Greenham ...26 C2
Green Hammerton 95 D7
Greenhaugh ...116 F3
Greenhead ...109 C6
Greenhill Falk ...119 B7
Kent ...31 C5
Leics ...63 C8
London ...40 F4
Greenhills ...118 D3
Greenhithe ...29 B6
Greenholm ...118 F5
Greenholme ...99 D7
Greenhow Hill ...94 C4
Greenigoe ...159 H5
Greenland ...158 D4
Greenlands ...39 F7
Green Lane ...59 E8
Greenlaw Aberds ...153 C6
Borders ...122 E3
Greenlea ...107 B7
Greenloaning ...127 D7
Greenmount ...87 C5
Greenmow ...160 L6
Greenock ...118 B2
Greenock West ...118 B2
Greenodd ...99 F5
Green Ore ...23 D7
Greenrow ...107 D8
Green St Green ...29 C5
Greenside ...110 C4
Greensidehill ...117 C5
Greens Norton ...52 E4
Greenstead Green .42 B4
Greensted ...41 D8
Green Street ...40 E4
Greenwich ...28 B4
Greet ...50 F5
Greete ...49 B7
Greetham Lincs ...79 B6
Rutland ...65 C6
Greetland ...87 B8
Gregg Hall ...99 E6
Gregson Lane ...86 B3
Greinetobht ...148 A3
Greinton ...23 F6
Gremista ...160 J6
Grenaby ...84 E2
Grendon N Nhants ...53 C6
Warks ...63 D6
Grendon Common 63 E6
Grendon Green ...49 D7
Grendon
Underwood ...39 B6
Grenofen ...6 B2
Grenoside ...88 E4
Greosabhagh ...154 H6
Gresford ...73 D7
Gresham ...81 D7
Greshornish ...149 C8
Gressenhall ...68 C2
Gressingham ...93 C5
Gresty Green ...74 D4
Greta Bridge ...101 C5
Gretna ...108 C3
Gretna Green ...108 C3
Gretton Glos ...50 F5
N Nhants ...65 E5
Shrops ...60 E5
Grewelthorpe ...94 B5
Greygarth ...94 B4
Grey Green ...89 D8
Greynor ...33 D6
Greysouthen ...98 B2
Greystoke ...108 F4
Greystone Angus ...135 E5
Dumfries ...107 B6
Greywell ...26 D5
Griais ...155 C9
Grianan ...155 D9
Gribthorpe ...96 F3
Gridley Corner ...9 E5
Griff ...63 F7
Griffithstown ...35 E6
Grimbister ...159 G4
Grimblethorpe ...91 F6
Grimeford Village ...86 C4
Grimethorpe ...88 D5
Griminis ...148 C2
Grimister ...160 D6
Grimley ...50 C3
Grimness ...159 J5
Grimoldby ...91 F7
Grimpo ...60 B3
Grimsargh ...93 F5
Grimsbury ...52 E2
Grimsby ...91 C6
Grimscote ...52 D4
Grimscott ...8 D4
Grimston E Yorks ...97 F8
Leics ...64 B3
Norf ...80 E3
Grimstone ...12 E4
Grinacombe Moor ...9 E6
Grindale ...97 B7
Grindigar ...159 H6
Grindiscol ...160 K6
Grindle ...61 D7
Grindleford ...76 B2
Grindleton ...93 E7
Grindley ...62 B4
Grindley Brook ...74 E2
Grindlow ...75 B8
Grindon Northumb 122 E5
Staffs ...75 D7
Grindonmoor Gate 75 D7
Gringley on the
Hill ...89 E8
Grinsdale ...108 D3
Grinshill ...60 B5
Grinton ...101 E5
Griomsidar ...155 E8
Grishipoll ...146 F4
Gristhorpe ...103 F8
Griston ...68 E2
Gritley ...159 H6
Grittenham ...37 F7
Grittleton ...37 F5
Grizebeck ...98 F4
Grizedale ...99 E5
Grobister ...159 F7
Groby ...64 D2
Groes Conwy ...72 C4
Neath ...34 F1
Groes-faen ...34 F4
Groesffordd Marli ...72 B4
Groeslon Gwyn ...82 E5
Gwyn ...82 F4
Groes-lwyd ...60 C2
Grogport ...143 D9
Gromford ...57 D7
Gronant ...72 A4
Groombridge ...18 B2
Grosmont Mon ...35 B8
N Yorks ...103 D6
Groton ...56 E3
Grougfoot ...120 B3
Grouville ...17 I3
Grove Dorset ...12 G5
Kent ...31 C6
Notts ...77 B7
Oxon ...38 E4
Grove Park ...28 B5
Grovesend ...33 D6
Grove Vale ...62 E4
Grudie ...150 E6
Gruids ...157 J8
Gruinard House ...150 B2
Grula ...149 F8
Gruline ...147 G8
Grunasound ...160 K5
Grundisburgh ...57 D6
Grunsagill ...93 D7
Gruting ...160 J4
Grutness ...160 N6
Gualachulain ...131 E5
Gualin House ...156 D6
Guardbridge ...129 C6
Guarlford ...50 E3
Guay ...133 E7
Guestling Green ...19 D5
Guestling Thorn ...19 D5
Guestwick ...81 E6
Guestwick Green ...81 E6
Guide ...86 B5
Guide Post ...117 F8
Guilden Morden ...54 E3
Guilden Sutton ...73 C8
Guildford ...27 E7
Guildtown ...133 F8
Guilsborough ...52 B4
Guilsfield ...60 C2
Guilton ...31 D6
Guineaford ...20 F4
Guisborough ...102 C4
Guiseley ...94 E4
Guist ...81 E5
Guith ...159 E6
Guiting Power ...37 B7
Gulberwick ...160 K6
Gullane ...129 F6
Gulval ...2 C3
Gulworthy ...6 B2
Gumfreston ...32 D2
Gumley ...64 E3
Gummow's Shop ...4 D3
Gunby E Yorks ...96 F3
Lincs ...65 B6
Gundleton ...26 F4
Gun Hill ...18 D2
Gunn ...20 F5
Gunnerside ...100 E4
Gunnerton ...110 B2
Gunness ...90 C2
Gunnislake ...6 B2
Gunnista ...160 J6
Gunthorpe Norf ...81 D6
Pboro ...65 D8
Gunthorpe Notts ...77 E6
Gunville ...15 F5
Gunwalloe ...3 D5
Gurnard ...15 E5
Gurnett ...75 B6
Gurney Slade ...23 E8
Gurnos ...34 D1
Gussage All Saints 13 C8
Gussage St
Michael ...13 C7
Guston ...31 E7
Gutcher ...160 D7
Guthrie ...135 D5
Guyhirn ...66 D3
Guyhirn Gull ...66 D3
Guy's Head ...66 B4
Guy's Marsh ...13 B6
Guyzance ...117 D8
Gwaenysgor ...72 A4
Gwalchmai ...82 D3
Gwaun-Cae-
Gurwen ...33 C8
Gwaun-Leision ...33 C8
Gwbert ...45 E3
Gweek ...3 D6
Gwehelog ...35 D7
Gwenddwr ...48 E2
Gwennap ...3 C6
Gwenter ...3 E6
Gwernaffield ...73 C6
Gwernesney ...35 D8
Gwernogle ...46 F4
Gwernymynydd ...73 C6
Gwersyllt ...73 D7
Gwespyr ...85 F2
Gwithian ...2 B4
Gwredog ...82 C4
Gwyddelwern ...72 E4
Gwyddgrug ...46 F3
Gwydyr Uchaf ...83 E7
Gwynfryn ...73 D6
Gwystre ...48 C2
Gwytherin ...83 E8

Gyfelia ...73 E7
Gyffi ...83 D7
Gyre ...159 H4
Gyrn-goch ...70 C5

H

Habberley ...60 D3
Habergham ...93 F8
Habrough ...90 C5
Haceby ...78 F3
Hacheston ...57 D7
Hackbridge ...28 C3
Hackenthorpe ...88 F5
Hackford ...68 D3
Hackforth ...101 E7
Hackland ...159 F4
Hackleton ...53 D6
Hackness N Yorks ...103 E7
Orkney ...159 J4
Hackney ...41 F6
Hackthorn ...90 F3
Hackthorpe ...99 B7
Haconby ...65 B8
Hacton ...41 F8
Hadden ...122 F3
Haddenham Bucks ...39 D7
Cambs ...55 B5
Haddington
E Loth ...121 B8
Lincs ...78 C2
Haddiscoe ...69 E7
Haddon Cambs ...65 E8
Ches E ...75 C6
Hade Edge ...88 D2
Hademore ...63 D5
Hadfield ...87 E8
Hadham Cross ...41 C7
Hadham Ford ...41 B7
Hadleigh Essex ...42 F4
Suff ...56 E4
Hadley ...61 C6
Hadley End ...62 B5
Hadlow ...29 E7
Hadlow Down ...18 C2
Hadnall ...60 C5
Hadstock ...55 E6
Hady ...76 B3
Hadzor ...50 C4
Haffenden Quarter 30 E2
Hafod-Dinbych ...83 F8
Hafod-Iom ...83 D8
Haggate ...93 F8
Haggbeck ...108 B4
Haggerston ...123 E6
Haggrister ...160 F5
Hagley Hereford ...49 E7
Worcs ...62 F3
Hagworthingham ...79 C6
Haigh Gtr Man ...86 D4
S Yorks ...88 C3
Haigh Moor ...88 B3
Haighton Green ...93 F5
Haile ...98 D2
Hailes ...50 F5
Hailey Herts ...41 C6
Oxon ...38 C3
Hailsham ...18 E2
Hail Weston ...54 C2
Haimer ...158 D3
Hainault ...41 E7
Hainford ...68 C5
Hainton ...91 F5
Hairmyres ...119 D6
Haisthorpe ...97 C7
Hakin ...44 E3
Halam ...77 D6
Halbeath ...128 F3
Halberton ...10 C5
Halcro ...158 D4
Hale Gtr Man ...87 F5
Halton ...86 F2
Hants ...14 C2
Hale Bank ...86 F2
Halebarns ...87 F5
Hales Norf ...69 E6
Staffs ...74 F4
Halesfield ...61 D7
Halesgate ...66 B3
Halesowen ...62 F3
Hales Place ...30 D5
Hale Street ...29 E7
Halesworth ...57 B7
Halewood ...86 F2
Halford Shrops ...60 F4
Warks ...51 E7
Halfpenny Furze ...32 C3
Halfpenny Green ...62 E2
Halfway Carms ...47 F7
W Berks ...26 C2
Halfway Bridge ...16 B3
Halfway House ...60 C3
Halfway Houses ...30 B3
Halifax ...87 B8
Halket ...118 D4
Halkirk ...158 E3
Halkyn ...73 C6
Halland ...18 D2
Hallaton ...64 E4
Hallatrow ...23 D8
Hallbankgate ...109 D5
Hallen ...36 F2
Hall Dunnerdale ...98 E4
Hall Green W Mid ...62 F4
S Yorks ...88 C4
Halliburton ...122 E2
Hallin ...148 C7
Halling ...29 C8
Hallington Lincs ...91 F7
Northumb ...110 B2
Halliwell ...86 C5
Hall of
Tankerness ...159 H6
Hall of the Forest ...60 F2
Halloughton ...77 D6
Hallow ...50 D3
Hallrule ...115 C8
Halls ...122 B2
Hallsands ...7 F6
Hall's Green ...41 B5
Hallthwaites ...98 F3
Hallworthy ...8 F3
Hallyburton
House ...134 F2
Hallyne ...120 E4
Halmer End ...74 E4

Halmore ...36 D3
Halmyre Mains ...120 E4
Halnaker ...16 D3
Halsall ...85 C4
Halse Som ...11 B6
W Nhants ...52 E3
Halsetown ...2 C4
Halsham ...91 B6
Halsinger ...20 F4
Halstead Essex ...56 F2
Kent ...29 C5
Leics ...64 D4
Halstock ...12 D3
Haltham ...78 C5
Haltoft End ...79 E6
Halton Bucks ...40 C1
Halton ...86 F3
Lancs ...92 C5
Northumb ...110 C2
Wrex ...73 F7
W Yorks ...95 F6
Halton East ...94 D3
Halton Gill ...93 B8
Halton Holegate ...79 C7
Halton Lea Gate ...109 D6
Halton West ...93 D8
Haltwhistle ...109 C7
Halvergate ...69 D7
Halwell ...7 D5
Halwill ...9 E6
Halwill Junction ...9 E6
Ham Devon ...11 D7
Glos ...36 E3
Highld ...158 C4
Kent ...31 D7
London ...28 B2
Shetland ...160 K1
Wilts ...25 C8
Hambleden ...39 F7
Hambledon Hants ...15 C7
Sur ...27 F7
Hamble-le-Rice ...15 D5
Hambleton Lancs ...92 E3
N Yorks ...95 F6
Hambridge ...11 B8
Hambrook S Glos ...23 B8
W Sus ...15 D8
Ham Common ...13 B6
Hameringham ...79 C6
Hamerton ...54 B2
Ham Green
Hereford ...50 E2
Kent ...19 C5
Kent ...30 C2
N Som ...23 B7
Worcs ...50 C5
Hamilton ...119 D7
Hammer ...27 F6
Hammerpot ...16 D4
Hammersmith ...28 B3
Hammerwich ...62 D4
Hammerwood ...28 F5
Hammond Street ...41 D6
Hammoon ...13 C6
Hamnavoe
Shetland ...160 E4
Shetland ...160 E6
Shetland ...160 F6
Shetland ...160 K5
Hampden Park ...18 E3
Hamperden End ...55 F6
Hampnett ...37 C7
Hampole ...89 C6
Hampreston ...13 E8
Hampstead ...41 F5
Hampstead
Norreys ...26 B3
Hampsthwaite ...95 D5
Hampton London ...28 C2
Shrops ...61 F7
Worcs ...50 E5
Hampton Bishop ...49 F7
Hampton Heath ...73 E8
Hampton in Arden ...63 F6
Hampton Loade ...61 F7
Hampton Lovett ...50 C3
Hampton Lucy ...51 D7
Hampton on the
Hill ...51 C7
Hampton Poyle ...39 C5
Hamrow ...80 E5
Hamsey ...17 C8
Hamsey Green ...28 D4
Hamstall Ridware ...62 C5
Hamstead IoW ...14 E5
W Mid ...62 E4
Hamstead
Marshall ...26 C2
Hamsterley
Durham ...110 D4
Durham ...110 F4
Hamstreet ...19 B7
Ham Street ...23 F7
Hamworthy ...13 E7
Hanbury Staffs ...63 B5
Worcs ...50 C4
Hanbury Woodend 63 B5
Hanby ...78 F3
Hanchurch ...74 E5
Handbridge ...73 C8
Handcross ...17 B6
Handforth ...87 F6
Handley ...73 D8
Handsacre ...62 C4
Handsworth
S Yorks ...88 F5
W Mid ...62 E4
Handy Cross ...9 B6
Hanford ...75 E5
Hanging Langford ...24 F5
Hangleton ...16 D4
Hanham ...23 B8
Hankelow ...74 E3
Hankerton ...37 E6
Hankham ...18 E3
Hanley ...75 E5
Hanley Castle ...50 E3
Hanley Child ...49 C8
Hanley Swan ...50 E3
Hanley William ...49 C8
Hanlith ...94 C2
Hanmer ...73 F8
Hannah ...79 B8
Hannington Hants ...26 D3
Swindon ...38 E1
W Nhants ...53 B6
Hannington Wick ...38 E1
Hansel Village ...118 F3

Hanslope 53 E6
Hanthorpe 65 B7
Hanwell London 40 F4
  Oxon 52 E2
Hanwood 60 D4
Hanworth London 28 B2
  Norf 81 D7
Happendon 119 F8
Happisburgh 69 A6
Happisburgh
  Common 69 B6
Hapsford 73 B8
Hapton Lancs 93 F7
  Norf 68 E4
Harberton 7 E5
Harbertonford 7 D5
Harbledown 30 D5
Harborne 62 F4
Harborough
  Magna 52 B2
Harbottle 117 D5
Harbury 51 D8
Harby Leics 77 F7
  Notts 77 B8
Harcombe 11 E6
Harden W Mid 62 D4
  W Yorks 94 F3
Hardenhuish 24 B4
Hardgate 141 D6
Hardham 16 C4
Hardingham 68 D3
Hardingstone 53 D5
Hardington 24 D2
Hardington
  Mandeville 12 C3
Hardington Marsh .12 D3
Hardley 14 D5
Hardley Street 69 D6
Hardmead 53 E7
Hardrow 100 E3
Hardstoft 76 C4
Hardway Hants 15 D7
  Som 24 F2
Hardwick Bucks 39 C8
  Cambs 54 D4
  N Nhants 53 C6
  Norf 67 C6
  Norf 68 F5
  Notts 77 B6
  Oxon 38 D3
  Oxon 39 B5
  W Mid 62 E4
Hardwicke Glos 36 C4
  Glos 37 B6
  Hereford 48 E4
Hardy's Green 43 B5
Hareby 79 C6
Hareden 93 D6
Harefield 40 E3
Hare Green 43 B6
Hare Hatch 27 B6
Harehills 95 F6
Harehope 117 B6
Haresceugh 109 E6
Harescombe 37 C5
Haresfield 37 C5
Hareshaw 119 C8
Hareshaw Head 116 F4
Hare Street 41 B6
Harewood 95 E6
Harewood End 36 B2
Harford Carms 46 E5
  Devon 6 D4
Hargate 68 E4
Hargatewall 75 B8
Hargrave Ches W 73 C8
  N Nhants 53 B8
  Suff 55 D8
Harker 108 C3
Harkland 160 E6
Harkstead 57 F5
Harlaston 63 C6
Harlaw House 141 B6
Harlaxton 77 F8
Harlech 71 D6
Harlequin 77 F6
Harlescott 60 C5
Harlesden 41 F5
Harleston Devon 7 E5
  Norf 68 F5
  Suff 56 D4
Harlestone 52 C5
Harle Syke 93 F8
Harley Shrops 61 D5
  S Yorks 88 E4
Harleyholm 120 F2
Harlington C Beds 53 F8
  London 27 B8
  S Yorks 89 D5
Harlosh 149 D7
Harlow 41 C7
Harlow Hill
  Northumb 110 C3
  N Yorks 95 D5
Harlthorpe 96 F3
Harlton 54 D4
Harman's Cross 13 F7
Harmby 101 F6
Harmer Green 41 C5
Harmer Hill 60 B4
Harmondsworth 27 B8
Harmston 78 C2
Harnham 110 B3
Harnhill 37 D7
Harold Hill 41 E8
Haroldston West 44 D3
Haroldswick 160 B8
Harold Wood 41 E8
Harome 102 F4
Harpenden 40 C4
Harpford 11 E5
Harpham 97 C6
Harpley Norf 80 E3
  Worcs 49 C8
Harpole 52 C4
Harpsden 39 F7
Harpswell 90 F3
Harpurhey 87 D6
Harpur Hill 75 B7
Harraby 108 D4
Harrapool 149 F11
Harrier 160 J1
Harrietfield 133 B7
Harrietsham 30 D2
Harrington Cumb 98 B1
  Lincs 79 B6
  N Nhants 64 F4
Harringworth 65 E6

Harris 146 B6
Harrogate 95 D6
Harrold 53 D7
Harrow 40 F4
Harrowbarrow 5 C8
Harrowden 53 E8
Harrowgate Hill 101 C7
Harrow on the Hill .40 F4
Harrow Street 56 F3
Harrow Weald 40 E4
Harston Cambs 54 D5
  Leics 77 F8
Harswell 96 E4
Hart 111 F7
Hartburn
  Northumb 117 F6
  Stockton 102 C2
Hart Common 86 D4
Hartest 56 D2
Hartfield 29 F5
Hartford Cambs 54 B3
  Ches W 74 B3
Hartfordbridge 27 D5
Hartford End 42 C2
Hartforth 101 D6
Harthill Ches W 74 D2
  N Lanark 120 C2
  S Yorks 89 F5
Hart Hill 40 B4
Hartington 75 C8
Hartland 8 B4
Hartlebury 50 B3
Hartlepool 111 F8
Hartley Cumb 100 D2
  Kent 18 B4
  Kent 29 C7
  Northumb 111 B6
Hartley Westpall 26 D4
Hartley Wintney 27 D5
Hartlip 30 C2
Hartoft End 103 E5
Harton N Yorks 96 C3
  Shrops 60 F4
  T&W 111 C6
Harpury 36 B4
Hartshead 88 B2
Hartshill 63 E7
Hartshorne 63 B7
Hartsop 99 C6
Hart Station 111 F7
Hartwell 53 D5
Hartwood 119 D8
Harvieston 126 F4
Harvington 51 E5
Harvington Cross ..51 E5
Harwell 38 F4
Harwich 57 F6
Harwood Durham ..109 F8
  Gtr Man 86 C5
Harwood Dale 103 E7
Harworth 89 E7
Hasbury 62 F3
Hascombe 27 E7
Haselbech 52 B5
Haseley
  Plucknett 12 C2
Haseley 51 C7
Haselor 51 D6
Hasfield 37 B5
Hasguard 44 E3
Haskayne 85 D4
Hasketon 57 D6
Hasland 76 C3
Haslemere 27 F7
Haslingden 87 B5
Haslingfield 54 D5
Haslington 74 D4
Hassall 74 D4
Hassall Green 74 D4
Hassall Street 30 E4
Hassendean 115 B8
Hassingham 69 D6
Hassocks 17 C6
Hassop 76 B2
Hastigrow 158 D4
Hastingleigh 30 E4
Hastings 18 E5
Hastingwood 41 D7
Hastoe 40 D2
Haswell 111 E6
Haswell Plough 111 E6
Hatch C Beds 54 E2
  Hants 26 D4
  Wilts 13 B7
Hatch Beauchamp .11 B8
Hatch End 40 E4
Hatchet Gate 14 D4
Hatch Green 11 C8
Hatching Green 40 C4
Hatchmere 74 B2
Hatcliffe 91 D6
Hatfield Hereford ...49 D7
  Herts 41 D5
  S Yorks 89 D7
  Worcs 50 D3
Hatfield Broad
  Oak 41 C8
Hatfield Garden
  Village 41 D5
Hatfield Heath 41 C8
Hatfield Hyde 41 C5
Hatfield Peverel 42 C3
Hatfield
  Woodhouse 89 D7
Hatford 38 E3
Hatherden 25 D8
Hatherleigh 9 D7
Hathern 63 B8
Hatherop 38 D1
Hathersage 88 F3
Hathershaw 87 D7
Hatherton Ches E 74 E3
  Staffs 62 C3
Hatley St George ...54 D3
Hatt 5 C8
Hattingley 26 F4
Hatton Aberds 153 E10
  Derbys 63 B6
  Lincs 78 B4
  Shrops 60 E4
  Warks 51 C7
  Warr 86 F3
Hatton Castle 153 D7
Hattoncrook 141 B7
Hatton Heath 73 C8
Hatton of Fintray ..141 C7
Haugh E Ayrs 112 B4
  Gtr Man 87 C7
  Lincs 79 B7

Haugham 91 F7
Haugh Head 117 B6
Haughley 56 C4
Haughley Green 56 C4
Haugh of Glass 152 E4
Haugh of Urr 106 C5
Haughs of
  Clinterty 141 C7
Haughton Notts 77 B6
  Shrops 60 B3
  Shrops 61 C5
  Shrops 61 D7
  Shrops 61 E6
  Staffs 62 B2
Haughton Castle ...110 B2
Haughton Green 87 E7
Haughton Moss 74 D2
Haultwick 41 B6
Haunn Argyll 146 G6
  W Isles 148 G2
Haunton 63 C6
Hauxley 117 D8
Hauxton 54 D5
Havant 15 D8
Haven 49 D6
Haven Bank 78 D5
Haven Side 91 B5
Havenstreet 15 E6
Havercroft 88 C4
Haverfordwest
  = Hwlffordd 44 D4
Haverhill 55 E7
Havering 92 B1
Havering-atte-
  Bower 41 E8
Haveringland 81 E7
Haversham 53 E6
Haverthwaite 99 F5
Haverton Hill 102 B2
Hawarden
  = Penarlâg 73 C7
Hawcoat 92 B2
Hawen 46 E2
Hawes 100 F3
Hawes' Green 68 E5
Hawes Side 92 F3
Hawford 50 C3
Hawick 115 C8
Hawkchurch 11 D8
Hawkedon 55 D8
Hawkenbury Kent ...18 B3
  Kent 30 E2
Hawkeridge 24 D3
Hawkerland 11 F5
Hawkesbury S Glos ..36 F4
  Warks 63 F7
Hawkesbury Upton .36 F4
Hawkes End 63 F7
Hawk Green 87 F7
Hawkhill 117 C8
Hawkhurst 18 B4
Hawkinge 31 F6
Hawkley 15 B8
Hawkridge 21 F7
Hawkshead 99 E5
Hawkshead Hill 99 E5
Hawksland 119 F8
Hawkswick 94 B2
Hawksworth Notts ..77 E7
  W Yorks 94 E4
  W Yorks 95 F5
Hawkwell 42 E4
Hawley Hants 27 D6
  Kent 29 B6
Hawling 37 B7
Hawnby 102 F3
Haworth 94 F3
Hawstead 56 D2
Hawthorn Durham ..111 E7
  Rhondda 35 F5
  Wilts 24 C3
Hawthorn Hill
  Brack 27 B6
  Lincs 78 D5
Hawthorpe 65 B7
Hawton 77 D7
Haxby 96 D2
Haxey 89 D8
Haydock 86 E3
Haydon 12 C4
Haydon Bridge 109 C8
Haydon Wick 37 F8
Haye 5 C8
Hayes London 28 C5
  London 40 F4
Hayfield Derbys 87 F8
  Fife 128 E4
Hay Green 66 C5
Hayhill 112 C4
Hayhillock 135 E5
Hayle 2 C4
Haynes 53 E8
Haynes Church
  End 53 E8
Hay-on-Wye
  = Y Gelli Gandryll ..48 E4
Hayscastle 44 C3
Hayscastle Cross ...44 C4
Hayshead 135 E6
Hay Street 41 B6
Hayton Aberdeen ...141 D8
  Cumb 107 D8
  Cumb 108 D5
  E Yorks 96 E4
  Notts 89 F8
Hayton's Bent 60 F5
Haytor Vale 7 B5
Haywards Heath 17 B7
Haywood 89 C6
Haywood Oaks 77 D6
Hazelbank 119 E8
Hazelbury Bryan ...12 D5
Hazeley 26 D5
Hazel Grove 87 F7
Hazelhurst 87 D7
Hazelslade 62 C4
Hazel Street 18 B3
Hazelton 37 C7
Hazelton Walls 128 B5
Hazelwood 76 E3
Hazlemere 40 E1
Hazlerigg 110 B5
Hazlewood 94 D3
Hazon 117 D7
Heacham 80 D2
Headbourne
  Worthy 26 F2
Headbrook 48 D5
Headcorn 30 E2

Headingley 95 F5
Headington 39 D5
Headlam 101 C6
Headless Cross 50 C5
Headley Hants 26 F1
  Hants 27 F6
  Sur 28 D3
Head of Muir 127 F7
Headon 77 B7
Heads 119 E7
Heads Nook 108 D4
Heage 76 D3
Healaugh N Yorks ...101 E5
  N Yorks 95 E7
Heald Green 87 F6
Heale Devon 20 E5
  Som 23 D8
Healey Gtr Man 87 C6
  Northumb 110 D3
  N Yorks 101 F6
Healing 91 C6
Heamoor 2 C3
Heanish 146 G3
Heanor 76 E4
Heanton
  Punchardon 20 F4
Heapham 90 F2
Hearthstane 114 B4
Heasley Mill 21 F6
Heast 149 G11
Heath Cardiff 22 B3
  Derbys 76 C4
Heath and Reach ..40 B2
Heathcote 75 C8
Heath End Hants 27 E6
  Sur 27 E6
  Warks 51 C7
Heather 63 C7
Heatherfield 149 D9
Heathfield Devon 7 B6
  E Sus 18 C2
  Som 11 B6
Heathhall 107 B6
Heath Hayes 62 C4
Heath Hill 61 C7
Heath House 23 E6
Heathrow Airport ...27 B8
Heathstock 11 D7
Heathton 62 E2
Heath Town 62 E3
Heatley 86 F5
Heaton Lancs 92 C4
  Staffs 75 C6
  T&W 111 C5
  W Yorks 94 F4
Heaton Moor 87 E6
Heaverham 29 D6
Heaviley 87 F7
Heavitree 10 E4
Hebburn 111 C6
Hebden 94 C3
Hebden Bridge 87 B7
Hebron Anglesey ...82 C4
  Carms 32 B2
  Northumb 117 F7
Heck 114 F3
Heckfield 26 C5
Heckfield Green 57 B5
Heckfordbridge 43 B5
Heckington 78 E4
Heckmondwike 88 B3
Heddington 24 C4
Heddle 159 G4
Heddon-on-the-
  Wall 110 C4
Hedenham 69 E6
Hedge End 15 C5
Hedgerley 40 F2
Hedging 11 B8
Hedley on the
  Hill 110 D3
Hednesford 62 C4
Hedon 91 B5
Hedsor 40 F2
Hedworth 111 C6
Hegdon Hill 49 D7
Heggerscales 100 C3
Heglibister 160 H5
Heighington Darl ...101 B7
  Lincs 78 C3
Heights of Brae 151 E8
Heights of
  Kinlochewe 150 E3
Heilam 156 C7
Heiton 122 F3
Hele Devon 10 D4
  Devon 20 E4
Helensburgh 145 E11
Helford 3 D6
Helford Passage 3 D6
Helhoughton 80 E4
Helions
  Bumpstead 55 E7
Hellaby 89 E6
Helland 5 B5
Hellesdon 68 C5
Hellidon 52 D3
Hellifield 93 D8
Hellingly 18 D2
Hellington 69 D6
Hellister 160 J5
Helm
  Newmarket 108 F3
Helmdon 52 E3
Helmingham 57 D5
Helmington Row ...110 F4
Helmsdale 157 H13
Helmshore 87 B5
Helmsley 102 F4
Helperby 95 C7
Helperthorpe 97 B5
Helpringham 78 E4
Helpston 65 D8
Helsby 73 B8
Helsey 79 B8
Helston 3 D5
Helstone 5 B5
Helton 99 B7
Helwith Bridge 93 C8
Hemblington 69 C6
Hemel Hempstead ..40 D3
Hemingbrough 96 F2
Hemingby 78 B5
Hemingford
  Abbots 54 B3
Hemingford Grey ...54 B3
Hemingstone 57 D5
Hemington Leics ...63 B8
  N Nhants 65 F7
  Som 24 D2

Hemley 57 E6
Hemlington 102 C3
Hemp Green 57 C7
Hempholme 97 D6
Hempnall 68 E5
Hempnall Green 68 E5
Hempriggs
  House 158 F5
Hempstead Essex ...55 F7
  Medway 29 C8
  Norf 69 B7
  Norf 81 D7
Hempsted 37 C5
Hempton Norf 80 E5
  Oxon 52 F2
Hemsby 69 C7
Hemswell 90 E3
Hemswell Cliff 90 F3
Hemsworth 88 C5
Hemyock 11 C6
Henbury Bristol 23 B7
  Ches E 75 B5
Hendon London 41 F5
  T&W 111 D7
Hendre 73 C5
Hendre-ddu 83 E8
Hendreforgan 34 F3
Hendy 33 D6
Heneglwys 82 D4
Hen-feddau fawr ...45 F4
Henfield 17 C6
Henford 9 E5
Henghurst 19 B6
Hengoed Caerph 35 E5
  Powys 48 D4
  Shrops 73 F6
Hengrave 56 C2
Henham 41 B8
Heniarth 59 D8
Henlade 11 B7
Henley Shrops 49 B7
  Som 23 F6
  Suff 57 D5
  W Sus 16 B2
Henley-in-Arden ...51 C6
Henley-on-
  Thames 39 F7
Henley's Down 18 D4
Henllan Ceredig ...46 E2
  Denb 72 C4
Henllan Amgoed ...32 B2
Henllys 35 E6
Henlow 54 F2
Hennock 10 F3
Henny Street 56 F2
Henryd 83 D7
Henry's Moat 32 B1
Hensall 89 B6
Henshaw 109 C7
Hensingham 98 C1
Henstead 69 F7
Henstridge 12 C5
Henstridge Ash 12 B5
Henstridge Marsh .12 B5
Henton Oxon 39 D7
  Som 23 E6
Henwood 5 B7
Heogan 160 J6
Heol-las 33 E7
Heol Senni 34 B3
Heol-y-Cyw 34 F3
Hepburn 117 B6
Hepple 117 D5
Hepscott 117 F8
Heptonstall 87 B7
Hepworth Suff 56 B3
  W Yorks 88 D2
Herbrandston 44 E3
Hereford 49 E7
Heriot 121 D6
Hermiston 120 B4
Hermitage
  Borders 115 D8
  Dorset 12 D4
  W Berks 26 B3
  W Sus 15 D8
Hermon Anglesey ...82 E3
  Carms 33 B7
  Carms 46 F2
  Pembs 45 F4
Herne 31 C5
Herne Bay 31 C5
Herner 9 B7
Hernhill 30 C4
Herodsfoot 5 C7
Herongate 42 E2
Heronsford 104 A5
Herriard 26 E4
Herringfleet 69 E7
Herringswell 55 B8
Hersden 31 C6
Hersham Corn 8 D4
  Sur 28 C2
Herstmonceux 18 D3
Herston 159 J5
Hertford 41 C6
Hertford Heath 41 C6
Hertingfordbury ...41 C6
Hesket
  Newmarket 108 F3
Heskin Green 86 C3
Hesleden 111 F7
Hesleyside 116 F4
Heslington 96 D2
Hessay 95 D8
Hessenford 5 D8
Hessett 56 C3
Hessle 90 B4
Hest Bank 92 C4
Heston 28 B2
Hestwall 159 G3
Heswall 85 F3
Hethe 39 B5
Hethersett 68 D4
Hethersgill 108 C4
Hethpool 116 B4
Hett 111 F5
Hetton 94 D2
Hetton-le-Hole 111 E6
Hetton Steads 123 F6
Heugh 110 B3
Heugh-head 140 C2
Heveningham 57 B7
Hever 29 E5
Heversham 99 F6
Hevingham 81 E7
  Som 24 D1

Hewelsfield 36 D2
Hewish N Som 23 C6
  Som 12 D2
Heworth 96 D2
Hexham 110 C2
Hextable 29 B6
Hexton 54 F2
Hexworthy 6 B4
Hey 93 E8
Heybridge Essex ...42 D4
  Essex 42 E2
Heybridge Basin ...42 D4
Heydon Cambs 54 E5
  Norf 81 E7
Heydour 78 F3
Heylipol 146 G2
Heylor 160 E4
Heysham 92 C4
Heyshott 16 C2
Heyside 87 D7
Heytesbury 24 E4
Heythrop 38 B3
Heywood Gtr Man ..87 C6
  Wilts 24 D3
Hibaldstow 90 D3
Hickleton 89 D5
Hickling Norf 69 B7
  Notts 64 B3
Hickling Green 69 B7
Hickling Heath 69 B7
Hickstead 17 B6
Hidcote Boyce 51 E6
High Ackworth 88 C5
Higham Derbys 76 D3
  Kent 29 B8
  Lancs 93 F8
  Suff 55 C8
  Suff 56 F4
Higham Dykes 110 B4
Higham Ferrers 53 C7
Higham Gobion 54 F2
Higham on the Hill .63 E7
Highampton 9 D6
Higham Wood 29 E6
High Angerton 117 F6
High Bankhill 109 E5
High Barnes 111 D6
High Beach 41 E7
High Bentham 93 C6
High Bickington 9 B8
High Birkwith 93 B7
High Blantyre 119 D6
High
  Bonnybridge 119 B8
High Bradfield 88 E3
High Bray 21 F5
Highbridge Highld ..136 F4
  Som 22 E5
High Brooms 29 E6
High Bullen 9 B7
Highburton 88 C2
Highbury 23 E8
High Buston 117 D8
High Callerton 110 B4
High Catton 96 D3
Highclere 26 C2
Highcliffe 14 E3
High Cogges 38 D3
High Coniscliffe ...101 C7
High Cross Herts ...41 C6
  Hants 15 B8
High Easter 42 C2
High Eggborough ..89 B6
High Ellington 101 F6
Higher Ansty 13 D5
Higher Ashton 10 F3
Higher Ballam 92 F3
Higher Bartle 92 F5
Higher Boscaswell ..2 C2
Higher
  Burwardsley 74 D2
Higher Clovelly 8 B5
Higher End 86 D3
Higher Kinnerton ...73 C7
Higher
  Penwortham 86 B3
Higher Town 2 E4
Higher Walreddon ...6 B2
Higher Walton
  Lancs 86 B3
  Warr 86 F3
Higher Wheelton ...86 B4
Higher Whitley 86 F4
Higher Wincham ...74 B3
Higher Wych 73 E8
High Etherley 101 B6
Highfield E Yorks ...96 F3
  Gtr Man 86 D5
  N Ayrs 118 D3
  Oxon 39 B5
  S Yorks 88 F4
  T&W 110 D4
Highfields Cambs ...54 D4
  Northants 65 F6
High Garrett 42 B3
Highgate 41 F5
High Grange 110 F4
High Green Norf 68 D4
  S Yorks 88 E4
  Worcs 50 E3
High Halden 19 B5
High Halstow 29 B8
High Ham 23 F6
High Harrington ...98 B2
High Hatton 61 B6
High Hawsker 103 D7
High Hesket 108 E4
High Hesleden 111 F7
High Hoyland 88 C3
High Hunsley 97 F5
High Hurstwood ...17 B8
High Hutton 96 C3
High Ireby 108 F2
High Kelling 81 C7
High Kilburn 95 B8
High Lands 101 B6
High Lane Gtr Man ..87 F7
  Worcs 49 C8
High Laver 41 D8
Highlaws 107 E7
Highleadon 36 B4
High Legh 86 F5
Highleigh 16 E2
High Leven 102 C2

Highley 61 F7
High Littleton 23 D8
High Lorton 98 B3
High Marishes 96 B4
High Melton 89 D6
High Mickley 110 C3
High Mindork 105 D7
Highmoor Cross 39 F7
Highmoor Hill 36 F1
Highnam 36 C4
Highnam Green 36 B4
High Newton-by-the-
  Sea 117 B8
High Nibthwaite 98 F4
High Offley 61 B7
High Ongar 42 D1
High Onn 62 C2
High Roding 42 C2
High Row 108 F3
High Salvington 16 D5
High Sellafield 98 D2
High Shaw 100 E3
High Spen 110 D4
Highsted 30 C3
High Stoop 110 E4
High Street Corn 4 D4
  Kent 18 B4
  Suff 56 E2
  Suff 57 B8
  Suff 57 D8
Highstreet Green ...55 F8
High Street Green ..56 D4
Hightae 107 B7
High Throston 111 F7
Hightown Ches E 75 C5
  Mers 85 D4
Hightown Green 56 D3
High Toynton 79 C5
High Trewhitt 117 D6
High Valleyfield 128 F2
Highway 24 B5
Highweek 7 B6
High Westwood 110 D4
Highworth 38 E2
High Wray 99 E5
High Wych 41 C7
High Wycombe 40 E1
Hilborough 67 D8
Hilcote 76 D4
Hilcott 25 D6
Hildenborough 29 E6
Hilden Park 29 E6
Hildersham 55 E6
Hilderstone 75 F6
Hilderthorpe 97 C7
Hilfield 12 D4
Hilgay 67 E6
Hill S Glos 36 E3
  W Mid 62 E5
  Warks 52 C3
Hillam 89 B6
Hillbeck 100 C2
Hillborough 31 C6
Hillbrae Aberds 141 B6
  Aberds 152 D6
Hill Brow 15 B8
Hillbutts 13 D7
Hillclifflane 76 E2
Hillcommon 11 B6
Hill Dale 86 C2
Hill Dyke 79 E6
Hillend 128 F3
Hill End Durham 110 F3
  Fife 128 E2
  N Yorks 94 D3
Hillerton 10 E2
Hillesden 39 B6
Hillesley 36 F4
Hillfarrance 11 B6
Hillhead Aberds 152 E5
  Devon 7 D7
  S Ayrs 112 C4
Hillhead of
  Auchentumb 153 C9
Hillhead of
  Cocklaw 153 D10
Hillhouse 121 D8
Hilliclay 158 D3
Hillingdon 40 F3
Hillington Glasgow ..118 C5
  Norf 80 E3
Hillmorton 52 B3
Hill Mountain 44 E4
Hillockhead
  Aberds 140 C3
  Aberds 140 D2
Hill of Beath 128 E3
Hill of Fearn 151 D11
Hill of
  Mountblairy 153 C6
Hill Ridware 62 C4
Hillside Aberds 141 E8
  Angus 135 C7
  Mers 85 C4
  Orkney 159 J5
  Shetland 160 G6
Hillswick 160 F4
Hill Top Durham 100 B4
  Hants 14 D5
  W Mid 62 E3
  W Yorks 88 C4
Hill View 13 E7
Hillway 15 F7
Hillwell 160 M5
Hilmarton 24 B5
Hilperton 24 D3
Hilsea 15 D7
Hilston 97 F8
Hilton Aberds 153 E9
  Cambs 54 C3
  Cumb 100 B2
  Derbys 76 F2
  Dorset 13 D5
  Highld 151 C10
  Shrops 61 E7
  Stockton 102 C2

Hinderwell 103 C5
Hindford 73 F7
Hindhead 27 F6
Hindley 86 D4
Hindley Green 86 D4
Hindlip 50 D3
Hindolveston 81 E6
Hindringham 81 D5
Hingham 68 D3
Hinstock 61 B6
Hintlesham 56 E4
Hinton Hants 14 E3
  Hereford 48 F5
  S Glos 24 B2
  Shrops 60 D3
  W Nhants 52 D3
Hinton Ampner 15 B6
Hinton Blewett 23 D7
Hinton
  Charterhouse 24 D2
Hinton-in-the-
  Hedges 52 F3
Hinton Martell 13 D8
Hinton on the
  Green 50 E5
Hinton Parva 38 F2
Hinton St George ...12 C2
Hinton St Mary 13 C5
Hinton Waldrist 38 E3
Hints Shrops 49 B8
  Staffs 63 D5
Hinwick 53 C7
Hinxhill 30 E4
Hinxton 55 E5
Hinxworth 54 E3
Hipperholme 88 B2
Hipswell 101 E6
Hirael 83 D5
Hiraeth 32 B2
Hirn 141 D6
Hirnant 59 B7
Hirst N Lanark 119 C8
  Northumb 117 F8
Hirst Courtney 89 B7
Hirwaen 72 C5
Hirwaun 34 D3
Hiscott 9 B7
Histon 54 C5
Hitcham 56 D3
Hitchin 40 B4
Hither Green 28 B4
Hittisleigh 10 E2
Hive 96 F4
Hixon 62 B4
Hoaden 31 D6
Hoaldalbert 35 B7
Hoar Cross 62 B5
Hoarwithy 36 B2
Hoath 31 C6
Hobarris 48 B5
Hobbister 159 H4
Hobkirk 115 C8
Hobson 110 D4
Hoby 64 C3
Hockering 68 C3
Hockerton 77 D7
Hockley 42 E4
Hockley Heath 51 B6
Hockliffe 40 B2
Hockwold cum
  Wilton 67 F7
Hockworthy 10 C5
Hoddesdon 41 D6
Hoddlesden 86 B5
Hoddomcross 107 B8
Hoddom Mains 107 B8
Hodgeston 32 E1
Hodley 59 E8
Hodnet 61 B6
Hodthorpe 76 B5
Hoe Hants 15 C6
  Norf 68 C2
Hoe Gate 15 C7
Hoff 100 C1
Hoggard's Green 56 D2
Hoggeston 39 B8
Hogha Gearraidh .148 A2
Hoghton 86 B4
Hognaston 76 D2
Hog Patch 27 E6
Hogsthorpe 79 B8
Holbeach 66 B3
Holbeach Bank 66 B3
Holbeach Clough ...66 B3
Holbeach Drove 66 C3
Holbeach Hurn 66 B3
Holbeach St Johns ..66 C3
Holbeach St Marks .79 F6
Holbeach St
  Matthew 79 F7
Holbeck Notts 76 B5
  W Yorks 95 F5
Holberrow Green ...50 D5
Holbeton 6 D4
Holborn 41 F6
Holbrook Derbys 76 E3
  Suff 57 F5
  S Yorks 88 F5
Holburn 123 F6
Holbury 14 D5
Holcombe Devon 7 B7
  Som 23 E8
Holcombe Rogus ...11 C5
Holcot 53 C5
Holden 93 E7
Holdenby 52 C4
Holdenhurst 14 E2
Holdgate 61 F5
Holdingham 78 E3
Holditch 11 D8
Holefield 122 F4
Holehouses 74 B4
Hole-in-the-Wall ...36 B3
Holemoor 9 D6
Holestane 113 E8
Holford 22 E3
Holgate 95 D8
Holker 92 B3
Holkham 80 C4
Hollacombe 9 D5
Holland Orkney 159 C5
  Orkney 159 F7
Holland Fen 78 E5
Holland-on-Sea 43 B8
Hollandstoun 159 C8
Hollee 108 C2

Hollesley 57 E7
Hollicombe 7 C6
Hollingbourne 30 D2
Hollington Derbys ..76 F2
  E Sus 18 D4
  Staffs 75 F7
Hollington Grove ...76 F2
Hollingworth 87 E8
Hollins 87 D6
Hollinsclough 75 C7
Hollins Green 86 E4
Hollins Lane 92 D4
Hollinwood
  Gtr Man 87 D7
  Shrops 74 F2
Hollocombe 9 C8
Holloway 76 D3
Hollowell 52 B4
Hollow Meadows ...88 F3
Hollybush Caerph ...35 D5
  E Ayrs 112 C3
  Worcs 50 F2
Holly End 66 D4
Holly Green 50 E3
Hollym 91 B7
Hollywood 51 B5
Holmbridge 88 D2
Holmbury St Mary .28 E2
Holmbush 4 D5
Holmcroft 62 B3
Holme Cambs 65 F8
  Cumb 92 B5
  Notts 77 D8
  N Yorks 102 F1
  W Yorks 88 D2
Holme Chapel 87 B6
Holme Green 95 E8
Holme Hale 67 D8
Holme Lacy 49 F7
Holme Marsh 48 D5
Holme next the
  Sea 80 C3
Holme-on-Spalding-
  Moor 96 F4
Holme on the
  Wolds 97 E5
Holme Pierrepont ..77 F6
Holmer 49 E7
Holmer Green 40 E2
Holme St
  Cuthbert 107 E7
Holmes Chapel 74 C4
Holmesfield 76 B3
Holmeswood 86 C2
Holmewood 76 C4
Holme Wood 94 F4
Holmfirth 88 D2
Holmhead
  Dumfries 113 F7
  E Ayrs 113 B5
Holmisdale 148 D6
Holmpton 91 B7
Holmrook 98 E2
Holmsgarth 160 J6
Holmwrangle 108 E5
Holne 6 C5
Holnest 12 D4
Holsworthy 8 D5
Holsworthy Beacon .9 D5
Holt Dorset 13 D8
  Norf 81 D6
  Wilts 24 C3
  Worcs 50 C3
  Wrex 73 D8
Holtby 96 D2
Holt End Hants 26 F4
  Worcs 51 C5
Holt Fleet 50 C3
Holt Heath 50 C3
Holton Oxon 39 D6
  Som 12 B4
  Suff 57 B7
Holton cum
  Beckering 90 F5
Holton Heath 13 E7
Holton le Clay 91 D6
Holton le Moor 90 E4
Holton St Mary 56 F4
Holt Park 95 E5
Holwell Dorset 12 C5
  Herts 54 F2
  Leics 64 B4
  Oxon 38 D2
Holwick 100 B4
Holworth 13 F5
Holy Cross 50 B4
Holyhead
  = Caergybi 82 C2
Holy Island 123 E7
Holymoorside 76 C3
Holyport 27 B6
Holystone 117 D5
Holytown 119 C7
Holywell Cambs 54 B4
  Corn 4 D2
  Dorset 12 D3
  E Sus 18 F2
  Northumb 111 B6
Holywell
  = Treffynnon 73 B5
Holywell Green 87 C8
Holywell Lake 11 B6
Holywell Row 55 B8
Holywood 114 F2
Homer 61 D6
Homersfield 69 F5
Hom Green 36 B2
Homington 14 B2
Honeyborough 44 E4
Honeybourne 51 E6
Honeychurch 9 D8
Honey Hill 30 C5
Honey Street 25 C6
Honey Tye 56 F3
Honiley 51 B7
Honing 69 B6
Honingham 68 C4
Honington Lincs 78 E2
  Suff 56 B3
  Warks 51 E7
Honiton 11 D6
Honley 88 C2
Hood Green 88 D3
Hooe E Sus 18 E3
  Plym 6 D3

Hooe Common 18 D3
Hoo Green 86 F5
Hook E Yorks 89 B8
　Hants. 26 D5
　London. 28 C2
　Pembs 44 D4
　Wilts 37 F7
Hooke 12 E3
Hookgate 74 F4
Hook Green Kent . . . 18 B3
　Kent. 29 C7
Hook Norton 51 F8
Hookway 10 E3
Hookwood 28 E3
Hoole 73 C8
Hooley 28 D3
Hoop 36 D2
Hoo St Werburgh . . 29 B8
Hooton 73 B7
Hooton Levitt 89 E6
Hooton Pagnell 89 D5
Hooton Roberts 89 E5
Hope Derbys 88 F2
　Devon 6 F4
　Highld 156 B7
　Powys 60 D2
　Shrops 60 D3
　Staffs. 75 D8
Hope = Yr Hôb 73 D7
Hope Bagot 49 B7
Hope Bowdler 60 E4
Hope End Green . . . 42 B1
Hope Green 87 F7
Hopeman 152 B1
Hope Mansell 36 C3
Hopesay 60 F3
Hope's Green 42 F3
Hope under
　Dinmore 49 D7
Hopley's Green 48 D5
Hopperton 95 D7
Hop Pole 65 C8
Hopton Shrops 60 B3
　Shrops 61 B5
　Staffs. 62 B3
　Suff 56 B3
Hopton Cangeford . 60 F5
Hopton Castle 49 B5
Hoptonheath 49 B5
Hopton on Sea 69 D8
Hopton Wafers 49 B8
Hopwas 63 D5
Hopwood Gtr Man . . 87 D6
　Worcs 50 B5
Horam 18 D2
Horbling 78 F4
Horbury 88 C3
Horcott 38 D1
Horden 111 E7
Horderley 60 F4
Hordle 14 E3
Hordley 73 F7
Horeb Carms 33 B6
　Carms 33 D5
　Ceredig 46 E2
Horfield 23 B8
Horham 57 B6
Horkesley Heath. . . 43 B5
Horkstow 90 C3
Horley Oxon. 52 E2
　Sur 28 E3
Hornblotton Green 23 F7
Hornby Lancs 93 C5
　N Yorks. 101 E2
　N Yorks. 102 D1
Horncastle 79 C5
Hornchurch 41 F8
Horncliffe 122 E5
Horndean Borders 122 E4
　Hants. 15 C8
Horndon 6 B3
Horndon on the
　Hill 42 F2
Horne 28 E4
Horniehaugh 134 C4
Horning 69 C6
Horninghall 64 E5
Horninglow 63 B6
Horningsea 55 C5
Horningsham 24 E3
Horningtoft 80 E5
Hornsby 108 D5
Horns Corner 18 C4
Horns Cross Devon . .9 B5
　E Sus 18 C5
Hornsea 97 E8
Hornsea Bridge . . . 97 E8
Hornsey 41 F6
Hornton 51 E8
Horrabridge 6 C3
Horringer 56 C2
Horringford 15 F6
Horsebridge Devon . .9 D7
　Hants. 25 F8
Horse Bridge 75 D6
Horsebrook 62 C2
Horsehay 61 D6
Horseheath 55 E7
Horsehouse 101 F5
Horsell 27 D7
Horseman's Green . 73 E8
Horseway 66 F4
Horsey 69 B7
Horsford 68 C4
Horsforth 94 F5
Horsham Worcs . . . 50 D2
　W Sus 28 F2
Horsham St Faith . . 68 C5
Horsington Lincs . . 78 C4
　Som 12 B5
Horsley Derbys 76 E3
　Glos. 37 E5
　Northumb 110 C3
　Northumb 116 E4
Horsley Cross 43 B7
Horsleycross
　Street 43 B7
Horsleyhill 115 C8
Horsleyhope 110 E3
Horsley
　Woodhouse 76 E3
Horsmonden 29 E7
Horspath 39 D5
Horstead 69 C5
Horsted Keynes . . . 17 B7

Horton Bucks 40 C2
　Dorset. 13 D8
　Lancs. 93 D8
　S Glos. 36 F4
　Shrops. 60 B4
　Som 11 C8
　Staffs. 75 D6
　Swansea 33 F5
　Wilts 25 C5
　Windsor. 27 B8
　W Nhants. 53 D6
Horton-cum-
　Studley 39 C5
Horton Green 73 E8
Horton Heath 15 C5
Horton in
　Ribblesdale 93 B8
Horton Kirby 29 C6
Hortonlane 60 C4
Horwich 86 C4
Horwich End 87 F8
Horwood 9 B7
Hose. 64 B4
Hoselaw 122 F4
Hoses 98 E4
Hosh. 127 B7
Hosta 148 A2
Hoswick 160 L6
Hotham 96 F4
Hothfield 30 E3
Hoton. 64 B2
Houbie 160 D8
Houdston 112 E1
Hough Ches E 74 D4
　Ches E 75 B5
Hougham 77 E8
Hough Green. 86 F2
Hough-on-the-
　Hill 78 E2
Houghton Cambs . . 54 B3
　Cumb 108 D4
　Hants. 25 F8
　Pembs 44 E4
　W Sus 16 C4
Houghton
　Conquest 53 E8
Houghton Green
　E Sus 19 C6
　Warr 86 E4
Houghton-le-
　Side 101 B7
Houghton-le-
　Spring 111 E6
Houghton on the
　Hill 64 D3
Houghton Regis . . . 40 B3
Houghton St Giles . 80 D5
Houlland Shetland 160 F7
　Shetland 160 H5
Houlsyke 103 D5
Hound 15 D5
Hound Green. 26 D5
Houndslow 122 E2
Houndwood 122 C4
Hounslow 28 B2
Hounslow Green . . 42 C2
Housay 160 F8
House of Daviot .151 G10
House of
　Glenmuick 140 E2
Housetter 160 E5
Houss. 160 K5
Houston 118 C4
Houstry 158 G3
Houton 159 H4
Hove. 17 D6
Hoveringham 77 E6
Hoverton 69 C6
Hovingham 96 B2
How 108 D5
Howbrook 88 E4
How Caple 49 F8
Howden Borders . 116 B2
　E Yorks. 89 B8
Howden-le-Wear 110 F4
Howe Highld 158 D5
　Norf. 69 D5
　N Yorks. 101 F8
Howe Bridge 86 D4
Howe Green. 42 D3
Howell 78 E4
How End 53 E8
Howe of Teuchar . 153 D7
Howe Street Essex . 42 C2
　Essex. 55 F7
Howey 48 D2
Howgate 120 D5
How Green 29 E5
Howick 117 C8
Howle Durham . . . 101 B5
　Telford. 61 B6
Howlett End 55 F6
Howley 11 D7
Hownam 116 C3
Hownam Mains . . 116 B3
Howpasley 115 D6
Howsham N Lincs . . 90 D4
　N Yorks. 96 C3
Howslack 114 D3
Howtel 122 F4
Howton 35 B8
Howtown 99 C6
Howwood 118 C3
Hoxne 57 B5
Hoy 159 H3
Hoylake 85 F3
Hoyland 88 D4
Hoylandswaine . . . 88 D3
Hubberholme 94 B2
Hubbert's Bridge . . 79 E5
Huby N Yorks 95 C8
　N Yorks. 95 E5
Hucclecote 37 C5
Hucking 30 D2
Hucknall 76 E5
Huddersfield 88 C2
Huddington 50 D4
Hudswell 101 D6
Huggate 96 D4
Hugglescote 63 C8
Hughenden Valley . 40 E1
Hughley 61 E5
Hugh Town 2 E4
Huish Devon 9 C7
　Wilts 25 C6
Huish
　Champflower . . . 11 B5
Huish Episcopi . . . 12 B2
Huisinis 154 F4

Hulcott 40 C1
Hulland 76 E2
Hulland Ward 76 E2
Hullavington 37 F5
Hullbridge 42 E4
Hulme 87 E6
Hulme End 75 D8
Hulme Walfield . . . 74 C5
Hulverstone 14 F4
Hulver Street 69 F7
Humber. 49 D7
Humber Bridge. . . . 90 B4
Humberston 91 D7
Humbie 121 C7
Humbleton E Yorks . 97 F8
　Northumb 117 B5
Humby 78 F3
Hume 122 E3
Humshaugh 110 B2
Huna 158 C5
Huncoat 93 F7
Huncote 64 E2
Hundalee 116 B2
Hunderthwaite . . 100 B4
Hundleby 79 C6
Hundle Houses . . . 79 D5
Hundleton 44 E4
Hundon 55 E8
Hundred Acres . . . 15 C6
Hundred End 86 B2
Hundred House . . . 48 D3
Hungarton 64 D3
Hungerford Hants . 14 C3
　W Berks. 25 C8
Hungerford
　Newtown 25 B8
Hungerton 65 B5
Hungladder 149 A8
Hunmanby 97 B6
Hunmanby Moor . . 97 B7
Hunningham 51 C8
Hunny Hill 15 F5
Hunsdon 41 C7
Hunsingore 95 D7
Hunslet 95 F6
Hunsonby 109 F5
Hunspow 158 C4
Hunstanton 80 C2
Hunstanworth . . . 110 E2
Hunsterson 74 E3
Hunston Suff. 56 C3
　W Sus 16 D2
Hunstrete 23 C8
Hunt End 50 C5
Hunter's Quay . . . 145 F10
Hunthill Lodge . . 134 B4
Huntingdon 54 B3
Huntingfield 57 B7
Huntingford. 24 F3
Huntington E Loth 121 B7
　Hereford. 48 D4
　Staffs. 62 C3
　York. 96 D2
Huntingtower 128 B2
Huntley 36 C4
Huntly 152 E5
Huntlywood 122 E2
Hunton Kent 29 E8
　N Yorks. 101 E6
Hunt's Corner 68 F3
Hunt's Cross 86 F2
Huntsham 10 B5
Huntspill 22 E5
Huntworth 22 F5
Hunwick 110 F4
Hunworth 81 D6
Hurdsfield 75 B6
Hurley Warks 63 E6
　Windsor. 39 F8
Hurlford 118 F4
Hurliness 159 K3
Hurn 14 E2
Hurn's End 79 E7
Hursley 14 B5
Hurst N Yorks 101 D5
　Som 12 C2
　Wokingham 27 B5
Hurstbourne
　Priors 26 E2
Hurstbourne
　Tarrant 25 D8
Hurst Green E Sus . 18 C4
　Lancs. 93 F6
Hurstpierpoint . . . 17 C6
Hurst Wickham . . . 17 C6
Hurstwood 93 F8
Hurtmore 27 E7
Hurworth Place . . 101 D7
Hury 100 C4
Husabost 148 C7
Husbands
　Bosworth 64 F3
Husborne Crawley . 53 F7
Husthwaite 95 B8
Hutchwns 21 B7
Huthwaite 76 D4
Huttoft 79 B8
Hutton Borders . . 122 D5
　Cumb 99 B6
　Essex. 42 E2
　E Yorks. 97 D6
　Lancs. 86 B2
　N Som 22 D5
Hutton Buscel . . . 103 F7
Hutton Conyers . . . 95 B6
Hutton Cranswick . 97 D6
Hutton End 108 F4
Hutton Gate 102 C3
Hutton Henry 111 F7
Hutton-le-Hole . . 103 E5
Hutton Magna . . . 101 C6
Hutton Roof Cumb . 93 B5
　Cumb 108 F3
Hutton Rudby . . . 102 D2
Hutton Sessay 95 B7
Hutton Village . . . 102 C3
Hutton Wandesley . 95 D8
Huxley 74 C2
Huxter Shetland . . 160 G7
　Shetland 160 H5
Huxton 122 C4
Huyton 86 E2
Hwlffordd
　= Haverfordwest . . 44 D4
Hycemoor 98 F2
Hyde Glos. 37 D5
　Gtr Man 87 E7
　Hants. 14 C2
Hyde Heath 40 D2

Hyde Park 89 D6
Hydestile 27 E7
Hylton Castle. . . . 111 D6
Hyndford Bridge . 120 E2
Hynish 146 H2
Hythe Hants 14 D5
　Kent. 19 B8
Hythe End. 27 B8
Hythie 153 C10

I

Ibberton 13 D5
Ible 76 D2
Ibsley 14 D2
Ibstock 63 C8
Ibstone 39 E7
Ibthorpe 25 D8
Ibworth 26 D3
Ichrachan 125 B6
Ickburgh 67 E8
Ickenham 40 F3
Ickford 39 D6
Ickham 31 D6
Ickleford 54 F2
Icklesham 19 D5
Ickleton 55 E5
Icklingham 55 B8
Ickwell Green 54 E2
Icomb 38 B2
Idbury 38 C2
Iddesleigh 9 D7
Ide 10 E3
Ideford 7 B6
Ide Hill 29 D5
Iden 19 C6
Iden Green Kent. . . 18 B4
　Kent. 18 B5
Idle 94 F4
Idlicote 51 E7
Idmiston 25 F6
Idole 33 C5
Idridgehay 76 E2
Idrigill 149 B8
Idstone 38 F2
Idvies 135 E5
Iffley 39 D5
Ifield 28 F3
Ifold 27 F8
Iford 17 D8
Ifton Heath 73 F7
Ightfield 74 F2
Ightham 29 D6
Iken 57 D8
Ilam 75 D8
Ilchester 12 B3
Ilderton 117 B6
Ilford 41 F7
Ilfracombe 20 E4
Ilkeston 76 E4
Ilketshall St
　Andrew. 69 F6
Ilketshall St
　Lawrence. 69 F6
Ilketshall St
　Margaret 69 F6
Ilkley 94 E4
Illey 62 F3
Illingworth 87 B8
Illogan 3 B5
Illston on the Hill . . 64 E4
Ilmer 39 D7
Ilmington 51 E7
Ilminster 11 C8
Ilsington 7 B5
Ilston 33 E6
Ilton N Yorks 94 B4
　Som 11 C8
Imachar 143 D9
Imeraval 142 D4
Immingham 91 C5
Impington 54 C5
Ince 73 B8
Ince Blundell. 85 D4
Ince in Makerfield . 86 D3
Inchbare 135 C6
Inchberry 152 C3
Inchbraoch 135 D7
Incheril 150 E3
Inchgrundle 134 B4
Inchina 150 B2
Inchinnan 118 C4
Inchkinloch 157 E8
Inchlaggan. 136 D4
Inchlumpie 151 D8
Inchmore 150 G6
Inchnacardoch
　Hotel 137 C6
Inchnadamph . . . 156 G5
Inch of Arnhall . . 135 B6
Inchree 130 C4
Inchture 128 B4
Inchyra 128 B3
Indian Queens. 4 D4
Inerval 142 D4
Ingatestone 42 D2
Ingbirchworth . . . 88 D3
Ingestre 62 B3
Ingham Lincs 90 F3
　Norf. 69 B6
　Suff 56 B2
Ingham Corner . . . 69 B6
Ingleborough 66 C4
Ingleby Derbys . . . 63 B7
Ingleby Arncliffe . 102 D2
Ingleby Barwick . 102 C2
Ingleby
　Greenhow 102 D3
Inglemire 97 F6
Inglesbatch 24 C2
Inglesham 38 E2
Ingleton Durham . 101 B6
　N Yorks. 93 B6
Inglewhite 92 E5
Ingliston 120 B4
Ingoe 110 B3
Ingol 92 F5
Ingoldisthorpe . . . 80 D2
Ingoldmells 79 C8
Ingoldsby 78 F3
Ingon 51 D7
Ingram 117 C6
Ingrow 94 F3
Ings 99 E6
Ingst 36 F2
Ingworth 81 E7

Inham's End. 66 E2
Inkberrow 50 D5
Inkpen. 25 C8
Inkstack 158 C4
Inn 99 D6
Innellan. 145 F10
Innerleithen 121 F6
Innerleven 129 D5
Innermessan 104 C4
Innerwick E Loth . . 122 B3
　Perth 132 E2
Innis Chonain . . . 125 C7
Insch 140 B5
Insh 138 D4
Inshore 156 C6
Inskip. 92 F4
Instoneville 89 C6
Instow 20 F3
Intake. 89 D6
Inver Aberds 139 E8
　Highld 151 C11
　Perth 133 E7
Inverailort 147 C10
Inveraldie 134 F4
Inverallign 149 C13
Inverallochy. 153 B10
Inveran 151 B8
Inveraray 125 E6
Inverarish 149 E10
Inverarity 134 E4
Inverarnan 126 C2
Inverasdale 155 J13
Inverbeg. 126 E2
Inverbervie 135 B8
Inverboyndie 153 B6
Inverbroom 150 C4
Invercassley. 156 J7
Invercauld House . 139 E7
Invercharnan 131 E5
Inverchoran 150 F5
Invercreran 130 E4
Inverdruie. 138 C5
Inverebrie. 153 E9
Invereck 145 E10
Inverernan
　House 140 C2
Invereshie House . 138 D4
Inveresk 121 B6
Inverey. 139 F6
Inverfarigaig 137 B8
Invergarry 137 D6
Invergelder 139 E8
Invergeldie 127 B6
Invergordon. 151 E10
Invergowrie 134 F3
Inverguseran. 149 H12
Inverhadden 132 D3
Inverharroch 152 E3
Inverherive 126 B2
Inverie 147 B10
Inverinan 125 D5
Inverinate. 136 B2
Inverkeilor 135 E6
Inverkeithing. . . . 128 F3
Inverkeithny 153 D6
Inverkip. 118 B2
Inverkirkaig 156 H3
Inverlael 150 C4
Inverlochlarig. . . . 126 C3
Inverlochy Argyll . 125 C7
　Highld 131 B5
Inverlussa 144 E5
Inver Mallie 136 F4
Invermark Lodge . 147 D9
Invermoidart 147 D9
Invermoriston . . . 137 C7
Invernaver 157 C10
Inverneill 145 E7
Inverness 151 G9
Invernettie 153 D11
Invernoaden 125 F7
Inveroran Hotel . . 131 E6
Inverpolly Lodge . 156 H3
Inverquharity 134 D4
Inverquhomery . . 153 D10
Inverroy. 137 F5
Inversanda 130 D3
Invershiel 136 C2
Invershin 151 B8
Inversnaid Hotel . 126 D2
Inveruglas 126 D2
Inveruglass 138 D4
Inverurie 141 B6
Invervar 132 E3
Inverythan 153 D7
Inwardleigh 9 E7
Inworth 42 C4
Iochdar 148 D2
Iping 16 B2
Ipplepen 7 C6
Ipsden 39 F6
Ipsley 50 C5
Ipstones 75 D7
Ipswich 57 E5
Irby 85 F3
Irby in the Marsh . . 79 C7
Irby upon Humber . 91 D5
Irchester 53 C7
Ireby Cumb. 108 F2
　Lancs. 93 B6
Ireland Orkney . . . 159 H4
　Shetland 160 K5
Ireland's Cross . . . 74 E4
Ireleth 92 B2
Ireshopeburn 109 F8
Irlam 86 E5
Irnham 65 B7
Iron Acton 36 F3
Iron Bridge 61 D6
Iron Cross. 51 D5
Irongray 107 B6
Ironmacannie . . . 106 B3
Ironside 153 C8
Ironville 76 D4
Irstead 69 B6
Irthington 108 C4
Irthlingborough . . 53 B7
Irton 103 F7
Irvine 118 F3
Isauld 157 C12
Isbister Orkney . . . 159 F3
　Orkney 159 G4
　Shetland 160 F5
　Shetland 160 G7
Isfield 17 C8
Isham 53 B6
Isle Abbotts 11 B8

Isle Brewers 11 B8
Isleham 55 B7
Isle of Whithorn . 105 F8
Isleornsay 149 G12
Islesburgh 160 G5
Islesteps 107 B6
Isleworth 28 B2
Isley Walton 63 B8
Islibhig 154 E4
Islington 41 F6
Islip N Nhants 53 B7
　Oxon 39 C5
Istead Rise 29 C7
Isycoed 73 D8
Itchen 14 C5
Itchen Abbas 26 F3
Itchen Stoke 26 F3
Itchingfield 16 B5
Itchington 36 F3
Itteringham 81 D7
Itton 9 E8
Itton Common . . . 36 E1
Ivegill 108 E4
Iver 40 F3
Iver Heath. 40 F3
Iveston 110 D4
Ivinghoe 40 C2
Ivinghoe Aston . . . 40 C2
Ivington 49 D6
Ivington Green . . . 49 D6
Ivy Chimneys 41 D7
Ivychurch 19 C7
Ivy Cross. 13 B6
Ivy Hatch 29 D6
Iwade 30 C3
Iwerne Courtney or
　Shroton 13 C6
Iwerne Minster . . . 13 C6
Ixworth 56 B3
Ixworth Thorpe . . 56 B3

J

Jack Hill 94 D5
Jack in the Green . . 10 E5
Jacksdale 76 D4
Jackstown 153 E7
Jacobstow 8 E3
Jacobstowe 9 D7
Jameston 32 E1
Jamestown
　Dumfries 115 E6
　Highld 150 F7
　W Dunb 126 F2
Jarrow 111 C6
Jarvis Brook 18 C2
Jasper's Green . . . 42 B3
Java 124 B3
Jawcraig 119 B8
Jaywick 43 C7
Jealott's Hill 27 B6
Jedburgh 116 B2
Jeffreyston 32 D1
Jellyhill 119 B6
Jemimaville 151 E10
Jersey Farm 40 D4
Jesmond 111 C5
Jevington 18 E2
Jockey End. 40 C3
Johnby 108 F4
John o'Groats. . . . 158 C5
John's Cross 18 C4
Johnshaven 135 C7
Johnston E Renfs . . 118 C4
　Pembs 44 D4
Johnstonebridge . 114 E3
Johnstown Carms . 33 C5
　Wrex 73 E7
Joppa Edin. 121 B6
　S Ayrs. 112 C4
Jordans 40 E2
Jordanthorpe 88 F4
Jump 88 D4
Jumpers Green . . . 14 E2
Juniper Green . . . 120 C4
Jurby East 84 C3
Jurby West 84 C3

K

Kaber 100 C2
Kaimend 120 E2
Kaimes 121 C5
Kalemouth 116 B3
Kames Argyll 124 D4
　Argyll 145 F8
　E Ayrs 113 B6
Kea 3 B7
Keadby 90 C2
Keal Cotes 79 C6
Kearsley 87 D5
Kearstwick 99 F8
Kearton 100 E4
Kearvaig 156 B5
Keasden 93 C7
Keckwick. 86 F3
Keddington 91 F7
Kedington 55 E8
Kedleston 76 E3
Keelby 91 C5
Keele 74 E5
Keeley Green 53 E8
Keeston 44 D4
Keevil 24 D4
Kegworth 63 B8
Kehelland. 2 B5
Keig 140 C5
Keighley 94 E3
Keil. 143 H7
Keilarsbrae 127 E7
Keilhill 153 C7
Keillmore 144 E5
Keillor 134 E2
Keillour 127 B8
Keills 142 B5
Keils 144 G4
Keinton
　Mandeville 23 F7
Keir Mill 113 E8
Keisby 65 B7
Keiss 158 D5
Keith 152 C4
Keith Inch 153 D11
Keithock. 135 C6
Kelbrook 94 E2
Kelby 78 E3

Keld Cumb 99 C7
　N Yorks. 100 D3
Keldholme 103 F5
Kelfield N Lincs . . . 90 D2
　N Yorks. 95 F8
Kelham 77 D7
Kellan 147 G8
Kellas Angus 134 F4
　Moray 152 C1
Kellaton 7 F6
Kelleth. 100 D1
Kelleythorpe 97 D5
Kelling 81 C6
Kellingley. 89 B6
Kellington 89 B6
Kelloe 111 F6
Kelloholm 113 C7
Kelly 9 F5
Kelly Bray 5 B8
Kelmarsh 52 B5
Kelmscot 38 E2
Kelsale 57 C7
Kelsall 74 C2
Kelsall Hill 74 C2
Kelshall 54 F4
Kelsick 107 D8
Kelso 122 F3
Kelstedge 76 C3
Kelstern 91 E6
Kelston 24 C2
Keltneyburn 132 E4
Kelton 107 B6
Kelty 128 E3
Kelvedon 42 C4
Kelvedon Hatch . . 42 E1
Kelvin 119 D6
Kelvinside 119 C5
Kemback 129 C6
Kemberton 61 D7
Kemble 37 E6
Kemerton 50 F4
Kemeys
　Commander 35 D7
Kemnay 141 C6
Kempley 36 B3
Kempsey 50 E3
Kempsford 38 E1
Kemps Green. 51 B6
Kempshott 26 D4
Kempston
　Hardwick 53 E8
Kempton 60 F3
Kemp Town. 17 D7
Kemsing 29 D6
Kemsley 30 C3
Kenardington 19 B6
Kenchester 49 E6
Kencot 38 D2
Kendal 99 E7
Kendoon 113 F6
Kendray 88 D4
Kenfig 34 F2
Kenfig Hill 34 F2
Kenilworth 51 B7
Kenknock 132 F1
Kenley London . . . 28 D4
　Shrops 61 D5
Kenmore Highld . 149 C12
　Perth 132 E4
Kenn Devon 10 F4
　N Som 23 C6
Kennacley 154 H6
Kennacraig 145 G7
Kennerleigh. 10 D3
Kennet 127 E8
Kennethmont . . . 140 B4
Kennett 55 C7
Kennford 10 F4
Kenninghall 68 F3
Kenninghall Heath 68 F3
Kennington Kent . . 30 E4
　Oxon 39 D5
Kennoway 129 D5
Kenny Hill 55 B7
Kennythorpe 96 C3
Kenovay 146 G2
Kensaleyre 149 C9
Kensington 40 C3
Kensworth
　Common 40 C3
Kentallen 130 D4
Kentchurch 35 B8
Kentford 55 C8
Kentisbeare 11 D5
Kentisbury 20 E5
Kentisbury Ford . . 20 E5
Kentmere 99 D6
Kenton Devon . . . 10 F4
　Suff 57 C5
　T&W 110 C5
Kenton Bankfoot . 110 C5
Kentra 147 E9
Kents Bank 92 B3
Kent's Green 36 B4
Kent's Oak 14 B4
Kent Street E Sus . 18 D4
　Kent 29 D7
　W Sus 17 B6
Kenwick 73 F8
Kenwyn 3 B7
Keoldale 156 C6
Keppanach 130 C4
Keppoch 136 B2
Keprigan 143 G7
Kepwick 102 E2
Kerchesters 122 F3
Keresley 63 F7
Kernborough 7 E5
Kerne Bridge 36 C2
Kerris 2 D3
Kerry 59 F8
Kerrycroy 145 G10
Kerry's Gate 49 F5
Kersall 77 C7
Kersey 56 E4
Kershopefoot . . . 115 F7
Kersoe 50 F4
Kerswell 11 D5
Kerswell Green . . . 50 E3
Kesgrave 57 E6
Kessingland 69 F8
Kessingland Beach 69 F8
Kessington 119 B5
Kestle 3 B8
Kestle Mill 4 D3

Keston 28 C5
Keswick Cumb 98 B4
　Norf. 68 D5
　Norf. 81 D9
Ketley 61 C6
Ketley Bank 61 C6
Ketsby 79 B6
Kettering 53 B6
Ketteringham 68 D4
Kettins 134 F2
Kettlebaston 56 D3
Kettlebridge. 128 D5
Kettleburgh 57 C6
Kettlehill 128 D5
Kettleholm 107 B8
Kettleness 103 C6
Kettleshume 75 B6
Kettlesing Bottom . 94 D5
Kettlesing Head . . 94 D5
Kettlestone 81 D5
Kettlethorpe 77 B8
Kettletoft 159 E7
Kettlewell 94 B2
Ketton 65 D6
Kew 28 B2
Kew Bridge 28 B2
Kewstoke 22 C5
Kexbrough 88 D4
Kexby Lincs 90 F2
　York 96 D3
Key Green 75 C5
Keyham 64 D3
Keyhaven 14 E4
Keyingham 91 B6
Keymer 17 C7
Keynsham 23 C8
Keysoe 53 C8
Keysoe Row 53 C8
Keyston 53 B8
Keyworth 77 F6
Kibblesworth 110 D5
Kibworth
　Beauchamp. . . . 64 E3
Kibworth Harcourt 64 E3
Kidbrooke 28 B5
Kiddemore Green . 62 D2
Kidderminster . . . 50 B3
Kiddington 38 C4
Kidlington 38 C4
Kidmore End 26 B4
Kidsgrove 74 D5
Kidstones 100 F4
Kidwelly
　= Cydweli 33 C5
Kiel Crofts 124 B5
Kielder 116 E2
Kierfield Ho. 159 G3
Kilbagie 127 E8
Kilbarchan 118 C4
Kilbeg 149 H11
Kilberry 144 G6
Kilbirnie 118 D3
Kilbride Argyll . . 124 C4
　Argyll 124 C5
　Highld 149 F10
Kilburn Angus . . . 134 C4
　Derbys. 76 E3
　London 41 F5
　N Yorks. 95 B8
Kilby 64 E3
Kilchamaig 145 G7
Kilchattan 144 D2
Kilchattan Bay . . 145 H10
Kilchenzie 143 F7
Kilcheran. 124 B4
Kilchiaran 142 B3
Kilchoan Argyll . . 124 D3
　Highld 146 E7
Kilchoman 142 B3
Kilchrenan 125 C6
Kilconquhar 129 D6
Kilcot 36 B3
Kilcoy 151 F8
Kilcreggan. 145 E11
Kildale 102 D4
Kildalloig 143 G8
Kildary 151 D10
Kildermorie
　Lodge 151 D8
Kildonan 143 F11
Kildonan Lodge .157 G12
Kildonnan 146 C7
Kildrummy 140 C3
Kildwick 94 E3
Kilfinan 145 F8
Kilfinnan 137 E5
Kilgetty 32 D2
Kilgwrrwg
　Common 36 E1
Kilham E Yorks . . . 97 C6
　Northumb 122 F4
Kilkenneth 146 G2
Kilkerran 143 G8
Kilkhampton 8 C5
Killamarsh 89 F5
Killay 33 E7
Killbeg 147 G9
Killean 143 D7
Killearn 126 F4
Killen 151 F9
Killerby 101 C6
Killichonan 132 D2
Killiechonate . . . 136 F5
Killiechronan . . . 147 G8
Killiecrankie 133 C6
Killiemor 146 H7
Killiemore House . 146 J7
Killilan 150 H2
Killimster 158 E5
Killin 132 F2
Killinallan 142 A4
Killinghall 95 D5
Killingholme 91 C5
Killinghurst 27 F7
Killington 99 F8
Killingworth 111 B5
Killin Lodge 137 D8
Killmahumaig. . . . 144 D6
Killochyett 121 E6
Killocraw 143 E7
Killundine 147 G8
Kilmacolm 118 C3
Kilmaha 124 E5
Kilmahog 126 D5
Kilmalieu. 130 D2
Kilmaluag. 149 A9
Kilmany 129 B5
Kilmarie 149 G10
Kilmarnock 118 F4
Kilmaron Castle . 129 C5
Kilmartin 124 F4

Kilmaurs. 118 E4
Kilmelford 124 D4
Kilmeny 142 B4
Kilmersdon 23 D8
Kilmeston 15 B6
Kilmichael 143 F7
Kilmichael of
　Glassary 145 D7
Kilmichael of
　Inverlussa 144 E6
Kilmington Devon . 11 E7
　Wilts 24 F2
Kilmonivaig 136 F4
Kilmorack 150 G7
Kilmore Argyll . . . 124 C4
　Highld 149 H11
Kilmory Argyll . . . 144 F6
　Highld 147 D8
　Highld 149 H8
　N Ayrs 143 F10
Kilmuir Highld . . 148 D7
　Highld 149 A8
　Highld 151 D10
　Highld 151 G9
Kilmun Argyll . . . 124 E5
　Argyll 145 E10
Kilncadzow 119 E8
Kilndown. 18 B4
Kilnhurst 89 E5
Kilninian 146 G6
Kilninver 124 C4
Kiln Pit Hill 110 D3
Kilnsea 91 C8
Kilnsey 94 C2
Kilnwick 97 E5
Kilnwick Percy . . 96 D4
Kiloran 144 D2
Kilpatrick 143 F10
Kilpeck 49 F6
Kilphedir 157 H12
Kilpin 89 B8
Kilpin Pike. 89 B8
Kilrenny 129 D7
Kilsby 52 B3
Kilspindie 128 B4
Kilsyth 119 B7
Kiltarlity 151 G8
Kilton Notts 77 B5
　Som 22 E3
Kilton Thorpe . . . 102 C4
Kilvaxter 149 B8
Kilve 22 E3
Kilvington 77 E7
Kilwinning 118 E3
Kimberley Norf. . . 68 D3
　Notts 76 E5
Kimberworth 88 E5
Kimble Wick 39 D8
Kimbolton Cambs . 53 C8
　Hereford. 49 C7
Kimcote 64 F2
Kimmeridge 13 G7
Kimmerston 123 F5
Kimpton Hants . . 25 E7
　Herts. 40 C4
Kinbrace 157 F11
Kinbuck 127 D6
Kincaple 129 C6
Kincardine Fife . . 127 F8
　Highld 151 C9
Kincardine
　Bridge 127 F8
Kincardine O'Neil 140 E4
Kinclaven. 134 F1
Kincorth 141 D8
Kincorth House . 151 E13
Kincraig 138 D4
Kincraigie 133 E6
Kindallachan 133 E6
Kineton Glos. 37 B7
　Warks 51 D8
Kinfauns 128 B3
Kingairloch 130 D2
Kingarth 145 H9
King Edward 153 C7
Kingerby 90 E4
Kingham 38 B2
Kingholm Quay . . 107 B6
Kinghorn 128 F4
Kingie 136 D4
Kinglassie 128 E4
King's Acre 49 E6
Kingsand 6 D2
Kingsbarns 129 C7
Kingsbridge Devon . .7 E5
　Som 21 F8
King's Bromley . . 62 C5
Kingsburgh 149 C8
Kingsbury London . 41 F5
　Warks 63 E6
Kingsbury
　Episcopi 12 B2
King's Caple 36 B2
Kingsclere 26 D3
King's Cliffe 65 E7
Kingscote 37 E5
Kingscott 9 C7
King's Coughton . 51 D5
Kingscross 143 F11
Kingsdon 12 B3
Kingsdown 31 E7
Kingseat 128 E3
Kingsey 39 D7
Kingsfold 28 F2
Kingsford E Ayrs . . 118 E4
　Worcs 62 F2
Kingsforth 90 C4
King's Green 50 F2
Kingsheanton . . . 20 F4
Kings Hedges . . . 55 C5
King's Heath. 62 F4
Kings Hedges . . . 55 C5
King's Hill 29 D7
Kingshouse
　Hotel 131 D6
Kingside Hill . . . 107 D8
Kingskerswell 7 C6
Kingskettle 128 D5
Kingsland Anglesey . 82 C2
　Hereford. 49 C6
Kings Langley . . . 40 D3
Kingsley Ches W . . 74 B2
　Hants. 27 F5
　Staffs. 75 E7
Kingsley Green . . 27 F6
Kingsley Holt . . . 75 E7
Kingsley Park . . . 53 C5

King's Lynn 67 B6
King's Meaburn ... 99 B8
King's Mills 73 E2
Kingsmuir Angus .. 134 E4
Fife 129 D7
Kings Muir 121 F5
King's Newnham .. 52 B2
King's Newton 63 B7
Kingsnorth 19 B7
King's Norton Leics 64 D3
W Mid 51 B5
King's Nympton ... 9 C8
King's Pyon 49 D6
King's Ripton 54 B3
King's Somborne .. 25 F8
King's Stag 12 C5
King's Stanley 37 D5
King's Sutton 52 F2
Kingstanding 62 E4
Kingsteignton 7 B6
King Sterndale ... 75 B7
King's Thorn 49 F7
Kingsthorpe 53 C5
Kingston Cambs ... 54 D4
Devon 6 E4
Dorset 13 D5
Dorset 13 G7
E Loth 129 F7
Hants 14 D2
IoW 15 F5
Kent 31 D5
Moray 152 B3
Kingston Bagpuize 38 E4
Kingston Blount .. 39 E7
Kingston by Sea .. 17 D6
Kingston Deverill . 24 F3
Kingstone Hereford . 11 C8
Som 11 C8
Staffs 62 B4
Kingston Gorse ... 16 D4
Kingston Lisle ... 38 F3
Kingston Maurward 12 E5
Kingston near Lewes 17 D7
Kingston on Soar . 64 B2
Kingston Russell . 12 E3
Kingston St Mary . 11 B7
Kingston Seymour 23 C6
Kingston upon Hull 90 B4
Kingston upon Thames 28 C2
Kingston Vale 28 B3
Kingstown 108 D3
King's Walden 40 B4
Kingswear 7 D6
Kingswells 141 D7
Kingswinford 62 F2
Kingswood Bucks . 39 C6
Glos 36 E4
Hereford 48 D4
Kent 30 D2
Powys 60 D2
S Glos 28 D3
Sur 28 D3
Warks 51 B6
Kings Worthy 26 F2
Kingthorpe 78 B4
Kington Hereford . 48 D4
Worcs 50 D4
Kington Langley . 24 B4
Kington Magna ... 13 B5
Kington St Michael 24 B4
Kingussie 138 D3
Kingweston 23 F7
Kininvie House ... 152 D3
Kinkell Bridge ... 127 C8
Kinknockie 153 D10
Kinlet 61 F7
Kinloch Fife 128 C4
Highld 146 B6
Highld 149 G11
Highld 156 F6
Perth 133 E8
Perth 134 E2
Kinlochan 130 C2
Kinlochard 126 C3
Kinlochbeoraid .147 C11
Kinlochbervie ... 156 D5
Kinlocheil 130 B3
Kinlochewe 150 E3
Kinloch Hourn ... 136 D2
Kinloch Laggan .. 137 F8
Kinlochleven 131 C5
Kinloch Lodge ... 157 D8
Kinlochmoidart .147 D10
Kinlochmorar ...147 B11
Kinlochmore 131 C5
Kinloch Rannoch .132 D3
Kinlochspelve .. 124 C2
Kinloid 147 C9
Kinloss 151 E13
Kinmel Bay 72 A3
Kinmuck 141 C7
Kinmundy 141 C7
Kinnadie 153 D9
Kinnaird 128 B4
Kinnaird Castle .. 135 D6
Kinneff 135 B8
Kinnelhead 114 D3
Kinnell 135 D6
Kinnerley 60 B3
Kinnersley Hereford 48 E5
Worcs 50 E3
Kinnerton 48 C4
Kinnesswood ... 128 D3
Kinninvie 101 B5
Kinnordy 134 D3
Kinoulton 77 F6
Kinross 128 D3
Kinrossie 134 F1
Kinsbourne Green .40 C4
Kinsey Heath ... 74 E3
Kinsham Hereford 49 C5
Worcs 50 F4
Kinsley 88 C5
Kinson 13 E8
Kintbury 25 C8
Kintessack 151 E12
Kintillo 128 C3
Kintocher 140 D4
Kinton Hereford . 49 B6
Shrops 60 C3
Kintore 141 C6
Kintour 142 C5
Kintra Argyll ... 142 D4
Argyll 146 J6

Kintraw 124 E4
Kinuachdrachd ...124 F3
Kinveachy 138 C5
Kinver 62 F2
Kippax 95 F7
Kippen 127 E5
Kippford or Scaur 106 D5
Kirbister Orkney .159 F3
Orkney 159 H4
Kirbuster 159 F3
Kirby Bedon 69 D5
Kirby Bellars ... 64 C4
Kirby Cane 69 E6
Kirby Cross 43 B8
Kirby Grindalythe 96 C5
Kirby Hill N Yorks 95 C6
N Yorks 101 D6
Kirby Knowle ... 102 F2
Kirby-le-Soken .. 43 B8
Kirby Misperton . 96 B3
Kirby Muxloe ... 64 D2
Kirby Row 69 E6
Kirby Sigston ... 102 E2
Kirby Underdale .96 C4
Kirby Wiske 102 F1
Kirdford 16 B4
Kirk 158 E4
Kirkabister 160 K6
Kirkandrews ... 106 E3
Kirkandrews upon Eden 108 D3
Kirkbampton .. 108 D3
Kirkbean 107 D6
Kirk Bramwith .. 89 C7
Kirkbride 108 D2
Kirkbuddo 135 E5
Kirkburn Borders 121 F5
E Yorks 97 D5
Kirkburton 88 C2
Kirkby Lincs 90 E4
N Yorks 86 E2
Kirkby Fleetham .101 E7
Kirkby Green ... 78 D3
Kirkby-in-Ashfield 76 D5
Kirkby-in-Furness 98 F4
Kirkby la Thorpe .78 E3
Kirkby Lonsdale . 93 B6
Kirkby Malham .. 93 C8
Kirkby Mallory .. 63 D8
Kirkby Malzeard . 94 B5
Kirkby Mills 103 F5
Kirkbymoorside . 102 F4
Kirkby on Bain . 78 C5
Kirkby Overflow . 95 E6
Kirkby Stephen .. 100 D2
Kirkby Thore 99 B8
Kirkby Underwood 65 B7
Kirkby Wharfe .. 95 E8
Kirkcaldy 128 E4
Kirkcambeck ... 108 C5
Kirkcarswell ... 106 E4
Kirkcolm 104 C4
Kirkconnel 113 C7
Kirkconnell 107 C6
Kirkcowan 105 D7
Kirkcudbright .. 106 D3
Kirkdale 85 E4
Kirk Deighton .. 95 D6
Kirk Ella 90 B4
Kirkfieldbank .. 119 E8
Kirkgunzeon ... 107 C5
Kirk Hallam 76 E4
Kirkham Lancs .. 92 F4
N Yorks 96 C3
Kirkhamgate ... 88 B3
Kirk Hammerton .95 D7
Kirkharle 117 F6
Kirkheaton Northumb 110 B3
W Yorks 88 C2
Kirkhill Angus .. 135 C6
Highld 151 G8
Midloth 120 C5
Moray 152 E2
Kirkhope 115 B6
Kirkhouse 121 F6
Kirkiboll 157 D8
Kirkibost 149 G10
Kirkinch 134 E3
Kirkinner 105 D8
Kirkintilloch ... 119 B6
Kirk Ireton 76 D2
Kirkland Cumb .. 98 C2
Cumb 109 F6
Dumfries 113 C7
Dumfries 113 E8
Kirk Langley ... 76 F2
Kirkleatham ... 102 B3
Kirklevington .. 102 D2
Kirkley 69 E8
Kirklington Notts .77 D6
N Yorks 101 F8
Kirklinton 108 C4
Kirkliston 120 B4
Kirkmaiden ... 104 F5
Kirk Merrington .111 F5
Kirkmichael Perth .133 D7
S Ayrs 112 D3
Kirk Michael ... 84 C3
Kirkmuirhill ... 119 E7
Kirknewton Northumb 122 F5
W Loth 120 C4
Kirkney 152 E5
Kirk of Shotts .. 119 C8
Kirkoswald Cumb .108 E5
S Ayrs 112 D2
Kirkpatrick Durham 106 B4
Kirkpatrick-Fleming 108 B2
Kirk Sandall 89 D7
Kirksanton 98 F3
Kirk Smeaton .. 89 C6
Kirkstall 95 F5
Kirkstead 78 C4
Kirkstile 152 E5
Kirkstyle 158 C5
Kirkton Aberds .140 B5
Aberds 153 D6
Angus 134 E4
Angus 134 F4
Borders 115 C8
Dumfries 114 F2
Fife 129 B5
Highld 149 F13
Highld 150 G2

Kirkton continued
Highld 151 B10
Highld 151 F10
Perth 127 C8
S Lanark 114 B2
Stirling 126 D4
Kirktonhill 121 D7
Kirkton of Airlie .134 D3
Kirkton of Auchterhouse .134 F3
Kirkton of Auchterless ..153 D7
Kirkton of Barevan 151 G11
Kirkton of Bourtie 141 B7
Kirkton of Collace 134 F1
Kirkton of Craig .135 D7
Kirkton of Culsalmond .153 E6
Kirkton of Durris .141 E6
Kirkton of Glenbuchat ..140 C2
Kirkton of Glenisla ... 134 C2
Kirkton of Kingoldrum .134 D3
Kirkton of Largo .129 D6
Kirkton of Lethendy 133 E8
Kirkton of Logie Buchan 141 B8
Kirkton of Maryculter ..141 E7
Kirkton of Menmuir 135 C5
Kirkton of Monikie 135 F5
Kirkton of Oyne .141 B5
Kirkton of Rayne .153 F6
Kirkton of Skene .141 D7
Kirkton of Tough .140 C5
Kirktown 153 C10
Kirktown of Alvah 153 B6
Kirktown of Deskford 152 B5
Kirktown of Fetteresso ...141 F7
Kirktown of Mortlach 152 E3
Kirktown of Slains 141 B9
Kirkurd 120 E4
Kirkwall 159 G5
Kirkwhelpington .117 F5
Kirk Yetholm .. 116 B4
Kirmington 90 C5
Kirmond le Mire . 91 E5
Kirn 145 F10
Kirriemuir 134 D3
Kirstead Green . 69 E5
Kirtlebridge ... 108 B2
Kirtleton 115 F5
Kirtling 55 D7
Kirtling Green .. 55 D7
Kirtomy 157 C10
Kirton Lincs ... 79 F6
Notts 77 C6
Suff 57 F6
Kirton End 79 E5
Kirton Holme ... 79 E5
Kirton in Lindsey 90 E3
Kislingbury 52 D4
Kites Hardwick .52 C2
Kittisford 11 B5
Kittle 33 F6
Kitt's Green ... 63 F5
Kitt's Moss 87 F6
Kittybrewster .. 141 D8
Kitwood 26 F4
Kivernoll 49 F6
Kiveton Park ... 89 F5
Knaith 90 F2
Knaith Park ... 90 F2
Knap Corner .. 13 B6
Knaphill 27 D7
Knapp Perth .. 134 F2
Som 11 B8
Knapthorpe ... 77 D7
Knapton Norf .. 81 D9
York 95 D8
Knapton Green .49 D6
Knapwell 54 C4
Knaresborough . 95 D6
Knarsdale 109 D6
Knauchland ... 152 C5
Knaven 153 D8
Knayton 102 F2
Knebworth ... 41 B5
Knedlington .. 89 B8
Kneesall 77 C7
Kneesworth .. 54 E4
Kneeton 77 E7
Knelston 33 F5
Knenhall 75 F6
Knettishall 68 F2
Knightacott .. 21 F5
Knightcote ... 51 D8
Knightley Dale . 62 B2
Knighton Devon . 6 E3
Leicester 64 D2
Staffs 61 B7
Staffs 74 E4
Knighton = Tref-y-Clawdd .. 48 B4
Knightswood ..118 C5
Knightwick 50 D2
Knill 48 C4
Knipton 77 F8
Knitsley 110 E4
Kniveton 76 D2
Knock Argyll ..147 H4
Cumb 100 B1
Moray 152 C5
Knockally 158 H3
Knockan 156 H5
Knockandhu .. 139 B8
Knockando ... 152 D1
Knockando House 152 D2
Knockbain 151 F9
Knockbreck ... 148 B7
Knockbrex ... 106 E3
Knockdee 158 D3
Knockdolian ..104 A5

Knockenkelly ...143 F11
Knockentiber ... 118 F3
Knockespock House 140 B4
Knockfarrel 151 F8
Knockglass 104 D4
Knockholt 29 D5
Knockholt Pound .29 D5
Knockie Lodge .137 C7
Knockin 60 B3
Knockinlaw 118 F4
Knocklearn ... 106 B4
Knocknaha 143 G7
Knocknain 104 C3
Knockrome 144 F4
Knocksharry .. 84 D2
Knodishall 57 C8
Knolls Green .. 74 B5
Knolton 73 F7
Knolton Bryn .. 73 F7
Knook 24 E4
Knossington .. 64 D5
Knott End-on-Sea 92 E3
Knotting 53 C8
Knotting Green . 53 C8
Knottingley ... 89 B6
Knotts Cumb ... 99 B6
Lancs 93 D7
Knotty Ash 86 E2
Knotty Green .. 40 E2
Knowbury 49 B7
Knowe 105 B7
Knowehead ... 113 E6
Knowesgate ... 117 F5
Knowes of Elrick .152 C6
Knoweton 119 D7
Knowhead 153 C9
Knowle Bristol . 23 B8
Devon 10 D2
Devon 11 F5
Devon 20 F3
Shrops 49 B7
W Mid 51 B6
Knowle Green .. 93 F6
Knowle Park ... 94 E3
Knowl Hill 27 B6
Knowlton Dorset . 13 C8
Kent 31 D6
Knowsley 86 E2
Knowstone ... 10 B3
Knox Bridge .. 29 E8
Knucklas 48 B4
Knuston 53 C7
Knutsford 74 B4
Knutton 74 E5
Knypersley ... 75 D5
Kuggar 3 E6
Kyleakin 149 F12
Kyle of Lochalsh .149 F12
Kylerhea 149 F12
Kylesknoydart ..147 B11
Kylesku 156 F5
Kylesmorar ..147 B11
Kylestrome ... 156 F5
Kyllachy House .138 B3
Kynaston 60 B3
Kynnersley ... 61 C6
Kyre Magna .. 49 C8

L
Labost 155 C7
Lacasaidh 155 E8
Lacasdal 155 D9
Laceby 91 D6
Lacey Green .. 39 E8
Lach Dennis .. 74 B4
Lackford 55 B8
Lacock 24 C4
Ladbroke 52 D2
Laddingford .. 29 E7
Lade Bank ... 79 D7
Ladock 4 D3
Lady 159 D7
Ladybank 128 C5
Ladykirk 122 E4
Ladysford 153 B9
La Fontenelle . 16 I2
Laga 147 E9
Lagalochan ... 124 D4
Lagavulin 142 D5
Lagg Argyll ... 144 F4
N Ayrs 143 F10
Laggan Argyll . 142 C3
Highld 137 E5
Highld 138 E2
Highld 147 D10
S Ayrs 112 F2
Lagganulva ... 146 G7
Laide 155 H13
Laigh Fenwick .118 E4
Laigh Glengall .112 C3
Laighmuir 118 E4
Laindon 42 F2
Lair 150 G3
Lairg 157 J8
Lairg Lodge .. 157 J8
Lairgmore 151 H8
Lairg Muir 157 J8
Laisterdyke ... 94 F4
Laithes 108 F4
Lake IoW 15 F6
Wilts 25 F6
Lakenham 68 D5
Lakenheath .. 67 F7
Lakesend 66 E5
Lakeside 99 F5
Laleham 27 C8
Laleston 21 B7
Lamarsh 56 F2
Lamas 81 E8
Lambden 122 E3
Lamberhurst .. 18 B3
Lamberhurst Quarter 18 B3
Lamberton ... 123 D5
Lambeth 28 B4
Lambhill 119 C5
Lambley Northumb .109 D6
Notts 77 E6
Lamborough Hill 38 D4
Lambourn 25 B8
Lambourne End .41 E7
Lambs Green . 28 F3
Lambston ... 44 D4
Lambton 111 D5
Lamerton 6 B2
Lamesley 111 D5

Laminess 159 E7
Lamington Highld 151 D10
S Lanark 120 F2
Lamlash 143 E11
Lamloch 112 E5
Lamonby 108 F4
Lamorna 2 D3
Lamorran 3 B7
Lampardbrook .57 C6
Lampeter = Llanbedr Pont Steffan 46 E4
Lampeter Velfrey 32 C2
Lamphey 32 D1
Lamplugh 98 B2
Lamport 53 B5
Lamyatt 23 F8
Lana 8 E5
Lanark 119 E8
Lancaster 92 C4
Lanchester ... 110 E4
Lancing 17 D5
Landbeach ... 55 C5
Landcross 9 B6
Landerberry ..141 D6
Landford 14 C3
Landford Manor 14 C3
Landimore ... 33 E5
Landkey 20 F4
Landore 33 E7
Landrake 5 D8
Landscove ... 7 C5
Landshipping . 32 C1
Landshipping Quay 32 C1
Landulph 6 C2
Landwade ... 55 C7
Landywood .. 62 D3
Lane 4 C3
Laneast 8 F4
Lane End Bucks . 39 E8
Cumb 98 E3
Dorset 13 E6
Hants 15 B6
IoW 15 F7
Lancs 93 F7
N Yorks 94 F2
Laneham 77 B8
Lanehead Durham .109 E8
Northumb 116 F3
Lane Head Derbys . 75 B8
Durham 101 C6
Gtr Man 86 E4
W Yorks 88 D2
Lanercost 109 C5
Laneshaw Bridge .94 E2
Lane Side 87 B5
Lanfach 35 E6
Langar 77 F7
Langbank 118 B3
Langbar 94 D3
Langburnshiels .115 D8
Langcliffe ... 93 C8
Langdale 157 E9
Langdale End .103 E7
Langdon 8 F4
Langdon Beck .109 F8
Langdon Hills . 42 F2
Langdyke 128 D5
Langenhoe ... 43 C6
Langford C Beds . 54 E2
Devon 10 D5
Essex 42 D4
Notts 77 D8
Oxon 38 D2
Langford Budville 11 B6
Langham Essex . 56 F4
Norf 81 C6
Rutland 64 C5
Suff 56 C3
Langhaugh ... 120 F5
Langho 93 F7
Langholm 115 F6
Langleeford .. 117 B5
Langley Ches E . 75 B6
Hants 14 D5
Herts 41 B5
Kent 30 D2
Northumb 109 C8
Slough 27 B8
Warks 51 C6
W Sus 16 B2
Langley Burrell . 24 B4
Langley Common 76 F2
Langley Heath .. 30 D2
Langley Lower Green 54 F5
Langley Marsh . 11 B5
Langley Park .. 110 E5
Langley Street .69 D6
Langley Upper Green 54 F5
Langney 18 E3
Langold 89 F6
Langore 8 F5
Langport 12 B2
Langrick 79 E5
Langridge ... 24 C2
Langridge Ford . 9 B7
Langrigg 107 E8
Langrish 15 B8
Langsett 88 D3
Langshaw ... 121 F8
Langside 127 C6
Langskaill ... 159 D5
Langstone Hants . 15 D8
Newport 35 E7
Langthorne .. 101 E7
Langthorpe .. 95 C6
Langthwaite . 101 D5
Langtoft E Yorks . 97 C6
Lincs 65 C8
Langton Durham .101 C6
Lincs 78 C5
Lincs 79 C6
N Yorks 96 C3
Langton by Wragby 78 B4
Langton Green Kent 18 B2
Suff 56 B5
Langton Herring 12 F4
Langton Matravers . 13 G8
Langtree 9 C6
Langwathby ..109 F5
Langwell House .158 H3
Langwell Lodge 156 J4

Langwith 76 C5
Langwith Junction 76 C5
Langworth ... 78 B3
Lanivet 4 C5
Lanjeth 3 D8
Lanlivery 5 D5
Lanner 3 C6
Lanreath 5 D6
Lansallos 5 D6
Lansdown 37 B6
Lanteglos Highway 5 D6
Lanton Borders .116 B2
Northumb 122 F5
Lapford 10 D2
Laphroaig ... 142 D4
Lapley 62 C2
Lapworth 51 B6
Larachbeg ...147 G9
Larbert 127 F7
Larden Green . 74 D2
Largie 152 E6
Largiemore ..145 E8
Largoward ... 129 D6
Largs 118 D2
Largybeg 143 F11
Largymore ..143 F11
Larkfield 118 B2
Larkhall 119 D7
Larkhill 25 E6
Larling 68 F2
Larriston ... 115 E8
Lartington .. 101 C5
Lary 140 D2
Lasham 26 E4
Lashenden .. 30 E2
Lassington .. 36 B4
Lassodie 128 E3
Lastingham .. 103 E5
Latcham 23 E6
Latchford Herts . 41 B6
Warr 86 F4
Latchingdon . 42 D4
Latchley 6 B2
Lately Common 86 E4
Lathbury 53 E6
Latheron 158 G3
Latheronwheel 158 G3
Latheronwheel House 158 G3
Lathones 129 D6
Latimer 40 E3
Latteridge ... 36 F3
Lattiford 12 B4
Latton 37 E7
Latton Bush . 41 D7
Lauchintilly ..141 C6
Lauder 121 E8
Laugharne ... 32 C4
Laughterton .. 77 B8
Laughton E Sus . 18 D2
Leics 64 F3
Lincs 78 F3
Lincs 90 E2
Laughton Common 89 F6
Laughton en le Morthen 89 F6
Launcells 8 D4
Launceston .. 8 F5
Launton 39 B6
Laurencekirk .135 B7
Laurieston Dumfries 106 C3
Falk 120 B2
Lavendon 53 D7
Lavenham 56 E3
Laverhay 114 E4
Laversdale .. 108 C4
Laverstock .. 25 F6
Laverstoke .. 26 E2
Laverton Glos . 51 F5
N Yorks 94 B5
Som 24 D2
Lavister 73 D7
Law 119 D8
Lawers Perth . 127 B6
Perth 127 C5
Lawford 56 F4
Lawhitton ... 8 F5
Lawkland ... 93 C7
Lawley 61 D6
Lawnhead ... 62 B2
Lawrenny ... 32 D1
Lawshall 56 D2
Lawton 49 D6
Laxey 84 D4
Laxfield 57 B6
Laxfirth Shetland .160 H6
Shetland 160 J6
Laxford Bridge .156 E5
Laxo 160 G6
Laxobigging . 160 F6
Laxton E Yorks . 89 B8
N Nhants 65 E6
Notts 77 C7
Laycock 94 E3
Layer Breton . 43 C5
Layer de la Haye 43 C5
Layer Marney . 43 C5
Layham 56 E4
Laylands Green 25 C8
Laytham ... 96 F3
Layton 92 F3
Lazenby 102 B3
Lazonby ... 108 F5
Lea Derbys .. 76 D3
Hereford 36 B3
Lincs 90 F2
Shrops 60 D4
Shrops 60 F3
Wilts 37 F6
Leabrooks .. 76 D4
Leac a Li ... 154 H6
Leachkin 151 G9
Leadburn ... 120 D5
Leaden Roding .42 C1
Leadgate Cumb .109 E7
Durham 110 D4
T&W 110 D4
Leadhills ... 113 C8
Leafield 38 C3
Leagrave 40 B3
Leake 102 F2
Leake Commonside 79 D6
Lealholm ... 103 D5
Lealt Argyll . 124 E3
Highld 149 B10
Lea Marston . 63 E6

Leamington Hastings 52 C2
Leamonsley ... 62 D5
Leamside ... 111 E6
Leanaig 151 F8
Leargybreck ..144 F4
Leasgill 99 F6
Leasingham .. 78 E3
Leasingthorne 101 B7
Leasowe 85 E3
Leatherhead . 28 D2
Leatherhead Common 28 D2
Leathley 94 E5
Leaton 60 C4
Lea Town 92 F4
Leaveland ... 30 D4
Leavening ... 96 C3
Leaves Green . 28 C5
Leazes 110 D4
Lebberston ..103 F8
Lechlade-on-Thames 38 E2
Leck 93 B6
Leckford 25 F8
Leckfurin 157 D10
Leckgruinart .142 B3
Leckhampstead Bucks 52 F5
W Berks 26 B2
Leckhampstead Thicket 26 B2
Leckhampton . 37 C6
Leckie 150 E3
Leckmelm ... 150 B4
Leckwith 22 B3
Leconfield ... 97 E6
Ledaig 124 B5
Ledburn 40 B2
Ledbury 50 F2
Ledcharrie .. 126 B4
Ledgemoor .. 49 D6
Ledicot 49 C6
Ledmore 156 H5
Lednagullin ..157 C10
Ledsham Ches W . 73 B7
W Yorks 89 B5
Ledston 88 B5
Ledston Luck . 95 F7
Ledwell 38 B4
Lee Argyll ... 146 J7
Devon 20 E3
Hants 14 C4
Lancs 93 D5
Shrops 73 F8
Leeans 160 J5
Leebotten ... 160 L6
Leebotwood . 60 E4
Lee Brockhurst 60 B5
Leece 92 C2
Leechpool ... 44 D4
Lee Clump ... 40 D2
Leeds Kent .. 30 D2
W Yorks 95 F5
Leedstown .. 2 C5
Leek 75 D6
Leekbrook .. 75 D6
Leek Wootton . 51 C7
Lee Mill 6 D4
Leeming 101 F7
Leeming Bar .101 E7
Lee Moor ... 6 C3
Lee-on-the-Solent 15 D6
Lees Derbys .. 76 F2
Gtr Man 87 D7
W Yorks 94 F3
Leeswood ... 73 C6
Legbourne ... 91 F7
Legerwood ..121 E8
Legsby 90 F5
Leicester ... 64 D2
Leicester Forest East 64 D2
Leigh Dorset . 12 D4
Glos 37 B5
Gtr Man 86 D4
Kent 29 E6
Shrops 60 D3
Sur 28 E3
Wilts 37 E7
Worcs 50 D2
Leigh Beck ... 42 F4
Leigh Common 12 B5
Leigh Delamere 24 B3
Leigh Green .. 19 B6
Leigh on Sea . 42 F4
Leigh Park .. 15 D8
Leigh Sinton . 50 D2
Leighswood .. 62 D4
Leighterton .. 37 E5
Leighton N Yorks .94 B4
Powys 60 D2
Shrops 61 D6
Som 24 E2
Leighton Bromswold .. 54 B2
Leighton Buzzard 40 B2
Leigh upon Mendip 23 E8
Leigh Woods .. 23 B7
Leinthall Earls .49 C6
Leinthall Starkes .49 C6
Leintwardine .. 49 B6
Leire 64 E2
Leirinmore ..156 C7
Leiston 57 C8
Leitfie 134 E2
Leith 121 B5
Leitholm 122 E3
Lelant 2 C4
Lelley 97 F8
Lem Hill 50 B2
Lemington .. 110 C4
Lemington Hall .117 C7
Lempitlaw ... 122 F3
Lenchwick .. 50 E5
Lendalfoot ... 112 F1
Lendrick Lodge 126 D4
Lenham 30 D2
Lenham Heath . 30 E3
Lennel 122 E4
Lennoxtown ..119 B6
Lenton Lincs .. 78 F3
Nottingham 77 F5
Lentran 151 G8
Lenwade 68 C3
Leny House .. 126 D5
Lenzie 119 B6
Leoch 134 F3

Leochel-Cushnie .140 C4
Leominster ... 49 D6
Leonard Stanley 37 D5
Leorin 142 D4
Lepe 15 E5
Lephin 148 D6
Lephinchapel .145 D8
Lephinmore ..145 D8
Le Planel 16 I2
Leppington .. 96 C3
Lepton 88 C3
Lerryn 5 D6
Lerwick 160 J6
Lesbury 117 C8
Le Skerne Haughton 101 C8
Leslie Aberds .140 B4
Fife 128 D4
Lesmahagow ..119 F8
Lesnewth 8 E3
Lessendrum ..152 D5
Lessingham .. 69 B6
Lessonhall .. 108 D2
Leswalt 104 C4
Letchmore Heath .40 E4
Letchworth .. 54 F3
Letcombe Bassett 38 F3
Letcombe Regis 38 F3
Letham Angus .135 E5
Falk 127 F7
Fife 128 C5
Perth 128 B3
Letham Grange .135 E6
Lethenty 153 D8
Letheringham . 57 D6
Letheringsett . 81 D6
Lettaford 10 F2
Lettan 159 D8
Letterewe ...150 D2
Letterfearn ..149 F13
Letterfinlay ..137 E5
Lettermorar ..147 C10
Lettermore .. 146 G7
Letters 150 C4
Letterston .. 44 C4
Lettoch Highld .139 C6
Highld 151 H13
Letton Hereford . 48 E5
Hereford 49 B5
Thurrock 29 B7
Lingague 84 E2
Lingards Wood . 87 C8
Lingbob 94 F3
Lingdale 102 C4
Lingen 49 C5
Lingfield 28 E4
Lingreabhagh .154 J5
Lingwood ... 69 D6
Linicro 149 B8
Linkenholt .. 25 D8
Linkhill 18 C5
Linkinhorne . 5 B8
Linklater 159 K5
Linksness ...159 H3
Linktown ... 128 E4
Linley 60 E3
Linley Green . 49 D8
Linlithgow ..120 B3
Linlithgow Bridge 120 B2
Linshiels 116 D4
Linsiadar ... 154 D7
Linsidemore .151 B8
Linslade 40 B2
Linstead Parva 57 B7
Linstock 108 D4
Linthwaite .. 88 C2
Lintlaw 122 D4
Lintmill 152 B5
Linton Borders .116 B3
Cambs 55 E6
Derbys 63 C6
Hereford 36 B3
Kent 29 E8
N Yorks 94 C2
W Yorks 95 E6
Linton-on-Ouse .95 C7
Linwood Hants . 14 D2
Lincs 90 F5
Renfs 118 C4
Lionacleit 148 D2
Lional 155 A10
Liphook 27 F6
Liscard 85 E4
Liscombe 21 F7
Liskeard 5 C7
L'Islet 16 I2
Liss 15 B8
Lissett 97 D7
Liss Forest .. 15 B8
Lissington .. 90 F5
Lisvane 35 F5
Liswerry 35 F7
Litcham 67 C8
Litchborough . 52 D4
Litchfield ... 26 D2
Litherland .. 85 E4
Litlington Cambs . 54 E4
E Sus 18 E2
Little Abington . 55 E6
Little Addington 53 B7
Little Alne 51 C6
Little Altcar . 85 D4
Little Asby .. 100 D1
Little Assynt .156 G4
Little Aston . 62 D4
Little Atherfield 15 F5
Little Ayre .. 159 J4
Little-ayre .. 160 G5
Little Ayton . 102 C3
Little Baddow . 42 D3
Little Badminton 37 F5
Little Ballinluig .133 D6
Little Bampton 108 D2
Little Bardfield . 55 F7
Little Barford . 54 D2
Little Barningham 81 D7
Little Barrington 38 C2
Little Barrow . 73 B8
Little Barugh . 96 B3
Little Bavington .117 F6
Little Bealings . 57 E6
Littlebeck .. 103 D6
Little Bedwyn . 25 C7
Little Bentley . 43 B7
Little Berkhamsted 41 D5
Little Billing . 53 C6
Little Birch . 49 F7

Letty Green .. 41 C5
Letwell 89 F6
Leuchars 129 B6
Leuchars House 152 B2
Leumrabhagh .155 F8
Levan 118 B2
Levanap 160 G6
Levedale 62 C2
Leven E Yorks . 97 E7
Fife 129 D6
Levencorroch .143 F11
Levens 99 F6
Levens Green . 41 B6
Levenshulme . 87 E6
Levenwick ...160 L6
Leverburgh = An t-Ob .. 154 J5
Leverington .. 66 C4
Leverton 79 E7
Leverton Highgate 79 E7
Leverton Lucasgate 79 E7
Leverton Outgate 79 E7
Le Villocq ... 16 I2
Levington ... 57 F6
Levisham ... 103 E6
Levishie 137 C7
Lew 38 D3
Lewannick ... 8 F4
Lewdown 9 F6
Lewes 17 C8
Leweston ... 44 C4
Lewisham .. 28 B4
Lewiston ... 137 B8
Lewistown .. 34 F3
Lewknor 39 E7
Leworthy Devon . 9 D5
Devon 21 F5
Lewtrenchard . 9 F6
Lexden 43 B5
Ley Aberds ...140 C4
Corn 5 C6
Leybourne .. 29 D7
Leyburn 101 E6
Leyfields 63 D6
Leyhill 40 D2
Leyland 86 B3
Leylodge 141 C6
Leymoor 88 C2
Leys Aberds ..153 C10
Perth 134 F2
Leys Castle ..151 G9
Leys of Cossans 134 E3
Leysmill 135 E6
Leysters Pole . 49 C7
Leyton 41 F6
Leytonstone . 41 F6
Lezant 5 B8
Leziate 67 C6
Lhanbryde .. 152 B2
Liatrie 150 H5
Libanus 34 B3
Libberton ...120 E2
Liberton 121 C5
Liceasto 154 H6
Lichfield ... 62 D5
Lickey 50 B4
Lickey End .. 50 B4
Lickfold 16 B3
Liddel 159 K5
Liddesdale .. 130 D1
Liddington .. 38 F2
Lidgate 55 D8
Lidget 89 D7
Lidget Green . 94 F4
Lidgett 77 C6
Lidlington .. 53 F7
Lidstone ... 38 B3
Lieurary ... 158 D2
Liff 134 F3
Lifton 9 F5
Liftondown .. 9 F5
Lighthorne .. 51 D8
Lightwater .. 27 C7
Lightwood .. 75 E6
Lightwood Green Ches E .. 74 E3
Wrex 73 E7

Lilbourne ... 52 B3
Lilburn Tower .117 B6
Lilleshall ... 61 C7
Lilley Herts .. 40 B4
W Berks 26 B2
Lilliesleaf .. 115 B8
Lillingstone Dayrell . 52 F5
Lillingstone Lovell. 52 E5
Lillington Dorset . 12 C4
Warks 51 C8
Lilliput 13 E8
Lilstock 22 E3
Lilyhurst ... 61 C7
Limbury 40 B3
Limebrook .. 49 C5
Limefield ... 87 C6
Limekilnburn .119 D7
Limekilns .. 128 F2
Limerigg ... 119 B8
Limerstone . 14 F5
Limington .. 12 B3
Limpenhoe .. 69 D6
Limpley Stoke 24 C2
Limpsfield .. 28 D5
Limpsfield Chart 28 D5
Linby 76 D5
Linchmere .. 27 F6
Lincoln 78 B2
Lincomb ... 50 C3
Lincombe ... 6 D5
Lindale 99 F6
Lindal in Furness 92 B2
Lindean 121 F7
Lindfield ... 17 B7
Lindford ... 27 F6
Lindifferon .128 C5
Lindley 88 C2
Lindley Green . 94 E5
Lindores ... 128 C4
Lindridge .. 49 C8
Lindsell ... 42 B2
Lindsey ... 56 E3
Linford Hants . 14 D2

Little Blakenham .. 56 E5
Little Blencow .. 108 F4
Little Bollington .. 86 F5
Little Bookham .. 28 D2
Littleborough
  Gtr Man 87 C7
  Notts 90 F2
Littlebourne 31 D6
Little Bowden 64 F4
Little Bradley 55 D7
Little Brampton 60 F3
Little Brechin 135 C5
Littlebredy 12 F3
Little Brickhill 53 F7
Little Brington 52 C4
Little Bromley 43 B6
Little Broughton .. 107 F7
Little Budworth ... 74 C2
Little Burstead 42 E2
Littlebury 55 F6
Littlebury Green ... 55 F5
Little Bytham 65 C7
Little Carlton
  Lincs 91 F7
  Notts 77 D7
Little Casterton ... 65 D7
Little Cawthorpe .. 91 F7
Little Chalfont 40 E2
Little Chart 30 E3
Little Chesterford .. 55 E6
Little Cheverell ... 24 D4
Little Chishill 54 F5
Little Clacton 43 C7
Little Clifton 98 B2
Little Colp 153 D7
Little Comberton .. 50 E4
Little Common 18 E4
Little Compton 51 F7
Little Cornard 56 F2
Little Cowarne 49 D8
Little Coxwell 38 E2
Little Crakehall .. 101 E7
Little Cressingham 67 D8
Little Crosby 85 D4
Little Dalby 64 C4
Little Dawley 61 D6
Littledean 36 C3
Little Dens 153 D10
Little Dewchurch .. 49 F7
Little Downham 66 F5
Little Driffield ... 97 D6
Little Dunham 67 C8
Little Dunkeld ... 133 E7
Little Dunmow 42 B2
Little Easton 42 B2
Little Eaton 76 E3
Little Eccleston ... 92 E4
Little Ellingham .. 68 E3
Little End 41 D8
Little Eversden ... 54 D4
Little Faringdon .. 38 D2
Little Fencote ... 101 E7
Little Fenton 95 F8
Littleferry 151 B11
Little Finborough .. 56 D4
Little Fransham ... 68 C2
Little Gaddesden .. 40 C2
Little Gidding 65 F8
Little Glemham 57 D7
Little Glenshee .. 133 F6
Little Gransden ... 54 D3
Little Green 24 E2
Little Grimsby 91 E7
Little Gruinard .. 150 C2
Little Habton 96 B3
Little Hadham 41 B7
Little Hale 78 E4
Little Hallingbury 41 C7
Littleham Devon.... 9 B6
  Devon 10 F5
Little Hampden 40 D1
Littlehampton 16 D4
Little Harrowden .. 53 B6
Little Haseley 39 D6
Little Hatfield 97 E7
Little Hautbois ... 81 E8
Little Haven 44 D3
Little Hay 62 D5
Little Hayfield ... 87 F8
Little Haywood 62 B4
Little Heath 63 F7
Littlehempston 7 C6
Little Hereford ... 49 C7
Little Horkesley .. 56 F3
Little Horsted 17 C8
Little Horton 94 F4
Little Horwood 53 F5
Littlehoughton .. 117 C6
Little Houghton
  S Yorks. 88 D5
  W Nhants 53 D6
Little Hucklow ... 75 B8
Little Hulton 86 D5
Little Humber 91 B5
Little Hungerford .. 26 B3
Little Irchester ... 53 C7
Little Kimble 39 D8
Little Kineton ... 51 D8
Little Kingshill .. 40 E1
Little Langdale ... 99 D5
Little Langford ... 25 F5
Little Laver 41 D8
Little Leigh 74 B3
Little Leighs 42 C3
Little Lever 87 D5
Little London Bucks 39 C6
  E Sus 18 D2
  Hants 25 E8
  Hants 26 D4
  Lincs 66 B2
  Lincs 66 B4
  Norf 81 E7
  Powys 59 F7
Little Longstone .. 75 B8
Little Lynturk 140 C4
Little Malvern 50 E2
Little Maplestead .. 56 F2
Little Marcle 49 F8
Little Marlow 40 F1
Little Marsden ... 93 F8
Little Massingham 80 E3
Littlemill Aberds. 140 E2
  E Ayrs. 112 C4
  Highld 151 F12
  Northumb 117 C8
Little Mill 35 D7

Little Milton 39 D6
Little Missenden .. 40 E2
Littlemoor 12 F4
Littlemore 39 D5
Little Musgrave .. 100 C2
Little Ness 60 C4
Little Neston 73 B6
Little Newcastle .. 44 C4
Little Newsham ... 101 C6
Little Oakley Essex 43 B8
  N Nhants 65 F5
Little Orton 108 D3
Little Ouseburn .. 95 C7
Littleover 76 F3
Little Paxton 54 C2
Little Petherick 4 B4
Little Pitlurg ... 152 D4
Little Plumpton ... 92 F3
Little Plumstead .. 69 C6
Little Ponton 78 F2
Littleport 67 F5
Little Raveley 54 B3
Little Reedness ... 90 B2
Little Ribston 95 D6
Little Rissington .. 38 C1
Little Ryburgh ... 81 E5
Little Ryle 117 C6
Little Salkeld ... 109 F5
Little Sampford ... 55 F7
Little Sandhurst .. 27 C6
Little Saxham 55 C8
Little Scatwell .. 150 F6
Little Sessay 95 B7
Little Shelford ... 54 D5
Little Singleton .. 92 F3
Little
  Skillymarno ... 153 C9
Little Smeaton ... 89 C6
Little Snoring 81 D5
Little Sodbury 36 F4
Little Somborne .. 25 F8
Little Somerford .. 37 F6
Little Stainforth .. 93 C8
Little Stainton .. 101 B8
Little Stanney ... 73 B8
Little Staughton .. 54 C2
Little Steeping ... 79 C7
Little Stoke 75 F6
Littlestone on Sea 19 C7
Little Stonham ... 56 C5
Little Stretton Leics 64 D3
  Shrops. 60 E4
Little Strickland .. 99 C7
Little Stukeley ... 54 B3
Little Sutton 73 B7
Little Tew 38 B3
Little Thetford ... 55 B6
Little Thirkleby .. 95 B7
Littlethorpe Leics 64 E2
  N Yorks. 95 C6
Little Thurlow ... 55 D7
Little Thurrock ... 29 B7
Littleton Ches W 73 C8
  Hants 26 F2
  Perth 134 F2
  Som 23 F6
  Sur 27 C8
  Sur 27 E7
Littleton Drew ... 37 F5
Littleton-on-
  Severn 36 F2
Littleton Pannell .. 24 D5
Little Torboll ... 151 B10
Little Torrington .. 9 C6
Little Totham 42 C4
Little Toux 152 C5
Littletown 111 E6
Little Town Cumb 98 C4
  Lancs 93 F6
Little Urswick ... 92 B2
Little Wakering ... 43 F5
Little Walden 55 E6
Little Waldingfield 56 E3
Little Walsingham 80 D5
Little Waltham ... 42 C3
Little Warley 42 E2
Little Weighton .. 97 F5
Little Weldon 65 F6
Little Welnetham .. 56 C2
Little Wenlock ... 61 D6
Little Whittingham
  Green 57 B6
Littlewick Green .. 27 B6
Little Wilbraham .. 55 D6
Little Wishford ... 25 F5
Little Witley 50 C2
Little Wittenham .. 39 E5
Little Wolford ... 51 F7
Littleworth Bedford. 53 E8
  Glos. 37 D5
  Oxon 38 E3
  Staffs. 62 C4
  Worcs 50 D3
Little Wratting ... 55 E7
Little Wymington .. 53 C7
Little Wymondley .. 41 B5
Little Wyrley 62 D4
Little Yeldham ... 55 F8
Litton Derbys. ... 75 B8
  N Yorks. 94 B2
  Som 23 D7
Litton Cheney ... 12 E3
Liurbost 155 E8
Liverpool 85 E4
Liverpool Airport 86 F2
Liversedge 88 B3
Liverton Devon....... 7 B6
  Redcar 103 C5
Livingston 120 C3
Livingston
  Village 120 C3
Lixwm 73 B5
Lizard 3 E6
Llaingoch 82 C2
Llaithddu 59 F7
Llan 59 D5
Llanaber 58 C3
Llanaelhaearn 70 C4
Llanafan 47 B5
Llanafan-fawr 47 D8
Llanallgo 82 C4
Llanandras
  = Presteigne. .. 48 C5
Llanarmon 70 D5
Llanarmon Dyffryn
  Ceiriog 73 F5
Llanarmon-yn-Ial . 73 D5
Llanarth Ceredig. 46 D3
  Mon 35 C7

Llanarthne 33 B6
Llanasa 85 F2
Llanbabo 82 C3
Llanbadarn Fawr . 58 F3
Llanbadarn Fynydd 48 B3
Llanbadarn-y-
  Garreg 48 E3
Llanbadoc 35 E7
Llanbadrig 82 B3
Llanbeder 35 E7
Llanbedr Gwyn ... 71 E6
  Powys 35 B6
  Powys 48 E3
Llanbedr-Dyffryn-
  Clwyd 72 D5
Llanbedrgoch 82 C5
Llanbedrog 70 D4
Llanbedr Pont Steffan
  = Lampeter. 46 E4
Llanbedr-y-cennin 83 E7
Llanberis 83 E6
Llanbethery 22 C2
Llanbister 48 B3
Llanblethian 21 B8
Llanboidy 32 B3
Llanbradach 35 E5
Llanbrynmair 59 D5
Llancarfan 22 B2
Llancayo 35 D7
Llancloudy 36 B1
Llancynfelyn 58 E3
Llandaff 22 B3
Llandanwg 71 E6
Llandarcy 33 E8
Llandawke 32 C3
Llanddaniel Fab .. 82 D4
Llanddarog 33 C6
Llanddeiniol 46 B4
Llanddeiniolen ... 82 E5
Llandderfel 72 F3
Llanddeusant
  Anglesey 82 C3
  Carms 34 B1
Llanddew 48 F2
Llanddewi 33 F5
Llanddewi-Brefi .. 47 D5
Llanddewi'r Cwm . 48 E2
Llanddewi
  Rhydderch 35 C7
Llanddewi Velfrey 32 C2
Llanddoged 83 E8
Llanddona 83 D5
Llanddowror 32 C3
Llanddulas 72 B3
Llanddwywe 71 E6
Llanddyfynan 82 D4
Llandefaelog Fach 48 F2
Llandefaelog-
  tre'r'graig 35 B5
Llandefalle 48 F3
Llandegai 83 D5
Llandegfan 83 D5
Llandegla 73 D5
Llandegley 48 C3
Llandegveth 35 E7
Llandegwning 70 D3
Llandeilo 33 B7
Llandeilo Graban . 48 E2
Llandeilo'r Fan .. 47 F7
Llandeloy 44 C3
Llandenny 35 D8
Llandevenny 35 F8
Llandewednock 3 E6
Llandewi
  Ystradenny 48 C3
Llandinabo 36 B2
Llandinam 59 F7
Llandissilio 32 B2
Llandogo 36 D2
Llandough V Glam 21 B8
  V Glam 22 B3
Llandovery
  = Llanymddyfri 47 F6
Llandow 21 B8
Llandre Carms 47 E5
  Ceredig 58 F3
Llandrillo 72 F4
Llandrillo-yn-
  Rhos 83 C8
Llandrindod
  = Llandrindod
  Wells 48 C2
Llandrindod Wells
  = Llandrindod .. 48 C2
Llandrinio 60 C2
Llandudno 83 C7
Llandudno Junction
  = Cyffordd
  Llandudno 83 D7
Llandwrog 82 F4
Llandybie 33 C7
Llandyfaelog 33 C5
Llandyfan 33 C7
Llandyfriog 46 E2
Llandyfrydog 82 C4
Llandygwydd 45 E4
Llandynan 73 E5
Llandyrnog 72 C5
Llandysilio 60 C2
Llandyssil 59 E8
Llandysul 46 E3
Llanedeyrn 35 F6
Llanedi 33 D6
Llaneglwys 48 F2
Llanegryn 58 D2
Llanegwad 33 B6
Llaneilian 82 B4
Llanelian-yn-Rhos 83 D8
Llanelidan 72 D5
Llanelieu 48 F3
Llanellen 35 C7
Llanelli 33 E6
Llanelltyd 58 C4
Llanelly 35 C6
Llanelly Hill 35 C6
Llanelwedd 48 D2
Llanelwy
  = StAsaph. 72 B4
Llanenddwyn 71 E6
Llanengan 70 E3
Llanerchymedd ... 82 C4
Llanerfyl 59 D7
Llanfachraeth 82 C3
Llanfachreth 71 E8
Llanfaelog 82 D3
Llanfaelrhys 70 E3
Llanfaenor 35 C8
Llanfaes Anglesey 83 D6
  Powys 34 B4

Llanfaethlu 82 C3
Llanfaglan 82 E4
Llanfair 71 E6
Llanfair-ar-y-bryn 47 F7
Llanfair
  Caereinion 59 D8
Llanfair Clydogau 46 D5
Llanfair-Dyffryn-
  Clwyd 72 D5
Llanfairfechan ... 83 D6
Llanfair
  Kilgheddin 35 D7
Llanfair-Nant-
  Gwyn 45 F3
Llanfairpwllgwyngyll
  .... 82 D5
Llanfair Talhaiarn 72 B3
Llanfair Waterdine 48 B4
Llanfair-ym-Muallt
  = Builth Wells. 48 D2
Llanfairyneubwll . 82 D3
Llanfairynghornwy 82 B3
Llanfallteg 32 C2
Llanfaredd 48 D2
Llanfarian 46 B4
Llanfechain 59 B8
Llanfechan 47 D8
Llanfechell 82 B3
Llanfendigaid 58 D2
Llanferres 73 C5
Llan Ffestiniog .. 71 C8
Llanfflewyn 82 C3
Llanfihangel-
  ararth 46 F3
Llanfihangel-
  Crucorney 35 B7
Llanfihangel Glyn
  Myfyr 72 E3
Llanfihangel Nant
  Bran 47 F8
Llanfihangel-nant-
  Melan 48 D3
Llanfihangel
  Rhydithon 48 C3
Llanfihangel
  Rogiet 35 F8
Llanfihangel Tal-y-
  llyn 35 B5
Llanfihangel-uwch-
  Gwili 33 B5
Llanfihangel-y-
  Creuddyn 47 B5
Llanfihangel-yn-
  Ngwynfa 59 C7
Llanfihangel yn
  Nhowyn 82 D3
Llanfihangel-
  ypennant
  Gwyn 58 D3
  Gwyn 71 C6
Llanfihangel-
  ytraethau 71 D6
Llanfilo 48 F3
Llanfoist 35 C6
Llanfor 72 F3
Llanfrechfa 35 E7
Llanfrothen 71 C7
Llanfrynach 34 B4
Llanfwrog Anglesey 82 C3
  Denb 72 D5
Llanfyllin 59 C8
Llanfynydd Carms 33 B6
  Flint 73 D6
Llanfyrnach 45 F4
Llangadfan 59 C7
Llangadog 33 B8
Llangadwaladr
  Anglesey 82 E3
  Powys 73 F5
Llangaffo 82 E4
Llangain 32 C4
Llangammarch
  Wells 47 E8
Llangan 21 B8
Llangarron 36 B2
Llangasty Tallyllyn 35 B5
Llangathen 33 B6
Llangattock 35 C6
Llangattock
  Lingoed 35 B7
Llangattock nigh
  Usk. 35 C7
Llangattock-Vibon-
  Avel 36 C1
Llangedwyn 59 B8
Llangefni 82 D4
Llangeinor 34 F3
Llangeitho 46 D5
Llangeler 46 F2
Llangelynin 58 D2
Llangendeirne 33 C5
Llangennech 33 E6
Llangenny 35 C6
Llangernyw 83 E8
Llangian 70 E3
Llanglydwen 32 B2
Llangoed 83 D6
Llangoedmor 45 E3
Llangollen 73 E6
Llangolman 32 B2
Llangors 35 F6
Llangovan 36 D1
Llangower 72 F3
Llangrannog 46 D2
Llangristiolus ... 82 D4
Llangrove 36 C2
Llangua 35 B7
Llangunllo 48 B4
Llangunnor 33 C5
Llangurig 47 B8
Llangwm Conwy ... 72 E3
  Mon 35 D8
  Pembs 44 E4
Llangwnnadl 70 D3
Llangwyfan 72 C5
Llangwyfan-isaf . 82 E3
Llangwyllog 82 D4
Llangwyryfon 46 B4
Llangybi Ceredig . 46 D5
  Gwyn 70 C5
  Mon 35 E7
Llangyfelach 33 E7
Llangynhafal 72 C5
Llangynidr 35 C5
Llangyniew 59 D8
Llangynin 32 C3
Llangynog Carms . 32 C4
  Powys 59 B7
Llangynwyd 34 F2

Llanhamlach 34 B4
Llanharan 34 F4
Llanharry 34 F4
Llanhennock 35 E7
Llanhilleth
  = Llanhilleth. . 35 D6
Llanidloes 59 F6
Llaniestyn 70 D3
Llanifyny 59 F5
Llanigon 48 F4
Llanilar 47 B5
Llanilid 34 F3
Llanilltud Fawr
  = Llantwit Major 21 C8
Llanishen Cardiff . 35 F5
  Mon 36 D1
Llanllawddog 33 B5
Llanllechid 83 E6
Llanllowell 35 E7
Llanllugan 59 D7
Llanllwch 32 C4
Llanllwchaiarn ... 59 E8
Llanllwni 46 F3
Llanllyfni 82 F4
Llanmadoc 33 E5
Llanmaes 21 C8
Llanmartin 35 F7
Llanmihangel 21 B8
Llanmorlais 33 E5
Llannefydd 72 B3
Llannon 33 D6
Llannor 70 D4
Llanover 35 D7
Llanpumsaint 33 B5
Llanreithan 44 C3
Llanrhaeadr 72 C4
Llanrhaeadr-ym-
  Mochnant 59 B8
Llanrhian 44 B3
Llanrhidian 33 E5
Llanrhos 83 C7
Llanrhyddlad 82 C3
Llanrhystud 46 C4
Llanrosser 48 F4
Llanrothal 36 C1
Llanrug 82 E5
Llanrumney 35 F6
Llanrwst 83 E8
Llansadurnen 32 C3
Llansadwrn
  Anglesey 83 D5
  Carms 47 F5
Llansaint 32 D4
Llansamlet 33 E7
Llansanffraid-ym-
  Mechain 60 B2
Llansannan 72 C3
Llansannor 21 B8
Llansantffraed
  Ceredig 46 C4
  Powys 35 B5
Llansantffraed
  Cwmdeuddwr. ... 47 C8
Llansantffraed-in-
  Elvel 48 D2
Llansawel 46 F5
Llansilin 60 B2
Llansoy 35 D8
Llanspyddid 34 B4
Llanstadwell 44 E4
Llansteffan 32 C4
Llanstephan 48 E3
Llantarnam 35 E7
Llanteg 32 C2
Llanthony 35 B6
Llantilio
  Crossenny 35 C7
Llantilio
  Pertholey 35 C7
Llantood 45 E3
Llantrisant Anglesey 82 C3
  Mon 35 E7
  Rhondda 34 F4
Llantrithyd 22 B2
Llantwit Fardre .. 34 F4
Llantwit Major
  = Llanilltud Fawr 21 C8
Llanuwchllyn 72 F2
Llanvaches 35 E8
Llanvair Discoed . 35 E8
Llanvapley 35 C7
Llanvetherine ... 35 C7
Llanveynoe 48 F5
Llanvihangel
  Gobion 35 C7
Llanvihangel-Ystern-
  Llewern 35 C8
Llanwarne 36 B2
Llanwddyn 59 C7
Llanwenog 46 E3
Llanwern 35 F7
Llanwinio 32 B3
Llanwnda Gwyn ... 82 F4
  Pembs 44 B4
Llanwnnen 46 E4
Llanwnog 59 E7
Llanwrda 47 F6
Llanwrin 58 D4
Llanwrthwl 47 C8
Llanwrtud
  = Llanwrtyd Wells 47 E7
Llanwrtyd 47 E7
Llanwrtyd Wells
  = Llanwrtud 47 E7
Llanwyddelan 59 D7
Llanyblodwel 60 B2
Llanybri 32 C4
Llanybydder 46 E4
Llanycefn 32 B1
Llanychaer 44 B4
Llanycil 72 F3
Llanycrwys 46 E5
Llanymawddwy ... 59 C6
Llanymddyfri
  = Llandovery ... 47 F6
Llanymynech 60 B2
Llanynghenedl ... 82 C3
Llanynys 72 C5
Llan-y-pwll 73 D7
Llanyre 48 C2
Llanystumdwy.... 71 D5
Llanywern 35 B5
Llawhaden 32 C1
Llawnt 73 F6
Llawr Dref 70 E3
Llawryglyn 59 E6

Llay 73 D7
Llechcynfarwy 82 C3
Llecheiddior 71 C5
Llechfaen 34 B4
Llechryd Caerph.. 35 C5
  Ceredig 45 E4
Llechrydau 73 F6
Llechwedd 59 E8
Lledrod 46 B5
Llenmerewig 59 E8
Llethrid 33 E6
Llidiad Nenog 46 F4
Llidiardau 72 F2
Llidiart-y-parc .. 72 E5
Llithfaen 70 C4
Llong 73 C6
Llowes 48 E3
Llundain-fach 46 D4
Llwydcoed 34 D3
Llwydiarth 59 C7
Llwyn 60 F2
Llwyncelyn 46 D3
Llwyndafydd 46 D2
Llwynderw 60 D2
Llwyn-du 35 C6
Llwyndyrys 70 C4
Llwyngwril 58 D2
Llwyn-hendy 33 E6
Llwynmawr 73 F6
Llwyn-têg 33 D6
Llwyn-y-brain 32 C2
Llwyn-y-groes 46 D4
Llwynypia 34 E3
Llynclys 60 B2
Llynfaes 82 D4
Llysfaen 83 D8
Llyswen 48 F3
Llysworney 21 B8
Llys-y-frân 32 B1
Llywel 47 F7
Loan 120 B2
Loanend 122 D5
Loanhead 121 C5
Loans 118 F3
Loans of Tullich 151 D11
Lobb 20 F3
Loch a'
  Ghaimmhich ... 155 E7
Lochailort 147 C10
Lochaline 147 G9
Lochanhully 138 B5
Lochans 104 D4
Locharbriggs 114 F2
Lochassynt
  Lodge 156 G4
Lochavich House 124 D5
Lochawe 125 C7
Loch Baghasdail
  = Lochboisdale 148 G2
Lochboisdale = Loch
  Baghasdail 148 G2
Lochbuie 124 C2
Lochcarron 149 E13
Loch Choire
  Lodge 157 F9
Lochdhu 157 E13
Lochdochart
  House 126 B3
Lochdon 124 B3
Lochdrum 150 D5
Lochead 144 F6
Lochearnhead 126 B4
Lochee 134 F3
Lochend Highld . 151 H8
  Highld 158 D4
Locherben 114 E2
Loch Euphoirt .. 148 B3
Lochfoot 107 B5
Lochgair 145 D8
Lochgarthside ... 137 C8
Lochgelly 128 E3
Lochgilphead ... 145 E7
Lochgoilhead 125 E8
Loch Head 105 E7
Lochhill 152 B2
Lochindorb
  Lodge 151 H12
Lochinver 156 G3
Lochlane 127 B7
Lochluichart 150 E6
Loch Loyal Lodge 157 E9
Lochmaben 114 F3
Lochmaddy = Loch
  nam Madadh ... 148 B4
Lochmore
  Cottage 158 F2
Lochmore Lodge 156 F5
Loch nam Madadh
  = Lochmaddy .. 148 B4
Lochore 128 E3
Lochportain 148 A4
Lochs Crofts 152 B3
Loch Sgioport .. 148 E3
Lochside Aberds . 135 C7
  Highld 151 F11
  Highld 151 F11
  Highld 157 F11
Lochslin 151 C11
Lochstack Lodge 156 F5
Lochton 141 E6
Lochty Angus.... 135 C5
  Fife 129 D7
  Perth 128 B2
Lochuisge 130 D1
Lochurr 113 F7
Lochwinnoch 118 D3
Lochwood 114 E3
Lochyside 131 B5
Lockengate 4 C5
Lockerbie 114 F4
Lockeridge 25 C6
Lockerley 14 B3
Locking 23 D5
Lockinge 38 F4
Lockington E Yorks 97 E5
  Leics 63 B8
Lockleywood 61 B6
Locks Heath 15 D6
Lockton 103 E6
Lockwood 88 C2
Loddington Leics 64 D4
  N Nhants 53 B6
Loddiswell 6 E5
Loddon 69 E6
Lode 55 C6
Loders 12 E2
Lodsworth 16 B3
Lofthouse N Yorks 94 B4
  W Yorks 88 B4

Loftus 103 C5
Logan 113 B5
Loganlea 120 C2
Logan Mains 104 E4
Loggerheads 74 F4
Logie Angus.... 135 C6
  Fife 129 B6
  Moray 151 F13
Logiealmond
  Lodge 133 F6
Logie Coldstone 140 D3
Logie Hill 151 D10
Logie Newton ... 153 E6
Logie Pert 135 C6
Logierait 133 D6
Login 32 B2
Lolworth 54 C4
Lonbain 149 C11
Londesborough .. 96 E4
London Colney ... 40 D4
Londonderry 101 F8
Londonthorpe ... 78 F2
Londubh 155 J13
Lonemore 151 C10
Long Ashton 23 B7
Long Bennington . 77 E8
Longbenton 111 C5
Longborough 38 B1
Long Bredy 12 E3
Longbridge Warks 51 C7
  W Mid 50 B5
Longbridge
  Deverill 24 E3
Long Buckby 52 C4
Longburton 12 C4
Long Clawson ... 64 B4
Long Common 15 C6
Long Compton
  Staffs. 62 B2
  Warks 51 F7
Longcot 38 E2
Long Crendon ... 39 D6
Long Crichel 13 C7
Longcroft 119 B7
Longden 60 D4
Long Ditton 28 C2
Longdon Staffs . 62 C4
  Worcs 50 F3
Longdon Green .. 62 C4
Longdon on Tern 61 C6
Longdown 10 E3
Longdowns 3 C6
Long Drax 89 B7
Long Duckmanton 76 B4
Long Eaton 76 F4
Longfield Kent .. 29 C7
  Shetland 160 M5
Longford Derbys . 76 F2
  Glos. 37 B8
  London. 27 B8
  Shrops. 74 F3
  Telford 61 C7
  W Mid 63 F7
Longformacus ... 122 D2
Longframlington 117 D7
Long Green 50 F3
Longham Dorset . 13 E8
  Norf 68 C2
Long Hanborough 38 C4
Longhaven 153 E11
Longhill 153 C9
Longhirst 117 F8
Longhope Glos. .. 36 C3
  Orkney 159 J4
Longhorsley 117 E7
Longhoughton .. 117 C8
Long Itchington 52 C2
Longlane Derbys . 76 F2
  W Berks 26 B2
Long Lawford ... 52 B2
Longlevens 37 B5
Longley 88 D2
Longley Green ... 50 D2
Long Load 12 B2
Longmanhill 153 B7
Long Marston
  Herts 40 C1
  N Yorks. 95 D8
  Warks 51 E6
Long Marton 100 B1
Long Melford ... 56 E2
Longmoor Camp .. 27 F5
Longmorn 152 C2
Long Newnton ... 37 E6
Longnewton
  Borders 115 B8
  Stockton 102 C1
Long Newton ... 121 C8
Longney 36 C4
Longniddry 121 B7
Longnor Shrops . 60 D4
  Staffs. 75 C7
Longparish 26 E2
Longport 75 E5
Long Preston ... 93 D8
Longridge Lancs 93 F6
  Staffs. 62 C3
  W Loth 120 C2
Longriggend 119 B8
Long Riston 97 E7
Longsdon 75 D6
Longshaw 86 D3
Longside 153 D10
Long Sight 87 D7
Longstanton 54 C4
Longstock 25 F8
Longstone 32 D2
Longstowe 54 D4
Long Stratton ... 68 E4
Long Street 53 E5
Long Sutton Hants 26 E5
  Lincs 66 B4
  Som 12 B2
Longthorpe 65 E8
Long Thurlow ... 56 C4
Longthwaite 99 B6
Longton Lancs .. 86 B2
  Stoke 75 E6
Longtown Cumb . 108 C4
  Hereford 35 B7
Longview 86 E2
Longville in the
  Dale 60 E5
Long Whatton ... 63 B8
Longwick 39 D7

Long Wittenham . 39 E5
Longwitton 117 F6
Longwood 61 D6
Longworth 38 E3
Longyester 121 C8
Lonmay 153 C10
Lonmore 148 D7
Looe 5 D7
Loose 29 D8
Loosley Row 39 D8
Lopcombe Corner . 25 F7
Lopen 12 C2
Loppington 60 B4
Lopwell 6 C2
Lorbottle 117 D6
Lorbottle Hall .. 117 D6
Lornty 134 E1
Loscoe 76 E4
Losgaintir 154 H5
Lossiemouth 152 A2
Lossit 142 C2
Lostford 74 F3
Lostock Gralam .. 74 B3
Lostock Green ... 74 B3
Lostock Hall 86 B3
Lostock Junction 86 D4
Lostwithiel 5 D6
Loth 159 E7
Lothbeg 157 H12
Lothersdale 94 E2
Lothmore 157 H12
Loudwater 40 E2
Loughborough ... 64 C2
Loughor 33 E6
Loughton Essex . 41 E7
  M Keynes 53 F6
  Shrops. 61 F6
Lound Lincs 65 C7
  Notts 89 F7
  Suff 69 E8
Lount 63 C7
Louth 91 F7
Love Clough 87 B6
Lovedean 15 C7
Lover 14 B3
Loversall 89 E6
Loves Green 42 D2
Lovesome Hill .. 102 E1
Loveston 32 D1
Lovington 23 F7
Low Ackworth ... 89 C5
Low Barlings 78 B3
Low Bentham 93 C6
Low Bradfield ... 88 E3
Low Bradley 94 E3
Low Braithwaite 108 E4
Lowbridge House . 99 D7
Low Brunton 110 B2
Low Burnham 89 D8
Low Burton 101 F7
Low Buston 117 D8
Low Catton 96 D3
Low Clanyard ... 104 F5
Low Coniscliffe 101 C7
Low Crosby 108 D4
Low Dalby 103 F6
Lowdham 77 E6
Low Dinsdale ... 101 C8
Lowe 74 F2
Low Ellington .. 101 F7
Lower Aisholt ... 22 F4
Lower Arncott .. 39 C6
Lower Ashton ... 10 F3
Lower Assendon . 39 F7
Lower Badcall .. 156 E4
Lower Bartle ... 92 F4
Lower Basildon . 26 B4
Lower Beeding .. 17 B6
Lower Benefield . 65 F6
Lower Boddington 52 D2
Lower Brailes ... 51 F8
Lower Breakish 149 F11
Lower Broadheath 50 D3
Lower Bullingham 49 F7
Lower Cam 36 D4
Lower Chapel ... 48 F2
Lower Chute 25 D8
Lower Cragabus 142 D4
Lower Crossings 87 F8
Lower
  Cumberworth.. 88 D3
Lower Darwen ... 86 B4
Lower Dean 53 C8
Lower Diabaig . 149 B12
Lower Dicker ... 18 D2
Lower Dinchope . 60 F4
Lower Down 60 F3
Lower Drift 2 D3
Lower Dunsforth 95 C7
Lower Egleton .. 49 E8
Lower Elkstone . 75 D7
Lower End 40 B2
Lower Everleigh . 25 D6
Lower Farringdon 26 F5
Lower Foxdale .. 84 E2
Lower Frankton . 73 F7
Lower Froyle ... 27 E5
Lower Gledfield 151 B8
Lower Green 81 D5
Lower Hacheston 57 D7
Lower Halistra 148 C7
Lower Halstow .. 30 C2
Lower Hardres .. 31 D5
Lower Hawthwaite 98 F4
Lower Heath 75 C5
Lower
  Hempriggs 151 E14
Lower Hergest .. 48 D4
Lower Heyford .. 38 B4
Lower Higham ... 29 B8
Lower Holbrook . 57 F5
Lower Hordley .. 60 B3

Lower Midway 63 B7
Lower Milovaig . 148 C6
Lower Moor 50 E4
Lower Nazeing ... 41 D6
Lower Netchwood 61 E6
Lower Ollach .. 149 E10
Lower Penarth .. 22 B3
Lower Penn 62 E2
Lower Pennington 14 E4
Lower Peover ... 74 B4
Lower Pexhill ... 75 B5
Lower Place 87 C7
Lower Quinton .. 51 E6
Lower Rochford . 49 C8
Lower Seagry ... 37 F6
Lower Shelton .. 53 E7
Lower Shiplake .. 27 B5
Lower
  Shuckburgh 52 C2
Lower Slaughter . 38 B1
Lower Stanton St
  Quintin 37 F6
Lower Stoke 30 B2
Lower Stondon .. 54 F2
Lower Stow Bedon 68 E2
Lower Street Norf 69 C6
  Norf 81 D8
Lower Strensham 50 E4
Lower Stretton .. 86 F4
Lower Sundon ... 40 B3
Lower Swanwick 15 D5
Lower Swell 38 B1
Lower Tean 75 F7
Lower Thurlton . 69 E7
Lower Tote 149 B10
Lower Town 44 B4
Lower Tysoe 51 E8
Lower Upham 15 C6
Lower Vexford .. 22 F3
Lower Weare 23 D6
Lower Welson ... 48 D4
Lower Whitley .. 74 B3
Lower Wield 26 E4
Lower
  Winchendon.. .. 39 C7
Lower Withington 74 C5
Lower Woodend .. 39 F8
Lower Woodford . 25 F6
Lower Wyche 50 E2
Lowesby 64 D4
Lowestoft 69 E8
Loweswater 98 B3
Low Etherley ... 101 B6
Low Fell 111 D5
Lowford 15 C5
Low Fulney 66 B2
Low Garth 103 D5
Low Gate 110 C2
Lowgill Cumb 99 E8
  Lancs 93 C6
Low Grantley ... 94 B5
Low Habberley .. 50 B3
Low Ham 12 B2
Low Hanwdde.... 50 B2
Low Hawsker ... 103 D7
Low Hesket 108 E4
Low Hesleyhurst 117 E6
Low Hutton 96 C3
Lowick N Nhants 65 F6
  Northumb 123 F6
Lowick Bridge .. 98 F4
Lowick Green ... 98 F4
Low Laithe 94 C4
Lowlands 35 E6
Low Leighton ... 87 F8
Low Lorton 98 B3
Low Marishes ... 96 B4
Low Marnham ... 77 C8
Low Mill 102 E4
Low Moor Lancs . 93 E7
  W Yorks 88 B3
Lowmoor Row ... 99 B8
Low Moorsley .. 111 E6
Low Newton 99 F6
Low Newton-by-the-
  Sea 117 B8
Lownie Moor ... 134 E4
Low Row Cumb .. 108 F3
  Cumb 109 D5
  N Yorks. 100 E4
Low Salchrie ... 104 C4
Low Smerby 143 F8
Low Torry 128 F2
Low Worsall ... 102 D1
Low Wray 99 D5
Loxbeare 10 C4
Loxhill 27 F8
Loxhore 20 F5
Loxley 51 D7
Loxton 23 D5
Loxwood 27 F8
Lubcroy 156 J6
Lubenham 64 F4
Luccombe 21 E8
Luccombe Village . 15 G6
Lucker 123 F7
Luckett 5 B8
Luckington 37 F5
Lucklawhill 129 B6
Luckwell Bridge . 21 F8
Lucton 49 C6
Ludag 148 G2
Ludborough 91 E6
Ludchurch 32 C2
Luddenden 87 B8
Luddenden Foot . 87 B8
Luddesdown 29 C7
Luddington N Lincs 90 C2
  Warks 51 D6
Luddington in the
  Brook 65 F8
Lude House 133 C5
Ludford Lincs ... 91 F6
  Shrops. 49 B7
Ludgershall Bucks. 39 C6
  Wilts 25 D7
Ludgvan 2 C4
Ludham 69 C6
Ludlow 49 B7
Ludwell 13 B7
Ludworth 111 E6
Luffincott 8 E5
Lugar 113 B5
Luggate Burn .. 122 B2
Lugg Green 49 C6
Luggiebank 119 B7

Lugton 118 D4
Lugwardine 49 E7
Luib 149 F10
Lulham 49 E6
Lullenden 28 E5
Lullington Derbys . . 63 C6
Som 24 D2
Lulsgate Bottom . 23 C7
Lulsley 50 D2
Lumb 87 B8
Lumby 95 F7
Lumloch 119 C6
Lumphanan 140 D4
Lumphinnans . . . 128 E3
Lumsdaine 122 C4
Lumsden 140 B3
Lunan 135 D6
Lunanhead 134 D4
Luncarty 128 B2
Lund E Yorks 97 E5
N Yorks 96 F2
Shetland 160 C7
Lunderton 153 D11
Lundie Angus . . . 134 F2
Highld 136 C4
Lundin Links . . . 129 D6
Lunga 124 E3
Lunna 160 G6
Lunning 160 G7
Lunnon 33 F6
Lunsford's Cross . 18 D4
Lunt 85 D4
Luntley 49 D5
Luppitt 11 D6
Lupset 88 C4
Lupton 99 F7
Lurgashall 16 B3
Lusby 79 C6
Lusta 149 C7
Lustleigh 10 F2
Luston 49 C6
Luthermuir 135 C6
Luthrie 128 C5
Luton Devon 7 B7
Luton 40 B3
Medway 29 C8
Lutterworth 64 F2
Lutton Devon 6 D3
Lincs 66 B4
N Hants 65 F8
Lutworthy 10 C2
Luxborough 21 F8
Luxulyan 5 D5
Lybster 158 G4
Lydbury North . . . 60 F3
Lydcott 21 F5
Lydd 19 C7
Lydden 31 E6
Lyddington 65 E5
Lydd on Sea 19 C7
Lydeard St
Lawrence 22 F3
Lyde Green 26 D5
Lydford 9 F7
Lydgate 87 B7
Lydham 60 E3
Lydiard Green . . . 37 F7
Lydiard Millicent . 37 F7
Lydiate 85 D4
Lydney 36 D3
Lydstep 32 E1
Lye 62 F3
Lye Green Bucks . . 40 D2
E Sus 18 B2
Lyford 38 E3
Lymbridge Green . 30 E5
Lyme Regis 11 E8
Lyminge 31 E5
Lymington 14 E4
Lyminster 16 D4
Lymm 86 F4
Lymore 14 E3
Lympne 19 B8
Lympsham 22 D5
Lympstone 10 F4
Lynchat 138 D3
Lyndale House . . 149 C8
Lyndhurst 14 D4
Lyndon 65 D6
Lyne 27 C8
Lyneal 73 F8
Lyne Down 49 F8
Lyneham Oxon . . . 38 B2
Wilts 24 B5
Lynemore 139 B6
Lynemouth 117 E8
Lyne of
Gorthleck 137 B8
Lyne of Skene . . 141 C6
Lyness 159 J4
Lyng Norf 68 C3
Som 11 B8
Lynmouth 21 E6
Lynsted 30 C3
Lynton 21 E6
Lyon's Gate 12 D4
Lyonshall 48 D5
Lytchett Matravers 13 E7
Lytchett Minster . 13 E7
Lyth 158 D4
Lytham 85 B4
Lytham St Anne's . 85 B4
Lythe 103 C6
Lythes 159 K5

M

Mabe Burnthouse . . 3 C6
Mabie 107 B6
Mablethorpe 91 F9
Macclesfield 75 B6
Macclesfield
Forest 75 B6
Macduff 153 B7
Mace Green 56 E5
Macharioch 143 H6
Machen 35 F6
Machrihanish . . . 143 F7
Machynlleth 58 D4
Machynys 33 E6
Mackerel's
Common 16 B4
Mackworth 76 F3

Macmerry 121 B7
Madderty 127 B8
Maddiston 120 B2
Madehurst 16 C3
Madeley Staffs . . 74 E4
Telford 61 D6
Madeley Heath . . 74 E4
Madeley Park . . . 74 E4
Madingley 54 C4
Madley 49 F6
Madresfield 50 E3
Madron 2 C3
Maenaddwyn . . . 82 C4
Maenclochog . . . 32 B1
Maendy 22 B2
Maentwrog 71 C7
Maen-y-groes . . . 46 D2
Maer 74 F4
Maerdy Conwy . . . 72 E4
Rhondda 34 E3
Maesbrook 60 B2
Maesbury 60 B3
Maesbury Marsh . 60 B3
Maesgwyn-Isaf . . 59 C8
Maesgwynne . . . 32 B3
Maeshafn 73 C6
Maes Llyn 46 E2
Maesmynis 48 E2
Maesteg 34 E2
Maestir 46 E4
Manswood 13 D7
Manthorpe Lincs . 65 C7
Lincs 78 F2
Manton N Lincs . . 90 D3
Notts 77 B5
Rutland 65 D5
Wilts 25 C6
Manuden 41 B7
Maperton 12 B4
Maplebeck 77 C7
Maple Cross 40 E3
Mapledurham . . . 26 B4
Mapledurwell . . . 26 D4
Maplehurst 17 B5
Maplescombe . . . 29 C6
Mapleton 75 E8
Mapperley 76 E4
Mapperley Park . . 77 E5
Mapperton 12 E3
Mappleborough
Green 51 C5
Mappleton 97 E8
Mappowder 12 D5
Maraig 154 G6
Marazanvose 4 D3
Marazion 2 C4
Marbhig 155 F9
Marbury 74 E2
March Cambs . . . 66 E4
S Lanark 114 C2
Marcham 38 E4
Marchamley 61 B5
Marchington 75 F8

Manmoel 35 D5
Marlingford 68 D4
Mar Lodge 139 E6
Marloes 44 E2
Marlow Bucks . . . 39 F8
Hereford 49 B7
Marlow Bottom . . 40 F1
Marlpit Hill 28 E5
Marlpool 76 E4
Marnhull 13 C5
Marnoch 152 C5
Marnock 119 C7
Marple 87 F7
Marple Bridge . . . 87 F7
Marr 89 D6
Marrel 157 H13
Marrick 101 E5
Marrister 160 G7
Marros 32 D3
Marsden T&W . . . 111 C6
W Yorks 87 C8
Marsett 100 F4
Marsh Devon 11 C7
W Yorks 94 F3
Marshall's Heath . 40 C4
Marshalsea 11 D8
Marshalswick . . . 40 D4
Marsham 81 E7
Marshaw 93 D5
Marshborough . . . 31 D7
Marshbrook 60 F4
Marshchapel 91 E7
Marshfield Newport 35 F6
S Glos 24 B2
Marshgate 8 E3
Marsh Gibbon . . . 39 B6
Marsh Green Devon 10 E5
Kent 28 E5
Staffs 75 D5
Marshland St
James 66 D5
Marsh Lane 76 B4
Marshside 85 C4
Marsh Street . . . 21 E8
Marshwood 11 E8
Marske 101 D6
Marske-by-the-
Sea 102 B4
Marston Ches W . 74 B3
Hereford 49 D5
Lincs 77 E8
Oxon 39 D5
Staffs 62 B3
Staffs 62 C2
Warks 63 E6
Wilts 24 D4
Marston Doles . . 52 D2
Marston Green . . 63 F5
Marston Magna . . 12 B3
Marston Meysey . 37 E8
Marston
Montgomery . . 75 F8
Marston
Moretaine 53 E7
Marston on Dove . 63 B6
Marston St
Lawrence 52 E3
Marston Stannett . 49 D7
Marston Trussell . 64 F3
Marstow 36 C2
Marsworth 40 C2
Marten 25 D7
Marthall 74 B5
Martham 69 C7
Martin Hants 13 C8
Kent 31 E7
Lincs 78 C4
Lincs 78 D4
Martin Dales . . . 78 C4
Martin Drove End . 13 B8
Martinhoe 21 E5
Martinhoe Cross . 21 E5
Martin
Hussingtree . . . 50 C3
Martin Mill 31 E7
Martinscroft 86 F4
Martinstown 12 F4
Martlesham 57 E6
Martlesham Heath 57 E6
Martletwy 32 C1
Martley 50 D2
Martock 12 C2
Marton Ches E . . 75 C5
E Yorks 97 F7
Lincs 90 F2
Mbro 102 C3
N Yorks 95 C7
N Yorks 103 F5
Shrops 60 B4
Shrops 61 C5
Warks 52 C2
Marton-le-Moor . 95 B6
Martyr's Green . . 27 D8
Martyr Worthy . . . 26 F3
Marwick 159 F3
Marwood 20 F4
Maryburgh 151 F8
Maryhill 119 C5
Marykirk 135 C6
Marylebone 86 D3
Marypark 152 E1
Maryport Cumb . . 107 F7
Dumfries 104 F5
Mary Tavy 9 F7
Maryton 135 D6
Marywell Aberds . 141 E6
Aberds 141 E8
Angus 135 E6
Masham 101 F7
Mashbury 42 C2
Masongill 93 B6
Masonhill 112 B3
Mastin Moor 76 B4
Mastrick 141 D7
Matching 41 C8
Matching Green . . 41 C8
Matching Tye . . . 41 C8
Matfen 110 B3
Matfield 29 E7
Mathern 36 E2
Mathon 50 E2
Mathry 44 B3
Matlaske 81 D7
Matlock 76 C2
Matlock Bath . . . 76 C2
Matson 37 C5
Matterdale End . . 99 B5

Mattersey 89 F7
Mattersey Thorpe . 89 F7
Mattingley 26 D5
Mattishall 68 C3
Mattishall Burgh . 68 C3
Mauchline 112 B4
Maud 153 D9
Maugersbury . . . 38 B2
Maughold 84 C4
Mauld 150 H7
Maulden 53 F8
Maulds Meaburn . 99 C8
Maunby 102 F1
Maund Bryan . . . 49 D7
Maundown 11 B5
Mautby 69 C7
Mavis Enderby . . 79 C6
Mawbray 107 E7
Mawdesley 86 C2
Mawdlam 34 F2
Mawgan 3 D6
Maw Green 74 D4
Mawla 3 D6
Mawnan 3 D6
Mawnan Smith . . . 3 D6
Mawsley 53 B6
Maxey 65 D8
Maxstoke 63 F6
Maxton Borders . 122 F2
Kent 31 E7
Maxwellheugh . . 122 F3
Maxwelltown . . . 107 B6
Maxworthy 8 E4
Mayals 33 E7
May Bank 75 E5
Maybole 112 D3
Mayfield E Sus . . 18 C2
Midloth 121 C6
Staffs 75 E8
W Loth 120 C2
Mayford 27 D7
Mayland 43 D5
Maynard's Green . 18 D2
Maypole Mon . . . 36 C1
Scilly 2 E4
Maypole Green
Essex 43 B5
Norf 69 E7
Suff 57 C6
Maywick 160 L5
Meadle 39 D8
Meadowtown . . . 60 D3
Meaford 75 F5
Mealabost 155 D9
Mealabost
Bhuirgh 155 B9
Meal Bank 99 E7
Mealsgate 108 E2
Meanwood 95 F5
Mearbeck 93 C8
Meare 23 E6
Meare Green . . . 11 B8
Mears Ashby . . . 53 C6
Measham 63 C7
Meath Green . . . 28 E3
Meathop 99 F6
Meaux 97 F6
Meavy 6 C3
Medbourne 64 E4
Medburn 110 B4
Meddon 8 C4
Meden Vale 77 C5
Medlam 79 D6
Medmenham . . . 39 F8
Medomsley 110 D4
Medstead 26 F4
Meerbrook 75 C6
Meer End 51 B7
Meers Bridge . . . 91 F8
Meesden 54 F5
Meeth 9 D7
Meggethead . . . 114 B4
Meidrim 32 B3
Meifod Denb 72 D4
Powys 59 C8
Meigle N Ayrs . . 118 C3
Perth 134 E2
Meikle Earnock . 119 D7
Meikle Ferry . . . 151 C10
Meikle Forter . . 134 C1
Meikle Gluich . . 151 C9
Meikleour 134 F1
Meikle Pinkerton . 122 B3
Meikle Strath . . . 135 B6
Meikle Tarty . . . 141 B8
Meikle Wartle . . . 153 E7
Meinciau 33 C5
Meir 75 E6
Meir Heath 75 E6
Melbourn 54 E4
Melbourne Derbys . 63 B7
E Yorks 96 E3
S Lanark 120 E3
Melbury Abbas . . 13 B6
Melbury Bubb . . . 12 D3
Melbury Osmond . 12 D3
Melbury Sampford 12 D3
Melby 160 H3
Melchbourne . . . 53 C8
Melcombe
Bingham 13 D5
Melcombe Regis . 12 F4
Meldon Devon 9 E7
Northumb 117 F7
Meldreth 54 E4
Meldrum House . 141 B7
Melfort 124 D4
Melgarve 137 E7
Meliden 72 A4
Melin-y-coed . . . 83 E8
Melin-y-ddôl . . . 59 D7
Melin-y-grug . . . 59 D7
Melin-y-Wig 72 E4
Melkinthorpe . . . 99 B7
Melkridge 109 C7
Melksham 24 C4
Melldalloch . . . 145 F8
Melling Lancs . . . 93 B5
Mers 85 D4
Melling Mount . . 86 D2
Mellis 56 B5
Mellon Charles . 155 H13
Mellon Udrigle . 155 H13
Mellor Gtr Man . . 87 F7
Lancs 93 F6
Mellor Brook . . . 93 F6
Mells 24 E2
Melmerby Cumb . 109 F6
N Yorks 95 B6
N Yorks 101 F5
Melplash 12 E2
Melrose 121 F8
Melsetter 159 K3
Melsonby 101 D6
Meltham 88 C2
Melton 57 D6
Meltonby 96 D3
Melton Constable . 81 D6
Melton Mowbray . 64 C4
Melton Ross 90 C4
Melvaig 155 J12
Melverley 60 C3
Melverley Green . 60 C3
Melvich 157 C11
Membury 11 D7
Memsie 153 B9
Memus 134 D4
Menabilly 5 D5
Menai Bridge
= Porthaethwy . 83 D5
Mendham 69 F5
Mendlesham 56 C5
Mendlesham
Green 56 C4
Menheniot 5 C7
Mennock 113 D8
Menston 94 E4
Menstrie 127 E7
Menthorpe 96 F2
Mentmore 40 C2
Meoble 147 C10
Meole Brace . . . 60 C4
Meols 85 E3
Meonstoke 15 C7
Meopham 29 C7
Meopham
Station 29 C7
Mepal 66 F4
Meppershall 54 F2
Merbach 48 E5
Mere Ches E 86 F5
Wilts 24 F3
Mere Brow 86 C2
Mereclough 93 F8
Mere Green 62 E5
Mereside 92 F3
Mereworth 29 D7
Mergie 141 F6
Meriden 63 F6
Merkadale 149 E8
Merkland Dumfries 106 B4
S Ayrs 112 E2
Merkland Lodge . 156 G7
Merley 13 E8
Merlin's Bridge . . 44 D4
Merrington 60 B4
Merrion 44 F4
Merriott 12 C2
Merrivale 6 B3
Merrow 27 D8
Merrymeet 5 C7
Mersham 19 B7
Merstham 28 D3
Merston 16 D2
Merstone 15 F6
Merther 3 B7
Merthyr 32 B4
Merthyr Cynog . . 47 F8
Merthyr-Dyfan . . 22 C3
Merthyr Mawr . . . 21 B7
Merthyr Tudful
= Merthyr Tydfil . 34 D4
Merthyr Tydfil
= Merthyr Tudful . 34 D4
Merthyr Vale . . . 34 E4
Merton Devon 9 C7
London 28 B3
Norf 68 E2
Oxon 39 C5
Mervinslaw 116 C2
Meshaw 10 C2
Messing 42 C4
Messingham 90 D2
Metfield 69 F5
Metherell 6 C2
Metheringham . . 78 C3
Methil 129 E5
Methlem 70 D2
Methley 88 B4
Methlick 153 E8
Methven 128 B2
Methwold 67 E7
Methwold Hythe . 67 E7
Mettingham 69 F6
Mevagissey 3 B9
Mewith Head . . . 93 C7
Mexborough 89 D5
Mey 158 C4
Meysey Hampton . 37 E8
Miabhag W Isles . 154 H5
W Isles 154 G5
Miabhig 154 D5
Michaelchurch . . 36 B2
Michaelchurch
Escley 48 F5
Michaelchurch on
Arrow 48 D4
Michaelston-le-
Pit 22 B3
Michaelston-y-
Fedw 35 F6
Michaelstow 5 B5
Micheldever 26 F3
Michelmersh 14 B4
Mickfield 56 C5
Micklebring 89 E6
Mickleby 103 C6
Mickleham 28 D2
Mickleover 76 F3
Micklethwaite . . . 94 E4
Mickleton Durham 100 B4
Glos 51 E6
Mickletown 88 B4
Mickley 95 B5
Mickley Square . 110 C3
Mid Ardlaw 153 B9
Mid Auchinloch . . 119 B6
Midbea 159 D5
Mid Beltie 140 D5
Mid Calder 120 C3
Mid Cloch Forbie 153 C7
Mid Clyth 158 G4
Middle Assendon . 39 F7
Middle Aston . . . 38 B4

Middle Barton . . 38 B4
Middlebie 108 B2
Middle
Cairncake . . . 153 D7
Middle Claydon . . 39 B7
Middle Drums . . 135 D5
Middleforth Green 86 B3
Middleham 101 F6
Middle Handley . . 76 B4
Middlehope 60 F4
Middle Littleton . . 51 E5
Middlemarsh . . . 12 D4
Middle Mill 44 C3
Middlemuir 141 B8
Middle Rasen . . . 90 F4
Middle Rigg . . . 128 D2
Middlesbrough . 102 B2
Middleshaw Cumb . 99 F7
Dumfries 107 B8
Middlesmoor . . . 94 B3
Middlestone . . . 111 F5
Middlestone
Moor 110 F5
Middlestown . . . 88 C3
Middlethird . . . 122 E2
Middleton Aberds 141 C7
Argyll 146 G2
Cumb 99 F8
Derbys 75 C8
Derbys 76 D2
Essex 56 F2
Gtr Man 87 D6
Hants 26 E2
Hereford 49 C7
Lancs 92 D4
Midloth 121 D6
N Hants 64 F5
Norf 67 C6
Northumb 117 F6
Northumb 123 F7
N Yorks 94 E4
N Yorks 103 F5
Perth 128 D3
Perth 133 E8
Shrops 49 B7
Shrops 60 B3
Shrops 60 E2
Suff 57 C8
Swansea 33 F5
Warks 63 E5
W Yorks 88 B3
Middleton Cheney . 52 E2
Middleton Green . 75 F6
Middleton Hall . . 117 B5
Middleton-in-
Teesdale 100 B4
Middleton Moor . 57 C8
Middleton One
Row 102 C1
Middleton-on-
Leven 102 D2
Middleton-on-Sea 16 D3
Middleton on the
Hill 49 C7
Middleton-on-the-
Wolds 96 E5
Middleton Priors . 61 E6
Middleton
Quernham . . . 95 B6
Middleton St
George 101 C8
Middleton Scriven 61 F6
Middleton Stoney . 39 B5
Middleton Tyas . 101 D7
Middletown Cumb . 98 D1
Powys 60 C3
Middle Tysoe . . . 51 E8
Middle Wallop . . 25 F7
Middlewich 74 C3
Middle Winterslow 25 F7
Middle Woodford . 25 F6
Middlewood
Green 56 C4
Middlezoy 23 F5
Midfield 157 C8
Midge Hall 86 B3
Midgeholme . . . 109 D6
Midgham 26 C3
Midgley W Yorks . 87 B8
W Yorks 88 C3
Midhopestones . . 88 E3
Midhurst 16 B2
Mid Lavant 16 D2
Midlem 115 B8
Mid Main 150 H7
Midmar 141 D5
Midsomer Norton . 23 D8
Midton 118 B2
Midtown Highld . 155 J13
Highld 157 C8
Midtown of
Buchromb . . . 152 D3
Mid Urchany . . 151 G11
Midville 79 D6
Mid Walls 160 H4
Mid Yell 160 D7
Migdale 151 B9
Migvie 140 D3
Milarrochy 126 E3
Milborne Port . . 12 C4
Milborne St
Andrew 13 E6
Milborne Wick . . 12 B4
Milbourne 110 B4
Milburn 100 B1
Milbury Heath . . 36 E3
Milcombe 52 F2
Milden 56 E3
Mildenhall Suff . . 55 B8
Wilts 25 C7
Milebrook 48 B5
Milebush 29 E8
Mile Cross 68 C5
Mile Elm 24 C4
Mile End Essex . . 43 B5
Glos 36 C2
Mileham 68 C2
Mile Oak 17 D6
Milesmark 128 F2
Milfield 122 F5
Milford Derbys . . 76 E3
Devon 8 B4
Powys 59 E7
Staffs 62 B3
Sur 27 E7
Wilts 14 B2

Milford Haven
= Aberdaugleddau 44 E4
Milford on Sea . . 14 E3
Milkwall 36 D2
Milkwell 13 B7
Milland 16 B2
Millarston 118 C4
Millbank Aberds . 153 D11
Highld 158 D3
Mill Bank 87 B8
Millbeck 98 B4
Millbounds 159 E6
Millbreck 153 D10
Millbridge 27 E6
Corn 6 D2
Soton 14 C4
Millbrook C Beds . 53 F8
Dumfries 107 B8
Millcorner 18 C5
Milldale 75 D8
Millden Lodge . . 135 B5
Milldens 135 D5
Mill End Bucks . . 39 F7
Herts 54 F4
Millerhill 121 C6
Miller's Dale . . . 75 B8
Miller's Green . . 76 D2
Millgreen 61 B6
Mill Green Essex . 42 D2
Norf 68 F4
Suff 56 E3
Millhalf 48 E4
Millhayes 11 D7
Millheugh 119 D7
Mill Hill 41 E5
Millholme 99 F7
Millhouse Argyll . 145 F8
Cumb 108 F3
Millhousebridge . 114 F4
Millhouse Green . 88 D3
Millhouses 88 F4
Millikenpark . . . 118 C4
Millin Cross 44 D4
Millington 96 D4
Mill Lane 27 D5
Millmeece 74 F5
Mill of
Kingoodie . . . 141 B7
Mill of Muiresk . 153 D6
Mill of Sterin . . 140 E2
Mill of Uras . . . 141 F7
Millom 98 F3
Millook 8 E3
Mill Place 90 D3
Millpool 5 B6
Millport 145 H10
Millquarter 113 F6
Mill Side 99 F6
Mill Street 68 C3
Millthorpe 78 F4
Millthrop 100 E1
Milltimber 141 D7
Milltown Corn . . . 5 D6
Derbys 76 C3
Devon 20 F4
Dumfries 108 B3
Milltown of
Aberdalgie . . . 128 B2
Milltown of
Auchindoun . . 152 D3
Milltown of
Craigston . . . 153 C7
Milltown of
Edinvillie . . . 152 D2
Milltown of
Kildrummy . . . 140 C3
Milltown of
Rothiemay . . . 152 D5
Milltown of
Towie 140 C3
Milnathort 128 D3
Milner's Heath . . 73 C8
Milngavie 119 B5
Milnrow 87 C7
Milnshaw 87 B5
Milnthorpe 99 F6
Milo 33 C6
Milson 49 B8
Milstead 30 D3
Milston 25 E6
Milton Angus . . 134 E3
Cambs 55 C5
Cumb 109 C5
Derbys 63 B7
Dumfries 105 D6
Dumfries 106 B5
Dumfries 113 F8
Highld 150 F6
Highld 150 F7
Highld 151 D10
Highld 151 G8
Highld 158 E5
Moray 152 B5
N Som 22 C5
Oxon 38 E4
Oxon 52 F2
Pembs 32 D1
Perth 127 C8
Ptsmth 15 E7
Stirling 126 D4
Stoke 75 D6
W Dunb 118 B4
Milton Abbas . . . 13 D6
Milton Abbot 6 B2
Milton Bridge . . 120 C5
Milton Bryan . . . 53 F7
Milton Clevedon . 23 F8
Milton Coldwells . 153 E9
Milton Combe . . . 6 C2
Milton Damerel . . 9 C5
Milton End 37 D8
Milton Ernest . . . 53 D8
Milton Green . . . 73 D8
Miltonhill 151 E13
Milton Hill 38 E4
Milton
Keynes 53 F6
Milton Keynes
Village 53 F6
Milton Lilbourne . 25 C6
Milton Malsor . . 52 D5
Milton Morenish . 132 F3

Milton of
Balgonie 128 D5
Milton of
Buchanan . . . 126 E3
Milton of
Campfield . . . 140 D5
Milton of
Campsie 119 B6
Milton of
Corsindae . . . 141 D5
Milton of
Cushnie 140 C4
Milton of
Dalcapon . . . 133 D6
Milton of
Edradour . . . 133 D6
Milton of
Gollanfield . . 151 F10
Milton of
Lesmore 140 B3
Milton of Logie . 140 D3
Milton of Murtle . 141 D7
Milton of Noth . . 140 B4
Milton of Tullich . 140 E2
Milton Regis . . . 30 C3
Milton under
Wychwood . . . 38 C2
Milverton Som . . 11 B6
Warks 51 C8
Milwich 75 F6
Minard 125 F5
Minchinhampton . 37 D5
Mindrum 122 F4
Minehead 21 E8
Minera 73 D6
Minety 37 E7
Minffordd Gwyn . . 58 C4
Gwyn 71 D6
Gwyn 83 D5
Miningsby 79 C6
Minions 5 B7
Minishant 112 C3
Minllyn 59 C5
Minnes 141 B8
Minngearraidh . . 148 F2
Minnigaff 105 C8
Minnonie 153 B7
Minskip 95 C6
Minstead 14 C3
Minsted 16 B2
Minster Kent . . . 30 B3
Kent 31 C7
Minsterley 60 D3
Minster Lovell . . 38 C3
Minsterworth . . . 36 C4
Minterne Magna . 12 D4
Minting 78 B4
Mintlaw 153 D9
Minto 115 B8
Minton 60 E4
Minwear 32 C1
Minworth 63 E5
Mirbister 159 F4
Mirehouse 98 C1
Mireland 158 D5
Mirfield 88 C3
Miserden 37 D6
Miskin 34 F4
Misson 89 E7
Misterton Leics . . 64 F2
Notts 89 E8
Som 12 D2
Mistley 56 F5
Mitcham 28 C3
Mitcheldean 36 C3
Mitchel Troy . . . 36 C1
Mitcheltroy
Common 36 D1
Mitford 117 F7
Mithian 4 D2
Mitton 62 C2
Mixbury 52 F4
Moat 108 B4
Moats Tye 56 D4
Mobberley Ches E . 74 B4
Staffs 75 E7
Moccas 49 E5
Mochdre Conwy . . 83 D8
Powys 59 F7
Mochrum 105 E7
Mockbeggar 14 D2
Mockerkin 98 B2
Modbury 6 D4
Moddershall 75 F6
Moelfre Anglesey . 82 C5
Powys 59 B8
Moffat 114 D3
Moggerhanger . . 54 E2
Moira 63 C7
Molash 30 D4
Mol-chlach . . . 149 G9
Mold
= Yr Wyddgrug . 73 C6
Moldgreen 88 C2
Molehill Green . . 42 B1
Molescroft 97 E6
Molesden 117 F7
Molesworth 53 B8
Moll 149 E10
Molland 10 B3
Mollington ChesW . 73 B7
Oxon 52 E2
Mollinsburn . . . 119 B7
Monachty 46 C4
Monachylemore . 126 C3
Monar Lodge . . 150 G5
Monaughty 48 C4
Monboddo House 135 B7
Mondynes 135 B7
Monevechadan . 125 E7
Monewden 57 D6
Moneydie 128 B2
Moniaive 113 E7
Monifieth 134 F4
Monikie 135 F4
Monimail 128 C4
Monington 45 E3
Monk Bretton . . . 88 D4
Monken Hadley . . 41 E5
Monk Fryston . . . 89 B6
Monkhopton . . . 61 E6
Monkland 49 D6
Monkleigh 9 B6
Monknash 21 B8

Monkokehampton . . 9 D7
Monkseaton 111 B6
Monks Eleigh 56 E3
Monk's Gate 17 B6
Monks Heath 74 B5
Monk Sherborne . . 26 D4
Monkshill 153 D7
Monksilver 22 F2
Monks Kirby 63 F8
Monk Soham 57 C6
Monkspath 51 B6
Monks Risborough 39 D8
Monk Street 42 B2
Monkswood 35 D7
Monkton Devon . . . 11 D6
Kent 31 C6
Pembs 44 E4
S Ayrs 112 B3
Monkton Combe . . 24 C2
Monkton Deverill . . 24 F3
Monkton Farleigh . 24 C3
Monkton Heathfield 11 B7
Monkton Up Wimborne 13 C8
Monkwearmouth . 111 D6
Monkwood 26 F4
Monmouth = Trefynwy 36 C2
Monmouth Cap 35 B7
Monnington on Wye 49 E5
Monreith 105 E7
Monreith Mains . . 105 E7
Montacute 12 C2
Montcoffer House 153 B6
Montford Argyll . . 145 G10
Shrops 60 C4
Montford Bridge . . 60 C4
Montgarrie 140 C4
Montgomery = Trefaldwyn 60 E2
Montrave 129 D5
Montrose 135 D7
Mont Saint 16 I2
Montsale 43 E6
Monxton 25 E8
Monyash 75 C8
Monymusk 141 C5
Monzie 127 B7
Monzie Castle 127 B7
Moodiesburn 119 B6
Moonzie 128 C5
Moor Allerton 95 F5
Moorby 79 C5
Moor Crichel 13 D7
Moordown 13 E8
Moore 86 F3
Moorend 36 D4
Moor End E Yorks . . . 96 F4
York 96 D2
Moorends 89 C7
Moorgate 88 E5
Moorgreen 76 E4
Moorhall 76 B3
Moorhampton 49 E5
Moorhead 94 F4
Moorhouse Cumb . 108 D3
Notts 77 C7
Moorlinch 23 F5
Moor Monkton 95 D8
Moor of Granary . 151 F13
Moor of Ravenstone 105 E7
Moor Row 98 C2
Moorsholm 102 C4
Moorside 87 D7
Moor Street 30 C2
Moorthorpe 89 C5
Moortown Hants . . . 14 D2
IoW 14 F5
Lincs 90 E4
Morangie 151 C10
Morar 147 B9
Morborne 65 E8
Morchard Bishop . . 10 D2
Morcombelake 12 E2
Morcott 65 D6
Morda 60 B2
Morden Dorset 13 E7
London 28 C3
Mordiford 49 F7
Mordon 101 B8
More 60 E3
Morebath 10 B4
Morebattle 116 B3
Morecambe 92 C4
Morefield 150 B4
Moreleigh 7 D5
Morenish 132 F2
Moresby 98 B1
Moresby Parks 98 C1
Morestead 15 B6
Moreton Dorset 13 F6
Essex 41 D8
Mers 85 E3
Oxon 39 D6
Staffs 61 C7
Moreton Corbet . . . 61 B5
Moretonhampstead 10 F2
Moreton-in-Marsh 51 F7
Moreton Jeffries . . 49 E8
Moreton Morrell . . 51 D8
Moreton on Lugg . . 49 E7
Moreton Pinkney . . 52 E3
Moreton Say 74 F3
Moreton Valence . . 36 D4
Morfa Carms 33 C6
Carms 33 E6
Morfa Bach 32 C4
Morfa Bychan 71 D6
Morfa Dinlle 82 F4
Morfa Glas 34 D2
Morfa Nefyn 70 C3
Morfydd 72 E5
Morgan's Vale 14 B2
Moriah 46 B5
Morland 99 B7
Morley Derbys 76 E3
Durham 101 B6
W Yorks 88 B3
Morley Green 87 F6
Morley St Botolph . 68 E3
Morningside Edin . 120 B5
Morningside continued
N Lanark 119 D8
Morningthorpe 68 E5
Morpeth 117 F8
Morphie 135 C7
Morrey 62 C5
Morris Green 55 F8
Morriston 33 E7
Morston 81 C6
Mortehoe 20 E3
Mortimer 26 C4
Mortimer's Cross . . 49 C6
Mortimer West End 26 C4
Mortlake 28 B3
Morton Cumb 108 D3
Derbys 76 C4
Lincs 65 B7
Lincs 77 C8
Lincs 90 E2
Norf 68 C4
Notts 77 D7
S Glos 36 E3
Shrops 60 B2
Morton Bagot 51 C6
Morton-on-Swale 101 E8
Morvah 2 C3
Morval 5 D7
Morvich Highld . . . 136 B2
Highld 157 J10
Morville 61 E6
Morville Heath 61 E6
Morwenstow 8 C4
Mosborough 88 F5
Moscow 118 E4
Mosedale 108 F3
Moseley W Mid 62 E3
W Mid 62 F4
Worcs 50 D3
Moss Argyll 146 G2
Highld 147 E9
S Yorks 89 C6
Wrex 73 D7
Mossat 140 C3
Mossbank 160 F6
Moss Bank 86 E3
Mossbay 98 B1
Mossblown 112 B4
Mossbrow 86 F5
Mossburnford 116 C2
Mossdale 106 B3
Moss Edge 92 E4
Mossend 119 C7
Moss End 27 B6
Mosser 98 B3
Mossfield 151 D9
Mossgiel 112 B4
Mosside 134 D4
Mossley Ches E 75 C5
Gtr Man 87 D7
Mossley Hill 85 F4
Moss of Barmuckity 152 B2
Moss Pit 62 B3
Moss-side 151 F11
Moss Side 92 F3
Mosstodloch 152 B3
Mosston 135 E5
Mossy Lea 86 C3
Mosterton 12 D2
Moston Gtr Man 87 D6
Shrops 61 B5
Moston Green 74 C4
Mostyn 85 F2
Mostyn Quay 85 F2
Motcombe 13 B6
Mothecombe 6 E4
Motherby 99 B6
Motherwell 119 D7
Mottingham 28 B5
Mottisfont 14 B4
Mottistone 14 F5
Mottram in Longdendale 87 E7
Mottram St Andrew 75 B5
Mouilpied 16 I2
Mouldsworth 74 B2
Moulin 133 D6
Moulsecoomb 17 D7
Moulsford 39 F5
Moulsoe 53 E7
Moulton Ches W 74 C3
Lincs 66 B3
N Yorks 101 D7
Suff 55 C7
V Glam 22 B2
W Nhants 53 C5
Moulton Chapel . . . 66 C2
Moulton Eaugate . . 66 C3
Moulton St Mary . . 69 D6
Moulton Seas End . 66 B3
Mounie Castle . . . 141 B6
Mount Corn 4 D2
Corn 5 C6
Highld 151 G12
Mountain 94 F3
Mountain Ash = Aberpennar 34 E4
Mountain Cross . . 120 E4
Mountain Water . . . 44 C4
Mountbenger 115 B6
Mount Bures 56 F3
Mount Canisp . . . 151 D10
Mountfield 18 C4
Mountgerald 151 E8
Mount Hawke 3 B6
Mountjoy 4 C3
Mountnessing 42 E2
Mounton 36 E2
Mount Pleasant Ches E 74 D5
Derbys 63 C6
Derbys 76 E3
Flint 73 B6
Hants 14 E3
W Yorks 88 B3
Mountsorrel 64 C2
Mount Sorrel 13 B8
Mount Tabor 87 B8
Mousehole 2 D3
Mousen 123 F7
Mouswald 107 B7
Mow Cop 75 D5
Mowhaugh 116 B4
Mowsley 64 F3
Moxley 62 E3
Moy Highld 137 F7
Moy continued
Highld 151 H10
Moy Hall 151 H10
Moy House 151 E13
Moyles Court 14 D2
Moylgrove 45 E3
Moy Lodge 137 F7
Muasdale 143 D7
Muchalls 141 E8
Much Birch 49 F7
Much Cowarne 49 E8
Much Dewchurch . . 49 F6
Muchelney 12 B2
Much Hadham 41 C7
Much Hoole 86 B2
Muchlarnick 5 D7
Much Marcle 49 F8
Muchrachd 150 H5
Much Wenlock 61 D6
Muckernich 151 F8
Mucking 42 F2
Muckleford 12 E4
Mucklestone 74 F4
Muckleton 61 B5
Muckletown 140 B4
Muckley Corner . . . 62 D4
Muckton 91 F7
Mudale 157 F8
Muddiford 20 F4
Mudeford 14 E2
Mudford 12 C3
Mudgley 23 E6
Mugdock 119 B5
Mugeary 149 E9
Mugginton 76 E2
Muggleswick 110 E3
Muie 157 J9
Muir 139 F6
Muirden 153 C7
Muirdrum 135 F5
Muirhead Angus . . . 134 F3
Fife 128 D4
N Lanark 119 C6
S Ayrs 118 F3
Muirhouselaw 116 B2
Muirhouses 128 F2
Muirkirk 113 B6
Muirmill 127 F6
Muir of Fairburn . . 150 F7
Muir of Fowlis 140 C4
Muir of Ord 151 F8
Muir of Pert 134 F4
Muirshearlich 136 F4
Muirskie 141 E7
Muirtack 153 E9
Muirton Highld . . . 151 E10
Perth 127 C8
Perth 128 B3
Muirton Mains 150 F7
Muirton of Ardblair 134 E1
Muirton of Ballochy 135 C6
Muiryfold 153 C7
Muker 100 E4
Mulbarton 68 D4
Mulben 152 C3
Mulindry 142 C4
Mullardoch House 150 H5
Mullion 3 E5
Mullion Cove 3 E5
Mumby 79 B8
Munderfield Row . . 49 D8
Munderfield Stocks 49 D8
Mundesley 81 D9
Mundford 67 E8
Mundham 69 E6
Mundon 42 D4
Mundurno 141 C8
Munerigie 137 D5
Muness 160 C8
Mungasdale 150 B2
Mungrisdale 108 F3
Munlochy 151 F9
Munsley 49 E8
Munslow 60 F5
Murchington 9 F8
Murcott 39 C5
Murkle 158 D3
Murlaggan Highld . . 136 E3
Highld 137 F6
Murra 159 H3
Murrayfield 120 B5
Murrow 66 D3
Mursley 39 B8
Murthill 134 D4
Murthly 133 F7
Murton Cumb 100 B2
Durham 111 E6
Northumb 123 E5
York 96 D2
Musbury 11 E7
Muscoates 102 F4
Musdale 124 C5
Musselburgh 121 B6
Muston Leics 77 F8
N Yorks 97 B6
Mustow Green 50 B3
Mutehill 106 E3
Mutford 69 F7
Muthill 127 C7
Mutterton 10 D5
Muxton 61 C7
Mybster 158 E3
Myddfai 34 B1
Myddle 60 B4
Mydroilyn 46 D3
Myerscough 92 F4
Mylor Bridge 3 C7
Mynachlog-ddu . . . 45 F3
Myndtown 60 F3
Mynydd Bach 47 B6
Mynydd-bach 36 E1
Mynydd Bodafon 82 C4
Mynydd Isa 73 C6
Mynyddygarreg . . . 33 D5
Mynytho 70 D4
Myrebird 141 E6
Myrelandhorn 158 E4
Myreside 128 B4
Myrtle Hill 47 F6
Mytchett 27 D6
Mytholm 87 B7
Mytholmroyd 87 B8
Myton-on-Swale . . 95 C7
Mytton 60 C4
N
Naast 155 J13
Naburn 95 E8
Nackington 31 D5
Nacton 57 E6
Nafferton 97 D6
Na Gearrannan . . . 154 C6
Nailbridge 36 C3
Nailsbourne 11 B7
Nailsea 23 B6
Nailstone 63 D8
Nailsworth 37 E5
Nairn 151 F11
Nalderswood 28 E3
Nancegollan 2 C5
Nancledra 2 C3
Nanhoron 70 D3
Nannau 71 E8
Nannerch 73 C5
Nanpantan 64 C2
Nanpean 4 D4
Nanstallon 4 C5
Nant-ddu 34 C4
Nanternis 46 D2
Nantgaredig 33 B5
Nantgarw 35 F5
Nant-glas 47 C8
Nantglyn 72 C4
Nantgwyn 47 B8
Nantlle 82 F5
Nantmawr 60 B2
Nantmel 48 C2
Nantmor 71 C7
Nant Peris 83 F6
Nant Uchaf 72 D4
Nantwich 74 D3
Nant-y-Bai 47 E6
Nant-y-cafn 34 D2
Nantycaws 33 C5
Nant-y-derry 35 D7
Nant-y-ffin 46 F4
Nantyffyllon 34 E2
Nantyglo 35 C5
Nant-y-moel 34 E3
Nant-y-pandy 83 D6
Naphill 39 E8
Nappa 93 D8
Napton on the Hill . 52 C2
Narberth = Arberth . 32 C2
Narborough Leics . . 64 E2
Norf 67 C7
Nasareth 82 F4
Naseby 52 B4
Nash Bucks 53 F5
Hereford 48 C5
Newport 35 F7
Shrops 49 B8
Nash Lee 39 D8
Nassington 65 E7
Nasty 41 B6
Nateby Cumb 100 D2
Lancs 92 E4
Natland 99 F7
Naughton 56 E4
Naunton Glos 37 B8
Worcs 50 F3
Naunton Beauchamp 50 D4
Navenby 78 D2
Navestock Heath . . 41 E8
Navestock Side 42 E1
Navidale 157 H13
Nawton 102 F4
Nayland 56 F3
Nazeing 41 D7
Neacroft 14 E2
Neal's Green 63 F7
Neap 160 H7
Near Sawrey 99 E5
Neasham 101 C8
Neath = Castell-Nedd . . . 33 E8
Neath Abbey 33 E8
Neatishead 69 B6
Nebo Anglesey 82 B4
Ceredig 46 C4
Conwy 83 F8
Gwyn 82 F4
Necton 67 D8
Nedd 156 F4
Nedderton 117 F8
Nedging Tye 56 E4
Needham 68 F5
Needham Market . . 56 D4
Needingworth 54 B4
Needwood 63 B5
Neen Savage 49 B8
Neen Sollars 49 B8
Neenton 61 F6
Nefyn 70 C4
Neilston 118 D4
Neinthirion 59 D6
Neithrop 52 E2
Nelly Andrews Green 60 D2
Nelson Caerph 35 E5
Lancs 93 F8
Nelson Village 111 B5
Nemphlar 119 E8
Nempnett Thrubwell 23 C7
Nene Terrace 66 D2
Nenthall 109 E7
Nenthead 109 E7
Nenthorn 122 F2
Nerabus 142 C3
Nercwys 73 C6
Nerston 119 D6
Nesbit 123 F5
Ness 73 B7
Nesscliffe 60 C3
Neston Ches W 73 B6
Wilts 24 C3
Nether Alderley . . . 74 B5
Netheravon 25 E6
Nether Blainslie . . 121 E8
Nether Booth 88 F2
Netherbrae 153 C7
Netherbrough 159 G4
Nether Broughton 64 B3
Netherburn 119 E8
Nether Burrow 93 B6
Netherbury 12 E2
Netherby Cumb . . . 108 B3
N Yorks 95 E6
Nether Cerne 12 E4
Nether Compton . . 12 C3
Nethercote 52 C3
Nethercott 20 F3
Nether Crimond . . 141 B7
Nether Dalgliesh . 115 D5
Nether Dallachy . . 152 B3
Netherend 36 D2
Nether Exe 10 D4
Netherfield 18 D4
Nether Glasslaw . . 153 C8
Netherhampton 14 B2
Nether Handwick . 134 E3
Nether Haugh 88 E5
Nether Heage 76 D3
Nether Heyford 52 D4
Nether Hindhope . 116 C3
Nether Howecleuch 114 C3
Nether Kellet 92 C5
Nether Kinmundy 153 D10
Nether Langwith . . 76 B5
Netherlaw 106 E4
Nether Leask 153 E10
Nether Lenshie . . . 153 D6
Netherley Aberds . . 141 E7
Mers 86 F2
Nethermill 114 F3
Nether Monynut . . 122 C3
Nethermuir 153 D9
Nether Padley 76 B2
Nether Park 153 C10
Netherplace 118 D5
Nether Poppleton . 95 D8
Netherseal 63 C6
Nether Silton 102 E2
Nether Stowey 22 F3
Netherthird 113 C5
Netherthong 88 D2
Netherthorpe 89 F6
Netherton Angus . . 135 D5
Devon 7 B6
Hants 25 D8
Mers 85 D4
Northumb 117 D5
Oxon 38 E4
Perth 133 D8
Stirling 119 B5
W Mid 62 F3
Worcs 50 E4
W Yorks 88 C2
W Yorks 88 C3
Nethertown Cumb . . 98 D1
Highld 158 C5
Nether Urquhart . . 128 D3
Nether Wallop 25 F8
Nether Wasdale . . . 98 D3
Nether Whitacre . . . 63 E6
Netherwitton 117 E7
Netherwood 113 B6
Nether Worton 52 F2
Nethy Bridge 139 B6
Netley 15 D5
Netley Marsh 14 C4
Netteswell 41 C7
Nettlebed 39 F7
Nettlebridge 23 E8
Nettlecombe 12 E3
Nettleden 40 C3
Nettleham 78 B3
Nettlestead 29 D7
Nettlestead Green . 29 D7
Nettlestone 15 E7
Nettlesworth 111 E5
Nettleton Lincs 90 D5
Wilts 24 B3
Neuadd 33 B7
Nevendon 42 E3
Nevern 45 E2
New Abbey 107 C6
New Aberdour 153 B8
New Addington . . . 28 C4
Newall 94 E4
New Alresford 26 F3
New Alyth 134 E2
Newark Orkney . . . 159 D8
Pboro 66 D2
Newark-on-Trent . 77 D7
New Arley 63 F6
Newarthill 119 D7
New Ash Green 29 C7
New Barn 29 C7
New Barnetby 90 C4
Newbarns 92 B2
New Barton 53 C6
Newbattle 121 C6
New Bewick 117 B6
Newbiggin Cumb . . . 92 C2
Cumb 98 E2
Cumb 99 B6
Cumb 99 B8
Cumb 109 E5
Durham 100 B4
N Yorks 100 E4
N Yorks 100 F4
Newbiggin-by-the-Sea 117 F9
Newbigging Angus . 134 E2
Angus 134 F4
Angus 134 F4
S Lanark 120 E3
Newbiggin-on-Lune 100 D2
New Bilton 52 B2
Newbold Derbys 76 B3
Leics 63 C8
Newbold on Avon . . 52 B2
Newbold on Stour . 51 E7
Newbold Pacey 51 D7
Newbold Verdon . . . 63 D8
New Bolingbroke . . 79 D6
Newborough Anglesey 82 E4
Pboro 66 D2
Staffs 62 B5
Newbottle T&W 111 D6
W Nhants 52 F3
New Boultham 78 B2
Newbourne 57 E6
New Bradwell 53 E6
New Brancepeth . . 110 E5
Newbridge Caerph . . 35 E6
Ceredig 46 D4
Corn 2 C3
Corn 5 C8
Dumfries 107 B6
Edin 120 B4
Hants 14 C3
IoW 14 F5
Newbridge continued
Pembs 44 B4
New Bridge 73 E6
Newbridge Green . . 50 F3
Newbridge-on-Usk 35 E7
Newbridge on Wye 48 D2
New Brighton Flint . 73 C6
Mers 85 E4
New Brinsley 76 D4
Newbrough 109 C8
New Broughton 73 D7
New Buckenham . . 68 E3
Newbuildings 10 D2
Newburgh Aberds . 141 B8
Aberds 153 C9
Borders 115 C6
Fife 128 C4
Lancs 86 C2
Newburn 110 C4
Newbury 26 C2
Newbury Park 41 F7
Newby Cumb 99 B7
Lancs 93 E8
N Yorks 93 B7
N Yorks 102 C3
N Yorks 103 E8
Newby Bridge 99 F5
Newby East 108 D4
New Byth 153 C8
Newby West 108 D3
Newby Wiske 102 F1
Newcastle Mon 35 C8
Shrops 60 F2
Newcastle Emlyn = Castell Newydd Emlyn 46 E2
Newcastleton or Copshaw Holm . . 115 F7
Newcastle-under-Lyme 74 E5
Newcastle upon Tyne 110 C5
New Catton 68 C5
Newchapel Pembs . . 45 F4
Powys 59 F6
Staffs 75 D5
Sur 28 E4
New Cheriton 15 B6
Newchurch Carms . . 32 B4
IoW 15 F6
Kent 19 B7
Lancs 93 F8
Mon 36 E1
Powys 48 D4
Staffs 62 B5
New Costessey 68 C4
Newcott 11 D7
New Cowper 107 E8
Newcraighall 121 B6
New Cross Ceredig . . 46 B5
London 28 B4
New Cumnock 113 C6
New Deer 153 D8
New Delaval 111 B5
Newdigate 28 E2
New Duston 52 C5
New Earswick 96 D2
New Edlington 89 E6
New Elgin 152 B2
New Ellerby 97 F7
Newell Green 27 B6
New Eltham 28 B5
New End 51 D5
Newenden 18 C5
Newent 36 B4
Newerne 36 D3
New Farnley 94 F5
New Ferry 85 F4
Newfield Durham . . 110 F5
Highld 151 D10
Newford 2 E4
Newfound 26 D3
New Fryston 89 B5
Newgale 44 C3
New Galloway 106 B3
Newgate 81 C6
Newgate Street 41 D6
New Gilston 129 D6
New Grimsby 2 E3
New Hainford 68 C5
Newhall Ches E 74 E3
Derbys 63 B6
Newhall House . . . 151 E9
Newhall Point . . . 151 E10
Newham 117 B7
Newham Hall 117 B7
New Hartley 111 B6
Newhaven Derbys . . 75 D8
Edin 121 B5
E Sus 17 D8
New Haw 27 C8
New Hedges 32 D2
New Herrington . . 111 D6
Newhey 87 C7
New Hinksey 39 D5
New Holkham 80 D4
New Holland 90 B4
Newholm 103 C6
New Houghton Derbys 76 C4
Norf 80 E3
Newhouse 119 C7
New Houses 93 B8
New Humberstone 64 D3
New Hutton 99 E7
New Hythe 29 D8
Newick 17 B8
Newingreen 19 B8
Newington Kent 19 B8
Kent 30 C2
Kent 31 C7
Notts 89 E7
Oxon 39 E6
Shrops 60 F4
New Inn Carms 46 F3
Mon 36 D1
Pembs 45 F2
Torf 35 E7
New Invention Shrops 48 B4
W Mid 62 D3
New Kelso 150 G2
New Kingston 64 B2
New Lanark 119 E8
Newland Glos 36 D2
Hull 97 F6
N Yorks 89 B7
Newland continued
Worcs 50 E2
Newlandrig 121 C6
Newlands Borders . 115 E8
Highld 151 G10
Moray 152 C3
Northumb 110 D3
Newland's Corner . 27 E8
Newlandsmuir . . . 119 D6
Newlands of Geise 158 D2
Newlands of Tynet 152 B3
Newlands Park 82 C2
New Lane 86 C2
New Lane End 86 E4
New Leake 79 D7
New Leeds 153 C9
New Longton 86 B3
Newlot 159 G6
New Luce 105 C5
Newlyn 2 D3
Newmachar 141 C7
Newmains 119 D8
New Malden 28 C3
Newmarket Suff 55 C7
W Isles 155 D9
New Marske 102 B4
New Marton 73 F7
New Micklefield . . . 95 F7
Newmill Borders . . 115 C7
Corn 2 C3
Moray 152 C4
New Mill Aberds . . . 141 F6
Herts 40 C2
Wilts 25 C6
W Yorks 88 D2
Newmill of Inshewan 134 C4
New Mills Ches E 87 F5
Corn 4 D3
Derbys 87 F7
Powys 59 D7
Newmills of Boyne 152 C5
Newmiln 133 F8
Newmilns 118 F5
New Milton 14 E3
New Moat 32 B1
Newnham Cambs . . . 54 D5
Glos 36 C3
Hants 26 D5
Herts 54 F3
Kent 30 D3
W Nhants 52 D3
Newnham Bridge . . . 49 C8
New Ollerton 77 C6
New Oscott 62 E4
Newpark 129 C6
New Park 95 D5
New Pitsligo 153 C8
New Polzeath 4 B4
Newport Devon 20 F4
Essex 55 F6
E Yorks 96 F4
Highld 158 H3
IoW 15 F6
Norf 69 C8
Telford 61 C7
Newport = Casnewydd 35 F7
Newport = Trefdraeth 45 F2
Newport-on-Tay . 129 B6
Newport Pagnell . . 53 E6
Newpound Common 16 B4
Newquay 4 C3
New Quay = Ceinewydd 46 D2
New Rackheath 69 C5
New Radnor 48 C4
New Rent 108 F4
New Ridley 110 D3
New Road Side 94 E2
New Romney 19 C7
New Rossington . . . 89 E7
New Row Ceredig . . . 47 B6
Lancs 93 F6
N Yorks 102 C4
New Sarum 25 F6
Newsbank 74 C5
Newseat Aberds . . 153 D10
Aberds 153 E7
Newsham Northumb 111 B6
N Yorks 101 C6
N Yorks 102 F1
Newsholme E Yorks 89 B8
Lancs 93 D8
New Silksworth . . 111 D6
Newsome 88 C2
Newstead Borders . 121 F8
Northumb 117 B7
Notts 76 D5
New Stevenston . . 119 D7
New Street 75 D7
New Street Lane . . . 74 F3
New Swanage 13 F8
Newthorpe 95 F7
Newton Argyll 125 F6
Borders 116 B2
Bridgend 21 B7
Cambs 54 E5
Cambs 66 C4
Cardiff 22 B4
Ches W 73 C8
Ches W 74 B2
Ches W 74 D2
Cumb 92 B2
Derbys 76 D4
Dorset 13 C5
Dumfries 108 B2
Dumfries 114 E4
Gtr Man 87 E7
Hereford 48 F5
Hereford 49 D7
Highld 151 E10
Highld 151 G10
Highld 156 F5
Highld 158 F5
Lancs 92 F4
Lancs 93 B5
Lancs 93 D6
Lincs 78 F3
Moray 152 B1
N Nhants 65 F5
Norf 67 C8
Newton continued
Northumb 110 C3
Notts 77 E6
Perth 133 F5
S Lanark 119 C6
S Lanark 120 F2
Staffs 62 B4
Suff 56 E3
Swansea 33 F7
S Yorks 89 D6
Warks 52 B3
Wilts 14 B3
W Loth 120 B3
Newton Abbot 7 B6
Newtonairds 113 F8
Newton Arlosh . . . 107 D8
Newton Aycliffe . . 101 B7
Newton Bewley . . 102 B2
Newton Blossomville 53 D7
Newton Bromswold 53 C7
Newton Burgoland 63 D7
Newton by Toft 90 F4
Newton Ferrers 6 E3
Newton Flotman . . . 68 E5
Newtongrange . . . 121 C6
Newton Hall 110 C3
Newton Harcourt . . 64 E3
Newton Heath 87 D6
Newtonhill Aberds . 141 E8
Highld 151 G8
Newton House . . . 141 B5
Newton Kyme 95 E7
Newton-le-Willows Mers 86 E3
N Yorks 101 F7
Newton Longville . . 53 F6
Newton Mearns . . 118 D5
Newtonmill 135 C6
Newtonmore 138 E3
Newton Morrell . . 101 D7
Newton Mulgrave 103 C5
Newton of Ardtoe 147 D9
Newton of Balcanquhal 128 C3
Newton of Falkland 128 D4
Newton on Ayr . . . 112 B3
Newton on Ouse . . . 95 D8
Newton-on-Rawcliffe 103 E6
Newton-on-the-Moor 117 D7
Newton on Trent . . . 77 B8
Newton Park 145 G10
Newton Poppleford 11 F5
Newton Purcell 52 F4
Newton Regis 63 D6
Newton Reigny . . . 108 F4
Newton St Cyres . . . 10 E3
Newton St Faith . . . 68 C5
Newton St Loe 24 C2
Newton St Petrock . 9 C6
Newton Solney 63 B6
Newton Stacey 26 E2
Newton Stewart . . 105 C8
Newton Tony 25 E7
Newton Tracey 9 B7
Newton under Roseberry 102 C3
Newton upon Derwent 96 E3
Newton Valence . . . 26 F5
New Totley 76 B3
Newtown Argyll . . . 125 E6
BCP 13 E8
Ches W 74 B2
Corn 3 D6
Cumb 107 E7
Cumb 108 C5
Derbys 87 F7
Devon 10 B2
Glos 36 D3
Glos 50 F4
Hants 14 B4
Hants 14 C3
Hants 15 C6
Hants 15 C7
Hants 15 D5
Hants 26 C2
Hereford 49 E8
Highld 137 D6
IoM 84 E3
IoW 14 E5
Northumb 117 B6
Northumb 117 D6
Northumb 123 F5
Shrops 73 F8
Staffs 75 C6
Staffs 75 C7
Wilts 13 B7
New Town 121 B7
Newtown = Y Drenewydd 59 E8
Newtown Linford . . 64 D2
Newtown St Boswells 121 F8
Newtown Unthank . 63 D8
New Tredegar = Tredegar Newydd 35 D5
New Trows 119 F8
Newtyle 134 E2
New Ulva 144 E6
New Walsoken 66 D4
New Waltham 91 D6
New Whittington . . 76 B3
New Wimpole 54 E4
New Winton 121 B7
New Yatt 38 C3
New York Lincs 78 D5
N Yorks 94 C4
Neyland 44 E4
Niarbyl 84 E2
Nibley 36 F3
Nibley Green 36 E4
Nibon 160 F5
Nicholashayne 11 C6
Nicholaston 33 F6
Nidd 95 C6
Nigg Aberdeen . . . 141 D8
Highld 151 D11
Nigg Ferry 151 E10
Nightcott 10 B3
Nilig 72 D4
Nine Ashes 42 D1
Ninebanks 109 D7
Nine Mile Burn . . . 120 D4
Nine Wells 44 C2
Ninfield 18 D4
Ningwood 14 F4
Nisbet 116 B2
Nisthouse Orkney . . 159 G4
Shetland 160 G7
Niton 15 G6
Nitshill 118 C5
Noak Hill 41 E8
Noblethorpe 88 D3
Nobottle 52 C4
Nocton 78 C3
Noke 39 C5
Nolton 44 D3
Nolton Haven 44 D3
No Man's Heath Ches W 74 E2
Warks 63 D6
Nomansland Devon . 10 C3
Wilts 14 C3
Noneley 60 B4
Nonikiln 151 D9
Nonington 31 D6
Noonsbrough 160 H4
Norbreck 92 E3
Norbridge 50 E2
Norbury Ches E 74 E2
Derbys 75 E8
Shrops 60 E3
Staffs 61 B7
Nordelph 67 D5
Norden 87 C6
Norden Heath 13 F7
Nordley 61 E6
Norham 122 E5
Norley 74 B2
Norleywood 14 E4
Normanby N Lincs . . 90 C2
N Yorks 103 F5
Redcar 102 C3
Normanby-by-Spital 90 F4
Normanby by Stow . 90 F2
Normanby le Wold . 90 E5
Norman Cross 65 E8
Normandy 27 D7
Norman's Bay 18 E3
Norman's Green . . . 11 D5
Normanstone 69 E8
Normanton Derby . . . 76 F3
Leics 77 E8
Lincs 78 E2
Notts 77 D7
Rutland 65 D6
W Yorks 88 B4
Normanton le Heath 63 C7
Normanton on Soar 64 B2
Normanton-on-the-Wolds 77 F6
Normanton on Trent 77 C7
Normoss 92 F3
Norney 27 E7
Norrington Common 24 C3
Norris Green 85 E4
Norris Hill 63 C7
Northacre 68 E2
Northallerton 102 E1
Northam Devon 9 B6
Soton 14 C5
Northampton 53 C5
North Anston 89 F6
North Aston 38 B4
Northaw 41 D5
North Baddesley . . . 14 C4
North Ballachulish 130 C4
North Barrow 12 B4
North Barsham 80 D5
Northbeck 78 E3
North Benfleet 42 F3
North Bersted 16 D3
North Berwick 129 F7
North Boarhunt 15 C7
Northborough 65 D8
Northbourne 31 D7
North Bovey 10 F2
North Bradley 24 D3
North Brentor 9 F6
North Brewham 24 F2
Northbridge Street 18 C4
North Buckland 20 E3
North Burlingham . 69 C6
North Cadbury 12 B4
North Cairn 104 B3
North Carlton 78 B2
North Carrine 143 H7
North Cave 96 F4
North Cerney 37 D7
Northchapel 16 B3
North Charford 14 C2
North Charlton 117 B7
North Cheriton 12 B4
Northchurch 40 D2
North Cliff 97 E8
North Cliffe 96 F4
North Clifton 77 B8
North Cockerington 91 E7
North Coker 12 C3
North Collafirth . . 160 E5
North Common 17 B7
North Connel 124 B5
North Cornelly 34 F2
North Cotes 91 D7
Northcott 8 E5
North Cove 69 F7
North Cowton 101 D7
North Crawley 53 E7
North Cray 29 B5
North Creake 80 D4
North Curry 11 B8
North Dalton 96 D5
North Dawn 159 H5
North Deighton 95 D6
Northdown 31 B7
North Duffield 96 F2
Northdyke 159 F3
North Elkington . . . 91 E6
North Elmham 81 E5
North Elmshall 89 C5
Northend Bath 24 C2

North**end** *continued*
Bucks 39 E7
Warks 51 E7
North End Bucks 39 B8
Essex 42 C2
E Yorks 97 F8
Hants 26 C2
Lincs 78 E5
N Som 23 C6
Ptsmth 15 D7
Som 11 B7
W Sus 16 D5
Northenden 87 E6
North Erradale . . 155 J12
North Fambridge 42 E4
North Fearns . . 149 E10
North
  Featherstone . . 88 B5
North Ferriby 90 B3
Northfield
  Aberdeen 141 D8
  Borders 122 C5
  E Yorks 90 B4
  W Mid 50 B5
Northfields 65 D7
Northfleet 29 B7
North Frodingham 97 D7
Northgate 65 B8
North Gluss 160 F5
North Gorley 14 C2
North Green Norf . . 68 F5
  Suff 57 C7
North Greetwell . . 78 B3
North Grimston . . 96 C4
North Halley . . . 159 H6
North Halling 29 C8
North Hayling . . . 15 D8
North Hazelrigg 123 F6
North Heasley . . . 21 F6
North Heath 16 B4
North Hill Cambs 55 B5
  Corn 5 B7
North Hinksey . . . 38 C4
North Holmwood 28 E2
Northhouse 115 D7
North Howden . . . 96 F3
North Huish 6 D5
North Hykeham . . 78 C2
Northiam 18 C5
Northill 54 E2
Northington 26 F3
North Johnston . . 44 D4
North Kelsey 90 D4
North Kelsey Moor 90 D4
North Kessock . . 151 G9
North
  Killingholme . . . 90 C5
North Kilvington . 102 F2
North Kilworth . . . 64 F3
North Kirkton . . . 153 C11
North Kiscadale 143 F11
North Kyme 78 D4
North Lancing . . . 16 D5
Northlands 79 D6
Northlea 111 D7
Northleach 37 C8
North Lee 39 C7
Northleigh 11 E6
North Leigh 38 C3
North Leverton with
  Habblesthorpe . . 89 F8
Northlew 9 E7
North Littleton . . . 51 E5
North Lopham . . . 68 F3
North Luffenham 65 D6
North Marden . . . 16 C2
North Marston . . 39 B7
North Middleton
  Midloth 121 D6
  Northumb 117 B6
North Molton 10 B2
Northmoor 38 D4
Northmoor Green or
  Moorland 22 F5
North Moreton . . . 39 F5
Northmuir 134 D3
North Mundham . 16 D2
North Muskham . . 77 D7
North Newbald . . 96 F5
North Newington 52 F2
North Newnton . . 25 D6
North Newton . . . 22 F4
Northney 15 D8
North Nibley 36 E4
North Oakley 26 D3
North Ockendon . 42 F1
Northolt 40 F4
Northop 73 C6
Northop Hall 73 C6
North Ormesby . . 102 B3
North Ormsby . . . 91 E6
Northorpe Lincs . . 65 C7
  Lincs 78 F5
  Lincs 90 E2
North
  Otterington . . . 102 F1
Northover Som . . 12 B3
  Som 12 C4
North Owersby . . 90 E4
Northowram 88 B2
North Perrott . . . 12 D2
North Petherton . 22 F4
North Petherwin . . 8 F4
North Pickenham . 67 D8
North Piddle 50 D4
North Poorton . . . 12 E3
Northport 13 F7
North Port 125 C6
Northpunds 160 L6
North
  Queensferry . . 128 F3
North Radworthy . 21 F6
North Rauceby . . 78 E3
Northrepps 81 D8
North Reston 91 F7
North Rigton 95 D5
North Rode 75 C5
North Roe 160 E5
North Runcton . . . 67 C6
North Sandwick . 160 D8
North Scale 92 C1
North Scarle 77 C8
North Seaton . . . 117 F8
North Shian 130 E3
North Shields . . . 111 C6
North Shoebury . . 43 F5
North Shore 92 F3
North Side Cumb . 98 B2
  Pboro 66 E2

North Skelton . . . 102 C4
North Somercotes 91 E8
North Stainley . . . 95 B5
North Stainmore 100 C3
North Stifford . . . 42 F2
North Stoke Bath . . 24 C2
  Oxon 39 F6
  W Sus 16 C4
Northstowe 54 C5
North Street Hants 26 F4
  Kent 30 D4
  Medway 30 B2
  W Berks 26 B4
North
  Sunderland . . . 123 F8
North Tamerton . . . 8 E5
North Tawton 9 D8
North Thoresby . . 91 E6
North Tidworth . . 25 E7
North Togston . . . 117 D8
Northtown 159 J5
North Tuddenham 68 C3
North Walbottle . . 110 C4
North Walsham . . 81 D8
North Waltham . . . 26 E3
North
  Warnborough . . 26 D5
North Water
  Bridge 135 C6
North Watten . . . 158 E4
Northway 50 F4
North Weald
  Bassett 41 D7
North Wheatley . . 89 F8
North Whilborough 7 C6
Northwich 74 B3
Northwick 36 F2
North Wick 23 C7
North Willingham 91 F5
North Wingfield . . 76 C4
North Witham . . . 65 B6
Northwold 67 E7
Northwood Derbys 76 C2
  IoW 15 E5
  Kent 31 C7
  London 40 E3
  Shrops 73 F8
Northwood Green 36 C4
North Woolwich . . 28 B5
North Wootton
  Dorset 13 C5
  Norf 67 B6
  Som 23 E7
North Wraxall . . . 24 B3
North Wroughton 38 F1
Norton E Sus 17 D8
  Glos 37 B5
  Halton 86 F3
  Herts 54 F3
  IoW 14 F4
  Mon 35 C8
  Notts 77 B5
  Powys 48 C5
  Shrops 60 F4
  Shrops 61 D5
  Shrops 61 D7
  Stockton 102 B2
  Suff 56 C3
  S Yorks 89 C6
  Wilts 37 F5
  W Nhants 52 C4
  Worcs 50 D3
  Worcs 50 E5
  W Sus 16 D3
  W Sus 16 D3
Norton Bavant . . . 24 E4
Norton Bridge . . . 75 F5
Norton Canes . . . 62 D4
Norton Canon . . . 49 E5
Norton Corner . . . 81 E6
Norton Disney . . . 77 D8
Norton East 62 D4
Norton Ferris 24 F2
Norton Fitzwarren 11 B6
Norton Green 14 F4
Norton Hawkfield 23 C7
Norton Heath 42 D2
Norton in Hales . . 74 F4
Norton-in-the-
  Moors 75 D5
Norton-Juxta-
  Twycross 63 D7
Norton-le-Clay . . 95 B7
Norton Lindsey . . 51 C7
Norton Malreward 23 C8
Norton Mandeville 42 D1
Norton-on-
  Derwent 96 B3
Norton St Philip . . 24 D2
Norton sub
  Hamdon 12 C2
Norton Woodseats 88 F4
Norwell 77 C7
Norwell
  Woodhouse . . . 77 C7
Norwich 68 D5
Norwick 160 B8
Norwood 89 F5
Norwood Hill 28 E3
Norwoodside 66 E4
Noseley 64 E4
Noss 160 M5
Noss Mayo 6 E3
Nosterfield 101 F7
Nostie 149 F13
Notgrove 37 B8
Nottage 21 B7
Nottingham 77 F5
Nottington 12 F4
Notton Wilts 24 C4
  W Yorks 88 C4
Nounsley 42 C3
Noutard's Green . 50 C2
Novar House . . . 151 E9
Nox 60 C4
Nuffield 39 F6
Nunburnholme . . 96 E4
Nuncargate 76 D5
Nuneaton 63 E7
Nuneham
  Courtenay 39 E5
Nun Hills 87 B6
Nun Monkton . . . 95 D8
Nunney 24 E2
Nunnington 96 B2
Nunnykirk 117 E6
Nunsthorpe 91 D6
Nunthorpe Mbro . 102 C3
  York 96 D2

Nunton 14 B2
Nunwick 95 B6
Nupend 36 D4
Nursling 14 C4
Nursted 15 B8
Nutbourne W Sus . 15 D8
  W Sus 16 C4
Nutfield 28 D4
Nuthall 76 E5
Nuthampstead . . . 54 F5
Nuthurst 17 B5
Nutley E Sus 17 B8
  Hants 26 E4
Nutwell 89 D7
Nybster 158 D5
Nyetimber 16 E2
Nyewood 16 B2
Nymet Rowland . . 10 D2
Nymet Tracey . . . 10 D2
Nympsfield 37 D5
Nynehead 11 B6
Nyton 16 D3

O

Oadby 64 D3
Oad Street 30 C2
Oakamoor 75 E7
Oakbank 120 C3
Oak Cross 9 E7
Oakdale 35 E5
Oake 11 B6
Oaken 62 D2
Oakenclough 92 E5
Oakengates 61 C7
Oakenholt 73 B6
Oakenshaw
  Durham 110 F5
  W Yorks 88 B2
Oakerthorpe 76 D3
Oakes 88 C2
Oakfield 35 E7
Oakford Ceredig . . 46 D3
  Devon 10 B4
Oakfordbridge . . . 10 B4
Oakgrove 75 C6
Oakham 65 D5
Oakhanger 27 F5
Oakhill 23 E8
Oakhurst 29 D6
Oakington 54 C5
Oaklands Herts . . 41 C5
  Powys 48 D2
Oakle Street 36 C4
Oakley BCP 13 E8
  Bedford 53 D8
  Bucks 39 C6
  Fife 128 F2
  Hants 26 D3
  Oxon 39 D7
  Suff 57 B5
Oakley Green 27 B7
Oakley Park 59 F6
Oakmere 74 C2
Oakridge Glos . . . 37 D6
  Hants 26 D4
Oaks 60 D4
Oaksey 37 E6
Oaks Green 75 F8
Oakthorpe 63 C7
Oakwoodhill 28 F2
Oakworth 94 F3
Oape 156 J7
Oare Kent 30 C4
  Som 21 E7
  W Berks 26 B3
  Wilts 25 C6
Oasby 78 F3
Oathlaw 134 D4
Oatlands 95 D6
Oban Argyll 124 C4
  Highld 147 C11
Oborne 12 C4
Obthorpe 65 C8
Occlestone Green 74 C3
Occold 57 B5
Ochiltree 112 B5
Ochtermuthill . . . 127 C7
Ochtertyre 127 B7
Ockbrook 76 F4
Ockham 27 D8
Ockle 147 D8
Ockley 28 F2
Ocle Pychard . . . 49 E7
Octon 97 C6
Octon Cross
  Roads 97 C6
Odcombe 12 C3
Odd Down 24 C2
Oddendale 99 C7
Odder 78 B2
Oddingley 50 D4
Oddington Glos . . 38 B2
  Oxon 39 C5
Odell 53 D7
Odie 159 F7
Odiham 26 D5
Odstock 14 B2
Odstone 63 D7
Offchurch 51 C8
Offenham 51 E5
Offham E Sus 17 C7
  Kent 29 D7
  W Sus 16 D4
Offord Cluny 54 C3
Offord Darcy 54 C3
Offton 56 E4
Offwell 11 E6
Ogbourne Maizey 25 B6
Ogbourne St
  Andrew 25 B6
Ogbourne St
  George 25 B7
Ogil 134 C4
Ogle 110 B4
Ogmore 21 B7
Ogmore-by-Sea . . 21 B7
Ogmore Vale 34 E3
Okeford Fitzpaine 13 C6
Okehampton 9 E7
Okehampton Camp 9 E7
Okraquoy 160 K6
Old 53 B5
Old Aberdeen . . . 141 D8
Old Alresford 26 F3
Oldany 156 F4
Old Arley 63 E6
Old Basford 76 E5

Old Basing 26 D4
Oldberrow 51 C6
Old Bewick 117 B6
Old Bolingbroke . . 79 C6
Old Bramhope . . . 94 E5
Old Brampton . . . 76 C3
Old Bridge of Tilt 133 C5
Old Bridge of Urr 106 C4
Old Buckenham . . 68 E3
Old Burghclere . . 26 D2
Oldbury Shrops . . 61 E7
  Warks 63 E7
  W Mid 62 F3
Oldbury-on-
  Severn 36 E3
Oldbury on the Hill 37 F5
Old Byland 102 F3
Old Cassop 111 F6
Oldcastle Bridgend . 21 B8
  Mon 35 B7
Old Castleton . . . 115 E8
Old Catton 68 C5
Old Clee 91 D6
Old Cleeve 22 E2
Old Clipstone . . . 77 C6
Old Colwyn 83 D8
Oldcotes 89 F6
Old Coulsdon . . . 28 D4
Old Crombie 152 C5
Old Dailly 112 E2
Old Dalby 64 B3
Old Deer 153 D9
Old Denaby 89 E5
Old Edlington . . . 89 E6
Old Eldon 101 B7
Old Ellerby 97 F7
Oldfallow 62 C3
Old Felixstowe . . 57 F7
Oldfield 50 C3
Old Fletton 65 E8
Old Glossop 87 E8
Old Goole 89 B8
Old Hall 59 F6
Oldham 87 D7
Oldhamstocks . . 122 B3
Old Heath 43 B6
Old Heathfield . . . 18 C2
Old Hill 62 F3
Old Hunstanton . . 80 C2
Old Hurst 54 B3
Old Hutton 99 F7
Old Kea 3 C7
Old Kilpatrick . . . 118 B4
Old Kinnernie . . . 141 D6
Old Knebworth . . 41 B5
Oldland 23 B8
Old Langho 93 F7
Old Laxey 84 D4
Old Leake 79 D7
Old Malton 96 B3
Oldmeldrum 141 B7
Old Micklefield . . 95 F7
Old Milton 14 E3
Old Milverton . . . 51 C7
Old Monkland . . . 119 C7
Old Netley 15 D5
Old Philpstoun . . 120 B3
Old Quarrington . 111 F6
Old Radnor 48 D4
Old Rattray 153 C10
Old Rayne 141 B5
Old Romney 19 C7
Oldshore Beg . . . 156 D4
Oldshoremore . . 156 D5
Old Sodbury 36 F4
Old Somerby 78 F2
Oldstead 102 F3
Old Stratford . . . 53 E5
Old Thirsk 102 F2
Oldtown 140 B4
Old Town Cumb . . 99 F7
  Northumb 116 B4
  Scilly 2 E4
Oldtown of Ord . . 152 C6
Old Trafford 87 E6
Old Tupton 76 C3
Old Warden 54 E2
Oldway 33 F6
Oldways End 10 B3
Old Weston 53 B8
Oldwhat 153 C8
Old Whittington . . 76 B3
Old Wick 158 E5
Old Windsor 27 B7
Old Wives Lees . . 30 D4
Old Woking 27 D8
Old Woodhall . . . 78 C5
Olgrinmore 158 E2
Oliver's Battery . . 15 B5
Ollaberry 160 E5
Ollerton Ches E . . 74 B4
  Notts 77 C6
  Shrops 61 B6
Olmarch 46 D5
Olney 53 D6
Olrig House 158 D3
Olton 62 F5
Olveston 36 F3
Olwen 46 E4
Ombersley 50 C3
Ompton 77 C6
Onchan 84 E3
Onecote 75 D7
Onen 35 C8
Ongar Hill 67 B5
Ongar Street 49 C5
Onibury 49 B6
Onich 130 C4
Onllwyn 34 C2
Onneley 74 E4
Onslow Village . . 27 E7
Onthank 118 E4
Openwoodgate . . 76 E3
Opinan Highld . . 149 A12
  Highld 155 H13
Orange Lane . . . 122 E3
Orange Row 66 B5
Orasaigh 155 F8
Orbliston 152 C3
Orbost 148 D7
Orby 79 C7
Orchard Hill 9 B6
Orchard Portman . 11 B7
Orcheston 25 E5
Orcop 36 B1
Orcop Hill 36 B1

Ord 149 G11
Ordhead 141 C5
Ordie 140 D3
Ordiequish 152 C3
Ordsall 89 F7
Ore 18 D5
Oreton 61 F6
Orford Suff 57 E8
  Warr 86 E4
Orgreave 63 C5
Orlestone 19 B6
Orleton Hereford . 49 C6
  Worcs 49 C8
Orlingbury 53 B6
Ormesby 102 C3
Ormesby St
  Margaret 69 C7
Ormesby St
  Michael 69 C7
Ormiclate Castle . 148 E2
Ormiscaig 155 H13
Ormiston 121 C7
Ormsaigbeg 146 E7
Ormsaigmore . . . 146 E7
Ormsary 144 F6
Ormsgill 92 B1
Ormskirk 86 D2
Orpington 29 C5
Orrell Gtr Man . . . 86 D3
  Mers 85 E4
Orrisdale 84 C3
Orroland 106 E4
Orsett 42 F2
Orslow 62 C2
Orston 77 E7
Orthwaite 108 F2
Ortner 92 D5
Orton Cumb 99 D8
  N Nhants 64 F5
Orton Longueville 65 E8
Orton-on-the-Hill 63 D7
Orton Waterville . 65 E8
Orwell 54 D4
Osbaldeston 93 F6
Osbaldwick 96 D2
Osbaston 60 B3
Osbournby 78 F3
Oscroft 74 C2
Ose 149 D8
Osgathorpe 63 C8
Osgodby Lincs . . . 90 E4
  N Yorks 96 F3
  N Yorks 103 F8
Oskaig 149 E10
Oskamull 146 G7
Osmaston Derby . 76 F3
  Derbys 76 E2
Osmington 12 F5
Osmington Mills . 12 F5
Osmotherley 102 E2
Ospisdale 151 C10
Ospringe 30 C4
Ossett 88 B3
Ossington 77 C7
Ostend 43 E5
Oswaldkirk 96 B2
Oswaldtwistle . . . 86 B5
Oswestry 60 B2
Otford 29 D6
Otham 29 D8
Othery 23 F5
Otley Suff 57 D6
  W Yorks 94 E5
Otterbourne 15 B5
Otterburn
  Northumb 116 E4
  N Yorks 93 D8
Otterburn Camp . 116 E4
Otter Ferry 145 E8
Otterham 8 E3
Otterhampton . . . 22 E4
Otterswick 160 E7
Otterton 11 F5
Ottery St Mary . . 11 E6
Ottinge 31 E5
Ottringham 91 B6
Oughterby 108 D2
Oughtershaw . . . 100 F3
Oughterside 107 E8
Oughtibridge 88 E4
Oughtrington . . . 86 F4
Oulston 95 B8
Oulton Cumb . . . 108 D2
  Norf 81 E7
  Staffs 75 F6
  Suff 69 E8
  W Yorks 88 B4
Oulton Broad 69 E8
Oulton Street . . . 81 E7
Oundle 65 F7
Ousby 109 F6
Ousdale 158 H2
Ousefleet 90 B2
Ouston Durham . . 111 D5
  Northumb 110 B3
Outertown 159 G3
Outgate 99 E5
Outhgill 100 D2
Outlane 87 C8
Out Newton 91 B7
Out Rawcliffe . . . 92 E4
Outwell 66 D5
Outwick 14 C2
Outwood Sur 28 E4
  W Yorks 88 B4
Outwoods 61 C7
Ovenden 87 B8
Ovenscloss 121 F7
Over Cambs 54 B4
  Ches W 74 C3
  S Glos 36 F2
Overbister 159 D7
Overbury 50 F4
Overcombe 12 F4
Over Compton . . . 12 C3
Overgreen 76 B3
Over Green 63 E5
Over Haddon 76 C2
Over Hulton 86 D4
Over Kellet 92 B5
Over Kiddington . 38 B4
Over Knutsford . . 74 B4
Overleigh 23 F6
Overley Green . . . 51 D5
Over Monnow . . . 36 C2
Over Norton 38 B3
Over Peover 74 B4

Overpool 73 B7
Overscaig Hotel . 156 G7
Overseal 63 C6
Over Silton 102 E2
Oversland 30 D4
Overstone 53 C6
Over Stowey 22 F3
Overstrand 81 C8
Over Stratton . . . 12 C2
Overthorpe 52 E2
Overton Aberdeen 141 C7
  Ches W 74 B2
  Dumfries 107 C6
  Hants 26 E3
  Lancs 92 D4
  N Yorks 95 D8
  Shrops 49 B7
  Swansea 33 F5
  W Yorks 88 C3
Overton = *Owrtyn* 73 E7
Overton Bridge . . 73 E7
Overtown 119 D8
Over Wallop 25 F7
Over Whitacre . . . 63 E6
Over Worton 38 B4
Oving Bucks 39 B7
  W Sus 16 D3
Ovingdean 17 D7
Ovingham 110 C3
Ovington Durham . 101 C6
  Essex 55 E8
  Hants 26 F3
  Norf 68 D2
  Northumb 110 C3
Ower 14 C4
Owermoigne 13 F5
Owlbury 60 E3
Owler Bar 76 B2
Owlerton 88 F4
Owl's Green 57 C6
Owlswick 39 D7
Owmby 90 D4
Owmby-by-Spital 90 F4
Owrtyn = Overton 73 E7
Owslebury 15 B6
Owston Leics 64 D4
  S Yorks 89 C6
Owston Ferry . . . 90 D2
Owstwick 97 F8
Owthorpe 77 F6
Oxborough 67 D7
Oxcombe 79 B6
Oxenholme 99 F7
Oxenhope 94 F3
Oxen Park 99 F5
Oxenton 50 F4
Oxenwood 25 D8
Oxford 39 D5
Oxhey 40 E4
Oxhill 51 E8
Oxley 62 D3
Oxley Green 43 C5
Oxley's Green . . . 18 C3
Oxnam 116 C2
Oxshott 28 C2
Oxspring 88 D3
Oxted 28 D4
Oxton Borders . . 121 D7
  Notts 77 D6
Oxwich 33 F5
Oxwick 80 E5
Oykel Bridge . . . 156 J6
Oyne 141 B5

P

Pabail Iarach . . . 155 D10
Pabail Uarach . . . 155 D10
Pace Gate 94 D4
Packington 63 C7
Padanaram 134 D4
Padbury 52 F5
Paddington 41 F5
Paddlesworth . . . 19 B8
Paddockhaugh . . 152 C2
Paddockhole 115 F5
Paddock Wood . . 29 E7
Padfield 87 E8
Padiham 93 F7
Padog 83 B8
Padside 94 D4
Padstow 4 B4
Padworth 26 C4
Page Bank 110 F5
Pagham 16 E2
Paglesham
  Churchend 43 E5
Paglesham
  Eastend 43 E5
Paibeil 148 B2
Paible 154 H5
Paignton 7 C6
Pailton 63 F8
Painscastle 48 E3
Painshawfield . . . 110 C3
Painsthorpe 96 D4
Painswick 37 D5
Pairc Shiaboist . . 154 C7
Paisley 118 C4
Pakefield 69 E8
Pakenham 56 C3
Pale 72 F3
Palestine 25 E7
Paley Street 27 B6
Palfrey 62 E4
Palgowan 112 F3
Palgrave 56 B5
Pallion 111 D6
Palmarsh 19 B8
Palnackie 106 D5
Palnure 105 C8
Palterton 76 C4
Pamber End 26 D4
Pamber Green . . . 26 D4
Pamber Heath . . . 26 C4
Pamhill 13 D7
Pampisford 55 E5
Pan 159 J4
Panbride 135 F5
Pancrasweek 8 D4
Pandy Gwyn 58 D3
  Mon 35 B7
  Powys 59 D6
  Wrex 73 F5
Pandy Tudur 83 E8
Panfield 42 B3

Penparc *continued*
  Pembs 44 B3
Penparcau 58 F2
Penperlleni 35 D7
Penpillick 5 D5
Penpol 3 C7
Penpoll 5 D6
Penpont Dumfries 113 E8
  Powys 34 B3
Penrherber 45 F4
Penrhiwceiber . . . 34 E4
Penrhiw goch . . . 33 C6
Penrhiw-llan 46 E2
Penrhiw-pâl 46 E2
Penrhos 70 D4
Penrhôs 35 C8
Penrhos 34 C1
Penrhosfeilw 82 C2
Penrhyn Bay 83 C8
Penrhyn-coch . . . 58 F3
Penrhyndeudraeth 71 D7
Penrhynside 83 C8
Penrice 33 F5
Penrith 108 F5
Penrose 4 B3
Penruddock 99 B6
Penryn 3 C6
Pensarn Carms . . 33 C5
  Conwy 72 B3
Pen-sarn Gwyn . . 70 C5
  Gwyn 71 E6
Pensax 50 C2
Pensby 85 F3
Penselwood 24 F2
Pensford 23 C8
Penshaw 111 D6
Penshurst 29 E6
Pensilva 5 C7
Penston 121 B7
Pentewan 3 B9
Pentir 83 E5
Pentire 4 C2
Pentlow 56 E2
Pentney 67 C7
Penton Mewsey . 25 E8
Pentraeth 82 D5
Pentre Carms . . . 33 C6
  Powys 59 F7
  Powys 60 D2
  Rhondda 34 E3
  Shrops 60 C3
  Wrex 72 F5
  Wrex 73 E6
Pentrebach M Tydf . 34 D4
  Swansea 33 D7
Pentre-bâch 46 E4
Pentre-bach 47 F8
Pentrebeirdd 59 C8
Pentre Berw 82 D4
Pentre-bont 83 F7
Pentrecagal 46 E2
Pentre-celyn Denb 72 D5
  Powys 59 D5
Pentre-chwyth . . 33 E7
Pentre-cwrt 46 F2
Pentre Dolau-
  Honddu 47 E8
Pentredwr 73 E5
Pentre-dwr 33 E7
Pentrefelin Carms . 33 B6
  Ceredig 46 E5
  Conwy 83 D8
  Gwyn 71 D6
Pentrefoelas 83 F8
Pentre-galar 45 F3
Pentregat 46 D2
Pentre-Gwenlais . 33 C7
Pentre Gwynfryn . 71 E6
Pentre Halkyn . . . 73 B6
Pentre-Isaf 83 E8
Pentre
  Llanrhaeadr . . . 72 C4
Pentre-llwyn-
  ll yd 47 D8
Pentre-llyn 46 B5
Pentre-llyn
  cymmer 72 D3
Pentre Meyrick . . 35 F6
Pentre-poeth 35 F6
Pentre'r Felin . . . 83 E8
Pentre'r-felin . . . 47 F8
Pentre-rhew 47 D5
Pentre-tafarn-y-
  fedw 83 E8
Pentre-ty-gwyn . . 47 F7
Pentrich 76 D3
Pentridge 13 C8
Pen-twyn 36 D2
Pentyrch 35 F5
Penuchadre 21 B7
Penuwch 46 C4
Penwithick 4 D5
Penwyllt 34 C2
Penybanc 33 C7
Penybont 48 C3
Pen-y-banc 33 B7
Penybont Carms . 32 B4
  Gwyn 58 D4
  Gwyn 71 E7
Pen-y-Bont Ar Ogwr
  = Bridgend 21 B8
Penybontfawr . . . 59 B7
Pen-y-bryn Gwyn . 58 C3
  Pembs 45 E3
Penycae 34 C2
Pen-y-cae 34 C2
Pen-y-cae-mawr . 35 E8
Pen-y-cefn 72 B5
Pen-y-clawdd . . . 36 D1
Pen-y-coedcae . . 34 F4
Penycwm 44 C3
Pen-y-fai 34 F2
Penyffordd 73 C7
Pen-y-ffridd 82 E5
Pen-y-garn Carms . 46 F4
  Ceredig 58 F3
Penygarnedd 59 B8
Pen-y-garnedd . . 82 D5
Pen-y-graig 70 D2
Penygraig 34 E3
Penygroes Gwyn . 82 F4
  Pembs 45 F3
Pen-y-groes 33 C6

Pen-y-groeslon...70 D3
Pen-y-Gwryd Hotel...83 F6
Penyrheol...35 F5
Pen-yr-heol...35 C8
Pen-yr-Heolgerrig...34 D4
Penysarn...82 B4
Pen-y-stryt...73 D5
Penywaun...34 D3
Penzance...2 C1
Peopleton...50 D4
Peover Heath...74 B4
Peper Harow...27 E7
Perceton...118 C3
Percie...140 E4
Percyhorner...153 B9
Periton...21 E8
Perivale...40 F4
Perkinsville...111 D5
Perlethorpe...77 B6
Perranarworthal...4 D2
Perranporth...4 D2
Perranuthnoe...2 D4
Perranzabuloe...4 D2
Perry Barr...62 E4
Perryfoot...88 F2
Perry Green Herts...41 C7
  Wilts...37 F6
Perry Street...29 B7
Pershall...74 F5
Pershore...50 E4
Pert...135 C6
Pertenhall...53 C8
Perth...128 B3
Perthy...73 F7
Perton...62 E2
Pertwood...24 F3
Peterborough...65 E8
Peterburn...155 J12
Peterchurch...48 F5
Peterculter...141 D7
Peterhead...153 D11
Peterlee...111 E7
Petersfield...15 B8
Peter's Green...40 C4
Peters Marland...9 C6
Peterstone Wentlooge...35 F6
Peterston-super-Ely...22 B2
Peterstow...36 B2
Peter Tavy...6 B3
Petertown...159 H4
Petham...30 D5
Petrockstow...9 D7
Pett...19 D5
Pettaugh...57 D5
Petteridge...29 E7
Pettinain...120 E2
Pettistree...57 D6
Petton Devon...10 B5
  Shrops...60 B4
Petts Wood...28 C5
Petty...153 E7
Pettycur...128 F4
Pettymuick...141 B8
Petworth...16 B3
Pevensey...18 E3
Pevensey Bay...18 E3
Pewsey...25 C6
Philham...8 B4
Philiphaugh...115 B7
Phillack...2 C1
Philleigh...3 C7
Philpstoun...120 B3
Phocle Green...36 B3
Phoenix Green...27 D5
Pica...98 B2
Piccotts End...40 D3
Pickering...103 F5
Picket Piece...25 E8
Picket Post...14 D2
Pickhill...101 F8
Picklescott...60 E4
Pickletillem...129 B6
Pickmere...74 B3
Pickney...11 B6
Pickstock...61 B7
Pickwell Devon...20 E3
  Leics...64 C4
Pickworth Lincs...78 F3
  Rutland...65 D6
Picton Ches W...73 B8
  Flint...85 F2
  N Yorks...102 D2
Piddinghoe...17 D8
Piddington Oxon...39 C6
  W Nhants...53 D6
Piddlehinton...12 E5
Piddletrenthide...12 E5
Pidley...54 B4
Piercebridge...101 C7
Pierowall...159 D6
Pigdon...117 F7
Pikehall...75 D8
Pilgrims Hatch...42 E1
Pilham...90 E2
Pill...23 B7
Pillaton...5 C8
Pillerton Hersey...51 E8
Pillerton Priors...51 E7
Pilleth...48 C4
Pilley Hants...14 E4
  S Yorks...88 D4
Pilling...92 E4
Pilling Lane...92 E3
Pillowell...36 D3
Pillwell...13 C5
Pilning...36 F2
Pilsbury...75 C8
Pilsdon...12 E2
Pilsgate...65 D7
Pilsley Derbys...76 B3
  Derbys...76 C4
Pilton Devon...20 F4
  N Nhants...65 F7
  Rutland...65 D6
  Som...23 F7
Pilton Green...33 F5
Pimperne...13 D7
Pinchbeck...66 B2
Pinchbeck Bars...65 B8
Pinchbeck West...66 B2
Pincheon Green...89 C7
Pinehurst...38 F1

Pinfold...85 C4
Pinged...33 D5
Pinhoe...10 E4
Pinkneys Green...40 F1
Pinley...51 B8
Pin Mill...57 F6
Pinminnoch...112 E1
Pinmore...112 E2
Pinmore Mains...112 E2
Pinner...40 F4
Pinvin...50 E4
Pinwherry...112 F1
Pinxton...76 D4
Pipe and Lyde...49 E7
Pipe Gate...74 E4
Piperhill...151 F11
Piper's Pool...8 F4
Pipewell...64 F5
Pippacott...20 F4
Pipton...48 F3
Pirbright...27 D7
Pirnmill...143 D9
Pirton Herts...54 F2
  Worcs...50 E3
Pisgah Ceredig...47 B5
  Stirling...127 D6
Pishill...39 F7
Pistyll...70 C4
Pitagowan...133 C5
Pitblae...153 B9
Pitcairngreen...128 B2
Pitcalnie...151 D11
Pitcaple...141 B6
Pitch Green...39 D7
Pitchcombe...37 D5
Pitchcott...39 B7
Pitchford...60 D5
Pitch Green...39 D7
Pitch Place...27 D7
Pitcombe...23 F8
Pitcorthie...129 D7
Pitcox...122 B2
Pitcur...134 F2
Pitfichie...141 C5
Pitforthie...135 B8
Pitgrudy...151 B10
Pitkennedy...135 D5
Pitkevy...128 D4
Pitkierie...129 D7
Pitlessie...128 D5
Pitlochry...133 D6
Pitmachie...141 B5
Pitmain...138 D3
Pitmedden...141 B7
Pitminster...11 C7
Pitmuies...135 E5
Pitmunie...141 C5
Pitney...12 B2
Pitscottie...129 C6
Pitsea...42 F3
Pitsford...53 C5
Pitsmoor...88 F4
Pitstone...40 C2
Pitstone Green...40 C2
Pittendreich...152 B1
Pittentrail...157 J10
Pittenweem...129 D7
Pittington...111 E6
Pittodrie...141 B5
Pitton...25 F7
Pittswood...29 E7
Pittulie...153 B9
Pityme...4 B4
Pity Me...111 E5
Pityoulish...138 C5
Pixey Green...57 B6
Pixham...28 D2
Pixley...49 E8
Place Newton...96 B4
Plains...119 C7
Plaish...60 E5
Plaistow...27 F8
Plaitford...14 C3
Plank Lane...86 E4
Plas-canol...58 F2
Plas Gogerddan...58 F3
Plas Llwyngwern...58 D4
Plas Nantyr...73 F5
Plastow Green...26 C3
Plas-yn-Cefn...72 B4
Platt...29 D7
Platt Bridge...86 D4
Platts Common...88 D4
Plawsworth...111 E5
Plaxtol...29 D7
Playden...19 C6
Playford...57 E6
Play Hatch...26 B5
Playing Place...3 B7
Playley Green...50 F2
Plealey...60 D4
Plean...127 F7
Pleasington...86 B4
Pleasley...76 C5
Pleckgate...93 F6
Plenmeller...109 C7
Pleshey...42 C2
Plockton...149 E13
Plocrapol...154 H6
Ploughfield...49 E5
Plowden...60 F3
Ploxgreen...60 D3
Pluckley...30 E3
Pluckley Thorne...30 E3
Plumbland...107 F8
Plumley...74 B4
Plumpton Cumb...108 F4
  E Sus...17 C7
Plumpton Green...17 C7
Plumpton Head...108 F4
Plumstead London...29 B5
  Norf...81 D7
Plumtree...77 F6
Plungar...77 F7
Plush...12 D5
Plwmp...46 D2
Plymouth...6 D2
Plympton...6 D3
Plymstock...6 D3
Plymtree...11 D5
Pockley...102 F4
Pocklington...96 E4
Pode Hole...66 B2
Podimore...12 B3
Podmore...74 F4
Point Clear...43 C6
Pointon...78 F4
Pokesdown...14 E2

Pol a Charra...148 G2
Polbae...105 B6
Polbain...156 H2
Polbathic...5 D8
Polbeth...120 C3
Polchar...138 D4
Polebrook...65 F7
Pole Elm...50 E3
Polegate...18 E2
Poles...151 B10
Polesworth...63 D6
Polgigga...2 D1
Polglass...156 J3
Polgooth...4 D4
Poling...16 D4
Polkerris...5 D5
Polla...156 D6
Pollard's Green...89 C7
Polloch...130 C1
Pollok...118 C5
Pollokshields...119 C5
Polmassick...3 B8
Polmont...120 B2
Polnessan...112 C4
Polnish...147 C10
Polperro...5 D7
Polruan...5 D6
Polsham...23 E7
Polstead...56 F3
Poltalloch...124 F4
Poltimore...10 E4
Polton...121 C5
Polwarth...122 D3
Polyphant...8 F4
Polzeath...4 B4
Pondersbridge...66 E2
Ponders End...41 E6
Pondtail...27 D6
Ponsanooth...3 C6
Ponsonby...98 D2
Ponsworthy...6 B5
Pont Aber...33 B8
Pont Aber-Geirw...71 E8
Pontamman...33 C7
Pontantwn...33 C5
Pontardawe...33 D8
Pontarddulais...33 D6
Pont ar-gothi...33 B6
Pont ar Hydfer...34 B2
Pont-ar-llechau...33 B8
Pontarsais...33 B5
Pontblyddyn...73 C6
Pontbren Araeth...33 B7
Pontbren Llwyd...34 D3
Pont Cwm Pydew...72 F4
Pont Cyfyng...83 F7
Pont Cysyllte...73 E6
Pont Dolydd Prysor...71 D8
Pontefract...89 B5
Ponteland...110 B4
Ponterwyd...58 F4
Pontesbury...60 D3
Pontfadog...73 F6
Pont-faen...46 F2
Pont-faen...47 F8
Pont Fronwydd...58 B5
Pont-gareg...45 E3
Pontgarreg...46 D2
Pont-Henri...33 D5
Ponthir...35 E7
Ponthirwaun...45 E4
Pontllanfraith...35 E5
Pontlliw...33 D7
Pont-Llogel...59 C7
Pontllyfni...82 F4
Pontlottyn...35 D5
Pontneddfechan...34 D3
Pontnewydd...35 E6
Pont Pen-y-benglog...83 E6
Pontrhydfendigaid...47 C6
Pont Rhyd-goch...83 E6
Pont-Rhyd-sarn...59 B5
Pont Rhyd-y-cyff...34 F2
Pontrhydyfen...34 E1
Pont-rhyd-y-groes...47 B6
Pontrilas...35 B7
Pontrobert...59 C8
Pont-rug...82 E5
Pont Senni = Sennybridge...34 B3
Ponts Green...18 D3
Pontshill...36 B3
Pont-siân...46 E3
Pontsticill...34 C4
Pontwgan...83 D7
Pontyates...33 D5
Pontyberem...33 C6
Pontyclun...34 F4
Pontycymer...34 E3
Pontyglasier...45 F3
Pont-y-gwaith...34 E4
Pont-y-pant...83 F7
Pont y Pennant...59 B6
Pontypool = Pont-y-pŵl...35 D6
Pontypridd...34 F4
Pont-y-pŵl = Pontypool...35 D6
Pont yr Afon-Gam...71 C8
Pont-yr-hafod...44 C4
Pontywaun...35 E6
Pooksgreen...14 C4
Pool Corn...3 B5
  W Yorks...94 E5
Poole...13 E8
Poole Keynes...37 E6
Poolend...75 D6
Poolewe...155 J13
Pooley Bridge...99 B6
Poolfold...75 D5
Poolhill...36 B4
Pool o'Muckhart...128 D2
Pool Quay...60 C2
Poolsbrook...76 B4
Pootings...29 E5
Pope Hill...44 D4
Popeswood...27 C6
Popham...26 E3
Poplar...41 F6
Popley...26 D4
Porchester...77 E5
Porchfield...14 E5
Porin...150 F6
Poringland...69 D5
Porkellis...3 C6
Porlock...21 E7
Porlock Weir...21 E7

Portachoillan...144 H6
Port Ann...145 E8
Port Appin...130 E3
Port Arthur...160 K5
Port Askaig...142 B5
Portavadie...145 G8
Portbury...23 B7
Port Carlisle...108 C2
Port Charlotte...142 C3
Portchester...15 D7
Portclair...137 C7
Port Clarence...102 B2
Port Driseach...145 F8
Port Ellen...142 D4
Port Elphinstone...141 C6
Portencalzie...118 E1
Portencross...118 E1
Port Erin...84 F1
Port Erroll...153 E10
Portesham...12 F4
Portessie...152 B4
Port e Vullen...84 C4
Port-Eynon...33 F5
Portfield Gate...44 D4
Portgate...9 F6
Port Gaverne...4 B4
Port Glasgow...118 B3
Portgordon...152 B3
Portgower...157 H13
Porth...34 E4
  Rhondda...34 E4
Porthaethwy = Menai Bridge...83 D5
Porthallow Corn...3 D6
  Corn...5 D7
Porthcawl...21 B7
Porthcothan...4 B3
Porthcurno...2 D2
Port Henderson...149 A12
Porthgain...44 B3
Porthill...60 C4
Porthkerry...22 C2
Porthleven...2 D5
Porthllechog...82 B4
Porthmadog...71 D6
Porthmeor...2 C3
Porth Navas...3 D6
Portholland...3 B8
Porthoustock...3 D7
Porthpean...4 D5
Porthtowan...3 B5
Porth Tywyn = Burry Port...33 D5
Porthyrhyd Carms...33 C6
  Carms...47 F6
Porth-y-waen...60 B2
Portincaple...145 D11
Portington...96 F3
Portinnisherrich...125 D5
Portinscale...98 B4
Port Isaac...4 A4
Portishead...23 B6
Portkil...145 E11
Portknockie...152 B4
Port Lamont...145 F9
Portlethen...141 E8
Portling...107 D5
Port Lion...44 E4
Portloe...3 C8
Port Logan...104 E4
Portmahomack...151 C12
Portmeirion...71 D6
Portmellon...3 B9
Port Mholair...155 D10
Port Mor...146 D7
Portmore...14 E4
Port Mulgrave...103 C5
Portnacroish...130 E3
Portnahaven...142 C2
Portnalong...149 E8
Portnaluchaig...147 C9
Portnancon...156 C7
Port Nan Giùran...155 D10
Port nan Long...148 A3
Portnellan...126 B3
Port Nis...155 A10
Portobello...121 B6
Port of Menteith...126 D4
Porton...25 F6
Portpatrick...104 D4
Port Quin...4 A4
Port Ramsay...130 E2
Portreath...3 B5
Portree...149 D9
Port St Mary...84 F2
Portscatho...3 C7
Portsea...15 D7
Portskerra...157 C11
Portskewett...36 F2
Portslade...17 D6
Portslade-by-Sea...17 D6
Portsmouth Ptsmth...15 D7
  W Yorks...87 B7
Portsonachan...125 C6
Portsoy...152 B5
Port Sunlight...85 F4
Portswood...14 C5
Port Talbot...34 E1
Porttanachy...152 B3
Port Tennant...33 E7
Portuairk...146 E7
Portway Hereford...49 F6
  Worcs...51 B5
Port Wemyss...142 C2
Port William...105 E7
Portwrinkle...5 D8
Posenhall...61 D6
Poslingford...55 E8
Postbridge...6 B4
Postcombe...39 E7
Postling...19 B8
Postwick...69 D5
Potholm...115 F6
Potsgrove...40 B2
Pott End...40 D3
Potten End...40 D3
Potter Brompton...97 B5
Potterhanworth...78 C3
Potterhanworth Booths...78 C3
Potter Heigham...69 C7
Potterne...24 D4
Potterne Wick...24 D5
Potternewton...95 F6
Potters Bar...41 D5
Potter's Cross...62 F2
Potterspury...53 E5
Potter Street...41 D7
Potterton Aberds...141 C8

Potterton continued
  W Yorks...95 F7
Potto...102 D2
Potton...54 E3
Pott Row...80 E3
Pott Shrigley...75 B6
Poughill Corn...8 D4
  Devon...10 D3
Poulshot...24 D4
Poulton Glos...37 D8
  Mers...85 E4
Poulton-le-Fylde...92 F3
Pound Bank...50 B2
Poundbury...12 E4
Poundfield...18 B2
Pound Green
  E Sus...18 C2
  IoW...14 F4
  Worcs...50 B2
Pound Hill...28 F3
Poundland...112 F1
Poundon...39 B6
Poundsgate...6 B5
Poundstock...8 E4
Powburn...117 C6
Powderham...10 F4
Powerstock...12 E3
Powfoot...107 C8
Powick...50 D3
Powmill...128 E2
Poxwell...12 F5
Poyle...27 B8
Poynings...17 C6
Poyntington...12 C4
Poynton...87 F7
Poynton Green...61 C5
Poystreet Green...56 D3
Praa Sands...2 D4
Pratt's Bottom...29 C5
Praze...2 C4
Praze-an-Beeble...2 C5
Predannack Wollas...3 E5
Prees...74 F2
Preesall...92 E3
Prees Green...74 F2
Preesgweene...73 F6
Prees Heath...74 F2
Prees Higher Heath...74 F2
Prees Lower Heath...74 F2
Prendergast...44 D4
Prendwick...117 C6
Prengwyn...46 E3
Prenteg...71 C6
Prenton...85 F4
Prescot...86 E2
Prescott...60 B4
Pressen...122 F4
Prestatyn...72 A4
Prestbury Ches E...75 B6
  Glos...37 B6
Presteigne = Llanandras...48 C5
Presthope...61 E5
Prestleigh...23 E8
Preston Borders...122 D3
  Brighton...17 D7
  Devon...7 B6
  Dorset...12 F5
  E Loth...121 B8
  E Yorks...97 F7
  Glos...37 D7
  Glos...49 F8
  Herts...40 B4
  Kent...30 C4
  Kent...31 C6
  Lancs...86 B3
  Northumb...117 B7
  Rutland...65 D5
  Shrops...60 C5
  Wilts...24 B5
  Wilts...25 B7
Preston Bagot...51 C6
Preston Bissett...39 B6
Preston Bowyer...11 B6
Preston Brockhurst...60 B5
Preston Brook...86 F3
Preston Candover...26 E4
Preston Capes...52 D3
Preston Crowmarsh...39 E6
Preston Gubbals...60 C4
Prestonmill...107 D6
Preston on Stour...51 E7
Preston on the Hill...86 F3
Preston on Wye...49 E5
Prestonpans...121 B6
Preston Plucknett...12 C3
Preston St Mary...56 D3
Preston-under-Scar...101 E5
Preston upon the Weald Moors...61 C6
Preston Wynne...49 E7
Prestwich...87 D6
Prestwick Northumb...110 B4
  S Ayrs...112 B3
Prestwood...40 D1
Price Town...34 E3
Prickwillow...67 F5
Priddy...23 D7
Priesthaugh...115 D7
Priest Hutton...92 B5
Priest Weston...60 E2
Primethorpe...64 E2
Primrose Green...68 C3
Primrosehill...40 D3
Primrose Valley...97 B7
Princes Gate...32 C2
Princes Risborough...39 D8
Princethorpe...52 B2
Princetown Caerph...35 C5
  Devon...6 B3
Prion...72 C4
Prior Muir...129 C7
Prior Park...123 D5
Priors Frome...49 F7
Priors Hardwick...52 D2
Priorslee...61 C7
Priors Marston...52 D2
Priory Wood...48 E4
Pristow Green...68 F4
Prittlewell...42 F4
Privett...15 B7
Prixford...20 F4

Probus...3 B7
Proncy...151 B10
Prospect...107 E8
Prudhoe...110 C3
Ptarmigan Lodge...132 E1
Pubil...132 E1
Puckeridge...41 B6
Puckington...11 C8
Pucklechurch...23 B8
Pucknall...14 B4
Puckrup...50 F3
Puddinglake...74 C4
Puddington Ches W...73 B7
  Devon...10 C3
Puddledock...68 E3
Puddletown...13 E5
Pudleston...49 D7
Pudsey...94 F5
Pulborough...16 C4
Puleston...61 B7
Pulford...73 D7
Pulham...12 D5
Pulham Market...68 F4
Pulham St Mary...68 F5
Pulloxhill...53 F8
Pumpherston...120 C3
Pumsaint...47 E5
Puncheston...32 B1
Puncknowle...12 F3
Punnett's Town...18 C3
Purbrook...15 D7
Purewell...14 E2
Purfleet...29 B6
Puriton...22 E5
Purleigh...42 D4
Purley London...28 C4
  W Berks...26 B4
Purlogue...48 B4
Purls Bridge...66 F4
Purse Caundle...12 C4
Purslow...60 F3
Purston Jaglin...88 C5
Purton Glos...36 D3
  Glos...36 D3
  Wilts...37 F7
Purton Stoke...37 E7
Pury End...52 E5
Pusey...38 E3
Putley...49 F8
Putney...28 B3
Putsborough...20 E3
Puttenham Herts...40 C1
  Sur...27 E7
Puxton...23 C6
Pwll...33 D5
Pwllcrochan...44 E4
Pwll-glas...72 D5
Pwllgloyw...48 F2
Pwllheli...70 D4
Pwllmeyric...36 E2
Pwll-trap...32 C3
Pwll-y-glaw...34 E1
Pyecombe...17 C6
Pye Corner...35 F7
Pye Green...62 C3
Pyewipe...91 C6
Pyle...15 G5
Pyle = Y Pîl...34 F2
Pylle...23 F8
Pymoor...66 F4
Pyrford...27 D8
Pyrton...39 E6
Pytchley...53 B6
Pyworthy...8 D5

Q
Quabbs...60 F2
Quadring...78 F5
Quainton...39 C7
Quarley...25 E7
Quarndon...76 E3
Quarrier's Homes...118 C3
Quarrington...78 E3
Quarrington Hill...111 F6
Quarry Bank...62 F3
Quarryford...121 C8
Quarryhill...151 C10
Quarrywood...152 B1
Quarter...119 D7
Quatford...61 E7
Quatt...61 F7
Quebec...110 E4
Quedgeley...37 C5
Queen Adelaide...67 F5
Queenborough...30 B3
Queen Camel...12 B3
Queen Charlton...23 C8
Queen Dart...10 C3
Queenhill...50 F3
Queen Oak...24 F2
Queensbury...94 F4
Queensferry Edin...120 B4
  Flint...73 C7
Queensferry Crossing...120 B4
Queen's Head...60 B3
Queen's Park Bedford...53 E8
  W Nhants...53 C5
Queenstown...92 F3
Queen Street Kent...29 E7
  Wilts...37 F7
Queenzieburn...119 B6
Quemerford...24 C5
Quendale...160 M5
Quendon...55 F6
Queniborough...64 C3
Quenington...37 D8
Quernhead...92 D5
Quernmore...92 D5
Quethiock...5 C8
Quholm...159 G3
Quicks Green...26 B3
Quidenham...68 F3
Quidhampton Hants...26 D3
  Wilts...25 F6
Quilquox...153 E9
Quina Brook...74 F2
Quindry...159 J5
Quinton W Mid...62 F3
  W Nhants...53 D5
Quintrell Downs...4 C3
Quixhill...75 E8
Quoditch...9 E6
Quoig...127 B7

Quorndon...64 C2
Quothquan...120 F2
Quoyloo...159 F3
Quoyness...159 H3
Quoys Shetland...160 B8
  Shetland...160 G6

R
Raasay House...149 E10
Rabbit's Cross...29 E8
Raby...73 B7
Rachan Mill...120 F4
Rachub...83 E6
Rackenford...10 C3
Rackham...16 C4
Rackheath...69 C5
Racks...107 B7
Rackwick Orkney...159 D5
  Orkney...159 J3
Radbourne...76 F2
Radcliffe Gtr Man...87 D5
  Northumb...117 D8
Radcliffe on Trent...77 F6
Radclive...52 F4
Radcot...38 E2
Raddery...151 F10
Radernie...129 D6
Radford Semele...51 C8
Radipole...12 F4
Radlett...40 E4
Radley...39 E5
Radmanthwaite...76 C5
Radmoor...61 B6
Radmore Green...74 D2
Radnage...39 E7
Radstock...23 D8
Radstone...52 E3
Radway...51 E8
Radway Green...74 D4
Radwell Bedford...53 D8
  Herts...54 F3
Radwinter...55 F7
Radyr...35 F5
Rafford...151 F13
Ragdale...64 C3
Raglan...35 D8
Ragnall...77 B8
Rahane...145 E11
Rainford...86 D2
Rainford Junction...86 D2
Rainham London...41 F8
  Medway...30 C2
Rainhill...86 E2
Rainhill Stoops...86 E3
Rainow...75 B6
Rainton...95 B6
Rainworth...77 D6
Raisbeck...99 D8
Raise...109 E7
Rait...128 B4
Raithby Lincs...79 C6
  Lincs...91 F7
Rake...16 B2
Rakewood...87 C7
Ram...46 E4
Ramasaig...148 D6
Rame Corn...3 C6
  Corn...6 E2
Rameldry Mill Bank...128 D5
Ram Lane...30 E3
Ramnageo...160 C8
Rampisham...12 D3
Rampside...92 C2
Rampton Cambs...54 C5
  Notts...77 B7
Ramsbottom...87 C5
Ramsbury...25 B7
Ramscraigs...158 H3
Ramsdean...15 B8
Ramsdell...26 D3
Ramsden...38 C3
Ramsden Bellhouse...42 E3
Ramsden Heath...42 E3
Ramsey Cambs...66 F2
  Essex...57 F6
  IoM...84 C4
Ramsey Forty Foot...66 F3
Ramsey Heights...66 F2
Ramsey Island...43 D5
Ramsey Mereside...66 F2
Ramsey St Mary's...66 F2
Ramsgate...31 C7
Ramsgill...94 B4
Ramshorn...75 E7
Ramsnest Common...27 F7
Ranais...155 E9
Ranby Lincs...78 B5
  Notts...89 F7
Rand...78 B4
Randwick...37 D5
Ranfurly...118 C3
Rangag...158 F3
Rangemore...63 B5
Rangeworthy...36 F3
Rankinston...112 C4
Ranmoor...88 F4
Ranmore Common...28 D2
Rannerdale...98 C2
Rannoch Station...131 D8
Ranochan...147 C11
Ranskill...89 F7
Ranton...62 B2
Ranworth...69 C6
Raploch...127 E6
Rapness...159 D6
Rascal Moor...96 F4
Rascarrel...106 E4
Rashiereive...141 B8
Raskelf...95 B7
Rassau...35 C5
Ratagan...136 C2
Ratby...64 D2
Ratcliffe Culey...63 E7
Ratcliffe on Soar...63 B8
Ratcliffe on the Wreake...64 C3
Rathen...153 B10
Rathillet...129 B5
Rathmell...93 D8
Ratho...120 B4
Ratho Station...120 B4
Rathven...152 B4

Ratley...51 E8
Ratlinghope...60 E4
Rattar...158 C4
Ratten Row...92 E4
Rattery...6 C5
Rattlesden...56 D3
Rattray...134 E1
Raughton Head...108 E3
Raunds...53 B7
Ravenfield...89 E5
Ravenglass...98 E2
Raveningham...69 E6
Ravenscar...103 D7
Ravenscraig...118 B2
Ravensdale...84 C3
Ravensden...53 D8
Ravenseat...100 D3
Ravenshead...77 D5
Ravensmoor...74 D3
Ravensthorpe W Nhants...52 B4
  W Yorks...88 B3
Ravenstone Leics...63 C8
  M Keynes...53 D6
Ravenstonedale...100 D2
Ravenstown...92 B3
Ravensworth...101 D6
Raw...103 D7
Rawcliffe E Yorks...89 B7
  York...95 D8
Rawcliffe Bridge...89 B7
Rawdon...94 F5
Rawmarsh...88 E5
Rawreth...42 E3
Rawridge...11 D7
Rawtenstall...87 B6
Raxton...153 E8
Raydon...56 F4
Raylees...117 E5
Rayleigh...42 E4
Rayne...42 B3
Rayners Lane...40 F4
Raynes Park...28 C3
Reach...55 C6
Read...93 F7
Reading...26 B5
Reading Street...19 B6
Reagill...99 C8
Rearquhar...151 B10
Rearsby...64 C3
Reaster...158 D4
Reawick...160 J5
Reay...157 C12
Reculver...31 C6
Redberth...32 D1
Redbourn...40 C4
Redbourne...90 E3
Redbrook Mon...36 C2
Redburn Highld...151 E13
  Highld...151 G12
  Northumb...109 C7
Redcar...102 B4
Redcastle Highld...151 G8
  Angus...135 D6
Redding...120 B2
Reddingmuirhead...120 B2
Reddish...87 E6
Redditch...50 C5
Rede...56 D2
Redenhall...69 F5
Redesdale Camp...116 E4
Redesmouth...116 F4
Redford Aberds...135 B7
  Angus...135 E5
  Durham...110 F3
Redfordgreen...115 C6
Redgorton...128 B2
Redgrave...56 B4
Redhill Aberds...153 E6
  N Som...23 C7
  Sur...28 D3
Red Hill...51 D6
Redhouse...145 G7
Redhouses...142 B4
Red Houses...17 I3
Redisham...69 F7
Redland Bristol...23 B7
  Orkney...159 F4
Redlingfield...57 B5
Red Lodge...55 B7
Redlynch Som...23 F9
  Wilts...14 B3
Redmarley D'Abitot...50 F2
Redmarshall...102 B1
Redmile...77 F7
Redmire...101 E5
Redmoor...5 C5
Rednal...50 B4
Redpath...121 F8
Redpoint...149 B12
Red Rail...36 B2
Red Rock...86 D3
Red Roses...32 C3
Red Row...117 E8
Redruth...3 B5
Red Street...74 D5
Redvales...87 D6
Red Wharf Bay...82 C5
Redwick Newport...35 F8
  S Glos...36 F2
Redworth...101 B7
Reed...54 F4
Reedham...69 D7
Reedness...89 B8
Reeds Beck...78 C5
Reepham Lincs...78 B3
  Norf...81 E6
Reeth...101 E5
Regaby...84 C4
Regoul...151 F11
Reiff...156 H2
Reigate...28 D3
Reighton...97 B7
Reighton Gap...97 B7
Reinigeadal...154 G7
Reiss...158 E5
Rejerrah...4 D2
Releath...3 C5
Relubbus...2 C4
Relugas...151 G12
Remenham...39 F7

Remenham Hill...39 F7
Remony...132 E4
Rempstone...64 B2
Rendcomb...37 D7
Rendham...57 C7
Rendlesham...57 D7
Renfrew...118 C5
Renhold...53 D8
Renishaw...76 B4
Rennington...117 C8
Renton...118 B3
Renwick...109 E5
Repps...69 C7
Repton...63 B7
Reraig...149 E13
Rescobie...135 D5
Resipole...147 E10
Resolis...151 E9
Resolven...34 D2
Reston...122 C4
Reswallie...135 D5
Retew...4 D4
Retford...89 F8
Rettendon...42 E3
Rettendon Place...42 E3
Revesby...79 C5
Revesby Bridge...79 C6
Rew...10 E4
New Street...15 E5
Rewe...10 E4
Reydon...57 B8
Reydon Smear...57 B8
Reymerston...68 D3
Reynalton...32 D1
Reynoldston...33 E5
Rezare...5 B8
Rhaeadr Gwy = Rhayader...47 C8
Rhandirmwyn...47 E6
Rhayader = Rhaeadr Gwy...47 C8
Rhedyn...70 D3
Rhemore...147 F8
Rhencullen...84 C3
Rhes-y-cae...73 B5
Rhewl Denb...72 C5
  Denb...73 E5
Rhian...157 H8
Rhicarn...156 G3
Rhiconich...156 D5
Rhicullen...151 D9
Rhidorroch House...150 B4
Rhifail...157 E10
Rhigos...34 D3
Rhilochan...157 J10
Rhiroy...150 C4
Rhisga = Risca...35 E6
Rhiw...70 E3
Rhiwabon = Ruabon...73 E7
Rhiwbina...35 F5
Rhiwbryfdir...71 C7
Rhiwderin...35 F6
Rhiwlas Gwyn...72 F3
  Gwyn...83 E5
  Powys...73 F5
Rhodes...87 D6
Rhodesia...77 B5
Rhodes Minnis...31 E5
Rhodiad...44 C2
Rhondda...34 E3
Rhonehouse or Kelton Hill...106 D4
Rhoose = Y Rhws...22 C2
Rhôs Carms...46 F2
  Neath...33 D8
Rhosaman...33 C8
Rhosbeirio...82 B3
Rhoscefnhir...82 D5
Rhoscolyn...82 D2
Rhoscrowther...44 E4
Rhosesmor...73 C6
Rhos-fawr...70 D4
Rhosgadfan...82 F5
Rhosgoch...82 C4
Rhos-goch...48 E3
Rhos-hill...45 E3
Rhoshirwaun...70 E2
Rhoslan...71 C5
Rhoslefain...58 D2
Rhosllanerchrugog...73 E6
Rhosmaen...33 B7
Rhosmeirch...82 D4
Rhosneigr...82 D3
Rhosnesni...73 D7
Rhos-on-Sea...83 C8
Rhosrobin...73 D7
Rhossili...33 F5
Rhosson...44 C2
Rhostryfan...82 F4
Rhostyllen...73 E7
Rhosybol...82 C4
Rhos-y-brithdir...59 B8
Rhos-y-garth...46 B5
Rhos-y-gwaliau...72 F3
Rhos-y-llan...70 D3
Rhos-y-Madoc...73 E7
Rhos-y-meirch...48 C4
Rhu Argyll...145 E11
  Argyll...145 G7
Rhuallt...72 B4
Rhuddall Heath...74 C2
Rhuddlan Ceredig...46 E3
  Denb...72 B4
Rhue...150 B3
Rhulen...48 E3
Rhunahaorine...143 D8
Rhuthun = Ruthin...72 D5
Rhyd Gwyn...71 C7
  Powys...59 D6
Rhydaman = Ammanford...33 C7
Rhydargaeau...33 B5
Rhydcymerau...46 F4
Rhydd...50 E3
Rhyd-Ddu...83 F5
Rhydding...33 E8
Rhydfudr...46 C4
Rhydlewis...46 E2
Rhydlios...70 D2
Rhydlydan...83 F8
Rhyd-moel-ddu...48 B2
Rhydness...48 E3
Rhydowen...46 E3
Rhyd-Rosser...46 C4
Rhydspence...48 E4
Rhydtalog...73 D6
Rhyd-uchaf...72 F3

Rhyd-wen 58 C4
Rhydwyn 82 C3
Rhyd-y-clafdy . . . 70 D2
Rhydycroesau . . . 73 F6
Rhydyfelin Ceredig . 46 B4
  Rhondda 34 F4
Rhyd-y-foel 72 B3
Rhyd-y-fro 33 D8
Rhyd-y-gwin 33 D7
Rhydymain 58 B5
Rhyd-y-meirch . . . 35 D7
Rhyd-y-meudwy . . 72 D5
Rhydymwyn 73 C6
Rhyd-y-pandy . . . 33 D7
Rhyd-yr-onen . . . 58 D3
Rhyd-y-sarn 71 C7
Rhyl = Y Rhyl . . . 72 A4
Rhymney
  = Rhymni . . . 35 D5
Rhymni
  = Rhymney . . 35 D5
Rhynd Fife 129 B6
  Perth 128 B3
Rhynie Aberds. . . 140 B3
  Highld 151 D11
Ribbesford 50 B2
Ribblehead 93 B7
Ribbleton 93 F5
Ribchester 93 F6
Ribigill 157 D8
Riby 91 D5
Riby Cross Roads . 91 D5
Riccall 96 F2
Richards Castle . . 49 C6
Richings Park . . . 27 B8
Richmond London . 28 B2
  N Yorks. 101 D6
Rickarton 141 F7
Rickinghall 56 B4
Rickleton 111 D5
Rickling 55 F5
Rickmansworth . . 40 E3
Riddings Cumb. . . 108 B4
  Derbys. 76 D4
Riddlecombe 9 C8
Riddlesden 94 E3
Riddrie 119 C6
Ridge Dorset 13 F7
  Hants. 14 C4
  Wilts 24 F4
Ridgebourne 48 C2
Ridge Green 28 E4
Ridgehill 23 C7
Ridge Lane 63 E6
Ridgewell 55 E8
Ridgewood 17 C8
Ridgmont 53 F7
Riding Mill 110 C3
Ridleywood 73 D8
Ridlington Norf . . . 69 A6
  Rutland 64 D5
Ridsdale 116 F5
Riechip 133 E7
Riemore 133 E7
Rienachait 156 F3
Rievaulx 102 F3
Rift House 111 F7
Rigg 108 C2
Riggend 119 B7
Rigsby 79 B7
Rigside 119 F8
Riley Green 86 B4
Rileyhill 62 C5
Rilla Mill 5 B7
Rillington 96 B4
Rimington 93 E8
Rimpton 12 B4
Rimswell 91 B7
Rinaston 44 C4
Ringasta 160 M5
Ringford 106 D3
Ringinglow 88 F3
Ringland 68 C4
Ringles Cross 17 B8
Ringmer 17 C8
Ringmore 6 E4
Ringorm 152 D2
Ring's End 66 D3
Ringsfield 69 F7
Ringsfield Corner . . 69 F7
Ringshall Herts . . . 40 C2
  Suff 56 D4
Ringshall Stocks . . 56 D4
Ringstead N Nhants . 53 B7
  Norf 80 C3
Ringwood 14 D2
Ringwould 31 E7
Rinmore 140 C3
Rinnigill 159 J4
Rinsey 2 D4
Riof 154 D6
Ripe 18 D2
Ripley Derbys 76 D3
  Hants. 14 E2
  N Yorks. 95 C5
  Sur. 27 D8
Riplingham 97 F5
Ripon 95 B6
Rippingale 65 B7
Ripple Kent 31 E7
  Worcs 50 F3
Ripponden 87 B8
Rireavach 150 B3
Risabus 142 D4
Risbury 49 D7
Risby 55 C8
Risca = Rhisga . . . 35 E6
Rise 97 E7
Riseden 18 B3
Risegate 66 B2
Riseholme 78 B2
Riseley Bedford. . . 53 C8
  Wokingham . . . 26 C5
Rishangles 57 C5
Rishton 93 F7
Rishworth 87 B8
Rising Bridge 87 B5
Risley Derbys. 76 F4
  Warr. 86 E4
Risplith 94 C5
Rispond 156 C7
Rivar 25 C8
Rivenhall End 42 C4
River Bank 55 C6
Riverhead 29 D6
Rivington 86 C4
Roachill 10 B3

Roade 53 D5
Road Green 69 E5
Roadhead 108 B5
Roadmeetings 119 E8
Roadside 158 D3
Roadside of
  Catterline 135 B8
Roadside of
  Kinneff 135 B8
Roadwater 22 F2
Roag 149 D7
Roa Island 92 C2
Roath 22 B3
Roberton Borders . . 115 C7
  S Lanark. 114 B2
Robertsbridge 18 C4
Roberttown 88 B2
Robeston Cross . . . 44 E3
Robeston Wathen . . 32 C1
Robin Hood 88 B4
Robin Hood's
  Bay. 103 D7
Roborough Devon . . 6 C3
  Devon 9 C7
Roby 86 E2
Roby Mill 86 D3
Rocester 75 F8
Roch 44 C3
Rochdale 87 C6
Roche 4 C4
Rochester Medway . 29 C8
  Northumb 116 E4
Rochford 42 E4
Roch Gate 44 C3
Rock Corn 4 B4
  Northumb 117 B8
  Worcs 50 B2
  W Sus 16 C5
Rockbeare 10 E5
Rockbourne 14 C2
Rockcliffe Cumb. . . 108 C3
  Dumfries 107 D5
Rock Ferry 85 F4
Rockfield Highld. . . 151 C12
  Mon 36 C1
Rockford 14 D2
Rockhampton 36 E3
Rockingham 65 E5
Rockland All
  Saints 68 E2
Rockland St Mary . 69 D6
Rockland St Peter . 68 E2
Rockley 25 B6
Rockwell End 39 F7
Rockwell Green . . . 11 B6
Rodborough 37 D5
Rodbourne Swindon . 37 F7
  Wilts 37 F6
Rodbourne Cheney . 37 F7
Rodd 48 C5
Roddam 117 B6
Rodden 12 F4
Rode 24 D3
Rodeheath 75 C5
Rode Heath 74 D5
Roden 61 C5
Rodhuish 22 F2
Rodington 61 C5
Rodley Glos 36 C4
  W Yorks. 94 F5
Rodmarton 37 E6
Rodmell 17 D8
Rodmersham 30 C3
Rodney Stoke 23 D6
Rodsley 76 E2
Rodway 22 F4
Rodwell 12 G4
Roecliffe 95 C6
Roe Green 54 F4
Roehampton 28 B3
Roesound 160 G5
Roffey 28 F2
Rogart 157 J10
Rogart Station . . . 157 J10
Rogate 16 B2
Rogerstone 35 F6
Roghadal 154 J5
Rogiet 36 F1
Rogue's Alley 66 D3
Roke 39 E6
Roker 111 D7
Rollesby 69 C7
Rolleston Leics. . . . 64 D4
  Notts 77 D7
Rolleston-on-
  Dove 63 B6
Rolston 97 E8
Rolvenden 18 B5
Rolvenden Layne . . 18 B5
Romaldkirk 100 B4
Romanby 102 E1
Romannobridge . . 120 E4
Romansleigh 10 B2
Romford 41 F8
Romiley 87 E7
Romsey 14 B4
Romsey Town 55 D5
Romsley Shrops . . . 50 B2
  Worcs 50 B4
Ronague 84 E2
Rookhope 110 E2
Rookley 15 F6
Rooks Bridge 23 D5
Roos 97 F8
Roosebeck 92 C2
Rootham's Green . . 54 D2
Rootpark 120 D2
Ropley 26 F4
Ropley Dean 26 F4
Ropsley 78 F2
Rora 153 C10
Rorandle 141 C5
Rorrington 60 D3
Roscroggan 3 B5
Rose 4 D2
Roseacre Kent 29 D8
  Lancs. 92 F4
Rose Ash 10 B2
Rosebank 119 E8
Rosebrough 117 B7
Rosebush 32 B1
Rosecare 8 E3
Rosedale Abbey . . 103 E5
Roseden 117 B6
Rosefield 151 F1
Rose Green 16 E3
Rose Grove 93 F8
Rosehall 156 J7
Rosehaugh Mains 151 F9

Rosehearty 153 B9
Rosehill 74 F3
Rose Hill E Sus . . . 17 C8
  Lancs. 93 F8
  Suff 57 E5
Roseisle 152 B1
Roselands 18 E3
Rosemarket 44 E4
Rosemarkie 151 F10
Rosemary Lane. . . . 11 C6
Rosemount 134 E1
Rosenannon 4 C4
Rosewell 121 C5
Roseworth 102 B2
Roseworthy 2 C5
Rosgill 99 C7
Roshven 147 D10
Roskhill 149 D7
Roskill House 151 F9
Rosley 108 E3
Roslin 121 C5
Rosliston 63 C6
Rosneath 145 E11
Ross Dumfries 106 E3
  Northumb 123 F7
  Perth 127 B6
Rossett 73 D7
Rossett Green 95 D6
Rossie Ochill 128 C2
Rossie Priory. 134 F2
Rossington 89 E7
Rosskeen 151 E9
Rossland 118 B4
Ross-on-Wye 36 B3
Roster 158 G4
Rostherne 86 F5
Rosthwaite 98 C4
Roston 75 E8
Rosyth 128 F3
Rothbury 117 D6
Rotherby 64 C3
Rotherfield 18 C2
Rotherfield Greys . 39 F7
Rotherfield
  Peppard 39 F7
Rotherham 88 E5
Rothersthorpe . . . 52 D5
Rotherwick 26 D5
Rothes 152 D2
Rothesay 145 G9
Rothiebrisbane . . . 153 E7
Rothienorman 153 E7
Rothiesholm 159 F7
Rothley Leics. 64 C2
  Northumb 117 F6
Rothley Shield
  East 117 E6
Rothmaise 153 E6
Rothwell Lincs 91 E5
  N Nhants 64 F5
  W Yorks 88 B4
Rothwell Haigh . . . 88 B4
Rotsea 97 D6
Rottal 134 C3
Rotten End 57 C7
Rottingdean 17 D7
Rottington 98 C1
Roud 15 F6
Rougham Norf 80 E4
  Suff 56 C3
Rougham Green . . . 56 C3
Roughburn 137 F6
Rough Close 75 F6
Rough Common . . . 30 D5
Roughlee 93 E8
Roughley 62 E5
Roughsike 108 B5
Roughton Lincs . . . 78 C5
  Norf 81 D8
  Shrops. 61 E7
Roughton Moor . . . 78 C5
Roundhay 95 F6
Roundstonefoot . . 114 D4
Roundstreet
  Common 16 B4
Roundway 24 C5
Rousdon 11 E7
Rous Lench 50 D5
Routenburn 118 C1
Routh 97 E6
Row Corn 5 B5
  Cumb 99 F6
Rowanburn 108 B4
Rowardennan 126 E2
Rowde 24 C4
Rowen 83 D7
Rowfoot 109 C6
Row Heath 43 C7
Rowhedge 43 B6
Rowhook 28 F2
Rowington 51 C7
Rowland 76 B2
Rowlands Castle . . 15 C8
Rowlands Gill 110 D4
Rowledge 27 E6
Rowlestone 35 B7
Rowley E Yorks . . . 97 F5
  Shrops. 60 D3
Rowley Hill 88 C2
Rowley Regis 62 F3
Rowly 27 E8
Rowney Green . . . 50 B5
Rownhams 14 C4
Rowrah 98 C2
Rowsham 39 C8
Rowsley 76 C2
Rowstock 38 F4
Rowston 78 D3
Rowton ChesW . . . 73 C8
  Shrops. 60 C3
  Telford 61 C6
Roxburgh 122 F3
Roxby N Lincs 90 C3
  N Yorks. 103 C5
Roxton 54 D2
Roxwell 42 D2
Royal Leamington
  Spa 51 C8
Royal Oak Darl . . . 101 B7
  Lancs. 86 D2
Royal Tunbridge
  Wells 18 B2
Royal Wootton
  Bassett 37 F7
Roybridge 137 F5
Roydhouse 88 C3
Roydon Essex 41 D7
  Norf 68 F3
  Norf 80 E4

Roydon Hamlet . . . 41 D7
Royston Herts. 54 E4
  S Yorks. 88 C4
Royton 87 D7
Rozel 17 I3
Ruabon
  = Rhiwabon . . . 73 E7
Ruaig 146 G3
Ruan Lanihorne . . . 3 B8
Ruan Minor 3 E6
Ruarach 136 B2
Ruardean 36 C3
Ruardean
  Woodside 36 C3
Rubery 50 B4
Ruckcroft 108 E5
Ruckhall 49 F6
Ruckinge 19 B7
Ruckland 79 B6
Ruckley 60 D5
Rudbaxton 44 C4
Rudby 102 D2
Ruddington 77 F5
Rudford 36 B4
Rudge Shrops 62 E2
  Som 24 D3
Rudgeway 36 F3
Rudgwick 27 F8
Rudhall 36 B3
Rudheath 74 B3
Rudley Green 42 D4
Rudry 35 F5
Rudston 97 C6
Rudyard 75 D6
Rufford 86 C2
Rufforth 95 D8
Rugby 52 B3
Rugeley 62 C4
Ruglen 112 D2
Ruilick 151 G8
Ruishton 11 B7
Ruisigearraidh . . . 154 J4
Ruislip 40 F3
Ruislip Common . . 40 F3
Rumbling
  Bridge. 128 E2
Rumburgh 69 F6
Rumford 4 B3
Rumney 22 B4
Runcorn 86 F3
Runcton 16 D2
Runcton Holme . . . 67 D6
Rundlestone 6 B3
Runfold 27 E6
Runhall 68 D3
Runham Norf 69 C7
  Norf 69 D8
Runnington 11 B6
Runsell Green 42 D3
Runswick Bay 103 C6
Runwell 42 E3
Ruscombe 27 B5
Rushall Hereford . . 49 F8
  Norf 68 F4
  Wilts 25 D6
  W Mid 62 D4
Rushbrooke 56 C2
Rushbury 60 E5
Rushden Herts 54 F4
  N Nhants 53 C7
Rushenden 30 B3
Rushford 68 F2
Rush Green 41 F8
Rush-head 153 D8
Rushlake Green . . . 18 D3
Rushmere 69 F7
Rushmere St
  Andrew. 57 E6
Rushmoor 27 E6
Rushock 50 B3
Rusholme 87 E6
Rushton ChesW . . . 74 C2
  N Nhants 64 F5
  Shrops. 61 D6
Rushton
  Spencer 75 C6
Rushwick 50 D3
Rushyford 101 B7
Ruskie 126 D5
Ruskington 78 D3
Rusland 99 F5
Rusper 28 F3
Ruspidge 36 C3
Russell's Water . . . 39 F7
Russel's Green . . . 57 B6
Rusthall 18 B2
Rustington 16 D4
Ruston 103 F7
Ruston Parva 97 C6
Ruswarp 103 D6
Rutherford 122 F2
Rutherglen 119 C6
Ruthernbridge . . . 4 C5
Ruthin = Rhuthun . 72 D5
Ruthrieston 141 D8
Ruthven Aberds . . . 152 D5
  Angus 134 E2
  Highld 138 E3
  Highld 151 H11
Ruthven House . . . 134 E3
Ruthvoes 4 C4
Ruthwell 107 C7
Ruyton-
  XI-Towns 60 B3
Ryal 110 B3
Ryal Fold. 86 B4
Ryall 12 E2
Ryarsh 29 D7
Rydal 99 D5
Ryde 15 E6
Rye 19 C6
Ryecroft Gate 75 C6
Rye Foreign 19 C5
Rye Harbour 19 D6
Ryehill 91 B6
Rye Park 41 C6
Rye Street 50 F2
Ryhall 65 C7
Ryhill 88 C4
Ryhope 111 D7
Rylstone 94 D2
Ryme Intrinseca . . 12 C3
Ryther 95 F8
Ryton Glos 50 F2
  N Yorks. 96 B3
  Shrops. 61 D7
  T&W 110 C4
Ryton-on-
  Dunsmore 51 B8

S

Sabden 93 F7
Sacombe 41 C6
Sacriston 110 E5
Sadberge 101 C8
Saddell 143 E8
Saddington 64 E3
Saddle Bow 67 C6
Saddlescombe . . . 17 C6
Sadgill 99 D6
Saffron Walden . . . 55 F6
Sageston 32 D1
Saham Hills 68 D2
Saham Toney 68 D2
Saighdinis 148 B3
Saighton 73 C8
St Abbs 122 C5
St Abb's Haven . . . 122 C5
St Agnes Corn. . . . 4 D2
  Scilly 2 F3
St Albans 40 D4
St Allen 4 D3
St Andrews 129 C6
St Andrew's Major . 22 B3
St Anne 16 I1
St Annes 85 B4
St Ann's 114 E3
St Ann's Chapel
  Corn. 6 B2
  Devon 6 E4
St Anthony-in-
  Meneage 3 D6
St Anthony's Hill . . 18 E3
St Arvans 36 E2
St Asaph
  = Llanelwy 72 B4
St Athan 22 C2
St Aubin 17 I3
St Austell 4 D5
St Bees 98 C1
St Blazey 5 D5
St Boswells 121 F8
St Brelade 17 I3
St Breock 4 B4
St Breward 5 B5
St Briavels 36 D2
St Bride's 44 D3
St Brides Major . . 21 B7
St Bride's
  Netherwent . . . 35 F8
St Brides-super-
  Ely 22 B2
St Brides
  Wentlooge. . . . 35 F6
St Budeaux 6 D2
Saintbury 51 F6
St Buryan 2 D3
St Catherine 24 B2
St Catherine's . . . 125 E7
St Clears
  = Sanclêr 32 C3
St Cleer 5 C7
St Clement 3 B7
St Clements 17 I3
St Clether 8 F4
St Colmac 145 G9
St Columb Major . . 4 C4
St Columb Minor . . 4 C3
St Columb Road . . 4 D4
St Combs 153 B10
St Cross South
  Elmham 69 F5
St Cyrus 135 C7
St David's 127 B8
St David's
  = Tyddewi 44 C2
St Day 3 B6
St Dennis 4 D4
St Devereux 49 F6
St Dogmaels 45 E3
St Dogwells 44 C4
St Dominick 6 C2
St Donat's 21 C8
St Edith's 24 C4
St Endellion 4 B4
St Enoder 4 D3
St Erme 4 D3
St Erney 5 D8
St Erth 2 C4
St Ervan 4 B3
St Eval 4 C3
St Ewe 3 B8
St Fagans 22 B3
St Fergus 153 C10
St Fillans 127 B5
St Florence 32 D1
St Genny's 8 E3
St George 72 B3
St George's 22 B2
St Germans 5 D8
St Giles 78 B2
St Giles in the
  Wood 9 C7
St Giles on the
  Heath 9 E5
St Harmon 47 B8
St Helena 63 D6
St Helen
  Auckland 101 B6
St Helens IoW 15 F7
  Mers 86 E3
St Helen's 18 D5
St Helier Jersey . . 17 I3
  London 28 C3
St Hilary Corn 2 C4
  V Glam 22 B2
Saint Hill 28 F4
St Illtyd 35 D6
St Ippollytts 40 B4
St Ishmael's 44 E3
St Issey 4 B4
St Ive 5 C8
St Ives Cambs 54 B4
  Corn. 2 B4
  Dorset 14 D2
St James South
  Elmham 69 F6
St Jidzey 4 C4
St John 6 D2
St John's IoM 84 D2
  Jersey 17 I3
  Sur. 27 D7
  Worcs 50 D3
St John's Chapel . 109 F8
St John's Fen End . 66 C5
St John's
  Highway. 66 C5

St John's Town of
  Dalry 113 F6
St Judes 84 C3
St Just 2 C2
St Just in Roseland . 3 C7
St Katherine's . . . 153 E7
St Keverne 3 D6
St Kew 4 B5
St Kew Highway . . 4 B5
St Keyne 5 C7
St Lawrence Corn . . 4 C5
  Essex 43 D5
  IoW 15 G6
St Leonards Dorset . 14 D2
  E Sus. 18 E4
  S Lanark. 119 D6
St Leonard's 40 D2
St Levan 2 D2
St Lythans. 22 B3
St Mabyn 4 B5
St Madoes 128 B3
St Margarets 41 C6
St Margaret's 49 F5
St Margaret's at
  Cliffe 31 E7
St Margaret's
  Hope 159 J5
St Margaret South
  Elmham 69 F6
St Mark's 84 E2
St Martin 5 D7
St Martins Corn . . 3 D6
  Perth 134 F1
St Martin's Jersey . 17 I3
  Shrops. 73 F7
St Mary Bourne . . 26 D2
St Mary Church. . . 22 B2
St Mary Cray 29 C5
St Mary Hill 21 B8
St Mary Hoo 30 B2
St Mary in the
  Marsh 19 C7
St Mary's Jersey. . 17 I3
  Orkney 159 H5
St Mary's Bay . . . 19 C7
St Maughans 36 C1
St Mawes 3 C7
St Mawgan 4 C3
St Mellion 5 C8
St Mellons 35 F6
St Merryn 4 B3
St Mewan 4 D4
St Michael
  Caerhays. 3 B8
St Michael Penkevil . 3 B7
St Michaels 49 C7
St Michael's 19 B5
St Michael's on
  Wyre 92 E4
St Michael South
  Elmham 69 F6
St Minver 4 B4
St Monans 129 D7
St Neot 5 C6
St Neots 54 C2
St Newlyn East . . . 4 D3
St Nicholas Pembs. . 44 B3
  V Glam 22 B2
St Nicholas at
  Wade 31 C6
St Ninians 127 E6
St Osyth 43 C7
St Osyth Heath . . . 43 C7
St Ouens 17 I3
St Owens Cross . . 36 B2
St Paul's Cray . . . 29 C5
St Paul's Walden . 40 B4
St Peter Port 16 I2
St Peter's Jersey . . 17 I3
  Kent 31 C7
St Petrox 44 F4
St Pinnock 5 C7
St Quivox 112 B3
St Ruan 3 E6
St Sampson 16 I2
St Stephen 4 D4
St Stephens Corn. . 6 D2
  Herts 40 D4
St Stephen's 8 F5
St Teath 8 F2
St Thomas 10 E4
St Tudy 5 B5
St Twynnells 44 F4
St Veep 5 D6
St Vigeans 135 E6
St Wenn 4 C4
St Weonards 36 B1
Saintfield 89 D8
Salcombe 6 F5
Salcombe Regis . . 11 F6
Salcott 43 C5
Sale 87 E5
Saleby 79 B7
Sale Green 50 D4
Salehurst 18 C4
Salem Carms 33 B7
  Ceredig 58 F3
Salen Argyll 147 G8
  Highld 147 E9
Salesbury 93 F6
Salford C Beds. . . . 53 F7
  Gtr Man 87 E6
  Oxon 38 B2
Salford Priors . . . 51 D5
Salfords 28 E3
Salhouse 69 C6
Saline 128 E2
Salisbury 14 B2
Sallachan 130 C3
Sallachy Highld. . . 150 H2
  Highld 157 J8
Salle 81 E7
Salmonby 79 B6
Salmond's Muir . . 135 F5
Salperton 37 B7
Salph End 53 D8
Salsburgh 119 C8
Salt 62 B3
Saltaire 94 F4
Saltash 6 D2
Saltburn 151 E10
Saltburn-by-the-
  Sea. 102 B4
Saltby 65 B5
Saltcoats Cumb . . . 98 E2
  N Ayrs 118 E2
Saltdean 17 D7
Salt End 91 B5
Salter 93 C6
Salterforth 93 E8

Salterswall. 74 C3
Saltfleet 91 E8
Saltfleetby All
  Saints 91 E8
Saltfleetby St
  Clements 91 E8
Saltfleetby St
  Peter 91 F8
Salford 23 C8
Salthouse 81 C6
Saltmarshe 89 B8
Saltney 73 C7
Salton 96 B3
Saltwood 19 B8
Salum 146 G3
Salvington 16 D5
Salwarpe 50 C3
Salwayash 12 E2
Sambourne 51 C5
Sambrook 61 B7
Samhla 148 B2
Samlesbury 93 F5
Samlesbury
  Bottoms 86 B4
Sampford Arundel . 11 C6
Sampford Brett. . . 22 E2
Sampford
  Courtenay 9 D8
Sampford Peverell . 10 C5
Sampford Spiney . . 6 B3
Sampool Bridge . . 99 F6
Samuelston 121 B7
Sanachan 149 D13
Sanaigmore 142 A3
Sanclêr = St Clears . 32 C3
Sancreed 2 D3
Sancton 96 F5
Sand Highld 150 B2
  Shetland 160 J5
Sandaig 149 H12
Sandale 108 E2
Sandbach 74 C4
Sandbank 145 E10
Sandbanks 13 F8
Sandend 152 B5
Sanderstead 28 C4
Sandfields 37 B6
Sandford Cumb. . . 100 C2
  Devon 10 D3
  Dorset 13 F7
  IoW 15 F6
  N Som 23 D6
  Shrops. 74 F2
  S Lanark. 119 E7
Sandfordhill 153 D11
Sandford on
  Thames 39 D5
Sandford Orcas . . 12 B4
Sandford St
  Martin 38 B4
Sandgate 19 B8
Sandgreen 106 D2
Sandhaven 153 B9
Sandhead 104 E4
Sandhills 27 F7
Sandhoe 110 C2
Sand Hole 96 F4
Sandholme E Yorks . 96 F4
  Lincs 79 F6
Sandhurst Brack . . 27 C6
  Glos 37 B5
  Kent 18 C4
Sandhurst Cross . . 18 C4
Sand Hutton 96 D2
Sandhutton 102 F1
Sandiacre 76 F4
Sandilands Lincs . . 91 F9
  S Lanark. 119 F8
Sandiway 74 B3
Sandleheath 14 C2
Sandling 29 D8
Sandlow Green . . . 74 C4
Sandness 160 H3
Sandon Essex 42 D3
  Herts 54 F4
  Staffs. 75 F6
Sandown 15 F6
Sandplace 5 D7
Sandridge Herts . . 40 C4
  Wilts 24 C4
Sandringham 67 B6
Sandsend 103 C6
Sandside
  House. 157 C12
Sandsound 160 J5
Sandtoft 89 D8
Sandway 30 D2
Sandwell 62 F4
Sandwich 31 D7
Sandwick Cumb . . . 99 C6
  Orkney 159 K5
  Shetland 160 L6
Sandwith 98 C1
Sandy Carms 33 D5
  C Beds. 54 E2
Sandy Bank 79 D5
Sandycroft 73 C7
Sandyford
  Dumfries 114 E5
  Stoke 75 D5
Sandygate 84 C3
Sandy Haven 44 E3
Sandyhills 107 D5
Sandylands 92 C4
Sandy Lane Wilts . . 24 C4
  Wrex 73 E7
Sandypark 10 F2
Sangobeg 156 C7
Sangomore 156 C7
Sanna 146 E7
Sanndabhaig
  W Isles 148 D3
  W Isles 155 D9
Sannox 143 D11
Sanquhar 113 D7
Santon Bridge. . . . 98 D3
Santon Downham . 67 F8
Sapcote 63 E8
Sapey Common . . . 50 C2
Sapiston 56 B3
Sapley 54 B3
Sapperton Glos . . . 37 D6
  Lincs 78 F3
Saracen's Head . . 66 B3
Sarclet 158 F5

Sardis 33 D6
Sarn Bridgend 34 F3
  Powys 60 E2
Sarnau Carms 32 C4
  Ceredig 46 D2
  Gwyn 72 F3
  Powys 48 F2
  Powys 60 C2
Sarn Bach 70 E4
Sarnesfield 49 D5
Sarn Meyllteyrn . . 70 D3
Saron Carms 33 C7
  Carms 46 F2
  Denb 72 C4
  Gwyn 82 E5
  Gwyn 82 F4
Sarratt 40 E3
Sarre 31 C6
Sarsden 38 B2
Sarsgrum 156 C6
Satley 110 E4
Satron 100 E4
Satterleigh 9 B8
Satterthwaite . . . 99 E5
Satwell 39 F7
Sauchen 141 C5
Saucher 134 F1
Sauchie 127 E7
Sauchieburn 135 C6
Saughall 73 B7
Saughtree 115 E8
Saul 36 D4
Saundby 89 F8
Saundersfoot 32 D2
Saunderton 39 D7
Saunton 20 F3
Sausthorpe 79 C6
Saval 157 J8
Savary 147 G9
Savile Park 87 B8
Sawbridge 52 C3
Sawbridgeworth . . 41 C7
Sawdon 103 F7
Sawley Derbys . . . 76 F4
  Lancs 93 E7
  N Yorks. 94 C5
Sawston 55 E5
Sawtry 65 F8
Saxby Leics 64 C5
  Lincs 90 F4
Saxby All Saints . . 90 C3
Saxelbye 64 B4
Saxham Street . . . 56 C4
Saxilby 77 B8
Saxlingham 81 D6
Saxlingham Green . 68 E5
Saxlingham
  Nethergate . . . 68 E5
Saxlingham
  Thorpe 68 E5
Saxmundham 57 C7
Saxondale 77 F6
Saxon Street 55 D7
Saxtead 57 C6
Saxtead Green . . . 57 C6
Saxthorpe 81 D7
Saxton 95 F7
Sayers Common . . 17 C6
Scackleton 96 B2
Scadabhagh 154 H6
Scaftworth 89 E7
Scagglethorpe . . . 96 B4
Scaitcliffe 87 B5
Scalasaig 144 D2
Scalby E Yorks . . . 90 B2
  N Yorks. 103 E8
Scaldwell 53 B5
Scaleby 108 C4
Scaleby Hill 108 C4
Scale Houses 109 E5
Scales Cumb 92 B2
  Cumb. 99 B5
  Lancs. 92 F4
Scalford 64 B4
Scaling 103 C5
Scallastle 124 B2
Scalloway 160 K6
Scalpay 154 H7
Scalpay House . . . 149 F11
Scalpsie 145 H9
Scamadale 147 B10
Scamblesby 79 B5
Scamodale 130 B2
Scampston 96 B4
Scampton 78 B2
Scapa. 159 H5
Scapegoat Hill . . . 87 C8
Scar 159 D7
Scarborough 103 F8
Scarcliffe 76 C4
Scarcroft 95 E6
Scarcroft Hill 95 E6
Scardroy 150 F5
Scarff. 160 E4
Scarfskerry 158 C4
Scargill 101 C5
Scarinish 146 G3
Scarisbrick 85 C4
Scarning 68 C2
Scarrington 77 E7
Scartho 91 D6
Scarwell 159 F3
Scatness 160 M5
Scatraig 151 H10
Scawby 90 D3
Scawsby 89 D6
Scawton 102 F3
Scayne's Hill 17 B7
Scethrog 35 B5
Scholar Green . . . 74 D5
Scholes W Yorks . . 88 B2
  W Yorks 88 D2
  W Yorks 95 F6
School Green 74 C3
Scleddau 44 B4
Scofton 89 F7
Scole 56 B5
Scolpaig 148 A2
Scone 128 B3
Sconser 149 E10
Scoonie 129 D5
Scoor 146 K7
Scopwick 78 D3
Scoraig 150 B3
Scorborough 97 E6
Scorrier 3 B6
Scorton Lancs 92 E5
  N Yorks. 101 D7
Sco Ruston 81 E8

Scotbheinn 148 C3
Scotby 108 D4
Scotch Corner . . . 101 D7
Scotforth 92 C4
Scothern 78 B3
Scotland Gate . . . 117 F8
Scotlandwell 128 D3
Scotsburn 151 D10
Scotscalder
  Station 158 E2
Scotscraig 129 B6
Scots' Gap 117 F6
Scotston Aberds. . . 135 B7
  Perth 133 E6
Scotstown 118 C5
Scotstown 130 C2
Scotswood 110 C4
Scottas 149 H12
Scotter 90 D2
Scotterthorpe . . . 90 D2
Scottlethorpe . . . 65 B7
Scotton Lincs 90 E2
  N Yorks. 95 D6
  N Yorks. 101 E6
Scottow 81 E8
Scoughall 129 F8
Scoulag 145 H10
Scoulton 68 D2
Scourie 156 E4
Scourie More 156 E4
Scousburgh 160 M5
Scrabster 158 C2
Scrafield 79 C6
Scrainwood 117 D5
Scrane End 79 E6
Scraptoft 64 D3
Scratby 69 C8
Scrayingham 96 C3
Scredington 78 E3
Scremby 79 C7
Scremerston 123 E6
Screveton 77 E7
Scrivelsby 79 C5
Scriven 95 D6
Scrooby 89 E7
Scropton 75 F8
Scrub Hill 78 D5
Scruton 101 E7
Sculcoates 97 F6
Sculthorpe 80 D4
Scunthorpe 90 C2
Scurlage 33 F5
Seaborough 12 D2
Seacombe 85 E4
Seacroft Lincs 79 C8
  W Yorks 95 F6
Seadyke 79 F6
Seafield S Ayrs . . . 112 B3
  W Loth. 120 C3
Seaford 17 E8
Seaforth 85 E4
Seagrave 64 C3
Seaham 111 E7
Seahouses 123 F8
Seal 29 D6
Sealand 73 C7
Seale 27 E6
Seamer N Yorks . . . 102 C2
  N Yorks. 103 F8
Seamill 118 E2
Sea Palling 69 B7
Searby 90 D4
Seasalter 30 C4
Seascale 98 D2
Seathorne 79 C8
Seathwaite Cumb . . 98 C4
  Cumb. 98 E4
Seatoller 98 C4
Seaton Corn 5 D8
  Cumb. 107 F7
  Devon 11 F7
  Durham 111 D6
  E Yorks. 97 E7
  Northumb 111 B6
  Rutland 65 E6
Seaton Burn 110 B5
Seaton Carew . . . 102 B3
Seaton Delaval . . 111 B6
Seaton Ross 96 E3
Seaton Sluice . . . 111 B6
Seatown Aberds. . . 152 B5
  Dorset 12 E2
Seave Green 102 D3
Seaview 15 E7
Seaville 107 D8
Seavington St
  Mary 12 C2
Seavington St
  Michael 12 C2
Sebergham 108 E3
Seckington 63 D6
Second Coast . . . 150 B2
Sedbergh 100 E1
Sedbury 36 E2
Sedbusk 100 E3
Sedgeberrow 50 F5
Sedgebrook 77 F8
Sedgefield 102 B1
Sedgeford 80 D3
Sedgehill 13 B6
Sedgley 62 E3
Sedgwick 99 F7
Sedlescombe 18 D4
Sedlescombe
  Street 18 D4
Seend 24 C4
Seend Cleeve . . . 24 C4
Seer Green 40 E2
Seething 69 E6
Sefton 85 D4
Seghill 111 B5
Seifton 60 F4
Seighford 62 B2
Seilebost 154 H5
Seion 82 E5
Seisdon 62 E2
Seisiadar 155 D10
Selattyn 73 F6
Selborne 26 F5
Selby 96 F2
Selham 16 B3
Selhurst 28 C4
Selkirk 115 B7
Sellack 36 B2
Sellafirth 160 D7
Sellibister 159 D8

Sellindge 19 B7
Sellindge Lees 19 B8
Selling 30 D4
Sells Green 24 C4
Selly Oak 62 F4
Selmeston 18 E2
Selsdon 28 C4
Selsey 16 E2
Selsfield Common 28 F4
Selsted 31 E6
Selston 76 D4
Selworthy 21 E8
Semblister 160 H5
Semer 56 E3
Semington 24 C3
Semley 13 B6
Send 27 D8
Send Marsh 27 D8
Senghenydd 35 E5
Sennen 2 D2
Sennen Cove 2 D2
Sennybridge
= Pont Senni 34 B3
Serlby 89 F7
Sessay 95 B7
Setchey 67 C6
Setley 14 D4
Setter Shetland 160 L6
Shetland 160 H5
Shetland 160 J7
Settiscarth 159 G4
Settle 93 C8
Settrington 96 B4
Sevenhampton 37 B7
Seven Kings 41 F7
Sevenoaks 29 D6
Sevenoaks Weald 29 E6
Seven Sisters 34 D2
Severn Beach 36 F2
Severnhampton 38 E2
Severn Stoke 50 E3
Sevington 30 E4
Sewards End 55 F6
Sewardstone 41 E6
Sewardstonebury 41 E6
Sewerby 97 C7
Seworgan 3 C6
Sewstern 65 B5
Sezincote 51 F6
Sgarasta Mhor 154 H5
Sgiogarstaigh 155 A10
Shabbington 39 D6
Shackerstone 63 D7
Shackleford 27 E7
Shade 87 B7
Shadforth 111 E6
Shadingfield 69 F7
Shadoxhurst 19 B6
Shadsworth 86 B5
Shadwell Norf 68 F2
W Yorks 95 F6
Shaftesbury 13 B6
Shafton 88 C4
Shalbourne 25 C8
Shalcombe 14 F4
Shalden 26 E4
Shaldon 7 B7
Shalfleet 14 F5
Shalford Essex 42 B3
Sur 27 E8
Shalford Green 42 B3
Shallowford 21 E6
Shalmsford Street 30 D4
Shalstone 52 F4
Shamley Green 27 E8
Shandon 145 E11
Shandwick 151 D11
Shangton 64 E4
Shankhouse 111 B5
Shanklin 15 F6
Shanquhar 152 E5
Shanzie 134 D2
Shap 99 C7
Shapwick Dorset 13 D7
Som 23 F6
Shardlow 76 F4
Shareshill 62 D3
Sharlston 88 C4
Sharlston
Common 88 C4
Sharnbrook 53 D7
Sharnford 63 E8
Sharoe Green 92 F5
Sharow 95 B6
Sharpenhoe 53 F8
Sharperton 117 D5
Sharpness 36 D3
Sharp Street 69 B6
Sharpthorne 28 F4
Sharrington 81 D6
Shatterford 61 F7
Shaugh Prior 6 C3
Shavington 74 D4
Shaw Gtr Man 87 D7
W Berks 26 C2
Wilts 24 C3
Shawbury 61 B5
Shawdon Hall 117 C6
Shawell 64 F2
Shawford 15 B5
Shawforth 87 B6
Shaw Green 86 C3
Shawhead 107 B5
Shawhill 108 C2
Shaw Mills 95 C5
Shawton 119 E6
Shawtonhill 119 E6
Shear Cross 24 E3
Shearington 107 C7
Shearsby 64 E3
Shebbear 9 D6
Shebdon 61 B7
Shebster 157 C13
Sheddens 119 D5
Shedfield 15 C6
Sheen 75 C8
Sheepscar 95 F6
Sheepscombe 37 C5
Sheepstor 6 C3
Sheepwash 9 D6
Sheepway 23 B6
Sheepy Magna 63 D7
Sheepy Parva 63 D7
Sheering 41 C8
Sheerness 30 B3
Sheet 15 B8

Sheffield 88 F4
Sheffield Bottom 26 C4
Sheffield Green 17 B8
Shefford 54 F2
Shefford
Woodlands 25 B8
Sheigra 156 C4
Sheinton 61 D6
Shelderton 49 B6
Sheldon Derbys 75 C8
Devon 11 D6
W Mid 63 F5
Sheldwich 30 D4
Shelf 88 B2
Shelfanger 68 F4
Shelfield Warks 51 C6
W Mid 62 D4
Shelford 77 E6
Shellacres 122 E4
Shelley Essex 42 D1
Suff 56 F4
W Yorks 88 C3
Shellingford 38 E3
Shellow Bowells 42 D2
Shelsley
Beauchamp 50 C2
Shelsley Walsh 50 C2
Shelthorpe 64 C2
Shelton Bedford 53 C8
Norf 68 E5
Notts 77 E7
Shrops 60 C4
Shelton Green 68 E5
Shelve 60 E3
Shelwick 49 E7
Shenfield 42 E2
Shenington 51 E8
Shenley 40 D4
Shenley Brook End 53 F6
Shenleybury 40 D4
Shenley Church
End 53 F6
Shenmore 49 F5
Shennanton 105 C7
Shenstone Staffs 62 D5
Worcs 50 B3
Shenton 63 D7
Shenval Highld 137 B7
Moray 139 B8
Shepeau Stow 66 C3
Shephall 41 B5
Shepherd's Green 39 F7
Shepherd's Port 80 D2
Shepherdswell 31 E6
Shepley 88 D2
Shepperdine 36 E3
Shepperton 27 C8
Shepreth 54 E4
Shepshed 63 C8
Shepton
Beauchamp 12 C2
Shepton Mallet 23 E8
Shepton Montague 23 F8
Shepway 29 D8
Sheraton 111 F7
Sherborne Dorset 12 C3
Glos 38 C1
Sherborne St
John 26 D4
Sherbourne 51 C7
Sherburn Durham 111 E6
N Yorks 97 B5
Sherburn Hill 111 E6
Sherburn in Elmet 95 F7
Shere 27 E8
Shereford 80 E4
Sherfield English 14 B3
Sherfield on
Loddon 26 D4
Sherford 7 E5
Sheriffhales 61 C7
Sheriff Hutton 96 C2
Sheringham 81 C7
Sherington 53 E6
Shernal Green 50 C4
Shernborne 80 D3
Sherrington 24 F4
Sherston 37 F5
Sherwood Green 9 B7
Shettleston 119 C6
Shevington 86 D3
Shevington Moor 86 C3
Shevington Vale 86 D3
Sheviock 5 D8
Shide 15 F5
Shiel Bridge 136 C2
Shieldaig Highld 149 A13
Highld 149 C13
Shieldhill Dumfries 114 F3
Falk 119 B8
S Lanark 120 C3
Shielfoot 147 E9
Shielhill Angus 134 D4
Invclyd 118 B2
Shifford 38 D3
Shifnal 61 D7
Shilbottle 117 D7
Shildon 101 B7
Shillingford Devon 10 B4
Oxon 39 E5
Shillingford St
George 10 F4
Shillingstone 13 C6
Shillington 54 F2
Shillmoor 116 D4
Shilton Oxon 38 D2
Warks 63 F8
Shilvington 117 F7
Shimpling Norf 68 F4
Suff 56 D2
Shimpling Street 56 D2
Shincliffe 111 E5
Shiney Row 111 D6
Shinfield 26 C5
Shingham 67 D7
Shingle Street 57 E7
Shinner's Bridge 7 C5
Shinness 157 H8
Shipbourne 29 D6
Shipdham 68 D2
Shipham 23 D6
Shiphay 7 C6
Shiplake 27 B5
Shipley Derbys 76 E4
Northumb 117 C7
Shrops 62 E2
W Sus 16 B5
W Yorks 94 F4
Shipley Shiels 116 E3

Shipmeadow 69 F6
Shippea Hill
Station 67 F6
Shippon 38 E4
Shipston-on-
Stour 51 E7
Shipton Glos 37 C7
N Yorks 95 D8
Shrops 61 E5
Shipton Bellinger 25 E7
Shipton Gorge 12 E2
Shipton Green 16 D2
Shipton Moyne 37 F5
Shipton on
Cherwell 38 C4
Shipton Solers 37 C7
Shiptonthorpe 96 E4
Shipton-under-
Wychwood 38 C2
Shirburn 39 E6
Shirdley Hill 85 C4
Shirebrook 76 C5
Shiregreen 88 E4
Shirehampton 23 B7
Shiremoor 111 B6
Shirenewton 36 E1
Shireoaks 89 F6
Shirkoak 19 B6
Shirland 76 D3
Shirley Derbys 76 E2
London 28 C4
Soton 14 C5
W Mid 51 B6
Shirl Heath 49 D6
Shirrell Heath 15 C6
Shirwell 20 F4
Shirwell Cross 20 F4
Shiskine 143 F10
Shobdon 49 C6
Shobnall 63 B6
Shobrooke 10 D3
Shoby 64 C3
Shocklach 73 E8
Shoeburyness 43 F5
Sholden 31 D7
Sholing 14 C5
Shoot Hill 60 C4
Shop Corn 4 B3
Corn 8 C4
Shop Corner 57 F6
Shoreditch 41 F6
Shoreham 29 C6
Shoreham-by-Sea 17 D6
Shore Mill 151 E10
Shoresdean 123 E5
Shoreswood 122 E5
Shoreton 151 E9
Shorncote 37 E7
Shorne 29 B7
Shortacombe 9 F7
Shortgate 17 C8
Short Heath 62 D3
Shortlanesend 3 B7
Shortles 118 F4
Shortstown 53 E8
Shorwell 15 F5
Shoscombe 24 D2
Shotesham 69 E5
Shotgate 42 E3
Shotley 57 F6
Shotley Bridge 110 D3
Shotleyfield 110 D3
Shotley Gate 57 F6
Shottenden 30 D4
Shottermill 27 F6
Shottery 51 D6
Shotteswell 52 E2
Shottisham 57 E7
Shottle 76 E3
Shottlegate 76 E3
Shotton Durham 111 F7
Flint 73 C7
Northumb 122 F4
Shotton Colliery 111 E6
Shotts 119 C8
Shotwick 73 B7
Shouldham 67 D6
Shouldham
Thorpe 67 D6
Shoulton 50 D3
Shover's Green 18 B3
Shrawardine 60 C4
Shrawley 50 C3
Shrewley Common 51 C7
Shrewsbury 60 C4
Shrewton 25 E5
Shripney 16 D3
Shrivenham 38 F2
Shropham 68 E2
Shrub End 43 B5
Shucknall 49 E7
Shudy Camps 55 E7
Shulishadermor 149 D9
Shurdington 37 C6
Shurlock Row 27 B6
Shurrery 157 D13
Shurrery Lodge 157 D13
Shurton 22 E4
Shustoke 63 E6
Shute Devon 10 D3
Devon 11 E7
Shutford 51 E8
Shuthonger 50 F3
Shutlanger 52 D5
Shuttington 63 D6
Shuttlewood 76 B4
Siabost bho
Dheas 154 C7
Siabost bho
Thuath 154 C7
Siadar 155 B8
Siadar Iarach 155 B8
Siadar Uarach 155 B8
Sibbaldbie 114 F4
Sibbertoft 64 F3
Sibdon Carwood 60 F4
Sibford Ferris 51 F8
Sibford Gower 51 F8
Sible Hedingham 55 F8
Sibsey 79 D6
Sibson Cambs 65 E7
Leics 63 D7
Sibthorpe 77 E7
Sibton 57 C7
Sibton Green 57 B7
Sicklesmere 56 C2
Sicklinghall 95 E6
Sid 11 F6

Sidbury Devon 11 E6
Shrops 61 F6
Sidcot 23 D6
Sidcup 29 B5
Siddick 107 F7
Siddington Ches E 74 B5
Glos 37 E7
Sidemoor 50 B4
Sidestrand 81 D8
Sidford 11 E6
Sidlesham 16 E2
Sidley 18 E4
Sidlow 28 E3
Sidmouth 11 F6
Sigford 7 B5
Sigglesthorne 97 E7
Sighthill 120 B4
Sigingstone 21 B8
Signet 38 C2
Silchester 26 C4
Sildinis 155 F7
Sileby 64 C2
Silecroft 98 F3
Silfield 68 E4
Silian 46 D4
Silk Willoughby 78 E3
Silkstone 88 D3
Silkstone
Common 88 D3
Silloth 107 D8
Sills 116 D4
Sillyearn 152 C5
Siloh 47 F6
Silpho 103 E7
Silsden 94 E3
Silsoe 53 F8
Silverburn 120 C5
Silverdale Lancs 92 B4
Staffs 74 E5
Silver End 42 C4
Silvergate 81 E7
Silverhill 18 D4
Silverley's Green 57 B6
Silverstone 52 E4
Silverton 10 D4
Silvington 49 B8
Silwick 160 J4
Simmondley 87 E8
Simonburn 109 B8
Simonsbath 21 F6
Simonstone 93 F7
Simprim 122 E4
Simpson 53 F6
Simpson Cross 44 D3
Sinclair's Hill 122 D4
Sinclairston 112 C4
Sinderby 101 F8
Sinderhope 109 D8
Sindlesham 27 C5
Singdean 115 D8
Singleborough 53 F5
Singleton Lancs 92 F3
W Sus 16 C2
Singlewell 29 B7
Sinkhurst Green 30 E2
Sinnahard 140 C3
Sinnington 103 F5
Sinton Green 50 C3
Sipson 27 B8
Sirhowy 35 C5
Sisland 69 E6
Sissinghurst 18 B4
Sisterpath 122 E3
Siston 23 B8
Sithney 2 D5
Sittingbourne 30 C2
Six Ashes 61 F7
Sixhills 91 F5
Six Hills 64 B3
Six Mile Bottom 55 D6
Sixpenny Handley 13 C7
Sizewell 57 C8
Skail 157 E10
Skaill Orkney 159 E5
Orkney 159 G3
Orkney 159 H6
Skares 113 C5
Skateraw 122 B3
Skaw 160 F7
Skeabost 149 D9
Skeabrae 159 F3
Skeeby 101 D7
Skeffington 64 D4
Skeffling 91 C7
Skegby 76 C4
Skegness 79 C8
Skelberry 160 M5
Skelbo 151 B10
Skelbrooke 89 C6
Skeldyke 79 F6
Skellingthorpe 78 B2
Skellister 160 H6
Skellow 89 C6
Skelmanthorpe 88 C3
Skelmersdale 86 D2
Skelmonae 153 E8
Skelmorlie 118 C1
Skelmuir 153 D9
Skelpick 157 D10
Skelton Cumb 108 F4
E Yorks 89 B8
N Yorks 101 D5
Redcar 102 C4
York 95 D8
Skelton-on-Ure 95 C6
Skelwick 159 D5
Skelwith Bridge 99 D5
Skendleby 79 C7
Skene House 141 D6
Skenfrith 36 B1
Skerne 97 D6
Skeroblingarry 143 F8
Skerray 157 C9
Skerton 92 C4
Sketchley 63 E8
Sketty 33 E7
Skewen 33 E8
Skewsby 96 B2
Skeyton 81 E8
Skiag Bridge 156 G5
Skibo Castle 151 C10
Skidbrooke 91 E8
Skidbrooke North
End 91 E8
Skidby 97 F6
Skilgate 10 B4
Skillington 65 B5
Skinburness 107 D8
Skinflats 127 F8

Skinidin 148 D7
Skinningrove 103 B5
Skinnet 157 C8
Skipness 145 H7
Skippool 92 E3
Skipsea 97 D7
Skipsea Brough 97 D7
Skipton 94 D2
Skipton-on-Swale 95 B6
Skipwith 96 F2
Skirbeck 79 E6
Skirbeck Quarter 79 E6
Skirlaugh 97 F7
Skirling 120 F3
Skirmett 39 F7
Skirpenbeck 96 D3
Skirwith 109 F6
Skirza 158 D5
Skulamus 149 F11
Skullomie 157 C9
Skyborry Green 48 B4
Skye of Curr 139 B5
Skyreholme 94 C3
Slackhall 87 F8
Slackhead 152 B4
Slad 37 D5
Slade Devon 20 E4
Pembs 44 D4
Slade Green 29 B6
Slaggyford 109 D6
Slaidburn 93 D7
Slaithwaite 87 C8
Slaley 110 D2
Slamannan 119 B8
Slapton Bucks 40 B2
Devon 7 E6
W Nhants 52 E4
Slatepit Dale 76 C3
Slattocks 87 D6
Slaugham 17 B6
Slaughterford 24 B3
Slawston 64 E4
Sleaford Hants 27 F6
Lincs 78 E3
Sleagill 99 C7
Sleapford 61 C6
Sledge Green 50 F3
Sledmere 96 C5
Sleightholme 100 C4
Sleights 103 D6
Slepe 13 E7
Slickly 158 D4
Sliddery 143 F10
Sligachan Hotel 149 F9
Slimbridge 36 D4
Slindon Staffs 74 F5
W Sus 16 D3
Slinfold 28 F2
Sling 36 D2
Slingsby 96 B2
Slioch 152 E5
Slip End C Beds 40 C3
Herts 54 F3
Slipton 53 B7
Slitting Mill 62 C4
Slochd 138 B4
Slockavullin 124 F4
Sloley 81 E8
Sloothby 79 B7
Slough 27 B7
Slough Green 17 B6
Sluggan 138 B4
Slumbay 149 E13
Slyfield 27 D7
Slyne 92 C4
Smailholm 122 F2
Smallbridge 87 C7
Smallburgh 69 B6
Smallburn
Aberds 153 D10
E Ayrs 113 B6
Small Dole 17 C6
Smalley 76 E4
Smallfield 28 E4
Small Hythe 19 B5
Smallridge 11 D8
Smannell 25 E8
Smardale 100 D2
Smarden 30 E2
Smarden Bell 30 E2
Smeatharpe 11 C6
Smeeth 19 B7
Smeeton Westerby 64 E3
Smercleit 148 G2
Smerral 158 G3
Smethcott 60 E4
Smethwick 62 F4
Smirisary 147 D9
Smisby 63 C7
Smithfield 108 C4
Smith Green 92 D4
Smithincott 11 C5
Smith's Green 42 B1
Smithstown 149 A12
Smithton 151 G10
Smithy Green 74 B4
Smockington 63 F8
Smoogro 159 H4
Smythe's Green 43 C5
Snaigow House 133 E7
Snailbeach 60 D3
Snailwell 55 C7
Snainton 103 F7
Snaith 89 B7
Snape N Yorks 101 F7
Suff 57 D7
Snape Green 85 C4
Snarestone 63 D7
Snarford 90 F4
Snargate 19 C6
Snave 19 C7
Sneath Common 68 F4
Sneaton 103 D6
Sneatonthorpe 103 D7
Snelland 90 F4
Snelston 75 E8
Snettisham 80 D2
Sniseabhal 148 E2
Snitter 117 D6
Snitterby 90 E3
Snitterfield 51 D7
Snittlegarth 108 F2
Snitton 49 B7
Snodhill 48 E5
Snodland 29 C7
Snowden Hill 88 D3
Snowdown 31 D6
Snowshill 51 F5
Snydale 88 C5
Soar Anglesey 82 D3

Soar continued
Carms 33 B7
Devon 6 F5
Soar-y-Mynydd 47 D6
Soberton 15 C7
Soberton Heath 15 C7
Sockbridge 99 B7
Sockburn 101 D8
Soham 55 B6
Soham Cotes 55 B6
Solas 148 A3
Soldon Cross 8 C5
Soldridge 26 F4
Sole Street Kent 29 C7
Kent 30 E4
Solihull 51 B6
Sollers Dilwyn 49 D6
Sollers Hope 49 F8
Sollom 86 C2
Solva 44 C2
Somacotes 76 D4
Somerby Leics 64 C4
Lincs 90 D4
Somercotes 76 D4
Somerford 14 E2
Somerford Keynes 37 E7
Somerley 16 E2
Somerleyton 69 E7
Somersal Herbert 75 F8
Somersby 79 B6
Somersham Cambs 54 B4
Suff 56 E4
Somerton Oxon 38 B4
Som 12 B2
Sompting 17 D5
Sonning 27 B5
Sonning Common 39 F7
Sonning Eye 27 B5
Sontley 73 E7
Sopley 14 E2
Sopwell 40 D4
Sopworth 37 F5
Sorbie 105 E8
Sordale 158 D3
Sorisdale 146 E5
Sorn 113 B5
Sornhill 118 F5
Sortat 158 D4
Sotby 78 B5
Sots Hole 78 C4
Sotterley 69 F7
Soudley 61 B7
Soughton 73 C6
Soulbury 40 B1
Soulby 100 C2
Souldern 52 F3
Souldrop 53 C7
Sound Ches E 74 E3
Shetland 160 H5
Shetland 160 J6
Sound Heath 74 E3
Soundwell 23 B8
Sourhope 116 B4
Sourin 159 E5
Sourton 9 E7
Soutergate 98 F4
South Acre 67 C8
Southall 40 F4
South Allington 7 F5
South Alloa 127 E7
Southam Glos 37 B6
Warks 52 C2
South Ambersham 16 B3
Southampton 14 C5
South Anston 89 F6
South Ascot 27 C7
South
Ballachulish 130 D4
South Balloch 112 E3
South Bank 102 B3
South Barrow 12 B4
South Beach 70 D4
South Benfleet 42 F3
South Bersted 16 D3
Southborough 29 E6
Southbourne BCP 14 E2
W Sus 15 D8
South Brent 6 C4
South Brewham 24 F2
South Broomhill 117 E8
Southburgh 68 D3
South Burlingham 69 D6
Southburn 97 D5
South Cadbury 12 B4
South Cairn 104 C3
South Carlton 78 B2
South Cave 96 F5
South Cerney 37 E7
South Chard 11 D8
South Charlton 117 B7
South Cheriton 12 B4
Southchurch 43 F5
South Cliffe 96 F4
South Clifton 77 B8
South
Cockerington 91 F7
South Cornelly 34 F2
Southcott 25 D6
Southcourt 39 C8
South Cove 69 F7
South Creagan 130 E3
South Creake 80 D4
South Croston 64 C3
South Crosland 28 C4
South Dalton 97 E5
South Darenth 29 C6
Southdean 116 D2
Southdene 86 E2
South Duffield 96 F2
Southease 17 D8
South Elkington 91 F6
South Elmsall 89 C5
Southend Argyll 143 H7
W Berks 26 B3
Wilts 25 B6
South End Bucks 40 B1
Cumb 92 C2
N Lincs 90 B5
Southend-on-Sea 42 F4
Southernden 30 E2
Southerndown 21 B7
Southerness 107 D6
South Erradale 149 A12
Southery 67 E6
South Fambridge 42 E4
South Fawley 38 F3
South Ferriby 90 B3
Southfield 111 B5
Southfleet 29 B7
South Garth 160 D7

South Garvan 130 B3
Southgate Ceredig 46 B4
London 41 E5
Norf 81 E7
Swansea 33 F6
South Glendale 148 G2
South Godstone 28 E4
South Gorley 14 C2
South Green Essex 42 E2
Kent 30 C2
South-haa 160 E5
South Ham 26 D4
South
Hanningfield 42 E3
South Harting 15 C8
South Hatfield 41 D5
South Hayling 15 E8
South Hazelrigg 123 F6
South Heath 40 D2
South Heighton 17 D8
South Hetton 111 E6
South Hiendley 88 C4
South Hill 5 B8
South Hinksey 39 D5
South Hole 8 B4
South Holme 96 B2
South Holmwood 28 E2
South Hornchurch 41 F8
South Hykeham 78 C2
South Hylton 111 D6
Southill 54 E2
South Kelsey 90 E4
South Kessock 151 G9
South
Killingholme 91 C5
South Kilvington 102 F2
South Kilworth 64 F3
South Kirkby 88 C5
South Kirkton 141 D6
South Kiscadale 143 F11
South Kyme 78 E4
South Lancing 17 D5
Southleigh 11 E7
South Leigh 38 D3
South Leverton 89 F8
South Littleton 51 E5
South Lopham 68 F3
South Luffenham 65 D6
South Malling 17 C8
South Marston 38 F1
South Middleton 117 B5
South Milford 95 F7
South Millbrex 153 D8
South Milton 6 E5
South Mimms 41 D5
South Molton 10 B2
Southmoor 38 E3
South Moreton 39 F5
South Mundham 16 D2
South Muskham 77 D7
South Newbald 96 F5
South Newington 52 F2
South Newton 25 F5
South Normanton 76 D4
South Norwood 28 C4
South Nutfield 28 E4
South Ockendon 42 F1
Southoe 54 C2
Southolt 57 C5
South Ormsby 79 B6
Southorpe 65 D7
South
Otterington 102 F1
South Owersby 90 E4
Southowram 88 B2
South Oxhey 40 E4
South Perrott 12 D2
South Petherton 12 C2
South Petherwin 8 F5
South Pickenham 67 D8
South Pool 7 E5
Southport 85 C4
South Port 125 C6
Southpunds 160 L6
South Radworthy 21 F6
South Rauceby 78 E3
South Raynham 80 E4
Southrepps 81 D8
South Reston 91 F8
Southrey 78 C4
Southrop 38 D1
South Runcton 67 D6
South Scarle 77 C8
Southsea 15 E7
South Shian 130 E3
South Shields 111 C6
South Shore 92 F3
South Somercotes 91 E8
South Stainley 95 C6
South Stainmore 100 C3
South Stifford 29 B7
Southstoke 24 C2
South Stoke Oxon 39 F5
W Sus 16 D4
South Street E Sus 17 C7
Kent 30 C4
Kent 30 D4
London 28 C5
South Tawton 9 E8
South Thoresby 79 B7
South Tidworth 25 E7
Southtown Norf 69 D8
Orkney 159 J5
South Town 26 F4
South View 26 D4
Southwaite 108 E4
South Walsham 69 C6
Southwark 28 B4
South
Warnborough 26 E5
Southwater 17 B5
Southwater Street 17 B5
Southway 23 E7
South Weald 42 E1
Southwell Dorset 12 G4
Notts 77 D6
South Weston 39 E7
South Wheatley
Corn 8 E4
Notts 89 F8
Southwick Hants 15 D7
N Nhants 65 E7
T&W 111 D6
Wilts 24 D3
W Sus 17 D6
South Widcombe 23 D7

South Wigston 64 E2
South Willingham 91 F5
South Wingfield 76 D3
South Witham 65 C6
Staines-upon-
Thames 27 B8
Stainfield Lincs 78 B4
Lincs 78 B4
Stainforth N Yorks 93 C8
S Yorks 89 C7
Staining 92 F3
Stainland 87 C8
Stainsacre 103 D7
Stainsby 76 C4
Stainton Cumb 99 B6
Cumb 99 F7
Durham 101 C5
Mbro 102 C2
N Yorks 101 E6
S Yorks 89 E6
Stainton by
Langworth 78 B3
Staindale 103 E7
Stainton le Vale 91 E5
Stainton with
Adgarley 92 B2
Stair Cumb 98 B4
E Ayrs 112 B4
Stairhaven 105 D6
Staithes 103 C5
Stakeford 117 F8
Stake Pool 92 E4
Stalbridge 12 C5
Stalbridge Weston 12 C5
Stalham 69 B6
Stalham Green 69 B6
Stalisfield Green 30 D3
Stallingborough 91 C5
Stalling Busk 100 F4
Stalmine 92 E3
Stalybridge 87 E7
Stambourne 55 F8
Stambourne Green 55 F8
Stamford 65 D7
Stamford Bridge
Ches W 73 C8
E Yorks 96 D3
Stamfordham 110 B3
Stanah 99 C5
Stanborough 41 C5
Stanbridge C Beds 40 B2
Dorset 13 D8
Stanbrook 50 E3
Stanbury 94 F3
Stand Gtr Man 87 D5
N Lanark 119 C7
Standburn 120 B2
Standeford 62 D3
Standen 30 E2
Standford 27 F6
Standingstone 107 F7
Standish 86 C3
Standlake 38 D3
Standon Hants 14 B5
Herts 41 B6
Staffs 74 F5
Stane 119 D8
Stanfield 80 E5
Stanford C Beds 54 E2
Kent 19 B8
Stanford Bishop 49 D8
Stanford Bridge 50 C2
Stanford Dingley 26 B3
Stanford in the
Vale 38 E3
Stanford-le-Hope 42 F2
Stanford on Avon 52 B3
Stanford on Soar 64 B2
Stanford on Teme 50 C2
Stanfree 76 B4
Stanghow 102 C4
Stanground 66 E2
Stanhoe 80 D4
Stanhope Borders 114 B4
Durham 110 F2
Stanion 65 F6
Stanley Derbys 76 E4
Durham 110 D4
Lancs 86 D2
Perth 133 F8
Staffs 75 D6
W Yorks 88 B4
Stanley Common 76 E4
Stanley Gate 86 D2
Stanley Hill 49 E8
Stanlow 73 B8
Stanmer 17 D7
Stanmore Hants 15 B5
London 40 E4
W Berks 26 B2
Stannergate 134 F4
Stanningley 94 F5
Stannington
Northumb 110 B5
S Yorks 88 F4
Stansbatch 48 C5
Stansfield 55 D8
Stanstead 56 E2
Stanstead Abbotts 41 C6
Stansted 29 C7
Stansted Airport 42 B1
Stansted
Mountfitchet 41 B8
Stanton Glos 51 F5
Mon 35 B7
Northumb 117 F7
Staffs 75 E8
Suff 56 B3
Stanton by Bridge 63 B7
Stanton-by-Dale 76 F4
Stanton Drew 23 C7
Stanton
Fitzwarren 38 E1
Stanton Harcourt 38 D4
Stanton Hill 76 C4
Stanton in Peak 76 C2
Stanton Lacy 49 B6
Stanton Long 61 E5
Stanton-on-the-
Wolds 77 F6
Stanton Prior 23 C8
Stanton St
Bernard 25 C5
Stanton St John 39 D5
Stanton St Quintin 24 B4
Stanton Street 56 C3
Stanton under
Bardon 63 C8
Stanton upon Hine
Heath 61 B5

Stanton Wick 23 C8
Stanwardine in the
  Fields 60 B4
Stanwardine in the
  Wood 60 B4
Stanway Essex . . . 43 B5
  Glos 51 F5
Stanway Green . . . 57 B6
Stanwell 27 B8
Stanwell Moor 27 B8
Stanwick 53 B7
Stanwick-St-
  John 101 C6
Stanwix 108 D4
Stanydale 160 H4
Staoinebrig 148 E2
Stape 103 E5
Stapehill 13 D8
Stapeley 74 E3
Stapenhill 63 B6
Staple Kent 31 D6
  Som 22 E3
Staple Cross 18 C4
Staplefield 17 B6
Staple Fitzpaine . . 11 C7
Stapleford Cambs . 55 D5
  Herts 41 C6
  Leics 64 C5
  Lincs 77 D8
  Notts 76 F4
  Wilts 25 F5
Stapleford Abbotts 41 E8
Stapleford Tawney 41 E8
Staplegrove 11 B7
Staplehay 11 B7
Staplehurst 29 E8
Staplers 15 F6
Stapleton Bristol . 23 B8
  Cumb 108 B5
  Hereford 48 C5
  Leics 63 E8
  N Yorks 101 C7
  Shrops 60 D4
  Som 12 B2
Stapley 11 C6
Staploe 54 C2
Staplow 49 E8
Star Fife 128 D5
  Pembs 45 F4
  Som 23 D6
Stara 159 F3
Starbeck 95 D6
Starbotton 94 B2
Starcross 10 F4
Stareton 51 B8
Starkholmes 76 D3
Starlings Green . . . 55 F5
Starston 68 F5
Startforth 101 C5
Startley 37 F6
Stathe 11 B8
Stathern 77 F7
Station Town 111 F6
Staughton Green . . 54 C2
Staughton
  Highway 54 C2
Staunton Glos 36 B4
  Glos 36 C2
Staunton in the
  Vale 77 E8
Staunton on
  Arrow 49 C5
Staunton on Wye . . 49 E5
Staveley Cumb . . . 99 E6
  Cumb 99 F5
  Derbys 76 B4
  N Yorks 95 C6
Staverton Devon . . 7 C5
  Glos 37 B5
  Wilts 24 C3
  W Nhants 52 C3
Staverton Bridge . . 37 B5
Stawell 23 F5
Staxigoe 158 E5
Staxton 97 B6
Staylittle 59 E5
Staynall 92 E3
Staythorpe 77 D7
Stean 94 B3
Stearsby 96 B2
Steart 22 E4
Stebbing 42 B2
Stebbing Green . . . 42 B2
Stedham 16 B2
Steele Road 115 E8
Steen's Bridge . . . 49 D7
Steep 15 B8
Steeple Dorset . . . 13 F7
  Essex 43 D5
Steeple Ashton . . . 24 D4
Steeple Aston 38 B4
Steeple Barton . . . 38 B4
Steeple
  Bumpstead 55 E7
Steeple Claydon . . 39 B6
Steeple Gidding . . 65 F8
Steeple Langford . . 24 F5
Steeple Morden . . 54 E3
Steep Marsh 15 B8
Steeton 94 E3
Stein 148 C7
Steinmanhill 153 D7
Stelling Minnis . . . 30 E5
Stemster 158 D3
Stemster House . . 158 D3
Stenalees 4 D5
Stenhousemuir . . . 127 F7
Stenigot 91 F6
Stenness 160 F4
Stenscholl 149 B9
Stenso 159 F4
Stenson 63 B7
Stenton E Loth . . . 122 B2
  Fife 128 E4
Stenwith 77 F8
Stepaside 32 D2
Stepping Hill 87 F7
Steppingley 53 F8
Stepps 119 C6
Sterndale Moor . . . 75 C8
Sternfield 57 C7
Sterridge 20 E4
Stert 24 D5
Stetchworth 55 D7
Stevenage 41 B5
Stevenston 118 E3
Steventon Hants . . 26 E3
  Oxon 38 E4
Stevington 53 D7

Stewartby 53 E8
Stewarton Argyll . 143 G7
  E Ayrs 118 E4
Stewkley 40 B1
Stewton 91 F7
Steyne Cross 15 F7
Steyning 17 C5
Steynton 44 E4
Stibb 8 C4
Stibbard 81 E5
Stibb Cross 9 C6
Stibb Green 25 C7
Stibbington 65 E7
Stichill 122 F3
Sticker 4 D4
Stickford 79 D6
Sticklepath 9 E8
Stickney 79 D6
Stiffkey 81 C5
Stifford's Bridge . . 50 E2
Stillingfleet 95 E8
Stillington N Yorks . 95 C8
  Stockton 102 B1
Stilton 65 F8
Stinchcombe 36 E4
Stinsford 12 E5
Stirchley 61 D7
Stirkoke House . . . 158 E5
Stirling Aberds . . 153 D11
  Stirling 127 E6
Stisted 42 B3
Stithians 3 C6
Stittenham 151 D9
Stivichall 51 B8
Stixwould 78 C4
Stoak 73 B8
Stobieside 119 F6
Stobo 120 F4
Stoborough 13 F7
Stoborough Green . 13 F7
Stobshiel 121 C7
Stobswood 117 E8
Stock 42 E2
Stockbridge 25 F8
Stockbury 30 C2
Stockcross 26 C2
Stockdalewath 64 E5
Stock Green 50 D4
Stockheath 15 D8
Stockiemuir 126 F4
Stockingford 63 E7
Stocking Pelham . . 41 B7
Stockland 11 D7
Stockland Bristol . . 22 E4
Stockleigh English 10 D3
Stockleigh
  Pomeroy 10 D3
Stockley 24 C5
Stocklinch 11 C8
Stockport 87 E6
Stocksbridge 88 E3
Stocksfield 110 C3
Stockton Hereford . 49 C7
  Norf 69 E6
  Shrops 60 D2
  Shrops 61 E7
  Warks 52 C2
  Wilts 24 F3
Stockton Heath . . . 86 F4
Stockton-on-
  Tees 102 C2
Stockton on Teme . 50 C2
Stockton on the
  Forest 96 D2
Stock Wood 50 D5
Stodmarsh 31 C6
Stody 81 D6
Stoer 156 G3
Stoford Som 12 C3
  Wilts 25 F5
Stogumber 22 F2
Stogursey 22 E4
Stoke Devon 8 B4
  Hants 15 D8
  Hants 26 D2
  Medway 30 B2
  Suff 57 E5
Stoke Abbott 12 D2
Stoke Albany 64 F5
Stoke Ash 56 B5
Stoke Bardolph . . . 77 E6
Stoke Bliss 49 C8
Stoke Bruerne 52 E5
Stoke by Clare 55 E8
Stoke-by-Nayland . 56 F3
Stoke Canon 10 E4
Stoke Charity 26 F2
Stoke Climsland . . . 5 B8
Stoke D'Abernon . . 28 D2
Stoke Doyle 65 F7
Stoke Dry 65 E5
Stoke Farthing . . . 13 B8
Stoke Ferry 67 E7
Stoke Fleming 7 E6
Stokeford 13 F6
Stoke Gabriel 7 D6
Stoke Gifford 23 B8
Stoke Golding 63 E7
Stoke Goldington . 53 E6
Stoke Green 40 F2
Stokeham 77 B7
Stoke Hammond . . 40 B1
Stoke Heath 61 B6
Stoke Holy Cross . . 68 D5
Stokeinteignhead . . 7 B7
Stoke Lacy 49 E8
Stoke Lyne 39 B5
Stoke Mandeville . . 39 C8
Stokenchurch 39 E7
Stoke Newington . . 41 F6
Stokenham 7 E6
Stoke on Tern 61 B6
Stoke-on-Trent . . . 75 E5
Stoke Orchard 37 B6
Stoke Poges 40 F2
Stoke Prior
  Hereford 49 D7
  Worcs 50 C4
Stoke Rivers 20 F5
Stoke Rochford . . . 65 B6
Stoke Row 39 F6
Stoke St Gregory . . 11 B8
Stoke St Mary 11 B7
Stoke St Michael . . 23 E8
Stoke St
  Milborough 61 F5
Stokesay 60 F4
Stokesby 69 C7

Stokesley 102 D3
Stoke sub
  Hamdon 12 C2
Stoke Talmage . . . 39 E6
Stoke Trister 12 B5
Stoke Wake 13 D5
Stolford 22 E4
Stondon Massey . . 42 D1
Stone Bucks 39 C7
  Glos 36 E3
  Kent 19 C6
  Kent 29 B6
  Staffs 75 F6
  S Yorks 89 F6
  Worcs 50 B3
Stone Allerton 23 D6
Ston Easton 23 D8
Stone Bridge
  Corner 66 D2
Stonebroom 76 D4
Stone Chair 88 B2
Stone Cross E Sus . 18 E3
  Kent 31 D7
Stone-edge Batch . 23 B6
Stoneferry 97 F7
Stonefield 119 D6
Stonegate E Sus . . 18 C3
  N Yorks 103 D5
Stonegrave 96 B2
Stonehaugh 109 B7
Stonehaven 141 F7
Stonehouse Glos . . 37 D5
  Northumb 109 D6
  S Lanark 119 E7
Stone House 100 F2
Stoneleigh 51 B8
Stonely 54 C2
Stoner Hill 15 B8
Stonesby 64 B5
Stonesfield 38 C3
Stone's Green 43 B7
Stone Street Kent . 29 D6
  Suff 56 F3
  Suff 69 F6
Stonethwaite 98 C4
Stoneybreck 160 N8
Stoneyburn 120 C2
Stoney Cross 14 C3
Stoneygate
  Aberds 153 E10
  Leicester 64 D3
Stoneyhills 43 E5
Stoneykirk 104 D4
Stoney Middleton . 76 B2
Stoney Stanton . . . 63 E8
Stoney Stoke 24 F2
Stoney Stratton . . . 23 F8
Stoney Stretton . . . 60 D3
Stoneywood
  Aberdeen 141 C7
  Falk 127 F6
Stonganess 160 C7
Stonham Aspal . . . 56 D5
Stonnall 62 D4
Stonor 39 F7
Stonton Wyville . . . 64 E4
Stony Cross 50 E2
Stonyfield 151 D9
Stony Stratford . . . 53 E5
Stoodleigh 10 C4
Stopes 88 F3
Stopham 16 C4
Stopsley 40 B4
Stores Corner 57 E7
Storeton 85 F4
Stornoway 155 D9
Storridge 50 E2
Storrington 16 C4
Storrs 99 E5
Storth 99 F6
Storwood 96 E3
Stotfield 152 A2
Stotfold 54 F3
Stottesdon 61 F6
Stoughton Leics . . 64 D3
  Sur 27 D7
  W Sus 16 C2
Stoul 147 B10
Stoulton 50 E4
Stourbridge 62 F3
Stourpaine 13 D6
Stourport on
  Severn 50 B3
Stour Provost 13 B5
Stour Row 13 B6
Stourton Staffs . . . 62 F2
  Warks 51 F7
  Wilts 24 F2
Stourton
  Caundle 12 C5
Stove Orkney 159 E7
  Shetland 160 L6
Stoven 69 F7
Stow Borders 121 E7
  Lincs 78 F3
  Lincs 90 F2
Stow Bardolph 67 D6
Stow Bedon 68 E2
Stowbridge 67 D6
Stow cum Quy 55 C6
Stowe 48 B5
Stowe-by-
  Chartley 62 B4
Stowe Green 36 D2
Stowell 12 B4
Stowford 9 F6
Stowlangtoft 56 C3
Stow Longa 54 B2
Stow Maries 42 E4
Stowmarket 56 D4
Stow-on-the-
  Wold 38 B1
Stowting 30 E5
Stowupland 56 D4
Straad 145 G9
Strachan 141 E5
Stradbroke 57 B6
Stradishall 55 D8
Stradsett 67 D6
Stragglethorpe . . . 78 D2
Straid 112 E1
Straith 113 F8
Straiton Edin 121 C5
  S Ayrs 112 D3
Straloch Aberds . . 141 B7
  Perth 133 C7
Stramshall 75 F7
Strang 84 E3
Stranraer 104 C4

Stratfield
  Mortimer 26 C4
Stratfield Saye . . . 26 C4
Stratfield Turgis . . 26 D4
Stratford 41 F6
Stratford St
  Andrew 57 C7
Stratford St Mary . 56 F4
Stratford Sub
  Castle 25 F6
Stratford Tony 13 B8
Stratford-upon-
  Avon 51 D6
Strath Highld . . . 149 A12
  Highld 158 E4
Strathan Highld . . 136 E2
  Highld 156 G3
  Highld 157 C8
Strathaven 119 E7
Strathblane 119 B5
Strathcanaird . . . 156 J4
Strathcarron 150 G2
Strathcoil 124 B2
Strathdon 140 C2
Strathellie 153 B10
Strathkinness . . . 129 C6
Strathmashie
  House 137 E8
Strathmiglo 128 C4
Strathmore
  Lodge 158 F3
Strathpeffer 150 F7
Strathrannoch . . . 150 D6
Strathtay 133 D6
Strathvaich
  Lodge 150 D6
Strathwhillan . . . 143 E11
Strathy 157 C11
Strathyre 126 C4
Stratton Corn 8 D4
  Dorset 12 E4
  Glos 37 D7
Stratton Audley . . . 39 B6
Stratton on the
  Fosse 23 D8
Stratton St
  Margaret 38 F1
Stratton St
  Michael 68 E5
Stratton Strawless 81 E8
Stravithie 129 C7
Streat 17 C7
Streatham 28 B4
Streatley C Beds . . 40 B3
  W Berks 39 F5
Street Lancs 92 D5
  N Yorks 103 D5
  Som 23 F6
Street Dinas 73 F7
Street End Kent . . . 30 D5
  W Sus 16 E2
Street Gate 110 D5
Streethay 62 C5
Streetlam 101 E8
Streetly 62 E4
Street Lydan 73 F8
Streetly End 55 E7
Strefford 60 F4
Strelley 76 E5
Strensall 96 C2
Stretcholt 22 E4
Strete 7 E6
Stretford 87 E6
Strethall 55 F5
Stretham 55 B6
Strettington 16 D2
Stretton Ches W . . 73 D8
  Derbys 76 C3
  Rutland 65 C6
  Staffs 62 C2
  Staffs 63 B6
  Warr 86 F4
Stretton
  Grandison 49 E8
Stretton-on-
  Dunsmore 52 B2
Stretton-on-Fosse 51 F7
Stretton Sugwas . . 49 E6
Stretton under
  Fosse 63 F8
Stretton
  Westwood 61 E5
Strichen 153 C9
Strines 87 F7
Stringston 22 E3
Strixton 53 C7
Stroat 36 E2
Stromeferry 149 E13
Stromemore 149 E13
Stromness 159 H3
Stronaba 136 F5
Stronachlachar . . 126 C3
Stronchreggan . . . 130 B4
Stronchrubie 156 H5
Strone Argyll . . . 145 E10
  Highld 136 F4
  Highld 137 B8
  Invclyd 118 B2
Stronmilchan 125 C7
Strontian 130 C2
Strood 29 C8
Strood Green Sur . 28 E3
  W Sus 16 B4
  W Sus 28 F2
Stroud Glos 37 D5
  Hants 15 B8
Stroud Green 42 E4
Stroxton 78 F2
Struan Highld . . . 149 E8
  Perth 133 C5
Strubby 91 F8
Strumpshaw 69 D6
Strutherhill 119 E7
Struy 150 H6
Stryd-issa 73 D6
Stryt-issa 73 E6
Stuartfield 153 D9
Stubbington 15 D6
Stubbins 87 C5
Stubbs Cross 19 B6
Stubb's Green 69 E5
Stubhampton 13 C7
Stubton 77 E8
Stuckgowan 126 D2
Stuckton 14 C2
Stud Green 27 B6
Studham 40 C3
Studland 13 F8

Studley Warks . . . 51 C5
  Wilts 24 B4
Studley Roger 95 B5
Stump Cross 55 E6
Stuntney 55 B6
Sturbridge 74 F5
Sturmer 55 E7
Sturminster
  Marshall 13 D7
Sturminster
  Newton 13 C5
Sturry 31 C5
Sturton 90 D3
Sturton by Stow . . 90 F2
Sturton le Steeple . 89 F8
Stuston 56 B5
Stutton N Yorks . . . 95 E7
  Suff 57 F5
Styal 87 F6
Styrrup 89 E7
Suainebost 155 A10
Suardail 155 D9
Succoth Aberds . . 152 E4
  Argyll 125 E7
Suckley 50 D2
Suckquoy 159 K5
Sudborough 65 F6
Sudbourne 57 D8
Sudbrook Lincs . . . 78 E2
  Mon 36 F2
Sudbrooke 78 B3
Sudbury Derbys . . . 75 F8
  London 40 F4
  Suff 56 E2
Suddie 151 F9
Sudgrove 37 D6
Suffield Norf 81 D8
  N Yorks 103 E7
Sugnall 74 F4
Suladale 149 C8
Sulaisiadar 155 D10
Sulby 84 C3
Sulgrave 52 E3
Sulham 26 B4
Sulhamstead 26 C4
Sulland 159 D6
Sullington 16 C4
Sullom 160 F5
Sullom Voe Oil
  Terminal 160 F5
Sully 22 C3
Sumburgh 160 N6
Summer Bridge . . 94 C5
Summercourt 4 D3
Summerfield 80 D3
Summergangs . . . 97 F7
Summer-house . . 101 C7
Summerleaze 35 F8
Summersdale 16 D2
Summerseat 87 C5
Summertown 39 D5
Summit 87 D7
Sunbury-on-
  Thames 28 C2
Sundaywell 113 F8
Sunderland Argyll 142 B3
  Cumb 107 F8
  T&W 111 D6
Sunderland
  Bridge 111 F5
Sundhope 115 B6
Sundon Park 40 B3
Sundridge 29 D5
Sunk Island 91 C6
Sunningdale 27 C7
Sunninghill 27 C7
Sunningwell 38 D4
Sunniside Durham . 110 F4
  T&W 110 D5
Sunnyhurst 86 B4
Sunnylaw 127 E6
Sunnyside 28 F4
Sunton 25 D7
Surbiton 28 C2
Surby 84 E2
Surfleet 66 B2
Surfleet Seas End . 66 B2
Surlingham 69 D6
Sustead 81 D7
Susworth 90 D2
Sutcombe 8 C5
Suton 68 E3
Sutors of
  Cromarty 151 E11
Sutterby 79 B6
Sutterton 79 F5
Sutton Cambs 54 B5
  C Beds 54 E3
  Kent 31 E7
  London 28 C3
  Mers 86 E3
  Norf 69 B6
  Notts 77 F7
  Notts 89 F7
  N Yorks 89 B5
  Oxon 38 D4
  Pboro 65 E7
  Shrops 61 F7
  Shrops 74 F3
  Som 23 F8
  Staffs 61 B7
  Suff 57 E7
  Sur 27 E8
  S Yorks 89 C6
  W Sus 16 C3
Sutton at Hone . . . 29 B6
Sutton Bassett . . . 64 E4
Sutton Benger . . . 24 B4
Sutton Bonington . 64 B2
Sutton Bridge 66 B4
Sutton Cheney . . . 63 D8
Sutton Coldfield . . 62 E5
Sutton Courtenay . 39 E5
Sutton Crosses . . . 66 B4
Sutton Grange . . . 95 B5
Sutton Green 27 D8
Sutton Howgrave . 95 B6
Sutton in Ashfield . 76 D4
Sutton-in-Craven . 94 E3
Sutton Ings 97 F7
Sutton in the Elms 64 E2
Sutton Lane Ends . 75 B6
Sutton Leach 86 E3
Sutton Maddock . . 61 D7
Sutton Mallet 23 F5
Sutton Mandeville . 13 B7
Sutton Manor 86 E3
Sutton Montis 12 B4

Sutton on Hull . . . 97 F7
Sutton on Sea 91 F9
Sutton-on-the-
  Forest 95 C8
Sutton on the Hill . 76 F2
Sutton on Trent . . 77 C7
Sutton St Edmund 66 C3
Sutton St James . . 66 C3
Sutton St Nicholas 49 E7
Sutton Scarsdale . 76 C4
Sutton Scotney . . . 26 F2
Sutton under
  Brailes 51 F8
Sutton-under-
  Whitestonecliffe
  . . . . 102 F2
Sutton upon
  Derwent 96 E3
Sutton Valence . . . 30 E2
Sutton Veny 24 E3
Sutton Waldron . . . 13 C6
Sutton Weaver . . . 74 B2
Sutton Wick 23 D7
Swaby 79 B6
Swadlincote 63 C7
Swaffham 67 D8
Swaffham Bulbeck 55 C6
Swaffham Prior . . . 55 C6
Swafield 81 D8
Swainby 102 D2
Swainshill 49 E6
Swainsthorpe 68 D5
Swainswick 24 C2
Swalcliffe 51 F8
Swalecliffe 30 C5
Swallow 91 D5
Swallowcliffe 13 B7
Swallowfield 26 C5
Swallownest 89 F5
Swallows Cross . . . 42 E2
Swanage 13 G8
Swanbister 159 H4
Swanbourne 39 B8
Swan Green
  Ches W 74 B4
  Suff 57 B6
Swanland 90 B3
Swanley 29 C6
Swanley Village . . 29 C6
Swanmore 15 C6
Swannington Leics 63 C8
  Norf 68 C4
Swanscombe 29 B7
Swansea
  = Abertawe 33 E7
Swanton Abbott . . 81 E8
Swanton Morley . . 68 C3
Swanton Novers . . 81 D6
Swanton Street . . 30 D2
Swanwick Derbys . 76 D4
  Hants 15 D6
Swarby 78 E3
Swardeston 68 D5
Swarister 160 E7
Swarkestone 63 B7
Swarland 117 D7
Swarland Estate . 117 D7
Swarthmoor 92 B2
Swathwick 76 C3
Swaton 78 F4
Swavesey 54 C4
Sway 14 E3
Swayfield 65 B6
Swaythling 14 C5
Sweet Green 49 C8
Sweetham 10 E3
Sweethouse 5 C5
Swefling 57 C7
Swepstone 63 C7
Swerford 51 F8
Swettenham 74 C5
Swetton 94 B4
Swffryd 35 E6
Swiftsden 18 C4
Swilland 57 D5
Swillington 95 F6
Swimbridge 9 B8
Swimbridge
  Newland 20 F5
Swinbrook 38 C2
Swinderby 77 C8
Swindon Glos 37 B6
  Staffs 62 E2
  Swindon 38 F1
Swine 97 F7
Swinefleet 89 B8
Swineshead
  Bedford 53 C8
  Lincs 78 E5
Swineshead
  Bridge 78 E5
Swiney 158 G4
Swinford Leics . . . 52 B3
  Oxon 38 D4
Swingate 76 E5
Swingfield Minnis . 31 E6
Swingfield Street . 31 E6
Swinhoe 117 B8
Swinhope 91 E6
Swining 160 G6
Swinithwaite 101 F5
Swinnow Moor . . . 94 F5
Swinscoe 75 E8
Swinside Hall . . . 116 C3
Swinstead 65 B7
Swinton Borders . . 122 E4
  Gtr Man 87 D5
  N Yorks 94 B5
  N Yorks 96 B3
  S Yorks 88 E5
Swintonmill 122 E4
Swithland 64 C2
Swordale 151 E8
Swordland 147 B10
Swordly 157 C10
Sworton Heath . . . 86 F4
Swydffynnon 47 C5
Swynnerton 75 F5
Swyre 12 F3
Sychtyn 59 D6
Syde 37 C6
Sydenham London . 28 B4
  Oxon 39 D7
Sydenham Damerel 6 B2
Syderstone 80 D4
Sydling St
  Nicholas 12 E4
Sydmonton 26 D2
Syerston 77 E7

Syke 87 C6
Sykehouse 89 C7
Sykes 93 D6
Syleham 57 B6
Sylen 33 D6
Symbister 160 G7
Symington S Ayrs . 118 F3
  S Lanark 120 F2
Symonds Green . . 41 B5
Symondsbury 12 E2
Symonds Yat 36 C2
Synod Inn 46 D3
Syre 157 E9
Syreford 37 B7
Syresham 52 E4
Syston Leics 64 C3
  Lincs 78 E2
Sytchampton 50 C3
Sywell 53 C6

T

Taagan 150 E3
Tàbost 155 A10
Tabost 155 F8
Tackley 38 B4
Tacleit 154 D6
Tacolneston 68 E4
Tadcaster 95 E7
Taddington 75 B8
Taddiport 9 C6
Tadley 26 C4
Tadlow 54 E3
Tadmarton 51 F8
Tadworth 28 D3
Tafarnau-bach . . . 35 C5
Tafarn-y-gelyn . . . 73 C5
Taff's Well 35 F5
Tafolwern 59 D5
Tai 83 E7
Taibach 34 F1
Tai-bach 59 B8
Taigh a
  Ghearraidh . . . 148 A2
Tai-mawr 72 E3
Tain Highld 151 C10
  Highld 158 D4
Tainant 73 E6
Tainlon 82 F4
Tairbeart
  = Tarbert 154 G6
Tai'r-Bull 34 B3
Tairgwaith 33 C8
Tai-Ucha 72 D4
Takeley 42 B1
Takeley Street . . . 41 B8
Talachddu 48 F2
Talacre 85 F2
Talardd 59 B5
Talaton 11 E5
Talbenny 44 D3
Talbot Green 34 F4
Talbot Village . . . 13 E8
Tale 11 D5
Talerddig 59 D6
Talgarreg 46 D3
Talgarth 48 F3
Talisker 149 E8
Talke 74 D5
Talkin 109 D5
Talladale 150 D2
Talla Linnfoots . . 114 B4
Tallarn Green 73 E8
Tallentire 107 F8
Talley 46 F5
Tallington 65 D7
Talmine 157 C8
Talog 32 B4
Talsarn 34 B1
Tal-sarn 46 D4
Talsarnau 71 D7
Talskiddy 4 C4
Talwrn Anglesey . . 82 D4
  Wrex 73 E6
Tal-y-bont Ceredig 58 F3
  Conwy 83 E7
  Gwyn 71 E6
  Gwyn 83 D6
Talybont-on-Usk . 35 B5
Tal-y-cafn 83 D7
  London 28 B2
Tal-y-llyn 58 D4
Talyllyn 35 B5
Tal-y-sarn 82 F4
Tal-y-wern 58 D5
Tame Bridge 102 D3
Tamerton Foliot . . . 6 C2
Tamworth 63 D6
Tan Hinon 59 F5
Tankersley 88 D4
Tankerton 30 C5
Tan-lan Conwy . . . 83 E7
  Gwyn 71 C7
Tannach 158 F5
Tannachie 141 F6
Tannadice 134 D4
Tannington 57 C6
Tansley 76 D3
Tansley Knoll 76 C3
Tansor 65 E7
Tantobie 110 D4
Tanton 102 D3
Tanworth-in-
  Arden 51 B6
Tan-y-bwlch 71 C7
Tan-y-fron 72 C3
Tan-y-graig
  Anglesey 82 D5
  Gwyn 70 D4
Tanygrisiau 71 C7
Tan-y-groes 45 E4
Tan-y-pistyll 59 B7
Tan-yr-allt 82 F4
Tanyrhydiau 47 C6
Taobh a Chaolais 148 G2
Taobh a'Ghlinne . 155 F8

Taobh a Thuath Loch
  Aineort 148 F2
Taobh a Tuath Loch
  Baghasdail . . . 148 F2
Taobh Tuath 154 J4
Taplow 40 F2
Tapton 76 B3
Tarbat House . . . 151 D10
Tarbert Argyll . . . 143 C7
  Argyll 144 E5
  Argyll 145 G7
Tarbert
  = Tairbeart . . . 154 G6
Tarbet Argyll 126 D2
  Highld 147 B10
  Highld 156 E4
Tarbock Green . . . 86 F2
Tarbolton 112 B4
Tarbrax 120 D3
Tardebigge 50 C5
Tarfside 134 B4
Tarland 140 D3
Tarleton 86 B2
Tarlogie 151 C10
Tarlscough 86 C2
Tarlton 37 E6
Tarnbrook 93 D5
Tarporley 74 C2
Tarr 22 F3
Tarrant Crawford . 13 D7
Tarrant Gunville . . 13 C7
Tarrant Hinton . . . 13 C7
Tarrant Keyneston 13 D7
Tarrant
  Launceston . . . 13 D7
Tarrant Monkton . 13 D7
Tarrant Rawston . 13 D7
Tarrant Rushton . 13 D7
Tarrel 151 C11
Tarring Neville . . . 17 D8
Tarrington 49 E8
Tarsappie 128 B3
Tarskavaig 149 H10
Tarves 153 E8
Tarvie Highld 150 F7
  Perth 133 C7
Tarvin 73 C8
Tasburgh 68 E5
Tasley 61 E6
Taston 38 B3
Tatenhill 63 B6
Tathall End 53 E6
Tatham 93 C6
Tathwell 91 F7
Tatling End 40 F3
Tatsfield 28 D5
Tattenhall 73 D8
Tattenhoe 53 F6
Tatterford 80 E4
Tattersett 80 D4
Tattershall 78 D5
Tattershall Bridge 78 D4
Tattershall Thorpe 78 D5
Tattingstone 56 F5
Tatworth 11 D8
Taunton 11 B7
Taverham 68 C4
Tavernspite 32 C2
Tavistock 6 B2
Taw Green 9 E8
Tawstock 9 B7
Taxal 75 B7
Tay Bridge 129 B6
Tayinloan 143 D7
Taymouth Castle . 132 E4
Taynish 144 E6
Taynton Glos 36 B4
  Oxon 38 C2
Taynuilt 125 B6
Tayport 129 B6
Tayvallich 144 E6
Tealby 91 E5
Tealing 134 F4
Teangue 149 H11
Teanna Mhachair 148 B2
Tebay 99 D8
Tebworth 40 B2
Tedburn St Mary . 10 E3
Teddington Glos . . 50 F4
  London 28 B2
Tedstone
  Delamere 49 D8
Tedstone Wafre . . 49 D8
Teeton 52 B4
Teffont Evias 24 F4
Teffont Magna . . . 24 F4
Tegryn 45 F4
Teigh 65 C5
Teigncombe 9 F8
Teigngrace 7 B6
Teignmouth 7 B7
Telford 61 D6
Telham 18 D4
Tellisford 24 D3
Telscombe 17 D8
Telscombe Cliffs . 17 D8
Templand 114 F3
Temple Corn 5 B6
  Glasgow 118 C5
  Midloth 121 D6
Temple Balsall . . . 51 B7
Temple Bar Carms . 33 C6
  Ceredig 46 D4
Temple Cloud 23 D8
Temple Combe . . . 12 B5
Temple Ewell 31 E6
Temple Grafton . . 51 D6
Temple Guiting . . . 37 B7
Templehall 128 E4
Temple
  Herdewyke 51 D8
Temple Hirst 89 B7
Temple
  Normanton 76 C4
Temple Sowerby . . 99 B8
Templeton Devon . 10 C3
  Pembs 32 C2
Templeton Bridge . 10 C3
Templetown 110 D4
Tempsford 54 D2
Tenbury Wells . . . 49 C7
Tenby
  = Dinbych-y-Pysgod 32 D2
Tendring 43 B7
Tendring Green . . 43 B7
Ten Mile Bank . . . 67 E6
Tenston 159 G3
Tenterden 19 B5
Terling 42 C3

Ternhill 74 F3
Terregles Banks . 107 B6
Terrick 39 D8
Terrington 96 B2
Terrington St
  Clement 66 C5
Terrington St
  John 66 C5
Teston 29 D8
Testwood 14 C4
Tetbury 37 E5
Tetbury Upton . . . 37 E5
Tetchill 73 F7
Tetcott 8 E5
Tetford 79 B6
Tetney 91 D7
Tetney Lock 91 D7
Tetsworth 39 D6
Tettenhall 62 E2
Teuchan 153 E10
Teversal 76 C4
Teversham 55 D5
Teviothead 115 D7
Tewel 141 F7
Tewin 41 C5
Tewkesbury 50 F3
Teynham 30 C3
Thackthwaite 98 B3
Thainston 135 B6
Thakeham 16 C5
Thame 39 D7
Thames Ditton . . . 28 C2
Thames Haven . . . 42 F3
Thamesmead 41 F7
Thanington 30 D5
Thankerton 120 F2
Tharston 68 E4
Thatcham 26 C3
Thatto Heath 86 E3
Thaxted 55 F7
The Aird 149 C9
Theakston 101 F8
Thealby 90 C2
Theale Som 23 E6
  W Berks 26 B4
The Arms 67 E8
Thearne 97 F6
The Bage 48 E4
The Balloch 127 C7
The Barony 159 F3
Theberton 57 C8
The Bog 60 E3
The Bourne 27 E6
The Braes 149 E10
The Broad 49 C6
The Butts 24 E2
The Camp Glos . . 37 D6
  Herts 40 D4
The Chequer 73 E8
The City 39 E7
The Common 25 F7
The Craigs 150 B7
The Cronk 84 C3
Theddingworth . . 64 F3
Theddlethorpe All
  Saints 91 F8
Theddlethorpe St
  Helen 91 F8
The Dell 69 E7
The Den 118 D3
The Eals 116 F3
The Eaves 36 D3
The Flatt 109 B5
The Four Alls 74 F3
The Garths 160 B8
The Green Cumb . 98 F3
  Wilts 24 F3
The Grove 107 B6
The Hall 160 D8
The Haven 27 F8
The Heath Norf . . 81 E8
  Suff 56 F5
The Hill 98 F3
The Howe Cumb . . 99 F6
  IoM 84 F1
The Hundred 49 C7
Thelbridge Barton . 10 C2
The Lee 40 D2
The Lhen 84 B3
Thelnetham 56 B4
Thelveton 68 F4
Thelwall 86 F4
The Marsh Powys . 60 E3
  Wilts 37 F7
Themelthorpe . . . 81 E6
The Middles 110 D5
The Moor 18 C4
The Mumbles
  = Y Mwmbwls . . 33 F7
The Murray 119 D6
The Neuk 141 E6
Thenford 52 E3
The Oval 24 C2
The Pole of Itlaw . 153 C6
The Quarry 36 E4
Therfield 54 F4
The Rhos 32 C1
The Rock 61 D6
The Ryde 41 D5
The Sands 27 E6
The Stocks 19 C5
Thetford Lincs . . . 65 C8
  Norf 67 F8
The Throat 27 C6
The Vauld 49 E7
The Wyke 61 D7
Theydon Bois 41 E7
Thickwood 24 B3
Thimbleby Lincs . . 78 C5
  N Yorks 102 E2
Thingwall 85 F3
Thirdpart 118 E1
Thirlby 102 F2
Thirlestane 121 E8
Thirn 101 F7
Thirsk 102 F2
Thirtleby 97 F7
Thistleton Lancs . 92 F4
  Rutland 65 C6
Thistley Green . . . 55 B7
Thixendale 96 C4
Thockrington . . . 110 B2
Tholomas Drove . . 66 D3
Tholthorpe 95 C7
Thomas Chapel . . 32 D2
Thomas Close . . . 108 E4

Thomastown 152 E5
Thompson 68 E2
Thomshill 152 C2
Thong 29 B7
Thongsbridge 88 D2
Thoralby 101 F5
Thoresway 91 E5
Thorganby Lincs 91 E6
　N Yorks 96 E2
Thorgill 103 E5
Thorington 57 B8
Thorington Street .56 F4
Thorlby 94 D2
Thorley 41 C7
Thorley Street
　Herts 41 C7
　IoW 14 F4
Thormanby 95 B7
Thornaby-on-
　Tees 102 C2
Thornage 81 D6
Thornborough
　Bucks 52 F5
　N Yorks 95 B5
Thornbury Devon 9 D6
　Hereford 49 D8
　S Glos 36 E3
　W Yorks 94 F4
Thornby 52 B4
Thorncliffe 75 D7
Thorncombe
　Dorset 11 D8
　Dorset 13 D6
Thorncombe
　Street 27 E8
Thorncote Green .54 E2
Thorncross 14 F5
Thorndon 56 C5
Thorndon Cross 9 E7
Thorne 89 C7
Thorner 95 E6
Thorne St
　Margaret 11 B5
Thorney Notts 77 B8
　Pboro. 66 D2
Thorney Crofts 91 B6
Thorney Green 56 C4
Thorney Hill 14 E2
Thorney Toll 66 D3
Thornfalcon 11 B7
Thornford 12 C4
Thorngumbald 91 B6
Thornham 80 C3
Thornham Magna .56 B5
Thornham Parva ..56 B5
Thornhaugh 65 D7
Thornhill Cardiff... 35 F5
　Cumb. 98 D2
　Derbys. 88 F2
　Dumfries 113 E8
　Soton. 15 C5
　Stirling. 127 E6
　W Yorks 88 C3
Thornhill Edge 88 C3
Thornhill Lees.... 88 C3
Thornholme 97 C7
Thornley Durham . 110 F4
　Durham 111 F6
Thornliebank 118 D5
Thorns 55 D8
Thornsett 87 F8
Thorns Green 87 F5
Thornthwaite Cumb 98 D4
　N Yorks 94 D4
Thornton Angus ..134 E3
　Bucks. 53 F5
　E Yorks 96 E3
　Fife 128 E4
　Lancs. 92 E3
　Leics. 63 D8
　Lincs. 78 C5
　Mbro. 102 C2
　Mers. 85 D4
　Northumb. 123 E5
　Pembs. 44 E4
　W Yorks 94 F4
Thornton Curtis ...90 C4
Thorntonhall.... 119 D5
Thornton Heath ...28 C4
Thornton Hough .. 85 F4
Thornton in
　Craven 94 E2
Thornton-le-
　Beans 102 E1
Thornton-le-Clay . 96 C2
Thornton-le-
　Dale 103 F6
Thornton le Moor . 90 E4
Thornton-le-
　Moor 102 F1
Thornton-le-
　Moors 73 B8
Thornton-le-
　Street 102 F2
Thorntonloch ...122 B3
Thorntonpark 122 E5
Thornton Rust ...100 F4
Thornton
　Steward 101 F6
Thornton
　Watlass 101 F7
Thornwood
　Common 41 D7
Thornydykes 122 E2
Thoroton 77 E7
Thorp Arch 95 E7
Thorpe Derbys ...75 D8
　E Yorks 97 E5
　Lincs 91 F8
　Norf. 69 E7
　Notts 77 E7
　N Yorks 94 C3
　Sur. 27 C8
Thorpe Abbotts ...57 B5
Thorpe Acre 64 B2
Thorpe Arnold 64 B4
Thorpe Bassett ...96 B4
Thorpe Bay 43 F5
Thorpe by Water .65 E5
Thorpe Common . 57 F6
Thorpe
　Constantine 63 D6
Thorpe Culvert ...79 C7
Thorpe End 69 C5
Thorpe Fendykes . 79 C7

Thorpe Green
　Essex....43 B7
　Suff 56 D3
Thorpe Hesley 88 E4
Thorpe in Balne .. 89 C6
Thorpe in the
　Fallows....90 F3
Thorpe Langton ...64 E4
Thorpe Larches ..102 B1
Thorpe-le-Soken .43 B7
Thorpe le Street ..96 E4
Thorpe Malsor 53 B6
Thorpe Mandeville 52 E3
Thorpe Market 81 D8
Thorpe Marriott ...68 C4
Thorpe Morieux ...56 D3
Thorpeness 57 D8
Thorpe on the Hill .78 C2
Thorpe St Andrew .69 D5
Thorpe St Peter ...79 C7
Thorpe Salvin 89 F6
Thorpe Satchville .64 C4
Thorpe Thewles ..102 B2
Thorpe Tilney 78 D4
Thorpe
　Underwood....95 D7
Thorpe Waterville .65 F7
Thorpe Willoughby 95 F8
Thorrington 43 C6
Thorverton 10 D4
Thrandeston 56 B5
Thrapston 53 B7
Thrashbush 119 C7
Threapland Cumb .107 F8
　N Yorks 94 C2
Threapwood
　Ches W....73 E8
　Staffs....75 E7
Three Ashes 36 B2
Three Bridges 28 F3
Three Burrows....3 B6
Three Chimneys ..18 B5
Three Cocks 48 F3
Three Crosses 33 E6
Three Cups
　Corner 18 C3
Threehammer
　Common 69 C6
Three Holes 66 D5
Threekingham 78 F3
Three Leg Cross ..18 B3
Three Legged
　Cross 13 D8
Threemile Cross .. 26 C5
Threemilestone....3 D6
Threemiletown ..120 B3
Three Oaks 18 D5
Threlkeld 99 B5
Threshfield 94 C2
Thrigby 69 C7
Thringarth 100 B4
Thringstone 63 C8
Thrintoft 101 E8
Thriplow 54 E5
Throckenholt 66 D3
Throcking 54 F4
Throckley 110 C4
Throckmorton 50 E4
Throphill 117 F7
Thropton 117 D6
Throsk 127 E7
Throwleigh....9 E8
Throwley 30 D3
Thrumpton 76 F5
Thrumster 158 F5
Thrunton 117 C6
Thrupp Glos 37 D5
　Oxon 38 C4
Thrushelton....9 E6
Thrussington 64 C3
Thruxton Hants ...25 E7
　Hereford 49 F6
Thrybergh 89 E5
Thulston 76 F4
Thundergay 143 D9
Thundersley 42 F3
Thundridge 41 C6
Thurcaston 64 C2
Thurcroft 89 F5
Thurgarton Norf ...81 D7
　Notts 77 E6
Thurgoland 88 D3
Thurlaston Leics ..64 E2
　Warks 52 B2
Thurlbear 11 B7
Thurlby Lincs 65 C8
　Lincs 78 C2
Thurleigh 53 D8
Thurlestone....6 E4
Thurloxton 22 F4
Thurlstone 88 D3
Thurlton 69 E7
Thurlwood 74 D5
Thurmaston 64 D3
Thurnby 64 D3
Thurne 69 C7
Thurnham Kent ...30 D2
　Lancs. 92 D4
Thurning N Nhants .65 F7
　Norf. 81 E6
Thurnscoe 89 D5
Thurnscoe East ...89 D5
Thursby 108 D3
Thursford 81 D5
Thursley 27 F7
Thurso 158 D3
Thurso East 158 D3
Thurstaston 85 F3
Thurston 56 C3
Thurstonfield ...108 D3
Thurstonland 88 C2
Thurton 69 D6
Thurvaston 76 F2
Thuxton 68 D3
Thwaite N Yorks ..100 E3
　Suff 56 C5
Thwaite Head 99 E5
Thwaites 94 E3
Thwaite St Mary .. 69 E6
Thwaites Brow 94 E3
Thwing 97 B6
Tibbermore 128 B2
Tibberton Glos ...36 B4
　Telford 61 B6
　Worcs 50 D4
Tibenham 68 F4
Tibshelf 76 C4
Tibthorpe 97 D5
Ticehurst 18 B3
Tichborne 26 F3

Tickencote....65 D6
Tickenham 23 B6
Tickhill 89 E6
Ticklerton 60 E4
Ticknall 63 B7
Tickton 97 E6
Tidcombe 25 D7
Tiddington Oxon .39 D6
　Warks 51 D7
Tidebrook 18 C3
Tideford....5 D8
Tideford Cross....5 C8
Tidenham 36 E2
Tideswell 75 B8
Tidmarsh 26 B4
Tidmington 51 F7
Tidpit 13 C8
Tidworth 25 E7
Tiers Cross 44 D4
Tiffield 52 D4
Tifty 153 D7
Tigerton 135 C5
Tigh-na-Blair 127 C6
Tighnabruaich ...145 F8
Tighnafiline 155 J13
Tigley....7 C5
Tilbrook 53 C8
Tilbury 29 B7
Tilbury Juxta Clare 55 E8
Tile Cross 63 F5
Tile Hill 51 B7
Tilehurst 26 B4
Tilford 27 E6
Tilgate 28 F3
Tilgate Forest Row 28 F3
Tillathrowie 152 E4
Tilley 60 B5
Tillicoultry 127 E8
Tillingham 43 D5
Tillington Hereford .49 E6
　W Sus 16 B3
Tillington
　Common 49 E6
Tillyarblet 135 C5
Tillybirloch 141 D5
Tillycorthie 141 B8
Tillydrine 140 E5
Tillyfour 140 C4
Tillyfourie 140 C5
Tillygarmond 140 E5
Tillygreig 141 B7
Tillykerrie 141 B7
Tilmanstone 31 D7
Tilney All Saints ..67 C5
Tilney High End ...67 C5
Tilney St
　Lawrence 66 C5
Tilshead 24 E5
Tilstock 74 F2
Tilston 73 D8
Tilstone Fearnall .74 C2
Tilsworth 40 B2
Tilton on the Hill .64 D4
Timberland 78 D4
Timbersbrook 75 C5
Timberscombe 21 E8
Timble 94 D4
Timperley 87 F5
Timsbury Bath ...23 D8
　Hants. 14 B4
Timsgearraidh ...154 D5
Timworth Green... 56 C2
Tincleton 13 E5
Tindale 109 D6
Tingewick 52 F4
Tingley 88 B3
Tingrith 53 F8
Tingwall 159 F4
Tinhay....9 F5
Tinshill 95 F5
Tinsley 88 E5
Tintagel....8 F2
Tintern Parva 36 D2
Tintinhull 12 C3
Tintwistle 87 E8
Tinwald 114 F3
Tinwell 65 D7
Tipperty 141 B8
Tipsend 66 E5
Tipton 62 E3
Tipton St John 11 E5
Tiptree 42 C4
Tirabad 47 E7
Tiraghoil 146 J6
Tirley 37 B5
Tirphil 35 D5
Tir-y-dail 33 C7
Tisbury 13 B7
Tisman's Common 27 F8
Tissington 75 D8
Titchberry....8 B4
Titchfield 15 D6
Titchmarsh 53 B8
Titchwell 80 C3
Tithby 77 F6
Titley 48 C5
Titlington 117 C7
Titsey 28 D5
Tittensor 75 F5
Tittleshall 80 E4
Tiverton Ches W ..74 C2
　Devon 10 C4
Tivetshall St
　Margaret 68 F4
Tivetshall St Mary .68 F4
Tividale 62 E3
Tivy Dale 88 D3
Tixall 62 B3
Tixover 65 D6
Toab Orkney 159 H6
　Shetland 160 M5
Toadmoor 76 D3
Tobermory 147 F8
Toberonochy 124 E3
Tobha Mor 148 E2
Tobhtarol 154 D6
Tobson 154 D6
Tocher 153 E6
Tockenham 37 F7
Tockenham Wick .37 F7
Tockholes 86 B4
Tockington 36 F3
Tockwith 95 D7
Todber 13 B6
Toddington C Beds .40 B3
　Glos. 50 F5
Todenham 51 F7

Todhills 108 C3
Todlachie 141 C5
Todmorden 87 B7
Todrig 115 C7
Todwick 89 F5
Toft Cambs 54 D4
　Lincs 65 C7
Toft Hill Durham ..101 B6
　Lincs 78 C5
Toft Monks 69 E7
Toft next Newton ..90 F4
Toftrees 80 E4
Tofts 158 D5
Toftwood 68 C2
Togston 117 D8
Tokavaig 149 G11
Tokers Green 26 B5
Tolastadh a
　Chaolais.... 154 D6
Tolastadh bho
　Thuath 155 C10
Tolland 22 F3
Tollard Royal 13 C7
Toll Bar 89 D6
Tollbar End 51 B8
Toll End 62 E3
Toller Fratrum 12 E3
Toller Porcorum ..12 E3
Tollerton Notts ...77 F6
　N Yorks 95 C8
Tollesbury 43 C5
Tolleshunt D'Arcy .43 C5
Tolleshunt Major .. 43 C5
Toll of Birness ...153 E10
Tolm 155 D9
Tolpuddle 13 E5
Tolvah 138 E4
Tolworth 28 C2
Tomatin 138 B4
Tombreck 151 H9
Tomchrasky 137 C5
Tomdoun 136 D4
Tomich Highld 137 B6
　Highld 151 D9
Tomich House ... 151 G8
Tomintoul Aberds .139 E7
　Moray 139 C7
Tomnaven 152 E4
Tomnavoulin 139 B8
Tonbridge 29 E6
Tondu 34 F2
Tonfanau 58 D2
Tong Shrops 61 D7
　W Yorks 94 F5
Tonge 63 B8
Tongham 27 E6
Tongland 106 D3
Tong Norton 61 D7
Tongue 157 D8
Tongue End 65 C8
Tongwynlais 35 F5
Tonna 34 E1
Ton-Pentre 34 E3
Tonwell 41 C6
Tonypandy 34 E3
Tonyrefail 34 F4
Toot Baldon 39 D5
Toothill 14 C4
Toot Hill 41 D8
Topcliffe 95 B7
Topcroft 69 E5
Topcroft Street ...69 E5
Top of Hebers 87 D6
Toppesfield 55 F8
Toppings 86 C5
Topsham 10 F4
Torbeg 143 F10
Torboll Farm 151 B10
Torbrex 127 E6
Torbryan....7 C6
Torcross....7 E6
Tore 151 F9
Torinturk 145 G7
Torksey 77 B8
Torlum 148 C2
Torlundy 131 B5
Tormarton 24 B2
Tormisdale 142 C2
Tormitchell 112 E2
Tormore 143 E9
Tornagrain 151 G10
Tornahaish 139 D8
Tornaveen 140 D5
Torness 137 B8
Toronto 110 F4
Torpenhow 108 F2
Torphichen 120 B2
Torphins 140 D5
Torpoint....6 D2
Torquay....7 C7
Torquhan 121 E7
Torran Argyll 124 E4
　Highld 149 D10
　Highld 151 D10
Torrance 119 B6
Torrans 146 J7
Torranyard 118 E3
Torre....7 C7
Torridon 150 F2
Torridon House .149 C13
Torrin 149 F10
Torrisdale-
　Square 143 E8
Torrish 157 H12
Torrisholme 92 C4
Torroble 157 J8
Torry Aberdeen ...141 D8
　Aberds. 152 E4
Torryburn 128 F2
Torterston 153 D10
Torthorwald 107 B7
Tortington 16 D4
Tortworth 36 E4
Torver 99 E4
Torwood 127 F7
Torworth 89 F7
Tosberry....8 B4

Totland 14 F4
Totnes....7 C6
Toton 76 F5
Totronald 146 F4
Totscore 149 B8
Tottenham 41 E6
Tottenhill 67 C6
Tottenhill Row 67 C6
Totteridge 41 E5
Totternhoe 40 B2
Tottington 87 C5
Totton 14 C4
Touchen End 27 B6
Tournaig 155 J13
Toux 153 C9
Tovil 29 D8
Toward 145 G10
Towcester 52 E4
Towednack....2 C3
Tower End 67 C6
Towersey 39 D7
Towie Aberds 140 C3
　Aberds. 153 B8
Towiemore 152 D3
Tow Law 110 F4
Townend 118 B4
Town End Cambs ..66 F4
　Cumb. 99 F6
Towngate 65 C8
Townhead Cumb ..108 F5
　Dumfries 106 E3
　S Ayrs. 112 D1
　S Yorks. 88 D2
Townhead of
　Greenlaw 106 C4
Townhill 128 F3
Town Row 18 B2
Townsend Bucks ..39 D7
　Herts. 40 D4
Townshend....2 C4
Town Yetholm ...116 B4
Towthorpe 96 D2
Towton 95 F7
Towyn 72 B3
Toxteth 85 F4
Toynton All Saints .79 C6
Toynton Fen Side .79 C6
Toynton St Peter ..79 C7
Toy's Hill 29 D5
Trabboch 112 B4
Traboe....3 D6
Tradespark
　Highld 151 F11
　Orkney 159 H5
Trafford Park 87 E5
Trallong 34 B3
Tranent 121 B7
Tranmere 85 F4
Trantlebeg 157 D11
Trantlemore 157 D11
Tranwell 117 F7
Trapp 33 C7
Traprain 121 B8
Traquair 121 F6
Trawden 94 F2
Trawsfynydd 71 D8
Trealaw 34 E4
Treales 92 F4
Trearddur 82 D2
Treaslane 149 C8
Trebanog 34 E4
Trebanos 33 D8
Trebartha....5 B7
Trebarwith....8 F2
Trebetherick....4 B4
Treborough 22 F2
Trebudannon....4 C3
Trebullett....5 B8
Treburley....5 B8
Trebyan....5 C5
Trecastle 34 B2
Trecenydd 35 F5
Trecwn 44 B4
Tredavoe....2 D3
Treddiog 44 C3
Tredegar 35 D5
Tredegar = Newydd
　New Tredegar ...35 D5
Tredington Glos ...37 B6
　Warks 51 E7
Tredinnick....4 B4
Tredomen 48 F3
Tredunnock 35 E7
Tredustan 48 F3
Treen....2 D2
Treeton 88 F5
Trefaldwyn
　= Montgomery...60 E2
Trefasser 44 B3
Trefdraeth 82 D4
Trefdraeth
　= Newport 45 F2
Trefecca 48 F3
Trefechan 58 F2
Trefeglwys 59 E6
Trefenter 46 C5
Treffgarne 44 C4
Treffynnon
　= Holywell 73 B5
Trefgarn Owen 44 C3
Trefi 44 B3
Trefil 35 C5
Trefilan 46 D4
Treflach 60 B2
Trefnanney 60 C2
Trefnant 72 B4
Trefonen 60 B2
Trefor Anglesey ...82 C3
　Gwyn. 70 C4
Treforest 34 F4
Trefriw 83 E7
Tref-y-Clawdd
　= Knighton 48 B4
Trefynwy
　= Monmouth 36 C2
Tregadillett....8 F4
Tregaian 82 D4
Tregare 35 C8
Tregaron 47 D5
Tregarth 83 E6
Tregeare....8 F4
Tregeiriog 73 F5
Tregele 82 B3
Tre-Gibbon 34 D3
Tregidden....3 D6
Treglemais 44 C3
Tregole....8 E3

Tregonetha....4 C4
Tregony....3 B8
Tregoss 4 C4
Tregoyd 48 F4
Tregroes 46 E3
Tregurrian....4 C3
Tregynon 59 E7
Trehafod 34 E4
Treharris 34 E4
Treherbert 34 E3
Trekenner....5 B8
Treknow....8 F2
Trelan....3 E6
Trelash....8 E3
Trelassick....4 D3
Trelawnyd 72 B4
Trelech 45 F4
Treleddyd-fawr ...44 C2
Trelewis 35 E5
Treligga....8 F2
Trelights....4 B4
Trelill....4 B5
Trelissick....3 C7
Trellech 36 D2
Trelleck Grange ..36 D1
Trelogan 85 F2
Trelystan 60 D2
Tremadog 71 C6
Tremail....8 F3
Tremain 45 E4
Tremaine....8 F4
Tremar....5 C7
Trematon....5 D8
Tremeirchion 72 B4
Trenance....4 C3
Trenarren....3 B9
Trench 61 C6
Treneglos....8 F4
Trenewan....5 D7
Trent 12 C3
Trentham 75 E5
Trentishoe 20 E5
Trent Vale 75 E5
Treoes 21 B8
Treorchy = Treorci.34 E3
　Treorci = Treorchy.34 E3
Tre'r-ddôl 58 E3
Trerulefoot....5 D8
Tresaith 45 E4
Tresawle....3 B7
Trescott 62 E2
Trescowe....2 C4
Tresham 36 E4
Tresillian....3 B7
Tresinwen 44 A4
Treskinnick Cross..8 E4
Tresmeer....8 F4
Tresparrett....8 E3
Tresparrett Posts...8 E3
Tressait 133 C5
Tresta Shetland ...160 D8
　Shetland 160 H5
Treswell 77 B7
Tretio....44 C2
Tretire 36 B2
Tretower 35 B5
Treuddyn 73 D6
Trevalga....8 F2
Trevalyn 73 D7
Trevanson....4 B4
Trevarren....4 C4
Trevarrick....3 B8
Trevaughan 32 C2
Tre-vaughan 32 B4
Treveighan....5 B5
Trevellas....4 D2
Treverva....3 C6
Trevethin 35 D6
Trevigro....5 C8
Trevone....4 B3
Trewarmett....8 F2
Trewassa....8 F3
Trewellard....2 C2
Trewen....8 F4
Trewennack....3 D5
Trewern 60 C2
Trewethern....4 B5
Trewidland....5 D7
Trewint Corn....8 E4
　Corn.....8 C7
Trewithian....3 C7
Trewoofe....2 D3
Trewoon....3 D8
Treworga....3 B7
Treworlas....3 C7
Tre-wyn 35 B7
Treyarnon 16 C2
Treyford 16 C2
Trezaise....4 D4
Triangle 87 B8
Trickett's Cross ...13 D8
Triffleton 44 C4
Trimdon 111 F6
Trimdon Colliery ..111 F6
Trimdon Grange .. 111 F6
Trimingham 81 D8
Trimley Lower
　Street 57 F6
Trimley St Martin .57 F6
Trimley St Mary ...57 F6
Trimpley 50 B3
Trimsaran 33 D5
Trimstone 20 E3
Trinafour 132 C4
Trinant 35 D6
Tring 40 C2
Tring Wharf 40 C2
Trinity Angus 135 C6
　Jersey 17 I3
Trisaig 147 B9
Trislaig 130 B4
Trispen....4 D3
Tritlington 117 E8
Trochry 133 E6
Trodigal 143 F7
Troed-rhiwdalar .47 D8
Troedyraur 46 E2
Troedyrhiw 34 D4
Tromode 84 E3
Trondavoe 160 F5
Troon Corn.....3 C5
　S Ayrs. 118 F3
Trosaraidh 148 G2
Trossachs Hotel ..126 D4

Troston 56 B2
Trottiscliffe 29 C7
Trotton 16 B2
Troutbeck Cumb ..99 B5
　Cumb. 99 D6
Troutbeck Bridge ..99 D6
Trow Green 36 D2
Trowbridge 24 D3
Trowell 76 F4
Trowle Common ..24 D3
Trowley Bottom ...40 C3
Trows 122 F2
Trowse Newton ...68 D5
Trudoxhill 24 E2
Trull 11 B7
Trumaisgearraidh
　....148 A3
Trumpan 148 B7
Trumpet 49 F8
Trumpington 54 D5
Trunch 81 D8
Trunnah 92 E3
Truro 3 B7
Trusham 10 F3
Trusley 76 F2
Trusthorpe 91 F9
Trysull 62 E2
Tubney 38 E4
Tuckenhay....7 D6
Tuckhill 61 F7
Tuckingmill....3 B5
Tuddenham 55 B8
Tuddenham St
　Martin 57 E5
Tudeley 29 E7
Tudhoe 111 F5
Tudorville 36 B2
Tudweiliog 70 D3
Tuesley 27 E7
Tuffley 37 C5
Tufton Hants 26 E2
　Pembs. 32 B1
Tugby 64 D4
Tugford 61 F5
Tullibardine 127 C8
Tullibody 127 E7
Tullich Argyll 125 D6
　Highld 138 B2
Tullich Muir 151 D10
Tulliemet 133 D6
Tulloch Aberds ...135 B7
　Aberds. 153 E8
　Perth 128 B2
Tulloch Castle 151 E8
Tullochgorm 125 F5
Tulloes 135 E5
Tullybannocher ..127 B6
Tullybelton 133 F7
Tullyfergus 134 E2
Tullymurdoch 134 D1
Tullynessle 140 C4
Tumble 33 C6
Tumby Woodside ..79 D5
Tummel Bridge ...132 D4
Tunga 155 D9
Tunstall E Yorks ...97 F9
　Kent 30 C2
　Lancs. 93 B6
　Norf. 69 D7
　N Yorks 101 E7
　Stoke 75 D5
　Suff 57 D7
　T&W 111 D6
Tunstead Derbys ..75 B8
　Gtr Man 87 D8
　Norf. 81 E8
Tunworth 26 E4
Tupsley 49 E7
Tupton 76 C3
Turgis Green 26 D4
Turin 135 D5
Turkdean 37 C8
Tur Langton 64 E4
Turleigh 24 C3
Turn 87 C6
Turnastone 49 F5
Turnberry 112 D2
Turnditch 76 E2
Turners Hill 28 F4
Turners Puddle ...13 E6
Turnford 41 D6
Turnhouse 120 B4
Turnworth 13 D6
Turriff 153 C7
Turton Bottoms ...86 C5
Turves 66 E3
Turvey 53 D7
Turville 39 E7
Turville Heath 39 E7
Turweston 52 F4
Tushielaw 115 C6
Tutbury 63 B6
Tutnall 50 B4
Tutshill 36 E2
Tuttington 81 E8
Tutts Clump 26 B3
Tuxford 77 B7
Twatt Orkney 159 F3
　Shetland 160 H5
Twechar 119 B7
Tweedmouth 123 D5
Tweedsmuir 114 B3
Twelve Heads....3 B6
Twelwe Green 74 C4
Twenty 65 B8
Twerton 24 C2
Twickenham 28 B2
Twigworth 37 B5
Twineham 17 C6
Twinhoe 24 D2
Twinstead 56 F2
Twinstead Green ..56 F2
Twiss Green 86 E4
Twiston 93 E8
Twitchen Devon ...21 F6
　Shrops. 49 B5
Two Bridges....6 B4
Two Dales 76 C2
Two Mills 73 B7
Twycross 63 D7
Twyford Bucks ...39 B6
　Derbys. 63 B7
　Hants. 15 B5
　Leics. 64 C4
　Lincs 65 B6
　Norf. 81 E6
　Wokingham 27 B5
Twyford Common .49 F7
Twyn-y-Sheriff ...35 D8
Twynholm 106 D3

Twyning 50 F3
Twyning Green 50 F4
Twynllanan 34 B1
Twynmynydd 33 C7
Twywell 53 B7
Tyberton 49 F5
Tyburn 62 E5
Tycroes 33 C7
Tycrwyn 59 C8
Tyddewi
　= St David's 44 C2
Tydd Gote 66 C4
Tydd St Giles 66 C4
Tydd St Mary 66 C4
Tyddyn-mawr 71 C6
Ty-draw 83 F8
Tye Green Essex ..41 C7
　Essex 42 B3
　Essex 55 F6
Ty-hen Carms 32 B4
　Gwyn. 70 D2
Tyldesley 86 D4
Tyler Hill 30 C5
Tylers Green 40 E2
Tylorstown 34 E4
Tylwch 59 F6
Ty-mawr 82 C4
Ty Mawr 46 E4
Ty Mawr Cwm 72 E3
Ty-nant Conwy ...72 E3
　Gwyn. 59 B6
Tyncelyn 46 C5
Tyndrum 131 F7
Tyneham 13 F6
Tynehead 121 D6
Tynemouth 111 C6
Tyne Tunnel 111 C6
Tynewydd 34 E3
Tyninghame 122 B2
Tynron 113 E8
Tyn-y-celyn 73 F5
Tyn-y-coed 60 B2
Tyn-y-fedwen 72 F5
Tyn-y-ffridd 72 F5
Tynygongl 82 C5
Tynygraig 47 C5
Tyn-y-graig 48 D2
Ty'n-y-maes 83 E6
Tyn-y-pwll 82 C4
Tyn-yr-eithin 47 C5
Tyrie 153 B9
Tyringham 53 E6
Tythecott....9 C6
Tythegston 21 B7
Tytherington
　Ches E 75 B6
　S Glos. 36 F3
　Som. 24 E2
　Wilts 24 E4
Tytherleigh 11 D8
Ty-uchaf 59 B7
Tywardreath....5 D5
Tywyn Conwy 83 D7

U

Uachdar 148 C2
Uags 149 E12
Ubbeston Green ..57 B7
Ubley 23 D7
Uckerby 101 D7
Uckfield 17 B8
Uckington 37 B6
Uddingston 119 C6
Uddington 119 F8
Udimore 19 D5
Udny Green 141 B7
Udny Station 141 B8
Udston 119 D6
Udstonhead 119 E7
Uffcott 25 B6
Uffculme 11 C5
Uffington Lincs ...65 D7
　Oxon 38 F3
　Shrops. 60 C5
Ufford Pboro 65 D7
　Suff 57 D6
Ufton 51 C8
Ufton Nervet 26 C4
Ugadale 143 F8
Ugborough....6 D4
Uggeshall 69 F7
Ugglebarnby 103 D6
Ughill 88 E3
Ugley 41 B8
Ugley Green 41 B8
Ugthorpe 103 C5
Uidh 148 J1
Uig Argyll 145 E10
　Highld 148 C6
　Highld 149 B8
Uigen 154 D5
Uigshader 149 D9
Uisken 146 K6
Ulbster 158 F5
Ulceby Lincs 79 B7
　N Lincs. 90 C5
Ulceby Skitter 90 C5
Ulcombe 30 E2
Uldale 108 F2
Uley 36 D4
Ulgham 117 E8
Ullapool 150 B4
Ullenhall 51 C6
Ullenwood 37 C6
Ulleskelf 95 E8
Ullesthorpe 64 F2
Ulley 89 F5
Ullingswick 49 E7
Ullinish 149 E8
Ullock 98 B2
Ulnes Walton 86 C3
Ulpha 98 E3
Ulrome 97 D7
Ulsta 160 E6
Ulva House 146 H7
Ulverston 92 B2
Ulwell 13 F8
Umberleigh 9 B8
Unapool 156 F5
Unasary 148 F2
Underbarrow 99 E6
Undercliffe 94 F4
Underhoull 160 C7

Underriver 29 D6
Underwood 76 D4
Undy 35 F8
Unifirth 160 H4
Union Cottage ...141 E7
Union Mills 84 E3
Union Street 18 B4
Unstone 76 B3
Unstone Green 76 B3
Unthank Cumb ...108 F4
　Cumb. 109 E6
Unthank End 108 F4
Upavon 25 D6
Up Cerne 12 D4
Upchurch 30 C2
Upcott 48 D5
Upend 55 D7
Up Exe 10 D4
Upgate 68 C4
Uphall 120 B3
Uphall Station ...120 B3
Upham Devon 10 D3
　Hants. 15 B6
Uphampton 50 C3
Up Hatherley 37 B6
Uphill 22 D5
Up Holland 86 D3
Uplawmoor 118 D4
Upleadon 36 B4
Upleatham 102 C4
Uplees 30 C3
Uploders 12 E3
Uplowman 10 C5
Uplyme 11 E8
Up Marden 15 C8
Up Nately 26 D4
Upnor 29 B8
Upottery 11 D7
Upper
　Affcot 60 F4
Upper
　Ardchronie 151 C9
Upper Arley 61 F7
Upper Arncott 39 C6
Upper Astrop 52 F3
Upper Badcall ...156 E4
Upper Basildon ...26 B3
Upper Beeding ...17 C5
Upper Benefield ..65 F6
Upper Bighouse .157 D11
Upper Boddington 52 D2
Upper Borth 58 F3
Upper Boyndlie ..153 B9
Upper Brailes 51 F8
Upper Breakish .149 F11
Upper Breinton ...49 E6
Upper Broadheath .50 D3
Upper Broughton ..64 B3
Upper Bucklebury 26 C3
Upper
　Burnhaugh 141 E7
Upperby 108 D4
Upper Caldecote ..54 E2
Upper Catesby ...52 D3
Upper Chapel 48 E2
Upper Church
　Village 34 F4
Upper Chute 25 D7
Upper Clatford ...25 E8
Upper Clynnog ...71 C5
Upper
　Cumberworth....88 D3
Upper Cwmbran ..35 E6
Upper Dallachy ..152 B3
Upper Dean 53 C8
Upper Denby 88 D3
Upper Denton 109 C6
Upper Derraid ...151 H13
Upper Dicker 18 E2
Upper Dovercourt .57 F6
Upper Druimfin ...147 F8
Upper Dunsforth .95 C7
Upper Eathie 151 E10
Upper Elkstone ...75 D7
Upper End 75 B7
Upper Farringdon .26 F5
Upper Framilode ..36 C4
Upper Glenfintaig 137 F5
Upper Gornal 62 E3
Upper Gravenhurst 54 F2
Upper Green Mon .35 C7
　W Berks. 25 C8
Upper Grove
　Common 36 B2
Upper Hackney ...76 C2
Upper Hale 27 E6
Upper Halistra ...148 C7
Upper Halling 29 C7
Upper Hambleton .65 D6
Upper Hardres
　Court 31 D5
Upper Hartfield ...29 F5
Upper Haugh 88 E5
Upper Heath 61 F5
Upper Hellesdon ..68 C5
Upper Helmsley ..96 D2
Upper Hergest 48 D4
Upper Heyford
　Oxon 38 B4
　W Nhants. 52 D4
Upper Hill 49 D6
Upper Hopton 88 C2
Upper
　Horsebridge 18 D2
Upper Hulme 75 C7
Upper Inglesham .38 E2
Upper
　Inverbrough ...151 H11
Upper Killay 33 E6
Upper
　Knockando 152 D1
Upper Lambourn .25 B8
Upper Leigh 75 F7
Upper Lenie 137 B8
Upper Lochton ...141 E5
Upper Longdon ...62 C4
Upper Lybster ...158 G4
Upper Maes-coed .48 F5
Upper Midway 63 B6
Upper Milovaig ..148 D6
Upper Minety 37 E7
Upper Mitton 50 B3
Upper North Dean 39 E8
Upper Obney 133 F7
Upper Ollach ...149 E10
Upper Padley 76 B2
Upper Pollicott ...39 C7

Upper Poppleton . . 95 D8
Upper Quinton . . . 51 E6
Upper Ratley 14 B4
Upper Rissington . . 38 C2
Upper Rochford . . . 49 C8
Upper Sandaig . . 149 G12
Upper Sanday . . . 159 H6
Upper Sapey 49 C8
Upper Saxondale . . 77 F6
Upper Seagry 37 F6
Upper Shelton . . . 53 E7
Upper
  Sheringham . . . 81 C7
Upper Skelmorlie 118 C2
Upper Slaughter . . 38 B1
Upper Soudley . . . 36 C3
Uppersound 160 J6
Upper Stondon . . . 54 F2
Upper Stowe 52 D4
Upper Stratton . . . 38 F1
Upper Street Hants. 14 C2
  Norf 69 C6
  Norf 69 C6
  Suff 56 F5
Upper Strensham . . 50 F4
Upper Sundon . . . 40 B3
Upper Swell 38 B1
Upper Tean 75 F7
Upperthong 88 D2
Upperthorpe 89 D8
Upper Tillyrie . . . 128 D3
Upperton 16 B3
Upper Tooting . . . 28 B3
Upper Tote 149 C10
Uppertown Derbys . 76 C3
  Highld 158 C5
  Orkney 159 J5
Upper Town 23 C7
Upper Treverward . 48 B4
Upper Tysoe 51 E8
Upper Upham 25 B7
Upper Wardington 52 E2
Upper Weald 53 F5
Upper Weedon . . . 52 D4
Upper Wield 26 F4
Upper
  Winchendon . . . 39 C7
Upper Witton 62 E4
Upper Woodend . 141 C5
Upper Woodford . . 25 F6
Upper Wootton . . . 26 D3
Upper Wyche 50 E2
Uppingham 65 E5
Uppington 61 D6
Upsall 102 F2
Upshire 41 D7
Up Somborne 25 F8
Upstreet 31 C6
Up Sydling 12 D4
Upthorpe 56 B3
Upton Bucks 54 B2
  Ches W 73 C8
  Corn 8 D4
  Dorset 12 F5
  Dorset 13 E7
  Hants 14 C4
  Hants 25 D8
  Leics 63 E7
  Lincs 90 F2
  Mers 85 F3
  Norf 69 C6
  Notts 77 B7
  Notts 77 D7
  Oxon 39 F5
  Pboro 65 D8
  Slough 27 B7
  Som 10 B4
  W Nhants 52 C5
  W Yorks 89 C5
Upton Bishop 36 B3
Upton Cheyney . . . 23 C8
Upton Cressett . . . 61 E6
Upton Cross 5 B7
Upton Grey 26 E4
Upton Hellions . . . 10 D3
Upton Lovell 24 E4
Upton Magna 61 C5
Upton Noble 24 F2
Upton Pyne 10 E4
Upton St
  Leonard's 37 C5
Upton Scudamore 24 E3
Upton Snodsbury . 50 D4
Upton upon
  Severn 50 E3
Upton Warren . . . 50 C4
Upwaltham 16 C3
Upware 55 B6
Upwell 66 D4
Upwey 12 F4
Upwood 66 F2
Uradale 160 K6
Urafirth 160 F5
Urchfont 24 D5
Urdimarsh 49 E7
Ure 160 F4
Ure Bank 95 B6
Urgha 154 H6
Urishay Common . . 48 F5
Urlay Nook 102 C1
Urmston 87 E5
Urpeth 110 D5
Urquhart Highld . 151 F8
  Moray 152 B2
Urra 102 D3
Urray 151 F8
Ushaw Moor 110 E5
Usk = Brynbuga . . 35 D7
Usselby 90 E4
Usworth 111 D6
Utkinton 74 C2
Utley 94 E3
Uton 10 E3
Utterby 91 E7
Uttoxeter 75 F7
Uwchmynydd 70 E2
Uxbridge 40 F3
Uyeasound 160 C7
Uzmaston 44 D4

V
Valley 82 D2
Valleyfield 106 D3
Valley Truckle 8 C2
Valsgarth 160 B8
Valtos 149 B10
Van 59 F6

Vange 42 F3
Varteg 35 D6
Vatten 149 D7
Vaul 146 G3
Vaynor 34 C4
Veensgarth 160 J6
Velindre 48 F3
Vellow 22 F2
Veness 159 F6
Venn Green 9 C5
Vennington 60 D3
Venn Ottery 11 E5
Venny Tedburn . . . 10 E3
Ventnor 15 G6
Vernham Dean . . . 25 D8
Vernham Street . . . 25 D8
Vernolds Common . 60 F4
Verwood 13 D8
Veryan 3 C8
Vicarage 11 F6
Vickerstown 92 C1
Victoria Corn. 4 D4
  S Yorks 88 D2
Vidlin 160 G6
Viewpark 119 C7
Vigo Village 29 C7
Vinehall Street . . . 18 C4
Vine's Cross 18 D2
Viney Hill 36 D3
Virginia Water . . . 27 C8
Virginstow 9 E5
Vobster 24 E2
Voe Shetland . . . 160 E5
  Shetland 160 G6
Vowchurch 49 F5
Voxter 160 F5
Voy 159 G3

W
Wackerfield 101 B6
Wacton 68 E4
Wadbister 160 J6
Wadborough 50 E4
Waddesdon 39 C7
Waddingham 90 E3
Waddington Lancs 93 E7
  Lincs 78 C2
Wadebridge 4 B4
Wadeford 11 C8
Wadenhoe 65 F7
Wadesmill 41 C6
Wadhurst 18 B3
Wadshelf 76 B3
Wadsley 88 E4
Wadsley Bridge . . 88 E4
Wadworth 89 E6
Waen Denb 72 C3
  Denb 72 C5
Waen Fach 60 C2
Waen Goleugoed . . 72 B4
Wag 157 G13
Wainfleet All
  Saints 79 D7
Wainfleet Bank . . 79 D7
Wainfleet St Mary . 79 D8
Wainfleet Tofts . . 79 D7
Wainhouse Corner . . 8 E3
Wainscott 29 B8
Wainstalls 87 B8
Waitby 100 D2
Waithe 91 D6
Wakefield 88 B4
Wake Lady Green . 102 E4
Wakerley 65 E6
Wakes Colne 42 B4
Walberswick 57 B8
Walberton 16 D3
Walbottle 110 C4
Walcot Lincs 78 F3
  N Lincs 90 B2
  Shrops 60 F3
  Swindon 38 F1
  Telford 61 C5
Walcote Leics . . . 64 F2
  Warks 51 D6
Walcott Lincs . . . 78 D4
  Norf 69 A6
Walden 101 F5
Walden Head . . . 100 F4
Walden Stubbs . . . 89 C6
Waldersey 66 D4
Walderslade 29 C8
Walderton 15 C8
Walditch 12 E2
Waldley 75 F8
Waldridge 111 D5
Waldringfield 57 E6
Waldringfield
  Heath 57 E6
Waldron 18 D2
Wales 89 F5
Walesby Lincs . . . 90 E5
  Notts 77 B6
Walford Hereford . 36 B2
  Hereford 49 B5
  Shrops 60 B4
Walford Heath . . . 60 C4
Walgherton 74 E3
Walgrave 53 B6
Walhampton 14 E4
Walkden 86 D5
Walker 111 C5
Walker Barn 75 B6
Walkerburn 121 F6
Walker Fold 93 E6
Walkeringham . . . 89 E8
Walkerith 89 E8
Walkern 41 B5
Walker's Green . . 49 E7
Walkerville 101 E7
Walkford 14 E3
Walkhampton 6 C3
Walkington 97 F5
Walkley 88 F4
Walk Mill 93 F8
Wall Northumb . . 110 C2
  Staffs 62 D5
Wallaceton 113 F8
Wallacetown
  S Ayrs 112 B3
  S Ayrs 112 D2
Wallands Park . . . 17 C8
Wallasey 85 E4
Wall Bank 60 E5
Wallcrouch 18 B3
Wall Heath 62 F2

Wallingford 39 F6
Wallington Hants . 15 D6
  Herts 54 F3
  London 28 C3
Wallis 32 B1
Walliswood 28 F2
Walls 160 J4
Wallsend 111 C5
Wallston 22 B3
Wall under
  Heywood 60 E5
Wallyford 121 B6
Walmer 31 D7
Walmer Bridge . . . 86 B2
Walmersley 87 C6
Walmley 62 E5
Walpole 57 B7
Walpole Cross
  Keys 66 C5
Walpole Highway . 66 C5
Walpole Marsh . . . 66 C4
Walpole
  St Andrew 66 C5
Walpole
  St Peter 66 C5
Walsall 62 E4
Walsall Wood 62 D4
Walsden 87 B7
Walsgrave on
  Sowe 63 F7
Walsham le
  Willows 56 B3
Walshaw 87 C5
Walshford 95 D7
Walsoken 66 C4
Walston 120 E3
Walsworth 54 F3
Walters Ash 39 E8
Walterston 22 B2
Walterstone 35 B7
Waltham Kent . . . 30 E5
  NE Lincs 91 D6
Waltham Abbey . . 41 D6
Waltham Chase . . 15 C6
Waltham Cross . . 41 D6
Waltham on the
  Wolds 64 B5
Waltham St
  Lawrence 27 B6
Walthamstow . . . 41 F6
Walton Cumb. . . 108 C5
  Derbys 76 C3
  Leics 64 F2
  Mers 85 E4
  M Keynes 53 F6
  Pboro 65 D8
  Powys 48 D4
  Som 23 F6
  Staffs 75 F5
  Suff 57 F6
  Telford 61 C5
  Warks 51 D7
  W Yorks 88 C4
  W Yorks 95 E7
Walton Cardiff . . . 50 F4
Walton East 32 B1
Walton-in-
  Gordano 23 B6
Walton-le-Dale . . 86 B3
Walton-on-
  Thames 28 C2
Walton on the Hill
  Staffs 62 B3
  Sur 28 D3
Walton-on-the-
  Naze 43 B8
Walton on the
  Wolds 64 C2
Walton-on-Trent . . 63 C6
Walton West 44 D3
Walwen 73 B6
Walwick 110 B2
Walworth 101 C7
Walworth Gate . . 101 B7
Walwyn's Castle . . 44 D3
Wambrook 11 D7
Wanborough Sur . . 27 E7
  Swindon 38 F2
Wandsworth 28 B3
Wangford 57 B8
Wanlockhead . . . 113 C8
Wansford E Yorks . 97 D6
  Pboro 65 E7
Wanstead 41 F7
Wanstrow 24 E2
Wanswell 36 D3
Wantage 38 F4
Wapley 24 B2
Wappenbury 51 C8
Wappenham 52 E4
Warbleton 18 D3
Warblington 15 D8
Warborough 39 E5
Warboys 66 F3
Warbreck 92 F3
Warbstow 8 E4
Warburton 86 F5
Warcop 100 C2
Warden Kent 30 B4
  Northumb 110 C2
Ward End 62 F5
Ward Green 56 C4
Wardhill 159 F7
Wardington 52 E2
Wardlaw 115 C5
Wardle Ches E . . . 74 D3
  Gtr Man 87 C7
Wardley 64 D5
Wardlow 75 B8
Wardy Hill 66 F4
Ware Herts 41 C6
  Kent 31 C6
Wareham 13 F7
Warehorne 19 B6
Warenford 117 B7
Waren Mill 123 F7
Warenton 123 F7
Wareside 41 C6
Waresley Cambs . . 54 D3
  Worcs 50 B3
Warfield 27 B6
Warfleet 7 D6
Wargrave 27 B5
Warham 80 C5

Warkworth
  Northumb 117 D8
  W Nhants 52 E2
Warlaby 101 E8
Warland 87 B7
Warleggan 5 C6
Warlingham 28 D4
Warmfield 88 B4
Warmingham 74 C4
Warmington
  N Nhants 65 E7
  Warks 52 E2
Warminster 24 E3
Warmlake 30 D2
Warmley 23 B8
Warmley Tower . . 23 B8
Warmonds Hill . . . 53 C7
Warmsworth 89 D6
Warmwell 13 F5
Warndon 50 D3
Warnford 15 B7
Warnham 28 F2
Warninglid 17 B6
Warren Ches E . . . 75 B5
  Pembs 44 F4
Warren Heath . . . 57 E6
Warren Row 39 F8
Warren Street . . . 30 D3
Warrington
  M Keynes 53 D6
  Warr 86 F4
Warsash 15 D5
Warslow 75 D7
Warter 96 D4
Warthermarske . . 94 B5
Warthill 96 D2
Wartling 18 E3
Wartnaby 64 B4
Warton Lancs 86 B2
  Lancs 92 B4
  Northumb 117 D6
  Warks 63 D6
Warwick 51 C7
Warwick Bridge . . 108 D4
Warwick on Eden . 108 D4
Wasbister 159 E4
Wasdale Head . . . 98 D3
Washaway 4 C5
Washbourne 7 D5
Wash Common . . . 26 C2
Washfield 10 C4
Washfold 101 D5
Washford 22 E2
Washford Pyne . . . 10 C3
Washingborough . . 78 B3
Washington T&W . 111 D6
  W Sus 16 C5
Wasing 26 C3
Waskerley 110 E3
Wasperton 51 D7
Wasps Nest 78 C3
Wass 95 B8
Watchet 22 E2
Watchfield Oxon . . 38 E2
  Som 22 E5
Watchgate 99 E7
Watchhill 107 E8
Watcombe 7 C7
Watendlath 98 C4
Water Devon 10 F2
  Lancs 87 B6
Waterbeach 55 C5
Waterbeck 108 B2
Waterden 80 D4
Water End E Yorks . 96 F3
  Herts 40 C3
  Herts 41 D5
Waterfall 75 D7
Waterfoot E Renf . 63 C6
  Lancs 87 B6
Waterford Hants . . 14 E4
  Herts 41 C6
Waterhead 99 D5
Waterheads 120 D5
Waterhouses
  Durham 110 E4
  Staffs 75 D7
Wateringbury 29 D7
Waterloo BCP . . . 13 E8
  Gtr Man 87 D7
  Highld 149 F11
  Mers 85 E4
  N Lanark 119 D8
  Norf 68 C5
  Perth 133 F7
Waterloo Port . . . 82 E4
Waterlooville 15 D7
Watermeetings . . 114 C2
Watermillock 99 B6
Water Newton . . . 65 E8
Water Orton 63 E5
Waterperry 39 D6
Waterrow 11 B5
Watersfield 16 C4
Waterside Aberds . 141 B9
  Blackburn 86 B5
  Cumb 108 E2
  E Ayrs 112 D4
  E Ayrs 118 E4
  E Dunb 119 B6
  E Renf 118 D5
Water's Nook 86 D4
Waterstock 39 D6
Waterston 44 E4
Water Stratford . . 52 F4
Waters Upton . . . 61 C6
Water Yeat 98 F4
Watford Herts . . . 40 E4
  W Nhants 52 C4
Watford Gap 62 D5
Wath N Yorks . . . 94 C4
  N Yorks 95 B6
  N Yorks 96 B3
Wath Brow 98 C2
Wath upon
  Dearne 88 D5
Watlington Norf . . 67 C6
  Oxon 39 E6
Watnall 76 E5
Watten 158 E4
Wattisfield 56 B4
Wattisham 56 D4
Wattlesborough
  Heath 60 C3
Watton E Yorks . . 97 D6
  Norf 68 D2
Watton at Stone . . 41 C6

Wattston 119 B7
Wattstown 34 E4
Wauchan 136 F2
Waulkmill Lodge . 159 H4
Waun 59 D5
Waunarlwydd . . . 33 E7
Waunclunda 47 F5
Waunfawr 82 F5
Waungron 33 D6
Waunlwyd 35 D5
Waun-y-clyn 33 D5
Wavendon 53 F7
Waverbridge 108 E2
Waverton Ches W . 73 C8
  Cumb 108 E2
Wavertree 85 F4
Wawne 97 F6
Waxham 69 B7
Waxholme 91 B7
Way 31 C7
Wayfield 29 C8
Wayford 12 D2
Waymills 74 E2
Wayne Green 35 C8
Way Village 10 C3
Wdig = Goodwick . 44 B4
Weachyburn 153 C6
Weald 38 D3
Wealdstone 40 F4
Weardley 95 E5
Weare 23 D6
Weare Giffard 9 B6
Wearhead 109 F8
Weasdale 100 D1
Weasenham All
  Saints 80 E4
Weasenham St
  Peter 80 E4
Weatherhill 28 E4
Weaverham 74 B3
Weaverthorpe . . . 97 B5
Webheath 50 C5
Wedderlairs 153 E8
Wedderlie 122 D2
Weddington 63 E7
Wedhampton 25 D5
Wedmore 23 E6
Wednesbury 62 E3
Wednesfield 62 D3
Weedon 39 C8
Weedon Bec 52 D4
Weedon Lois 52 E4
Weeford 62 D5
Week 10 C2
Weeke 26 F2
Weekley 65 F5
Week St Mary 8 E4
Weel 97 F6
Weeley 43 B7
Weeley Heath . . . 43 B7
Weem 133 E5
Weeping Cross . . . 62 B3
Weethley Gate . . . 51 D5
Weeting 67 F7
Weeton E Yorks . . 91 B7
  Lancs 92 F3
  N Yorks 95 E5
Weetwood Hall . . 117 B6
Weir 87 B6
Weir Quay 6 C2
Welborne 68 D3
Welbourn 78 D2
Welburn N Yorks . . 96 C3
  N Yorks 102 F4
Welbury 102 D1
Welby 78 F2
Welches Dam 66 F4
Welcombe 8 C4
Weld Bank 86 C3
Weldon 117 E7
Welford E Berks . . 26 B2
  W Nhants 64 F3
Welford-on-Avon . 51 D6
Welham Leics . . . 64 E4
  Notts 89 F8
Welham Green . . . 41 D5
Well Hants 27 E5
  Lincs 79 B7
  N Yorks 101 F7
Welland 50 E2
Wellbank 134 F4
Welldale 107 C8
Well End 40 E1
Wellesbourne . . . 51 D7
Well Heads 94 F3
Well Hill 29 C5
Welling 29 B5
Wellingborough . . 53 C6
Wellingham 80 E4
Wellingore 78 D2
Wellington Cumb . 98 D2
  Hereford 49 E6
  Som 11 B6
  Telford 61 C6
Wellington Heath . 50 E2
Wellington Hill . . 95 F6
Wellow Bath 24 D2
  IoW 14 F4
  Notts 77 C6
Wellpond Green . . 41 B7
Wells 23 E7
Wellsborough . . . 63 D7
Wells Green 74 D3
Wells-next-the-
  Sea 80 C5
Wellswood 7 C7
Well Town 10 D4
Wellwood 128 F2
Welney 66 E5
Welshampton . . . 73 F8
Welsh Bicknor . . . 36 C2
Welsh End 74 F2
Welsh Frankton . . 73 F7
Welsh Hook 44 C4
Welsh Newton . . . 36 C1
Welshpool
  = Y Trallwng . . 60 D2
Welsh St Donats . . 22 B2
Welton Cumb . . . 108 E3
  E Yorks 90 B3
  Lincs 78 B3
  W Nhants 52 C3
Welton Hill 90 F4
Welton le Marsh . 79 C7
Welton le Wold . . 91 F6
Welwick 91 B7
Welwyn 41 C5
Welwyn Garden
  City 41 C5

Wem 60 B5
Wembdon 22 F4
Wembley 40 F4
Wembury 6 E3
Wembworthy 9 D8
Wemyss Bay 118 C1
Wenallt Ceredig . . 47 B5
  Gwyn 72 E3
Wendens Ambo . . 55 F6
Wendlebury 39 C5
Wendling 68 C2
Wendover 40 D1
Wendron 3 C5
Wendy 54 E4
Wenfordbridge 5 B5
Wenhaston 57 B8
Wennington Cambs. 54 B3
  Lancs 93 B6
  London 41 F8
Wensley Derbys . . 76 C2
  N Yorks 101 F5
Wentbridge 89 C5
Wentnor 60 E3
Wentworth Cambs. 55 B5
  S Yorks 88 E4
Wenvoe 22 B3
Weobley 49 D6
Weobley Marsh . . 49 D6
Wereham 67 D6
Wergs 62 D2
Wern Powys 59 C6
  Powys 60 C2
Wernffrwd 33 E6
Wernyrheolydd . . 35 C7
Werrington Corn . . 8 F5
  Pboro 65 D8
  Staffs 75 E6
Wervin 73 B8
Wesham 92 F4
Wessington 76 D3
Westacott 20 F4
Wester Aberchalder 137 B8
West Acre 67 C7
West Adderbury . . 52 F2
West Allerdean . . 123 E5
West Alvington 6 E5
West Amesbury . . 25 E6
West Anstey 10 B3
West Ashby 79 B5
West Ashling 16 D2
West Ashton 24 D3
West Auckland . . 101 B6
West Ayton 103 F7
West Bagborough . 22 F3
West Barkwith . . . 91 F5
West Barnby 103 C6
West Barns 122 B2
West Barsham . . . 80 D5
West Bay 12 E2
West Beckham . . . 81 D7
West Bedfont . . . 27 B8
West Benhar . . . 119 C8
West Bergholt . . . 43 B5
West Bexington . . 12 F3
West Bilney 67 C7
West Blatchington . 17 D6
Westborough . . . 77 E8
West Bourne BCP . . 13 E8
  W Sus 15 D8
West Bowling . . . 94 F4
West Bradford . . . 93 E7
West Bradley 23 F7
West Bretton 88 C3
West Bridgford . . 77 F5
West Bromwich . . 62 E4
Westbrook 26 B2
West Buckland
  Devon 21 F5
  Som 11 B6
West Burrafirth . . 160 H4
West Burton
  N Yorks 101 F5
  W Sus 16 C3
Westbury Bucks . . 52 F4
  Shrops 60 D3
  Wilts 24 D3
Westbury Leigh . . 24 D3
Westbury-on-
  Severn 36 C4
Westbury on Trym 23 B7
Westbury-sub-
  Mendip 23 E7
West Butterwick . . 90 D2
Westby 92 F3
West Byfleet 27 C8
West Caister 69 C8
West Calder 120 C3
West Camel 12 B3
West Challow 38 F3
West Chelborough . 12 D3
West Chevington . 117 E8
West Chiltington . 16 C4
West Chiltington
  Common 16 C4
West Chinnock . . 12 C2
West Chisenbury . 25 D6
West Clandon . . . 27 D8
West Cliffe 31 E7
Westcliff-on-Sea . 42 F4
West Clyne 157 J11
West Clyth 158 G4
West Coker 12 C3
Westcombe 23 F8
West Compton
  Dorset 12 E3
  Som 23 E7
Westcote 38 B2
Westcott Bucks . . 39 C7
  Devon 10 D5
  Sur 28 E2
Westcott Barton . . 38 B4
West Cowick 89 B7
West Cranmore . . 23 E8
West Cross 33 F7
West Cullery . . . 141 D6
West Curry 8 E4
West Curthwaite . 108 E3
West Darlochan . . 143 F7
West Dean Wilts . . 14 B3
  W Sus 16 C2
West Deeping . . . 65 D8
West Dereham . . . 67 D6
West Derby 85 E4
West Didsbury . . . 87 E6
West Ditchburn . . 117 B7

West Drayton
  London 27 B8
  Notts 77 B7
West Ella 90 B4
West End Bedford . 53 D7
  E Yorks 96 F5
  E Yorks 97 F7
  Hants 15 C5
  Lancs 86 B5
  Norf 68 D2
  Norf 69 C8
  N Som 23 C6
  N Yorks 94 D4
  Oxon 38 D4
  S Lanark 120 E2
  Sur 69 F7
  S Yorks 89 D7
  Wilts 13 B7
  Wilts 24 B4
  W Sus 17 C6
West End Green . . 26 C4
Wester
  Aberchalder . . 137 B8
Wester Balgedie . 128 D3
Wester
  Culbeuchly . . . 153 B6
Westerdale Highld. 158 E3
  N Yorks 102 D4
Wester Dechmont 120 C3
Wester Denoon . . 134 E3
Westerfield
  Shetland 160 H5
  Suff 57 E5
Westergate 16 D3
Wester Fintray . . 141 C7
Wester Gruinards 151 B8
Westerham 28 D5
Westerhope 110 C4
Wester Lealty . . . 151 D9
Westerleigh 23 B9
Wester Milton . . 151 F12
Wester Newburn . 129 D6
Wester Quarff . . 160 K6
Wester Skeld . . . 160 J4
Westerton Angus . 135 D6
  Durham 110 F5
  W Sus 16 D2
Westerwick 160 J4
West Farleigh . . . 29 D8
West Felton 60 B3
West Fenton . . . 129 F6
West Ferry 134 F4
Westfield Cumb . . 98 B1
  E Sus 18 D5
  Hereford 50 E2
  Highld 158 D2
  N Lanark 119 B7
  Norf 68 D2
  W Loth 120 B2
Westfields 12 D5
Westfields of
  Rattray 134 E1
West Firle 17 D8
Westgate Durham . 110 F2
  N Lincs 89 D8
  Norf 80 C4
  Norf 81 C5
Westgate on Sea . 31 B7
West Ginge 38 F4
West Grafton 25 C7
West Green 26 D5
West
  Greenskares . . 153 B7
West Grimstead . . 14 B3
West Grinstead . . 17 B5
West Haddlesey . . 89 B6
West Haddon 52 B4
West Hagbourne . 39 F5
West Hagley 62 F3
West Hall 109 C5
West Hallam 76 E4
West Halton 90 B3
Westham Dorset . . 12 G4
  E Sus 18 E3
  Som 23 E6
West Ham 41 F7
Westhampnett . . . 16 D2
West Handley . . . 76 B3
West Hanney 38 E4
West Hanningfield . 42 E3
West Hardwick . . 88 C5
West Harnham . . 14 B2
West Harptree . . . 23 D7
West Hatch 11 B7
Westhay 23 E6
Westhead 86 D2
West Head 67 D5
West Heath Ches E . 74 C5
  Hants 26 D3
  Hants 27 D6
West Helmsdale . 157 H13
West Hendred . . . 38 F4
West Heslerton . . 96 B5
Westhide 49 E7
Westhill Aberds . 141 D7
  Highld 151 G10
West Hill Devon . . 11 E5
  E Yorks 97 C7
  N Som 23 B6
West Hoathly 28 F4
West Holme 13 F6
Westhope Hereford 49 D6
  Shrops 60 F4
West Horndon . . . 42 F2
Westhorpe Lincs . . 78 F5
  Suff 56 C4
West Horrington . 23 E7
West Horsley 27 D8
West Horton . . . 123 F6
West Hougham . . 31 E6
Westhoughton . . . 86 D4
West Houlland . . 160 H4
Westhouse 93 B6
Westhouses 76 D4
Westhumble 28 D2
West Huntington . 96 D2
West Hythe 19 B8
West Ilsley 38 F4
West Itchenor . . . 15 D8
West Keal 79 C6
West Kennett . . . 25 C6
West Kilbride . . . 118 E2
West Kingsdown . 29 C6
West Kington . . . 24 B3

West Kinharrachie 153 E9
West Kirby 85 F3
West Knapton . . . 96 B4
West Knighton . . . 12 F5
West Knoyle 24 F3
West Kyloe 123 E6
Westlake 6 D4
West Lambrook . . 12 C2
West Langdon . . . 31 E7
West Langwell . . 157 J9
West Lavington
  Wilts 24 D5
  W Sus 16 B2
West Layton . . . 101 D6
West Lea 111 E7
West Leake 64 B2
West Learmouth . 122 F4
Westleigh Devon . . 9 B6
  Devon 11 C5
  Gtr Man 86 D4
West Leigh 9 D8
Westleton 57 C8
West Lexham 67 C8
Westley Shrops . . 60 D3
  Suff 56 C2
Westley Waterless 55 D7
West Lilling 96 C2
Westlington 39 C7
Westlinton 108 C3
West Linton . . . 120 D4
West Liss 15 B8
West Littleton . . . 24 B2
West Looe 5 D7
West Luccombe . . 21 E7
West Lulworth . . 13 F6
West Lutton 96 C5
West Lydford . . . 23 F7
West Lyng 11 B8
West Lynn 67 B6
West Malling . . . 29 D7
West Malvern . . . 50 E2
West Marden . . . 15 C8
West Marina 18 E4
West Markham . . 77 B7
Westmarsh 31 C6
West Marsh 91 C6
West Marton 93 D8
West Meon 15 B7
West Mersea 43 C6
Westmeston 17 C7
Westmill 41 B6
West Milton 12 E3
Westminster 28 B4
West Minster 30 B3
West Molesey . . . 28 C2
West Monkton . . . 11 B7
West Moors 13 D8
West Morriston . . 122 E2
Westmuir 134 D3
West Muir 135 C5
Westness 159 F4
West Ness 96 B2
West Newham . . 110 B3
Westnewton Cumb 107 E8
  Northumb 122 F5
West Newton
  E Yorks 97 F7
  Norf 67 B6
West Norwood . . 28 B4
Westoe 111 C6
West Ogwell 7 B6
Weston Bath 24 C2
  Ches E 74 D4
  Devon 11 F6
  Dorset 12 G4
  Halton 86 F3
  Herts 54 F3
  Lincs 66 B2
  Notts 77 C7
  N Yorks 94 E4
  Shrops 61 B5
  Staffs 62 B3
  W Berks 26 B2
  W Nhants 52 E3
Weston Beggard . 49 E7
Westonbirt 37 F5
Weston by
  Welland 64 E4
Weston Colville . . 55 D7
Westoncommon . . 60 B4
Weston Coyney . . 75 E6
Weston Favell . . . 53 C5
Weston Green
  Cambs 55 D7
  Norf 68 C4
Weston Heath . . . 61 C7
Weston Hills 66 B2
Westoning 53 F8
Weston-in-
  Gordano 23 B6
Weston Jones . . . 61 B7
Weston Longville . 68 C4
Weston
  Lullingfields . . 60 B4
Weston-on-the-
  Green 39 C5
Weston-on-Trent . 63 B8
Weston Patrick . . 26 E4
Weston Rhyn 73 F6
Weston-sub-Edge 51 E6
Weston-super-
  Mare 22 C5
Weston Turville . . 40 C1
Weston under
  Lizard 62 C2
Weston under
  Penyard 36 B3
Weston under
  Wetherley 51 C8
Weston Underwood
  Derbys 76 E2
  M Keynes 53 D6
Westonzoyland . . 23 F5
West Orchard . . . 13 C6
West Overton . . . 25 C6
Westow 96 C3
West Park 111 F7
West Parley 13 E8
West Peckham . . . 29 D7
West Pelton 110 D5
West Pennard . . . 23 F7
West Pentire 4 C2
West Perry 54 C2
Westport Argyll . 143 F7
  Som 11 C8
West Putford 9 C5

West Quantoxhead 22 E3
West Rainton . . . 111 E6
West Rasen 90 F4
West Rayham . . . 80 E4
West Retford . . . 89 F7
Westrigg 120 C2
West Rounton . . 102 D2
West Row 55 B7
West Rudham . . . 80 E4
West Runton 81 C7
Westruther 122 E2
Westry 66 E3
West Saltoun . . . 121 C7
West Sandwick . . 160 E6
West Scrafton . . 101 F5
West Sleekburn . . 117 F8
West Somerton . . 69 C7
West Stafford . . . 12 F5
West Stockwith . . 89 E8
West Stoke 16 D2
West Stonesdale . 100 D3
West Stoughton . . 23 E6
West Stour 13 B5
West Stourmouth . 31 C6
West Stow 56 B2
West Stowell 25 C6
West Strathan . . 157 C8
West Stratton . . . 26 E3
West Street 30 D3
West Tanfield . . . 95 B5
West Taphouse . . . 5 C6
West Tarbert . . 145 G7
West Thirston . . 117 E7
West Thorney . . . 15 D8
West Thurrock . . 29 B6
West Tilbury 29 B7
West Tisted 15 B7
West Tofts Norf . . 67 E8
  Perth 133 F8
West Torrington . . 90 F5
West Town Hants . 15 E8
  N Som 23 C6
West Tytherley . . 14 B3
West Tytherton . . 24 B4
Westville 76 E5
West Walton 66 C4
West Walton
  Highway 66 C4
Westward 108 E2
Westward Ho! 9 B6
Westwell Kent . . . 30 E3
  Oxon 38 D2
Westwell Leacon . 30 E3
West Wellow 14 C3
West Wemyss . . . 128 E5
Westwick Cambs . 54 C5
  Durham 101 C5
  Norf 81 E8
West Wick 23 C5
West Wickham
  Cambs 55 E7
  London 28 C4
West Williamston . 32 D1
West Willoughby . 78 E2
West Winch 67 C6
West Winterslow . 25 F7
West Wittering . . 15 E8
West Witton . . . 101 F5
Westwood Devon . 10 E5
  Wilts 24 D3
West Woodburn . 116 F4
West Woodhay . . 25 C8
West Woodlands . 24 E2
Westwoodside . . . 89 E8
West Worldham . . 26 F5
West Worlington . 10 C2
West Worthing . . 16 D5
West Wratting . . 55 D7
West Wycombe . . 39 E8
West Wylam . . . 110 C4
West Yell 160 E6
Wetheral 108 D4
Wetherby 95 E7
Wetherden 56 C4
Wetheringsett . . . 56 C5
Wethersfield 55 F8
Wethersta 160 G5
Wetherup Street . 56 C5
Wetley Rocks . . . 75 E6
Wettenhall 74 C3
Wetton 75 D8
Wetwang 96 D5
Wetwood 74 F4
Wexcombe 25 D7
Wexham Street . . 40 F2
Weybourne 81 C7
Weybread 57 B6
Weybridge 27 C8
Weycroft 11 E8
Weydale 158 D3
Weyhill 25 E8
Weymouth 12 G4
Whaddon Bucks . . 53 F6
  Cambs 54 E4
  Glos 37 C5
  Wilts 14 B2
Whale 99 B7
Whaley 76 B5
Whaley Bridge . . 87 F8
Whaley Thorns . . 76 B5
Whaligoe 158 F5
Whalley 93 F7
Whalton 117 F7
Wham 93 C7
Whaplode 66 B3
Whaplode Drove . 66 C3
Whaplode St
  Catherine 66 B3
Wharfe 93 C7
Wharles 92 F4
Wharncliffe Side . 88 E3
Wharram le Street . 96 C4
Wharton 74 C3
Wharton Green . . 74 C3
Whashton 101 D6
Whatcombe 13 D6
Whatcote 51 E8
Whatley Som . . . 11 D8
  Som 24 E2
Whatlington 18 D4
Whatstandwell . . 76 D3
Whatton 77 F7
Whauphill 105 E8
Whaw 100 D4
Wheatacre 69 E7

Wheatcroft 76 D3
Wheathampstead 40 C4
Wheathill
 Shrops 61 F6
 Som 23 D8
Wheatley Devon 10 E4
 Hants 27 E5
 Oxon 39 D5
 S Yorks 89 D6
 W Yorks 87 B8
Wheatley Hill 111 F6
Wheaton Aston 62 C2
Wheddon Cross 21 F8
Wheelerstreet 27 E7
Wheelock 74 D4
Wheelock Heath 74 D4
Wheelton 86 B4
Wheen 134 B3
Wheldrake 96 E2
Whelford 38 E1
Whelpley Hill 40 D2
Whempstead 41 B6
Whenby 96 C2
Wherstead 57 E5
Wherwell 25 E8
Wheston 75 B8
Whetsted 29 E7
Whetstone 64 E2
Whicham 98 F3
Whichford 51 F8
Whickham 110 C5
Whiddon Down 9 E8
Whigstreet 134 E4
Whilton 52 C4
Whimble 9 D5
Whim Farm 120 D5
Whimple 10 E5
Whimpwell Green 69 B6
Whinburgh 68 D3
Whinnieligate 106 D4
Whinnyfold 153 E10
Whippingham 15 E6
Whipsnade 40 C3
Whipton 10 E4
Whirlow 88 F4
Whisby 78 C2
Whissendine 64 C5
Whissonsett 80 E5
Whistlefield
 Argyll 145 D10
 Argyll 145 D11
Whistley Green 27 B5
Whiston Mers 86 E2
 Staffs 62 C2
 Staffs 75 E7
 S Yorks 88 F5
 W Nhants 53 C6
Whitbeck 98 F3
Whitbourne 50 D2
Whitburn T&W 111 C7
 W Loth 120 C2
Whitburn Colliery 111 C7
Whitby Ches W 73 B7
 N Yorks 103 C6
Whitbyheath 73 B7
Whitchurch Bath 23 C8
 Bucks 39 B7
 Cardiff 35 F5
 Devon 6 B2
 Hants 26 E2
 Hereford 36 C2
 Oxon 26 B4
 Pembs 44 C2
 Shrops 74 E2
Whitchurch Canonicorum 11 E8
Whitchurch Hill 26 B4
Whitcombe 12 F5
Whitcott Keysett 60 F7
Whiteacen 152 D2
Whiteacre Heath 63 E6
Whitebridge 137 C7
Whitebrook 36 D2
Whiteburn 121 E8
Whitecairn 105 D6
Whitecairns 141 C8
Whitecastle 120 C3
Whitechapel 93 E5
Whitecleat 159 H6
White Coppice 86 C4
Whitecroft 121 B6
Whitecross Corn 4 B4
 Falk 120 B2
 Staffs 62 B2
Whiteface 151 C10
Whitefarland 143 D9
Whitefaulds 112 D2
Whitefield Gtr Man 87 D6
 Perth 134 F1
Whiteford 141 B6
Whitegate 74 C3
Whitehall Blackburn 86 B4
 W Sus 16 B5
Whitehall Village 159 F7
Whitehaven 98 C1
Whitehill 27 F5
Whitehills Aberds 153 B6
 S Lanark 119 D6
Whitehough 87 F8
Whitehouse
 Aberds 140 C5
 Argyll 145 G7
Whiteinch 118 C5
Whitekirk 129 F7
White Lackington 12 E5
White Ladies Aston 50 D4
Whitelaw 119 E6
Whiteleas 111 C6
Whiteley Bank 15 F6
Whiteley Green 75 B6
Whiteley Village 27 C8
White Lund 92 C4
Whitemans Green 17 B7
White Mill 33 C5
Whitemire 151 F12
Whitemoor 4 D4
Whitemore 75 C5
Whitenap 14 B4
White Ness 160 J5
White Notley 42 C3
Whiteoak Green 38 C3
Whiteparish 14 B3

White Pit 79 B6
White Post 77 D6
Whiterashes 141 B7
White Rocks 35 B8
White Roding 42 C1
Whiterow 158 F5
Whiteshill 37 D5
Whiteside
 Northumb 109 C7
 W Loth 120 C2
Whitesmith 18 D2
Whitestaunton 11 C7
Whitestone Devon 10 E3
 Devon 20 E3
 Warks 63 F7
Whitestones 153 C8
Whitestreet Green 56 F3
Whitewall Corner 96 B3
White Waltham 27 B6
Whiteway Glos 37 C6
 Glos 37 E5
Whitewell Aberds 153 B9
 Lancs 93 E6
Whitewell Bottom 87 B6
Whiteworks 6 B4
Whitfield Kent 31 E7
 Northumb 109 D7
 S Glos 36 E3
 W Nhants 52 F4
Whitford Devon 11 E7
 Flint 72 B5
Whitgift 90 B2
Whitgreave 62 B2
Whithorn 105 E8
Whiting Bay 143 F11
Whitkirk 95 F6
Whitland 32 C2
Whitletts 112 B3
Whitley N Yorks 89 B6
 Reading 26 B5
 Wilts 24 C3
Whitley Bay 111 B6
Whitley Chapel 110 D2
Whitley Lower 88 C3
Whitley Row 29 D5
Whitlock's End 51 B6
Whitminster 36 D4
Whitmore 74 E5
Whitnage 10 C5
Whitnash 51 C8
Whitney-on-Wye 48 E4
Whitrigg Cumb 108 D2
 Cumb 108 F2
Whitsbury 14 C2
Whitsome 122 D4
Whitson 35 F7
Whitstable 30 C5
Whitstone 8 E4
Whittingham 117 C6
Whittingslow 60 F4
Whittington Glos 37 B7
 Lancs 93 B6
 Norf 67 E7
 Shrops 73 F7
 Staffs 62 F2
 Staffs 63 D5
 Worcs 50 D3
Whittle-le-Woods 86 B3
Whittlebury 52 E4
Whittlesey 66 E2
Whittlesford 55 E5
Whittlestone Head 86 C5
Whitton Borders 116 B3
 N Lincs 90 B3
 Northumb 117 D6
 Powys 48 C4
 Shrops 49 B7
 Stockton 102 B1
 Suff 56 E5
Whittonditch 25 B7
Whittonstall 110 D3
Whitway 26 D2
Whitwell Derbys 76 B5
 Herts 40 B4
 IoW 15 G6
 N Yorks 101 E7
 Rutland 65 D6
Whitwell-on-the-Hill 96 C3
Whitwell Street 81 E7
Whitwick 63 C8
Whitwood 88 B5
Whitworth 87 C6
Whixall 74 F2
Whixley 95 D7
Whoberley 51 B8
Whorlton Durham 101 C6
 N Yorks 102 D2
Whygate 109 B7
Whyle 49 C7
Whyteleafe 28 D4
Wibdon 36 E2
Wibsey 88 A3
Wibtoft 63 F8
Wichenford 50 C2
Wichling 30 D3
Wick BCP 14 E2
 Devon 11 D6
 Highld 158 E5
 S Glos 24 B2
 Shetland 160 K6
 V Glam 21 B8
 Wilts 14 B2
 Worcs 50 E4
 W Sus 16 D3
Wick Hill 27 C5
Wicken Cambs 55 B6
 W Nhants 52 F5
Wicken Bonhunt 55 F5
Wickenby 90 F4
Wicken Green Village 80 D4
Wickersley 89 E5
Wickford 42 E3
Wickham Hants 15 C6
 W Berks 25 B8
Wickham Bishops 42 C4
Wickhambreaux 31 D6
Wickhambrook 55 D8
Wickhamford 51 E5
Wickham Market 57 D7
Wickhampton 69 D7
Wickham St Paul 56 F2
Wickham Skeith 56 C4
Wickham Street
 Suff 55 D8
 Suff 56 C4
Wick Hill 27 C5
Wicklewood 68 D3

Wickmere 81 D7
Wick St Lawrence 23 C5
Wickwar 36 F4
Widdington 55 F6
Widdrington 117 E8
Widdrington Station 117 E8
Widecombe in the Moor 6 B5
Widegates 5 D7
Widemouth Bay 8 D4
Wide Open 110 B5
Widewall 159 J5
Widford Essex 42 D2
 Herts 41 C7
Widham 37 F7
Widmer End 40 E1
Widmerpool 64 B3
Widnes 86 F3
Wigan 86 D3
Wiggaton 11 E6
Wiggenhall St Germans 67 C5
Wiggenhall St Mary Magdalen 67 C5
Wiggenhall St Mary the Virgin 67 C5
Wigginton Herts 40 C2
 Oxon 51 F8
 Staffs 63 D6
 York 95 D8
Wigglesworth 93 D8
Wiggonby 108 D2
Wiggonholt 16 C4
Wighill 95 E7
Wighton 80 D5
Wigley 14 C4
Wigmore Hereford 49 C6
 Medway 30 C2
Wigsley 77 B8
Wigsthorpe 65 F7
Wigston 64 E3
Wigthorpe 89 F6
Wigtoft 79 F5
Wigton 108 E2
Wigtown 105 D8
Wigtwizzle 88 E3
Wike 95 E6
Wike Well End 89 C7
Wilbarston 64 F5
Wilberfoss 96 E3
Wilberlee 87 C8
Wilburton 55 B5
Wilby N Nhants 53 C6
 Norf 68 F3
 Suff 57 B6
Wilcot 25 C6
Wilcott 60 C3
Wilcrick 35 F8
Wilday Green 76 B3
Wildboarclough 75 C6
Wilden Bedford 53 D8
 Worcs 50 B3
Wildhern 25 D8
Wildhill 41 D5
Wildmoor 50 B4
Wildsworth 90 E2
Wilford 77 F5
Wilkesley 74 E3
Wilkhaven 151 C12
Wilkieston 120 C4
Willand 10 C5
Willaston Ches E 74 D3
 Ches W 73 B7
Willen 53 E6
Willenhall W Mid 51 B8
 W Mid 62 E3
Willerby E Yorks 97 F6
 N Yorks 97 B6
Willersey 51 F6
Willersley 48 E5
Willesborough 30 E4
Willesborough Lees 30 E4
Willesden 41 F5
Willett 22 F3
Willey Shrops 61 E6
 Warks 63 F8
Willey Green 27 D7
Williamscott 52 E2
Willian 54 F3
Willingale 42 D1
Willingdon 18 E2
Willingham 54 B5
Willingham by Stow 90 F2
Willington Bedford 54 E2
 Derbys 63 B6
 Durham 110 F4
 T&W 111 C6
 Warks 51 F7
Willington Corner 74 C2
Willisham Tye 56 D4
Willitoft 96 F3
Williton 22 E2
Willoughbridge 74 E4
Willoughby Lincs 79 B7
 Warks 52 C3
Willoughby-on-the-Wolds 64 B3
Willoughby Waterleys 64 E2
Willoughton 90 E3
Willows Green 42 C3
Willsbridge 23 B8
Willslock 62 B4
Willsworthy 9 F7
Wilmcote 51 D6
Wilmington Devon 11 E7
 E Sus 18 E2
 Kent 29 B6
Wilminstone 6 B2
Wilmslow 87 F6
Wilnecote 63 D6
Wilpshire 93 F6
Wilsden 94 F3
Wilsford Lincs 78 E3
 Wilts 25 D6
 Wilts 25 F6
Wilsill 94 C4
Wilsley Pound 18 B4
Wilsom 26 F5
Wilson 63 B8
Wilsontown 120 D2
Wilstead 53 E8
Wilsthorpe 65 C7
Wilstone 40 C2
Wilton Borders 115 C7
 Cumb 98 C2

N Yorks 103 F6
 Redcar 102 C3
 Wilts 25 C7
 Wilts 25 F5
Wimbish 55 F6
Wimbish Green 55 F7
Wimblebury 62 C4
Wimbledon 28 B3
Wimblington 66 E4
Wimborne Minster 13 E8
Wimborne St Giles 13 C8
Wimbotsham 67 D6
Wimpson 14 C4
Wimpstone 51 E7
Wincanton 12 B5
Wincham 74 B3
Winchburgh 120 B3
Winchcombe 37 B7
Winchelsea 19 D6
Winchelsea Beach 19 D6
Winchester 15 B5
Winchet Hill 29 E8
Winchfield 27 D5
Winchmore Hill
 Bucks 40 E2
 London 41 E6
Wincle 75 C6
Wincobank 88 E4
Windermere 99 E6
Winderton 51 E8
Windhill 151 G8
Windhouse 160 D6
Windlehurst 87 F7
Windlesham 27 C7
Windley 76 E3
Windmill Hill
 E Sus 18 D3
 Som 11 C8
Windrush 38 C1
Windsor N Lincs 89 C8
 Windsor 27 B7
Windsoredge 37 D5
Windygates 128 D5
Windyknowe 120 C2
Windywalls 122 F3
Wineham 17 B6
Winestead 91 B6
Winewall 94 E2
Winfarthing 68 F4
Winford IoW 15 F6
 N Som 23 C7
Winforton 48 E4
Winfrith Newburgh 13 F6
Wing Bucks 40 B1
 Rutland 65 D5
Wingate 111 F7
Wingates Gtr Man 86 D4
 Northumb 117 E7
Wingerworth 76 C3
Wingfield C Beds 40 B2
 Suff 57 B6
 Wilts 24 D3
Wingham 31 D6
Wingmore 31 E5
Wingrave 40 C1
Winkburn 77 D7
Winkfield 27 B7
Winkfield Row 27 B6
Winkhill 75 D7
Winklebury 26 D4
Winkleigh 9 D8
Winksley 95 B5
Winkton 14 E2
Winlaton 110 C4
Winless 158 E5
Winmarleigh 92 E4
Winnal 49 F6
Winnall 15 B5
Winnersh 27 B5
Winscales 98 B2
Winscombe 23 D6
Winsford Ches W 74 C3
 Som 21 F8
Winsham 11 D8
Winshill 63 B6
Winskill 109 F5
Winslade 26 E4
Winsley 24 C3
Winslow 39 B7
Winson 37 D7
Winson Green 62 F4
Winsor 14 C4
Winster Derbys 76 C2
 Cumb 99 E6
Winston Durham 101 C6
 Suff 57 C5
Winstone 37 D6
Winston Green 57 C5
Winswell 9 C6
Winterborne Clenston 13 D6
Winterborne Herringston 12 F4
Winterborne Houghton 13 D6
Winterborne Kingston 13 E6
Winterborne Monkton 12 F4
Winterborne Stickland 13 D6
Winterborne Whitechurch 13 D6
Winterborne Zelston 13 E6
Winterbourne S Glos 36 F3
 W Berks 26 B2
Winterbourne Abbas 12 E4
Winterbourne Bassett 25 B6
Winterbourne Dauntsey 25 F6
Winterbourne Down 23 B8
Winterbourne Earls 25 F6
Winterbourne Gunner 25 F6
Winterbourne Monkton 25 B6
Winterbourne Steepleton 12 F4
Winterbourne Stoke 25 E5
Winter Gardens 42 F3

Winteringham 90 B3
Winterley 74 D4
Wintersett 88 C4
Wintershill 15 C6
Winterton 90 C3
Winterton-on-Sea 69 C7
Winthorpe Lincs 79 C8
 Notts 77 D8
Winton BCP 13 E8
 Cumb 100 C2
 N Yorks 102 E2
Wintringham 96 B4
Winwick Cambs 65 F8
 Warr 86 E4
 W Nhants 52 B4
Wirksworth 76 D2
Wirksworth Moor 76 D2
Wirswall 74 E2
Wisbech 66 D4
Wisbech St Mary 66 D4
Wisborough Green 16 B4
Wiseton 89 F7
Wishaw N Lanark 119 D7
 Warks 63 E5
Wisley 27 D8
Wispington 78 B5
Wissenden 30 E3
Wissett 57 B7
Wistanstow 60 F4
Wistanswick 61 B6
Wistaston 74 D3
Wistaston Green 74 D3
Wiston Pembs 32 C1
 S Lanark 120 F2
 W Sus 16 C5
Wistow Cambs 66 F2
 N Yorks 95 F8
Wiswell 93 F7
Witcham 66 F4
Witchampton 13 D7
Witchford 55 B6
Witham 42 C4
Witham Friary 24 E2
Witham on the Hill 65 C7
Withcall 91 F6
Withdean 17 D7
Witherenden Hill 18 C3
Witheridge 10 C3
Witherley 63 E7
Withern 91 F8
Withernsea 91 B7
Withernwick 97 E7
Withersdale Street 69 F5
Withersfield 55 E7
Witherslack 99 F6
Withiel 4 C4
Withiel Florey 21 F8
Withington Glos 37 C7
 Gtr Man 87 E6
 Hereford 49 E7
 Shrops 61 C5
 Staffs 75 F7
Withington Green 74 B5
Withleigh 10 C4
Withnell 86 B4
Withybrook 63 F8
Withycombe 22 E2
Withycombe Raleigh 10 F5
Withyham 29 F5
Withypool 21 F7
Witley 27 F7
Witnesham 57 D5
Witney 38 C3
Wittering 65 D7
Wittersham 19 C5
Witton Angus 135 B5
 Worcs 50 C3
Witton Bridge 69 A6
Witton Gilbert 110 E5
Witton-le-Wear 110 F4
Witton Park 110 F4
Wiveliscombe 11 B5
Wivelrod 26 F4
Wivelsfield 17 B7
Wivelsfield Green 17 B7
Wivenhoe 43 B6
Wivenhoe Cross 43 B6
Wiveton 81 C6
Wix 43 B7
Wixford 51 D5
Wixhill 61 B5
Wixoe 55 E8
Woburn 53 F7
Woburn Sands 53 F7
Wokefield Park 26 C4
Woking 27 D8
Wokingham 27 C6
Wolborough 7 B6
Woldingham 28 D4
Wold Newton
 E Yorks 97 B6
 NE Lincs 91 E6
Wolfclyde 120 F3
Wolferton 67 B6
Wolfhill 134 F1
Wolf's Castle 44 C4
Wolfsdale 44 C4
Woll 115 B7
Wollaston
 N Nhants 53 C7
 Shrops 60 C3
Wollaton 76 F5
Wollerton 74 F3
Wollescote 62 F3
Wolsingham 110 F3
Wolstanton 75 E5
Wolston 52 B2
Wolvercote 38 D4
Wolverhampton 62 E3
Wolverley Shrops 73 F8
 Worcs 50 B3
Wolverton Hants 26 D3
 M Keynes 53 E6
 Warks 51 C7
Wolverton Common 26 D3
Wolvesnewton 36 E1
Wolvey 63 F8
Wolviston 102 B2
Wombleton 102 F4
Wombourne 62 E2
Wombwell 88 D4
Womenswold 31 D6
Womersley 89 C6
Wonastow 36 C1
Wonersh 27 E8
Wonson 9 F8

Wonston 26 F2
Wooburn 40 F2
Wooburn Green 40 F2
Woodacott 9 D5
Woodale 94 B3
Woodbank 143 G7
Woodbastwick 69 C6
Woodbeck 77 B7
Woodborough
 Notts 77 E6
 Wilts 25 D6
Woodbridge Dorset 12 C5
 Suff 57 E6
Woodbury 10 F5
Woodbury Salterton 10 F5
Woodchester 37 D5
Woodchurch Kent 19 B6
 Mers 85 F3
Woodcombe 21 E8
Woodcote 39 F6
Woodcott 26 D2
Woodcroft 36 E2
Woodcutts 13 C7
Wood Dalling 81 E6
Woodditton 55 D7
Woodeaton 39 C5
Woodend Cumb 98 E3
 W Nhants 52 E4
 W Sus 16 D2
Wood End Herts 41 B6
 Warks 51 B6
 Warks 63 E6
Wood Enderby 79 C5
Woodend Green 52 F4
Woodfalls 14 B2
Woodfield S Ayrs 112 B3
 Oxon 39 B5
Wood Field 28 D2
Woodford Corn 8 C4
 Devon 7 E5
 Glos 36 E3
 Gtr Man 87 F6
 London 41 E7
 N Nhants 53 B7
Woodford Bridge 41 E7
Woodford Halse 52 D3
Woodgate Norf 68 C3
 Oxon 38 F2
 W Mid 62 F3
 Worcs 50 C4
 W Sus 16 D3
Woodgreen 14 C2
Wood Green 41 E6
Woodhall Herts 41 C5
 Inclyd 118 B3
 N Yorks 100 E4
Woodhall Spa 78 C4
Woodham 27 C8
Woodham Ferrers 42 E3
Woodham Mortimer 42 D4
Woodham Walter 42 D4
Woodhaven 129 B6
Wood Hayes 62 D3
Woodhead 153 E7
Woodhey 87 C5
Woodhill 61 F7
Woodhorn 117 F8
Woodhouse
 Leics 64 C2
 N Lincs 89 D8
 S Yorks 88 F5
 W Yorks 88 B4
Woodhouse Eaves 64 C2
Woodhouselee 120 C5
Woodhouselees 108 B3
Woodhouse Park 87 F6
Woodhouses 63 C5
Woodhurst 54 B4
Woodingdean 17 D7
Woodkirk 88 B3
Woodland Devon 7 C5
 Durham 101 B5
Woodlands Aberds 141 E6
 Dorset 13 D8
 Hants 14 C4
 Highld 151 E8
 N Yorks 95 D6
 S Yorks 89 D6
Woodlands Park 27 B6
Woodlands St Mary 25 B8
Woodlane 62 B5
Wood Lanes 87 F7
Woodleigh 6 E5
Woodlesford 88 B4
Woodley Gtr Man 87 E7
 Wokingham 27 B5
Woodmancote Glos 36 E4
 Glos 37 B6
 Glos 37 D7
 W Sus 16 C2
 W Sus 17 C6
Woodmancott 26 E3
Woodmansey 97 F6
Woodmansterne 28 D3
Woodminton 13 B8
Woodnesborough 31 D7
Woodnewton 65 E7
Wood Norton 81 E6
Woodplumpton 92 F5
Woodrising 68 D2
Wood's Green 18 B3
Woodseaves Shrops 74 F3
 Staffs 61 B7
Woodsend 25 B7
Woodsetts 89 F6
Woodsford 13 E5
Woodside
 Aberdeen 141 D8
 Aberds 153 D10
 Brack 27 B7
 Fife 129 D6
 Hants 14 E4
 Herts 41 D5
 Perth 134 F2
Woodside of Arbeadie 141 E6
Woodstock Oxon 38 C4
 Pembs 32 B1
Wood Street Norf 69 B6
 Sur 27 D7
Woodthorpe Derbys 76 B4
 Leics 64 C2
 Lincs 91 F8
 York 95 E8
Woodton 69 E5
Woodtown Devon 9 B6

Devon 9 B6
Woodvale 85 C4
Woodville 63 C7
Wood Walton 66 F2
Woodyates 13 C8
Woofferton 49 C7
Wookey 23 E7
Wookey Hole 23 E7
Wool 13 F6
Woolacombe 20 E3
Woolage Green 31 E6
Woolaston 36 E2
Woolavington 22 E5
Woolbeding 16 B2
Wooldale 88 D2
Wooler 117 B5
Woolfardisworthy
 Devon 8 B5
 Devon 10 D3
Woolfords Cottages 120 D3
Woolhampton 26 C3
Woolhope 49 F8
Woolhope Cockshoot 49 F8
Woolland 13 D5
Woollaton 9 C6
Woolley Bath 24 C2
 Cambs 54 B2
 Corn 8 C4
 Derbys 76 C3
 W Yorks 88 C4
Woolmer Green 41 C5
Woolmere Green 50 C4
Woolpit 56 C3
Woolscott 52 C2
Woolsington 110 C4
Woolstanwood 74 D3
Woolstaston 60 E4
Woolsthorpe Lincs 65 B6
 Lincs 77 F8
Woolston Devon 6 E5
 Shrops 60 B3
 Shrops 60 F4
 Soton 14 C5
 Warr 86 E4
Woolstone
 M Keynes 53 F6
 Oxon 38 F2
Woolton 86 F2
Woolton Hill 26 C2
Woolverstone 57 F5
Woolverton 24 D2
Woolwich 28 B5
Woolwich Ferry 28 B5
Woonton 49 D5
Wooperton 117 B6
Woore 74 E4
Wootten Green 57 B6
Wootton Bedford 53 E8
 Hants 14 E3
 Hereford 48 D5
 Kent 31 E6
 N Lincs 90 C4
 Oxon 38 C4
 Oxon 38 D4
 Shrops 49 B6
 Shrops 60 B3
 Staffs 62 B2
 Staffs 75 E8
 W Nhants 53 D5
Wootton Bridge 15 E6
Wootton Common 15 E6
Wootton Courtenay 21 E8
Wootton Fitzpaine 11 E8
Wootton Rivers 25 C6
Wootton St Lawrence 26 D3
Wootton Wawen 51 C6
Worcester 50 D3
Worcester Park 28 C3
Wordsley 62 F2
Worfield 61 E7
Work 159 G5
Workington 98 B1
Worksop 77 B5
Worlaby 90 C4
World's End 26 B2
Worle 23 C5
Worleston 74 D3
Worlingham 69 F7
Worlington 55 B7
Worlingworth 57 C6
Wormald Green 95 C6
Wormbridge 49 F6
Wormegay 67 C6
Wormelow Tump 49 F6
Wormhill 75 B8
Wormingford 56 F3
Worminghall 39 D6
Wormington 50 F5
Worminster 23 E7
Wormit 129 B5
Wormleighton 52 D2
Wormley Herts 41 D6
 Sur 27 F7
Wormley West End 41 D6
Wormshill 30 D2
Wormsley 49 E6
Worplesdon 27 D7
Worral 88 E4
Worsbrough 88 D4
Worsbrough Common 88 D4
Worsley 86 D5
Worstead 69 B6
Worsthorne 93 F8
Worston 93 E7
Worswell 6 E3
Worth Kent 31 D7
 W Sus 28 F4
Wortham 56 B4
Worthen 60 D3
Worthenbury 73 E8
Worthing Norf 68 C2
 W Sus 16 D5
Worthington 63 B8
Worth Matravers 13 G7

Wotton 28 E2
Wotton-under-Edge 36 E4
Wotton Underwood 39 C7
Woughton on the Green 53 F6
Wouldham 29 C8
Wrabness 57 F5
Wrafton 20 F3
Wragby Lincs 78 B4
 W Yorks 88 C5
Wragholme 91 E7
Wramplingham 68 D4
Wrangbrook 89 C5
Wrangham 153 E6
Wrangle 79 D7
Wrangle Bank 79 D7
Wrangle Lowgate 79 D7
Wrangway 11 C6
Wrantage 11 B8
Wrawby 90 D4
Wraxall Dorset 12 D3
 N Som 23 B6
 Som 23 E8
Wray 93 C6
Wraysbury 27 B8
Wrayton 93 B6
Wrea Green 92 F3
Wreay Cumb 99 B6
 Cumb 108 E4
Wrecclesham 27 E6
Wrecsam = Wrexham 73 D7
Wrekenton 111 D5
Wrelton 103 F5
Wrenbury 74 E2
Wrench Green 103 F7
Wreningham 68 E4
Wrentham 69 F7
Wrenthorpe 88 B4
Wrentnall 60 D4
Wressle E Yorks 96 F3
 N Lincs 90 D3
Wrestlingworth 54 E3
Wretham 68 F2
Wretton 67 E6
Wrexham = Wrecsam 73 D7
Wrexham Industrial Estate 73 E7
Wribbenhall 50 B2
Wrightington Bar 86 C3
Wrinehill 74 E4
Wrington 23 C6
Writhlington 24 D2
Writtle 42 D2
Wrockwardine 61 C6
Wroot 89 D8
Wrotham 29 D7
Wrotham Heath 29 D7
Wroughton 37 F8
Wroxall IoW 15 G6
 Warks 51 B7
Wroxeter 61 D5
Wroxham 69 C6
Wroxton 52 E2
Wyaston 75 E8
Wyberton 79 E6
Wyboston 54 D2
Wybunbury 74 E4
Wychbold 50 C4
Wych Cross 28 F5
Wyck 27 F5
Wyck Rissington 38 B1
Wycoller 94 F2
Wycomb 64 B4
Wycombe Marsh 40 E1
Wyddial 54 F4
Wye 30 E4
Wyesham 36 C2
Wyfordby 64 C4
Wyke Dorset 13 B5
 Shrops 61 D6
 Sur 27 D7
 W Yorks 88 B2
Wyke Regis 12 G4
Wykey 60 B3
Wylam 110 C4
Wylde Green 62 E5
Wyllie 35 E5
Wylye 24 F5
Wymering 15 D7
Wymeswold 64 B3
Wymington 53 C7
Wymondham Leics 65 C5
 Norf 68 D4
Wyndham 34 E3
Wynford Eagle 12 E3
Wyng 159 J4
Wynyard Village 102 B2
Wyre Piddle 50 E4
Wysall 64 B3
Wythall 51 B5
Wytham 38 D4
Wythburn 99 C5
Wythenshawe 87 F6
Wythop Mill 98 B3
Wyton 54 B3
Wyverstone 56 C4
Wyverstone Street 56 C4
Wyville 65 B5
Wyvis Lodge 150 D7

Y

Yaddlethorpe 90 D2
Yafford 14 F5
Yafforth 101 E7
Yalding 29 D7
Yanworth 37 C7
Yapham 96 D3
Yapton 16 D3
Yarburgh 91 E7
Yarcombe 11 D7
Yard 22 F2
Yardley 62 F5
Yardley Gobion 53 E5
Yardley Hastings 53 D6
Yardro 48 D4
Yarkhill 49 E8
Yarlet 62 B3
Yarlington 12 B4
Yarlside 92 C2

Yarm 102 C2
Yarmouth 14 F4
Yarnbrook 24 D3
Yarnfield 75 F5
Yarnscombe 9 B7
Yarnton 38 C4
Yarpole 49 C6
Yarrow 115 B6
Yarrow Feus 115 B6
Yarsop 49 E6
Yarwell 65 E7
Yate 36 F4
Yateley 27 C6
Yatesbury 25 B5
Yattendon 26 B3
Yatton Hereford 49 C6
 N Som 23 C6
Yatton Keynell 24 B3
Yaverland 15 F7
Yaxham 68 C3
Yaxley Cambs 65 E8
 Suff 56 B5
Yazor 49 E6
Y Bala = Bala 72 F3
Y Barri = Barry 22 C3
Y Bont-Faen
 = Cowbridge 21 B8
Y Drenewydd
 = Newtown 59 E8
Yeading 40 F4
Yeadon 94 E5
Yealand Conyers 92 B5
Yealand Redmayne 92 B5
Yealmpton 6 D3
Yearby 102 B4
Yearsley 95 B8
Yeaton 60 C4
Yeaveley 75 E8
Yedingham 96 B4
Yeldon 53 C8
Yelford 38 D3
Yelland 20 F3
Yelling 54 C3
Yelvertoft 52 B3
Yelverton Devon 6 C3
 Norf 69 D5
Yenston 12 B5
Yeoford 10 E2
Yeolmbridge 8 F5
Yeo Mill 10 B3
Yeovil 12 C3
Yeovil Marsh 12 C3
Yeovilton 12 B3
Yerbeston 32 D1
Yesnaby 159 G3
Yetlington 117 D6
Yetminster 12 C3
Yettington 11 F5
Yetts o'Muckhart 128 D2
Y Felinheli 82 E5
Y Fenni
 = Abergavenny 35 C6
Y Fflint = Flint 73 B6
Y Ffôr 70 D4
Y-Ffrith 72 A4
Y Gelli Gandryll
 = Hay-on-Wye 48 E4
Yieldshields 119 D8
Yiewsley 40 F3
Y Mwmbwls
 = The Mumbles 33 F7
Ynysboeth 34 E4
Ynysddu 35 E5
Ynysgyfflog 58 C3
Ynyshir 34 E4
Ynyslas 58 E3
Ynys-meudwy 33 D8
Ynystawe 33 D7
Ynysybwl 34 E4
Yockenthwaite 94 B2
Yockleton 60 C3
Yokefleet 90 B2
Yoker 118 C5
Yonder Bognie 152 D6
York 95 D8
Yorkletts 30 C4
Yorkley 36 D3
York Town 27 C6
Yorton 60 B5
Youlgreave 76 C2
Youlstone 8 C4
Youlthorpe 96 D3
Youlton 95 C7
Young's End 42 C3
Young Wood 78 B4
Yoxall 62 C5
Yoxford 57 C7
Y Pîl = Pyle 34 F2
Yr Hôb = Hope 73 D7
Y Rhws = Rhoose 22 C2
Y Rhyl = Rhyl 72 A4
Yr Wyddgrug
 = Mold 73 C6
Ysbyty-Cynfyn 47 B6
Ysbyty Ifan 72 E2
Ysbyty Ystwyth 47 B6
Ysceifiog 73 B5
Yspitty 33 E6
Ystalyfera 34 D1
Ystrad 34 E3
Ystrad Aeron 46 D4
Ystradfellte 34 C3
Ystradffin 47 E6
Ystradgynlais 34 C1
Ystradmeurig 47 C6
Ystradowen Carms 33 C8
 V Glam 22 B2
Ystumtuen 47 B6
Ythanbank 153 E9
Ythanwells 153 E6
Ythsie 153 E8

Z

Zeal Monachorum 10 D2
Zeals 24 F2
Zelah 4 D3
Zennor 2 C3